# Contract Law

WITHDRAWN

COVENTRY UNIVERSITY LONDON CAMPUS
East India House,
109-117 Middlesex Street, London, E1 7JF
Tel: 020 7247 3666 | Fax: 020 7375 3048
www.coventry.ac.uk/londoncampus

Tenth edition

# Contract Law

## Catherine Elliott and Frances Quinn

**PEARSON**

Harlow, England • London • New York • Boston • San Francisco • Toronto • Sydney
Auckland • Singapore • Hong Kong • Tokyo • Seoul • Taipei • New Delhi
Cape Town • São Paulo • Mexico City • Madrid • Amsterdam • Munich • Paris • Milan

**Pearson Education Limited**
Edinburgh Gate
Harlow CM20 2JE
United Kingdom
Tel: +44 (0)1279 623623
Web: www.pearson.com/uk

———————————————

First published 1996 (print)
Second edition 1999 (print)
Third edition 2001 (print)
Fourth edition 2003 (print)
Fifth edition 2005 (print)
Sixth edition 2007 (print)
Seventh edition 2009 (print)
Eighth edition 2011 (print)
Ninth edition 2013 (print and electronic)
**Tenth edition published 2015** (print and electronic)

ISBN: 978-1-292-06447-5 (print)
       978-1-292-06452-9 (PDF)
       978-1-292-06448-2 (eText)

**British Library Cataloguing-in-Publication Data**
A catalogue record for the print edition is available from the British Library

**Library of Congress Cataloging-in-Publication Data**
Elliott, Catherine, 1966-
   Contract law / Catherine Elliott and Frances Quinn. -- Tenth Edition.
      pages cm
   ISBN 978-1-292-06447-5
   1. Contracts--England.  I. Quinn, Frances, 1963-  II. Title.
   KD1554.E44 2015
   346.4202--dc23

                                                           2015006619

10 9 8 7 6 5 4 3 2 1
19 18 17 16 15

Cover image © Bax Walker/Alamy

Print edition typeset in 9/12.5pt Frutiger by 35
Print edition printed in Slovakia by Neografia

NOTE THAT ANY PAGE CROSS REFERENCES REFER TO THE PRINT EDITION

# Brief contents

# Contents

## Part 2 The contents of a contract

### Chapter 7 Terms of the contract

### Chapter 8 Unfair contract terms

# Preface

The tenth edition of this book aims to build on the strengths that have led to the success and popularity of the previous editions, which have been extremely well received by both teachers and students alike. It incorporates all the important legal developments that have taken place since the publication of the last edition. As with our previous editions, our aim has been to provide a clear explanation of the law of contract. As well as setting out the law itself, we look at the principles behind it, and discuss some of the issues and debates arising from contract law. We hope that the material will allow you to enter into some of that debate and develop your own views as to how the law should develop.

One of our priorities in writing this book has been to explain the material clearly, so that it is easy to understand, without lowering the quality of the content. Too often, law is avoided as a difficult subject, when the real difficulty is the vocabulary and style of legal textbooks. For that reason, we have aimed to use 'plain English' as far as possible, and explain the more complex legal terminology where it arises. There is also a glossary explaining common terms at the back of the book. In addition, chapters are structured so that material is in a systematic order for the purposes of both learning and revision, and clear subheadings make specific points easy to locate.

Although we hope that many readers will use this book to satisfy a general interest in the law, we recognise that the majority will be those who have to sit an examination in the subject. Therefore, each chapter features typical examination questions, with detailed guidance on answering them, using the material in the book. This is obviously useful at revision time, but we recommend that, when first reading the book, you take the opportunity offered by the questions sections to think through the material that you have just read and look at it from different angles. This will help you both to understand and to remember it. You will also find that the Appendix at the end of the book gives useful general advice on answering examination questions on contract law.

This book is part of a series that has been produced by the authors. The other books in the series are *English Legal System*, *Criminal Law* and *Tort Law*.

We would like to thank Elliot Schatzberger of Middlesex University for his help in updating this edition.

We have endeavoured to state the law as at 1 January 2015.

Catherine Elliott and Frances Quinn
London 2015

# Acknowledgements

We are grateful to the following for permission to reproduce the following copyright material:

## Figures

Figure 16.4 from *A Trader's Guide: The Law Relating to the Supply of Goods and Services*, DTI (2005) available at www.berr.gov.uk/files/file25486.pdf, Crown Copyright material is reproduced with permission under the terms of the Click-Use Licence.

## Text

Exam Board Questions on pp. 45, 242, 305, 336, 337 and 423 London External LLB, University of London, reproduced by permission of University of London International Academy; www. londoninternational.ac.uk; Exam Board Questions on pp. 46, 48, 114, 115, 218, 243, 281, 336 and 389 from Oxford/OCR,reproduced by permission of OCR, please note the model answers have not been seen or verified by OCR and are the work of the author(s); Exam Board Questions on pp. 47 and 424 from WJEC, reproduced by permission of WJEC; Exam Board Questions on pp. 149, 186, 282, 337, 387, 389, 392 and 425 from AQA, AQA examination questions are reproduced by permission of AQA, please note the model answers are the work of the author(s), have neither been provided or approved by AQA and they may not necessarily constitute the only possible solutions.

The examination boards are not responsible for any suggested answers to the questions.

In some instances we have been unable to trace the owners of copyright material and we would appreciate any information that would enable us to do so.

# Table of cases

# Table of statutes

# Table of statutory instruments

# Table of EC legislation

# Introduction

Ask most people to describe a contract, and they will talk about a piece of paper – the documents you sign when you start a job, buy a house or hire a television, for example. While it is certainly true that these documents are often contracts, in law the term has a wider meaning, covering any legally binding agreement, written or unwritten. In order to be legally binding, an agreement must satisfy certain requirements (which will be discussed in Part 1) but with a few exceptions, being in writing is not one of those requirements. We make contracts when we buy goods at the supermarket, when we get on a bus or train, and when we put money into a machine to buy chocolate or drinks – all without a word being written down, or sometimes even spoken.

## Why do we need contract law?

The obvious answer is because promises should be binding, but in fact the law only enforces certain types of promise, essentially those which involve some form of exchange. A promise for which nothing is given in return is called a gratuitous promise, and is not usually enforceable in law (the exception is where such a promise is put into a formal document called a deed).

Why then do we need laws specifically designed to enforce promises involving an exchange? The major reason appears to be the kind of society we live in, which is called a market capitalist society. In such a society, people buy and sell fairly freely, making their own bargains, both on the small scale of ordinary shoppers in supermarkets, and on the much bigger one of a project such as the construction of the Channel Tunnel, which involved many different parties, each buying and selling goods and services. Although, as we shall see, there are areas in which government intervenes, in general we choose what we want to buy, who from and, to some extent at least, at what price.

It would be impossible to run a society on this basis if promises were not binding. Long-term projects show this very clearly – contractors working on the Channel Tunnel, for example, would have been very reluctant to invest time and money on the project if they knew that the British and French Governments could suddenly decide that they did not want a tunnel after all, and not be expected to compensate the contractors. On a smaller scale, who would book a package holiday if the tour operator was free to decide not to fly you home at the end of it? How would manufacturers run their businesses if customers could simply withdraw orders, even though the goods had been made specially for them? A market economy will only work efficiently if its members can plan their business activities, and they can only do this if they know that they can rely on promises made to them.

In fact, contract law rarely forces a party to fulfil contractual promises, but what it does do is try to compensate innocent parties financially, usually by attempting to put them in the position they would have been in if the contract had been performed as agreed. This has the double function of helping parties to know what they can expect if the contract is not performed, and encouraging performance by ensuring that those who fail to perform cannot simply get away with their breach.

## The origins of contract law

In order to understand the rationale underlying contract law, it helps to know a little about its history. Although some principles of contract law go back three centuries, the majority of contract rules were established in the early nineteenth century. Before that, contract hardly existed as a separate branch of law, and took up very few pages in textbooks. Yet today, it is one of the core subjects which lawyers must study, and affects many areas of daily life. What caused the change?

The answer lies in the transformation of our society which occurred during the late eighteenth and early nineteenth centuries, a transformation which has been described as a move from status to contract. Today, we are very used to the important role that 'the market' plays in our society. We take it for granted that, for example, the price of food should generally be set by the manufacturer or retailer, with the customer choosing to take it or leave it. We may not actually negotiate a bargain in many areas of ordinary life, but we see the operation of the market in the fact that manufacturers have to set prices at which people will buy. We would be rather surprised if Parliament suddenly made it illegal to charge more than 50p for a loaf of bread.

Before the nineteenth century, however, there were many areas of life where free negotiation and bargaining were simply not an issue. An example is the market for what were regarded as essential foodstuffs, which included wheat, bread and beer. Although bakers and millers were entitled to make a profit, that did not mean they could sell at whatever price people would pay. Prices and quality standards for bread were fixed, according to the price the baker had had to pay for the wheat, so limiting their profits, and ensuring that they could not take advantage of shortages.

Activities such as buying goods and then selling them in the same market at a higher price, buying up supplies before they reached the market, and cornering the market by buying huge stocks of a particular commodity are all seen as good business practice now, but in the eighteenth-century market for essential foodstuffs, they were criminal offences, called regrating, forestalling and engrossing respectively. The basis for this approach was explained by Kenyon J in **R** v **Rusby**: 'Though in a status society some may have greater luxuries and comfort than others, all should have the necessaries of life.' In other words, there was a basic right to a reasonable standard of living, and nobody was expected to negotiate that standard for themselves.

A similar, though less humane, approach was taken to relationships between employer and employee – or master and servant, as they were called then. These days, we expect to have an employment contract detailing our hours of work, duties and pay, even though the amount of control we actually have in negotiating those areas may be negligible. In a status society, employment obligations were simply derived from whether you were a master or a servant; masters were entitled to ask servants to do more or less anything, and criminal sanctions could be used against an employee who disobeyed. Employers had obligations too (though rather less onerous than those of employees), which sometimes included supplying food or medical care. Both sets of obligations were seen as fixed for everyone who was either an employee or an employer, and not a matter for individual negotiation. Even wages were often set by local magistrates.

All this began to change in the eighteenth and nineteenth centuries. Society itself was undergoing huge changes, moving from an agricultural to an industrial economy, and with that came political changes, and changes in the way people saw society. With the rise of an economic doctrine called *laissez-faire* came a view that society was no more than a collection of self-interested individuals, each of whom was the best judge of their own interests, and should, as far as possible, be left alone to pursue those interests. If we apply this view to the market for bread, for example, it would suggest that bakers would sell bread for the highest price they could get, while consumers shopped around for the lowest, and the result should be a bargain suitable to both. The market would consist of hundreds and hundreds of similar transactions, with the result that everyone would be able to secure their own best interests, and the state would not need to intervene to do this for them – in fact it should not do so, because the parties should be left alone to decide what was best for them.

This *laissez-faire* approach carved out a very important place for contracts. As we have seen, where people make their own transactions, unregulated by the state, it is important that they keep their promises, and as a result, contract law became an increasingly important way of enforcing obligations.

# Freedom of contract

Its origins in the *laissez-faire* doctrine of the nineteenth century have had enormous influence on the development of contract law. Perhaps the most striking reflection of this is the importance traditionally placed on freedom of contract. This doctrine promotes the idea that since parties are the best judges of their own interests, they should be free to make contracts on any terms they choose – on the assumption that nobody would choose unfavourable terms. Once this choice is made, the job of the courts is simply to act as an umpire, holding the parties to their promises; it is not the courts' role to ask whether the bargain made was a fair one.

Some academics, notably Professor Atiyah (*The Rise and Fall of Freedom of Contract*, 1985), have suggested that this extreme position lasted only a short time, and that the courts were always concerned to establish some concept of fairness. His view has been challenged, but in any case, it is clear that over the last century, the courts have moved away from their reluctance to intervene, sometimes of their own accord, sometimes under the guidance of Parliament through legislation such as the Unfair Contract Terms Act 1977. However, as the basic principle still holds, decisions which actually have their basis in notions of fairness may be disguised behind more technical issues.

# Contract and fairness

Traditional contract law lays down rules which are designed to apply in any contractual situation, regardless of who the parties are, their relationship to each other, and the subject matter of a contract. This means that the law uses basically the same rules to analyse the contract that arises when you go into a supermarket to buy a tin of beans as it does to analyse the contract to build the Channel Tunnel.

The basis for this approach is derived from the *laissez-faire* belief that parties should be left alone to make their own bargains. This, it was thought, required the law simply to provide a framework, allowing parties to know what they had to do to make their agreements binding. This framework was intended to treat everybody equally, since to make different rules for one type of contracting party than for another would be to intervene in the fairness of the bargain. As a result, the same rules were applied to contracts in which both parties had equal bargaining power (between two businesses, for example) as to those where one party had significantly less economic power, or legal or technical knowledge, such as a consumer contract.

This approach, often called procedural fairness, or formal justice, was judged to be fair because it treats everybody equally, favouring no one. The problem with it is that if people are unequal to begin with, treating them equally simply maintains the inequality. This has obvious repercussions in contract law. Take, for example, an employment contract stating that if either party is dissatisfied with the other's performance, the dissatisfied party can terminate the contract at any time. This clearly amounts to treating both parties in exactly the same way, making them play by the same rules. But in doing so, it gives the more powerful employer the useful opportunity to sack the employee at any time, while the corresponding 'benefit' to the less powerful employee will in many cases amount to no more than the chance to become unemployed.

Over the last century the law has to some extent moved away from simple procedural fairness, and an element of what is called substantive fairness, or distributive justice, has developed. Substantive fairness aims to redress the balance of power between unequal parties, giving protection to the weaker one. So, for example, terms are now implied by law into employment contracts so that employers cannot simply dismiss employees without reasonable grounds for doing so. Similar protections have been given to tenants and to consumers, and in these three areas (and some others) traditional contract rules are overlaid with special rules applying only to particular types of contract. (You can see the way in which this approach operates in Chapter 16.)

The balance between substantive and procedural fairness in contract law is always an uneasy one, but major academics such as Treitel (*The Law of Contract*, 2007) and Atiyah believe that there has been, as Atiyah puts it, 'a move from principle to pragmatism'. He suggests that in modern cases, the courts have been less concerned with laying down general rules, and more with producing justice in individual cases. In fact, an examination of the cases, especially those between businesses, where bargaining power is assumed to be equal, shows that although the courts are often attempting to secure substantive justice, they still tend to hide that attempt behind what appears to be an application of the traditional rules. The cases on innominate terms (p. 145), and on reasonable notice, particularly **Interfoto** (see p. 161), have been seen as examples of this.

# The objective approach

Contract law claims to be about enforcing obligations which the parties have voluntarily assumed. Bearing in mind that contracts do not have to be in writing, and that even where they are, important points may be left out, it is clear that contract law faces a problem: how to find out what – or even whether – the parties agreed. For example, if I promise to clean your car, meaning that I will wash the outside, and you promise to give me £10 in return, assuming that I will vacuum the inside as well, what have we agreed?

Contract law's approach to this problem is to look for the appearance of consent. If my words and/or actions would suggest to a reasonable person that I was agreeing to clean the inside of your car as well as the outside, then that is what I will have to do before I get my £10. This approach was explained by Blackburn J in **Smith** v **Hughes** (1871): 'If, whatever a man's real intention may be, he so conducts himself that a reasonable man would believe he was assenting to the terms proposed by the other party, and that other party upon that belief enters into the contract with him, the man thus conducting himself would be equally bound as if he had intended to agree to the other party's terms.' This point was repeated by the Supreme Court in **RTS Flexible Systems** v **Molkerei Alois Müller** (2010) where it stated:

> Whether there is a binding contract between the parties and, if so, upon what terms depends upon what they have agreed. It depends not upon their subjective state of mind, but upon a consideration of what was communicated between them by words or conduct, and whether that leads objectively to a conclusion that they intended to create legal relations and had agreed upon all the terms which they regarded or the law requires as essential for the formation of legally binding relations.

In some cases, the basis for this approach is obvious. If you get into a taxi and simply state your destination, it is perfectly reasonable for the driver to assume you are agreeing to pay for the ride; it would not be right to allow you to claim at the end that although your behaviour might have suggested that, you had no such intention in your mind, and so are not obliged to pay. In practice, the principle has led to some potentially harsh results, such as the rule, established in a case called **L'Estrange** v **F Graucob Ltd** (1934), that a person who signs a contractual document is bound by it, even though they may not have understood or even read it.

# The Human Rights Act 1998

The Human Rights Act 1998 came into force on 2 October 2000. This Act incorporates the European Convention on Human Rights into English law so that rights contained in the Convention can be enforced by English courts. The Act has not yet had a major impact on contract law, and the extent of any future impact depends on how it is interpreted. Under s. 3 of the Act, legislation on the subject of contract law will have to conform with the Convention. This section states:

> So far as it is possible to do so, primary legislation and subordinate legislation must be read and given effect in a way which is compatible with Convention rights.

If legislation is found to be incompatible with Convention rights, then the courts may make a 'declaration of incompatibility' (s. 4).

Contracts are frequently made by private individuals and businesses, though some contracts are made with public authorities, such as a local council. Section 6 of the Act states that it is 'unlawful for a public authority to act in a way which is incompatible with a Convention right'. There has been considerable debate as to whether the Act would affect a contract which was only made between private individuals so that a public authority is not a party to the contract.

Many of the Convention rights are unlikely to be relevant to contracts, but one provision which could be important in this context is Article 1 of the First Protocol. This provides that 'every natural or legal person is entitled to the peaceful enjoyment of his possessions. No one shall be deprived of his possessions except in the public interest and subject to law'. The implications of this provision on contract law were considered by the Court of Appeal in **Shanshal** v **Al-Kishtaini** (2001) (which is discussed at p. 261).

## Topical Issue

### The influence of Europe

European law has had an increasing impact on contract law in England. A range of European directives have been passed, particularly in the field of consumer law. The aim of these directives has been to promote the development of an internal European market by harmonising the relevant law across Europe. But these directives have been quite narrow in scope and have been criticised for having an inconsistent drafting style. In addition, there have been significant differences in the way the directives have been implemented in the various European countries, so the aim of harmonisation has not been completely achieved. As a result, the European Commission published a *Communication on European Contract Law* (2001). This document considered whether the European Union needed to change its approach to contract law. It identified four options:

- do nothing, and leave the market to resolve any problems that arose;
- draw up common principles of contract law which would provide guidance to member states, but would not bind them;
- improve the existing European directives in the field to achieve greater consistency;
- adopt binding principles of contract law.

This document led to considerable debate and in 2003 the European Commission published an action plan. It concluded that Europe would continue to issue directives in the field. It would encourage the use of standard European contractual terms for certain types of contract. It would give further consideration as to whether in the future a code of European contract law should be drawn up which might or might not be binding in member states. For the time being it would focus on the development of a 'Common Frame of Reference for European Contract Law'. The final draft of the Common Frame of Reference containing recommendations on model rules, principles and definitions was published in December 2008.

In 2011 the European Commission published a proposed regulation for a Common European Sales Law (CESL). This draws heavily on the draft Common Frame of Reference. It is a proposed law for the sale of goods across Europe which could be applied to both business to consumer (B2C) transactions and business to business (B2B) transactions (where at least one business is a small or medium enterprise). It would not replace national law, but be an optional law that the trader could opt to use for its transactions. If it wanted a transaction to be governed by CESL, it would provide a leaflet to the consumer explaining this and the consumer would have to agree to this for the sale to proceed.

The aim of the CESL is to energise the EU economy by improving cross-border trade within the EU by removing legal barriers which increase the cost of doing business with other member states. The European Commission estimates that 500 million consumers in Europe are missing out on greater choice and cheaper prices on goods because businesses are not making cross-border offers. At the moment only 9 per cent of consumers in the EU buy goods from a trader located in another member state.

For consumers, internet shopping is the way in which they are most likely to buy goods across borders. The UK has one of the most developed internet economies in the world, but internet traders are often small enterprises run from home. Under a regulation known as Rome I, the current law provides that a trader which directs its activities to another EU member state must comply with the mandatory consumer protection laws of that state. There is uncertainty over when a trader will be viewed as 'directing activities' to a member state. It is a fine line between an English business setting up a website which is accessed by consumers in France and an English company getting regular orders from France and making changes to its website to facilitate those orders (such as quoting reviews from French customers and accepting orders in euros). In the latter scenario a company may be found to be 'directing activities' to France (**Peter Pammer** v **Reederei Karl Schlüter** (2011)). If the local consumer laws in France apply this would include the *Loi Toubon* which imposes a criminal sanction if websites are not translated into French.

Critics have argued that the CESL would add unnecessary confusion and legal complexity to consumer law. It is over 100 pages long and includes vague legal terms such as 'reasonableness', 'fair dealing' and 'good faith' which will leave a lot of discretion to the courts, which might interpret them differently in different member states. It gives consumers a right to reject faulty goods for up to two years from the date the consumer could be expected to be aware of the fault. Retailers fear that such a long period could be abused by consumers who simply no longer want the goods. While businesses could deduct money to reflect the consumer's use of the item, this calculation could be a source of dispute. Even if a common sales law existed across Europe, should litigation arise, language barriers and differences in national court procedures would remain a problem. The CESL would not cover every aspect of contract law, so knowledge of the local law of contract might still prove necessary, for example, on the issue of illegality and ownership of the goods.

The Law Commission has suggested that practical problems rather than legal differences are the real barrier to cross-border trade. Fear of fraud, language barriers, VAT complexities and problems with delivery and payment are more likely to be discouraging cross-border transactions than a lack of harmonisation in consumer law. The Law Commission has suggested that instead of the CESL, there should be an optional European distance selling code which would primarily apply to internet sales.

 ## Reading list

Adams and Brownsword, 'The ideologies of contract' (1987) 7 Legal Studies 205

Atiyah (1985) *The Rise and Fall of Freedom of Contract*, Oxford: Oxford University Press

Jansen and Zimmerman 'Restating the Acquis Communautaire? A critical examination of the "Principles of the Existing EC Contract Law"' (2008) 71(4) Modern Law Review 505

McKendrick, 'English contract law: a rich past, an uncertain future?' (1997) Current Legal Problems 25

Steyn, 'Contract law: fulfilling the reasonable expectations of honest men' (1997) 113 Law Quarterly Review 433

Treitel and Peel (2007) *Treitel on the Law of Contract*, London: Sweet and Maxwell

### Reading on the internet

The Human Rights Act 1998 is available on the website of the Office of Public Sector Information: http://www.opsi.gov.uk/acts/acts1998/19980042.htm

The *Communication on European Contract Law* (2001) issued by the European Commission is available on its website at:

http://ec.europa.eu/comm/consumers/cons_int/safe_shop/fair_bus_pract/cont_law/cont_law_02_en.pdf

# Part 1
## The formation of a contract

There are five basic requirements that need to be satisfied in order to make a contract:

- **An agreement** between the parties (which is usually shown by the fact that one has made an offer and the other has accepted it).
- **An intention** to be legally bound by that agreement (often called intent to create legal relations).
- **Certainty** as to the terms of the agreement.
- **Capacity** to contract.
- **Consideration** provided by each of the parties – put simply, this means that there must be some kind of exchange between the parties. If I say I will give you my car, and you simply agree to have it, I have voluntarily made you a promise (often called a gratuitous promise), which you cannot enforce in law if I change my mind. If, however, I promise to hand over my car and you promise to pay me a sum of money in return, we have each provided consideration.

In addition, in some cases, the parties must comply with certain formalities. Remember that, with a few exceptions, it is **not** necessary for a contract to be in writing – a contract is an agreement, not a piece of paper.

In this part of the book we will consider these different requirements for the creation of a contract.

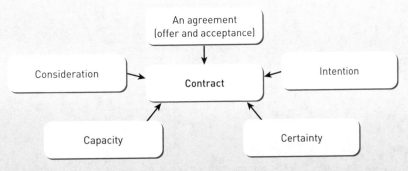

# Chapter 1
## Offer and acceptance

**This chapter discusses:**

- the formation of a contract by one party making an offer which is accepted by another party;
- the distinction between unilateral and bilateral contracts;
- the distinction between an offer and an invitation to treat;
- how long an offer lasts;
- what amounts to a valid acceptance; and
- the requirement that an acceptance must be communicated along with the postal rule exception.

For a contract to exist, usually one party must have made an offer, and the other must have accepted it. Once acceptance takes effect, a contract will usually be binding on both parties, and the rules of offer and acceptance are typically used to pinpoint when a series of negotiations has passed that point, in order to decide whether the parties are obliged to fulfil their promises. There is generally no halfway house – negotiations have either crystallised into a binding contract, or they are not binding at all.

# Unilateral and bilateral contracts

In order to understand the law on offer and acceptance, you need to understand the concepts of unilateral and bilateral contracts. Most contracts are bilateral. This means that each party takes on an obligation, usually by promising the other something – for example, Ann promises to sell something and Ben to buy it. (Although contracts where there are mutual obligations are always called bilateral, there may in fact be more than two parties to such a contract.)

By contrast, a unilateral contract arises where only one party assumes an obligation under the contract. Examples might be promising to give your mother £50 if she gives up smoking for a year, or to pay a £100 reward to anyone who finds your lost purse, or, as the court suggested in **Great Northern Railway Co** v **Witham** (1873), to pay someone £100 to walk from London to York. What makes these situations unilateral contracts is that only one party has assumed an obligation – you are obliged to pay your mother if she gives up smoking, but she has not promised in turn to give up smoking. Similarly, you are obliged to pay the reward to anyone who finds your purse, but nobody need actually have undertaken to do so.

A common example of a unilateral contract is that between estate agents and people trying to sell their houses – the seller promises to pay a specified percentage of the house price to the estate agent if the house is sold, but the estate agent is not required to promise in return to sell the house, or even to try to do so.

**Figure 1.1** Bilateral and unilateral contracts

# Offer

The person making an offer is called the offeror, and the person to whom the offer is made is called the offeree. A communication will be treated as an offer if it indicates the terms on which the offeror is prepared to make a contract (such as the price of the goods for sale), and gives a clear indication that the offeror intends to be bound by those terms if they are accepted by the offeree.

**Figure 1.2** Offeror and offeree

An offer may be express, as when Ann tells Ben that she will sell her CD player for £200, but it can also be implied from conduct – a common example is taking goods to the cash desk in a supermarket, which is an implied offer to buy those goods.

 ## Offers to the public at large

In most cases, an offer will be made to a specified person – as when Ann offers to sell her computer to Ben. However, offers can be addressed to a group of people, or even to the general public. For example, a student may offer to sell her old textbooks to anyone in the year below, or the owner of a lost dog may offer a reward to anyone who finds it.

### Key Case    Carlill v Carbolic Smoke Ball Co

In **Carlill v Carbolic Smoke Ball Co** (1893) the defendants were the manufacturers of 'smokeballs' which they claimed could prevent flu. They published advertisements stating that if anyone used their smokeballs for a specified time and still caught flu, they would pay that person £100, and that to prove they were serious about the claim, they had deposited £1,000 with their bankers.

Mrs Carlill bought and used a smokeball, but nevertheless ended up with flu. She therefore claimed the £100, which the company refused to pay. They argued that their advertisement could not give rise to a contract, since it was impossible to make a contract with the whole world, and that therefore they were not legally bound to pay the money. This argument was rejected by the court, which held that the advertisement did constitute an offer to the world at large, which became a contract when it was accepted by Mrs Carlill using the smokeball and getting flu. She was therefore entitled to the £100.

#### Legal Principle
Offers can be addressed to the general public and are accepted when the offer is acted upon by a member of the general public. Advertisements for unilateral contracts are generally treated as offers.

A more recent illustration is provided by the Court of Appeal in **Bowerman v Association of British Travel Agents Ltd** (1996). A school had booked a skiing holiday with a tour operator which was a member of the Association of British Travel Agents (ABTA). All members of this association display a notice provided by ABTA which states:

Where holidays or other travel arrangements have not yet commenced at the time of failure [of the tour operator], ABTA arranges for you to be reimbursed the money you have paid in respect of your holiday arrangements.

The tour operator became insolvent and cancelled the skiing holiday. The school was refunded the money they had paid for the holiday, but not the cost of the wasted travel insurance. The claimant brought an action against ABTA to seek reimbursement of the cost of this insurance. He argued, and the Court of Appeal agreed, that the ABTA notice constituted an offer which the customer accepted by contracting with an ABTA member.

A contract arising from an offer to the public at large, like that in **Carlill**, is usually a unilateral contract.

# Invitations to treat

Some kinds of transaction involve a preliminary stage in which one party invites the other to make an offer. This stage is called an invitation to treat.

 **Key Case**   Gibson *v* Manchester City Council

In **Gibson *v* Manchester City Council** (1979) a council tenant was interested in buying his house. He completed an application form and received a letter from the Council stating that it 'may be prepared to sell the house to you' for £2,180. Mr Gibson initially queried the purchase price, pointing out that the path to the house was in a bad condition. The Council refused to change the price, saying that the price had been fixed taking into account the condition of the property. Mr Gibson then wrote on 18 March 1971 asking the Council to 'carry on with the purchase as per my application'. Following a change in political control of the Council in May 1971, it decided to stop selling Council houses to tenants, and Mr Gibson was informed that the Council would not proceed with the sale of the house. Mr Gibson brought legal proceedings claiming that the letter he had received stating the purchase price was an offer which he had accepted on 18 March 1971. The House of Lords, however, ruled that the Council had not made an offer; the letter giving the purchase price was merely one step in the negotiations for a contract and amounted only to an invitation to treat. Its purpose was simply to invite the making of a 'formal application', amounting to an offer, from the tenant.

**Legal Principle**
Negotiations to enter into a contract can amount to an invitation to treat but not an offer.

Confusion can sometimes arise when what would appear, in the everyday sense of the word, to be an offer is held by the law to be only an invitation to treat. This issue arises particularly in the following areas.

**Figure 1.3** Gibson *v* Manchester City Council (1979)

## Advertisements

A distinction is generally made between advertisements for a unilateral contract, and those for a bilateral contract.

### Advertisements for unilateral contracts

These include advertisements such as the one in **Carlill** *v* **Carbolic Smoke Ball Co**, or those offering rewards for the return of lost property, or for information leading to the arrest or conviction of a criminal. They are usually treated as offers, on the basis that the contract can normally be accepted without any need for further negotiations between the parties, and the person making the advertisement intends to be bound by it.

### Advertisements for a bilateral contract

These are the type of advertisements which advertise specified goods at a certain price, such as those found at the back of newspapers and magazines. They are usually considered invitations to treat, on the grounds that they may lead to further bargaining – potential buyers might want to negotiate about the price, for example – and that since stocks could run out, it would be unreasonable to expect the advertisers to sell to everybody who applied.

In **Partridge** *v* **Crittenden** (1968), an advertisement in a magazine stated 'Bramblefinch cocks and hens, 25s each'. As the Bramblefinch was a protected species, the person who placed the advertisement was charged with unlawfully offering for sale a wild bird contrary to the Protection of Birds Act 1954, but his conviction was quashed on the grounds that the advertisement was not an offer but an invitation to treat.

It was held in **Grainger & Sons** *v* **Gough** (1896) that the circulation of a price-list by a wine merchant was not an offer to sell at those prices but merely an invitation to treat.

## Shopping

Price-marked goods on display on the shelves or in the windows of shops are generally regarded as invitations to treat, rather than offers to sell goods at that price. In **Fisher** *v* **Bell** (1960) the defendant had displayed flick knives in his shop window, and was convicted of the criminal offence of offering such knives for sale. On appeal, Lord Parker CJ stated that the display of an article with a price on it in a shop window was only an invitation to treat and not an offer, and the conviction was overturned.

Where goods are sold on a self-service basis, the customer makes an offer to buy when presenting the goods at the cash desk, and the shopkeeper may accept or reject that offer.

## Key Case — Pharmaceutical Society of Great Britain *v* Boots Cash Chemists (Southern) Ltd

In **Pharmaceutical Society of Great Britain *v* Boots Cash Chemists (Southern) Ltd** (1953) Boots were charged with an offence concerning the sale of certain medicines which could only be sold by or under the supervision of a qualified pharmacist. Two customers in a self-service shop selected the medicines, which were price-marked, from the open shelves, and placed them in the shop's wire baskets. The shelves were not supervised by a pharmacist, but a pharmacist had been instructed to supervise the transaction at the cash desk. The issue was therefore whether the sale had taken place at the shelves or at the cash desk.

The Court of Appeal decided the shelf display was like an advertisement for a bilateral contract, and was therefore merely an invitation to treat. The offer was made by the customer when medicines were placed in the basket and presented at the cash desk, and was only accepted by the shop at the cash desk. Since a pharmacist was supervising at that point no offence had been committed.

### Legal Principle
Where goods are sold on a self-service basis, the customer makes an offer to buy when presenting the goods at the cash desk.

There are two main practical consequences of this principle. First, shops do not have to sell goods at the marked price; so if a shop assistant wrongly marks a CD at £2.99 rather than £12.99, for example, you cannot insist on buying it at that price (though the shop may be committing an offence under the Trade Descriptions Act 1968 – see Chapter 16 on consumer contracts). Secondly, a customer cannot insist on buying a particular item on display – so you cannot make a shopkeeper sell you the sweater in the window even if there are none left inside the shop. Displaying the goods is not an offer, so a customer cannot accept it and thereby make a binding contract.

## Timetables and tickets for transport

The legal position here is rather unclear. Is a bus timetable an offer to run services at those times, or just an invitation to treat? Does the bus pulling up at a stop constitute an offer to carry you, which you accept by boarding the bus? Or, again, is even this stage just an invitation to treat, so that the offer is actually made by you getting on the bus or by handing over money for the ticket? These points may seem academic, but they become important when something goes wrong. If, for example, the bus crashes and you are injured, your ability to sue for breach of contract will depend on whether the contract had actually been completed when the accident occurred.

Although there have been many cases in this area, no single reliable rule has emerged, and it seems that the exact point at which a contract is made depends in each case on the particular facts. For example, in **Denton** v **GN Railway** (1856) it was said that railway company advertisements detailing the times at and conditions under which trains would run were offers. But in **Wilkie** v **London Passenger Transport Board** (1947) Lord Greene thought that a contract between bus company and passenger was made when a person intending to travel 'puts himself either on the platform or inside the bus'. The opinion was *obiter* but, if correct, it implies that the company makes an offer of carriage by running the bus or train and the passenger accepts when he or she gets properly on board, completing the contract. Therefore, if the bus crashed, an injured passenger could have a claim against the bus company for breach of contract despite not having yet paid the fare or been given a ticket.

However, in **Thornton** v **Shoe Lane Parking Ltd** (1971) it was suggested that the contract may be formed rather later. If the legal principles laid down in **Thornton** are applied to this factual situation, it would appear that passengers asking for a ticket to their destination are making an invitation to treat. The bus company makes an offer by issuing the tickets, and the passengers accept the offer by keeping the tickets without objection. Fortunately, these questions are not governed solely by the law of contract, as some legislation relevant to the field of public transport has since been passed.

There are other less common situations in which the courts will have to decide whether a communication is an offer or merely an invitation to treat. The test used is whether a person watching the proceedings would have thought the party concerned was making an offer or not (the objective approach discussed at p. 5).

# How long does an offer last?

An offer may cease to exist under any of the following circumstances.

## Specified time

Where an offeror states that an offer will remain open for a specific length of time, it lapses when that time is up (though it can be revoked before that – see p. 19 below).

## Reasonable length of time

Where the offeror has not specified how long the offer will remain open, it will lapse after a reasonable length of time has passed. Exactly how long this is will depend upon whether the means of communicating the offer were fast or slow and on its subject matter – for example, offers to buy perishable goods, or a commodity whose price fluctuates daily, will lapse quite quickly. Offers to buy shares on the stock market may last only seconds.

In **Ramsgate Victoria Hotel Ltd** v **Montefiore** (1866) the defendant, Montefiore, applied for shares in the company, paying a deposit into their bank. After hearing nothing from them for five months, he was then informed that the shares had been allotted to him, and asked to pay the balance due on them. He refused to do so, and the court upheld his argument that five months was not a reasonable length of time for acceptance of an offer to buy shares, which are a commodity with a rapidly fluctuating price. Therefore the offer had lapsed before the company tried to accept it, and there was no contract between them.

## Failure of a precondition

Some offers are made subject to certain conditions, and if such conditions are not in place, the offer may lapse. For example, a person might offer to sell their bike for £50 if they manage to buy a car at the weekend. In **Financings Ltd** *v* **Stimson** (1962) the defendant saw a car for sale at £350 by a second-hand car dealer on 16 March. He decided to buy it on hire-purchase terms. The way that hire purchase works in such cases is that the finance company buys the car outright from the dealer, and then sells it to the buyer, who pays in instalments. The defendant would therefore be buying the car from the finance company (the claimants), rather than from the dealer. The defendant signed the claimants' form, which stated that the agreement would be binding on the finance company only when signed on their behalf. The car dealer did not have the authority to do this, so it had to be sent to the claimants for signing. On 18 March the defendant paid the first instalment of £70. On 24 March the car was stolen from the dealer's premises. It was later found, badly damaged and the defendant no longer wanted to buy it. Not knowing this, on 25 March the claimants signed the written 'agreement'. They subsequently sued the defendant for failure to pay the instalments. The Court of Appeal ruled in favour of the defendant, as the so-called 'agreement' was really an offer to make a contract with the claimants, which was subject to the implied condition that the car remained in much the same state as it was in when the offer was made, until that offer was accepted. The claimants were arguing that they had accepted the offer by signing the document on 25 March. As the implied condition had been broken by then, the offer was no longer open so no contract had been concluded.

## Rejection

An offer lapses when the offeree rejects it. If Ann offers to sell Ben her car on Tuesday, and Ben says no, Ben cannot come back on Wednesday and insist on accepting the offer.

## Counter-offer

A counter-offer terminates the original offer.

### Key Case   Hyde *v* Wrench

In **Hyde** *v* **Wrench** (1840) the defendant offered to sell his farm for £1,000, and the claimant responded by offering to buy it at £950 – this is called making a counter-offer. The farm owner refused to sell at that price, and when the claimant later tried to accept the offer to buy at £1,000, it was held that this offer was no longer available; it had been terminated by the counter-offer. In this situation the offeror can make a new offer on exactly the same terms, but is not obliged to do so.

**Legal Principle**
A counter-offer terminates the original offer.

# Requests for information

A request for information about an offer (such as whether delivery could be earlier than suggested) does not amount to a counter-offer, so the original offer remains open. In **Stevenson Jaques & Co v McLean** (1880) the defendant made an offer on a Saturday to sell iron to the claimants at a cash-on-delivery price of 40 shillings, and stated that the offer would remain available until the following Monday. The claimants replied by asking if they could buy the goods on credit. They received no answer. On Monday afternoon they contacted the defendant to accept the offer, but the iron had already been sold to someone else.

When the claimants sued for breach of contract, it was held that their reply to the offer had been merely a request for information, not a counter-offer, so the original offer still stood and there was a binding contract.

# Death of the offeror

The position is not entirely clear, but it appears that if the offeree knows that the offeror has died, the offer will lapse; if the offeree is unaware of the offeror's death, it probably will not (**Bradbury v Morgan** (1862)). So if, for example, A promises to sell her video recorder to B, then dies soon after, and B writes to accept the offer not knowing that A is dead, it seems that the people responsible for A's affairs after death would be obliged to sell the video recorder to B, and B would be obliged to pay the price to the executors.

However, where an offer requires personal performance by the offeror (such as painting a picture, or appearing in a film) it will usually lapse on the offeror's death.

# Death of the offeree

There is no English case on this point, but it seems probable that the offer lapses and cannot be accepted after the offeree's death by the offeree's representatives.

# Withdrawal of offer

The withdrawal of an offer is sometimes described as the revocation of an offer. The old case of **Payne v Cave** (1789) establishes the principle that an offer may be withdrawn at any time up until it is accepted. In **Routledge v Grant** (1828) the defendant made a provisional offer to buy the claimant's house at a specified price, 'a definite answer to be given within six weeks from date'. It was held that, regardless of this provision, the defendant still had the right to withdraw the offer at any moment before acceptance, even though the time limit had not expired.

A number of rules apply in relation to the withdrawal of offers.

## Withdrawal must be communicated

It is not enough for offerors simply to change their mind about an offer; they must notify the offeree that it is being revoked.

**Key Case**   Byrne & Co *v* Leon Van Tienhoven

In **Byrne & Co *v* Leon Van Tienhoven** (1880) the defendants were a company based in Cardiff. On 1 October they posted a letter to New York offering to sell the claimants 1,000 boxes of tinplates. Having received the letter on 11 October, the claimants immediately accepted by telegram. Acceptances sent by telegram take effect as soon as they are sent (see p. 30 below for details of the postal rule).

In the meantime, on 8 October, the defendants had written to revoke their offer, and this letter reached the claimants on 20 October. It was held that there was a binding contract, because revocation could only take effect on communication, but the acceptance by telegram took effect as soon as it was sent – in this case nine days before the revocation was received. By the time the second letter reached the claimants, a contract had already been made.

**Legal Principle**
An offer can only be withdrawn if it is communicated.

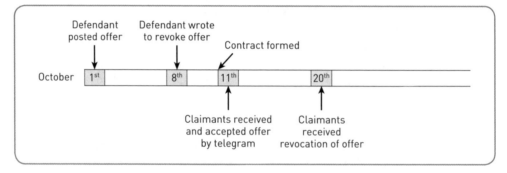

**Figure 1.4 Byrne *v* Van Tienhoven** (1880)

The revocation of an offer does not have to be communicated by the offeror; the communication can be made by some other reliable source.

**Key Case**   Dickinson *v* Dodds

In **Dickinson *v* Dodds** (1876) the defendant offered to sell a house to the claimant, the offer 'to be left open until Friday, June 12, 9 am'. On 11 June the defendant sold the house to a third party, Allan, and the claimant heard about the sale through a fourth man. Before 9 am on 12 June, the claimant handed the defendant a letter in which he said he was accepting the offer. It was held by the Court of Appeal that the offer had already been revoked by the communication from the fourth man, so there was no contract. By hearing the news from the fourth man, Dickinson 'knew that Dodds was no longer minded to sell the property to him as plainly and clearly as if Dodds had told him in so many words'.

**Legal Principle**
The revocation of an offer can be made by the offeror or some other reliable source.

An offeror who promises to keep an offer open for a specified period may still revoke that offer at any time before it is accepted, unless the promise to keep it open is supported by some consideration from the other party (by providing consideration the parties make a separate contract called an option).

An exception to the rule that the withdrawal must be communicated to the offeree exists where an offeree moves to a new address without notifying the offeror. In these circumstances, a withdrawal which is delivered to the offeree's last known address will be effective on delivery to that address. In the same way, where a withdrawal reaches the offeree, but the offeree simply fails to read it, the withdrawal probably still takes effect on reaching the offeree (see **The Brimnes** (1975) p. 30 below). This would be the position where a withdrawal by telex or fax reached the offeror's office during normal business hours, but was not actually seen or read by the offeree or by any of their staff until some time afterwards.

Many offices receive a lot of post every day. This post may not go directly to the person whose name is on the envelope, but is received, opened and sorted by clerical staff and then distributed to the relevant people. In these situations there may be some difficulty in pinpointing when the information in the letter is communicated for these purposes. Is it when the letter is received within the company, when it is opened, or when it is actually read by the relevant member of staff? There is no authority on the point but the approach of the courts would probably be that communication occurs when the letter is opened, even though there may in those circumstances be no true communication.

**Figure 1.5 Dickinson v Dodds** (1876)

In **Pickfords Ltd v Celestica Ltd** (2003) two offers were made by Pickfords, and the court had to decide whether the second offer had effectively withdrawn the first offer. Pickfords, the claimant, is a well-known furniture removal company. Celestica, the defendant, is an IT company which wished to use Pickfords services to move premises. The court observed:

> It is as if the facts of this case have been devised for an examination question on the law of contract for first year law students. They raise some basic questions in relation to offer and acceptance in the law of formation of contract.

The litigation turned on the meaning and effect of three documents. The first document was a fax that was dated 13 September 2001 and which estimated the cost of the removal as being £100,000, though the final cost would depend on how many vehicle loads would be required. The second document was more detailed and was sent to the defendant on 27 September 2001.

This contained a fixed quote for the removal of £98,760. The third document was a fax entitled 'Confirmation', which was sent by the defendant to the claimant and was dated 15 October 2001. This expressly referred to the fax dated 13 September 2001 and stated that the amount to be paid was 'not to exceed 100K'. The question for the court was whether the first offer on 13 September was capable of being accepted, or whether the second offer had withdrawn the first offer. The Court of Appeal concluded:

> In such a case, in my judgment, something more than the mere submission of the second quotation is required to indicate that [Pickfords] has withdrawn the first offer.

The question was whether the making of the second offer clearly indicated an intention on the part of the offeror to withdraw the first offer. The substantial differences between the two offers in this case went far beyond a mere difference in price which could have been explained as consistent with two alternative offers both being on the table for the defendant to choose which to accept. In the absence of any findings of fact as to the circumstances which gave rise to the second offer, the second offer superseded and revoked the first offer.

The fax was intended to be an acceptance of the first offer. Since the first offer had been revoked, the purported acceptance could not give rise to a contract. It was in law a counter-offer to accept the services offered by the claimant on the terms of the first offer, subject to the cap of £100,000. Since the work was carried out, this counter-offer must have been accepted by the claimant's conduct in carrying out the work.

## Withdrawal of an offer to enter into a unilateral contract

There are a number of special rules that apply in relation to the revocation of an offer to enter into a unilateral contract. An offer to enter into a unilateral contract cannot be revoked once the offeree has commenced performance.

**Key Case**   Errington *v* Errington

In **Errington** *v* **Errington** (1952) a father bought a house in his own name for £750, borrowing £500 of the price by means of a mortgage from a building society. He bought the house for his son and daughter-in-law to live in, and told them that if they met the mortgage repayments, the house would be signed over to them once the mortgage was paid off. The couple moved in, and began to pay the mortgage instalments, but they never in fact made a promise to continue with the payments until the mortgage was paid off, which meant that the contract was unilateral.

When the father later died, the people in charge of his financial affairs sought to withdraw the offer. The Court of Appeal held that it was too late to do so. The part-performance by the son and daughter-in-law prevented the offer from being withdrawn. The offer could only be withdrawn if the son and daughter-in-law ceased to make the payments.

**Legal Principle**
An offer for a unilateral contract cannot be revoked once the offeree has commenced performance.

In **Daulia Ltd** *v* **Four Millbank Nominees Ltd** (1978) the Court of Appeal stated that once an offeree had started to perform on a unilateral contract, it was too late for the offeror to revoke the offer. It should be noted that this statement was *obiter*, since the court found that the offeree in the case had in fact completed his performance before the supposed revocation.

There is an exception to this rule that part-performance following an offer to enter into a unilateral contract prevents revocation of the offer. This exception applies in the context of unilateral offers to enter into a contract with an estate agent to pay commission for the sale of a property. In **Luxor (Eastbourne) Ltd** *v* **Cooper** (1941) an owner of land had promised to pay an estate agent £10,000 in commission if the agent was able to find a buyer willing to pay £175,000 for the land. The arrangement was on the terms that are usual between estate agents and their clients, whereby the agent is paid commission if a buyer is found, and nothing if not. The House of Lords held that the owner in the case could revoke his promise at any time before the sale was completed, even after the estate agents had made extensive efforts to find a buyer or had stopped trying to do so.

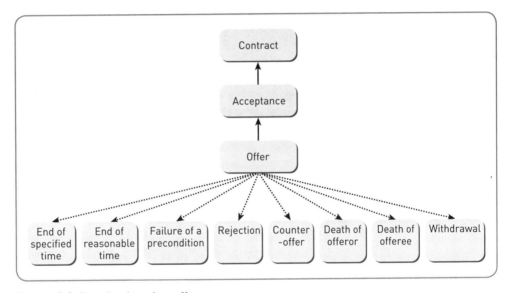

**Figure 1.6** Termination of an offer

Where a unilateral offer is made to the world at large, to be accepted by conduct, it can probably be revoked without the need for communication if the revocation takes place before performance has begun. For example, if you place a newspaper advertisement offering a reward for the return of something you have lost, and then decide you might actually be better off spending that money on replacing the item, it would probably be impossible for you to make sure that everyone who knew about the offer knows you are withdrawing it – even if you place a notice of withdrawal in the newspaper, you cannot guarantee that everyone concerned will see it. It seems to be enough for an offeror to take reasonable steps to bring the withdrawal to the attention of such persons, even though it may not be possible to ensure that they all know about it. Thus, in the American case of **Shuey** *v* **United States** (1875) it was held that an offer made by advertisement in a newspaper could be revoked by a similar advertisement, even though the second advertisement was not read by all the offerees.

# Acceptance

Acceptance of an offer means unconditional agreement to all the terms of that offer. Acceptance will often be oral or in writing, but in some cases an offeree may accept an offer by doing something, such as delivering goods in response to an offer to buy. The courts will only interpret conduct as indicating acceptance if it seems reasonable to infer that the offeree acted with the intention of accepting the offer.

In **Brogden** v **Metropolitan Rail Co** (1877) Brogden had supplied the railway company with coal for several years without any formal agreement. The parties then decided to make things official, so the rail company sent Brogden a draft agreement, which left a blank space for Brogden to insert the name of an arbitrator. After doing so and signing the document, Brogden returned it, marked 'approved'.

The company's employee put the draft away in a desk drawer, where it stayed for the next two years, without any further steps being taken regarding it. Brogden continued to supply coal under the terms of the contract, and the railway company to pay for it. Eventually a dispute arose between them, and Brogden denied that any binding contract existed.

The courts held that by inserting the arbitrator's name, Brogden added a new term to the potential contract, and therefore, in returning it to the railway company, he was offering (in fact counter-offering) to supply coal under the contract. But when was that offer accepted? The House of Lords decided that an acceptance by conduct could be inferred from the parties' behaviour, and a valid contract was completed either when the company first ordered coal after receiving the draft agreement from Brogden, or at the latest when he supplied the first lot of coal.

Merely remaining silent cannot amount to an acceptance, unless it is absolutely clear that acceptance was intended.

## Key Case     Felthouse v Bindley

In **Felthouse** v **Bindley** (1862) an uncle and his nephew had talked about the possible sale of the nephew's horse to the uncle, but there had been some confusion about the price. The uncle subsequently wrote to the nephew, offering to pay £30 and 15 shillings and saying, 'If I hear no more about him, I consider the horse mine at that price.' The nephew was on the point of selling off some of his property in an auction. He did not reply to the uncle's letter, but did tell the auctioneer to keep the horse out of the sale. The auctioneer forgot to do this, and the horse was sold. It was held that there was no contract between the uncle and the nephew. The court felt that the nephew's conduct in trying to keep the horse out of the sale did not necessarily imply that he intended to accept his uncle's offer – even though the nephew actually wrote afterwards to apologise for the mistake – and so it was not clear that his silence in response to the offer was intended to constitute acceptance. This can be criticised in that it is hard to see how there could have been clearer evidence that the nephew did actually intend to sell, but, on the other hand, there are many situations in which it would be undesirable and confusing for silence to amount to acceptance.

### Legal Principle
Merely remaining silent cannot amount to an acceptance, unless it is absolutely clear that acceptance was intended.

It has been pointed out by the Court of Appeal in **Re Selectmove Ltd** (1995) that an acceptance by silence could be sufficient if it was the offeree who suggested that their silence would be sufficient. Thus in **Felthouse**, if the nephew had been the one to say that if his uncle heard nothing more he could treat the offer as accepted, there would have been a contract.

## Acceptance of an offer to enter into a unilateral contract

Unilateral contracts are usually accepted by conduct. If I offer £100 to anyone who finds my lost dog, finding the dog will be an acceptance of the offer, making my promise binding – it is not necessary for anyone to contact me and say that they intend to take up my offer and find the dog.

There is no acceptance until the relevant act has been completely performed – so if Ann says to Ben that she will give Ben £5 if Ben washes her car, Ben would not be entitled to the money until the job is finished, and could not wash half the car and ask for £2.50.

## Acceptance must be unconditional

An acceptance must accept the precise terms of an offer. In **Tinn** v **Hoffman** (1873) one party offered to sell the other 1,200 tons of iron. It was held that the other party's order for 800 tons was not an acceptance.

## Negotiation and the 'battle of the forms'

Where parties carry on a long process of negotiation, it may be difficult to pinpoint exactly when an offer has been made and accepted. In such cases the courts will look at the whole course of negotiations to decide whether the parties have in fact reached agreement at all and, if so, when.

This process can be particularly difficult where the so-called 'battle of the forms' arises. Rather than negotiating terms each time a contract is made, many businesses try to save time and money by contracting on standard terms, which will be printed on company stationery such as order forms and delivery notes. The 'battle of the forms' occurs where one party sends a form stating that the contract is on their standard terms of business, and the other party responds by returning their own form and stating that the contract is on **their** terms.

The general rule in such cases is that the 'last shot' wins the battle. Each new form issued is treated as a counter-offer, so that when one party performs its obligation under the contract (by delivering goods for example), that action will be seen as acceptance by conduct of the offer in the last form. In **British Road Services** v **Arthur V Crutchley & Co Ltd** (1968) the claimants delivered some whisky to the defendants for storage. The BRS driver handed the defendants a delivery note, which listed his company's 'conditions of carriage'. Crutchley's employee stamped the note 'Received under [our] conditions' and handed it back to the driver. The court held that stamping the delivery note in this way amounted to a counter-offer, which BRS accepted by handing over the goods. The contract therefore incorporated Crutchley's conditions, rather than those of BRS.

However, a more recent case shows that the 'last shot' will not always succeed. In **Butler Machine Tool Ltd** v **Ex-Cell-O Corp (England) Ltd** (1979) the defendants wanted to buy a machine from the claimants, to be delivered ten months after the order. The claimants supplied a quotation (which was taken to be an offer), and on this document were printed their standard terms, including a clause allowing them to increase the price of the goods if the costs had risen by the date of delivery (known as a price-variation clause). The document also stated that their terms would prevail over any terms and conditions in the buyers' order. The buyers responded by placing an order, which was stated to be on their own terms and conditions, and these were listed on the order form. These terms did not contain a price-variation clause. The order form included a tear-off acknowledgement slip, which contained the words: 'we accept your order on the terms and conditions thereon' (referring to the order form). The sellers duly returned the acknowledgement slip to the buyers, with a letter stating that the order was being accepted in accordance with the earlier quotation. The acknowledgement slip and accompanying letter were the last forms issued before delivery.

**Figure 1.7** British Road Services *v* Arthur V Crutchley & Co Ltd (1968)

When the ten months were up, the machine was delivered and the sellers claimed an extra £2,892, under the provisions of the price-variation clause. The buyers refused to pay the extra amount, so the sellers sued them for it. The Court of Appeal held that the buyers' reply to the quotation was not an unconditional acceptance, and therefore constituted a counter-offer. The sellers had accepted that counter-offer by returning the acknowledgement slip, which referred back to the buyers' conditions. The sellers pointed out that they had stated in their accompanying letter that the order was booked in accordance with the earlier quotation, but this was interpreted by the Court of Appeal as referring back to the type and price of the machine tool, rather than to the terms listed on the back of the sellers' document. It merely confirmed that the machine in question was the one originally quoted for, and did not modify the conditions of the contract. The contract was therefore made under the buyers' conditions.

The Court of Appeal also contemplated what the legal position would have been if the slip had not been returned by the sellers. The majority thought that the usual rules of offer and counter-offer would have to be applied, which in many cases would mean that there was no contract until the goods were delivered and accepted by the buyer, with either party being free to withdraw before that. Lord Denning MR, on the other hand, suggested that the courts should take a much less rigid approach and decide whether the parties thought they had made a binding contract, and if it appeared that they did, the court should go on to examine the documents as a whole to find out what the content of their agreement might be.

**Figure 1.8** Butler Machine Tool Ltd *v* Ex-Cell-O Corp (England) Ltd (1979)

A recent case on the 'battle of the forms' is **GHSP Incorporated *v* AB Electronic Ltd** (2010). The case involved the manufacture and supply of car pedal sensors which were manufactured by the defendant, bought by the claimant and supplied to the car manufacturer Ford for use in its cars. The sensors proved defective and the claimant had to pay considerable compensation to Ford.

Orders for the sensors had been placed using the claimant's purchase order form which contained its standard terms with no limits on liability for defective goods. However, the defendant pointed out that it had sent an acknowledgement of the order which expressly incorporated and referred to its own contractual terms and in particular that its contractual liability was limited. It argued that this amounted to a counter-offer, which had been impliedly accepted.

The High Court held that, although the parties had entered into a contract, the terms of the contract were not to be found in either of the parties' respective standard terms of business. The negotiations between the parties made clear that neither party was willing to contract on the other's terms. Rather than conclude that no contract had been entered into, it was held that a contract had been concluded and the parties had acted under the contract by the goods being manufactured, delivered and paid for. But the contract was neither on the defendant's standard terms nor the claimant's standard terms. Instead, it was an unwritten contract containing the terms implied by the Sale of Goods Act 1979 (discussed on p. 404). In particular, s. 14(2) of that Act implies a term that the goods supplied will be of a satisfactory quality. There is no implied term limiting liability so this decision favoured the claimant. While it is no surprise that these terms were implied into the contract, what is surprising is that the contract consisted purely of these terms. This case seems to fit within Lord Denning's proposed approach to this type of case.

## Specified methods of acceptance

If an offeror states that his or her offer must be accepted in a particular way, then only acceptance by that method or an equally effective one will be binding. To be considered equally effective, a mode of acceptance should not be slower than the method specified in the offer, nor have any disadvantages for the offeror. It was stated in **Tinn** v **Hoffman** (1873) that where the offeree was asked to reply 'by return of post', any method which would arrive before return of post would be sufficient.

Where a specified method of acceptance has been included for the offeree's own benefit, however, the offeree is not obliged to accept in that way. In **Yates Building Co Ltd** v **R J Pulleyn & Sons (York) Ltd** (1975) the sellers stated that the option they were offering should be accepted by 'notice in writing . . . to be sent registered or recorded delivery'. The purchaser sent his acceptance by ordinary letter post, but the court held that the acceptance was still effective. The requirement of registered or recorded delivery was for the benefit of the offeree rather than the offeror (as it ensured that their acceptance was received and that they had proof of their acceptance) and was not therefore mandatory.

The case of **Felthouse** v **Bindley** (see p. 24 above) shows that, although the offeror can stipulate how the acceptance is to be made, he or she cannot stipulate that silence shall amount to acceptance. In the same way, if the offeror states that the performance of certain acts by the offeree will amount to an acceptance, and the offeree performs those acts, there will only be an acceptance if the offeree was aware of the terms of the offer and objectively intended their acts to amount to an acceptance. In **Inland Revenue Commissioners** v **Fry** (2001) the Inland Revenue claimed over £100,000 of unpaid tax from Mrs Fry. Following negotiations, Mrs Fry wrote to the Inland Revenue enclosing a cheque for £10,000. In her letter she said that if the Inland Revenue accepted her offer of £10,000 in full and final settlement, it should present the cheque for payment.

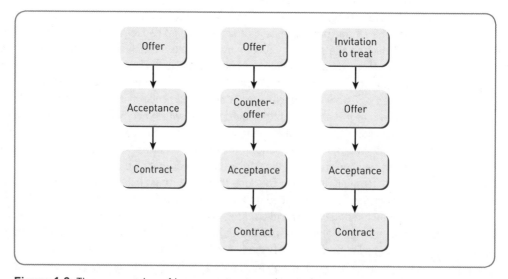

**Figure 1.9** Three examples of how a contract can be made

The Inland Revenue cashed the cheque but subsequently informed Mrs Fry that her offer was unacceptable. The High Court held that the Inland Revenue was entitled to the full amount of tax which it had claimed. The court explained that it was fundamental to the existence of a binding contract that there was a meeting of minds. An offer prescribing a mode of acceptance could be accepted by an offeree acting in accordance with that mode of acceptance. However, the Inland Revenue received thousands of cheques each day and there was no evidence that, when it cashed the cheque from Mrs Fry, it knew of the offer. The cashing of the cheque gave rise to no more than a rebuttable presumption of acceptance of the terms of the offer in the accompanying letter. On the evidence, that presumption had been rebutted, as a reasonable observer would not have assumed that the cheque was banked with the intention of accepting the offer in the letter.

An offeror who has requested the offeree to use a particular method of acceptance can always waive the right to insist on that method.

# Acceptance must be communicated

An acceptance does not usually take effect until it is communicated to the offeror. As Lord Denning explained in **Entores Ltd** v **Miles Far East Corporation** (1955), if A shouts an offer to B across a river but, just as B yells back an acceptance, a noisy aircraft flies over, preventing A from hearing B's reply, no contract has been made. A must be able to hear B's acceptance before it can take effect. The same would apply if the contract was made by telephone, and A failed to catch what B said because of interference on the line; there is no contract until A knows that B is accepting the offer. The principal reason for this rule is that, without it, people might be bound by a contract without knowing that their offer had been accepted, which could obviously create difficulties in all kinds of situations.

Where parties negotiate face to face, communication of the acceptance is unlikely to be a problem; any difficulties tend to arise where the parties are communicating at a distance, for example by post, telephone, telegram, telex, fax or messenger.

# Exceptions to the communication rule

There are some circumstances in which an acceptance may take effect without being communicated to the offeror.

## Terms of the offer

An offer may state or imply that acceptance need not be communicated to the offeror, although, as **Felthouse** v **Bindley** shows, it is not possible to state that the offeree will be bound unless he or she indicates that the offer is not accepted (in other words that silence will be taken as acceptance). This means that offerors are free to expose themselves to the risk of unknowingly incurring an obligation, but may not impose that risk on someone else. It seems to follow from this that if the horse in **Felthouse** v **Bindley** had been kept out of the sale for the uncle, and the uncle had then refused to buy it, the nephew could have sued his uncle, who would have been unable to rely on the fact that acceptance was not communicated to him.

Unilateral contracts do not usually require acceptance to be communicated to the offeror. In **Carlill** *v* **Carbolic Smoke Ball Co** (1893) the defendants argued that the claimant should have notified them that she was accepting their offer, but the court held that such a unilateral offer implied that performance of the terms of the offer would be enough to amount to acceptance.

## Conduct of the offeror

An offeror who fails to receive an acceptance through their own fault may be prevented from claiming that the non-communication means they should not be bound by the contract. In the **Entores** case (1955) it was suggested that this principle could apply where an offer was accepted by telephone, and the offeror did not catch the words of acceptance, but failed to ask for them to be repeated; and in *The Brimnes* (1975), where the acceptance is sent by telex during business hours, but is simply not read by anyone in the offeror's office.

## The postal rule

The general rule for acceptances by post is that they take effect when they are posted, rather than when they are communicated. The main reason for this rule is historical, since it dates from a time when communication through the post was even slower and less reliable than it is today. Even now, there is some practical purpose for the rule, in that it is easier to prove that a letter has been posted than to prove that it has been received or brought to the attention of the offeror.

 **Key Case** Adams *v* Lindsell

The postal rule was laid down in **Adams** *v* **Lindsell** (1818). On 2 September 1817, the defendants wrote to the claimants, who processed wool, offering to sell them a quantity of sheep fleeces, and stating that they required an answer 'in course of post'. Unfortunately, the defendants did not address the letter correctly, and as a result it did not reach the claimants until the evening of 5 September. The claimants posted their acceptance the same evening, and it reached the defendants on 9 September. It appeared that if the original letter had been correctly addressed, the defendants could have expected a reply 'in course of post' by 7 September. That date came and went, and they had heard nothing from the claimants, so on 8 September they sold the wool to a third party. The issue in the case was whether a contract had been made before the sale to the third party on 8 September. The court held that a contract was concluded as soon as the acceptance was posted, so that the defendants were bound from the evening of 5 September, and had therefore breached the contract by selling the wool to the third party. (Under current law there would have been a contract even without the postal rule, because the revocation of the offer could only take effect if it was communicated to the offeree – selling the wool to a third party without notifying the claimants would not amount to revocation. However, in 1818 the rules on revocation were not fully developed, so the court may well have considered that the sale was sufficient to revoke the offer, which was why an effective acceptance would have to take place before 8 September.)

**Legal Principle**
An acceptance by post takes effect when it is posted, rather than when it is communicated.

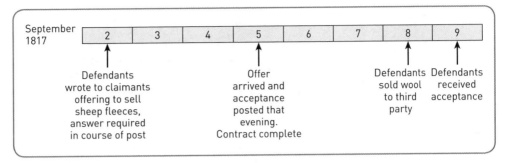

**Figure 1.10** Adams *v* Lindsell (1818)

## Application of the postal rule

The traditional title 'postal rule' has become slightly misleading because the rule does not only apply to the post but could also potentially apply to certain other non-instantaneous modes of communication. The postal rule was applied to acceptance by telegram in **Cowan *v* O'Connor** (1888), where it was held that an acceptance came into effect when the telegram was placed with the Post Office. These days the Post Office in England no longer offers a telegram service, but the same rule will apply to the telemessage service which replaced it.

Use of the postal service must be reasonable. Only when it is reasonable to use the post to indicate acceptance can the postal rule apply. If the offer does not dictate a method of acceptance, appropriate methods can be inferred from the means used to make the offer. An offer made by post may generally be accepted by post, but it may be reasonable to accept by post even though the offer was delivered in some other way. In **Henthorn *v* Fraser** (1892) the defendant was based in Liverpool and the claimant lived in Birkenhead. The defendant gave the claimant a document containing an offer in Liverpool, and the claimant accepted it by posting a letter from Birkenhead. It was held that, despite the offer having been handed over in person, acceptance by post was reasonable because the parties were based in different towns.

Where an offer is made by an instant method of communication, such as telex, fax or telephone, an acceptance by post would not usually be reasonable.

## Exceptions to the postal rule

### Offers requiring communication of acceptance

An offeror may avoid the postal rule by making it a term of their offer that acceptance will only take effect when it is communicated to them. In **Holwell Securities Ltd *v* Hughes** (1974) the defendants offered to sell some freehold property to the claimants but the offer stated that the acceptance had to be 'by notice in writing'. The claimants posted their acceptance, but it never reached the defendants, despite being properly addressed. The court held that 'notice' meant communication, and therefore it would not be appropriate to apply the postal rule.

### Instant methods of communication

When an acceptance is made by an instant mode of communication, such as telephone or telex, the postal rule does not apply. In such cases the acceptor will usually know at once that they have not managed to communicate with the offeror, and will need to try again.

**Figure 1.11** The postal rule

In **Entores** _v_ **Miles Far East Corporation** (1955) the claimants were a London company and the defendants were an American corporation with agents in Amsterdam. Both the London company and the defendants' agents in Amsterdam had telex machines, which allow users to type in a message, and have it almost immediately received and printed out by the recipient's machine. The claimants in London telexed the defendants' Amsterdam agents offering to buy goods from them, and the agents accepted, again by telex. The court case arose when the claimants alleged that the defendants had broken their contract and wanted to bring an action against them. The rules of civil litigation stated that they could only bring this action in England if the contract had been made in England. The Court of Appeal held that because telex allows almost instant communication, the parties were in the same position as if they had negotiated in each other's presence or over the telephone, so the postal rule did not apply and an acceptance did not take effect until it had been received by the claimants. Because the acceptance had been received in London, the contract was deemed to have been made there, and so the legal action could go ahead.

This approach was approved by the House of Lords in **Brinkibon** _v_ **Stahag Stahl** (1983). The facts here were similar, except that the offer was made by telex from Vienna to London, and accepted by a telex from London to Vienna. The House of Lords held that the contract was therefore made in Vienna.

In both cases the telex machines were in the offices of the parties, and the messages were received inside normal working hours. In **Brinkibon** the House of Lords said that a telex message sent outside working hours would not be considered instantaneous, so the time and place in which the contract was completed would be determined by the intentions of the parties, standard business practice and, if possible, by analysing where the risk should most fairly lie.

In **Thomas** _v_ **BPE Solicitors** (2010) the High Court stated that the postal rule would not apply to a contract made by e-mail. This statement was _obiter_ because it was not actually part of the reasoning for the decision itself and thus it is not a binding precedent on the point, but purely guidance on how the judges are likely to approach this issue in the future. E-mails were treated as similar to telex messages which were considered in **Entores** _v_ **Miles Far East Corporation**. So the ordinary rules of offer and acceptance apply and the contract will be formed when the acceptance is received. In looking at when the acceptance is received, the High Court in **Thomas** referred to **Brinkibon** _v_ **Stahag Stahl**. It concluded that an e-mail sent and received at 18.00 was an effective acceptance as in the context in which it was sent, this was not outside working hours; it was available to be read at the point of receipt, even though the potential recipient had actually gone home at 17.45.

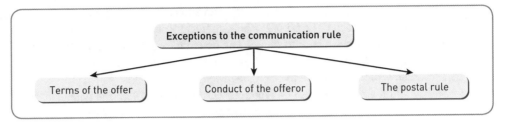

**Figure 1.12** Exceptions to the communication rule

### Misdirected acceptance

Where a letter of acceptance is lost or delayed because the offeree has wrongly or incompletely addressed it through their own carelessness, it seems reasonable that the postal rule should not apply, although there is no precise authority to this effect. Treitel, a leading contract law academic, suggests that a better rule might be that if a badly addressed acceptance takes effect at all, it should do so at the time which is least advantageous to the party responsible for the misdirection.

### Effect of the postal rule

The postal rule has three main practical consequences:

1 A postal acceptance can take effect when it is posted, even if it gets lost in the post and never reaches the offeror. In **Household Fire Insurance** *v* **Grant** (1879) Grant had applied for (and therefore offered to buy) shares in the claimant company. The shares were allotted to him and his name was put on the register of shareholders. The company did write to say that the shares had been allotted to Grant, but the letter was lost in the post and he never received it. Some time later the company went into liquidation, and the liquidator claimed from Grant the balance owing on the price of his shares. It was held that Grant was bound to pay the balance, because the contract had been completed when the company's letter was posted.

   It is likely that the same rule applies where the letter eventually arrives, but is delayed by postal problems.

2 Where an acceptance is posted after the offeror posts a revocation of the offer, but before that revocation has been received, the acceptance will be binding (posted acceptances take effect on posting, posted revocations on communication). This point is illustrated by the cases of **Byrne** *v* **Van Tienhoven** (1880) and **Henthorn** *v* **Fraser** (1892).

3 Where the postal rule applies, it seems unlikely that an offeree could revoke a postal acceptance by phone (or some other instant means of communication) before it arrives, though there is no English case on the point. A Scottish case, **Dunmore** *v* **Alexander** (1830), does appear to allow such a revocation, but the court's views were only *obiter* on this point.

# Ignorance of the offer

It is generally thought that a person cannot accept an offer of which they are unaware, because in order to create a binding contract, the parties must reach agreement. If their wishes merely happen to coincide, that may be very convenient for both, but it does not constitute a contract and cannot legally bind them. Thus, if Ann advertises a reward for the return of a lost cat and Ben, not having seen or heard of the advertisement, comes across the cat, reads Ann's address on its collar and takes it back to Ann, is Ann bound to pay Ben the reward? No English case has clearly decided this point, and the cases abroad conflict with the main English case. On general principles Ben is probably unable to claim the reward.

In the American case of **Williams** v **Carwardine** (1833) the defendant offered a $20 reward for information leading to the discovery of the murderer of Walter Carwardine, and leaflets concerning the reward were distributed in the area where the claimant lived. The claimant apparently knew about the reward, but when she gave the information it was not in order to receive the money. She believed she had only a short time to live, and thought that giving the information might ease her conscience. The court held that she was entitled to the reward: she was aware of the offer and had complied with its terms, and her motive for doing so was irrelevant. A second US case, **Fitch** v **Snedaker** (1868), stated that a person who gives information without knowledge of the offer of a reward cannot claim the reward.

The main English case on this topic is **Gibbons** v **Proctor** (1891). A reward had been advertised for information leading to the arrest or conviction of the perpetrator of a particular crime and the claimant attempted to claim the reward, even though he had not originally known of the offer. He was allowed to receive the money, but the result does not shed much light on the problem because the claimant did know of the offer of reward by the time the information was given on his behalf to the person named in the advertisement.

Following the Australian case of **R** v **Clarke** (1927), it would appear that if the offeree knew of the offer in the past but has completely forgotten about it, they are treated as never having known about it. In that case a reward was offered by the Australian Government for information leading to the conviction of the murderers of two policemen. The Government also promised that an accomplice giving such information would receive a free pardon. Clarke was such an accomplice, who panicked and provided the information required in order to obtain the pardon, forgetting, at the time, about the reward. He remembered it later, but it was held that he was not entitled to the money.

## Cross offers

These present a similar problem. If Ann writes to Ben offering to sell her television for £50, and by coincidence Ben happens to write offering to buy the television for £50, the two letters crossing in the post, do the letters create a contract between them? On the principles of offer and acceptance it appears not, since the offeree does not know about the offer at the time of the potential acceptance. The point has never been decided in a case but there are *obiter dicta* in **Tinn** v **Hoffman** (1873) which suggest there would be no contract.

## Time of the formation of the contract

Normally a contract is formed when an effective acceptance has been communicated to the offeror. An exception to this is the postal rule, where the contract is formed at the time the acceptance is posted and there is no need for communication. A further exception to the general rule has been created by s. 11 of the Electronic Communications Act 2000. This establishes the precise time at which an electronic contract is made. Electronic contracts are concluded when the customer has both

- received an acknowledgement that their acceptance has been received, and
- confirmed their receipt of that acknowledgement.

These communications are taken to be effective when the receiving party is able to access them. Section 11 applies unless the parties agree otherwise. Thus electronic contracts will normally be formed at a later stage than other contracts.

# Offer and acceptance implied by the court

Sometimes the parties may be in dispute as to whether a contract existed between them. They may never have signed any written agreement but one party may argue that the offer and acceptance had been made orally or through their conduct. Thus, in **Baird Textile Holdings Ltd** v **Marks & Spencer plc** (2001) Marks & Spencer had been in a business relationship with Baird Textile Holdings (BTH) for 30 years. BTH were based in the United Kingdom and had been a major supplier of clothes to Marks & Spencer over the years. In October 1999, Marks & Spencer advised BTH that it was ending all supply arrangements between them with effect from the end of the current production season. BTH brought a legal action against Marks & Spencer alleging that they had a contract with the company, and that a term of this contract had been breached by Marks & Spencer's terminating their supply arrangements in this way. The Court of Appeal held that there was no contract governing the relationship between the two litigants and that therefore Marks & Spencer were not in breach of a contract. It held that a contract should only be implied if it was necessary to do so 'to give business reality to a transaction and to create enforceable obligations between parties who are dealing with one another in circumstances in which one would expect that business reality and those enforceable obligations to exist'. It would not be necessary to imply such a contract if the parties might have acted in just the same way as they did without a contract. Marks & Spencer had preferred not to be bound by a contract so that they had maximum flexibility. For business reasons BTH had accepted this state of affairs.

In **West Bromwich Albion Football Club Ltd** v **El-Safty** (2006) the court held that there was no necessity to imply a contract between a football club and a doctor. In that case a footballer, Michael Appleton (known by his fans as 'Appy'), was signed by West Bromwich Albion Football Club for £750,000. Unfortunately, Appleton suffered a knee injury while training. The football club's physiotherapist said that he needed to see a surgeon. The football club telephoned the surgeon, El-Safty, who saw Appleton and recommended he undergo surgery. Appleton was unable to play football again after the surgery. It subsequently came to light that El-Safty's advice had been negligent and that the injury had only required minor treatment which would have allowed Appleton to be back on the football pitch within four months. The football club sued El-Safty. One argument put forward by the club was that the surgeon had been in breach of a contract with the football club. But the High Court held that, while there was a contract between the surgeon and the private insurance company BUPA which paid him, there was no contract between the football club and the surgeon. Such a contract could not be implied because the necessity test laid down in **Baird Textile Holdings Ltd** v **Marks & Spencer plc** had not been satisfied.

> ## Topical Issue
>
> ### Consumer's right to cancel
>
> Usually, once an offer has been accepted, the contract is binding and the acceptor cannot withdraw their acceptance. An exception to this general rule has been created for certain consumers entering into contracts made at a distance. Under the Consumer Protection (Distance Selling) Regulations 2000 a consumer entering into a contract at a distance has a 'cooling-off' period after the formation of the contract, during which they can change their mind and withdraw from the contract. The relevant contract must have been made under an organised distance-selling arrangement, and there must have been no face-to-face contact between the consumer and the seller: for example, in a shop. The contract is therefore likely to have been made over the telephone, through the post, on the internet or by using a catalogue. The cooling-off period allows the consumer to cancel the contract within seven working days of receiving the goods or concluding a contract for services. A large number of consumer contracts are excluded from this provision. Excluded contracts include those relating to financial services and the sale of land, vending machines, contracts for transport and leisure, and contracts to supply food for everyday consumption. Thus, if I buy an airplane ticket online or purchase some fast food from my local takeaway, these contracts will not incorporate a cooling-off period during which I could withdraw from the contract.

## Agreements to negotiate

An agreement to negotiate does not amount to a binding contract. In **Walford** v **Miles** (1992) the House of Lords considered that such agreements do not satisfy the requirement of certainty and no consideration will have been proffered to support these promises. In that case the parties were negotiating the sale of a business. The seller had orally agreed not to negotiate with any other party (known as a 'lock-out agreement'). A price was agreed 'subject to contract'. Despite this, the seller sold the business to someone else. The House of Lords ruled he was entitled to do so because 'a bare agreement to negotiate has no legal content'.

If, however, there is a binding contract and the parties have merely agreed to negotiate certain specific terms of the contract at a future date, then that agreement to negotiate a contractual term can form part of a binding contract (see **Foley** v **Classique Coaches** (1934) on p. 55).

The Court of Appeal in **Petromec Inc** v **Petroleo Brasileiro** (2005) distinguished **Walford**, describing the agreement in **Walford** as a 'bare agreement to negotiate'. The Court of Appeal suggested that an express contractual provision to negotiate in good faith was enforceable, and the fact that it would be difficult to determine whether action had been taken in good or bad faith ought not to prevent a court from enforcing such an obligation. A duty to negotiate in good faith may be enforceable where:

- it is part of a contractually binding agreement;
- it is express rather than implied; and
- the matter to be negotiated is capable of objective assessment by a third party.

# Agreements to agree, letters of intent and agreements 'subject to contract'

Sometimes parties choose to enter what can be described as 'agreements to agree' or 'letters of intent'. They are essentially promises that the parties intend to enter into an agreement at a future date, usually once negotiations have been completed. These agreements are sometimes described as 'subject to contract' on the basis that the parties do not intend to be bound until a formal written contract has been signed by both parties. The ordinary approach to these agreements to agree is that they are not binding.

If the parties are in a hurry to commence work on a project but are unable to finalise quickly the relevant contract for the work, they may decide to draw up a letter of intent under which the work can commence, with a view to finalising the contract shortly afterwards. In practice, once the work has started the parties might delay actually finalising the contract and disputes can arise as to the legal rights of the parties.

The legal status of letters of intent depends on the particular facts of each case; sometimes they can amount to contracts in their own right, sometimes they do not. The letters of intent may state the agreement is 'subject to contract' (see p. 42). To be a binding contract, the letter must have all the characteristics of a contract; in particular the parties must have provided consideration, have an intention to create legal relations and there must be sufficient certainty as to the contractual terms. The fact that work has been done following letters of intent being agreed is likely to be viewed by the court as an important factor when deciding whether or not the parties have actually concluded a binding contract.

In cases involving letters of intent the court has three options. First, to find that after the letter of intent was agreed a contract later arose and a remedy under contract is available. Second, to find that no contract has been concluded at any stage but a remedy will be available under restitution to the value of any work carried out subsequent to the letters of intent (see p. 374). Third, to reject the claim altogether. Which of these three options is chosen by the courts very much depends on the facts of each case.

In **RTS Flexible Systems** v **Molkerei Alois Müller** (2010) Müller manufactured dairy products, including yogurts. It wanted RTS Flexible Systems (RTS) to supply and install some machinery for packaging its products. A letter of intent was drawn up which was due to be in force for four weeks. The letter set out the contractual price for the machinery and stated that the final contract would be on Müller's contractual terms with amendments. The letter stated that the contract 'shall not become effective until each party has executed a counterpart and exchanged it with the other'. Thus the agreement in the letter was 'subject to contract'.

RTS commenced installing the machinery, but after the four-week period had expired the final contract had not been agreed. A dispute arose and RTS refused to finish installing the machinery. Müller refused to pay for the machinery and RTS brought legal proceedings for payment. The case went up to the Supreme Court which held that the parties' conduct after the letter of intent had expired suggested they intended to enter into a contract which they had effectively done even though no written document had been signed.

The Supreme Court stated that where a contract was being negotiated 'subject to contract' and work began before execution of a formal contract, there would not 'always or even usually' be a binding contract. The fact that work has been carried out is likely to be viewed by the court as an important factor when deciding whether or not the parties have concluded a binding contract. On the facts of this case, as substantial works had been carried out after all the terms had been agreed there was found to have been a contract. The 'subject to contract' clause had effectively been waived by the parties' conduct. Where there is no 'subject to contract' stipulation, the fact that work has been done and services rendered is likely to lead the courts to conclude there is a contract on the agreed terms.

If the parties have failed to reach agreement on terms which are of economic importance, the courts are inclined to find there is no contract.

In **British Steel Corporation** *v* **Cleveland Bridge & Engineering Co Ltd** (1984) work had begun at the request of the defendants, on the provision of some steel before all the elements of the contract for the steel had been agreed. Both sides confidently expected to reach agreement without difficulty. In fact, final agreement was never reached. The claimants successfully claimed a *quantum meruit* for the work they had done. This case was distinguished in **RTS Flexible Systems** on the basis that in **British Steel Corporation** each party's contractual terms were fundamentally different from each other on the important issue of liability for delay. On those facts, performance of the contract could not be equated with the existence of a contract between them.

The parties may initially intend that their oral agreement will be 'subject to contract', in other words not binding until a formal written agreement has been signed, but they may subsequently change their minds. If they change their minds the original agreement can become a binding contract. In **Grant** *v* **Bragg** (2009) the parties had reached an initial agreement 'subject to contract' but later only exchanged informal e-mails. The High Court ruled that the parties had subsequently changed their minds and intended to be bound by the original agreement regardless of whether that agreement was ever formally written and signed. The court stated:

> where parties are proceeding in anticipation of execution of a formal document then the normal inference will be that the parties will not be bound unless and until both of them sign the document. However, that inference will change if the facts change so that it can be objectively ascertained, on a balance of probabilities, that the continuing intention of the parties is, now, to be contractually bound immediately and not following formal execution of the document.

In **Cheverny Consulting** *v* **Whitehead Mann** (2006) the Court of Appeal noted that the more complicated the subject matter of the agreement, the more likely the parties would want it to be put down in writing before it became a binding contract:

> [T]he more complicated the subject matter the more likely the parties are to want to enshrine their contract in some written document to be prepared by their solicitors. This enables them to review all the terms before being committed to any of them. The commonest way of achieving this ability is to stipulate that the negotiations are 'subject to contract'. In such a case there is no binding contract until the formal written agreement has been duly executed . . . But it is not necessary that there should have been an express stipulation that the negotiations are to be 'subject to contract'.

In **Golden Ocean Group Ltd** *v* **Salgaocar Mining Industries** (2012) the Court of Appeal noted that even where a final e-mail between contracting parties might envisage that a formal contract would be drawn up, this did not on the facts indicate an intention not to be bound until that document was issued.

## Common types of contracts

The above rules of offer and acceptance apply to the sale of land and to sales by tender and auction, but it is useful to know how those rules apply in practice in these fairly common situations.

## Auction sales

The parties to an auction sale are the bidder and the owner of the goods. The auctioneer simply provides a service, and is not a party to the contract between buyer and seller. Under the Sale of Goods Act 1979 (s. 57(2)), the general rule is that the auctioneer's request for bids is an invitation to treat, and each bid is an offer. Each bidder's offer lapses as soon as a higher bid is made, and an offer is accepted by the auctioneer (on behalf of the seller) on the fall of the hammer. Any bidder may therefore withdraw a bid before the hammer falls, and the auctioneer may also withdraw the goods on behalf of the seller before that point.

### Advertisement of an auction

An advertisement that an auction is to take place at a certain time is a mere declaration of intention and is not an offer which those who attend at the specified time thereby accept. This was decided in **Harris** v **Nickerson** (1873), where the claimant failed to recover damages for travelling to an auction which was subsequently cancelled.

### Auction 'without reserve'

In many cases, sellers at an auction specify reserve prices – the lowest prices they will accept for their goods. If nobody bids at least that amount, the goods are not sold. An auction 'without reserve', on the other hand, means that the goods will be sold to the highest bidder, however low their bid. We have seen that an advertisement announcing that an auction will be held is an invitation to treat and not an offer, but in **Warlow** v **Harrison** (1859) it was held that if such an advertisement includes the words 'without reserve', it becomes an offer, from the auctioneers to the public at large, that if the auction is held they will sell to the highest bidder (though it does not oblige the auctioneers to hold the sale in the first place). The offer is accepted when a person makes a bid and when doing so assumes that there is no reserve. That acceptance completes a contract, which is separate from any contract that might be made between the highest bidder and the owner of the property being sold. An auctioneer who then puts a reserve price on any of the lots breaches this separate contract.

In **Barry** v **Davies** (2000) the defendant auctioneers were instructed to sell two engine analysers, which were specialist machines used in the motor trade. The claimant had been told the sale would be 'without reserve'. New machines would cost £14,000 each. The auctioneer attempted to start the bidding at £5,000, then £3,000, but the claimant was the only person interested in the machines and placed a bid of just £200 for each machine. The auctioneer refused to accept that bid and withdrew the machines from the sale. The claimant sought damages for breach of contract and he was awarded £27,600. The defendants' appeal was dismissed and the case of **Warlow** v **Harrison** was followed. A contract existed between the auctioneer and the bidder that the auction would be without reserve, and that contract had been breached.

## Tenders

When a large organisation, such as a company, hospital, local council or government ministry, needs to find a supplier of goods or services, it will often advertise for tenders. Companies wishing to secure the business then reply to the advertisement, detailing the price at which they are willing to supply the goods or services, and the advertiser chooses whichever is the more favourable quotation. Tenders can also be invited for the sale of goods, in much the same way as bids are made at an auction.

As a general rule, a request for tenders is regarded as an invitation to treat (**Spencer** v **Harding** (1870)), so there is no obligation to accept any of the tenders put forward. The tenders themselves are offers, and a contract comes into existence when one of them is accepted.

In exceptional cases, however, an invitation for tenders may itself be an offer, and submission of a tender then becomes acceptance of that offer. The main example of this is where the invitation to tender makes it clear that the lowest tender (or the highest in the case of tenders to buy) will be accepted. In **Harvela Investments Ltd** v **Royal Trust Co of Canada (CI) Ltd** (1985) the defendants telexed two parties inviting them to submit tenders for the purchase of some shares, stating in the invitation 'we bind ourselves to accept the [highest] offer'. The House of Lords said that the telex was a unilateral offer to accept the highest bid, which would be followed by a bilateral contract with the highest bidder.

An invitation to tender may also be regarded as an offer to consider all tenders correctly submitted, even if it is not an undertaking actually to accept one. In **Blackpool and Fylde Aero Club Ltd** v **Blackpool Borough Council** (1990) the Council invited tenders from people wishing to operate leisure flights from the local airport. Those who wished to submit a tender were to reply to the Town Hall, in envelopes provided, by a certain deadline. The claimant returned his bid before the deadline was up, but the Council mistakenly thought it had arrived late. They therefore refused to consider it, and accepted one of the other tenders.

The claim for breach of contract was upheld by the Court of Appeal. Although the Council was not obliged to accept any of the tenders, the terms of their invitation to tender constituted an offer at least to consider any tender which was submitted in accordance with their rules. That offer was accepted by anyone who put forward a tender in the correct manner, and their acceptance would create a unilateral contract, obliging the Council to consider the tender. The Council was in breach of this unilateral contract.

In some cases a tenderer makes what is called a 'referential' tender, offering to top anyone else's bid by a specified amount. This occurred in **Harvela Investments Ltd** v **Royal Trust Co of Canada (CI) Ltd** (1985). Some shares were for sale, and the claimants offered C$2,175,000 for them. Another party offered to pay C$2,100,000, or if this was not the highest bid, to pay C$101,000 'in excess of any other offer'. The House of Lords made it clear that the type of 'referential' tender made by the second party was not legally an offer, and was not permissible in such a transaction. Therefore the first defendants were bound to accept the claimants' bid. Their Lordships explained their decision on the grounds that the purpose of a sale by fixed bidding is to provoke the best price from purchasers regardless of what others might be prepared to pay, and that referential bids worked against this. Such bids would also present practical problems if allowed: if everyone made referential bids it would be impossible to define exactly what offer was being made, and if only some parties made bids in that way, the others would not have a valid opportunity to have their offers accepted.

## Selection of tenders

The implications of choosing to accept a tender depend on what sort of tender is involved.

### Specific tenders

Where an invitation to tender specifies that a particular quantity of goods is required on a particular date, or between certain dates, agreeing to one of the tenders submitted will constitute acceptance of an offer (the tender), creating a contract. This is the case even if delivery is to be in instalments as and when requested. If a company tenders to supply 100 wheelchairs to a hospital between 1 January and 1 June, their contract is completed when the hospital chooses the company's tender, and delivery must be made between those dates.

### Non-specific tenders

Some invitations to tender are not specific, and may simply state that certain goods may be required, up to a particular maximum quantity, with deliveries to be made 'if and when' requested. For example, an invitation to tender made by a hospital may ask for tenders to supply up to 1,000 test tubes, 'if and when' required. In such a case, taking up one of the tenders submitted does not amount to acceptance of an offer in the contractual sense, and there is no contract. Once the tender is approved, it becomes what is called a standing offer. The hospital may order no test tubes at all, may spread delivery over several instalments, or may take the whole 1,000 test tubes at once. If the hospital does buy the test tubes or some of them, whether in instalments or all at once, then each time it places an order it accepts the test tube manufacturer's offer, and a separate contract for the amount required is made on each occasion. The result is that when the hospital places an order, the company is bound to supply within the terms of the offer as required, but the company can revoke the offer to supply at any time, and will then only be bound by orders already placed.

This kind of situation would not oblige the hospital to order its test tubes only from the company whose tender it approved. In **Percival v LCC** (1918) Percival submitted a tender to the LCC for the supply of certain goods 'in such quantities and at such times and in such manner' as the Committee required. The tender was approved, but the LCC eventually placed its orders with other suppliers. Percival claimed damages for breach of contract, but the court held that acceptance of the non-specific tender did not constitute a contract, and the LCC were not obliged to order goods – although Percival was obliged to supply goods which were ordered under the terms of the standing offer, so long as the offer had not been revoked.

The nature of a standing offer was considered in **Great Northern Railway Co v Witham** (1873). The claimant had invited tenders for the supply of stores, and the defendant made a tender in these words: 'I undertake to supply the Company for twelve months with such quantities of [the specified articles] as the Company may order from time to time.' The railway company accepted this tender, and later placed some orders, which were met by the defendant. The court case arose when the railway company placed an order for goods within the scope of the tender, and the defendant refused to supply them. The court found that the supplying company was in breach of contract because the tender was a standing offer, which the railway company could accept each time it placed an order, thereby creating a contract each time. The standing offer could be revoked at any time, but the tenderer was bound by orders already made, since these were acceptances of his offer and thereby completed a contract.

**Figure 1.13** Tenders

# Sale of land

The standard rules of contract apply to the sale of land (which includes the sale of buildings such as houses), but the courts apply those rules fairly strictly, tending to require very clear evidence of an intention to be bound before they will state that an offer has definitely been made. The main reason for this is simply that land is expensive, and specific areas of land are unique and irreplaceable; damages are therefore often inadequate as a remedy for breach of contract in a sale of land, and it is better to avoid problems beforehand than put them right after a contract is made.

In **Harvey** v **Facey** (1893) the claimant sent the defendant a telegram asking: 'Will you sell us Bumper Hall Pen? Telegraph lowest cash price.' The reply arrived, stating: 'Lowest price for Bumper Hall Pen, £900.' The claimant then sent a telegram back saying: 'We agree to buy Bumper Hall Pen for £900 asked by you. Please send us your title deeds.' On these facts, the Privy Council held that there was no contract. They regarded the telegram from the defendant as merely a statement of what the minimum price would be if the defendant eventually decided to sell. It was therefore not an offer which could be accepted by the third telegram.

In practice, the normal procedure for sales involving land is as follows:

## Sale 'subject to contract'

First, parties agree on the sale, often through an estate agent. At this stage their agreement may be described as 'subject to contract', and although the effect of these words depends on the intention of the parties, there is a strong presumption against there being a contract at this stage (**Tiverton Estates Ltd** v **Wearwell Ltd** (1975)). The words 'subject to contract' usually suggest that no contract is formed until a formal written contract has been signed by the parties. If the parties sign a document at this point, it will normally be an agreement to make a more formal contract in the future, rather than a contract to go through with the sale. It was held in **Alpenstow Ltd** v **Regalian Properties plc** (1985) that there were some circumstances in which the courts may infer that the parties intended to be legally bound when signing the original document, even though it was said to be 'subject to contract', but such cases would arise only rarely.

The idea of making an agreement 'subject to contract' is to allow the buyers to check thoroughly all the details of the land (to make sure, for example, that there are no plans to build a new airport just behind the house they are thinking of buying, or that the house is not affected by subsidence).

## Exchange of contracts

The next stage is that the buyer and seller agree on the terms of the formal contract (usually through their solicitors, though there is no legal reason why the parties cannot make all the arrangements themselves). Both parties then sign a copy of the contract, and agree on a date on which the contracts will be exchanged, at which point the buyer usually pays a deposit of around 10 per cent of the sale price. Once the contracts are exchanged, a binding contract exists (though it is difficult to see this transaction in terms of offer and acceptance). However, if the contract is breached at this point the buyer can only claim damages – the buyer has no rights in the property itself.

After exchanging contracts, the parties may make further enquiries (checking, for example, that the seller really does own the property), and then the ownership of the land and house is transferred to the buyer, usually by means of a document known as a transfer. At this stage the buyer pays the balance of the purchase price to the seller. The buyer then has rights in the property – in the event of the seller breaching the contract, the buyer can have his or her property rights enforced in court, rather than just claiming damages.

These principles are illustrated by **Eccles** *v* **Bryant** (1947). After signing an agreement 'subject to contract', the parties consulted their solicitors, who agreed a draft contract. Each party signed the contract, and the buyer forwarded his copy to the seller's solicitor so that contracts could be exchanged. However, the seller changed his mind about the sale, and his solicitor informed the buyer's solicitor that the property had been sold to another buyer. The buyer tried to sue for breach of contract, but the Court of Appeal held that the negotiations were subject to formal contract, and the parties had not intended to be bound until they exchanged contracts. No binding obligations could arise before this took place. The court did not say when the exchange would be deemed to have taken place – that is, whether it was effective on posting of the contracts, or on receipt. In many cases a contract will specify when an exchange will be considered complete, by stating, for example, that the contract will be binding when the contracts are actually delivered.

# How important are offer and acceptance?

Although offer and acceptance can provide the courts with a useful technique for assessing at what point an agreement should be binding, what the courts are really looking to judge is whether the parties have come to an agreement, and there are some cases in which the rules on offer and acceptance give little help.

An example of this type of situation is **Clarke** *v* **Dunraven** (1897), which concerned two yacht owners who had entered for a yacht race. The paperwork they completed in order to enter included an undertaking to obey the club rules, and these rules contained an obligation to pay for 'all damages' caused by fouling. During the manoeuvring at the start of the race, one yacht, the *Satanita*, fouled another, the *Valkyrie*, which sank as a result. The owner of the *Valkyrie* sued the owner of the *Satanita* for the cost of the lost yacht, but the defendant claimed that he was under no obligation to pay the whole cost, and was only liable to pay the lesser damages laid down by a statute which limited liability to £8 for every ton of the yacht. The claimant argued that entering the competition in accordance with the rules had created a contract between the competitors, and this contract obliged the defendant to pay 'all damages'.

Clearly it was difficult to see how there could be an offer by one competitor and acceptance by the other, since their relations had been with the yacht club and not with each other. There was obviously an offer and an acceptance between each competitor and the club, but was there a contract between the competitors? The House of Lords held that there was, on the basis that 'a contract is concluded when one party has communicated to another an offer and that other has accepted it or when the parties have united in a concurrent expression of intention to create a legal obligation'. Therefore responsibility for accidents was governed by the race rules, and the defendant had to pay the full cost of the yacht.

There are problems in analysing the contract between the entrants to the race in terms of offer and acceptance. It seems rather far-fetched to imagine that, on starting the race, each competitor was making an offer to all the other competitors and simultaneously accepting their offers – and in any case, since the offers and acceptances would all occur at the same moment, they would be cross offers and would technically not create a contract.

As we have seen, contracts for the sale of land are also examples of agreements that do not usually fall neatly into concepts of offer and acceptance. We will also see later that the problems arising from the offer and acceptance analysis are sometimes avoided by the courts using the device of collateral contracts (see p. 300).

# Problems with offer and acceptance

## Artificiality

Clearly there are situations in which the concepts of offer and acceptance have to be stretched, and interpreted rather artificially, even though it is obvious that the parties have reached an agreement. In **Gibson** *v* **Manchester City Council** (1979) Lord Denning made it clear that he was in favour of looking at negotiations as a whole, in order to determine whether there was a contract, rather than trying to impose offer and acceptance on the facts, but his method has largely been rejected by the courts as being too uncertain and allowing too wide a discretion.

## Revocation of unilateral offers

The problem of whether a unilateral offer can be accepted by part-performance has caused difficulties for the courts. It can be argued that since the offeree has not promised to complete performance, they are free to stop at any time, so the offeror should be equally free to revoke the offer at any time. But this would mean, for example, that if A says to B, 'I'll pay you £100 if you paint my living room', A could withdraw the offer even though B had painted all but one square foot of the room, and pay nothing.

This is generally considered unjust, and various academics have expressed the view that in fact an offer cannot be withdrawn once there has been substantial performance. American academics have contended that the offeror can be seen as making two offers: the main offer that the price will be paid when the act is performed, and an implied accompanying offer that the main offer will not be revoked once performance has begun. On this assumption, the act of starting performance is both acceptance of the implied offer, and consideration for the secondary promise that the offer will not be withdrawn once performance begins. An offeror who does attempt to revoke the offer after performance has started may be sued for the breach of the secondary promise.

In England this approach has been considered rather artificial. Sir Frederick Pollock has reasoned that it might be more realistic to say that the main offer itself is accepted by beginning rather than completing performance, on the basis that acceptance simply means agreement to the terms of the offer, and there are many circumstances in which beginning performance will mean just that. Whether an act counts as beginning performance, and therefore accepting the offer, or whether it is just preparation for performing will depend on the facts of the case – so, for example, an offer of a reward for the return of lost property could still be revoked after someone had spent time looking for the property without success, but not after they had actually found it and taken steps towards returning it to the owner. This principle was adopted in 1937 by the Law Revision Committee.

## Revocation of offers for specific periods

The rule that an offer can be revoked at any time before acceptance even if the offeror has said it will remain open for a specified time could be considered unfairly biased in favour of the offeror, and makes it difficult for the offeree to plan their affairs with certainty.

In a Working Paper published in 1975, the Law Commission recommended that where an offeror promises not to revoke the offer for a specified time, that promise should be binding, without the need for consideration, and if it is broken the offeree should be able to sue for damages.

## An 'all or nothing' approach

The 'all or nothing' approach of offer and acceptance is not helpful in cases where there is clearly not a binding contract under that approach, and yet going back on agreements made would cause great hardship or inconvenience to one party. The problems associated with house-buying are well known – the buyer may go to all the expense of a survey and solicitor's fees, and may even have sold their own house, only to find that the seller withdraws the house from sale, sells it to someone else, or demands a higher price – generally known as 'gazumping'. So long as all this takes place before contracts are exchanged, the buyer has no remedy at all (though the Government is proposing to legislate to deal with some of these specific problems). Similarly, in a commercial situation, pressure of time may mean that a company starts work on a potential project before a contract is drawn up and signed. They will be at a disadvantage if in the end the other party decides not to contract.

## Objectivity

The courts claim that they are concerned with following the intention of the parties in deciding whether there is a contract, yet they make it quite clear that they are not actually seeking to discover what **was** intended, but what, looking at the parties' behaviour, an 'officious bystander' might assume they intended. This can mean that even though the parties were actually in agreement, no contract results, as was the case in **Felthouse** *v* **Bindley** – the nephew had asked for the horse to be kept out of the sale because he was going to sell it to his uncle, but because he did not actually communicate his acceptance, there was no contract.

## Answering questions

Alexander has four pet white rats which have been trained to dance together as a group. They escape from their cage. Alexander places an advertisement in the local newspaper describing the rats and promises to pay £1,000 for each rat to anyone who returns the rats to him. Beatrice, Alexander's neighbour, finds one of the rats. She keeps it warm and well fed in a shoe box overnight and then takes it to Alexander's house. Before she can reach the house, the rat escapes from the shoe box, runs away from her, and then wriggles through a hole back into Alexander's house. Charles searches diligently for the rats for two days. He spends £10 on bus fares travelling to different parts of the city. When he finds one of the rats, he takes it home with him and does not immediately return it. David finds another rat. Unfortunately, it has been savaged by a fox and is now dead. David takes the corpse to Alexander, who refuses to pay him anything. Ethel, Alexander's sister, finds another rat in her room. She gives the rat to Alexander, who refuses to pay her anything. Alexander decides that, as one of the rats is dead, there is no point in reassembling them as a dancing group. Accordingly, he places leaflets about the city cancelling the promise of a reward. Charles does not see the leaflets and returns the rat he found to Alexander later that day. Alexander refuses to pay him anything.

Advise Alexander. *London External LL.B*

Alexander has made an offer to enter into a unilateral contract: **Carlill** *v* **Carbolic Smoke Ball Co.** Has this offer been accepted by Beatrice, Charles, David or Ethel?

### Beatrice

Beatrice has failed to accept the offer because the rat ran away before she could return it to Alexander in accordance with the terms of his offer.

### Charles

Before Charles returns the rat, Alexander purports to withdraw his offer. Following the cases of **Daulia Ltd** v **Four Millbank Nominees Ltd** (1978) and **Errington** v **Errington** (1952), once an offeree has started to perform the act of acceptance, the offeror cannot withdraw their offer. It is a question of fact whether Charles has done enough to amount to starting to perform the act of acceptance. It will depend on whether this required Charles to have started to return the rat (which he had not done) or simply find the rat. In addition, in order for Alexander to effectively withdraw the offer, the withdrawal must be made by a method which reaches substantially the same audience as the original offer (**Shuey** v **United States**). Again, this will be a question of fact whether the leaflets satisfy this requirement, when the original offer was made by an advertisement in a local newspaper.

### David

David returns a dead rat. The advert makes no express statement that the rat had to be alive, but a court might be prepared to imply such a term (see p. 137).

### Ethel

Ethel returns the rat before the offer is withdrawn. But Ethel is a family member, and there will therefore be an issue as to whether Alexander had an intention to contract with Ethel: this is discussed at p. 61. On the facts, the court might be prepared to rebut the presumption against an intention to create legal relations between members of the family, because this was an offer to the world at large, with a general intention to create legal relations. In which case, Alexander would have to pay the reward to Ethel.

At 9.00 am on Monday 13 August, Maurice, a car dealer, sends a telex to Austin offering to sell him a rare vintage car for £50,000. Austin receives the telex at 9.15 am and telexes his acceptance at 1.00 pm. Austin is aware that Maurice's office is closed for lunch between 1.00 and 2.00 pm. On his return to the office, Maurice does not bother to check whether he has received a telex from Austin and at 2.30 pm receives an offer for the car from Ford, which he accepts. At 4.00 pm Austin hears from another car dealer that Maurice has sold the car to Ford. He is advised that it will cost him an additional £2,000 to buy a similar car and he immediately sends Maurice another telex demanding that the original car be sold to him. Maurice receives this telex at 5.00 pm, at the same time as he reads the acceptance telex.

Advise Austin of his legal position and what remedies, if any, are open to him. *Oxford*

Austin clearly wishes to establish that, at some point, he made a binding contract with Maurice; your task is to pinpoint when, if at all, that contract was made, using the rules of offer and acceptance. The clearest way to do this is to take each communication in turn, and consider its legal effect.

Maurice's first telex is clearly an offer; does Austin validly accept it? The general rule is that acceptance takes effect on communication; the application of this rule to telexed acceptances is contained in the cases of **Entores** and **Brinkibon**. Considering that the telex was sent outside working hours, when should it take effect, and considering the factors mentioned in **Brinkibon** – intentions of the parties, standard business practice – where should the risk lie? Obviously there is no clear answer, but in assessing where the risk should lie, you might take into account the fact that it seems reasonable for Austin to assume the telex would be read shortly after the lunch hour was finished, and to expect Maurice to check whether any reply had been received. This is relevant because in other cases on communication, the courts seem reluctant to bail out parties who fail to receive messages through their own fault (such as the requirement that telephone callers should ask for clarification if they cannot hear the other party – **Entores**). If Austin's telex acceptance is deemed to take effect when the telex is sent, a binding contract exists between them at that point, and this will take priority over the contract made with Ford. You should then consider the position if the rule that acceptance only takes effect on communication is strictly applied.

The next relevant communication is the other car dealer telling Austin that the car has been sold; **Dickinson** v **Dodds** makes it plain that information from a third party can amount to a revocation, and if this is the case, the offer ceases to be available and there is no contract between Austin and Maurice. However, in **Dickinson** v **Dodds** the message from the third party was such that the revocation was as clear as if the offeror had said it himself; if for any reason this was not the case here (if the dealer was known to be untrustworthy, for example), there would be no revocation, and the offer would still be available for acceptance at 5 pm, at which point the contract would be made.

The issue of remedies is discussed fully in Chapter 15, but, assuming a contract was made, Austin is likely to be limited to claiming damages. Maurice could only be forced to sell the car if the courts granted specific performance, and this is only done when damages would be an inadequate way of putting the claimant in the position they should have enjoyed if the contract had been performed as agreed. Here this could be done by allowing Austin to claim the difference between the car's price and the cost of a replacement.

Peter's car has been stolen. He places an advertisement in the Morriston *Evening News* stating that a reward of £1,000 will be given to any person who provides information leading to the recovery of the car – provided the reward is claimed by 1 January. Andrew, a policeman, finds the car, which has suffered severe accident damage. His best friend Kelvin tells him about the reward and Andrew applies for it by a letter posted on 30 December. The letter arrives at Peter's house on 2 January.

Advise Andrew whether he has a contractual right to the reward. *WJEC*

This question concerns the issue of offer and acceptance and consideration in unilateral contracts. You first need to consider whether Peter's advertisement is an offer. It is worth pointing out that not all advertisements are seen as offers, although in this case the issue is fairly straightforward as there are several cases in which advertisements proposing unilateral contracts, and specifically involving rewards, have been recognised as offers.

The fact that Andrew did not see the advertisement but was told about it by a friend seems to raise the issue of whether an offer can be accepted by someone who does not know about it. The cases on this matter are inconclusive, but the fact that Andrew does know about the reward by the time he applies for it would seem to avoid the problem.

The next issue is whether Andrew applies for the reward in time. As you know, acceptance does not usually take effect until it is communicated, but acceptances sent by post may take effect on posting – the postal rule. The postal rule will apply so long as it is reasonable to submit the application by post, and here there seems no reason why it should not be. This means that the offer is accepted in time, even though the letter arrives after the specified closing date.

However, there is another important issue to examine: consideration (discussed in Chapter 6). Since Andrew is a policeman, it could be argued that finding the car and informing the owner of its whereabouts is no more than his public duty. In order to have provided consideration for the reward, he would need to have gone beyond this, as explained in cases such as **Glasbrook Brothers** *v* **Glamorgan County Council** (1925) and **Harris** *v* **Sheffield United** (see p. 99).

---

 Critically evaluate what in law will amount to an 'offer'. *OCR*

 Your introduction could start with a definition of an offer, which is stated (at p. 12) to be a communication which indicates the terms on which the offeror is prepared to make a contract, and gives a clear indication that the offeror intends to be bound by those terms if they are accepted by the offeree. Your introduction could also put the concept of an offer into the wider context of the principle of freedom of contract. Contract law's emphasis on the requirement of an offer is an example of the belief that the parties should be free to make contracts on any terms they choose.

You could then move on to distinguishing the concept of an offer from an invitation to treat. You might start by looking at bilateral contracts and examine the approach of the courts to the specific scenarios of advertisements, shopping, timetables and tickets for transport, tenders (p. 39), auctions (p. 39) and the sale of land (p. 42). Offers for unilateral contracts could then be considered, and in particular the case of **Carlill** *v* **Carbolic Smoke Ball Co**.

The next stage of your answer could contain an examination of how long an offer lasts (p. 17).

The question requires you to 'critically evaluate' and it will therefore not be enough simply to describe the law. One of the problem areas has been the 'battle of the forms' (p. 25), and you could look closely at cases such as **Butler Machine Tool Ltd** *v* **Ex-Cell-O Corp**. The case of **Clarke** *v* **Dunraven** (p. 43) provides an example of the type of scenario which does not fit comfortably within the concept of offer (and acceptance). Other criticisms of the law on offers can be found (at p. 44) under the subheading 'Problems with offer and acceptance'.

**Summary of Chapter 1**

For a contract to exist, usually one party must have made an offer, and the other must have accepted it. Once acceptance takes effect, a contract will usually be binding on both parties.

## Unilateral and bilateral contracts

Most contracts are bilateral. This means that each party takes on an obligation, usually by promising the other something. By contrast, a unilateral contract arises where only one party assumes an obligation under the contract.

## Offer

The person making an offer is called the offeror, and the person to whom the offer is made is called the offeree. A communication will be treated as an offer if it indicates the terms on which the offeror is prepared to make a contract, and gives a clear indication that the offeror intends to be bound by those terms if they are accepted by the offeree. An offer may be express or implied.

## Offers to the public at large

In most cases, an offer will be made to a specified person, though offers can be addressed to a group of people, or even to the general public. A contract arising from an offer to the public at large, like that in **Carlill** v **Carbolic Smoke Ball Co** (1893), is usually a unilateral contract.

## Invitations to treat

Some kinds of transaction involve a preliminary stage in which one party invites the other to make an offer. This stage is called an invitation to treat. Confusion can sometimes arise when what would appear, in the everyday sense of the word, to be an offer is held by the law to be only an invitation to treat. This issue arises particularly in the following areas.

### Advertisements

Advertisements for unilateral contracts are usually treated as offers. Advertisements for a bilateral contract are generally considered invitations to treat.

### Shopping

Price-marked goods displayed on the shelves or in the windows of shops are generally regarded as invitations to treat, rather than offers to sell goods at that price: **Pharmaceutical Society of Great Britain** v **Boots Cash Chemists (Southern) Ltd** (1953).

### Timetables and tickets for transport

The legal position here is rather unclear; no single reliable rule has emerged, and it seems that the exact point at which a contract is made depends in each case on the particular facts.

### How long does an offer last?

An offer may cease to exist under any of the following circumstances.

### Specified time

Where an offeror states that an offer will remain open for a specific length of time, it lapses when that time is up.

### Reasonable length of time

Where the offeror has not specified how long the offer will remain open, it will lapse after a reasonable length of time has passed.

### Failure of a precondition

Some offers are made subject to certain conditions, and if such conditions are not in place, the offer may lapse.

### Rejection

An offer lapses when the offeree rejects it.

### Counter-offer

A counter-offer terminates the original offer: **Hyde** *v* **Wrench** (1840).

### Requests for information

A request for information about an offer (such as whether delivery could be earlier than suggested) does not amount to a counter-offer, so the original offer remains open.

### Death of the offeror

The position is not entirely clear, but it appears that if the offeree knows that the offeror has died, the offer will lapse; if the offeree is unaware of the offeror's death, it probably will not.

### Death of the offeree

There is no English case on this point, but it seems probable that the offer lapses and cannot be accepted after the offeree's death by the offeree's representatives.

## Withdrawal of offer

The withdrawal of an offer is sometimes described as the revocation of an offer. The old case of **Payne** *v* **Cave** (1789) establishes the principle that an offer may be withdrawn at any time up until it is accepted. A number of rules apply in relation to the withdrawal of offers.

### Withdrawal must be communicated

It is not enough for offerors simply to change their mind about an offer; they must notify the offeree that it is being revoked: **Byrne** *v* **Van Tienhoven** (1880). The revocation of an offer does not have to be communicated by the offeror; the communication can be made by some other reliable source: **Dickinson** *v* **Dodds** (1876).

### Withdrawal of an offer to enter into a unilateral contract

There are a number of special rules that apply in relation to the revocation of an offer to enter into a unilateral contract. An offer to enter into such a contract cannot be revoked once the offeree has commenced performance: **Errington** *v* **Errington** (1952).

## Acceptance

Acceptance of an offer means unconditional agreement to all the terms of that offer. Merely remaining silent cannot amount to an acceptance, unless it is absolutely clear that acceptance was intended: **Felthouse** *v* **Bindley** (1862).

### Acceptance of an offer to enter into a unilateral contract

Unilateral contracts are usually accepted by conduct. There is no acceptance until the relevant act has been completely performed.

### Acceptance must be unconditional

An acceptance must accept the precise terms of an offer.

### Negotiation and the 'battle of the forms'

Where parties carry on a long process of negotiation, it may be difficult to pinpoint exactly when an offer has been made and accepted. In such cases the courts will look at the whole course of negotiations to decide whether the parties have in fact reached agreement at all and, if so, when. This process can be particularly difficult where the so-called 'battle of the forms' arises. The general rule in such cases is that the 'last shot' wins the battle. Each new form issued is treated as a counter-offer, so that when one party performs its obligation under the contract (by delivering goods, for example), that action will be seen as acceptance by conduct of the offer in the last form.

### Specified methods of acceptance

If an offeror states that his or her offer must be accepted in a particular way, then only acceptance by that method or an equally effective one will be binding. Where a specified method of acceptance has been included for the offeree's own benefit, however, the offeree is not obliged to accept in that way.

### Acceptance must be communicated

An acceptance does not usually take effect until it is communicated to the offeror.

### Exceptions to the communication rule

There are some circumstances in which an acceptance may take effect without being communicated to the offeror.

#### Terms of the offer

An offer may state or imply that acceptance need not be communicated to the offeror.

#### Conduct of the offeror

An offeror who fails to receive an acceptance through their own fault may be prevented from claiming that the non-communication means they should not be bound by the contract.

#### The postal rule

The general rule for acceptances by post is that they take effect when they are posted, rather than when they are communicated: **Adams** *v* **Lindsell** (1818). The traditional title 'postal rule' has become slightly misleading because the rule does not only apply to the post but could also potentially apply to certain other non-instantaneous modes of communication. There are certain exceptions to the postal rule:

- offers requiring communication of acceptance;
- instant methods of communication;
- misdirected acceptance.

## Ignorance of the offer

It is generally thought that a person cannot accept an offer of which they are unaware, because in order to create a binding contract, the parties must reach agreement. If their wishes merely happen to coincide, that may be very convenient for both, but it does not constitute a contract and cannot legally bind them.

## Time of the formation of the contract

Normally, a contract is formed when an effective acceptance has been communicated to the offeree.

# Reading list

Beale and Dugdale, 'Contracts between businessmen' (1975) 2 British Journal of Law and Society 45

Burrows and Peel (2010) *Contract Formation and Parties*, Oxford: Oxford University Press

Evans, 'The Anglo-American mailing rule: some problems of offer and acceptance in contracts by correspondence' (1966) 15 International and Comparative Law Quarterly 553

Gardner, 'Trashing with Trollope: a deconstruction of the postal rules in contract' (1992) 12 Oxford Journal of Legal Studies 170

Graw, 'Puff, Pepsi and "That Plane" – the John Leonard Saga' (2000) 15 Journal of Contract Law 281

Rawlings, 'The battle of the forms' (1979) 42 Modern Law Review 715

Treitel and Peel (2007) *Treitel on the Law of Contract*, London: Sweet and Maxwell

### Reading on the internet

The Consumer Protection (Distance Selling) Regulations 2000 are available on the website of the Office of Public Sector Information at:

http://www.opsi.gov.uk/si/si2000/20002334.htm

The Office of Fair Trading provides a helpful guide to the distance-selling regulations on its website at:

http://www.oft.gov.uk/Business/Legal/DSR/default.htm

# Chapter 2
## Certainty

## This chapter explains:

- the legal requirement that the terms of the agreement must be certain in order for there to be a binding contract;
- an agreement can be sufficiently certain if it lays down how the terms can be clarified;
- clear terms can be implied by statute;
- terms can be clarified by the common law; and
- minor uncertain terms can simply be deleted.

In order to be a binding contract, an agreement must be certain – that is, it should not be unduly vague, or obviously incomplete. Two businessmen might orally reach an agreement over the telephone or during a business lunch. They might intend to put the agreement in writing at a later stage, but the oral agreement could be sufficiently certain (and made with an intention to create legal relations) so that it would itself immediately be a binding contract. Thus, in **Bear Stearns Bank plc** v **Forum Global Equity Ltd** (2007), Forum Global was owed money by the Parmalat group of companies which had collapsed in Italy in 2003. Under the subsequent insolvency procedures, it was expected to receive payment of a portion of the money owed. In a telephone conversation Forum Global agreed to sell the title to these loans to Bear Stearns for 2.9 million euros. Much of the detail of the agreement was left to be finalised at a later stage by the parties' lawyers. Forum Global later decided not to proceed with the sale and Bear Stearns brought civil proceedings. The High Court allowed the claim, finding that as the price and product had been agreed, there was a sufficiently certain agreement to bind the parties.

By contrast, in **Loftus** v **Roberts** (1902) Roberts engaged an actress to appear in a play at 'a West End salary to be mutually arranged between us'. The court held that there was no binding contract between them because the provision concerning payment was too vague.

Similarly, in **Scammell** v **Ouston** (1941), Ouston agreed to buy a van from Scammell, providing his old lorry in part-exchange and paying the balance 'on hire-purchase terms' over two years. Before the precise nature of those terms could be negotiated, Scammell decided not to go ahead with the deal, and claimed there was no contract between the parties. The House of Lords agreed, pointing out that although the courts aimed to uphold an agreement if there really was one, the terms used were too vague to signify any true agreement. The phrase 'hire-purchase terms' could be used to describe many different arrangements: it left open such questions as whether payments would be made on a weekly, monthly or yearly basis; whether there would be an initial deposit; and what the interest rate would be. Consequently, the parties could not be said to have made a sufficiently certain agreement to constitute a contract.

In **Baird Textile Holdings Ltd** v **Marks & Spencer plc** (2001) (discussed on p. 109) Baird Textile Holdings argued that they had a contract with Marks & Spencer under which Marks & Spencer 'would acquire garments from BTH in quantities and at prices which in all the circumstances were reasonable'. The Court of Appeal held that these terms would be too uncertain to be part of a valid contract.

The production of the highly successful television show, *Fame Academy*, gave rise to litigation in the courts in the case of **McNicholas Construction (Holdings) Ltd** v **Endemol UK plc** (2003). The claimants owned a house that the *Fame Academy* production company had been interested in renting. Following negotiations the house owners thought that a binding agreement had been reached, but the production company rented an alternative property. The claimants brought proceedings for the unpaid rent of £185,000, but their claim was rejected. The Chancery Division concluded that no binding contract had been formed to rent the property. One of the reasons for their decision was that the terms of any agreement had not been finalised, with a range of important terms still to be agreed.

The courts will usually look to see if there is any way to make an apparently vague or incomplete agreement more certain; as Lord Tomlin observed in **Hillas** v **Arcos** (1932) (below), they do not want to 'incur the reproach of being the destroyer of bargains'. The following are the main methods used.

# Provision for clarification

In some circumstances prices and other factors affecting a contract are likely to fluctuate, and the parties to an agreement will therefore be reluctant to commit themselves to a rigid arrangement concerning those factors. In such cases, contracts may leave such details vague, but contain provisions stating how they are to be clarified (such as by independent arbitration). Generally, an agreement to agree will not be binding, but where a mechanism has been provided to finalise the details of the contract, an agreement to agree can amount to a binding contract.

In **Foley** v **Classique Coaches** (1934) the claimant was the owner of a petrol station and some land adjoining it. The defendants ran a coach business, and the claimant sold them the land, on condition that they entered into an agreement to buy all the petrol they needed for the coaches from him, 'at a price to be agreed by the parties in writing and from time to time'. This agreement went ahead, but the defendants broke it, and argued that it was incomplete, and therefore not a binding contract, because the term regarding price was too vague. In fact, the contract provided that any dispute should be referred to arbitration in accordance with the Arbitration Act 1889 (now the Arbitration Act 1996). The Court of Appeal interpreted this as meaning that there was an implied term that the petrol should be sold at a reasonable price, with the arbitration clause being intended to sort out any dispute as to whether a price was reasonable. This meant that the contract was more certain than it looked at first glance, and the court decided that it was sufficiently certain to be binding on the parties.

## Topical Issue

### Budget airlines

In **Jet2.com** v **Blackpool Airport** (2012) the parties had entered into a contract for Jet2 to operate from Blackpool Airport for 15 years. Clause 1 of the contract stated that the parties would 'co-operate together and use their best endeavours to promote [Jet2's] low cost services' from the airport, and Blackpool would 'use all reasonable endeavours to provide a cost base that will facilitate [Jet2's] low cost pricing'.

The agreement said nothing about the times of the flights. Blackpool's normal opening hours were 7 am to 9 pm. However, for the first four years of the contract, Jet2 operated regular departures and arrivals outside the normal opening hours, inevitably causing the airport to incur additional costs in providing support services. Following a change of ownership, in October 2010, the airport gave Jet2 seven days' notice that it would not accept flights scheduled outside normal hours. Jet2 sued for breach of contract.

The Court of Appeal noted that there was a difference between:

- a clause that is so uncertain it cannot create a binding obligation; and
- a clause that does give rise to a binding obligation, the precise limits of which are difficult to define in advance, but which can nonetheless be given practical content.

An obligation to use best endeavours to promote another's business was of the latter sort. The court held that Blackpool Airport's obligation to use its 'best endeavours' to promote Jet2's low-cost services gave rise to an enforceable obligation to operate outside normal opening hours, as this was essential to Jet2's business model. The airport could not escape this obligation on the basis that to comply would be unprofitable.

## Terms implied by statute

In some cases, statutes provide that certain terms should be read into contracts of particular types, even though those terms have not actually been agreed between the parties. For example, under the Sale of Goods Act 1979 an agreement for the sale of goods can become binding as soon as the parties have agreed to buy and sell, with the details of the contract being laid down by law, or determined by the standard of reasonableness. In such a case, the parties do not even have to have agreed on a price – s. 8(2) of the Act provides that if the contract does not specify a price, the buyer is entitled to pay a reasonable price. We will look at terms implied by statute more fully in Chapter 7.

## Previous course of dealing

Where two parties have had dealings in the past, their previous agreements may be used to clarify uncertain terms in a contract.

 **Key Case**    Hillas *v* Arcos

In **Hillas *v* Arcos** (1932) Hillas had contracted to buy timber 'of fair specification' from Arcos in 1930. The agreement also included an option to purchase the following year, which did not detail the type or size of the wood to be bought. When Hillas tried to exercise the option, they discovered that Arcos had in fact already sold all the wood they had that year, and so Hillas sued for breach of contract. The House of Lords held that although the terms used were apparently unspecific, the parties were both very familiar with the way business was done in the timber industry, and had done a large amount of business with each other in the past. Consequently, the terms could be interpreted in the light of what they would usually mean in that industry and between those parties. They were therefore sufficiently certain to create a contract.

**Legal Principle**
Where two parties have had dealings in the past, their previous agreements may be used to clarify uncertain terms in a contract.

## Reasonableness

Sometimes the courts will clarify vague terms by relying on the principle of reasonableness. In **Sudbrook Trading Estate Ltd *v* Eggleton** (1983) leaseholders had the option to buy the premises 'at such price as may be agreed upon by two valuers', the parties being able to nominate one each. The landlord refused to appoint a valuer, and claimed that the agreement was not a binding contract because there was no provision detailing how the price would be reached if the two valuers disagreed. The House of Lords disagreed, stating that the important point was that the price was to be set by professional valuers. Such individuals would be obliged to apply professional and, by implication, reasonable standards in setting the price, and therefore the option was actually a definite agreement to sell at a reasonable price. The condition that each party should appoint one of the valuers was merely 'subsidiary and inessential'.

## Custom

Apparent vagueness can be resolved by custom – as we have seen, the customary way of dealing in the timber industry played a part in clarifying the terms in **Hillas** v **Arcos**, in combination with the parties' previous mutual dealings.

## The 'officious bystander'

A term may be implied by applying the 'officious bystander' test. Basically the court asks itself whether someone observing the making of a contract would have believed that a particular term was part of the contract. An example might be that if you heard your next-door neighbour offer to buy someone's car for 'a thousand' you would, assuming you were in Britain, presume that she meant £1,000, rather than the same amount in dollars or pesetas, even though the form of currency had not been specified. (See Chapter 7, p. 138 for more detail.)

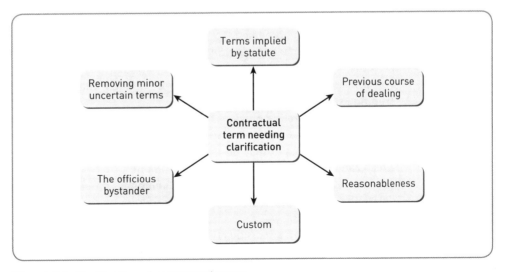

**Figure 2.1** Clarification of contractual terms

## Removing minor uncertain terms

In extreme cases, a minor term may be not only vague but also meaningless. Providing it is sufficiently unimportant, it can be struck out, allowing the courts to enforce the rest of the contract. Thus in **Nicolene** v **Simmonds** (1953) Nicolene ordered some steel bars from Simmonds. The terms of the agreement to buy were quite clear, except that the transaction was stated to be subject to 'the usual conditions of acceptance'. The parties later disagreed about the quality of the metal delivered, at which point Simmonds contended that there was no enforceable contract because the words 'usual conditions of acceptance' were too uncertain. The court agreed that the words were uncertain because there were in fact no 'usual conditions', but it held that, as the problematic term only concerned a subsidiary matter, they could be ignored.

## Answering questions

Albert is an importer and distributor of tea. Two years ago he bought five tonnes of tea from Louise, at a cost of £25,000. Last Monday, Albert ordered from Louise ten tonnes of Indian tea of 'standard grade' at £40,000. The tea was to be packed according to the 'established hygienic procedures'. Louise agreed to deliver the tea, but then later refused to do so. She argued that no contract existed between herself and Albert because there was no precise agreement as to the quality of the tea and there were no established hygienic procedures for packing tea.

In order for there to be a binding contract between Albert and Louise, an agreement must be certain, that is it should not be unduly vague or obviously incomplete. There are two aspects of this agreement which appear uncertain: the type of tea that was to be delivered and the requirement that the tea should have been packed under the established hygienic procedures. In practice, the courts will usually look to see if there is any way to make an apparently vague agreement more certain. Under the Sale of Goods Act 1979 an agreement for the sale of goods (here we have an agreement for the sale of tea) can become binding as soon as the parties have agreed to buy and sell, with the details of the contract being determined by the standard of reasonableness. This principle of reasonableness will also be applied under common law: **Sudbrook Trading Estate Ltd** v **Eggleton**.

In addition, there is a previous course of dealing between Albert and Louise, so the courts can look at their earlier agreement to clarify the meaning of these uncertain terms: **Hillas** v **Arcos**. It may be that there are also relevant customs in the tea trade which can clarify the meaning of the agreement.

Applying the principle in **Nicolene** v **Simmonds**, the court might be prepared to delete the term as to the usual hygienic procedures on the basis that it is a minor term that is meaningless.

In the light of this discussion it is likely that, in the business context, a court will find this agreement sufficiently certain to be binding on Louise.

# Summary of Chapter 2

In order to be a binding contract, an agreement must be certain – that is, it should not be unduly vague, or obviously incomplete. The courts will usually look to see if there is any way to make an apparently vague or incomplete agreement more certain.

## Provision for clarification

Contracts may leave certain details vague, but contain provisions stating how they are to be clarified.

## Terms implied by statute

In some cases, statutes provide that certain terms should be read into contracts of particular types, even though those terms have not actually been agreed between the parties.

## Previous course of dealing

Where two parties have had dealings in the past, their previous agreements may be used to clarify uncertain terms in a contract.

## Reasonableness

Sometimes the courts will clarify vague terms by relying on the principle of reasonableness.

## Custom

Apparent vagueness can be resolved by custom.

## The 'officious bystander'

A term may be implied by applying the 'officious bystander' test, under which the court asks whether someone observing the making of a contract would have believed that a particular term was part of the contract.

## Removing minor uncertain terms

In extreme cases, a minor term may be not only vague but also meaningless. Providing it is sufficiently unimportant, it can be struck out, allowing the courts to enforce the rest of the contract.

# Reading list

McLauchlan, 'Rethinking agreements to agree' (1998) 18 New Zealand Universities Law Review 77

# Chapter 3
## Intention to create legal relations

### This chapter explains:

- there is only a legally binding contract if both parties intend to create legal relations;
- there is a rebuttable presumption that parties do not intend to create legal relations when they enter into a domestic or social agreement; and
- there is a rebuttable presumption that parties do intend to create legal relations when they enter into a commercial agreement.

If two or more parties make an agreement without any intention of being legally bound by it, that agreement will not be regarded by the courts as a contract. It is important to remember with regard to this issue that the courts assess the parties' intentions objectively – so, if to onlookers their behaviour or words would suggest they intended to be bound, the fact that one secretly had reservations is irrelevant.

As far as intent to be legally bound is concerned, contracts can be divided into domestic and social agreements on the one hand and commercial transactions on the other. Where an agreement falls into the domestic and social category, there is a rebuttable presumption that the parties do not intend to create legal relations. The reverse applies in commercial agreements, where it is presumed that the parties do intend such agreements to be legally binding. Again, this principle can be rebutted if there is evidence that the parties did not intend their agreement to be legally enforceable.

# Social and domestic agreements

## Agreements between husband and wife

Where a husband and wife who are living together as one household make an agreement, courts will assume that they do not intend to be legally bound, unless there is evidence to the contrary.

**Key Case**   Balfour *v* Balfour

In **Balfour *v* Balfour** (1919) the defendant was a civil servant stationed in Ceylon (now Sri Lanka). While the couple were on leave in England, Mrs Balfour was taken ill, and it eventually became clear that her husband would have to return by himself. He promised to pay her a monthly maintenance allowance of £30. They later decided to separate, upon which the husband refused to make any more payments. The Court of Appeal decided he was not bound to pay the allowance because at the time when the agreement was made there was no intention to create legal relations. When this type of agreement was made between husband and wife, said Atkin LJ, it was a family matter in which the courts really had no place to interfere.

**Legal Principle**
Where a husband and wife living together as one household make an agreement, the courts will assume they do not intend to be legally bound, unless there is evidence to the contrary.

On its facts, **Balfour** might well be decided differently if it arose today; while the courts still seem reluctant to give effect to agreements made while spouses are still cohabiting, there have been a string of cases in which those who are separating or divorcing are treated as intending to create legal relations. In **Merritt** v **Merritt** (1969) Mr Merritt had left his wife to go and live with another woman, and subsequently met his spouse to resolve various financial arrangements. Sitting in Mr Merritt's car, they decided that he would pay his wife £40 a month, out of which she was to pay the outstanding mortgage payments on their house; he would transfer the house to her sole ownership when the mortgage was paid off. Mrs Merritt then refused to get out of the car until her husband put the agreement in writing. Eventually, he signed a piece of paper stating what they had agreed. The wife duly paid off the mortgage, but the husband then refused to transfer ownership of the house to her. The Court of Appeal upheld the wife's claim. Lord Denning pointed out that the presumption applied in **Balfour** v **Balfour**, that an agreement between husband and wife was 'a family arrangement', was not valid where the parties had separated or were about to do so. In such circumstances the parties 'do not rely on honourable understandings', but 'bargain keenly', and it could be safely presumed that any agreement between them was intended to be legally binding.

The US courts have shown themselves increasingly willing to give effect to domestic agreements, as shown by the case of **Morone** v **Morone** (1980), where an agreement between a cohabiting couple that the man would financially support the woman in return for her help in running their home and helping in his business was held to be binding.

## Agreements between parent and child

Agreements of a domestic nature between parents and children are also presumed not to be intended to be binding, though again the presumption can be rebutted.

**Key Case**   Jones v Padavatton

In **Jones** v **Padavatton** (1969) the claimant was a resident of Trinidad. Her daughter had a secretarial job in Washington, but her mother wanted her to give it up and train to be a barrister in England. The mother therefore volunteered to give her daughter a monthly allowance for the duration of her Bar studies. The daughter accepted the offer and went to England. Later on, the pair made a second agreement, under which the mother bought a house for the daughter to live in, and in which she could rent out rooms in order to support herself, instead of receiving the allowance. Neither agreement was ever put in writing. The daughter persistently failed to pass her Bar examinations and, five years after the original bargain was made, they quarrelled, and her mother sought possession of the house. On the facts of the case, the majority of the Court of Appeal considered that neither agreement was intended to create legal relations: they were merely family arrangements in which both parties, who had been close at the time, were happy to trust each other to keep the bargain. The mother was therefore entitled to possession of the house.

**Legal Principle**
Agreements of a domestic nature between parents and children are presumed not to be intended to be binding, although this presumption can be rebutted.

## Social agreements

The presumption that an agreement is not intended to be legally binding is also applied to social relationships between people who are not related. Again, it can be rebutted. In **Simpkins** *v* **Pays** (1955) the claimant enjoyed entering competitions run in Sunday newspapers. When he took lodgings in the defendant's house, she and her granddaughter began to do the competitions with him, sharing the cost of entry. The claimant filled in the forms in the name of the defendant, and she promised to share any winnings. Eventually, one of the entries was successful, and the defendant won £750. The claimant claimed a third of the sum as his share of the prize, but the defendant refused, claiming that she had not intended to be legally bound by the agreement. The court upheld the claimant's claim, considering that they had all contributed to the competition with the expectation that any prize would be shared.

## Topical Issue

### Winning the lottery

Many of us have dreamt of winning the national lottery and buy tickets every week at our local shop hoping to win the Saturday night draw – unfortunately we know that the odds are stacked against us winning. Some people buy lottery tickets with a group of friends or work colleagues and occasionally disputes can arise as to how the money should be shared. No cases have come to court directly relating to lottery tickets but a couple of interesting cases have arisen relating to purported agreements between women playing bingo to share any winnings. The same legal principles are likely to be applied to any future disputes relating to lottery winnings. Such agreements are viewed as social agreements by the courts for which there is a rebuttable presumption that the parties do not intend to create legal relations. In **Peck** *v* **Lateu** (1973) the court rebutted this presumption and found an intention to create legal relations where two women had agreed to share money won by either of them at bingo.

In **Wilson** *v* **Burnett** (2007) two women claimed they had reached an oral agreement with the defendant that if any of them won more than £10 at bingo they would share the winnings equally between them. The defendant admitted she had discussed this idea with the other two, but argued that no agreement had been reached. On the facts the judge concluded no such agreement had been reached, partly because there did not appear to be an intention to create legal relations.

In the light of these two cases, the starting point of the courts will be the presumption against an intention to create legal relations, and it will very much depend on the factual evidence before the court whether this presumption will be rebutted. In the first case it was; in the second case it was not.

# Commercial agreements

There is a strong presumption in commercial agreements that the parties intend to be legally bound, and, unless there is very clear contrary evidence, this presumption will not be rebutted.

## Key Case    Esso Petroleum Ltd *v* Customs and Excise Commissioners

In **Esso Petroleum Ltd *v* Customs and Excise Commissioners** (1976) Esso ran a sales promotion in which 'coins' showing members of the England football squad for the 1970 World Cup were to be given away free, one with every four gallons of petrol. The scheme was advertised on television and by posters at filling stations. The case arose when for tax purposes it became necessary to decide whether or not there was a contract of sale – did a motorist who bought four gallons of petrol have a contractual right to one of the coins? The House of Lords held, by a majority, that the coins were not being sold, and so were not liable for tax, but that there was intent to create legal relations. Lord Simon pointed out that 'the whole transaction took place in a setting of business relations', that it was undesirable to allow companies to make promises in advertisements that they were not bound to keep, and that Esso knew that, despite the coins' negligible monetary value, they would be attractive to motorists and Esso would therefore derive considerable commercial benefit from the scheme.

### Legal Principle

There is a strong presumption in commercial agreements that the parties intend to be legally bound, and, unless there is very clear contrary evidence, this presumption will not be rebutted.

In **J Evans & Son (Portsmouth) Ltd *v* Andrea Merzario Ltd** (1976) the claimants were machinery importers, who had regularly used the defendants, a firm of forwarding agents, to arrange transport of their goods. The machinery was prone to rust if stored on deck, and so it had always been agreed that it would be carried below decks. In 1967, in the course of a 'courtesy call' to the claimants, the defendants' representative put forward the idea of carrying the goods by container transport, assuring them that their containers would always be kept below decks because of the rust problem (many container ships are designed to have the containers stacked on deck). The claimants agreed to the change. About a year later, a container with one of the claimants' machines inside was carried on deck instead of below, and, not being properly secured, fell overboard as the ship left port and was lost. The claimants sued, and the defendants argued that the promise to store the containers below decks was not intended to be legally binding since it was made in the course of a courtesy call, was not related to any particular transaction, and its future duration was not specified. The Court of Appeal rejected this argument, saying that the background to the promise meant that an intent to be contractually bound could be inferred: the parties had previously done business together, in which goods were always transported below decks, and the claimants would not have agreed to the change in method if the promise had not been made.

In **Bear Stearns Bank plc *v* Forum Global Equity Ltd** (2007) (discussed at p. 54) involving a telephone conversation where the price and product were agreed, but the details were left to be decided at a later stage by the parties' lawyers, the High Court found that there was a sufficient intent to create legal relations. It reached this conclusion because the parties had made such statements as the deal was 'closed' and this type of deal was often made orally.

## Exceptions to the commercial agreements presumption

The presumption that parties to a commercial agreement intend to create legal relations may be rebutted where the words of a contract, or an offer, suggest that legal relations were not intended. There are three main situations where this will occur.

## 'Mere puffs'

Where an offer is extremely vague, or clearly not intended to be taken seriously, the law will not give its acceptance contractual effect. In **Weeks** v **Tybald** (1604) the defendant announced that he would give £100 to any suitable man who would marry his daughter, but it was held that his words were not intended to be taken seriously, and his promise was not legally binding.

This principle is sometimes applied to the extravagant language used in advertising and sales promotions, but only if there is no evidence of contractual intent. In **Carlill** v **Carbolic Smoke Ball Co** (1893) (discussed at p. 13), the defendants argued that their statement was 'a mere puff', an advertising gimmick which was never intended to be taken seriously. This contention was rejected by the court, pointing out that the advertisement stated that the company had deposited £1,000 with their bankers 'to show their sincerity', which was strong evidence that they had intended to be legally bound.

## Honour clauses

In **Rose and Frank** v **Crompton Bros** (1923) the claimants had been buying goods from the defendants for some time, and in 1913 the parties signed an agreement that this arrangement should continue for a specified period, with prices set for six months at a time. Though otherwise ordinary, the agreement contained one unusual term, the 'honourable pledge clause'. It stated: 'This agreement is not entered into . . . as a formal or legal agreement, and shall not be subject to legal jurisdiction in the law courts . . . but it is only a definite expression and record of the purpose and intention of the parties concerned, to which they each honourably pledge themselves.' In 1919, the defendants terminated the agreement without giving the specified notice. The claimants sued, making two separate claims. The first was for breach of the agreement contained in the written document of July 1913, that the buying and selling arrangement would continue for the specified period. This claim was rejected by the court, which held that the wording of the agreement placed neither side under any obligation to go on giving or accepting orders. Scrutton LJ commented: 'I can see no reason why, even in business matters, the parties should not intend to rely on each other's good faith and honour, and to exclude all idea of settling disputes by an outside intervention . . .'

The second claim concerned non-delivery of goods, which the claimants had ordered in accordance with the agreement before it was terminated. This claim was upheld on the basis that when each individual order was placed and accepted it constituted a new and separate contract, which was enforceable in its own right, without reference to the original document.

Similarly, where a football pools coupon states that it is 'binding in honour only', the pools company cannot be sued for payment by a winner: **Jones** v **Vernon's Pools** (1938).

## Agreement 'subject to contract'

Use of these words on an agreement is usually (though not always) taken to mean that the parties do not intend to be legally bound until formal contracts are exchanged (see p. 42). If the parties subsequently act upon the agreement, their conduct may be interpreted as amounting to an intention to create the final contract. In **Confetti Records** v **Warner Music UK Ltd** (2003) the claimants owned the copyright in a music track that the defendant wished to use on a compilation album. Terms were discussed between the parties and the defendant sent a fax to the claimants containing deal terms, but marked 'subject to contract'. The claimant signed this and faxed it back. The court held that this did not amount to a contract. However, shortly afterwards, the claimants sent the defendant a copy of the track and an invoice stating that it was licensed for 'three years non-exclusive'. The court held that this amounted to an offer which was accepted when the defendant started to record the album. It was therefore too late for the claimant subsequently to withdraw the track, as there was already a binding contract.

## Ambiguity

Where the words of a business agreement are ambiguous, the courts will favour the interpretation which suggests that the parties did intend to create legal relations, and therefore find that there is a contract. In **Edwards** v **Skyways Ltd** (1964) the claimant was a pilot employed by the defendants. As part of a redundancy agreement, Skyways promised to make an *ex gratia* payment of a specified amount in return for Mr Edwards not claiming his full pension rights. Later, the company refused to make the payment, claiming that the words '*ex gratia*' showed that there was no intention to create legal relations. The Court of Appeal rejected this argument, stating that this was a commercial agreement and there was therefore a strong presumption in favour of creating legal relations. The words '*ex gratia*' merely signified that the employers were not admitting any pre-existing liability to make the payment; it did not mean that they were not bound by the agreement.

## Collective bargaining agreements

There is one exception to the rule that the parties to a commercial agreement are presumed to intend to be legally bound. Under a collective bargaining agreement, an employer negotiates pay and conditions with the workforce as a whole (usually represented by a trade union), rather than on an individual basis. Such agreements are binding in most countries, but in **Ford Motor Co Ltd** v **Amalgamated Union of Engineering and Foundry Workers** (1969) it was held that in English law such an agreement was not intended to be legally binding. A carefully worded written agreement had been drawn up between Ford and various trade unions, including a clause stating that the unions should not call a strike unless specified negotiating procedures had been carried out first. The union breached this clause, and the claimants sought to prevent them calling the strike. The court, basing its decision on public policy, held that there was evidence that at the time, it was the general opinion in the industrial world that such agreements were not legally enforceable, and that both sides would have known this. Therefore, they could not be said to have intended to be legally bound by the collective agreement not to strike.

This approach is now contained in the Trade Union and Labour Relations (Consolidation) Act 1992, which states that collective agreements are conclusively presumed not to be intended to be legally binding unless they expressly state otherwise in writing. This presumption is rarely, if ever, displaced, and in the past few years has been relied upon by employers seeking to break agreements to negotiate with unions. Some of the terms of the collective agreement can be expressly incorporated into the employment contract and then they will be legally binding.

**Figure 3.1** Creating legal relations

# How important is intention to create legal relations?

In practice, it is rare for contract cases to involve problems with the requirement of intention to create legal relations. This is largely because in many of the situations in which the issue might be raised, particularly domestic and social ones, there is no consideration. The courts will only consider intent to create legal relations if offer and acceptance and consideration have already been established.

The US academic, Professor Williston, has suggested that in fact the common law does not demand any positive intention to create a legal obligation as an element of contract. In his view, the separate element of intention serves no purpose in our system, and is useful only in legal systems which do not have the test of consideration to help them to determine the boundaries of contract. He suggests that mere social arrangements will be enforced as contracts if the other requirements – offer and acceptance and consideration, for example – are present, and the issue of intention to be legally bound adds nothing to the decision of the court. But the case of **Balfour v Balfour** is an example of offer, acceptance and consideration existing but there still being no contract, and the only explanation for this lack of contract seems to be that there was no intention to be legally bound.

Feminists argue that the presumption against contractual intention in domestic agreements is in fact the law's way of saying that the work usually done by women is not to be regarded as important – it is seen as something done out of love for the family, rather than an economic contribution which ought to be paid for.

## Answering questions

Robert and Theresa are planning to divorce. They have spent their married life in a house which they bought in joint names, with the help of a mortgage which has six years still to run. Robert and Theresa agree that Robert will move out of the house, and if Theresa meets the mortgage repayments for the next six years, Robert will, at the end of that time, transfer sole ownership of the house to her. Theresa pays the mortgage for a year, at which point Robert says he has changed his mind, and does not intend to transfer his share of the house to her.

Advise Theresa. How, if at all, would your advice differ if Robert had changed his mind before Theresa had started paying the mortgage?

Here you first need to consider the question of intention to create legal relations, bearing in mind that this is a domestic agreement. Point out the presumption established in **Balfour**, and its rebuttal in **Merritt**, which seems to apply here. Assuming that there is intent to create legal relations, has there been an offer and an acceptance? It would seem that Robert made a unilateral offer, to be accepted by performance, in the form of Theresa repaying the mortgage, so the question arises of whether such an offer can be revoked once performance has started. As you know, the traditional assumption was that acceptance did not take effect until performance was complete, but the opposite conclusion was reached in **Errington v Errington**. This case seems to have clear application to the facts here, and suggests that Robert cannot revoke his offer unless Theresa stops paying the mortgage. However, if this is a unilateral offer, your advice might differ should Robert attempt to revoke before the payments start, since an offer can be revoked at any time before it is accepted, in this case by performance. If, on the other hand, the agreement was bilateral, and Theresa made a promise to pay the mortgage in return for Robert's promise to convey the house to her, that agreement would become binding when the promises were exchanged, and Robert's offer could not be revoked afterwards.

# Summary of Chapter 3

An agreement will only be legally binding if the parties intend it to be so. The courts assess the parties' intentions objectively. As far as intent to be legally bound is concerned, contracts can be divided into domestic and social agreements on the one hand and commercial transactions on the other. Where an agreement falls into the domestic and social category, there is a rebuttable presumption that the parties do not intend to create legal relations. The reverse applies in commercial agreements, where it is presumed that the parties do intend such agreements to be legally binding.

## Social and domestic agreements

### Agreements between husband and wife

Where a husband and wife who are living together as one household make an agreement, courts will assume that they do not intend to be legally bound, unless there is evidence to the contrary: **Balfour** v **Balfour** (1919).

### Agreements between parent and child

Agreements of a domestic nature between parents and children are also presumed not to be intended to be binding, though again the presumption can be rebutted: **Jones** v **Padavatton** (1969).

### Social agreements

The presumption that an agreement is not intended to be legally binding is also applied to social relationships between people who are not related.

## Commercial agreements

There is a strong presumption in commercial agreements that the parties intend to be legally bound, and, unless there is very clear contrary evidence, this presumption will not be rebutted.

### Exceptions to the commercial agreements presumption

There are three main situations where this presumption will be rebutted.

#### 'Mere puffs'

Where an offer is extremely vague, or clearly not intended to be taken seriously, the law will not give its acceptance contractual effect.

#### Honour clauses

In **Rose & Frank Co** v **Crompton Bros** (1923) Scrutton LJ commented: 'I can see no reason why, even in business matters, the parties should not intend to rely on each other's good faith and honour, and to exclude all idea of settling disputes by an outside intervention . . .'

### Agreement 'subject to contract'

Use of these words on an agreement is usually (though not always) taken to mean that the parties do not intend to be legally bound until formal contracts are exchanged.

### Ambiguity

Where the words of a business agreement are ambiguous, the courts will favour the interpretation which suggests that the parties did intend to create legal relations, and therefore find that there is a contract.

### Collective bargaining agreements

In English law, collective bargaining agreements are not intended to be legally binding.

 # Reading list

Hedley, 'Keeping contract in its place: *Balfour v Balfour* and the enforceability of informal agreements' (1985) 5 Oxford Journal of Legal Studies 391

Hepple, 'Intention to create legal relations' (1970) 20 Cambridge Law Journal 122

De Moor, 'Intention in the law of contract: elusive or illusory?' (1990) 106 Law Quarterly Review 632

# Chapter 4
## Capacity

**This chapter discusses:**

how some people and organisations are not considered in law to have the capacity to make contracts or only have a limited capacity to make contracts. These include:

- minors;
- people suffering from a mental incapacity; and
- corporations.

There are some categories of people whose power to make contracts is limited by law. The main categories are minors, and people considered incapable of contracting because of mental disorders or drunkenness.

Contracts are of course not only made between individual people. In many cases, one or both parties will actually be groups of people, such as companies, local authorities and other organisations. Such groups are generally called corporations, and the contracting capacity of a corporation depends on what type of corporation it is.

# Minors

Traditionally, anyone under 21 was regarded by the law as a minor (in fact the law usually called such people 'infants'). Their ability to make contracts was first limited by the common law, and then by the Infants Relief Act 1874, which introduced rather complicated provisions on the subject. In 1969, the Family Law Reform Act reduced the age of majority to 18, and replaced the term 'infant' with 'minor', and then in 1987, the Minors' Contracts Act repealed the Infants Relief Act 1874, and restored the common law, which still governs contracts made by minors today.

The basic common law rule is that contracts do not bind minors. There are, however, some types of contract which are binding on minors, or which are merely voidable.

## Contracts binding on a minor

The only contracts which are binding on a minor are contracts for the supply of necessaries. 'Necessaries' are interpreted as including not just the supply of necessary goods and services, but also contracts of service for the minor's benefit.

### Contracts for necessary goods and services

Under the Sale of Goods Act 1979, s. 3(2) 'necessaries' means 'goods suitable to the condition in life of the minor or other person concerned and to his actual requirements at the time of sale and delivery'. It therefore includes more than just such essentials as food, shelter and clothing, and in deciding the issue the courts can take into account the social status of the particular minor – items which might not be considered necessaries for a working-class child may nevertheless be necessaries for one from a wealthy background.

When deciding if a contract is one for necessaries, the courts first of all determine whether the goods or services are capable of amounting to necessaries in law, and then consider whether they are in fact necessaries as far as the minor before them is concerned. The tests are notoriously difficult to apply, but effectively mean that a minor will be bound by most consumer contracts, but usually not by commercial ones.

**Key Case**   Nash v Inman

In **Nash v Inman** (1908) a Savile Row tailor supplied a Cambridge undergraduate with 'eleven fancy waistcoats at two guineas each'. When the tailor sued for payment, the student claimed that the contract could not be enforced against him, as he was a minor (at this time people were considered minors until the age of 21). The Court of Appeal held that although the goods were suitable to the young man's 'condition in life' (he was 'the son of an architect of good position'), they did not satisfy the second limb of the statutory definition. They could not be regarded as suitable to his actual requirements at the time, because his father had given uncontradicted evidence that he already had a sufficient wardrobe of clothes. Therefore the contract was not binding.

**Legal Principle**

The only contracts binding on a minor are contracts for necessaries under the Sales of Goods Act 1979 s. 3(2).

Under common law, a similar approach is taken to contracts for services as for goods. In **Chapple v Cooper** (1844) an undertaker sued a widow, who was a minor, for the cost of her husband's funeral. It was held that this was a necessary service, and so the young woman was obliged to pay. In discussing what kind of goods and services could be considered necessaries, the court said, 'Articles of mere luxury are always excluded, though luxurious articles of utility are in some cases allowed.'

The Sale of Goods Act also provides that if necessaries are sold to a minor, but before receiving the goods the minor decides that they are no longer wanted, there is no obligation to accept and pay for them. Nor is a minor bound by a contract which contains oppressive or exceptionally onerous terms. Whether a term is sufficiently onerous to exclude liability will depend on the circumstances of each case. In **Fawcett v Smethurst** (1914) a minor was held not to be bound by a contract for the hire of a car, even though it was a necessary service in this case, because the contract included a term making him liable for damage to the car 'in any event' – that is, whether or not the damage was his fault.

Where there is a binding contract for necessaries, the minor is only bound to pay a reasonable price for them, which need not be the contract price.

## Contracts of service for the minor's benefit

Minors are also bound by contracts of service, providing these are on the whole beneficial to them. In practice this generally means contracts of employment under which a minor gains some training, experience or instruction for an occupation – an apprenticeship would be a common example. In **Clements v London and North Western Railway Co** (1894) a minor made an agreement under which he gave up his statutory right to personal injury benefit, but gained rights under an insurance scheme to which his employers would contribute. It was held that the rights gained were more beneficial than those given up, and so the contract was, on balance, for the minor's benefit and therefore binding.

Topical Issue

### Wayne Rooney: football dreams

We have all read in the newspapers about the huge sums that footballers can earn and we also know that as sportsmen, their careers start very young. This combination of youth, football and money can lead to some serious contractual disputes. The famous English football player Wayne Rooney entered into a contract when he was 15 years old with a company called Proform Sports Management Ltd (Proform). Under the contract, Rooney agreed that Proform would act as his representative for two years in any transfer negotiations during that period. At the time of making the contract, Rooney was already signed with Everton Football Club. Before the end of the two-year period, Rooney sought to terminate the contract. The High Court concluded that Rooney was entitled to do this, because the contract was a voidable contract with a minor. While Rooney's contract with Everton amounted to a contract for necessaries, the contract with Proform did not: **Proform Sports Management Ltd** *v* **Proactive Sports Management Ltd** (2006).

In **De Francesco** *v* **Barnum** (1890) a 14-year-old girl entered into a stage-dancing apprenticeship with De Francesco, under an agreement which was considerably more favourable to De Francesco than to the girl. She was not to marry during the seven years of the apprenticeship, could not take on professional engagements without his written consent and was completely subject to De Francesco's commands. He, on the other hand, made no commitment to employ her, and stated that if he did do so it would be at a very low rate of pay. The agreement also allowed him to send her abroad, and to put an end to the agreement at any time. Fry LJ concluded: 'Those are stipulations of an extraordinary and unusual character, which throw, or appear to throw, an inordinate power into the hands of the master without any correlative obligation.' Consequently, the court held that the contract was not for the minor's benefit, and could not therefore be enforced against her.

In some cases the courts have widened the concept of a contract of service beyond the usual employment situations. In **Doyle** *v* **White City Stadium Ltd** (1935) the claimant was a minor who entered into an agreement with the British Boxing Board to secure a fighter's licence. One of the terms of such a licence was that if a boxer was disqualified for committing a foul, he would not receive the 'purse' (fee) for the fight, only his travelling expenses. Doyle was contracted to take part in a fight, for which the purse was £3,000, and the contract was subject to British Boxing Board rules. He was disqualified for hitting below the belt, but tried to claim the £3,000 from the promoters and the Board. The court looked at the contract, and held that although boxing was not an occupation in which an ordinary apprenticeship was possible, the type of contract made with the Board could be compared with a contract of apprenticeship. Looked at as a whole, the contract was beneficial to the minor, and even the clause which deprived him of £3,000 was one which was designed to encourage clean fighting and thereby protect young, inexperienced boxers. He was thus bound by the contract and could not claim the £3,000.

There is no general principle that a contract for the benefit of a minor is automatically binding on him or her. For example, trading contracts are never binding on minors, even where they are for their benefit. Thus, in **Cowern** *v* **Nield** (1912) a minor was in business selling hay and straw. It was held that he was not liable to repay the price of a consignment of hay that he failed to deliver.

## Contracts voidable at common law

Apart from contracts for necessaries which bind the minor, the general rule at common law is that a minor's contracts are voidable. In other words, these contracts are not binding on the minor, but bind the other party. Thus, these contracts are valid when they are made, but can be terminated by a minor at any time before becoming 18 or within a reasonable time afterwards. This category covers contracts which involve a long-term interest in property such as land, shares or partnerships. If such a contract is terminated before any money is paid or obligations created, the position will be as if the contract had never been made in the first place, but problems can arise where obligations are incurred or money is paid, and then the minor terminates the contract. The law is somewhat unclear, but it seems likely that a minor would be liable to pay any debts arising before such a contract is terminated. Where a minor has already paid money under a contract, and then terminates it, whether that money can be recovered will depend on whether the minor got anything in return for it.

In **Corpe** v **Overton** (1833) a minor agreed to enter into a partnership, which was to be formed in the future. He paid a £100 deposit, knowing that he would lose it if he did not in the end go through with the partnership. Before the partnership was put into operation, the minor repudiated the agreement. The courts held that he was entitled to have his deposit back, because there was a total failure of consideration – at the time he terminated the contract, he had received nothing in return for it.

A contrasting case is **Steinberg** v **Scala (Leeds) Ltd** (1923). The claimant, a minor, bought shares in Scala. These shares were not fully paid up, which means that a company issuing such shares can subsequently demand from a shareholder payments up to the nominal value of the shares: for example, if a person pays £1 for a share which has a nominal value of £2.50, she can be asked to pay a further £1.50 at a later stage. Scala did make such a request, and Ms Steinberg paid a further £250. The court case arose because she later decided to reject the contract, and wanted her £250 back. Her claim failed: the court held that although terminating the contract meant she was free from any future obligation to make payment, she could not get the £250 back because there had not been a total failure of consideration. She had the shares, so she had got something in return for her money.

## Remedies against minors

Clearly the rules on minors and contracts have the potential to create injustice – for example, where an adult is unaware that the other party to a contract is a minor. Consequently, the equitable remedy of restitution, which is used to make anyone who has been unjustly enriched give back their profit, has been applied to minors. If a minor fraudulently obtains goods and then keeps them, an order for restitution can be made to make the minor give them back to the claimant.

In practice, this equitable remedy has become less important in the light of the power granted by s. 3 of the Minors' Contracts Act 1987. Under this Act, where an adult has entered into an unenforceable contract with a minor, or a contract which the minor has terminated, the courts may give any property acquired by the minor under the contract back to the adult, provided it is 'just and equitable' to do so. This provision goes further than the equitable remedy, in that it may be used even if the minor has not acted fraudulently. A young person who has already sold or exchanged the property may have to pay the cost of the goods, or give up any property received in exchange for them. However, a minor who no longer has the goods or any proceeds of their sale or exchange cannot be made to pay anything, as this would effectively enforce what is still an unenforceable agreement.

The equitable remedy of specific performance can never be used against a minor, nor can it be used by a minor, because the remedy requires mutuality between the parties (see p. 380).

If an adult realises that they are making a contract with a minor they may ask for a guarantee from an adult. Under s. 2 of the Minors' Contracts Act 1987, where a contract is unenforceable because it was made with a minor, a guarantee of that contract will be enforceable. Thus, the adult who provided that guarantee will have to compensate the other contracting party for their loss according to the terms of the guarantee. This arrangement is frequently used where loans are made to minors.

## Minors and tort

Minors can usually be liable under tort law so long as they are old enough to know the nature of what they are doing, but this rule cannot be used as an indirect way of enforcing a contract which would otherwise not be binding on a minor. In **Leslie Ltd** v **Sheill** (1914) a minor borrowed money, having lied about his age. The contract for the loan was an unenforceable one. In deliberately misrepresenting his age, the minor committed the tort of deceit, and knowing that he could not sue the minor for breach of contract to recover the money, the moneylender brought an action for damages in tort. The action was unsuccessful because the court held that it was merely an attempt to enforce a contract on which the minor was not liable.

## Very young children

The cases discussed so far generally concern older children. With very young children the courts may take the view that they lack the mental capacity to enter a contract, so that the rules on mental incapacity, discussed below, would apply. Thus, in **R** v **Oldham Metropolitan Borough Council,** *ex parte* **Garlick** (1993), the House of Lords considered that the laws on the validity of contracts made by minors could only apply if they were old enough to understand the nature of the transaction and the nature of any continuing obligations incurred. Thus, while a child well under the age of ten could buy sweets, a four-year-old could not contract for the occupation of residential premises.

## Problems with the law on minors

The law on minors and contracts is widely thought to be out of step with modern society. Many of the cases arose more than a hundred years ago, and often involved people between 18 and 21, who would now be considered adults. It is also strange that the age of full contractual capacity is 18, when an individual of 16 or 17 may legally be in full-time employment, married and even a parent. In addition, consumer protection laws may reduce the need for special protection for minors.

## Reform

In 1982, the Law Commission proposed that all contracts should be binding on minors who are 16 years or over. Below that age, contracts should be enforceable by minors, but not against them. A minor who misrepresents their age in order to secure a contract should be liable in tort for deceit, but in other cases of fraud a minor under 16 should not be liable if the effect of that liability would be to allow the other party to enforce indirectly an otherwise unenforceable contract.

# Mental incapacity

This category covers people suffering from mental disability (which appears to include both mental illness and mental handicap), and those who are drunk when the contract is made. In general, contracts made with someone in either state will be valid, unless, at the time when the contract is made, that person is incapable of understanding the nature of the transaction and the other party knows this. In such circumstances the contract is voidable: the party suffering from mental disability or drunkenness can choose whether or not to terminate it.

Where one party is incapable, through drunkenness or mental disability, of understanding the nature of the transaction, but the other party does not realise this, the courts will ignore the incapacity. In **Hart** v **O'Connor** (1985) the Privy Council held that a person of unsound mind was bound by his agreement to sell some land because, when the contract was made, the buyer did not realise that the seller had any mental incapacity.

The fact that a person has a poor understanding of the language in which the contract was made and is illiterate does not render them incapable of making a contract. The defendant in **Barclays Bank** v **Schwartz** (1995) was Romanian and had signed contracts rendering him liable for his company's debts of over £500,000. In an attempt to resist paying the money he argued that his poor English and illiteracy meant he lacked the capacity to make the contracts. This argument was rejected by the Court of Appeal, being described by the court as 'straight from the book of feeble excuses'. A person who was illiterate, or did not understand the language of a contract, was aware of this, and the obligation was on them to make sure that the contract was explained.

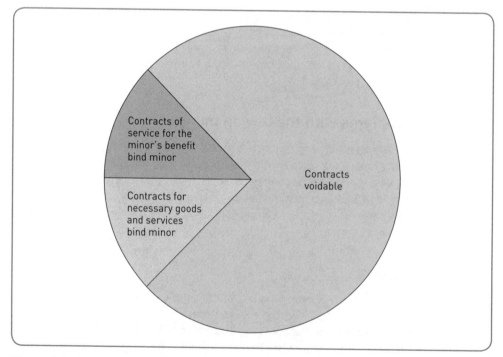

**Figure 4.1** Contracts with minors

There are no specific rules governing contracts made for necessaries by mentally incapable parties; they are subject to the general rules above, and also to s. 3 of the Sale of Goods Act 1979, which, as for minors, states that only a reasonable price need be paid for necessaries (regardless of whether the other party was unaware of the disability). In some cases, the Mental Health Act 1983 puts the property of a mentally disordered person under the control of the courts. Contracts made by such individuals are void.

# Corporations

A corporation is a legal entity, usually in fact a group of people, which is treated by the law as having a separate identity from the person or persons who constitute it. There are four main types of corporation: registered companies, statutory corporations, chartered corporations and limited liability partnerships. Each has a different level of contracting ability.

## Registered companies

These are companies registered under the Companies Act 1985 – in effect, most commercial companies. When registering, companies must supply a document called a memorandum of association, which carries information including an 'objects clause' laying down the range of activities in which that company will be allowed to engage. Before the Companies Act 1989 was passed, any contract that was outside a company's stated range of activities was invalid – it was said to be *ultra vires* (meaning outside the powers of the company). Under the 1989 Act, a company can be liable for a contract made outside its stated activities if the other party has acted in good faith. The reason for limiting the contractual capacity of registered companies is to provide shareholders and creditors with safeguards against directors who use company resources for their own unauthorised purposes.

## Statutory corporations

These corporations are created for particular purposes by Acts of Parliament – the Independent Broadcasting Authority is an example, as are local authorities. The statute creating each corporation will specify the purposes for which that corporation may make contracts, and any contract entered into which is outside the powers can be declared *ultra vires* and therefore void.

**Figure 4.2** Corporations

## Chartered corporations

These are corporations set up by Royal Charter, which means that their rights are officially granted by the Crown – examples are charities, and some universities and other educational institutions. They have the same contractual capacity as an adult human being of full capacity, and can enter into any kind of contract (although a charter may be withdrawn if such an institution becomes involved in activities which offend against the spirit of the charter).

## Limited liability partnerships

Limited liability partnerships were created by the Limited Liability Partnerships Act 2000. These are corporations, but they benefit from 'unlimited capacity' under s. 1(3) of the Act, so that they do not raise any problems of capacity in the context of contract law.

 # Answering questions

 Nadine and Olivia, both aged 17, are keen on dancing and theatre and both decide to pursue a career in this field.

Nadine gains a place at stage school, and begins her course with enthusiasm. However, she soon becomes annoyed at some of the terms to which she finds she has agreed, in particular one which prevents her from taking part in any professional productions during the school vacation, without permission from the school, and another which obliges her to hand over 30 per cent of any earnings from such productions during her time at the school. Nadine has been invited to take part in a professional play during the summer, and would now like to avoid these obligations.

Olivia's career takes a different course. She borrows money from Countrywide Bank to set up her own small but successful business, selling dance and stage clothing and equipment, the proceeds of which pay for singing and dancing lessons. After a few months, Olivia's main supplier finds out that she is only 17 and refuses to trade further with her. This leaves Olivia without enough business to pay for this month's lessons, and her teacher is pressing her to meet her obligations. She is also behind with the payments on her mobile telephone account, and has received a demand for payment.

Advise both Nadine and Olivia regarding the enforceability of any contracts which they may have made. *OCR*

This question is concerned with the capacity of minors in contract law. In your introduction you could point out that the basic common law rule is that contracts do not bind minors. There are, however, some types of contract which are binding on minors, or which are voidable.

You could structure your answer by dividing it into two parts, looking first at the position of Nadine and then the position of Olivia. Looking first at Nadine, we are told that she is 17 years old and we need to consider her capacity to make a contract with the stage school. As she is under 18, she is treated as a minor for the purposes of contract law. Minors are bound by contracts of service for the minor's benefit (see p. 72 above). You would need to look at such cases as **Clements** v **London and North**

**Western Railway Company, De Francesco** *v* **Barnum** and **Doyle** *v* **White City Stadium** to decide whether the contract with the stage school falls within this category. **De Francesco** *v* **Barnum** is most similar to the facts of this case, as it concerned a stage-dancing apprenticeship. In that case the contract was found to contain 'stipulations of an extraordinary and unusual character, which throw, or appear to throw, an inordinate power into the hands of the master without any correlative obligation'. The terms of this contract are not as extraordinary as those in **De Francesco** and it is not certain whether a court would find this contract to be for Nadine's benefit or not.

Turning now to Olivia, again she is 17 years old and treated as a minor for the purposes of contract law. She has made four contracts: a contract for a loan, a contract with a supplier of stage clothes and equipment, a contract for singing and dancing lessons and a contract for a mobile phone. Each contract needs to be considered separately. Looking first at the contract for a loan, this contract is voidable (p. 75). Olivia therefore has a right to terminate the contract if she decides she no longer wants the loan because she cannot make purchases from the supplier. On terminating the contract, she would probably have to return any money she had received under it. Olivia may have already paid interest on the loan and she is unlikely to be able to get this money back because she had the benefit of being able to buy stage clothes and equipment from her supplier with the money from the loan: **Steinberg** *v* **Scala (Leeds) Ltd**. If an adult had provided a guarantee for repayment of the loan, this guarantee will be enforceable under s. 2 of the Minors' Contracts Act 1987 (see p. 75).

The contract for the supply of stage clothes and equipment was not binding on Olivia because it was a trading contract (**Cowern** *v* **Nield**), but it was binding on the supplier. It will depend on the terms of the contract itself whether the supplier had a right to terminate supplies at the point in which he did, or whether he was in breach of contract. Any breach would give Olivia a right to damages, but she would not have a right to specific performance (see p. 75).

As regards the contract for the singing and dancing lessons, this is a contract of service for the minor's benefit and is therefore binding on Olivia. She will have to pay for the lessons.

The legal status of the contract for the mobile phone will depend on whether this is treated as a contract for a necessity under the Sale of Goods Act 1979 s. 3(2) in which case it would be binding (see p. 71). While owning a mobile phone is popular with young people, it is probably not a necessary item: **Nash** *v* **Inman**. The *dicta* in **Chapple** *v* **Cooper** could be considered where it was stated that 'Articles of mere luxury are always excluded, though luxurious articles of utility are in some cases allowed.' She could therefore terminate the contract for the mobile phone. Olivia will have to return the telephone, because under s. 3 of the Minors' Contracts Act 1987, where an adult has entered into an unenforceable contract with a minor, or a contract which the minor has terminated, the courts may give any property acquired by the minor under the contract back to the adult, provided it is 'just and equitable' to do so.

# Summary of Chapter 4

There are some categories of people whose power to make contracts is limited by law. The main categories are minors, and people considered incapable of contracting because of mental disorders or drunkenness. The contracting capacity of a corporation depends on what type of corporation it is.

## Minors

The basic common law rule is that contracts do not bind minors (children under 18 years old). There are, however, some types of contract which are binding on minors, or which are merely voidable.

### Contracts binding on a minor

The only contracts which are binding on a minor are contracts for the supply of necessaries. 'Necessaries' are interpreted as including not just the supply of necessary goods and services, but also contracts of service for the minor's benefit.

#### Contracts for necessary goods and services

Under the Sale of Goods Act 1979 s. 3(2) 'necessaries' means 'goods suitable to the condition in life of the minor or other person concerned and to his actual requirements at the time of sale and delivery'. This effectively means that a minor will be bound by most consumer contracts, but usually not by commercial ones.

The Sale of Goods Act also provides that if necessaries are sold to a minor, but before receiving the goods the minor decides that they are no longer wanted, there is no obligation to accept and pay for them. Nor is a minor bound by a contract which contains oppressive or exceptionally onerous terms.

Where there is a binding contract for necessaries, the minor is only bound to pay a reasonable price for them, which need not be the contract price.

#### Contracts of service for the minor's benefit

Minors are also bound by contracts of service, providing these are on the whole beneficial to them. In practice, this generally means contracts of employment under which a minor gains some training, experience or instruction for an occupation.

### Contracts voidable at common law

Apart from contracts for necessaries which bind the minor, the general rule at common law is that a minor's contracts are voidable. In other words, these contracts are not binding on the minor, but bind the other party. Thus, these contracts are valid when they are made, but can be terminated by a minor at any time before becoming 18 or within a reasonable time afterwards. This category covers contracts which involve a long-term interest in property such as land, shares or partnerships. If such a contract is terminated before any money is paid or obligations created, the position will be as if the contract had never been made in the first place, but problems can arise where obligations are incurred or money is paid, and then the minor terminates the contract. The law is unclear, but it seems likely that a minor would be liable to pay any debts arising before such a contract is terminated. Where a minor has already paid money under a contract, and then terminates it, whether that money can be recovered will depend on whether the minor got anything in return for it.

### Remedies against minors

Clearly, the rules on minors and contracts have the potential to create injustice – for example, where an adult is unaware that the other party to a contract is a minor. Consequently, the equitable remedy of restitution, which is used to make anyone who has been unjustly enriched give back their profit, has been applied to minors. If a minor fraudulently obtains goods and then keeps them, an order for restitution can be made to make the minor give them back to the claimant.

In practice, this equitable remedy has become less important in the light of the power granted by s. 3 of the Minors' Contracts Act 1987. Under this Act, where an adult has entered into an unenforceable contract with a minor, or a contract which the minor has terminated, the courts may give any property acquired by the minor under the contract back to the adult, provided it is 'just and equitable' to do so.

The equitable remedy of specific performance can never be used against a minor, nor can it be used by a minor, because the remedy requires mutuality between the parties.

If an adult realises that they are making a contract with a minor they may ask for a guarantee from another adult.

### Minors and tort

Minors can usually be liable under tort law so long as they are old enough to know the nature of what they are doing, but this rule cannot be used as an indirect way of enforcing a contract which would otherwise not be binding on a minor.

### Very young children

With very young children, the courts may take the view that they lack the mental capacity to enter a contract, so that the rules on mental incapacity would apply.

## Mental incapacity

This category covers people suffering from mental disability and those who are drunk when the contract is made. In general, contracts made with someone in either state will be valid, unless, at the time when the contract is made, that person is incapable of understanding the nature of the transaction and the other party knows this. In such circumstances, the contract is voidable: the party suffering from mental disability or drunkenness can choose whether or not to terminate it.

Where one party is incapable, through drunkenness or mental disability, of understanding the nature of the transaction, but the other party does not realise this, the courts will ignore the incapacity.

## Corporations

A corporation is a legal entity, usually in fact a group of people, which is treated by the law as having a separate identity from the person or persons who constitute it. There are four main types of corporation: registered companies; corporations established by statute; chartered corporations; and limited liability partnerships. Each has a different level of contracting ability.

### Registered companies

Under the Companies Act 1989, a company can be liable for a contract made outside its stated activities in the memorandum of association if the other party has acted in good faith.

### Statutory corporations

The statute creating each corporation will specify the purposes for which that corporation may make contracts, and any contract entered into which is outside those powers can be declared *ultra vires* and therefore void.

### Chartered corporations

These are corporations set up by Royal Charter. They have the same contractual capacity as an adult human being of full capacity, and can enter into any kind of contract.

### Limited liability partnerships

Limited liability partnerships benefit from 'unlimited capacity', so that they do not raise any problems of capacity in the context of contract law.

# Reading list

Hudson, 'Mental incapacity revisited' (1986) Conveyancer and Property Lawyer 178

## Reading on the internet

The Limited Liability Partnerships Act 2000 is available on the website of the Office of Public Sector Information at:

http://www.opsi.gov.uk/acts/acts2000/200000en12.htm

# Chapter 5
## Formalities

**This chapter explains:**

that most contracts can be made without any particular formalities being followed. However, a few contracts must be:

- made by deed;
- written; or
- evidenced in writing.

In addition, particular issues are raised when contracts are made over the internet and by e-mail.

As we have seen, the general rule of contract law is that an agreement does not have to take a specific written form in order to be deemed a binding contract. Often the contract will simply be oral. As it can be difficult to prove later what was said orally, there are practical advantages of putting a contract in writing, despite there being no legal requirements to do so. In **Hadley** *v* **Kemp** (1999) Gary Kemp was the songwriter in the pop group Spandau Ballet. He was sued by other members of the group for royalties received for the group's music. The basis of their claim was that there had been an oral agreement to share these royalties. They were unable to prove the existence of any oral agreement and so their action failed.

Of course most complex transactions are made in writing, and this clearly helps the parties prove their case if there is any disagreement, but usually lack of written formalities will not prevent a court from finding a contract. Following the Electronic Communications Act 2000, s. 8, legislation preventing the use of electronic communications such as e-mails for the formation of a contract can be removed by delegated legislation, and electronic signatures are legally recognised. There are some types of contract which currently require certain formalities to be followed to make them enforceable. They fall into three groups: those which must be made by deed, those which must be in writing and those which have to be evidenced in writing. The general aim of these requirements is to reduce the risk of fraud.

# Contracts that must be made by deed

Under the Law of Property Act 1925 a contract for a lease of three years or more must be made by deed, which basically means it must be put into a formal document, signed in front of witnesses. (A deed may also be used as a way of making binding what would otherwise be a gratuitous promise, without the need for consideration from the other party.)

# Contracts that must be in writing

Some statutes lay down that certain types of contract must be in writing. Contracts that need to be made in writing include those involving the transfer of shares in a limited company (Companies Act 1985); bills of exchange, cheques and promissory notes (Bills of Exchange Act 1882); and regulated consumer credit agreements, such as hire-purchase contracts (Consumer Credit Act 1974, s. 60).

Most contracts for the sale or disposition of an interest in land made since 27 September 1989 must be made in writing under s. 2 of the Law of Property (Miscellaneous Provisions) Act 1989. The section states:

> Section 2 (1) A contract for the sale or other disposition of an interest in land can only be made in writing and only by incorporating all the terms which the parties have expressly agreed and in one document or, where contracts are exchanged, in each.
>
> (2) The terms may be incorporated in a document either by being set out in it or by reference to some other document.

(3) The document incorporating the terms or, where contracts are exchanged, one of the documents incorporating them (but not necessarily the same one) must be signed by or on behalf of each party to the contract.

The document must be signed by each party or their representatives and must incorporate all the terms which the parties have expressly agreed. The aim of the 1989 Act is to reduce fraud and to prevent people from unintentionally entering into contracts for the transfer of rights over land. In **Ruddick** v **Ormston** (2005) the claimant had distributed leaflets offering to buy properties without charging for valuation, legal or estate agent's fees. The defendant had responded to one of these leaflets and the claimant had visited his flat. The claimant had agreed to buy the defendant's flat for £25,000. It was agreed that the sale should go through in seven days. They had written this agreement down in the claimant's diary, though no mention was made of the completion date, and both parties had put their signatures. The defendant had subsequently had his property valued to be worth £55,000 and he refused to proceed with the sale. The claimant took him to court for an order of specific performance of the contract. The court rejected this claim on the basis that there was no valid contract for the sale of the property, as the requirements in the 1989 Act had not been complied with. In particular, the written agreement did not incorporate the express term as to the completion date for the sale.

In **Cobbe** v **Yeoman's Row Management Ltd** (2008) the House of Lords accepted that an oral agreement for the transfer of an interest in land cannot be enforced. Where one party has reasonably acted upon that agreement, they will not be able to get a remedy which would reflect a proprietary interest in the land (such as a percentage of the land's increased value since the agreement was made). Instead, a person could get a remedy on the basis of 'quantum meruit' (see p. 374) for the value of the work they had carried out in reliance on the agreement. On the facts of the case, Mr Cobbe was a property developer and he had orally agreed to get planning permission for the demolition of a block of flats owned by Yeoman's Row Management Ltd. If Mr Cobbe succeeded in getting planning permission then the flats would be sold to him for £12 million. After he had succeeded in getting the planning permission, Yeoman's raised the price to £20 million, which Mr Cobbe considered to be commercially unacceptable. The original agreement could not be enforced because it amounted to an agreement to transfer land which was not in writing. However, he could be compensated for the work he had carried out in obtaining the planning permission.

This case has drawn some criticism on the basis that equity should not contradict the statute. A counter-argument is that equity is not contradicting the statute because it is not enforcing the contract, but simply sanctioning unconscionable conduct.

In **North Eastern Properties Ltd** v **Coleman** (2010) the Court of Appeal emphasised that Parliament did not intend s. 2 to be used as a tool to escape genuine contractual obligations. It stated that the section:

> was not intended to be a charter for those wishing to disown apparent contracts for the sale of property to go behind the document and search for statements made in pre-contract negotiations, then to claim that they were intended to be terms of the contract and thus bring the whole contractual edifice crashing to the ground.

The claimant was selling 11 flats to the defendant and went to court to enforce the sale. The defendant argued that the contracts for sale were not valid because they did not satisfy s. 2 as not all the terms of the contract had been reduced to writing. In particular, the written contract did not mention an agreed term of the sale that the sellers would pay the purchasers upon exchange a sum equal to 2 per cent of the advertised price for the flats (known as a finder's fee, as it was being paid as a reward for finding the buyers). The Court of Appeal rejected this argument. It pointed out that the written contracts included an entire agreement clause (see p. 142) so that everything about the land contract was actually included in the written contract in conformity with s. 2. The agreement about the finder's fee was a separate agreement which was contained in an oral contract, which was separately enforceable.

## Amendments

Section 2 of the Law of Property (Miscellaneous Provisions) Act 1989 must be satisfied when a contract for the sale or disposition of an interest in land is amended, otherwise the amendment will be ineffective. This issue arose in the case of **Keay v Morris Homes (West Midlands) Ltd** (2013). The appellant, Morris Homes, entered a written agreement to buy land from the respondent, Keay, for £4.5 million. Part of this agreement included that Morris Homes would build a medical centre, which Keay would then lease. About a year later, the parties entered into a written supplementary agreement reducing the purchase price to £3.8 million. Keay alleged that this reduction was agreed following an oral agreement that Morris Homes would speed up progress on the building works for the medical centre. Keay sought damages for an alleged breach of this oral agreement with delays in building the medical centre having allegedly caused them a loss of £2.7 million. Morris Homes argued in their defence that the oral agreement was void because it failed to comply with section 2. The Court of Appeal accepted this defence. It stated that the key issue was whether all the express terms for the sale of the land were incorporated in the written supplementary agreement. When the price of the sale was reduced, the parties were, in effect, entering into a new contract. A contract that amends an earlier contract must itself comply with s. 2 by being in writing, signed and containing all the expressly agreed terms of the agreement, including the terms of the original agreement. Because the supplemental agreement did not contain the terms of the oral agreement it was void for being in breach of s. 2. So Morris Homes did not have to pay damages for breach of the supplemental agreement because that agreement was void.

The irony of this decision is that s. 2 was aimed to provide certainty regarding the sale of land by requiring such transactions to be in writing, but s. 2 can actually create uncertainty as written contracts for the sale of land can be found to be void because they do not contain all the terms of the sale.

## E-mails

The 1989 Act was passed before e-mail had become a common means of communication. In **Green (Liquidator of Stealth Construction Ltd) v Ireland** (2011) the High Court suggested that an e-mail might, in some circumstances, satisfy the requirements in the 1989 Act and that typing one's name would be sufficient for a signature. On the facts of the case, no contract had been reached in the e-mail correspondence between two sisters. There had been an oral agreement that Mrs Ireland would lend her sister £300,000 at a rate of 15 per cent interest, with repayment to be paid in six monthly instalments. The sister had asked if £145,000 could be paid to a company's bank account. Mrs Ireland had e-mailed back: 'Do remind me tomorrow. Any news on the cooker?' The court concluded that this did not amount to a clear written acceptance and the two e-mails did not satisfy the requirements of the 1989 Act because they did not contain all the terms that had been orally agreed.

In **J. Pereira Fernandes** *v* **Mehta** (2006) the High Court stated that the appearance of the name of the sender in an e-mail did not, by itself, amount to a signature if it had been automatically generated by an internet service provider after the document had been transmitted. The name must be deliberately inserted by the sender to show that it was intended to give authenticity to the whole document.

In **Golden Ocean Group Ltd** *v* **Salgaocar Mining Industries** (2012) the Court of Appeal noted *obiter* that s. 2(2) of the 1989 Act recognises that some terms of the contract can be incorporated by reference to separate documents. The case itself was concerned with a contract made by a series of e-mails and so this dicta raises the possibility that a series of e-mails might in the future be treated as sufficient to satisfy the requirements of the 1989 Act. If wished, this could be avoided by the parties putting at the head of the e-mail correspondence 'subject to contract'.

# Contracts that must be evidenced in writing

A contract of guarantee is a contract under which one person (Ann) guarantees that if another person (Ben) does not pay back money owed, then Ann will pay the money instead. For example, a parent might guarantee a child's overdraft so that the bank will agree to lend money to the child under the overdraft facility. Contracts of guarantee are required by the Statute of Frauds 1677 to be 'evidenced in writing'. Section 4 of the 1677 Act states:

> S. 4. No action shall be brought whereby to charge the Defendant upon any special promise to answer for the debt default or miscarriage of another person unless the Agreement upon which such Action shall be brought or some Memorandum or Note thereof shall be in Writing and signed by the party to be charged therewith or some other person thereunto by him lawfully authorised.

In **J. Pereira Fernandes** *v* **Metha** (2006) the High Court held that this requirement had been satisfied where a contract was made by e-mail, though it was not enforceable on the facts because the claimant had not typed his name at the bottom of the e-mail to amount to a signature. Contracts for the sale or disposition of an interest in land made before 27 September 1989 are still covered by the old law prior to the Law of Property (Miscellaneous Provisions) Act 1989, and only have to be evidenced in writing.

'Evidenced in writing' essentially means that although the contract itself need not be a written one, there must be some written evidence of the transaction. The evidence must have existed before one party tried to enforce the contract against the other, and it must be signed by the party against whom the contract is to be enforced. If a note or memorandum containing the terms of a contract was signed only by one party to that contract, the contract could be enforced by the non-signer against the signer, but not *vice versa*. Such a note or memorandum does not have to have been created for the purpose of enforcing a contract, and in fact a string of documents can be added together to form evidence of a contract – if, for example, there is a document signed by the defendant which contains an express or implicit reference to another document, and that second document contains the terms of the contract. In **Golden Ocean Group Ltd** *v* **Salgaocar Mining Industries** (2012) the Court of Appeal held that a binding contractual guarantee had been entered into by e-mail. Golden Ocean had rented to T Ltd a ship for ten years (known as a ten-year charterparty). T Ltd stopped paying the rent before the ten-year period had ended and Golden Ocean said it had lost $54 million as a result. It believed that Salgaocar Mining Industries (SMI) had provided it with a guarantee for the ten-year charterparty, so claimed from it the $54 million. Golden Ocean argued that both the charterparty and the guarantee had been concluded in a series of e-mails. SMI counter-argued that it was not bound by this potential guarantee as there was no single document that could be identified as the contract of guarantee. The Court of Appeal held that typing a name at the bottom of an e-mail amounted to a signature. While this signature was only on one of the e-mails (and not the last one in the series) this was still sufficient authentication for the whole series of e-mails. The purpose of the Statute of Frauds Act was to ensure a person was not held liable as a guarantor on the basis of an oral utterance which was ill-considered, ambiguous or even completely fictitious. It was difficult to see why several documents together should not therefore satisfy the Act, particularly having regard to the manner in which commercial contracts are habitually reached in modern commerce. It would have been a serious failing of English commercial law if SMI could have avoided liability because its obligation had been written in two documents instead of one.

A House of Lords case on this subject is **Actionstrength Ltd** *v* **International Glass Engineering** (2003). The first defendants were builders who contracted to build a new factory for the second defendant in Yorkshire. The claimant, Actionstrength Ltd, was a recruitment agency based in Italy, which provided construction workers for its clients. The first defendants continually paid the recruitment agency late for its workforce, so that the recruitment agency threatened to withdraw its labour. The recruitment agency alleged that at this point the second defendant made a verbal promise that if the agency kept its workforce on site it would see that they were paid anything due, if necessary by paying the agency money that the second defendants were due to pay to the main contractor. Later the main contractor became insolvent, the work was abandoned, and the recruitment agency was owed over £1 million by the main contractor. The agency brought an action against the second defendant, seeking to rely on the alleged oral agreement to recover the money owed. The House of Lords rejected this claim because, even if the claimant's story was true, the contract involved was a contract of guarantee which was unenforceable as it had not been evidenced in writing as required under the Statute of Frauds. Justice might be better achieved if the Statute of Frauds was restricted to consumer contracts, and not applied between two businesses, as there is no justification for allowing a businessman who knowingly offers a guarantee to then avoid liability under the guarantee because it was not put in writing.

**Figure 5.1** Formalities

### Topical Issue

#### Internet shopping

Increasingly, contracts are being made over the internet. In particular, the internet is being used to order goods and services from suppliers. The European Union is keen to promote the development of a European internet industry. It has therefore passed the European Electronic Commerce Directive (2000). The Directive lays down some specific formalities that will need to be followed in order to make binding contracts over the internet. Thus, Article 10 imposes a general requirement on service providers to give a clear account, prior to the conclusion of a contract, of the steps which must be followed to complete the contract online, to ensure 'full and informed consent'. This part of the Directive has been brought into force in the United Kingdom by the Electronic Commerce (EC Directive) Regulations 2002. Under these Regulations companies must provide receipts for orders placed electronically without delay, allow customers to change an order easily before buying and provide information such as business e-mail addresses, though it is not necessary to provide a telephone number. Businesses which do not comply with the regulations face having to pay statutory damages to customers or receiving a 'stop now' order which will force them to change their procedures.

Article 9 of the Directive requires member states to ensure that their legal systems allow contracts to be concluded by electronic means. There must be nothing in the law of the member states to prevent or affect the validity of a contract concluded electronically just because it was so concluded. There is an exception to this in the case of contracts which require some act on the part of a notary or registration with a public authority for their validity. Contracts dealing with matters of succession or family law are also excluded.

The Electronic Communications Act 2000 has responded to this requirement. Section 8 of the Act contains a power to remove restrictions arising from legislation which currently prevent the use of electronic communications. Most contracts do not need to be made on paper and such contracts could already be made through electronic communications. But it has been seen that certain contracts require written documents. Under the 2000 Act, where necessary and desirable this legislation may be amended to allow for the use of electronic communications to make such contracts.

Part II of the Electronic Communications Act 2000 makes provision for the legal recognition of electronic signatures. For example, if electronic conveyancing was introduced, then it would no longer be possible for individuals to physically sign the legal documents, but instead electronic signatures could be used. Different forms of electronic signatures are possible, but in practice the most useful is likely to be the digital signature. This uses cryptography technology to convert information into disguised data so that the message sent is unique from the person sending the message and cannot be copied, in the same way that a written signature is unique to each individual.

## Answering questions

It is rare for an examination question to be concerned purely with the issue of formalities. The fourth question at the end of Chapter 6 raises the issue of formalities along with some other issues.

# Summary of Chapter 5

The general rule of contract law is that an agreement does not have to take a specific written form in order to be deemed a binding contract. There are, however, some types of contract which currently require certain formalities to be followed to make them enforceable. They fall into three groups: those which must be made by deed, those which must be in writing and those which have to be evidenced in writing.

## Contracts which must be made by deed

Under the Law of Property Act 1925, a contract for a lease of three years or more must be made by deed.

## Contracts which must be in writing

Some statutes lay down that certain types of contract must be in writing. Most contracts for the sale or disposition of an interest in land made since 27 September 1989 must be made in writing under the Law of Property (Miscellaneous Provisions) Act 1989. The document must be signed by each party or their representatives.

## Contracts which must be evidenced in writing

Contracts of guarantee (where one party guarantees the obligation of another, such as a parent guaranteeing a daughter's bank overdraft) are required by the Statute of Frauds 1677 to be 'evidenced in writing'. Contracts for the sale or disposition of an interest in land made before 27 September 1989 are still covered by the old law prior to the Law of Property (Miscellaneous Provisions) Act 1989, and only have to be evidenced in writing.

The European Electronic Commerce Directive lays down some specific formalities that will need to be followed in order to make binding contracts over the internet. Part II of the Electronic Communications Act 2000 makes provision for the legal recognition of electronic signatures.

# Reading on the internet

The House of Lords' judgment in **Actionstrength Ltd** v **International Glass Engineering** (2003) is available at:

http://www.parliament.the-stationery-office.co.uk/pa/ld200203/ldjudgmt/jd030403/action

The European Electronic Commerce Directive is available on the European Commission's website at:
http://eur-lex.europa.eu/LexUriServe/LexUriServe.do?uri=CELEX:32000L0031:EN:NOT

The Electronic Commerce (EC Directive) Regulations 2002 are available on the website of the Office of Public Sector Information at:
http://www.opsi.gov.uk/si/si2002/20022013.htm

The Electronic Communications Act 2000 is available on the website of the Office of Public Sector Information at:
http://www.opsi.gov.uk/acts/acts2000/20000007.htm

# Chapter 6
## Consideration

**This chapter discusses:**

the contractual requirement of consideration, which means that each party must give something in return for what is gained from the other party. In particular it notes that consideration:

- need not benefit the promisor;
- must not be past;
- must be sufficient;
- must be of economic value;
- can be a promise not to sue; and
- can occasionally exist through the performance of an existing duty.

Finally, the chapter looks at ways promises can be binding even in the absence of consideration.

In English law, an agreement is not usually binding unless it is supported by what is called consideration. Put simply, this means that each party must give something in return for what is gained from the other party, so if you wish to enforce someone's promise to you, you must prove that you gave something in return for that promise.

Consideration may be a thing or a service – I give you my car and you give me £1,000, or you clean my windows and I pay you £5. It may also take the form of promises – I promise to work for you and you promise to pay me a salary. A promise not supported by consideration is called a gratuitous promise: for example, if I simply say I will give you my car, without requiring anything in return. This type of promise is not usually enforceable in law.

Although up to now we have been talking about the requirements for making a contract in the first place, it is important to note that many of the problems concerning consideration arise not when a contract is made, but when one or the other party seeks to modify it – such as by paying a lower price than that agreed. A promise to accept such a modification was traditionally not binding unless supported by new consideration, but recent cases have changed the rules in such situations.

# What is consideration?

Consideration is usually described as being something which represents either some benefit to the person making a promise (the promisor) or some detriment to the person to whom the promise is made (the promisee), or both.

In **Dunlop** v **Selfridge** (1915) the House of Lords explained consideration in terms of purchase and sale – the claimant must show that he or she has bought the defendant's promise, by doing, giving or promising something in return for it.

Atiyah has suggested that consideration can simply be seen as 'a reason for the enforcement of promises', with that reason being 'the justice of the case'.

## Promisor and promisee

In most contracts, two promises will be exchanged, so each party is both a promisor and a promisee. In a contract case, the claimant will often be arguing that the defendant has broken the promise made to the claimant, and therefore the claimant will usually be the promisee, and the defendant will be the promisor. So if Ann contracts to paint Ben's bathroom and Ben promises to pay her £200 for doing it, there are two promises in this contract: Ann's promise to do the painting and Ben's promise to pay Ann £200. If Ann fails to paint the bathroom, Ben can sue her, and if the issue of consideration arises, Ben will seek to prove that his promise to pay £200 was consideration for Ann's promise to paint the bathroom. In that action, Ann will be the promisor, and Ben the promisee.

On the other hand, if Ann does the work but Ben does not pay the price, Ben can be sued by Ann and, if consideration is at issue, Ann will have to prove that her promise to paint the bathroom was consideration for Ben's promise to pay. In that action, Ann will be the promisee and Ben the promisor.

Ann's promise to paint the bathroom can be portrayed by the following diagram:

Ben's promise to pay £200 can be portrayed by the following diagram:

The contract between Ann and Ben can be portrayed by the following diagram:

## Consideration need not benefit the promisor

Consideration need not benefit the promisor – so there can be consideration where the promisee suffers some detriment at the promisor's request, but this gives no particular benefit to the promisor. For example, in **Jones** v **Padavatton** (see p. 62), the daughter's giving up her job would be consideration for the mother providing an allowance, even though it did not directly benefit the mother (though as we have seen, the mother's promise was not binding because there was no intention to create legal relations).

Another way in which consideration can be given by the promisee without benefiting the promisor is where contracts are made for the benefit of a third party – if, for example, Ann promises to pay Ben to give Ann's daughter driving lessons, Ben will be able to enforce this promise; although he has given no direct benefit to Ann, he has suffered some detriment in that he has provided the lessons.

## 'Executory' and 'executed' consideration

Consideration is often divided into two categories: executory and executed. Executory consideration is where something is to be done in the future after the contract has been formed. Executory consideration exists when the contracting parties make promises to each other because they are promising something for the future, after the contract has been made – on making the contract you promise to deliver some goods to me and I promise to pay for them when they arrive, for example. A bilateral contract usually involves executory consideration.

Executed consideration is where at the time of the formation of the contract the consideration has already been performed. If I promise to give £20 to anyone who finds my lost handbag, returning the bag is both acceptance of my offer (and thus the time when the contract is formed) and executed consideration for my promise. Executed consideration usually occurs in unilateral contracts.

## Consideration must not be past

Lawyers often say that consideration must not be past, but this is slightly confusing because the emphasis is not really about the time that the consideration was given, but more about whether the consideration was given in exchange for the other party's consideration. Consideration must be given **in return** for the promise or act of the other party; something done, given or promised for another reason will not count as consideration. If one party has completed performance before the other offered consideration, then as a matter of fact it is unlikely that the earlier performance was done in return for that consideration. So, if Ann looks after Ben's dog while Ben is on holiday, and when Ben returns he promises to give Ann some money, Ann cannot enforce that promise because she did not look after the dog in return for it – she had already looked after the dog.

## Key Case    Roscorla v Thomas

The defendant in **Roscorla v Thomas** (1842) sold the claimant a horse. After the sale was completed, the defendant told the claimant that the animal was 'sound and free from any vice'. This turned out to be rather far from the truth, and the claimant sued. The court held that the defendant's promise was unenforceable, because it was made after the sale. If the promise about the horse's condition had been made before, the claimant would have provided consideration for it by buying the horse. As it was made after the sale, the consideration was past, for it had not been given in return for the promise.

**Legal Principle**
Consideration must be given in return for the promise of the other party.

Whether or not consideration is past is a question of fact, and the wording of an agreement will not necessarily be conclusive. In **Re McArdle** (1951) a widow had been left the family home in her husband's will. The will allowed her to live in it for the rest of her life, and on her death it was to be inherited by their five children equally. During the mother's lifetime, one of her sons and his wife lived with her in the house and the daughter-in-law paid for some home improvements. When these were finished, the other four children signed a document which promised to pay her £488 for the work, 'in consideration of [her] carrying out certain alterations and improvements to the property'.

After the mother died, the daughter-in-law tried to claim the money, but her husband's brothers and sisters refused to pay. The Court of Appeal held that although the wording of the document suggested that the payment related to work to be done in the future, the facts of the case made it clear that the promise was given in return for something already done; it was therefore past consideration, and the promise was not binding.

There are two exceptions to the rule that past consideration is no consideration. The first is where the past consideration was provided at the promisor's request, and it was understood that payment would be made in return. This exception can be traced back to the old case of **Lampleigh v Brathwait** (1615).

## Key Case    Lampleigh v Brathwait

In **Lampleigh v Brathwait** (1615) Thomas Brathwait had been convicted of killing a man, and he asked Anthony Lampleigh to obtain a pardon for him from the King. After considerable trouble and expense, Lampleigh managed to do so. In the excitement of getting his pardon,

Brathwait promised to pay Lampleigh £100, but later refused to hand over the money, so Lampleigh sued.

It might appear that Lampleigh's consideration was past, since he had secured the pardon before the promise to pay was made. In fact, the court upheld Lampleigh's claim. It reasoned that Lampleigh had obtained the pardon at Brathwait's own request, and this request carried with it the unspoken understanding that the service would be paid for. Lampleigh obtained the pardon after, and in return for, this implied promise to pay, and so obtaining the pardon was good consideration for the promise to pay. The later promise, specifying that £100 would be paid, was said to be merely confirmation of the original, unspoken one.

This reasoning seems less odd when we consider that today there are many requests which carry with them unsaid promises to pay – when we ask a taxi driver to take us somewhere, or ask the milkman to leave an extra pint, we do not actually say that we will pay for those goods and services, but clearly it is understood by both parties that we will. It may well be that requests to secure royal pardons had the same well-understood effect in 1615.

**Legal Principle**
Past consideration is sufficient when it is provided at the promisor's request and it is understood that payment will be made in return.

A (slightly) more recent case on this principle is **Re Casey's Patents** (1892). The defendants owned some patent rights, and the claimant worked for them. They wrote to him, saying that in consideration of his services as manager in relation to the patents, they were going to give him a one-third interest in them. They later claimed that as their promise was made in relation to services which the claimant had already given, it was past consideration and therefore the promise was not binding. The court held, however, that the claimant's services were clearly always meant to be paid for, and the promise was merely putting this expectation into the form of a specified amount.

The second exception to the rule on past consideration is the bill of exchange. Under s. 27 of the Bills of Exchange Act 1882 an 'antecedent debt or liability' may be consideration for receipt of a bill of exchange.

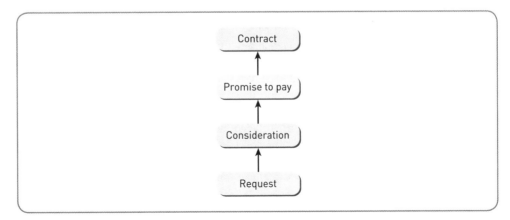

**Figure 6.1 Lampleigh *v* Brathwait**

## ◗ Consideration must be sufficient

Although consideration must provide some benefit to the promisor or detriment to the promisee, these do not have to amount to a great deal. This principle is usually described in the rather confusing phrase 'consideration must be sufficient but need not be adequate', which effectively means that the courts will not inquire into the adequacy of consideration, so long as there is some. Providing something is given in return for a promise, it does not matter that it is not much, or not what the promise would usually be considered to be worth. So if, for example, A promises to sell B her state-of-the-art CD player for £5, the consideration paid by B clearly provides very little benefit to A, and amounts to only a small loss to B, but nevertheless, the transaction will be binding because some consideration has been provided by both sides. It is often said that just one peppercorn can be good consideration – even if the promisee does not like pepper!

The reason for this rule is the old idea of freedom of contract, which required that the parties themselves should be allowed to make the bargains that suit them, without interference from the courts.

### Key Case  Thomas v Thomas

In **Thomas v Thomas** (1842) the claimant was a widow whose husband had stated that if he died before his wife, she should be allowed to live in his house for the rest of her life, after which it was to pass to his sons. When the man died, the defendant, who was his executor, agreed that the widow could continue to occupy the house in return for a promise that she would pay £1 a year and keep the house in good repair. Despite this, some time later, the defendant tried to evict the widow, so she sued for breach of contract. The defendant claimed that the earlier promise was not binding because of lack of consideration. However, the court held that the widow's promise to pay £1 and keep up the repairs was sufficient consideration to make the owner's promise binding.

**Legal Principle**
Consideration must be sufficient but need not be adequate.

The same principle was applied in **Chappell v Nestlé** (1959). Nestlé ran a special offer involving a record of a song called 'Rockin' Shoes' – customers could get a copy of the record by sending in 1s 6d (about seven and a half pence) and three wrappers from Nestlé's bars of chocolate. The copyright holders for the record brought an action against Nestlé, which among other things claimed that royalties should be paid on the price of the record.

To calculate the royalties due, it was necessary to establish what price Nestlé were charging for the record, and the copyright holder alleged that this price (which was the consideration for the promise to send the record) included the three wrappers. Nestlé, on the other hand, contended that the consideration was only the 1s 6d, and that they threw away the wrappers they received. The House of Lords held that the wrappers did form part of the consideration – the fact that they were of no real worth to Nestlé was irrelevant.

The interesting implication of this case is that if the fact that the wrappers were useless to Nestlé was irrelevant, presumably wrappers alone could have amounted to consideration – if, for example, Nestlé had just asked for three wrappers, and not requested money in addition.

## Consideration must be of economic value

It is sometimes said that consideration must have some 'economic' value, though, as the Nestlé case shows, this economic value may be negligible. What this principle basically seems to mean is that there must be some physical value, rather than just an emotional or sentimental one. In **Thomas** v **Thomas** (discussed above), for example, the claimant suggested that following her husband's wishes was part of the consideration, but the court rejected this argument because they said the husband's wishes had no economic value (though in the event this did not alter the outcome of the case, as the widow's own promise was consideration).

Similarly, in **White** v **Bluett** (1853), a father promised not to make his son repay money he had borrowed, if the son promised not to keep boring him with complaints. The court held that the son's promise was not sufficient consideration to make his father's promise binding, because it had no economic value.

## Consideration can be a promise not to sue

If one party has a possible civil claim against the other, a promise not to enforce that claim is good consideration for a promise given in return. If, for example, Ann crashes into Ben's car, Ben might agree that he will not sue Ann if Ann pays for the damage, and Ben's promise not to sue will be consideration for Ann's promise to pay.

In **Alliance Bank Ltd** v **Broom** (1864) Broom had an overdraft of £22,000 with the bank, and they asked him to provide some security. Mr Broom promised to do so, but never did, and as a result the bank sued him. Mr Broom argued that there was no consideration for his promise to provide security, but the court held that the consideration was provided by the bank's implied promise not to sue for a while, giving Mr Broom time to provide security, even though they did sue fairly shortly afterwards.

Where forbearing to enforce a legal claim is offered as consideration, there must have been some intention actually to bring proceedings. In **Miles** v **New Zealand Alford Estate Co** (1886) a company had bought some land which it was dissatisfied with. The seller later promised to make certain payments to the company, and the company alleged that it had provided consideration for this promise by not taking legal proceedings to rescind the contract when they found the problems with the land. This argument was rejected by the Court of Appeal, which held that there was no consideration for the vendor's promise, because there was no evidence that the buyers ever really intended to bring proceedings to rescind.

In the same case, it was pointed out that if the party who has the claim believes it to be legally valid, but it turns out not to be, the promise will still be good consideration if that party had honestly believed they had a valid claim – so in the car accident example above, even if it subsequently transpires that for some reason Ben could not have successfully sued Ann anyway, Ben's promise not to sue is still valid consideration, providing Ben honestly believes he has a claim against Ann.

One party's promise not to enforce an existing claim can only provide consideration if the promise given in return was actually induced by the promise not to enforce the claim. In **Combe** v **Combe** (1951) a husband and his wife were involved in divorce proceedings, during which he promised to pay her an annual allowance. She later brought an action to enforce this promise and argued, among other things, that she had given consideration for it by not exercising her right to apply to the court for a maintenance order. It was held that this could not be consideration because her husband had not asked her not to apply to the court, and therefore his promise had not been made in return for her promising not to do so.

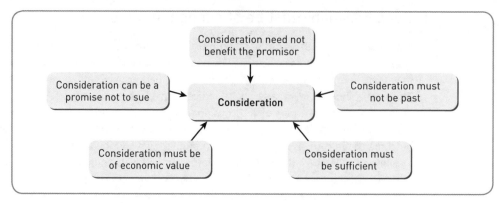

**Figure 6.2** Consideration

This principle can be a difficult one to apply. In **Alliance Bank** *v* **Broom** the defendant did not ask the bank not to sue, yet the bank's forbearance to do so was held to constitute consideration. However, the decision has been explained on the basis that by promising to supply security, the debtor was by implication asking the bank not to sue.

## Contracts (Rights of Third Parties) Act 1999

Following the Contracts (Rights of Third Parties) Act 1999, a term in a contract is sometimes enforceable by a third party. It is not necessary for consideration to have been given by the third party.

# Performance of an existing duty

Where a promisee already owes the promisor a legal duty, then in theory performing that duty should not in itself be consideration – if the promisee does nothing more than they are already obliged to do, they are suffering no detriment and the promisor is only getting a benefit to which he or she was already entitled. In most cases the courts have observed this principle, but as we shall see, in recent years they have discovered consideration in the performance of an existing duty, causing some controversy in the process.

Existing duties can be divided into three main categories: public duties; contractual duties to the promisor; and contractual duties to a third party.

## Existing public duty

Where a person is merely carrying out duties they are legally obliged to perform – such as a police officer protecting citizens, or a juror listening to evidence – doing that alone will not be consideration. In **Collins** *v* **Godefroy** (1831) the claimant had been summoned to give evidence in a court action. The defendant promised to give him six guineas for doing so, but later refused to pay. The claimant tried to enforce the promise, but it was held that since he was legally obliged to give the evidence, doing so could not be considered consideration for the promise. Clearly there are public policy reasons, as well as technical legal ones, for this principle.

However, where a promisee is under a public duty, but does something which goes beyond what they are bound to do under that duty, that extra act can amount to consideration. In **Glasbrook Brothers Ltd** v **Glamorgan County Council** (1925) Glasbrook Brothers were the owners of a coal mine in South Wales. Their employees went on strike and Glasbrook Brothers asked the police to place a guard at the coal mine during the strike. The police refused to do this as they considered that regular checks by a mobile police patrol would be sufficient to protect the mine. The mine owners therefore offered to pay the police £2,200 to cover the extra cost of having the police stationed at the mine full-time during the strike. When the strike was over, the mine owners refused to pay. They argued that the police had an existing duty to protect the mine and therefore had provided no consideration for their promise to pay. The House of Lords held that the police had provided an extra service which did amount to consideration. The police were merely under a public duty to maintain law and order and could choose how they achieved this. Viscount Cave LC said:

> If in the judgement of the police authorities, formed reasonably and in good faith, the garrison was necessary for the protection of life and property, then they were not entitled to make a charge for it.

As on the facts this was not the case, they were entitled to charge for the extra service.

In the later case of **Harris** v **Sheffield United Football Club Ltd** (1988) the football club sought to rely on the above reasoning to argue that they should not have to pay for police officers attending their ground at home matches. They argued that a big police presence was necessary to maintain law and order. But the case was distinguished. In **Glasbrook Brothers** the coal mine owners could not call off the strike, so the threat to law and order was not their fault. But in the present case, the football club chose to hold football matches on Saturday afternoons to get maximum attendance. This created a bigger risk to law and order so the necessity for the large police presence was self-induced. As a result the police services had to be paid for.

The case of **Ward** v **Byham** (1956) illustrates the willingness of the courts to find evidence of some consideration where public policy reasons seem to demand that a promise be binding. Ms Ward and Mr Byham lived together from 1949 to 1954, and in 1950 had a daughter. In 1954 Mr Byham threw Ms Ward out of the house, but kept their daughter with him. Some months later Ms Ward asked to take the child to live with her, and Mr Byham wrote to say that she could do so, and he would pay £1 a week maintenance, provided that she could 'prove that [the daughter] will be well looked after and happy', and that the little girl was allowed to decide for herself whether or not she wanted to go and live with her mother. Ms Ward duly took their daughter. Mr Byham paid the maintenance as agreed for seven months, but stopped when Ms Ward married another man. She sued for the money. Mr Byham alleged that there was no consideration because, as the mother of an illegitimate child, she was already under a statutory duty to maintain the little girl, so her promise to do so was not consideration. On the facts, the majority of the court held that there was a valid contract, because her promise to see that their daughter was happy, and to allow her to choose which parent she wanted to live with, went beyond her statutory duty, and could therefore be consideration for Mr Byham's promise to pay maintenance.

## Existing contractual duty to the promisor

The position on contractual duties and consideration has changed in recent years, and the implications of the change are still rather unclear. In the past, the rule was that performance of an existing contractual duty owed to a promisor was not consideration, as illustrated by two nineteenth-century shipping cases.

**Key Case**   Stilk *v* Myrick

In **Stilk *v* Myrick** (1809) two sailors deserted a ship during a voyage and the captain was unable to find replacements for them. The eight remaining crew members were promised extra wages for sailing the ship back home shorthanded, but when they arrived back in London, the captain refused to pay the extra money. The sailors sued for it, but the court held that there was no consideration for the captain's promise; the sailors had already contracted to sail to their destination and back, and that was all they had done.

**Legal Principle**
Performance of an existing contractual duty owed to a promisor is not normally consideration.

In **Hartley *v* Ponsonby** (1857) half the crew deserted a ship, and the rest were promised extra money to carry on working the ship to Bombay. Again, at the end of the voyage the captain refused to pay the extra money and the claimant sued. In this case the court held that there was consideration, because the crew had become so small that the remainder of the voyage was more dangerous than it had been when they made their contracts. In agreeing to carry on, the claimant was taking on duties beyond those in his original contract, and had therefore provided consideration for the promise to pay extra. In the light of the Court of Appeal case of **Williams *v* Roffey** (1990) a distinction now has to be drawn between contractual duties to supply goods or services and contractual duties to pay debts.

## Contractual duties to supply goods or services

**Key Case**   Williams *v* Roffey

In **Williams *v* Roffey** (1991) these principles were reconsidered by the Court of Appeal. Roffey were a building firm with a contract to refurbish a block of flats. They subcontracted the carpentry work on the project to Williams, agreeing to pay him £20,000 for the work. But before the work was finished, it became obvious that Williams had financial problems, which would prevent him finishing the work on time. Roffey's agreement with the owners of the flats contained a penalty clause, which meant Roffey would lose out if the complete project was not finished on time. Roffey agreed that the original contract price had been too low, and their representative approached Williams, offering an extra £10,300 on top of the agreed price of £20,000 in return for finishing the job on schedule. The agreement also included changes to the working arrangements: instead of Williams working on several flats at once, he would finish one at a time, so allowing other contractors doing different work to come in after him. When the carpentry work was done, Roffey refused to honour their promise to pay the extra £10,300, so Williams sued for breach of contract. The Court of Appeal found that Roffey's promise to pay extra was supported by valuable consideration: in return for Williams finishing the job on time, Roffey would avoid losing money under the penalty clause in their contract with the building's owners, and the cost and inconvenience of finding another contractor to finish the job, and had also benefited from the altered working arrangements. Even though Williams was only doing what he had originally contracted to do, Roffey was receiving extra benefit.

As a result of **Williams** v **Roffey**, the law now seems to be that if one party's promise to perform an existing contractual duty to supply goods or services confers an additional practical benefit on the other party, then, providing that no duress is involved, it will be sufficient consideration to make a promise given in return binding, even though in legal terms they are only agreeing to carry out their existing contractual duty. The case has caused much interest in the world of contract law, and some of its possible implications are discussed later in this chapter.

> **Legal Principle**
> If one party's promise to perform an existing contractual duty to supply goods or services confers an additional practical benefit on the other party, then, providing that no duress is involved, it will be sufficient consideration to make a promise given in return binding.

## Contractual duties to pay debts

Special rules apply to contractual duties regarding debts. Where someone owes another money and cannot pay the full amount, they will sometimes offer to pay a smaller sum, on condition that the creditor promises to accept it as full settlement for the debt – in other words, agrees not to sue later for the full amount. Even if such an agreement is made, it is only binding if the debtor provides some consideration for it by adding some extra element.

 **Key Case**   Pinnel's Case

In **Pinnel's Case** (1602) Pinnel sued Cole for £8 10s, which Cole owed on a bond (a promise under seal to pay money). The debt had become due on 11 November. Cole argued that at Pinnel's request, he had given him £5 2s 6d on 1 October, which Pinnel had accepted in full settlement of the debt. Pinnel actually won the case on a technicality, but the court made it clear that had it not been for that technicality, they would have found in favour of Cole, because of the fact that he had made payment earlier than the due date, and this amounted to fresh consideration for the promise to accept less than the full amount. The court stated: 'Payment of a lesser sum on the day in satisfaction of a greater cannot be any satisfaction for the whole but a change in time or mode of payment, or the addition by the debtor of a tomtit, or canary or the like will suffice to constitute consideration for the [creditor's promise to forgo his debt].' In other words, if the debtor pays early, or in a more convenient place, or gives something else as well as the part-payment, the creditor is receiving some benefit and the debtor some detriment, and this is fresh consideration for the creditor's new promise to accept part-payment and not insist on getting the whole amount. Suppose, for example, Ann lends Ben £100, and they agree that Ben will pay the money back in one month's time. If Ann arrives on the appointed date, to find that Ben only has £40, and will only hand over that amount if Ann agrees that it is in full settlement for the debt, Ann can agree to this, and still sue Ben for the other £60 later – Ben has given no consideration for Ann's promise to accept the part-payment, and so the promise is not binding. If, however, Ben pays the £40 before the month is up, or offers Ann £40 and a book, then if in either of these circumstances Ann agrees to accept the part-payment as full settlement, that promise will be binding because Ben has given consideration for it.

### Legal Principle

If a debtor offers to pay a reduced sum back to the lender in full and final settlement and the lender agrees to accept it, this agreement will only be binding if the debtor provides some extra element that can be treated as consideration.

The rule was approved in **Foakes** *v* **Beer** (1884). Mrs Beer was owed £2,090 by Dr Foakes, on what is known as a judgment debt. She could have obtained a court order for the seizure and sale of his property to pay the debt, but instead she agreed that he could give her £500 immediately, and pay the rest in instalments. If he did this, she said, she would not take legal action. Interest is usually payable on a judgment debt, but their agreement did not mention this. However, when Dr Foakes had paid off the debt, Mrs Beer asked for the interest as well. Dr Foakes refused to pay it, relying on their agreement. Mrs Beer sued, claiming that there was no consideration for the agreement. The House of Lords upheld her claim by applying the rule in **Pinnel's Case**: payment of part of the debt did not in itself constitute consideration for Mrs Beer's promise to forgo the balance.

This approach was confirmed more recently by the Court of Appeal in **Re Selectmove Ltd** (1995). The case concerned an alleged arrangement between the Inland Revenue and Selectmove under which it was alleged that it had been agreed that Selectmove could pay off its tax liabilities by instalments. Despite this alleged arrangement, the Inland Revenue later demanded immediate payment in full, and on failure to receive this payment sought to have the company wound up because of its continuing tax debts. Selectmove resisted this action on the basis that the previous arrangements for payment by instalments constituted a binding contract. The Inland Revenue argued that no contract could have been formed because, among other things, Selectmove had provided no consideration. Selectmove, relying on **Williams** *v* **Roffey**, argued that the consideration provided was the 'practical benefit' to the Inland Revenue of Selectmove remaining in business so that it could continue to make payments, rather than going into liquidation, which would reduce the Inland Revenue's chances of recovery of the money owed. The Court of Appeal found in favour of the Inland Revenue, concluding that there was no binding contract and one of the reasons given was because no consideration had been given. Thus, while in relation to promises to supply goods or services, a renewed promise to perform an existing obligation can amount to good consideration if the other party receives a 'practical benefit', this is not sufficient for promises for the part-payment of a debt.

## Exceptions to the rule in Pinnel's Case

### Disputed claims

The rule in **Pinnel's Case** does not apply if there is a genuine dispute about whether the debt is actually owed, or about the amount owed (**Cooper** *v* **Parker** (1885)). In such circumstances a part-payment by the debtor will be consideration for a promise not to enforce the rest of the alleged debt.

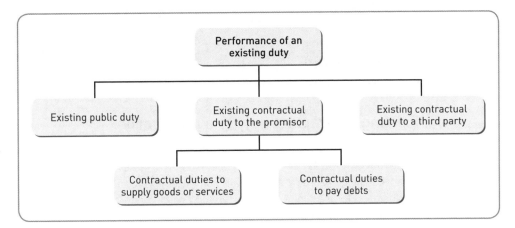

**Figure 6.3** Performance of an existing duty

## Unliquidated claims

A liquidated claim is one for a fixed amount – a sum of money lent, for example, or the agreed price of goods or services supplied. Where the amount of a claim is uncertain, as in a claim for damages, or in connection with a contract specifying 'reasonable remuneration', it is said to be unliquidated. In such circumstances the rule in **Pinnel's Case** does not apply. Because the value of the claim is not known, a sum offered in part-payment could actually turn out to be more than the claim was worth, and in any case gives the creditor the practical advantage of avoiding legal action, which is not guaranteed to succeed; these benefits provide consideration for a promise to accept the part-payment in full settlement.

## Composition agreements

A debtor who owes money to several different people, and cannot pay, may offer to pay each one a percentage of their claim, which is often expressed as so much in the pound, and known as a dividend. As an example, if A owes £10 to B, £50 to C and £100 to D, and cannot pay, her creditors may agree to accept a 'dividend' of 10p in the pound in settlement of each debt, which will amount to £1 to B, £5 to C and £10 to D. Such an arrangement is called a composition agreement, and the courts have long held such an agreement to be binding, so that none of the creditors can later sue for the full amount – although it is hard to see what in the arrangement could amount to consideration.

## Payment by a third party

A creditor who accepts part-payment from a third party, in full settlement of the debtor's liability, cannot then sue for the outstanding amount. This was the situation in **Hirachand Punamchand v Temple** (1911). An army officer owed money to a moneylender, and the officer's father sent a draft (which works in a similar way to a cheque) for a smaller amount, saying it was 'in full settlement' of the debt. The moneylender cashed the draft, and then went on to try to sue the son for the rest of the money owed. The Court of Appeal rejected this claim, considering that by accepting the draft, the claimant had agreed to the terms on which it was offered, and made an implied promise not to sue for the rest of the money. Although this implied promise was made to the father rather than the son, and the son had provided no consideration, the court stated that allowing the claimant to succeed would be a fraud on the father and thus an abuse of the process of the court.

### Promissory estoppel

(This is discussed on p. 105.)

## Existing contractual duty to a third party

In some cases two parties make a contract to provide a benefit to someone who is not a party to the contract, known as a third party. If one of them (X) makes a further promise to that third party, to provide the benefit they have already contracted to provide, that further promise can be good consideration for a promise made by the third party in return – even though nothing more than the contractual duty is being promised by X.

**Key Case**  Scotson v Pegg

In **Scotson v Pegg** (1861) Scotson contracted with A to supply a cargo of coal to A, or to anyone A nominated. Scotson was instructed by A to deliver the coal to Pegg who was a third party to the original contract between Scotson and A. Pegg promised to unload the coal at a stated rate of pay. He subsequently failed to do the agreed unloading. Scotson sued Pegg, claiming that their promise to deliver the coal to him was consideration for his promise to unload it. Pegg claimed this could not be consideration, since Scotson was already bound to supply the coal under the contract with A. The court upheld Scotson's claim: delivery of the coal was consideration because it was a benefit to Pegg, and a detriment to Scotson in that it prevented them from having the option of breaking their contract with A (in which case they would just pay damages to A) and having no liability to Pegg. However, there is some suggestion that Scotson had done more than he was bound to do under the earlier contract, and so provided additional consideration, and this means that the case is not entirely conclusive on the point we are discussing here.

#### Legal Principle
If a contracting party promises to provide a benefit to a third party which they are already bound to provide under the contract, this promise can still be good consideration for a promise made by the third party.

Another case on the issue is **Shadwell v Shadwell** (1860). The claimant, a young barrister, was engaged to marry, and his uncle wrote offering to give him £150 a year, until such time as the claimant was earning 600 guineas a year from his practice at the Bar. The claimant duly got married. He never actually reached the point where he was earning 600 guineas a year, but the allowance promised by his uncle was not always paid. When the uncle died, the claimant brought an action to recover the arrears from his uncle's personal representatives. They argued that there was no consideration for the promise; all the claimant had done was marry his fiancée, which he was bound to do before the uncle wrote his letter (at this time a promise to marry was considered legally binding, and could be sued upon if broken). However, a majority of the court held that marrying his fiancée was consideration. It was a detriment to the claimant, because it involved incurring financial responsibilities which could have been problematic without the uncle's allowance (although the court did accept that marriage did also provide some benefit to the claimant!). There was also some benefit to the uncle, in that he would be pleased about the marriage of such a near relative. The judgment is not entirely satisfactory, in that it does not address the fact that the claimant was already bound to marry his fiancée, nor the fact that the marriage of a near relative is merely a sentimental benefit, which as we have seen would not usually be sufficient consideration, because it has no economic value.

Although neither of these judgments is entirely satisfactory on this point, the rule on promises to a third party being good consideration has been confirmed in the more recent cases of **New Zealand Shipping Co** v **A M Satterthwaite & Co (*The Eurymedon*)** (1975), and **Pao On** v **Lau Yiu Long** (1980).

# Waiver and promissory estoppel

These doctrines are ways of making some kinds of promise binding even where there is no consideration. Waiver has traditionally applied where one party agrees not to enforce their strict rights under the contract by, for example, accepting delivery later than agreed. Subject to the usual principles of equity, that promise can be held binding, even without consideration.

An example of waiver in action is **Hickman** v **Haynes** (1875). A buyer asked the seller to deliver goods later than originally agreed, and then, when the delivery was made, refused to accept it. The seller sued for breach of contract, and the buyer responded by arguing that in fact the seller was in breach, for delivering later than specified in the original contract. The court rejected this argument on the grounds that the late delivery was made at the buyer's request.

In **Charles Rickards Ltd** v **Oppenheim** (1950) this principle was further developed. The defendant had asked the claimant to do some work on his Rolls-Royce, to be completed within 'six or seven months'. In fact, the work was not finished by this time, but the defendant agreed to wait a further three months. Even after that, the work was still unfinished, at which point the defendant gave the claimant notice that unless the work was done within another four weeks, the order would be cancelled. In the event, the work was not done for another three months, and the defendant then refused to accept the car. The claimant sued him.

The Court of Appeal decided that although originally the completion date had been an important term of the contract, the first extension of it operated as a waiver. This meant that if the car had been delivered within that time, the defendant would have been bound to accept it; he could not insist on the original delivery date. Once the defendant gave the claimant reasonable notice that delivery time was once again to be fixed, the claimant's failure to complete the work put him in breach of contract, and his action against the defendant failed.

Promissory estoppel is a somewhat newer doctrine than waiver, and could be said to be a development of it. It is derived from equity and is therefore sometimes known as equitable estoppel. The case of **Hughes** v **Metropolitan Railway Co** (1877), involving a landlord and his tenants, is usually seen as the starting point for the doctrine. Under the lease, the tenants were obliged to keep the premises in good repair, and in October 1874 the landlord gave them six months' notice to do some repairs, stating that if they were not done in that time, the lease would be forfeited. In November, the two parties began to negotiate the possibility of the tenants buying the lease, the tenants stating that in the meantime they would not carry out the repairs. By December, the negotiations had broken down, and at the end of the six-month notice period, the landlord claimed that the lease was forfeited because the tenants had not done the repairs. The House of Lords held, however, that the landlord's conduct was an implied promise to the tenants that he would not enforce the forfeiture at the end of the notice period, and in not doing the repairs, the tenants had been relying on this promise (the six-month notice period had started again from the date when the negotiations broke down). The promise was held to be binding.

Explaining the decision, Lord Cairns said:

> It is the first principle upon which all Courts of Equity proceed, that if parties who have entered into definite and distinct terms involving certain legal results – certain penalties or legal forfeit-ure – afterwards by their own act or with their own consent enter upon a course of negotiation which has the effect of leading one of the parties to suppose that the strict rights arising under the contract will not be enforced, or will be kept in suspense, or held in abeyance, the person who otherwise might have enforced those rights will not be allowed to enforce them where it would be inequitable having regard to the dealings which have thus taken place between the parties.

These principles were applied 70 years later by Denning J (later Lord Denning) in **Central London Property Trust Ltd** *v* **High Trees House Ltd** (1947).

## Key Case    Central London Property Trust Ltd *v* High Trees House Ltd

The claimant owned a block of flats. In September 1939, it had leased the block to the defendant, who planned to rent out the individual flats, use the income to cover the pay-ments on the lease, and make a profit on top. Unfortunately, these plans were rather spoilt by the fact that the Second World War had just broken out, and many people left London, making it difficult to find tenants. As a result, many of the flats were left empty. The claim-ant therefore agreed that the defendant could pay just half the ground rent stipulated in the lease. By 1945, the flats were full again, and the claimant sought the full ground rent for the last two quarters of 1945. The claimant stated that the agreement was only ever intended to last until the war was over, or the flats fully let, whichever was the sooner. Both events had happened by the time payment for the last two quarters of 1945 were due, and so the company believed it was entitled to full payment for that period.

The court accepted this argument, holding that the full rent was payable for the two quarters in question, and from then on. Of more importance is the fact that Denning J went on to state that the claimant would not have been entitled to recover the rent for the period 1940–45, even though there was no consideration for the promise to accept the reduced rent, because of the equitable principle laid down in **Hughes**. In fact, this reasoning (which was *obiter*, because the claimant was not actually seeking to recover all the past rent) went further than that put forward in **Hughes**. In the earlier case the landlord's rights had effect-ively been only temporarily suspended, but in **High Trees**, Denning J declared that the landlord's claim for its full contractual rights for the period 1940–45 had been destroyed – by accepting the reduced rent for the wartime period, it lost its right to claim for arrears of rent, rather than simply suspending this right until the tenant could afford to pay.

### Legal Principle
Under the doctrine of promissory estoppel, a contracting party who promises not to enforce a contractual right will not be able to enforce that right later if it would be inequitable to do so, and the promise has been relied upon by the other party.

The precise extent of the doctrine of promissory estoppel is still unclear. What is clear is that the following conditions must be fulfilled before the doctrine can be applied.

## A pre-existing contractual relationship

The cases suggest that there must already be a contractual relationship between the parties before promissory estoppel can be raised.

## A promise

There must be an obvious and unambiguous promise not to enforce a person's full legal rights. This promise may be implied from conduct, but silence, or failure to act, will not usually be sufficient. In **China-Pacific SA** *v* **Food Corp of India** (1980), the parties had been involved in a complex commercial dispute, entailing a great deal of correspondence and discussion. The defendants claimed that the contents of one of the letters, and remarks made during a discussion between the two parties' barristers, provided grounds for promissory estoppel. On the facts of the case, the claim was rejected, as no unambiguous promise had been made.

## Reliance

The promisee must have acted in reliance on the promise, in the sense that it must have influenced their conduct. In **High Trees**, for example, the lessees continued to rent out the flats, rather than, for example, trying to sell their leasehold interest to someone else.

It is not entirely clear whether or not an act of reliance has to be something which would put the promisee at a disadvantage if the promisor decided to reclaim their legal rights, or whether it can simply be some act which otherwise would not have happened. In **Hughes**, the tenants' failure to make repairs because they were relying on the landlord not to enforce the forfeiture clearly put them at a disadvantage, and in **Tool Metal Manufacturing** (see p. 108), Lord Tucker suggested that the act of reliance should involve such a disadvantage. On the other hand, there is no mention of such a requirement in **High Trees**, nor is it stated to be necessary in **Hughes**, even though there was in fact some disadvantage there. Where relying on the promise does not put the promisee at a disadvantage, it may be difficult to satisfy the next requirement described, that it must be inequitable for the promisor to go back on their word.

## Inequitable to enforce strict legal rights

As an equitable doctrine, promissory estoppel will only be applied where it would be inequitable for the promisor to go back on what was promised, and insist on their strict legal rights. If the party claiming promissory estoppel has acted in such a way that it would be inequitable to allow them to take advantage of it, the doctrine will not be applied. This was the situation in **D & C Builders** *v* **Rees** (1966).

**Key Case**    D & C Builders *v* Rees

The claimant in **D & C Builders** *v* **Rees** (1966) was a small firm of builders who did some work costing £732 on the premises of Mr and Mrs Rees. The defendants had paid £250 before the work was finished, but then stated that they would pay no more than a further £300, alleging (apparently falsely) that the work was defective. The builders were in severe financial trouble, which the defendants knew about, and faced bankruptcy if they failed to secure the full amount owed. They pressed for payment over several months, but received nothing. Eventually, Mrs Rees again offered a cheque of £300, saying that it was in final settlement, and that if it was refused, the builders would be paid nothing. The builders, still being pressed by their own creditors, reluctantly agreed. They later sued for the balance of the original debt, and the court gave judgment in their favour. The majority of the court held that it was a straightforward application of the rule in **Pinnel's Case**, but Lord Denning's judgment also raised the possibility of promissory estoppel, explaining that although it might otherwise have applied, Mr and Mrs Rees could not rely on it because of their own behaviour – they had deliberately taken advantage of the builders' financial problems, effectively holding them to ransom, and there was also evidence that they had misled the builders about their own financial position, suggesting that they could not afford the whole price when in fact they were well able to pay. Given such behaviour, it would be inequitable to allow them to rely on promissory estoppel.

> **Legal Principle**
> Lord Denning stated *obiter* that if the party claiming promissory estoppel has acted in such a way that it would be inequitable to allow him or her to take advantage of the doctrine, then the doctrine will not be applied.

In **Re Selectmove Ltd** (1995) (discussed at p. 102 above), Selectmove tried to rely on equitable estoppel to prevent the Inland Revenue reneging on an alleged agreement for the payment of unpaid tax by instalments. The Court of Appeal rejected this argument as, even if the agreement had existed, Selectmove had failed to make certain payments required by it. As a result of this failure, it would be perfectly equitable to allow the Inland Revenue to enforce its strict legal rights.

## Future rights not destroyed

Promissory estoppel can usually only be used to prevent rights being exercised for a period of time; it cannot destroy them for ever. This was stressed in **Tool Metal Manufacturing Co Ltd** *v* **Tungsten Electric Co Ltd** (1955). A licence for the use of a patent provided that the licensees had to pay 'compensation' if they manufactured more than the agreed number of items using the patent. In 1942, owing to the war, the patent owners agreed to forego their right to 'compensation' in the national interest, with a view to a new agreement being made after the war. When the war was over, the patent owners had problems getting the licensees to make a new agreement, and eventually claimed the compensation that would have been due from the time the war ended.

The court held that the patent owners' promise was binding during the specified period, so they could not get back any money that would have been due if the agreement had not been made; but they could revive their legal entitlement to receive the compensation payments after that period, on giving reasonable notice to the other party. In other words, rights can be revived for the future but not claimed back for the past.

## No new rights created

Promissory estoppel cannot be used to create entirely new rights or extend the scope of existing ones, only to prevent the enforcement of rights already held; it has been described as being 'a shield and not a sword'. This can be seen in **Combe** *v* **Combe** (1951) (see p. 97 above). Since there was no contract between them, Mrs Combe did not have a legal right to the payments her husband promised, even though she had relied on his promise in not applying for a maintenance order.

The doctrine of waiver clearly has a lot in common with promissory estoppel, and in fact some academics have suggested that they are the same thing. Actually, there appears to be at least one main distinction between the two: in a case of waiver, the party waiving their rights is really only waiving the right to claim damages for breach of contract, or to terminate for breach where applicable. They can still claim for any payments which would have been due during the waiver. In promissory estoppel, such payments could not be claimed back, as established in **High Trees**.

### Topical Issue

#### Marks & Spencer: a national treasure?

Marks & Spencer is one of the best known stores on the English high street and historically most of its goods were manufactured in the United Kingdom. It hit the headlines when, faced with fierce competition, it decided that it had to save money by manufacturing more of its goods abroad. As well as upsetting some of its traditional customers, this decision was a financial disaster for UK manufacturers which had been supplying clothes to Marks & Spencer for many years. One such manufacturer was Baird Textile Holdings (BTH) which had been an important supplier of clothes to Marks & Spencer for 30 years. It took Marks & Spencer to court and the case was reported as **Baird Textile Holdings Ltd** *v* **Marks & Spencer plc** (2001). One of the arguments submitted to the Court of Appeal was that Marks & Spencer should be estopped from terminating their business relationship without reasonable notice. It alleged that Marks & Spencer had induced BTH to assume that the relationship was long-term, and terminable only on reasonable notice. BTH said that they had allowed Marks & Spencer to control and influence their business; they had invested money to be highly responsive to Marks & Spencer's needs; and had foregone the chance to establish relationships with other retailers. Reversing the finding of the High Court, the Court of Appeal rejected this argument, pointing out that promissory estoppel could not create a cause of action. The Court of Appeal acknowledged that, in the light of certain Commonwealth decisions, the House of Lords might well develop the law of estoppel in the direction favoured by BTH, but it had not yet done so.

## Agreement by deed

There is one other way in which a promise can be made binding without consideration: it can be put into a document called a deed. An agreement by deed is often described as a 'formal' contract or a contract of 'speciality'; other types of contract are usually called 'simple' contracts. The procedure

**Table 6.1** Comparing consideration and promissory estoppel

| Consideration | Promissory estoppel |
|---|---|
| Rules contained in common law | Rules developed in equity |
| Reliance irrelevant | Doctrine only applies where one party relied on the promise of another |
| Creates and extinguishes rights | Only suspends rights, does not extinguish rights |
| Both a shield and a sword | A shield but not a sword |

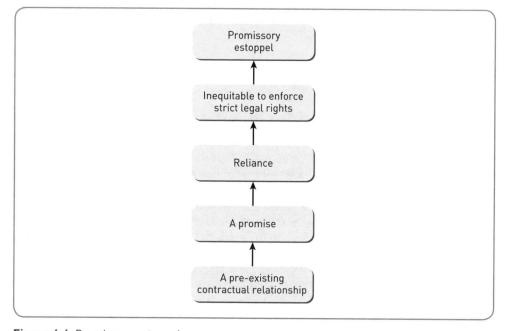

**Figure 6.4** Promissory estoppel

for making an agreement by deed is laid down in s. 1 of the Law of Property (Miscellaneous Provisions) Act 1989, and usually involves signing a formal document in the presence of a witness. Deeds are typically used to give binding legal effect to what might otherwise be a gratuitous gift, which would be unenforceable for lack of consideration.

# Consideration and conditional gifts

We already know that a gratuitous promise is not usually enforceable by law – if Ann promises to give Ben her lawnmower for nothing, there is no consideration and no contract. If Ben promises to give Ann £5 in return, there is consideration and, assuming all the other requirements of a contract are met, the agreement will be binding. But what is the situation if Ann promises to give Ben the lawnmower, and Ben goes and fetches it from Ann's garden shed? At first sight it might appear that fetching the lawnmower is consideration for the promise, but in law it is nothing more than a condition of Ann's gift. The lawnmower is not being 'sold' to Ben for the price of fetching it, but given on condition that Ben fetches it.

This is clearly a tricky distinction to draw, but one approach is that in interpreting words describing a condition, it is useful (though not foolproof) to ask whether the condition is a benefit to the promisor – if so, it is more likely to amount to consideration. If, for example, our imaginary lawnmower was actually in the repair shop, and the repairers were threatening to impose a storage charge because it had been left there so long, Ben fetching it from there could well be consideration for Ann's promise to let Ben keep it, as Ann would receive the benefit of avoiding the storage charges.

## Problems with consideration

The requirement for consideration can allow parties who make promises that ought, morally, to be binding, to escape liability. This has been one reason for the long history of judicial hostility to the doctrine. At the end of the eighteenth century, Lord Mansfield, a leading judge of the time, held that a moral obligation could amount to consideration. This view effectively destroyed the doctrine of consideration; by its very nature, making a promise implies a moral obligation to keep it, and so every promise would be supported by consideration. This approach was accepted for almost 60 years, but in **Eastwood** v **Kenyon** (1840) it was overruled and stated to be wrong.

Even today, the courts sometimes give a rather artificial interpretation to the principles of consideration, in order to prevent unjust avoidance of an agreement. This can be seen in cases such as **Ward** v **Byham** and **Shadwell** v **Shadwell**, above, where there were sound reasons of policy and justice for enforcing the promises, but the doctrine of consideration had to be considerably stretched in order to do so.

Rigid adherence to the requirement for consideration can mean that the parties' clear intentions are defeated – if there is an obvious agreement between two parties that they intended to be bound by their agreement, it seems unnecessary to impose a further requirement of consideration. In practice, the courts are reluctant to hold that mere lack of consideration prevents a business agreement, which has been satisfactory to the companies who made it, from being legally binding, and will stretch the doctrine as far as possible to accommodate such a situation – **New Zealand Shipping** v **Satterthwaite** (1974) is widely seen as an example of this (see p. 301).

The rules of consideration have also been criticised as highly artificial, and almost meaningless in many real-life situations. A gratuitous promise to give someone something is not binding, no matter how seriously it is made and how much the other party relies on it. Yet that same promise will be binding if the promisee hands over a peppercorn in return for it. To the parties concerned, the peppercorn adds nothing to the transaction, yet in legal terms it makes all the difference. The 'peppercorn' principle, and the fact that a promise can be made binding by putting it in a deed, also gives an enormous, and possibly unfair, advantage to a contracting party who can afford legal advice.

The rule that without consideration a promise to accept part-payment of a debt is not binding was criticised by Jessel MR in **Couldery** v **Bartrum** (1881):

According to English Common Law a creditor may accept anything in satisfaction of his debt except a lesser amount of money. He might take a horse, or a canary or a tom-tit if he chose, and that was accord and satisfaction; but by a most extraordinary peculiarity of the English Common Law, he could not take [part-payment].

The reason for the requirement of consideration in part-payment situations has been to protect those creditors who are 'held over a barrel' by debtors – where, for example, firms with cash flow problems are forced to agree to accept part-payment because they cannot hold out any longer for the full amount (as in **D & C Builders** v **Rees**). It has been argued that such protection is now better performed by the expanding concept of economic duress (which we will discuss later), so that the rule in **Pinnel's Case** no longer serves any useful purpose.

In **Foakes** v **Beer** Lord Blackburn criticised the rule in **Pinnel's Case**, on the ground that part-payment often offered more practical benefit to the creditors than strict insistence on their full legal rights. A small business with cash flow problems might stand to gain more from accepting part of what others owe to them, than from being able to sue for the full amount, given that suing costs money, and they may well go bust in the meantime.

A possible reform would be to extend the decision in **Williams** v **Roffey** to part-payment cases, so that an agreement to accept part-payment would be binding where it offered a practical benefit. This would make the law more consistent and more satisfactory in its practical operation, and take account of the real needs of businesses. So far, such a development seems unlikely. It was considered in **Re Selectmove Ltd** (1995), where we have seen that Selectmove argued that the Inland Revenue had promised to accept its tax payments in instalments, and that this promise should be binding because there was no practical benefit for the Inland Revenue in the fact that it was likely to receive more by accepting the instalments than by winding up the company, which was the only alternative. The Court of Appeal felt unable to accept Selectmove's argument, because to do so would leave the principle in **Foakes** v **Beer** without any application: it would always be the case that the creditor who agrees to payment by instalments will see a practical benefit in doing so. Although the court could see merit in making such a contract enforceable, it considered that this effective overruling of **Foakes** v **Beer** was a matter for the House of Lords, or Parliament, rather than the Court of Appeal.

## The future of consideration

Both promissory estoppel and the decision in **Williams** v **Roffey** have been seen as potentially major challenges to the requirement of consideration and there has been considerable speculation as to the future of consideration in contract law. When the doctrine of promissory estoppel first appeared, it was widely thought to have eliminated the need for consideration. However, it is now clear that that is not the case. The doctrine can only be used where a contract has already been created, for which consideration will have been required. Further, as **Combe** v **Combe** shows, the doctrine cannot create new rights. In addition, as an equitable doctrine, its protection cannot be claimed as of right.

The implications of **Williams** v **Roffey** are much less clear, as in legal terms it is still a very recent case, and the boundaries of the rule are yet to be established. It clearly redefines consideration, giving it a wider definition and in many ways reducing the barriers to making modifications binding. It has been suggested that consideration in the shape of a **Williams** v **Roffey** practical benefit is likely to be present in the majority of agreed modifications made to commercial contracts, since in such situations the parties are unlikely to agree to any change unless it has some benefit for them. The **Williams** v **Roffey** view of consideration also allows the courts more discretion than previous, tighter definitions, since they will clearly be able to find a practical benefit in situations where traditional consideration was not present because there was no legal benefit.

Hugh Collins (*The Law of Contract*, 1993) has suggested that the **Williams** v **Roffey** decision marks a new, and more realistic, approach to contracts, especially commercial ones. He argues that the traditional concept of consideration sees the parties' interests as diametrically opposed, whereas in reality there may be very good reasons why one party would accept what looks like less than was promised – the importance of maintaining good business relationships, and the possibility of losing a little on one contract, but gaining more business in the future, for example.

How far the doctrine will extend is still a matter for debate. Could a practical benefit be acceptable as consideration in the formation of a contract, for example? In theory there seems no reason why not. An interesting recent Privy Council case is **R** v **Attorney General for England and Wales** (2003) (discussed in detail at p. 271). In that case the appellant was a soldier who had been involved in a mission with the SAS during the Gulf War. Some other soldiers involved in the mission had published details of their activities. The Ministry of Defence had been concerned that this publicity might undermine the work of the Special Forces. It had therefore required the appellant to sign a confidentiality contract, and informed him that if he failed to do so he would be removed from the Special Forces and become an ordinary soldier. Later, the appellant had sought to publish details of his work in the Gulf. In holding that this publication would breach his contract with the Ministry of Defence, the Privy Council considered what consideration the Ministry had offered in return for the defendant's promise not to reveal his secrets. The Privy Council held that the consideration was the 'practical benefit' that he would not be demoted to an ordinary soldier.

**Williams** v **Roffey** could also affect the rules on waiver and promissory estoppel. In waiver, the party waiving their rights can decide to withdraw the waiver later, but if it was found that there was a practical benefit to them in waiving those rights, would the modification then be final? Similarly, if in a case like **High Trees** there was a practical benefit to the landlord in reducing the rent (such as avoiding ending up with a bankrupt tenant and no rent at all), would that bar him from later returning to his strict rights by giving reasonable notice? So far, we do not know the answers to any of these questions, and it remains for relevant cases to reach the higher courts and establish the boundaries.

In **South Caribbean Trading Ltd** v **Trafigura Beeheever BV** (2004) the High Court judge, Coleman J, was critical of the law in **Williams** v **Roffey**. He considered that the courts should always look for a legal benefit as opposed to just a practical benefit for any amendment to a contract and pointed out that the approach in **Williams** v **Roffey** directly conflicts with the established case of **Stilk** v **Myrick**.

# Reform

The following proposals for reform were made in 1937 by the Law Revision Committee:

- A written promise should be binding, with or without consideration.
- Past consideration should be valid.
- Consideration should no longer need to move from the promisee.
- Performance of an existing duty should always be good consideration for a promise.
- A creditor should be bound by a promise to accept part-payment of a debt as full settlement. The reason for this proposal is that the development of the doctrine of economic duress is thought to offer sufficient protection for creditors who are forced to accept part-payment 'over a barrel'.
- A promise to keep an offer open should be binding. The Law Commission thought that such an offer should be binding if it is made in the course of a business, and the offeror promises to keep it open for a definite period of not more than six years.

- In a unilateral contract, the promisor should not be allowed to revoke an offer after the promisee has started to perform (as we have seen in **Errington** v **Errington** (1952), this may already be the law).
- That where a promisor knows, or could reasonably be expected to know, that a promise will be relied upon by the promisee, and the promisee acts upon that promise to their own detriment, the promise should be binding. As was noted above, such promises already have a limited effect under the doctrine of promissory estoppel, but this proposal would make them fully binding as contracts.

The latter proposal has also been suggested by Professor Atiyah. It would cover situations such as where A promises to pay B £300 the following day and, relying on this promise, B goes shopping and spends £150, which without A's gift she cannot afford to spend. A's promise is clearly gratuitous, because nothing was given in return for it, but B clearly relied on it, and in certain circumstances it would obviously be reasonable for her to do so – if A seemed very serious about making the gift, for example, or frequently made such presents to B or anyone else, B would have every reason to believe that she was going to get the money. Atiyah has argued that reasonable reliance on a promise, resulting in the promisee's detriment, should give the promisee the right to enforce the promise (which in our example would allow B damages of £300), or at least to recover the amount she has lost by relying on the promise (damages to B of £150).

## Answering questions

To what extent will the doctrine of promissory estoppel prevent a party to a contract from enforcing his or her legal rights? *Oxford*

You should start your answer by describing what promissory estoppel is, citing the case of **High Trees**. Point out, with reference to **Tool Metal**, that promissory estoppel does not cancel rights for ever – they can be resumed by reasonable notice. Then, mentioning relevant cases, go through the situations in which promissory estoppel will not apply: where there is no pre-existing contract; where the promisee has not relied on the promise (discussing whether such reliance has to be detrimental); where it would be inequitable to allow promissory estoppel. Your conclusion could sum up the situation by pointing out that promissory estoppel has an important effect where it applies, but that the restrictions in its use limit the number of cases where it can apply.

How far is it true that performance of an existing contractual duty can never amount to consideration?

Start by discussing the reason why performance of an existing contractual duty should theoretically not amount to consideration – the idea that consideration must be something given in return for something else. Then point out the two different categories of existing contractual duty (to the promisor and to a third party), and discuss them in turn (note that existing public duty is not relevant here – you are asked to discuss **contractual** duty).

You may want to start with existing duties to a third party, as there is rather less to say on this – highlight the fact that there are clear cases where performance of an existing duty to a third party is held to be consideration.

The bulk of your essay is likely to be devoted to the effect of **Williams** v **Roffey**. Explain the rule before **Williams** v **Roffey**, and the new rule on practical benefit created by it. You should look at the possible future implications of the case, including the possibility it might eventually lead to a change to the rule in **Pinnel's Case** and **Foakes** v **Beer**, despite **Re Selectmove**. Your conclusion might say that not only is it already incorrect to say that performance of an existing duty will never amount to consideration, but also that the implications of **Williams** v **Roffey** suggest we may see even more exceptions to this rule in the future.

---

In August 1994 Idyllic Hotels employ Budget Builders to build a 50-bedroom luxury hotel for £20 million. The contract states that the hotel must be completed by 1 May 1996. After 12 months, work on the building has fallen behind and Budget Builders approach Idyllic Hotels to explain that they are in financial difficulties and will not be able to complete the hotel in time. The hotel is fully booked for the 1996 holiday season and Idyllic Hotels offer to pay an additional £125,000 to ensure that the hotel is built on time. Budget Builders agree to this arrangement and continue with the building work. In March 1996, just before the hotel is completed, Idyllic Hotels inform Budget Builders that they do not intend to pay the additional £125,000.

Advise Budget Builders. *Oxford*

Clearly Budget Builders (BB) want to establish that the promise made by Idyllic Hotels (IH) to pay extra was binding; this will only be the case if there is consideration for it. BB have not given consideration in the traditional sense, because they have not done anything they were not already obliged to do. However, since **Williams** v **Roffey**, there will be consideration if the promise to pay more created a practical benefit for IH, or protected them from a disbenefit, and the promise was not secured by duress. Duress is discussed in a later chapter, but essentially what the courts look for is some element of taking advantage of the other party's position; if BB's financial difficulties are genuine, there seems no sign of that here, so there is probably no duress.

Is there a practical benefit? At first sight, it seems obvious that there is – IH need the work finished on time, so that they can accept guests who have already booked. But the evidence is not as strong as that in **Williams** v **Roffey**. The original contract price in that case had been too low; the alternative to promising more money (finding new contractors and then suing the original ones for breach) was impractical for reasons of time, and there was an additional benefit in that changes to the arrangements for working made it easier for other contractors to operate. None of these is present here – in fact, given that there is at least eight months between the date on which BB approach IH and the date by which the building must be finished, it might have been possible for IH to take on new contractors to finish the work, and sue BB for breach. The fact that BB's breach was anticipatory means they could have taken this action immediately; they did not have to wait until full performance was due (see p. 328). These factors do not mean that the courts will not find a practical benefit – for example, finding new contractors might have been possible but much less convenient – but they could be used by IH as arguments against the application of **Williams** v **Roffey**, and so you need to discuss them. You then need to say whether, on balance, you think **Williams** v **Roffey** would apply; if it does, IH are bound to pay the money. BB can sue them for it without finishing the building, because IH's statement that they do not intend to pay the money is an anticipatory breach.

 Margaret has bought herself a new car. Greg had been her gardener for many years. She told him that as he had done such a good job in the garden that summer he could have her old car. Greg was delighted and sold his old car. Using the money from the sale of his old car he orally agreed to take out a four-year lease on a flat. The next week Margaret changed her mind and refused to give Greg the car.

Discuss.

 Greg does not appear to have provided consideration for Margaret's promise to give him her old car. The work he has done in her garden cannot amount to consideration because it is past: **Roscorla** v **Thomas**. Nor can Greg use the doctrine of promissory estoppel, because while he has acted in reliance on Margaret's promise, promissory estoppel can only act as a shield and not a sword: **Combe** v **Combe**. Thus he cannot bring an action against Margaret for delivery of the old car because that would be using promissory estoppel as a sword. However, Greg will be able to get out of the lease for the flat because this was a lease for more than three years and therefore should have been made by deed under the Law of Property Act 1925 (see p. 84).

# Summary of Chapter 6

An agreement is not usually binding unless it is supported by consideration. This means that each party must give something in return for what is gained from the other party.

## What is consideration?

Consideration may be a thing or a service. It is usually described as being something which represents either some benefit to the person making a promise (the promisor) or some detriment to the person to whom the promise is made (the promisee), or both.

## Promisor and promisee

In most contracts, two promises will be exchanged, so each party is both a promisor and a promisee.

## Consideration need not benefit the promisor

Consideration need not benefit the promisor – so there can be consideration where the promisee suffers some detriment at the promisor's request, but this gives no particular benefit to the promisor.

## 'Executory' and 'executed' consideration

Executory consideration is where something is to be done in the future after the contract has been formed. Executed consideration is where at the time of the formation of the contract the consideration has already been performed. Executed consideration usually occurs in unilateral contracts.

### Consideration must not be past

Lawyers often say that consideration must not be past, but this is slightly confusing because the emphasis is not really about the time that the consideration was given, but rather about whether the consideration was given in exchange for the other party's consideration. Consideration must be given *in return* for the promise or act of the other party: **Roscorla** *v* **Thomas** (1842).

There are two exceptions to the rule that past consideration is no consideration. The first is where the past consideration was provided at the promisor's request, and it was understood that payment would be made: **Lampleigh** *v* **Brathwait** (1615). The second exception to the rule on past consideration is the bill of exchange under s. 27 of the Bills of Exchange Act 1882.

### Consideration must be sufficient

Consideration must be sufficient but need not be adequate; the courts will not inquire into the adequacy of consideration, so long as there is some: **Thomas** *v* **Thomas** (1842).

### Consideration must be of economic value

Consideration must have some physical value, rather than just an emotional or sentimental one: **White** *v* **Bluett** (1853).

### Consideration can be a promise not to sue

If one party has a possible civil claim against the other, a promise not to enforce that claim is good consideration for a promise given in return: **Alliance Bank Ltd** *v* **Broom** (1864).

### Contracts (Rights of Third Parties) Act 1999

Following the Contracts (Rights of Third Parties) Act 1999, a term in a contract is sometimes enforceable by a third party. It is not necessary for consideration to have been given by the third party.

## Performance of an existing duty

Where a promisee already owes the promisor a legal duty, then in theory performing that duty should not in itself be consideration. Existing duties can be divided into three main categories: public duties; contractual duties to the promisor; and contractual duties to a third party.

### Existing public duty

Where a promisee is under a public duty, but does something which goes beyond what they are bound to do under that duty, that extra act can amount to consideration: **Glasbrook Brothers** *v* **Glamorgan County Council** (1925).

### Existing contractual duty to the promisor

In the past, the rule was that performance of an existing contractual duty owed to a promisor was not consideration: **Stilk** *v* **Myrick** (1809). In the light of the Court of Appeal case of **Williams** *v* **Roffey** (1990), a distinction now has to be drawn between contractual duties to supply goods or services and contractual duties to pay debts.

*Contractual duties to supply goods or services*

As a result of **Williams** *v* **Roffey**, the law now seems to be that if one party's promise to perform an existing contractual duty to supply goods or services confers an additional practical benefit on the other party, then, providing that no duress is involved, it will be sufficient consideration to make a promise given in return binding, even though in legal terms they are only agreeing to carry out their existing contractual duty.

*Contractual duties to pay debts*

Special rules apply to contractual duties regarding debts. Where someone owes another money and cannot pay the full amount, they will sometimes offer to pay a smaller sum, on condition that the creditor promises to accept it as full settlement for the debt – in other words, agrees not to sue later for the full amount. Even if such an agreement is made, it is only binding if the debtor provides some consideration for it by adding some extra element: **Pinnel's Case** (1602).

*Exceptions to the rule in **Pinnel's Case***

The rule in **Pinnel's Case** does not apply if there is a genuine dispute about whether the debt is actually owed, or about the amount owed (**Cooper** *v* **Parker** (1885)). The rule in **Pinnel's Case** does not apply to unliquidated damages. Composition agreements are binding. A creditor who accepts part-payment from a third party, in full settlement of the debtor's liability, cannot then sue for the outstanding amount. Promissory estoppel also constitutes an exception to the rule in **Pinnel's Case**.

### Existing contractual duty to a third party

In some cases, two parties make a contract to provide a benefit to someone who is not a party to the contract, known as a third party. If one of them (X) makes a further promise to that third party, to provide the benefit they have already contracted to provide, that further promise can be good consideration for a promise made by the third party in return – even though nothing more than the contractual duty is being promised by X: **Scotson** *v* **Pegg** (1861).

## Waiver and promissory estoppel

Waiver and promissory estoppel are both ways of making some kinds of promise binding even where there is no consideration. Promissory estoppel is a somewhat newer doctrine than waiver. It was developed by Lord Denning in **Central London Property Trust Ltd** *v* **High Trees House Ltd** (1947). The precise extent of the doctrine of promissory estoppel is still unclear. What is clear is that the following conditions must be fulfilled before the doctrine can be applied.

- A pre-existing contractual relationship.
- A promise.
- Reliance.
- Inequitable to enforce strict legal rights.
- Future rights not destroyed.
- No new rights created.

## Agreement by deed

There is one other way in which a promise can be made binding without consideration: it can be put into a document called a deed.

**Reading list**

Adams and Brownsword, 'Contract, consideration and the critical path' (1990) 55 Modern Law Review 536

Atiyah (1990) 'Consideration: a restatement', *Essays on Contract*, Oxford: Oxford University Press

Brinkworth and Powell, 'Contract and consideration: a new commercial reality?' (1991) 12 Business Law Review 5

Chen-Wishart (2010) 'A Bird in the Hand: Consideration and Contract Modification' in Burrows and Peel (eds) *Contract Formation and Parties*, Oxford: Oxford University Press

Cooke, 'Estoppel and the protection of expectations' (1997) 17 Legal Studies 258

Denning, 'Recent developments in the doctrine of consideration' (1952) 15 Modern Law Review 1

Hird and Blair, 'Minding your own business – *Williams v Roffey* re-visited: consideration reconsidered' (1996) Journal of Business Law 254

Mitchell and Phillips, 'The contractual nexus: is reliance essential?' (2002) 22 Oxford Journal of Legal Studies 115

O'Sullivan, 'In defence of *Foakes v Beer*' (1996) 55 Cambridge Law Journal 219

## Reading on the internet

The Privy Council decision **R** v **Attorney General for England and Wales** (2003) is available on its website (judgment No. 22) at:

http://www.privy-council.org.uk/output/Page331.asp

# Part 2
## The contents of a contract

Although there are some contract cases where the central issue is whether or not there was a valid contract, more often both parties agree that they have made a binding agreement, but disagree as to the content of the agreement. This is obviously more likely to occur when an agreement is purely oral, with nothing in writing; but as we shall see, even where there is a written contract, there may be arguments about what the written terms mean, and about whether the written document comprises the whole of the contract – if, for example, you are promised a company car during a job interview, but your written contract of employment does not mention the car, there may be a disagreement about whether you are contractually entitled to the car. In addition, the law tries to control the use of unfair contract terms, so that while a term might appear to be a part of the contract, the law may exclude it because it is unfair to one of the parties.

# Chapter 7
## Terms of the contract

### This chapter discusses:

how the terms of the contract set out the obligations on the parties under the agreement. Express terms can either be oral or in writing. The courts have developed rules on how to interpret these express terms. In addition terms can be implied into a contract and these terms can be divided into four groups:

- terms implied in fact;
- terms implied in law;
- terms implied by custom; and
- terms implied by trade usage.

The law also seeks to classify terms according to their importance, with the implications of a breach for the innocent party varying according to the type of term breached. From this perspective there are three types of contractual term:

- conditions;
- warranties; and
- innominate terms.

The terms of a contract describe the duties and obligations that each party assumes under their agreement. Sometimes the parties contract on standard contract terms: these are pre-existing contracts which are repeatedly used for different agreements. 'Boilerplate clauses' are those contractual terms which are not directly related to the subject matter of the contract but which are frequently cut and pasted into contracts to determine the general rules on contractual liability. These template clauses save drafters 'reinventing the wheel' each time they prepare such clauses. Sometimes the parties draw up a completely new contract to reflect the specific negotiations that have been undertaken to agree the contractual terms.

As well as the contractual terms laid down by the parties themselves, called express terms, the courts may find that a contract contains what are called implied terms – terms which are read into a contract because of the facts of the agreement and the apparent intention of the parties, or the law on specific types of contract. This chapter also examines the way contractual terms are interpreted.

# Express terms

Our analysis of express terms will look first at oral statements and then at written statements.

# Oral statements

In all but the simplest of transactions, there will be some negotiations before a contract is made. Companies making a deal for one to supply the other may hold detailed discussions about price, quality control and delivery; when hiring a firm to put in your central heating you might ask how long the job will take, what the price includes and who will do the work; and if you buy a tin of paint, a computer or a set of shelves, for example, you will want to know whether they are suitable for your particular purpose. In all these cases, oral statements will be made. Problems can arise when, although both parties agree that a certain statement was made, they disagree on whether that statement was part of the contract and therefore intended to be binding.

In looking at such questions, statements made during negotiations are classified by the courts as either representations or terms. A representation is a statement which may have encouraged one party to make the contract but is not itself part of that contract, while a term is a promise or undertaking that is part of the contract. Disputes generally centre around statements which have proved to be untrue: if that statement is a representation, it can give rise to an action for misrepresentation, whereas if it is a term, it can give rise to an action for breach of contract.

In some cases, a statement that was initially a misrepresentation later becomes incorporated into the contract as a term. In this situation the injured party has two possible causes of action: one for misrepresentation and the other for breach. In fact, although at one time the distinction was of major practical importance, developments in the law of misrepresentation (**Hedley Byrne** and the Misrepresentation Act 1967; see p. 204) mean it has less practical significance now.

Whether a statement is a representation or a term is largely a question of the parties' intentions. If the parties have indicated that a particular statement is a term of their contract, the court will carry out that intention. In other cases, the following guidelines may be used.

## Importance of the statement

A statement is likely to be seen as a term if the injured party has made the other party aware that had it not been for that statement, they would not have entered into the contract.

**Key Case**    Bannerman *v* White

In **Bannerman** *v* **White** (1861) White was considering buying hops from Bannerman, and asked whether they had been treated with sulphur, adding that if they had, he would not even bother to ask the price. Bannerman said there had been no such treatment (believing this to be the truth) and, after negotiations, a contract of sale was made. Later, though, it was discovered that sulphur had been used on some of the hops – 5 acres out of 300 – and when Bannerman sued for the price, White claimed that Bannerman's statement had been a term of the contract, and Bannerman had breached that contract, so he was justified in refusing to pay. The court agreed that the statement about the sulphur was indeed a term of the contract.

**Legal Principle**
A statement is likely to be seen as a term if the injured party has made the other party aware that, had it not been for that statement, he or she would not have entered into the contract.

## Special knowledge and skill

Where a statement is made by someone who has expert knowledge or skill that is relevant to the subject in hand, the courts will be more willing to deem that statement a term than if the same words were used by an amateur with no special expertise on the matter. This principle is illustrated by two cases involving the sale of cars. In **Dick Bentley Productions Ltd** *v* **Harold Smith (Motors) Ltd** (1965) the claimant had said they were looking for a 'well-vetted' Bentley car. The defendant, a car dealer, stated that the car he had for sale had had its engine and gearbox completely replaced, and had only done 20,000 miles since then. After the claimant bought the car, problems emerged, and it transpired that the car had in fact done almost 100,000 miles since the replacements. The Court of Appeal held that the dealer's statement was a term of the contract.

In the contrasting case of **Oscar Chess** *v* **Williams** (1957) the defendant, a private individual, wanted to trade in his old car and buy a new one. The price allowed for the old car depended on its age, and the defendant stated that it was a 1948 model, which was the year given in the vehicle's registration book (the equivalent of the car registration document used today). On this basis the claimant allowed £290 off the price of the new car. Later, they discovered that the registration book had been altered, presumably by a past owner: the car was in fact a 1939 model, which was only worth £175. The car dealer therefore sued the defendant for the difference in price between the two valuations, on the grounds that his assertion that the car was a 1948 model was a term of the contract, and he was therefore in breach. The Court of Appeal rejected their claim, pointing out that the seller was a private individual who had innocently trusted the registration book, but the buyers were experienced car dealers and therefore likely to be able, if anyone was, to spot the car's real age. Consequently, the defendant's statement was not a contractual term.

## Timing of the statement

In general, the more time that elapses between the statement being made and the contract being concluded, the less likely the courts will be to regard the statement as a term, though the cases show that this can only be an approximate guideline. In **Routledge** v **McKay** (1954) the parties had been discussing the sale of a motorbike. Both were private individuals without specialist knowledge of motorcycles, and the defendant, drawing his information from the registration book, stated that the motorbike under discussion was made in 1942. When a written contract was drawn up a week later, it did not mention the age of the motorbike. The motorbike turned out to be a 1930 model, and the buyer claimed that the date of manufacture was a term of the contract. His claim failed, because the interval between the statement being made and the contract concluded suggested that the statement was not a term.

In **Schawel** v **Reade** (1913) the claimant began to examine a horse that he was thinking of buying. The seller told him: 'You need not look for anything: the horse is perfectly sound', so the claimant did not make any further checks, and the sale was concluded three weeks later. When the horse in fact proved unsatisfactory, the House of Lords held the strength and importance of the seller's statement meant that it was a contractual term, despite the length of time between the statement being made and the contract being concluded.

## Agreements in writing

Where the parties put their eventual contract in writing, any statement that appears in the written contract will usually be regarded as a term. Any statement made before the written contract but not included in it is likely to be regarded as a representation, on the grounds that if the parties draw up a written contract which leaves out an earlier statement, it is likely that they did not regard that statement as an important one. The fact that the contract in **Routledge** (above) was made in writing, and did not include the date of the motorbike's manufacture, was seen as significant by the court.

### Topical Issue

#### Newcastle's football fans

Premier league football has become a world class business, but with its success has come tensions between the traditional fans, corporate interests and wealthy club owners. A dispute between some Newcastle United football supporters and their club was the subject of **Duffy** v **Newcastle United Football Co Ltd** (2000). In 1994 the club offered its season ticket holders the opportunity to buy what was described as a 'bond' for £500. This bond guaranteed a 'designated seat' for ten years, and the bondholder was entitled to have their name on the seat. Under the written terms and conditions of the bond, condition 9(b) stated:

> NUFC may determine at any time at its discretion that the Designated Seat shall no longer be available to the Bondholder (either for the balance of the current Season or any future Season) whereupon NUFC shall provide the Bondholder with an alternative seat in the Stadium and the Bondholder's Benefits shall apply in relation to such alternative seat.

Relying on this condition, the club sought to change the allocated seats of some of the bondholders to make way for a £42 million scheme to increase the capacity of the football stadium by 15,000. Under this scheme, more expensive seats with easy access to new bar facilities were going to be put where the bondholders currently sat.

Many bondholders objected strongly to the Club's attempts to move them. They argued that statements had been made, in the promotional material and media statements that had accompanied the issue of the bonds, that they would be guaranteed their seat for ten years. But the written terms and conditions of the bonds commenced by stating:

> The following Conditions should be read carefully and fully understood before you offer to purchase a United Bond from Newcastle United Football Company Limited. In offering to purchase a United Bond your offer will be deemed to incorporate all the Conditions listed herein and you will be required to sign an application form which acknowledges this fact.

The Court of Appeal concluded that the accompanying promotional material and media comments did not constitute terms of the contract: they were merely representations. These representations had not been false as there was nothing in any of the Club's literature or media statements which amounted to a binding representation that the claimants would have an absolute right to the use of their seats for the lifetime of the bond. The contract was interpreted by the court as allowing a seat relocation where the Club had 'good and sufficient reason'. On the facts, the stadium development scheme constituted a good and sufficient reason and the supporters' action failed.

## Strength of the inducement

The more emphatically a statement is made, the more likely the courts will be to regard it as a term. In **Ecay** v **Godfrey** (1947) the seller of a boat told the buyer that it was sound, but suggested that, nevertheless, the prospective buyer should have it surveyed. The court held that this suggested that the statement was never intended to be taken as a term of the contract. This result can be contrasted with that in **Schawel** v **Reade** (above), where the obvious strength and importance of the statement meant it was a term.

# Written terms

Written terms can be incorporated into a contract in three ways: by signature, by reasonable notice and by a previous course of dealing. This issue arises most often in connection with exclusion and limitation clauses (and so is discussed fully in Chapter 8) but it is important to remember that the rules apply to any written term.

## The parol evidence rule

Under this rule, where there is a written contract, extrinsic (parol) evidence cannot change the express terms laid down in that document. Extrinsic evidence includes oral statements, and written material such as draft contracts or letters, whether relating to pre-contract negotiations or the parties' post-contractual behaviour. The rule only prevents use of extrinsic evidence concerning the terms of a contract; where one side is seeking to prove whether or not a contract is valid (for example, by claiming that there was no consideration, or that there was misrepresentation), extrinsic evidence may be used even though the actual contract has been put in writing.

An example of the parol evidence rule in practice is **Henderson** v **Arthur** (1907). The claimant and the defendant were parties to a lease, which contained a covenant (a promise under seal) for the payment of rent quarterly in advance, although before the lease was drawn up, the parties had agreed that the rent could in fact be paid in arrears. When the tenant was sued for not making the payments in advance, he pointed out this prior oral agreement, but the Court of Appeal held that the terms of a prior oral agreement could not be substituted for the terms of a later formal contract concerning the same transaction. The written document effectively destroyed the previous oral agreement about the rent.

There are a number of exceptions to the parol evidence rule, with the following being the main ones:

## Rectification

Where a document is intended to record a previous oral agreement but fails to do that accurately, evidence of the oral agreement will be admitted.

## Partially written agreements

Where there is a written document, but the parties clearly intended it to be qualified by other written or oral statements, the parol evidence rule is again displaced.

## Key Case    Couchman v Hill

In **Couchman** v **Hill** (1947), the defendant's heifer was up for auction. The sale catalogue described her as 'unserved', and also stated that the sale was 'subject to the auctioneers' usual conditions' and that the auctioneers took no responsibility for mistakes in the catalogue. The 'usual conditions', on display at the auction, contained a clause that 'the lots were sold with all faults, imperfections and errors of description'.

Before making a bid, the claimant asked both the auctioneer and the defendant to confirm that the heifer was 'unserved', which they both did. On this understanding, the claimant successfully bid for the cow. The animal was later discovered to be in calf, and because it was too young to bear a calf, it eventually died. On these facts the Court of Appeal found that the claimant could recover damages for breach of contract. It held that the documents (the catalogue and the 'usual conditions') were only part of the contract, and the oral statements could be placed alongside them, so that together they formed one binding transaction.

### Legal Principle
Where there is a written document, but the parties clearly intend it to be qualified by an oral statement, the parol evidence rule does not apply.

## Implied terms

The parol evidence rule only applies where a party seeks to use extrinsic evidence to alter the express terms of a contract. Where a contract is of a type that is usually subject to terms implied by law, parol evidence may be given to support, or to rebut, the usual implication (see p. 141 below).

## Operation of the contract

The parol evidence rule does not apply to extrinsic evidence which shows that the written contract was intended to come into operation, or to cease to operate, in the event of a particular circumstance. In **Pym** v **Campbell** (1856) the parties drew up a written agreement concerning the sale of a share in an invention. Evidence was admitted that one party had stipulated orally that the agreement should not become operative until an independent expert had approved the invention.

## Evidence about the parties

Extrinsic evidence can be used to show the capacities in which the parties were acting when they made their contract – for example, where a person has apparently contracted as a principal (see p. 295), parol evidence is admissible in order to prove that he or she really acted as agent for someone else.

## Proving custom

Where it is suggested that a term should be read in the light of local or trade custom, evidence of that custom is admissible to add to or explain a written agreement, though not to contradict it. Thus in **Smith** v **Wilson** (1832) evidence was admitted to the effect that, under local custom, 1,000 rabbits meant 1,200 rabbits – a sort of 'bakers' dozen'.

The courts are now sometimes prepared to look at extrinsic evidence such as a custom to help them interpret a contract (see p. 130).

# Collateral contracts

There is a way in which an oral statement can be deemed binding, even though it conflicts with a written contract and does not fall within any of the exceptions to the parol rule. If one party says something to the effect that 'I will sign this document if you will assure me that it means . . .' the courts may find that two contracts have been created: the written agreement, and a collateral contract based on the oral statement.

In **City and Westminster Properties (1934) Ltd** v **Mudd** (1959) the terms of a lease included a condition that the premises could only be used for business purposes. However, the tenant was assured orally that the landlords would not object to his continuing to live on the premises (as he had been doing until that point), and on that basis, he signed the lease. Ten years later, the landlords attempted to make the tenant forfeit the lease, claiming he had broken its terms by living on the premises. Even though the oral statement contradicted the written lease, oral evidence of the statement was held admissible to prove that there was a collateral contract, which gave the tenant a defence for the breach of the lease.

It has been suggested that the device of finding a collateral contract based on an oral statement largely eliminates the parol evidence rule, and the above case does tend to support this view. Use of the device is, however, limited by the fact that a statement can only operate as a collateral contract if supported by separate consideration. This will often be provided by the act of entering into the main contract, as was the case in **City and Westminster Properties**. But entering the main contract will not be consideration for the collateral promise if that promise is made after the main contract is concluded; in that case entering the main contract will be past consideration, and therefore not valid.

# Oral and written statements

We have now seen that where parties enter into a written contract after one party has made oral assurances, there are at least three possibilities as to the status of those oral statements: the contract may be contained exclusively in the written document, with the oral statements being merely representations; the contract may be partly written and partly oral; or there may be two contracts, the main written one and a collateral one based on oral statements. However, it is important to know that different approaches can yield the same practical result. For example, in **J Evans & Son (Portsmouth) v Andrea Merzario** (1976) (see p. 65) some members of the Court of Appeal held that there was a partly written, partly oral contract, and others that the oral statements made constituted a separate, collateral contract. They were agreed that the result of either analysis was that the claimant could recover damages for breach of an oral promise, even though the written contract between the parties did not mention the subject matter of the promise.

# Interpretation of express terms

The courts sometimes have to determine the meaning of a contractual term. In doing this the judges try to discover what the parties appeared to intend the contract to mean. The task of ascertaining the intention of the parties has to be approached objectively. In a series of recent cases, Lord Hoffmann has significantly developed the law on this subject. The starting point is the contractual document itself. Where possible the words of the contract will be given their natural and ordinary meaning. But if a strict interpretation of the words gives them a meaning that goes against business common sense, then the courts will look beyond the words themselves. In **Sirius International Insurance Co Ltd v FAI General Insurance Ltd** (2004) the House of Lords gave an example developed by a nineteenth-century philosopher:

> The tendency should therefore generally speaking be against literalism. What is literalism? It will depend on the context. But an example is given in The Works of William Paley (1838 edition) . . . The moral philosophy of Paley influenced thinking on contract in the nineteenth century. The example is as follows. The tyrant Temures promised the garrison of Sebastia that no blood would be shed if they surrendered to him. They surrendered. He shed no blood. He buried them all alive. This is literalism. If possible it should be resisted in the interpretative process.

In **Mannai Investment Co Ltd v Eagle Star Life Assurance Co** (1997) Lord Hoffmann observed:

> It is of course true that the law is not concerned with the speaker's subjective intentions. But the notion that the law's concern is therefore with the 'meaning of his words' conceals an important ambiguity. The ambiguity lies in a failure to distinguish between the meaning of words and the question of what would be understood as the meaning of a person who uses words. The meaning of words, as they would appear in a dictionary, and the effect of their syntactical arrangement, as it would appear in a grammar, is part of the material which we use to understand a speaker's utterance. But it is only a part; another part is our knowledge of the background against which the utterance was made.

The Supreme Court emphasised in **Rainy Sky** v **Kookmin Bank** (2011) that business common sense must be applied when interpreting commercial contracts and where necessary the courts can ignore 'a chunk of the original contract wording'. Where possible, ambiguities in a contract should be resolved in a way that is consistent with business sense. It observed:

> If there are two possible constructions, the court is entitled to prefer the construction which is consistent with business common sense and to reject the other.

It was not necessary to conclude that a particular construction would produce an absurd or irrational result before proceedings to have regard to the commercial purpose of the agreement. The court noted that the language used by the parties to a commercial contract 'would often have more than one potential meaning'.

The facts of the case were that Rainy Sky was buying a ship from a shipbuilding company. The price of the ship was US$33.3 million. The Kookmin Bank provided an advance payment bond, effectively guaranteeing that if the ship was not delivered the bank would in certain circumstances refund any advance payments made. Rainy Sky paid the first two instalments for the ship. In 2009 the shipbuilding company became insolvent and Rainy Sky demanded an immediate refund of the money it had paid in advance with interest. The bank refused to pay.

The crucial provisions of the bonds were paragraphs (2) and (3):

> (2) Pursuant to the terms of the Contract, you are entitled, upon your rejection of the Vessel in accordance with the terms of the Contract, your termination, cancellation or rescission of the Contract or upon a Total Loss of the Vessel, to repayment of the pre-delivery instalments of the Contract Price paid by you prior to such termination . . . together with interest thereon at the rate of seven per cent (7%) per annum . . .
>
> (3) In consideration of your agreement to make the pre-delivery instalments under the Contract . . . we hereby, as primary obligor, irrevocably and unconditionally undertake to pay to you, your successors and assigns, on your first written demand, all such sums due to you under the Contract . . . PROVIDED THAT the total amount recoverable . . . under this Bond shall not exceed US$26,640,000. . . .

The key question for the court was to determine the meaning of 'all such sums' in paragraph (3). The bank argued that it was not required to pay under the bond. It said 'such sums' referred back to paragraph (2). Since paragraph (2) made no mention of insolvency, the bank argued that it did not have to pay anything to the claimants. By contrast, the claimants argued that 'such sums' simply referred back to the 'pre-delivery instalments' at the beginning of paragraph (3). This meant the bank's liability to pay would not be limited by the circumstances given in paragraph (2).

The Supreme Court rejected the bank's proposed interpretation of the contract. It said the bank's proposed interpretation did not make commercial sense. One of the key times when the buyers would have expected to rely on the bond was in exactly this situation: when the ship builder went into insolvency. It concluded that, of the two arguable constructions of paragraph (3) of the bond, 'the buyer's construction is to be preferred because it is consistent with the commercial purpose of the bond in a way which the bank's construction is not'.

Because of the parol evidence rule (discussed on p. 127), the courts have traditionally been limited to looking at the contract itself, and could not look at extrinsic evidence to determine the intention of the parties. Exceptions existed allowing such evidence to be considered where the terms were technical, ambiguous or absurd. Lord Wilberforce suggested in **Prenn** v **Simmonds** (1971) that in such situations extrinsic evidence would be admissible to show the background knowledge of the parties at the time of making the contract, so as to find out the purpose of the contract. The circumstances surrounding the making of the contract was described as the 'matrix of fact'.

Lord Hoffmann has encouraged the wider use of this matrix of fact in the interpretation of a contract. In **Investors Compensation Scheme Ltd** v **West Bromwich Building Society** (1998) he stated that this matrix of fact 'includes absolutely anything which would have affected the way in which the language of the document would have been understood by a reasonable man'.

In **Bank of Credit and Commerce International** v **Ali** (2001) Lord Hoffmann clarified that when he said the matrix of fact could consist of 'absolutely anything' he meant anything that might be considered relevant to the reasonable person. Thus, the court must seek 'the meaning which the document would convey to a reasonable person having all the background knowledge which would reasonably have been available to the parties in the situation in which they were at the time of the contract'.

In **Crema** v **Cenkos Securities plc** (2010) the Court of Appeal held that market practice can be taken into account as part of the factual matrix, even where this market practice is not 'notorious, certain and reasonable' for the purposes of amounting to a trade usage that could justify implying a contractual term (see p. 142). In that case Crema was an investment bank. It entered into a contract with Cenkos under which it was to find people willing to invest £18 million in a company called Green Park Ventures. Green Park had a separate contract with Cenkos that it would pay Cenkos 7 per cent of the £18 million raised (a commission). In Cenkos's contract with Crema it promised to pay it 70 per cent of this commission. Crema found the investors but Green Park Ventures went into liquidation before it had paid the commission. Crema sought its share of the commission and the Court of Appeal accepted that under the contract it was entitled to be paid in these circumstances. In reaching this conclusion the Court of Appeal stated that evidence of market practice could be used as an aid to contractual interpretation. Two experts had given evidence at the trial on when commission would generally be paid in these circumstances. Their evidence did not suggest there was a trade usage; however, the judge accepted that a 'market practice' existed which supported the position of Cenkos that the commission would not normally be paid to the sub-broker (Crema) until the main broker (Cenkos) had been paid.

The Supreme Court has stated that where there is a significant number of contractual parties, the factual matrix should be less important when interpreting that contract because 'it would be quite wrong to take account of circumstances which are not known to all of them': **Re Sigma Finance Corp (in administrative receivership)** (2009).

The courts have for many years taken the view that pre-contractual negotiations are not admissible when interpreting a contract, known as the 'exclusionary rule'. In **Prenn** v **Simmonds** (1971) it was stated that the courts will not look at the earlier negotiations of the parties to interpret a written contract. The courts consider that what is said in the course of negotiations does not necessarily reflect what the position was between the contracting parties when they later enter into the contract and may therefore be unhelpful. This case was applied in **P & S Platt Ltd** v **Crouch** (2003). The case concerned the interpretation of a contract for the sale of a hotel, and whether the sale included rights to moor boats alongside the hotel. The court was not prepared to look at the pre-contractual documentation, such as the valuation obtained for the bank and the claimant's business plan. The only pre-contractual documentation that can be looked at is documentation showing the 'genesis and aim' of the contract. On this basis the court was prepared to look at the particulars of sale. On the facts of the case the contract of sale was interpreted as including the right to moor boats alongside the hotel.

The impact of the exclusionary rule has been significantly narrowed by recent cases. In **Oceanbulk Shipping and Trading** v **TMT Asia** (2010) the Supreme Court held that without prejudice material could be used as an aid to interpretation of a compromise agreement. If that material relates to pre-contractual negotiations then the courts are drawing a fine distinction between objective background facts, which are admissible, and subjective statements, which are excluded under the exclusionary rule. The Supreme Court stated:

> Trial judges frequently have to distinguish between material which forms part of the pre-contractual negotiations which is part of the factual matrix and therefore admissible as an aid to interpretation and material which forms part of the pre-contractual negotiations but which is not part of the factual matrix and is not therefore admissible. This is often a straightforward task but sometimes it is not.

Therefore, objective facts communicated during the pre-contractual negotiations are part of the factual matrix and admissible when deciding an issue of contractual interpretation; anything subjective in those negotiations must be ignored. The subjective elements of any negotiation cannot be looked at as an aid to interpretation – because each party would have its own subjective view of the bargaining process. But the objective facts mentioned during the negotiations can be taken into account in interpreting the final agreement. This is possible even if those objective facts were part of the background to a negotiation which had been 'without prejudice' (which would normally mean they cannot be revealed to the court). Thus, when the courts are interpreting a contract they are allowed to look at without prejudice negotiations, an important exception to the usual rule that the courts should not look at without prejudice material.

Oceanbulk and TMT were in a contractual dispute because TMT had failed to make a payment that was due under the contract. A settlement was reached which was recorded in a written agreement. There was later a dispute as to how to interpret one of the terms of this contractual settlement. TMT sought to support its arguments by relying on comments made by Oceanbulk in the 48 hours before the signing of the settlement.

The Supreme Court applied **Chartbrook** v **Persimmon Homes** (2009) and said the contract should be interpreted by finding 'what a reasonable person having all the background knowledge which would have been available to the parties would have understood them to be using the language in the contract to mean'. The background knowledge could include 'objective facts communicated by one party to the other in the course of the negotiations' and it made no difference whether those negotiations were or were not made 'without prejudice'. TMT's appeal was therefore allowed. The Supreme Court stated 'only matters of fact raised during those negotiations can be raised to help explain what the contract was meant to mean'.

In practice, the full negotiations will be admissible in a claim for rectification and so the parties could choose to seek to argue in the alternative rectification. When technically the courts might have to ignore some of these negotiations for the purposes of contractual interpretation, in reality this is likely to be difficult to do.

In **Dean and Dean (solicitors)** v **Dionissiou and Moussaoui** (2011), having looked at this case law the Court of Appeal concluded:

> If a document is contractual, then in the absence of a plea of rectification, or an allegation that it has been replaced or revoked by a subsequent agreement, the role of the court is to construe the document. If it is alleged that the written agreement mistakenly failed to reflect an anterior oral agreement, so that the written agreement falls to be rectified, that earlier oral agreement must be clearly pleaded and proved. In the absence of a plea of rectification, communications preceding the written agreement may provide context and background, but they cannot be substituted for the terms of the written agreement itself.

Certain rules of construction have been formulated by the courts. Previously, these rules were applied rather rigidly. But Lord Hoffmann has advanced a more flexible approach, where these rules are treated simply as guidance to assist the judges to reach a reasonable interpretation of the parties' intentions. In **Investors Compensation Scheme Ltd** *v* **West Bromwich Building Society** (1998) Lord Hoffmann stated that the modern approach to construction is 'to assimilate the way in which [contractual] documents are interpreted by judges to the common-sense principles by which any serious utterance would be interpreted in ordinary life'.

Lord Hoffman summarised five principles which the courts follow when construing contracts:

1 The correct meaning is what the document would convey to a reasonable person with the relevant background knowledge.
2 The background includes everything in the '*matrix of fact*'.
3 The law excludes the prior negotiations of the parties.
4 The meaning of words in a document is not the same as the literal meaning of words, but the meaning one would reasonably understand against the relevant background.
5 The rule that words should be given their 'natural and ordinary meaning' reflects the common-sense proposition that it is not easily accepted that people have made linguistic mistakes, particularly in formal documents.

In **Bank of Credit and Commerce International SA** *v* **Ali** (2001) the House of Lords applied Lord Hoffmann's approach to the construction of a contract. The case was concerned with the interpretation of a redundancy agreement. Mr Naeem had been made redundant by the Bank of Credit and Commerce in 1990. The redundancy agreement contained a term that the money he received for his redundancy was 'in full and final settlement of all or any claims whether under statute, common law, or in equity of whatsoever nature that exist or may exist'. A year later the bank went into insolvent liquidation and it was discovered that a significant part of its business had been carried out in a corrupt and dishonest manner. Some former employees of the bank sought damages for the stigma of having been employed by the bank and the resulting difficulties in finding alternative employment. In the case of **Malik** *v* **Bank of Credit and Commerce International SA** (1997) (discussed on p. 141 below) the House of Lords had ruled that such claims could, in appropriate cases, succeed. Mr Naeem wanted to make such a claim in the present case, but the liquidators of the bank argued that his claim was barred because he had accepted that his redundancy package was in full and final settlement.

The House of Lords held that, on a proper construction of the redundancy agreement, Mr Naeem's claim was not barred. The majority cited with approval Lord Hoffmann's approach to the construction of contracts discussed above. Lord Bingham stated:

> A party may, at any rate in a compromise agreement supported by valuable consideration, agree to release claims or rights of which he is unaware and of which he could not be aware, even claims which could not on the facts known to the parties have been imagined, if appropriate language is used to make plain that that is his intention . . .
>
> . . . On a fair construction of this document I cannot conclude that the parties intended to provide for the release of rights and the surrender of claims which they could never have had in contemplation at all. If the parties had sought to achieve so extravagant a result they should in my opinion have used language which left no room for doubt and which might at least have alerted Mr Naeem to the true effect of what (on that hypothesis) he was agreeing.

Lord Hoffmann actually dissented in this case; while he agreed with the general rules of construction applied, he disagreed with the interpretation of the contractual terms.

The House of Lords has broadened the opportunities for the courts to correct contractual drafting errors through construction. In **Chartbrook** v **Persimmon Homes** (2009) the House encouraged the courts to use a purposive approach to the interpretation of contracts. Persimmon Homes were property developers who had agreed to buy land for development from Chartbrook. The price to be paid for the land included an 'Additional Residential Payment'. A dispute arose as to how the Additional Residential Payment was supposed to be calculated under the contract. Under a literal interpretation of the contract this would amount to almost £5 million. The House of Lords concluded that a literal interpretation was not appropriate on the facts because it made no commercial sense. Instead the House was entitled to correct a mistake in the contract by construction so that the amount payable was less than £1 million. To correct a mistake by construction two conditions had to be satisfied. First, there had to be a clear mistake on the face of the contract. Secondly, it must be obvious what correction should be made in order to cure the mistake. Where these conditions are satisfied the courts are entitled to significantly rewrite the contract. The courts are thereby trying to interpret the agreement in context to get as close as possible to its intended meaning. Lord Hoffmann concluded:

> All that is required is that it should be clear that something has gone wrong with the language and that it should be clear what a reasonable person would have understood the parties to have meant.

If these criteria are not satisfied then the parties could still seek the separate equitable remedy of rectification.

With regard to the first condition that there had to be a clear mistake on the face of the contract, the court has to take into account the 'matrix of facts' that formed the background or context of the formation of the contract. Persimmon Homes wanted the House of Lords to take into account two letters which had been written by the parties during the pre-contractual negotiations. The House concluded that these letters were not admissible because of the exclusionary rule that pre-contractual negotiations cannot be considered to interpret a contract. This rule excludes evidence of what the parties said or did during the course of negotiations for the purpose of drawing inferences about the meaning of the contract. It does not exclude the use of such evidence for other purposes: for example, to establish that a fact which may be relevant as background was known to the parties. Negotiations could only be relevant background in the exceptional cases where the negotiations shed light on what the parties would reasonably be taken to have meant by the language which they finally adopted to address their agreement.

In **ING Bank** v **Ros Roca** (2011) the Court of Appeal commented that a cautious approach should be taken to applying **Chartbrook**:

> Judges should not see in **Chartbrook** an 'open sesame' for reconstructing the parties' contract, but an opportunity to remedy by construction a clear error of language which could not have been intended.

Sir Richard Buxton (2010) has criticised the **Chartbrook** case on the basis that it confuses 'the meaning of what the parties said in the document with what they meant to say but did not say'. He has also pointed out how close the rules of construction are, and in particular Lord Hoffmann's fifth principle as enunciated in **Investors Compensation Scheme** and the rules on rectification. This reflects the fact that the rules on interpretation and on rectification are grappling with the same problems.

## Topical Issue

### Downloading music from the internet

**Pink Floyd Music Ltd** *v* **EMI Records** [2010] concerned the interpretation of a contract, known as a licence agreement, which gave the record company, EMI Records, the right to sell and distribute Pink Floyd's music. The licence agreement contained a contractual term that sale of the music would only be as full album song bundles, unless with the prior written consent of the claimants. The clause stated:

> [EMI] warrants undertakes and agrees with [PFM] . . . not to couple Records delivered hereunder with other master recordings or to sell in any form other than as the current Albums and to exploit the Albums in exactly the same form as to track listing and timing as are delivered hereunder (without limitation there are no rights to sell any or all of the Records as Single records other than with the Company's prior written consent which may be absolutely withheld).

Pink Floyd was seeking a declaration that this clause caught online sales and digital downloads, whereas EMI argued that its language was clearly confined to old-fashioned 'Albums', 'Records' and 'Single records'. Pink Floyd took the record company to court claiming that the record company had exploited the music in ways that were not allowed under the contract, including using parts of songs for ringtones and for downloading individual tracks. It contended that permitting single track downloads and the use of part of the tracks as ringtones was a breach of this contractual term. The purpose of the clause was to preserve the artistic integrity of its albums and therefore had to be interpreted as extending to digital sales. EMI, however, argued that the clause only related to old-fashioned physical records and did not apply to online sales.

The Court of Appeal said that applying established principles of construction, there had not been a clear mistake in the wording of the contract that would have justified rectification. The commercial purpose of the clause relating to the sale of whole albums had been to preserve the artistic integrity of the albums. The parties must have intended to give effect to this purpose for both physical and digital products. The purpose of the clause was clear but the language used was, unfortunately, unclear. The clause would be construed so as to give effect to its demonstrated purpose. The court concluded that the relevant contractual clause:

> . . . is not by any means a clearly drafted provision, whose effect is unambiguous as a matter of language, and that it is therefore quite permissible, indeed positively appropriate, to invoke commercial common sense to assist on the issue of clarifying a rather opaque provision. I also consider that the commercial common sense which Pink Floyd Music invokes for the purpose of interpreting clause 4.13 is simple and uncontroversial.

As a result, EMI was not entitled, under the licence agreement, to exploit the sale of albums by way of online distribution in any form other than the original, album, configuration.

### Tennis court brawl

An interesting example of a dispute over the meaning of a contract is **Martinez v Ellesse International SpA** (1999). Conchita Martinez was a top international tennis player. She had entered into a five-year sponsorship contract with Ellesse, a sportswear manufacturer, in 1995. The contract stated that if Martinez was ranked within the top ten professional singles players in each contract year, she was to be paid an annual retainer worth US$1,945,000 over the contract period. In addition, the contract stated that she would receive an annual bonus of US$550,000 if she reached number two in any month. It was the interpretation of the bonus clause that was the subject of the dispute, Martinez arguing that she was entitled to payment of the bonus for 1996 and Ellesse arguing that she was not. The contract stipulated that the ranking was to be based on 'the average of her best week's ranking in each month'. It was common ground that Martinez's best ranking added together and divided by 12 resulted in a figure of 2.5, and Martinez contended that she was therefore ranked second and entitled to a bonus. Ellesse argued that if the other players' rankings were averaged in the same way there were three other players ahead of her and Martinez was in fact fourth. It was this second interpretation that was accepted by the court of first instance and the Court of Appeal. Martinez was therefore not entitled to the bonus.

In **Cherry Tree Investments Ltd v Landmain Ltd** (2012) a distinction was drawn between the interpretation of commercial contracts and publicly registered contracts. The Court of Appeal stated that it would take a more restrictive approach to the interpretation of publicly registered contracts, particularly in the context of conveyancing, than 'ordinary contracts'. Little weight would be given to background material that did not appear on the register.

When interpreting employment contracts, the Supreme Court has said it is prepared to take a 'purposive approach'. In **Autoclenz v Belcher** (2011) a group of car cleaners argued they should be treated as workers entitled to the minimum wage and holiday pay. They worked for Autoclenz and their contracts with Autoclenz described them as self-employed. The Supreme Court held that it could disregard terms in the written contract and instead base its decision on their true intentions. In employment contracts the 'relative bargaining powers of the parties must be taken into account' and 'the true agreement will often have to be gleaned from all the circumstances of the case, of which the written agreement is only a part. This may be described as a purposive approach to the problem.'

# Implied terms

As well as the express terms laid down by the parties, further terms may in some circumstances be read into contracts by the courts. These implied terms may be divided into four groups: terms implied in fact; terms implied in law; terms implied by custom; and terms implied by trade usage.

# Terms implied in fact

These are terms which are not laid down in the contract, but which it is assumed both parties would have intended to include if they had thought about it – they may be left out by mistake, or because one or both parties thought them so obvious that they did not need to be spelt out. In **Equitable Life Assurance Society** *v* **Hyman** (2000) the House of Lords suggested that in deciding whether to imply a term into a contract, the courts will consider whether the proposed term would be:

- reasonable and equitable;
- capable of clear expression;
- compatible (not contradicting) any express terms of the contract;
- so obvious that it 'goes without saying' (the officious bystander test); and
- necessary to give business efficacy to the contract (the business efficacy test).

The officious bystander test and the business efficacy test are two overlapping tests which have been particularly important for the courts in determining the intention of the parties and will be discussed in more detail.

## The officious bystander test

This test was laid down by MacKinnon LJ in **Shirlaw** *v* **Southern Foundries** (1926). He said:

> ... that which in any contract is left to be implied and need not be expressed is something so obvious that it goes without saying; so that, if while the parties were making their bargain, an officious bystander were to suggest some express provision for it in the agreement, they would testily suppress him with a common 'Oh, of course!'

## The business efficacy test

This test covers terms which one side alleges must be implied in order to make the contract work – to give it business efficacy.

In order to imply a term for business efficacy, it was held in **BP Refinery (Westernport) Property Ltd** *v* **Shire of Hastings** (1978) that the court must be satisfied the term is:

- reasonable and equitable;
- necessary to give business efficacy to the contract (the term will not be implied if the contract is effective without it);
- so obvious that 'it goes without saying';
- capable of clear expression; and
- not contradicting any express term of the contract.

**Key Case**  *The Moorcock*

The leading case in this field is ***The Moorcock*** (1889). The defendants owned a wharf and jetty on the River Thames which people could pay to use to load and unload their boats. The defendants contracted with the claimants for the unloading of the claimants' boat, called *The Moorcock*, at their wharf. Both parties knew that the water level at the wharf was low and that the boat would have to rest on the river bed when the tide was down. This would be all right if the river bed was soft mud, but would damage the boat if it was hard ground.

In fact, the boat was damaged when it hit a ridge of hard ground at low tide. The contract did not expressly state that the boat would be moored safely. The claimants brought an action for compensation for the damage to the boat on the basis that there had been a breach of contract. The Court of Appeal implied a term into the contract that the boat would be moored safely at the jetty. Such a term was necessary to give the contract business efficacy. Otherwise the boat owner 'would simply be buying an opportunity of danger'. The term had been breached and the action for damages for breach of contract was therefore successful.

**Legal Principle**

A term can be implied into a contract in order to make the contract work – to give it business efficacy.

The principle laid down in **The Moorcock** has since been clarified, and its limits defined. In **Reigate v Union Manufacturing Co** (1918) Scrutton LJ said:

A term can only be implied if it is necessary in the business sense to give efficacy to the contract, i.e. if it is such a term that it can confidently be said that if at the time the contract was being negotiated someone had said to the parties: 'What will happen in such a case?' they would both have replied: 'Of course so and so will happen, we did not trouble to say that; it is too clear.'

Further definition was supplied by Lord Pearson in **Trollope & Colls Ltd v North West Regional Hospital Board** (1973):

An unexpressed term can be implied if, and only if, the court finds that the parties must have intended that term to form part of their contract: it is not enough for the court to find that such a term would have been adopted by the parties as reasonable men if it had been suggested to them: it must have been a term that went without saying, a term necessary to give business efficacy to the contract, a term which although tacit, formed part of the contract which the parties made for themselves.

This statement makes it clear that a term will only be implied if the contract will not work without it; it will not be implied simply because it makes the contract more sensible, fairer, or better in any other way. It also seems that since business efficacy terms are implied on the grounds that the parties must have intended them, a suggested term which is inconsistent with some express term agreed by the parties will not be implied.

A case which illustrates the principle of business efficacy is **Alpha Trading Ltd v Dunnshaw-Patten Ltd** (1981). In this case, one company was acting as agent for another (the principal) in promoting the sale of cement to a third party. The agent was to receive commission based on the tonnage sold. After contracting with the buyer, the principal then pulled out of the contract; since no sale took place, the agent stood to lose their commission. The cement company settled with the third party over their breach of the contract, but the Court of Appeal held that business efficacy required that there was an implied term that the principal would not withdraw from the contract so as to avoid the sale, and leave the agent without commission – without such a term, it would have been pointless for the agent to be a party to the contract. The cement company had breached this term and so their agent was entitled to recover damages.

## Both tests are subjective

Both the officious bystander and the business efficacy tests are subjective: they ask what the parties in the case would have agreed, and not what a reasonable person in their position would have agreed. Consequently, attempts to imply terms in fact commonly fail for one of two reasons.

First, a term will not be implied in fact where one of the parties is unaware of the subject matter of the suggested term to be implied, or the facts on which the implication of the term is based. In **Spring v NASDS** (1956) a trade union claimed that it was an implied term of its contract with each one of its members that the union would comply with the 'Bridlington agreement', which laid down the rules under which members transferred from one union to another. The court rejected this argument, on the grounds that if anyone had asked the member concerned whether he had agreed to allow the union to comply with the Bridlington agreement, he would have been very unlikely to reply 'Of course'; 'What's that?' would have been a more likely answer.

Secondly, a term will not be implied in fact if it is not clear that both parties would in fact have agreed to its inclusion in the contract; there may be many cases where a term that one party sees as obviously implied is strenuously rejected by the other party, who regards it as against their interests. In **Luxor (Eastbourne) Ltd v Cooper** (1941) the defendant had instructed an estate agent to sell two cinemas, with commission to be paid 'on completion of sale'. The agent introduced a potential buyer, who offered the asking price, but the cinema owner did not proceed with the sale, leaving the estate agent without commission, despite having done the work asked of him. The estate agent argued that the contract between himself and the seller contained an implied term that unless there was a very good reason, the defendant should not refuse to sell to a person introduced by the agent. This claim was rejected by the House of Lords, on the grounds that although the estate agent may have thought it was obvious that the contract contained such a term, it was not clear that the seller would have thought the same.

The House of Lords emphasised that they would only imply such terms where it was strictly necessary. In **Equitable Life Assurance Society v Hyman** (2000) the House of Lords was concerned with a dispute relating to payments made by Equitable Life on some of their life insurance policies. The directors claimed to have a discretion to pay low bonuses on the termination of the policy. Article 65 of the articles of association, which governed the activities of the directors of Equitable Life, appeared to give the directors a very broad discretion. It stated that they could distribute bonuses 'on such principles, and by such methods, as they may from time to time determine'.

The House of Lords stated that a distinction had to be drawn between interpretation and implication. The purpose of interpretation is to assign to the language of the text the most appropriate meaning that the words can legitimately bear. The language of Article 65 contained no relevant express restriction on the powers of the directors. It could therefore not be interpreted as restricting the directors' discretion.

But it went on to say that the critical question was whether any such restriction could be implied into Article 65:

> It is certainly not a case in which a term can be implied by law ... If a term is to be implied, it could only be a term implied from the language of article 65 read in its particular commercial setting. Such implied terms operate as *ad hoc* gap fillers ... Such a term may be imputed to parties: it is not critically dependent on proof of an actual intention of the parties ... This principle is sparingly and cautiously used and may never be employed to imply a term in conflict with the express terms of the text. The legal test for the implication of such a term is a standard of strict necessity ... In my judgement an implication precluding the use of the directors' discretion in

this way is strictly necessary. The supposition of the parties must be presumed to have been that the directors would not exercise their discretion in conflict with contractual rights. The implication is essential to give effect to the reasonable expectations of the parties.

# Terms implied in law

These are terms which the law dictates must be present in certain types of contract – in some cases, regardless of whether or not the parties want them.

## Key Case    Liverpool City Council *v* Irwin

In **Liverpool City Council *v* Irwin** (1977) the defendants lived in a council maisonette, which was part of a high-rise block in Liverpool. The whole building was in an extremely unpleasant condition, with unlit stairs, lifts that seldom worked and rubbish chutes that were frequently blocked, all owing largely to persistent vandalism. The defendants (and others in the block) protested against the conditions by withholding their rent and, when the case went to court, claimed that the Council were in breach of an implied term in the contract of tenancy that communal areas should be kept in repair and properly lit. The Council argued that there was no such implied term. When they took up their tenancy, the Irwin family had been given a copy of the Council rules for tenants, which contained a list of tenants' obligations; but there was no written document containing the Council's obligations as landlord. The House of Lords held that a landlord who let property containing several homes in one building must be under some implied obligation in law to provide proper access to the individual dwellings. They stated that the appropriate implied term in this case was that the landlord should take reasonable care to keep the common parts of the block in a reasonable state of repair, and their Lordships held that the Council had in fact taken reasonable care to do so, and could not be expected constantly to repair damage done by vandals and by the tenants themselves. Consequently, the claim failed.

### Legal Principle
A landlord who lets property containing several homes in one building is under an implied obligation in law to provide proper access to the individual dwellings.

Following **Spring *v* Guardian Assurance plc** (1994), most contracts of employment include an implied term that an employer will furnish an employee who leaves his employment with a reference based on facts compiled with due care. Contracts of employment also include an implied term that employer and employee will not engage in conduct 'likely to undermine the trust and confidence required if the employment relationship is to continue'. This was accepted by the House of Lords' judgment in **Malik *v* Bank of Credit and Commerce International** (1997), one of a string of cases following the collapse of Bank of Credit and Commerce International (BCCI). The claimants were employees of the bank who had been made redundant after it went into liquidation. They sought to be awarded, among other things, a payment that was described as 'stigma compensation'. They argued that their career prospects had been blighted by having worked over a long period for the bank. The House of Lords ruled that BCCI had breached the above-mentioned implied term in their employment contract by engaging in dishonest activities. Certain employees were therefore eligible for compensation; which employees would be a question of fact – for example, it was unlikely that a cleaner previously employed by BCCI would have any difficulties finding employment elsewhere, but this was not true of a banker.

Certain statutes imply terms into particular types of contract, and in some cases – notably consumer contracts – these terms must be read into the contract, regardless of either party's intentions. For example, under the combined provisions of the Sale of Goods Act 1979 and the Unfair Contract Terms Act 1977, goods sold to a consumer by someone acting in the course of a business must be of 'satisfactory quality', and it is not possible to exclude liability for breach of this term (for full details of the implied terms in consumer contracts, see Chapter 16). The Late Payment of Commercial Debts (Interest) Act 1998 provides that it is an implied term in commercial contracts that interest must be paid on certain debts, and a further £100 paid for late payment of debts worth over £10,000.

## Terms implied by custom

Terms can be implied into a contract if there is evidence that under local custom they would normally be there (see **Smith** v **Wilson**, p. 129 above).

## Terms implied by trade usage

Where a term would routinely be part of a contract made by parties involved in a particular trade or business, such a term may be implied by the courts. In **Cunliffe-Owen** v **Teather and Greenwood** (1967) the court said the trade usage would need to be 'notorious, certain and reasonable' and not illegal. If the trade practice does not satisfy this high threshold, then it will not form the basis of an implied term, but it can be of assistance in interpreting the contract, as part of the factual matrix (see p. 132). In **British Crane Hire Corp Ltd** v **Ipswich Plant Hire Ltd** (1975) the owner of a crane hired it to a contractor, who was engaged in the same sort of business. It held that the hirer was bound by the owner's usual terms, even though these were not actually stated at the time the contract was made. The owner's terms were based on a model supplied by a trade association, and were common in the trade, and could therefore be implied into the contract in much the same way as terms implied by custom.

## Entire agreement clauses

Some contracts contain entire agreement clauses which state that the written contract contains the entire agreement. The aim of such clauses is to prevent one party from arguing later that an earlier written or oral statement is also part of the contractual agreement. An entire agreement clause can be effective, though it cannot exclude liability for misrepresentation (discussed on

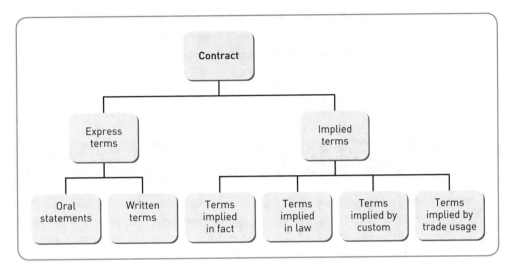

**Figure 7.1** Contractual terms

p. 196). Such a clause will prevent one of the parties from relying on statements made prior to the contract containing the entire agreement clause; however, it will not prevent statements made after that time being taken into account: **Lloyd** v **Sutcliffe** (2007).

The case of **Inntrepreneur Pub Co** v **East Crown Ltd** (2000) concerned the impact of an entire agreement clause in a contract. The contract was for the lease of a pub to the defendant. The defendant agreed to buy his beer for the pub from the claimant (this is known as a 'beer tie'). In this litigation, the defendant argued that the claimant had promised he would be released from this beer tie by 28 March 1998. The contract contained an entire agreement clause and so any promise on these lines made outside the written contract would not take effect. This clause prevented a party 'from threshing through the undergrowth and finding, in the course of negotiations, some (chance) remark or statement (often long forgotten or difficult to recall or explain) upon which to found a claim . . .'

The case of **Exxonmobil Sales and Supply Corp** v **Texaco Ltd** (2003) concerned a contract for the sale of diesel to Texaco. Upon delivery Texaco tested the diesel, concluded that its quality did not match the contractual requirements, and rejected the consignment. Exxonmobil pointed out that the diesel had been tested by an independent inspector prior to delivery and had been of the required standard. Texaco counter-argued that the contract included an implied term that a representative portion of the samples of diesel tested by the inspector would be retained. It submitted that such a term had to be implied in order to give business efficacy to the contract, so that the sample could be retested to check whether the independent inspector had made a mistake. Texaco contended in the alternative that there was usage or custom in the oil trade that such a sample would be kept.

The High Court rejected Texaco's submissions. The contract contained an entire agreement clause which stated:

> This instrument contains the entire agreement of the parties with respect to the subject matter hereof and there is no other promise, representation, warranty, usage or course of dealing affecting it.

The High Court concluded that the entire agreement clause was effective to exclude implied terms based upon usage or custom. The statement that 'there is no usage' affecting the agreement was a clear indication that the parties did not intend terms based upon usage or custom to be implied into the sale agreement. The entire agreement clause did not automatically prevent a clause being implied on the basis of business efficacy.

Entire agreement clauses and misrepresentation are discussed on p. 216.

# The relative importance of contractual terms

Different terms in a contract (both express and implied) will clearly vary in their level of importance. For example, if I offer to sell you my car with the engine in good condition, the paintwork unscratched and the ashtrays empty, clearly the first two terms are of rather more importance to you than the last, and my breaching that term will cause you less of a problem than violation of either of the others. Consequently, the law seeks to classify terms according to their importance, with the implications of a breach for the innocent party varying according to the type of term breached.

For these purposes, there are three types of contractual term: conditions, warranties, and innominate terms.

# Conditions

A term which is clearly an important one, in the sense that a breach of it would have very significant consequences for the innocent party, will usually be regarded by the courts as a condition. Where a condition is breached, the innocent party is entitled to regard the contract as repudiated, and so need not render any further performance, and can also sue for damages.

An example of a term deemed by the courts to be a condition can be found in **Bunge Corp v Tradax Export SA** (1981). A seller had contracted to ship 5,000 tons of US soya bean meal by the end of June 1975, with the buyer taking responsibility for arranging for the ship to transport the goods. The buyer was supposed to give 'at least 15 consecutive days' notice of probable readiness of vessel' but in fact only gave notice on 17 June. The seller might have been able to load in 13 days rather than 15. However, the House of Lords held that it was clear that the seller's obligation to ship the produce before the end of the month was a condition, so that the buyer could terminate if loading was not finished until 1 July. It therefore followed that the buyer's obligation to give notice was a condition, because in a contract of this kind it would be unfair to deprive sellers of their full period of notice.

In some cases, the parties themselves may have described particular terms as conditions in a written contract. As an examination of the cases on innominate terms will show, the courts will not always regard such terminology as decisive. In general, they look for evidence that the parties actually intended the term to have its precise legal meaning (see **Schuler AG v Wickman Machine Tool Sales Ltd**, p. 146 below).

Certain types of term are held by law to be conditions. For example, the Sale of Goods Act 1979 states that certain terms relating to title to goods and their quality are not only implied into consumer contracts for sale, but are usually also regarded as conditions, as opposed to warranties. Case law also lays down that certain terms are to be regarded as conditions whenever they appear.

**Key Case**   *The Mihalis Angelos*

In *The Mihalis Angelos* (1970) the owners of a ship hired it out by a charterparty (the name for the contract document in such a case). The document contained the clause 'expected ready to load under this charter about 1 July 1965'. In fact the ship could not have been ready by this time, and in the event was not ready until 23 July. The owners were obviously in breach of the term, but whether the charterers could terminate the contract depended on what sort of term it was. The House of Lords decided that an 'expected readiness' clause in charterparties was a condition. The judges based their decision on the fact that in previous sale of goods cases, similar undertakings had been construed as conditions, and that in commercial agreements, made by companies that bargain as equals, predictability and certainty are vital ingredients, and parties need to know the likely outcome of breaching any term before they can confidently agree to it.

> **Legal Principle**
> An 'expected readiness' clause in charterparties is a condition.

## Warranties

The word warranty usually describes a contractual term which can be broken without highly important consequences – such as our example of the car ashtray, above. The Sale of Goods Act 1979, s. 61 defines a warranty as a term 'collateral to the main purpose of [a contract of sale]'. If a warranty is breached the innocent party can sue for damages, but is not entitled to terminate the contract.

## Innominate terms

Also known as 'intermediate terms', these are terms which can be broken with either important or trivial consequences, depending on the nature of the breach. If the effects of the breach are serious, the term will act as a condition; if they are minor, it acts as a warranty.

**Key Case**   Hong Kong Fir Shipping Co Ltd *v* Kawasaki Ltd

Innominate terms were first described in **Hong Kong Fir Shipping Co Ltd *v* Kawasaki Ltd** (1962), in which the defendants had chartered a ship from the claimants for two years. Elderly engines and an inadequate and incompetent staff resulted in a total of 20 weeks of the charter being lost to breakdowns and repairs. The agreement contained a clause stating that the ship was 'in every way fitted for ordinary cargo service', so there was no doubt that the defendants were entitled to bring an action for damages for breach of contract, but instead of doing so, they decided to terminate the contract.

The claimants then brought an action for wrongful repudiation, claiming that their breach did not entitle the defendants to terminate, only to claim damages. The Court of Appeal agreed, stating that the question to be asked was whether the result of the breach had been to deprive the defendants of the whole of the benefit to which they were entitled under the contract. As this was not the case, the breach did not justify termination.

The real importance of the case is in the Court of Appeal's statement that some terms, and this was one of them, did not lend themselves to the traditional form of legal analysis: they could not be clearly defined before breach as conditions or warranties. Lord Diplock stated:

> The problem in this case is, in my view, neither solved nor soluble by debating whether the shipowner's express or implied undertaking to tender a seaworthy ship is a 'condition' or 'warranty'. The correct approach was to look at what had happened as a result of the breach and then decide if the charterers had been deprived of substantially the whole benefit which it was the intention of the parties they should obtain.

In other words, there were terms where the effect of a breach should depend on the importance of that breach. The term as to seaworthiness was such a term, because it could be broken in many different ways, with different levels of seriousness.

> **Legal Principle**
> Some terms cannot be defined before breach as conditions or warranties.

As a result of the decision in **Hong Kong Fir**, the courts have shown themselves ready to find that a term is innominate, even if the parties themselves describe it as a condition. In **Schuler AG v Wickman Machine Tool Sales Ltd** (1973) the parties made a contract in which one party agreed to visit certain manufacturers at least once every week. The written contract described this promise as a condition of the agreement. The term was clearly one which could be breached with serious consequences if, for example, the weekly visits were rarely undertaken, but could also be breached in a much less important way if just one visit was missed.

The House of Lords held that use of the word 'condition' was an indication that the parties intended that the innocent party should be allowed to terminate if that term was breached, but it was only an indication. It was still important to discover their intention by looking at the contract as a whole, and one relevant consideration would be whether imposing the strict legal meaning of condition created a very unreasonable result: 'The more unreasonable the result, the less likely it is that the party intended it.' In this case, their Lordships felt the result would be unreasonable, since the term could be breached in very minor ways; the term was held not to be a condition and Schuler were not entitled to terminate the contract.

In creating the innominate term, the **Hong Kong Fir** decision approaches the effect of breach from the opposite direction to that traditionally adopted by the courts. Conventionally, as we have seen, the courts sought to determine what the status of a particular term was at the time the parties made their contract; the importance of a term at that stage dictated the consequences. The **Hong Kong Fir** approach deduces the relative importance of a term only after it is breached, from the consequences of that breach.

This strategy is clearly very logical where terms can be broken in a wide number of ways, ranging from the trivial to the really serious, as it would seem unfair to allow termination for a very

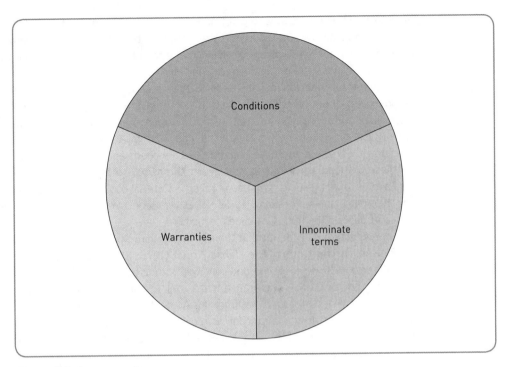

**Figure 7.2** Contractual terms

minor breach. In **Reardon Smith Line** *v* **Hansen Tangen** (1976) the respondents agreed to charter a tanker, which was in the process of being built. The contract identified the tanker as 'Osaka No. 354', and that name identified the shipyard which was to build the vessel. In the event, the Osaka yard was unable to do the work, and the ship was instead completed – quite satisfactorily – by another shipyard, who acted as sub-contractors, with the effect that the vessel was then known as 'Oshima 004'. By the time the ship was finished, the tanker market had hit problems, and the prospective charterers were apparently looking for a way out of the contract. In order to do this without penalty, they claimed that the vessel did not correspond with the contract description

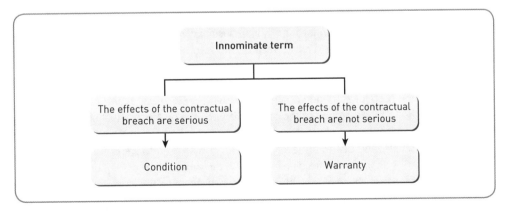

**Figure 7.3** Innominate terms

of it; they pointed out that the Sale of Goods Act, s. 13 requires goods to match up to any description of them. However, the House of Lords decided the words used were merely labels, and not a description in the sense meant by the Act. The term breached was therefore not a condition, and the appellants were not entitled to terminate the contract.

One problem with innominate terms is their potential for uncertainty; until a breach has occurred, it may not be clear what kind of term is involved. This is clearly a potential source of inconvenience, especially in business, where, in order to plan their affairs, parties need to know exactly what obligations they are assuming, and what will be the result if they do not fulfil those obligations. Consequently, in subsequent cases the courts appear to have decided not to give the doctrine too broad a scope, as we can see in **The Mihalis Angelos** (above). The term regarding readiness for loading could have been broken with trivial consequences – if the ship was ready a day later than planned, for example – as well as with serious results, yet in the interests of certainty the court decided the term should be a condition.

However, there is no doubt that the innominate term has its place. In **Cehave NV v Bremer Handelsgesellschaft mbH (The Hansa Nord)** (1975) a dispute arose over a contract to ship 12,000 tons of citrus pellets 'in good condition'. Some of the cargo became damaged, although apparently not seriously. It was argued that a contract for the sale of goods was governed by the Sale of Goods Act, and since it was from this Act that the modern distinction between conditions and warranties was derived, such contracts could not contain 'intermediate' or 'innominate' terms; terms must either be conditions or warranties. The Court of Appeal rejected this argument, holding that the clause was indeed an 'innominate' term, and because the breach was not serious, the buyers were not entitled to repudiate the contract.

# Criticism and reform

## Admissibility of pre-contractual negotiations

In **Chartbrook v Persimmon Homes** (2009) the House of Lords refused to budge from its established position that when interpreting a contract the courts cannot look at the pre-contractual negotiations. Lord Hoffmann acknowledged that the rule could mean that parties are sometimes held bound to a contract in terms which, if the negotiations were examined, no reasonable observer would take them to have been intended. But he felt that this was acceptable because it avoided the uncertainty that would result if the parties could not rely on the wording of the written contract. In favour of the exclusionary rule, the solicitor Alan Berg (2006) has argued that it enables lawyers to advise their clients as to how a court is likely to interpret a contract, without having to incur expenses to find out the background to the contract, which might in practice be impossible for the lawyer to find out during the pre-litigation stage. Without the exclusionary rule the costs of subsequent litigation would also increase as the parties would incur costs delving into the background of the contract. During the pre-contractual negotiations the parties' positions are changing; it is only the final contract which records the final agreement. The legal position is simpler and clearer if the written contract is allowed to speak for itself.

In an important academic article on the subject, the senior judge, Lord Nicholls (2005), has put forward a range of arguments in favour of changing the law to allow pre-contractual negotiations to be considered when interpreting contracts. Some other common law jurisdictions allow these negotiations to be considered. Even in the English courts, while pre-contractual negotiations are not admissible as evidence in determining how to interpret a contract, they are admissible when considering the equitable remedy of rectification when a mistake has been made in drafting the contract. Pre-contractual negotiations can also be considered when the court is considering the issue of estoppel or whether the parties habitually gave words an unusual meaning ('the private dictionary rule'), questions about the formation of oral contracts and claims for misrepresentation.

In **Oceanbulk Shipping and Trading** v **TMT Asia** (2010) the Supreme Court accepted that 'without prejudice' pre-contractual material could be used as an aid to interpreting a contract. This 'interpretation exception' to the 'without prejudice' rule has been criticised: the 'without prejudice' rule aims to encourage out of court settlements by allowing parties to speak freely without fear that the words spoken in private will be used later in evidence against them, and too many exceptions will undermine this public policy goal. The Supreme Court, however, stated:

> . . . if a party to negotiations knows that, in the event of a dispute about what a settlement contract means, objective facts which emerge during negotiations will be admitted in order to assist the court to interpret the agreement in accordance with the parties' true intentions, settlement is likely to be encouraged not discouraged.

# Answering questions

'The essential flexibility, or fatal uncertainty, of innominate terms stems from the fact that it is not possible to predict before the time of the breach what the legal effects of the breach of such a term will be.' (Downes)

Do you consider that innominate terms create an unacceptable level of uncertainty for contract law?

You need to define innominate terms and distinguish them from conditions and warranties, giving examples of each from case law. You then need to discuss the issues of flexibility and certainty, pointing out that both can have their place. Using the cases of **Schuler** v **Wickman** and **Reardon** v **Hansen**, you can highlight the potential unfairness of the traditional approach, and the way in which the innominate term deals with this. Then point out that the courts have also recognised that in some cases certainty will be more important, discussing **The Mihalis Angelos**, and explaining why contracting parties need to know the effect of a breach in advance. Your conclusion should state whether you think the use of innominate terms achieves the correct balance between the two, based on the points you have made.

Lisa saw a newspaper advertisement placed by M.J. Electrical in which VX48 video cassette recorders were available for £280 by mail order. Lisa sent a cheque for £280 but when she received the recorder, she discovered that it was a VX47. The next day, she received a letter from M.J. Electrical explaining that VX48 machines had become very difficult to obtain. The letter enclosed a cheque for £50, representing the difference in value between the two machines, and went on to say that, unless Lisa returned the VX47 within two weeks, it would be assumed that she was satisfied with the deal.

As she was going away for a two-week holiday on the day that she received the letter, Lisa did not have time to consider the matter further, but when she came back she decided to try the machine. She found that it was perfectly adequate in playing pre-recorded cassettes, but produced inferior quality recordings, no matter what brand of cassette tape she used.

Accordingly, she sent the machine back to M.J. Electrical, explaining in a note that it was not the machine she ordered. M.J. Electrical refused to accept the machine or to make any refund of the purchase price. They argued that she had failed to return the machine within the two weeks specified and further pointed to two clauses contained in the documents sent with the machine. The first said that, in any dispute as to the quality of the goods, M.J. Electrical reserved the right to repair or replace the goods at its discretion. The second said that no liability for the quality of the goods would be accepted if any unauthorised repair or inspection of the goods had been made.

Before Lisa sent the machine back, she had allowed her friend to open it up to examine the recording heads. However, though there was clear evidence that this had been done, her friend had not removed, replaced or repaired anything.

(a) Explaining the relevant rules on formation of contracts, consider whether a contract for the purchase of the VX47 was made between Lisa and M.J. Electrical. *(10 marks)*

(b) On the assumption that a contract did come into existence, explain what terms it would contain and consider whether any have been broken. *(10 marks)*

(c) Consider what remedies may be available to Lisa and discuss M.J. Electrical's claim not to be liable in any way. *(10 marks)*

(d) Ignoring any question of appeals, consider in which court(s) the dispute between Lisa and M.J. Electrical would eventually be resolved and comment on the procedure likely to be used. *(10 marks)*

(e) How satisfactory is the protection currently afforded by the law to persons such as Lisa in their dealings with those such as M.J. Electrical? *(10 marks) AQA*

 (a) The relevant rules here concern offer and acceptance (the requirements of intention to create legal relations and consideration pose no problems on these facts). You need to point out that what is needed for a contract to arise between Lisa and M.J. is an offer and an acceptance and then discuss whether these are present.

The first possible offer is the newspaper advertisement – as you know, in some cases these can be an offer (**Carlill** *v* **Carbolic Smoke Ball Co**), while in others they are deemed to be an invitation to treat (**Partridge** *v* **Crittenden**). You need to assess, by looking at the circumstances of the problem and comparing them with those in the cases, which side of the line you think this advertisement would fall.

Where, as here, the answer is not obvious, you should follow the two possible lines of argument through in turn. First, if the advertisement is an offer, it would seem to be accepted by Lisa sending her cheque – but the contract thus made was for a VX48, not a VX47. If the advertisement is not an offer, the offer might be Lisa's order, which could be accepted by sending the recorder (acceptance by performance). However, as acceptance must match the terms of the offer, sending a different machine becomes not acceptance, but a counter-offer. For there to be a contract, Lisa would have to accept this offer. M.J. seem to be claiming that her failure to return the machine within two weeks amounts to acceptance, but in contract law, mere silence never amounts to acceptance (**Felthouse** *v* **Bindley**), so it would appear that no contract for the sale of the VX47 was made.

(b) Where you are asked to define the terms of a contract, remember that terms may be implied as well as express, and deal with each in turn. In this case, it is probably simplest to deal with the implied terms first, since these will be the usual Sale of Goods Act terms (described in Chapter 16). It seems that several of these have been broken: the machine appears to be neither of satisfactory quality nor fit for its purpose. In each case, you should briefly state what the implied term requires, showing how they have been broken.

Then discuss the express terms. The first possibilities here are the statements in the advertisement: the price and the model number. If the advertisement is deemed to be an offer, these will clearly be part of the contract, and we know that the second has been broken. Then there are the two clauses contained in the documents sent with the machine; here you need to consider whether they have been incorporated. Clearly there has been neither signature nor, as far as we know, previous course of dealing (see Chapter 8), so the only possibility is reasonable notice.

(c) Lisa clearly wants to get her money back, and she has two ways to do this. First, she can claim that there was no contract, following the explanation of offer and acceptance detailed above. Secondly, she can claim for breach of contract, and this is where M.J.'s claim not to be liable comes in. They are clearly relying on the two clauses in the documents delivered with the video recorder. Lisa can try to defeat this either by arguing that the statements were not part of the contract (the issue you discussed in part (b)), or by establishing that they are inoperative as a result of either the Unfair Contract Terms Act 1977, or the Unfair Terms in Consumer Contracts Regulations 1999 (see Chapter 8). You need to examine each term in the light of these two.

(d) This part of the question raises issues that are outside the scope of this book, and which you will study as part of an English legal system course. A text by the same authors on the English legal system is available for this.

(e) This part requires an analysis of the law, rather than just description. You should aim to highlight any problems with the protection given by the law to consumers, and suggest any possible reforms (material on these issues is contained in Chapter 16).

## Summary of Chapter 7

The terms of a contract describe the duties and obligations that each party assumes under their agreement. As well as the contractual terms laid down by the parties themselves, called express terms, the courts may find that a contract contains implied terms.

### EXPRESS TERMS

Express terms can be divided up into oral statements and written statements.

### Oral statements

A representation is a statement which may have encouraged one party to make the contract but is not itself part of that contract, while a term is a promise or undertaking that is part of the contract. Whether a statement is a representation or a term is largely a question of the parties' intentions. If the parties have indicated that a particular statement is a term of their contract, the court will carry out that intention. In other cases, the following guidelines may be used.

### Importance of the statement

A statement is likely to be seen as a term if the injured party has made the other party aware that had it not been for that statement, they would not have entered into the contract: **Bannerman** v **White** (1861).

### Special knowledge and skill

Where a statement is made by someone who has expert knowledge or skill that is relevant to the subject in hand, the courts will be more willing to deem that statement a term than if the same words were used by an amateur with no special expertise on the matter. This principle is illustrated by two cases involving the sale of cars: **Dick Bentley Productions Ltd** v **Harold Smith (Motors) Ltd** (1965) and **Oscar Chess** v **Williams** (1957).

### Timing of the statement

In general, the more time that elapses between the statement being made and the contract being concluded, the less likely the courts will be to regard the statement as a term, though the cases show that this can only be an approximate guideline.

### Agreements in writing

Where the parties put their eventual contract in writing, any statement that appears in the written contract will usually be regarded as a term. A statement made before the written contract but not included in it is likely to be regarded as a representation: **Duffy** v **Newcastle United Football Co Ltd** (2000).

### Strength of the inducement

The more emphatically a statement is made, the more likely the courts will be to regard it as a term.

## Written terms

Written terms can be incorporated into a contract in three ways: by signature, by reasonable notice and by a previous course of dealing.

### The parol evidence rule

Under this rule, where there is a written contract, extrinsic (parol) evidence cannot change the express terms laid down in that document. Certain exceptions exist to the parol evidence rule.

#### Rectification

Where a document is intended to record a previous oral agreement but fails to do that accurately, evidence of the oral agreement will be admitted.

#### Partially written agreements

Where there is a written document, but the parties clearly intended it to be qualified by other written or oral statements, the parol evidence rule is again displaced: **Couchman** v **Hill** (1947).

### Implied terms

The parol evidence rule only applies where a party seeks to use extrinsic evidence to alter the express terms of a contract. Where a contract is of a type that is usually subject to terms implied by law, parol evidence may be given to support, or to rebut, the usual implication (see p. 141 above).

### Operation of the contract

The parol evidence rule does not apply to extrinsic evidence which shows that the written contract was intended to come into operation, or to cease to operate, in the event of a particular circumstance.

### Evidence about the parties

Extrinsic evidence can be used to show the capacities in which the parties were acting when they made their contract.

### Proving custom

Where it is suggested that a term should be read in the light of local or trade custom, evidence of that custom is admissible to add to or explain a written agreement, though not to contradict it.

## Collateral contracts

If one party says something to the effect that 'I will sign this document if you will assure me that it means . . .' the courts may find that two contracts have been created: the written agreement, and a collateral contract based on the oral statement.

## Construction of express terms

The courts sometimes have to determine the meaning of a contractual term. In doing this, the judges try to discover what the parties appeared to intend the contract to mean. The task of ascertaining the intention of the parties has to be approached objectively. The starting point is the contractual document itself. Where possible, the words of the contract will be given their natural and ordinary meaning. But Lord Hoffmann has warned against taking this rule too far.

Because of the parol evidence rule (discussed on p. 127), the courts have traditionally been limited to looking at the contract itself, and could not look at extrinsic evidence to determine the intention of the parties. Exceptions existed allowing such evidence to be considered where the terms were technical, ambiguous or absurd. Lord Wilberforce suggested in **Prenn** v **Simmonds** (1971) that in such situations extrinsic evidence would be admissible to show the background knowledge of the parties at the time of making the contract, so as to find out the purpose of the contract. The circumstances surrounding the making of the contract was described as the 'matrix of fact'. The law continues, however, to exclude the pre-contractual negotiations from the admissible background information.

Certain rules of construction have been formulated by the courts. Previously, these rules were applied rather rigidly. But Lord Hoffmann has advanced a more flexible approach, where these rules are treated simply as guidance to assist the judges to reach a reasonable interpretation of the parties' intentions.

## IMPLIED TERMS

Implied terms may be divided into four groups: terms implied in fact; terms implied in law; terms implied by custom; and terms implied by trade usage.

## Terms implied in fact

These are terms which are not laid down in the contract, but which it is assumed both parties would have intended to include if they had thought about it. In order to decide what the intention of the parties was, the courts have developed two overlapping tests: the officious bystander test (**Shirlaw** v **Southern Foundries** (1926)) and the business efficacy test (**The Moorcock** (1889)). Both tests are subjective: they ask what the parties in the case would have agreed, and not what a reasonable person in their position would have agreed.

## Terms implied in law

These are terms which the law dictates must be present in certain types of contract – in some cases, regardless of whether or not the parties want them: **Liverpool City Council** v **Irwin** (1977).

## Terms implied by custom

Terms can be implied into a contract if there is evidence that under local custom they would normally be there.

## Terms implied by trade usage

Where a term would routinely be part of a contract made by parties involved in a particular trade or business, such a term may be implied by the courts.

## Entire agreement clauses

Some contracts contain entire agreement clauses which state that the written contract contains the entire agreement. The aim of such clauses is to prevent one party from arguing later that an earlier written or oral statement is also part of the contractual agreement.

## THE RELATIVE IMPORTANCE OF CONTRACTUAL TERMS

There are three types of contractual term: conditions, warranties, and innominate terms.

## Conditions

A term which is clearly an important one will usually be regarded by the courts as a condition. Where a condition is breached, the innocent party is entitled to regard the contract as repudiated, and so need not render any further performance, and can also sue for damages.

## Warranties

The word warranty usually describes a contractual term which can be broken without highly important consequences. If a warranty is breached the innocent party can sue for damages, but is not entitled to terminate the contract.

## Innominate terms

Innominate terms can be broken with either important or trivial consequences, depending on the nature of the breach. If the effects of the breach are serious, the term will act as a condition; if they are minor, it acts as a warranty: **Hong Kong Fir Shipping Co Ltd** v **Kawasaki Ltd** (1962).

# Reading list

Berg, 'Thrashing through the undergrowth' (2006) 122 Law Quarterly Review 354

Bojczuk, 'When is a condition not a condition?' (1987) Journal of Business Law 353

Buxton, '"Construction" and rectification after *Chartbrook*' (2010) Cambridge Law Journal 253

Davenport, 'Thanks to the House of Lords' (1999) 115 Law Quarterly Review 11

Francis, 'Cracking the meaning' (2012) 162 New Law Journal 1279

Gee, 'The interpretation of commercial contracts' (2001) 117 Law Quarterly Review 358

Macdonald, 'Incorporation of contract terms by a "consistent course of dealing"' (1988) 8 Legal Studies 48

McMeel, 'Prior negotiations and subsequent conduct – the next step forward for contractual interpretation?' (2003) 119 Law Quarterly Review 272

Nicholls, Lord 'My kingdom for a horse: the meaning of words' (2005) 121 Law Quarterly Review 577

Pease, 'Wide-angle lens: courts continue to wrestle with the thorny issue of contract construction' (2012) 162 New Law Journal 1399

Staughton, 'How do the courts interpret commercial contracts?' (1999) Cambridge Law Journal 303

Steyn, 'Fulfilling the reasonable expectations of honest men' (1997) 113 Law Quarterly Review 433

Twomey, 'Spot the difference: the courts' approach to warranties and representations in share purchase agreements' (2013) 163 New Law Journal 263

## Reading on the internet

The House of Lords' judgment of **Mannai Investment Co Ltd** *v* **Eagle Star Life Assurance Co** (1997) is available on its website at:

http://www.publications.parliament.uk/pa/ld199798/ldjudgmt/jd970521/mann01.htm

The House of Lords' judgment of **Investors Compensation Scheme Ltd** *v* **West Bromwich Building Society** (1998) is available on its website at:

http://www.publications.parliament.uk/pa/ld199798/ldjudgmt/jd970619/invest01.htm

The House of Lords' judgment of **Bank of Credit and Commerce International** *v* **Ali** (2001) is available on its website at:

http://www.publications.parliament.uk/pa/ld200001/ldjudgmt/jd010301/credit-1.htm

# Chapter 8
## Unfair contract terms

**This chapter explains:**

that legal controls have developed to restrict the use of unfair contract terms. Under an exemption clause, one party to a contract seeks to limit their liability for certain breaches of the contract. Exemption clauses are controlled by:

- the common law; and
- statute, particularly the Unfair Contract Terms Act 1977.

In addition, the Unfair Terms in Consumer Contracts Regulations 1999 render ineffective certain unfair terms in contracts between sellers (or suppliers) and consumers.

Sometimes contract terms are considered to be so unfair to one of the contracting parties that the legislature or the courts have been prepared to intervene to prevent an injustice.

This has tended to arise in the context of exemption clauses and these are controlled both by the common law and by the Unfair Contract Terms Act 1977. The European Union has also intervened by making a Directive to prevent the use of unfair terms in contracts; such a term might be an exemption clause, but it might be another type of contractual clause. We will look first at the controls that are specific to exemption clauses, and then the more general controls provided as a result of the intervention by the European Union.

# Exemption clauses

In some cases, one party to a contract may seek to avoid incurring liability for certain breaches of the contract, or may specify that their liability for such a breach will be limited, usually to a certain amount in damages. For example, photographic processing companies often include a clause in their conditions of trading stating that if a film is lost or damaged, the compensation payable will be limited to the value of a replacement film. This is called a limitation clause.

A clause which seeks to exclude all liability for certain breaches is called an exclusion clause: an example might be the terms often imposed by holiday companies, which exclude liability for holiday problems caused by events beyond the company's control, such as war or natural disasters. The term 'exemption clause' is commonly used to cover both limitation and exclusion clauses, and we have used it in that sense here. Such clauses are usually, though not always, contained in standard form contracts (see p. 25). Over the past 40 years, the law has sought to control the use of these clauses, first by the efforts of the judges, and later by statutory intervention in the form of the Unfair Contract Terms Act 1977 (UCTA) and the Unfair Terms in Consumer Contracts Regulations 1999.

# Common law controls

Modern judges – notably Lord Denning – have expressed considerable disapproval of exemption clauses, which were frequently used by larger and more powerful contracting parties to impose harsh terms on smaller and weaker ones. In general, the courts have found two ways to regulate exclusion clauses: first, they may question whether a clause has actually been incorporated into the contract, in which case it is for the party seeking to rely on the clause to prove incorporation; and, secondly, they may question whether the words used in the clause can be construed as covering the alleged breach.

## Incorporation

There are three ways in which written exemption clauses (or in fact any other type of clause) may be incorporated into a contract: by signature; by reasonable notice; and by a previous course of dealing.

## Incorporation by signature

If a document is signed at the time of making the contract, its contents become terms of that contract, regardless of whether they have been read or understood. This principle is known as the rule in **L'Estrange** *v* **Graucob** (1934).

**Key Case**    L'Estrange *v* Graucob

The case of **L'Estrange** *v* **Graucob** concerned a woman who had signed a hire-purchase agreement for a cigarette vending machine, without reading it. The agreement contained, in very small print, a broad exemption from liability for the product. When the machine proved defective, it was held that signing the contract meant that the woman was bound by the exclusion clause, and therefore had no remedy.

**Legal Principle**
If a document is signed at the time of making the contract, its contents become terms of that contract, regardless of whether they have been read.

The rule does not apply where there is any misrepresentation as to the nature of the document signed.

**Key Case**    Curtis *v* Chemical Cleaning and Dyeing Co

In **Curtis** *v* **Chemical Cleaning and Dyeing Co** (1951) Ms Curtis took a wedding dress for cleaning, and was asked to sign a document exempting the cleaners from liability 'for any damage howsoever arising'. She queried the document, but was told it simply meant the cleaners would not accept liability for any sequins or beads on the dress. She then signed. When she collected the dress, it had a stain which was not there before, but the cleaners denied liability, relying on the exclusion clause. The Court of Appeal held that the statement made about sequins and beads misrepresented the effect of the clause, and therefore the cleaners could not rely on it, even though Ms Curtis had signed the document.

**Legal Principle**
The rule in **L'Estrange** *v* **Graucob** does not apply where there has been a misrepresentation as to the nature of the document signed.

Thus, in **Wilton** *v* **Farnworth** (1948) the court observed:

> In the absence of fraud or some other of the special circumstances of the character mentioned, a man cannot escape the consequences of signing a document by saying, and proving, that he did not understand it. Unless he was prepared to take the chance of being bound by the terms of the document, whatever they might be, it was for him to protect himself by abstaining from signing the document until he understood it and was satisfied with it. Any weakening of these principles would make chaos of every-day business transactions.

Professor Atiyah (1986) has observed:

> A signature is, and is widely recognized even by the general public as being a formal device, and
> its value would be greatly reduced if it could not be treated as a conclusive ground of contractual
> liability at least in all ordinary circumstances.

## Incorporation by reasonable notice

If separate written terms are presented at the time a contract is made – by handing over a ticket,
or listing them on a sign, for example – those terms only become part of the contract if it can be
said that the recipient had reasonable notice of them. Many of the rules on reasonable notice arise
out of what are called the 'ticket cases', which occurred during the nineteenth century with the
rise of companies providing public transport by rail.

**Key Case**   Parker *v* South Eastern Railway

The guiding principle regarding reasonable notice was laid down in **Parker *v* South Eastern
Railway** (1877). The claimant left his bag in a station cloakroom, paid the fee of 2d and
received a cloakroom ticket in return. On the front of the ticket was printed details such as
opening hours of the office, and also the words: 'See back'. On the back there was a clause
limiting to £10 the company's liability for the loss of property left with them. When the
claimant returned to collect his bag, it had been lost. The bag was worth £24 10s, so
Mr Parker claimed that amount from the railway company; the company maintained that
their liability was limited to £10. The Court of Appeal said that a party could be deemed to
have had reasonable notice if they knew of the clause, or if reasonable steps were taken to
bring the clause to their notice. On the facts of the case the limitation had been incorporated
into the contract, and the train company was only required to pay £10.

### Legal Principle
If separate written terms are presented at the time a contract is made, those terms only become
part of the contract if the recipient had reasonable notice of them.

In deciding whether reasonable steps have been taken, the courts will look at when the notice
was given, what form it took, and how serious and unusual the effect of the exemption clause is.

### Time of notice

As a rule, an exemption clause is only incorporated into the contract if notice is given before or at
the time of contracting. In **Olley *v* Marlborough Court Ltd** (1949) a married couple booked into
a hotel for a week, and then went to their allotted room. On the wall of the room they found a
notice stating that the hotel accepted no liability for loss of guests' property. While the couple
were out, Mrs Olley's fur coats were stolen. The hotel disclaimed liability, relying on the words of
the notice, but the Court of Appeal held that those words had not been incorporated into the
contract, because they came to the Olleys' notice too late. The contract was made at the reception
desk, and a new term could not then be imposed on them when they reached their room.

**Key Case** Thornton *v* Shoe Lane Parking

A similar issue arose in **Thornton *v* Shoe Lane Parking** (1971). The defendants ran a car park which motorists entered by taking a ticket from a machine, which triggered the raising of an automatic barrier. Mr Thornton did this, and parked his car, but when he returned to the car park later, there was an accident in which he was injured. The ticket stated that parking was subject to the conditions displayed on the premises, and various notices in the car park stated that the company did not accept responsibility for damage or personal injury. (The latter claim would be inoperative now under the Unfair Contract Terms Act 1977 (discussed on p. 167)).

When the claimant sued for damages, the defendants argued that they were exempt from liability, because of the clause. In deciding whether the clause was in fact part of the contract, Lord Denning analysed the transaction in terms of offer and acceptance, in order to decide when the contract was complete. He reasoned that the offer was made by the car park proprietors placing the machine ready to receive money. Acceptance took place when the customer drove up to the machine, and the contract was then complete. The terms printed on the ticket which was delivered a moment later by the machine therefore came too late.

**Legal Principle**
An exemption clause is only incorporated into the contract if notice is given before or at the time of contracting.

### Form of notice

The form in which notice is given is also important. In general, notice of an exemption clause will only be considered reasonable if it is given in a document which a reasonable person would expect to contain contractual terms. In **Chapelton *v* Barry UDC** (1940) the claimant wanted to hire two deckchairs on the beach. These were provided by the local council, which had posted a notice requesting those wanting chairs to obtain a ticket from the attendant and retain it for inspection.

The claimant bought two tickets, and put them into his pocket, without reading them. He then sat down on one of the chairs, which promptly collapsed, causing him some injury. He sued the Council, who relied on a term printed on the back of the ticket, which stated that they were not liable in the event of 'any accident or damage arising from the hire of the chair'. The Court of Appeal held that the clause was not part of the contract between Mr Chapelton and the Council, because such a ticket acted like a receipt – it merely acknowledged payment for the hire, and in most cases it would not be received until after the hirer had sat in the chair. A reasonable person would not have expected it to contain contractual terms.

A document will be considered to be contractual if the party to whom it is given knows it is intended to have this effect, or if the circumstances in which it was delivered provide reasonable notice of the fact that it contains conditions – so the mere fact that the document is called a receipt will not prevent it from having contractual effect if it is delivered in such a way as to allow reasonable notice of the terms within it.

Where an exemption clause is contained in a contractual document, it will usually be incorporated by reasonable notice if it is clearly set out or referred to on the front of the document. Notice is unlikely to be considered reasonable where an exemption clause is not on the front, and there are no words on the front referring to it. Equally, if a notice or ticket contains terms which are illegible or obscured in some way, the courts are likely to find that there was not reasonable notice. In **Sugar** *v* **LMS Railway Co** (1941) the ticket handed to a passenger carried the words 'For conditions see back' on the front, but these were hidden by the date stamp put on the ticket by the booking clerk. The court held that there had not been sufficient notice to incorporate the conditions into the contract.

## Effect of the clause

Modern cases have stressed that the more unusual or onerous a particular term is, the greater the degree of notice required to incorporate it. Highly unusual or onerous clauses cannot be incorporated simply by handing over or displaying a document containing the clause; the party seeking to impose the clause must take special steps to draw attention to it. This principle formed part of the reasoning in **Thornton**: although it was fairly common for car park conditions to exclude liability for damage to cars, exclusion of liability for personal injury was not a term that motorists would usually expect in such a transaction. Consequently, even though the steps taken by the proprietor might have been sufficient to incorporate the more usual clauses excluding or limiting liability for property damage, they could not be deemed to have given reasonable notice of the more unusual term concerning personal injury.

**Key Case**   Interfoto Picture Library *v* Stiletto Visual Programmes Ltd

This issue of the incorporation of unusual and onerous clauses was the subject of **Interfoto Picture Library** *v* **Stiletto Visual Programmes Ltd** (1988). The defendants were an advertising agency which borrowed some photographs from the claimants, a picture library. These libraries work by supplying photographic material to companies who have requested particular types of picture. The photographs are left with the client for a specified period for approval, with a reproduction fee to be paid if any of the pictures are published, and then returned to the library.

The Stiletto agency had not dealt with Interfoto before but, on request, the picture library delivered 47 photographs, along with a delivery note. This stated that the pictures should be returned within 14 days, and included a list of conditions, one of which was that companies who kept the pictures longer than 14 days would be charged a holding fee of £5 per picture per day until they were returned. The advertising agency, apparently without reading the conditions, decided that the pictures were unsuitable for their project, put them aside, and did not return them until almost a month later. When they did so, Interfoto submitted an invoice for £3,783.50, the holding fee.

The Court of Appeal held that Stiletto were not contractually bound to pay the charge, stating that as the term concerned was 'very onerous', the other party's attention had to be drawn to it very explicitly for it to be incorporated by reasonable notice. The court echoed a previous statement by Lord Denning that: 'Some clauses which I have seen would need to be printed in red ink on the face of the document with a red hand pointing to it before the notice could be considered sufficient.' In this case, although the clause was not hidden in any way – it was plainly printed on the delivery note – it was sufficiently onerous to require that the picture library should take action to ensure that the agency knew about it, rather than just assuming they would read it. Picture libraries frequently do impose charges for late return, but £5 per transparency per day would be considered expensive even today, let alone at the time when the case took place, and it seems that the high price made the court consider the term particularly onerous (in fact the claimant was allowed to recover £3.50 per week for each transparency returned late, as being a reasonable sum due on a *quantum meruit* – see p. 376).

### Legal Principle

The more unusual or onerous a particular term is, the greater the degree of notice required to incorporate it.

In **Kaye** *v* **Nu Skin UK Ltd** (2009) the High Court noted that the principle in **Interfoto** applied to commercial contracts as well as other types of contract. The judge observed:

I consider it is clear that the **Interfoto** principle is as applicable to commercial transactions as to any others, although, plainly, all relevant circumstances must be taken into account. In the case of a commercial transaction, that may have a significant bearing on whether a particular clause is onerous or unusual, and whether it was fairly brought to the attention of the other party.

### Topical Issue

#### Scratchcards

We have all tried our luck at one time or another with a scratchcard – not usually with any success. Few of us will have bothered to look closely at the tightly written words laying down the rules of the game. It was these rules which were the subject of litigation in **O'Brien** *v* **MGN Ltd** (2001). The *Daily Mirror* had launched a scratchcard game in 1995. The claimant had bought a newspaper that came with a game card. On the card was printed 'Full rules and how to claim see *Daily Mirror*'. Rule 5 provided: 'Should more prizes be claimed than are available in any prize category for any reason, a simple draw will take place for the prize.' The claimant bought another copy of the *Daily Mirror* a few weeks later which contained a scratchcard indicating two sums of £50,000. As was required, he telephoned a hotline and was informed by a message that he had won £50,000. Unfortunately, 1,472 people were also informed that they had won £50,000. The game had been designed to produce only one or two £50,000 prizes each week, but a person responsible for determining winning combinations had made a mistake. The newspaper announced that it would hold a special draw for one £50,000 prize and a further £50,000 would be shared by the other cardholders. As a result, the claimant only received £34, as his share of the second £50,000 prize. In the claimant's action to recover the full prize, the issue was whether the contract between the parties incorporated the newspaper's rules of the game. The Court of Appeal agreed with the trial judge that the rules were incorporated into the contract. The case of **Interfoto Picture Library Ltd** *v* **Stiletto Visual Programmes Ltd** (1989) was applied. The test was whether the newspaper could be said fairly and reasonably to have brought the rules to the notice of the claimant and whether those rules were particularly onerous or unusual. Rule 5, although it turned an apparent winner into a loser, was neither onerous nor outlandish. It merely deprived the claimant of a windfall for which he had done very little in return. In the particular context of the game, the court was satisfied that the newspaper had done just enough to bring the rules to the claimant's attention. There was a clear reference to the rules on the face of his card and they could be discovered from the newspaper office or from back issues of the paper.

## Incorporation by a previous course of dealing

If two parties have previously made a series of contracts between them, and those contracts contained an exemption clause, that clause may also apply to a subsequent transaction, even if the usual steps to incorporate the clause have not been taken. In **Spurling** v **Bradshaw** (1956) the parties had been doing business together for many years. The defendant delivered eight barrels of orange juice to the claimants, who were warehousemen, for storage. A few days later, he received a document from them, acknowledging receipt of the barrels. Words on the front of the document referred to clauses printed on the back, one of which exempted the claimants 'from any loss or damage occasioned by the negligence, wrongful act or default' of themselves or their employees.

When the defendant went to collect the barrels, they were empty. He consequently refused to pay the storage charges, so the claimants sued him. He counter-claimed for negligence and, in response, the claimants pleaded the exemption clause. The defendant argued that the clause could not affect his rights because it was only sent to him after the conclusion of the contract. However, he admitted that he had received similar documents during previous transactions, though he had never bothered to read them. The court held that the clause was incorporated into the contract by the course of the previous dealings.

A contrasting case is **Hollier** v **Rambler Motors (AMC) Ltd** (1972). The claimant left his car with a repairer, on whose premises it was destroyed by fire, owing to the defendant's negligence. The claimant had used the same garage three or four times in the previous five years, and each time had signed an invoice containing the words: 'The company is not responsible for damage caused by fire to customers' cars on the premises.' Although no invoice had been signed on the occasion in question, the defendants argued that this term was imported into the contract by the previous course of dealing. This was rejected by the Court of Appeal, which held that the previous course of dealing was not sufficient to justify the inclusion of such a clause.

## Interpreting exemption clauses

If it is established that an exemption clause has been incorporated into a contract, the courts will then check to see whether the clause actually covers the breach that has occurred. In doing so, they apply what is called the *contra proferentem* rule, which essentially means that where the words of an exemption clause are ambiguous, they will be interpreted in the way least favourable to the party relying on them. Since parties seeking to exempt themselves from liability will frequently use unclear and ambiguous language in order to conceal their purpose, the *contra proferentem* rule can be a useful tool.

Application of the rule can be seen in **Houghton** v **Trafalgar Insurance Co** (1954). The case centred on a car accident, involving a five-seater car which was carrying six people at the time.

The policy under which the car was insured excluded the insurer's liability where an excessive 'load' was being carried, but it was held by the Court of Appeal that the word 'load' should be given a narrow interpretation, referring to goods and not people; consequently the clause did not exclude the insurer's liability where the car was carrying too many people, rather than too much weight.

An exemption clause in an insurance policy was also given a narrow interpretation in **Middleton** v **Wiggins** (1995). The claimants owned a landfill site where waste was disposed of. The rotting of the waste produced gases which caused an explosion and destroyed a house nearby. They had to pay damages to the home owner and claimed this expense from their insurers. The insurance company refused to pay, relying on an exemption clause in the insurance policy which excluded liability for loss arising from the disposal of waste material. The Court of Appeal rejected this argument as the accident had not occurred from the disposal of the waste, but from the unforeseen escape of gas resulting from the process of decomposition.

Technically, the *contra proferentem* rule applies to all exemption clauses, but the courts tend to apply it less rigorously to those which merely limit liability, rather than exclude it completely. In **Ailsa Craig Fishing Co Ltd** v **Malvern Fishing Co Ltd and Securicor (Scotland) Ltd** (1983) Securicor had contracted to provide security services for certain ships moored in Aberdeen Harbour. As a result of their incompetence, two ships sank. A clause in the contract limited Securicor's liability to £1,000, but the shipowners claimed that the clause was ambiguous and should therefore be interpreted in their favour. The House of Lords, however, upheld Securicor's reliance on the clause, stating that limitation clauses did not need to be construed as strictly as exclusion clauses, because limitation clauses were usually made with reference to the risks to which the deal exposed the party putting forward the clause, the price that party receives, and the possibility of the other party taking out insurance against the breach. In other words, the courts feel that limitation clauses are more likely to express the genuine intentions of the parties, and to be considered as part of the bargain than exclusion clauses.

## Special applications of the *contra proferentem* rule

The *contra proferentem* rule is applied particularly strictly where a party relies on an exemption clause to protect them from liability for negligence. Many clauses purporting to exempt a party from liability for negligence are inoperative under the Unfair Contract Terms Act 1977 (UCTA), and even where it remains possible to exclude liability for negligence, extremely clear words must be used for this purpose. Where a clause expressly refers to negligence, or uses a term that means the same, it will be effective. Clauses written in general terms, without express reference to negligence, will only allow the party concerned to avoid liability for negligence if the clause could not be interpreted as referring to any other kind of liability.

In **White** v **John Warrick & Co Ltd** (1953) the claimant hired a bicycle from the defendants. The contract between them stated that 'nothing in this agreement shall render the owners liable for any personal injury'. While Mr White was riding the bike, its saddle tilted forward, and he was injured. By supplying the defective cycle, the defendants could have been held liable both for breach of contract and for the tort of negligence. The Court of Appeal held that the clause was ambiguous; therefore the *contra proferentem* rule was applied. Construing the clause in the sense least favourable to the defendants meant that it referred to contractual liability only; therefore the defendants were not protected if they were found to be negligent in tort.

A contrasting case is **Alderslade** v **Hendon Laundry Ltd** (1945). Articles sent by the claimant for laundering were lost, and the laundry company sought to rely on a clause exempting them from liability for 'lost or damaged' articles. The court held that such a clause did exempt them from responsibility for negligence, since there was no other way in which the wording could be interpreted.

Exclusion clauses do not apply to statutory implied conditions unless the term 'conditions' is actually used in the exclusion clause because conditions are fundamental obligations which should not easily be avoided. The Sale of Goods Act implies certain terms into contracts for the sale of goods. If a party wishes to exclude one of these important terms (conditions) from the contract, then the term 'condition' must actually be used in the exclusion clause. **KG Bominflot Bunkergesellschaft** *v* **Petroplus Marketing AG** (2010) was a case involving a contract for the sale of a cargo of gasoil. The gasoil was of a good standard when it started its journey, but deteriorated during transportation so that it was no longer of a satisfactory quality. A clause in the contract stated:

> There are no guarantees, warranties or representations, express or implied, on merchantability, fitness or suitability of the oil for any particular purpose or otherwise which extend beyond the description of the oil set forth in this agreement.

Exclusion clauses have to be interpreted strictly. While it was clear that this clause was intended to catch the implied conditions in the Sale of Goods Act about merchantability and fitness for purpose, it had not achieved this purpose because it did not use the term 'condition'. The sellers had argued that this rigid style of interpretation was out of date and the courts should take a more contextual approach, but this argument was rejected because the authorities on the point were clear and certainty was important in commercial law. The oil was not fit for purpose and the sellers could not avoid liability for this breach of contract.

## Fundamental breach

During the 1950s and 1960s, the courts developed the principle that as a matter of law no exclusion clause could protect a party from liability for a very serious breach of contract – even if the wording of the clause clearly covered the breach which had been committed. However, this 'doctrine of fundamental breach' was rejected by the House of Lords in **Suisse Atlantique Société d'Armement Maritime SA** *v* **NV Rotterdamsche Kolen Centrale** (1967). Their Lordships stated *obiter* that there was no rule of substantive law that an exclusion clause could never excuse liability for such a breach. Whether the clause covered the breach in question would always be a question of fact involving the interpretation of the contract.

This approach was confirmed in **Photo Production Ltd** *v* **Securicor Transport Ltd** (1980). Photo Production employed Securicor to protect their factory by means of a visiting patrol. A clause in their contract provided that 'under no circumstances shall the [defendant] company be responsible for any injurious act or default by any employee of the company'. One night, one of the Securicor guards lit a small fire inside the factory (for no rational reason so far as anyone could tell). The fire got completely out of control and destroyed the claimants' premises, at a cost of £615,000. The House of Lords held that there was no rule of law that a fundamental breach could not be covered by an exclusion clause, and pointed out that since the **Suisse Atlantique** case, the Unfair Contract Terms Act 1977 had been passed, ensuring that exemption clauses could not be freely applied in consumer contracts. In commercial agreements, their Lordships pointed out, the parties were likely to be of roughly equal bargaining power, and to be able to cover their own risks by insurance (as in this case, where the case was actually being fought to decide which of the parties' insurance companies should pay for the damage). Therefore there was no need for a doctrine of fundamental breach. On the facts of the case, their Lordships decided that the exclusion clause clearly covered negligence, and so the defendants were allowed to rely on it.

## Other common law controls

There are a number of other common law limitations on the effectiveness of exemption clauses. Although their importance is much reduced by the statutory provisions to be discussed later, they still have some practical importance in cases to which the statutory limitations do not apply.

### Misrepresentation

Where the party putting forward an exemption clause misrepresents its effect, the clause will not be binding on the other party (see **Curtis** v **Chemical Cleaning & Dyeing Co Ltd**, p. 158 above).

### Inconsistent oral promise

An exclusion clause can be made wholly or partly ineffective by an oral promise, given at or before the time of the contract, that conflicts with it. In **Mendelssohn** v **Normand Ltd** (1970) a customer was told by a garage attendant to leave his car unlocked. This instruction was held to override an exclusion clause disclaiming liability for goods stolen, so that the garage were not protected by the clause when valuables were stolen from the claimant's car.

### Third parties

As a result of the doctrine of privity, which states that only the parties to a contract can sue on it (see Chapter 13), the courts have held that a person who is not party to a contract (called a third party) cannot be protected by an exemption clause in that contract, even if the clause is stated to apply to them. The leading case in this area is the House of Lords' decision in **Scruttons Ltd** v **Midland Silicones Ltd** (1962). The law on this subject is discussed at p. 300.

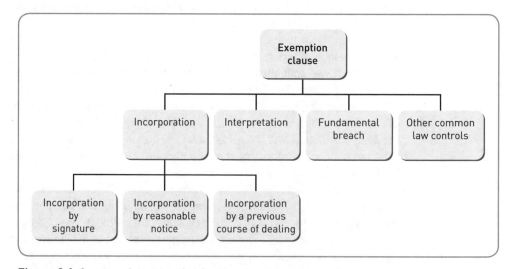

**Figure 8.1** Common law controls of exemption clauses

Following the enactment of the Contracts (Rights of Third Parties) Act 1999 (discussed at pp. 292–4), it is now possible under this legislation for the benefit of an exemption clause to be given to a third party. So third parties will be able to avoid the difficulties in the common law.

# Statutory controls

The most important limitations on exemption clauses are statutory, and most are contained in the Unfair Contract Terms Act 1977 (UCTA).

## Unfair Contract Terms Act 1977

In some ways, the title of the Act is misleading, since it does not aim to provide a general standard of fair or unfair contract terms. Its basic purpose is to control the use of clauses excluding or limiting liability for breach of contract, particularly where one of the parties is a consumer.

### Dealing as a consumer

Many of the provisions of the Act only apply where one of the contracting parties was dealing as a consumer. Section 12 explains that a party is 'dealing as a consumer' where they are not making the contract in the course of a business, and do not suggest that they are doing so, and the other party does act in the course of a business. Thus, in a contract where both parties are consumers, neither would be regarded as dealing as a consumer for the purposes of UCTA. In addition, where goods are supplied they must be of a type commonly supplied for private use (s. 12 also specifically states that anyone buying at auction or by competitive tender cannot be treated as a consumer).

The Court of Appeal has made it clear that the fact that a party is itself a business does not necessarily prevent it from 'dealing as a consumer' for the purposes of UCTA.

**Key Case** R & B Customs Brokers Co Ltd *v* United Dominions Trust Ltd

In **R & B Customs Brokers Co Ltd *v* United Dominions Trust Ltd** (1988) the claimant was a shipping company, owned and controlled by a Mr and Mrs Bell. The company bought a second-hand car from the defendants, for both business and personal use by the Bells; they had made two or three similar purchases in the past. The UCTA provision on which they sought to rely would only apply if they were dealing as consumers.

Despite the fact that the purchase was made by the company, and the car would be used partly for business purposes, the Court of Appeal held that the Bells were dealing as consumers. They stated that the question to ask was whether the transaction concerned was actually an integral part of the business, or merely incidental to it. If a contract related to the main purpose of a company (shipping goods in this case), the company concerned was acting 'in the course of a business' and could not be dealing as a consumer. However, if the contract was incidental to the company's main purpose, it would not be made 'in the course of a business', unless it was clearly something which the company did regularly.

The Bells' company was not in the business of buying cars, since it only bought one car at a time and had only previously bought one or two cars, so the court held that, regarding the contract in question, they were acting as consumers. If, for example, the Bells had been car dealers, or if the contract had been concerned with buying packing cases, or some other equipment required for their main purpose, that of shipping goods, the result would have been different.

> **Legal Principle**
> The fact that a party is itself a business does not prevent it from 'dealing as a consumer' for the purposes of UCTA.

Some doubt has been thrown on this narrow interpretation of the phrase 'in the course of a business' by the case of **Stevenson** v **Rogers** (1999) (which is discussed at p. 405). However, it was applied by the Court of Appeal in **Feldaroll Foundry plc** v **Hermes Leasing (London) Ltd** (2004). A company had bought a Lamborghini Diablo second-hand car for its company director at the price of £64,995. The managing director signed a hire-purchase agreement stating that all express and implied terms as to description, merchantability, quality and fitness for purpose were excluded. The contract also included a declaration that the car was to be used for business purposes. The car was found to have a defect with the steering which made it unpleasant to drive and potentially dangerous. The company sought to reject the car. The Court of Appeal held that the company was contracting as a consumer and therefore the exclusion clause could not apply.

## Other limitations on UCTA

UCTA does not apply to contracts concerning land, contracts which create or transfer most forms of intellectual property (such as patents or copyright), contracts relating to the formation or dissolution of a company, or any contract of insurance. The latter exclusion means that the Act has no application to a very important consumer area, where the imbalance of negotiating power is significant – insurance contracts are generally standard forms, and are notorious for exemption and limitation clauses which can be difficult to understand.

UCTA does not usually apply to employment contracts. In **Keen** v **Commerzbank** (2007), the claimant had been employed by a bank, but had been made redundant before receiving his annual bonus. He brought an unsuccessful claim for the unpaid bonus. His employment contract stated:

|  | Consumer | Acting in the course of a business |
|---|---|---|
| **Consumer** | Not a consumer contract | Consumer contract |
| **Acting in the course of a business** | Consumer contract | Not a consumer contract |

**Figure 8.2** UCTA and dealing as a consumer

The decision as to whether or not to award a bonus, the amount of any award and the timing and form of the award are at the discretion of the [bank].

The Court of Appeal held that the employment contract fell outside the protection of UCTA.

## Impact of UCTA

UCTA uses two methods of controlling exemption clauses: declaring them ineffective, and making them subject to reasonableness. Clauses which are ineffective under UCTA simply do not apply, even if they are written into a contract; the courts decide their verdict as if the clause was not there. As far as reasonableness is concerned, the Act gives some guidelines on what is reasonable, and others have been provided by case law which will be discussed later.

## Main provisions of UCTA

The following are the more important provisions of UCTA.

### Liability for negligence (s. 2)

Liability for death or personal injury resulting from negligence cannot be excluded or limited – clauses purporting to do so will simply be ineffective (s. 2(1)). This includes liability for negligence in tort as well as contract.

Responsibility for negligence which causes some harm short of death or personal injury can only be limited or excluded where it is reasonable to do so (s. 2(2)). Both these provisions apply, regardless of whether one party is dealing as a consumer.

Negligence is defined under s. 1 as the breach of any express or implied contractual obligation 'to take reasonable care or to exercise reasonable skill in the performance of the contract' or 'of the common duty of care imposed by the Occupiers' Liability Act 1957'.

### Non-performance (s. 3)

In a consumer contract, or when dealing on one party's standard business terms, a contract term cannot exclude or restrict liability for non-performance or for performance which is substantially different from what was agreed, unless it is reasonable to do so (s. 3). For example, a term in a contract for a package holiday which seeks to allow the tour operator to alter the date of the holiday or the accommodation would fall within this provision.

It is a question of fact and degree whether the courts will find that a party is dealing on another's written standard terms of business. In **St Albans City and District Council** v **International Computers Ltd** (1996) the Court of Appeal stated that a party still deals on another's standard terms even if there were pre-contractual negotiations, if these only resulted in minor changes. This issue arose in **Yuanda (UK) Co Ltd** v **WW Gear Construction Ltd** (2010). The relevant contract was clearly written, the dispute was whether it was 'standard'. The High Court stated:

the conditions have to be standard in that they are terms which the company in question uses for all, or nearly all, of its contracts of a particular type without alteration (apart from blanks which have to be completed showing the price, name of the other contracting party and so on).

In deciding this issue, the courts consider how far the party putting forward the 'standard terms' is prepared to agree changes to these terms and the extent and nature of any agreed alterations to the 'standard terms' made as a result of the negotiations between the parties. If there is a significant difference between the terms proffered and the terms of the final contract, then the contract will not have been made on one party's written standard terms of business.

This provision (s. 3 of UCTA) applied in **Timeload Ltd** *v* **British Telecommunications plc** (1995). Timeload was setting up a free telephone enquiry service and had obtained the number 0800 192 192 from BT. After Timeload had begun to market its service, BT sought to withdraw the use of that number because 192 was the number for directory enquiries. BT relied on a clause of the contract on its standard terms which allowed for termination of the service. The Court of Appeal accepted that this clause fell within s. 3 of UCTA, as it would permit termination without good cause when Timeload would reasonably expect termination only with good cause. That is to say, it allowed a performance which was different from that reasonably expected and was therefore subject to the test of reasonableness. On the facts of the case, BT's interpretation of the clause would make the clause unreasonable.

### Indemnity clauses (s. 4)

An indemnity clause is one which provides that one party will reimburse (indemnify) the other in the event of any loss arising from the contract. The effect of an indemnity clause is often to transfer liability away from the party who would normally be liable. Under s. 4 of UCTA such clauses in consumer contracts are only valid if they are reasonable. For example, contracts for the hire of a lorry and driver sometimes contain a clause by which the hirer promises to indemnify the owner for any injury, loss or damage caused by the negligence of the driver; if there is an accident and the lorry owner has to pay for repairs to their own or any other vehicle, they can claim the money spent from the hirer. This indemnity clause would only be valid if it was found to be reasonable.

### 'Guarantees' of consumer goods (s. 5)

Sometimes manufacturers issue what they call a 'guarantee' of their goods. While this guarantee might offer a quick remedy for minor problems, occasionally it seeks to exclude liability for more serious matters, such as personal injury caused by the product. Under s. 5 of UCTA such exemptions in consumer guarantees are ineffective.

### Implied terms in sale and hire-purchase contracts (s. 6)

Legislation, such as the Sale of Goods Act 1979 discussed on p. 406, implies certain terms into contracts for the sale of goods and hire-purchase contracts. Exclusion of these terms is controlled by s. 6 of UCTA. The implied condition that the seller has the right to sell the goods in s. 12 of the Sale of Goods Act 1979 can never be excluded. Other terms implied by ss. 13–15 of the Sale of Goods Act cannot be excluded if one party deals as a consumer. Where neither of the parties is dealing as a consumer the exclusion clause will be subject to a requirement of reasonableness.

### Implied terms in miscellaneous contracts (s. 7)

For certain contracts which are not contracts for the sale of goods or hire-purchase contracts, such as building contracts, s. 7 of UCTA contains similar controls as those contained in s. 6.

### Misrepresentation (s. 8)

Contractual terms in any type of contract which seek to exempt a contracting party from liability for misrepresentation are subject to a test of reasonableness.

**Table 8.1** Exclusion clauses and the Sale of Goods Act 1979

| Implied term | One party dealing as a consumer | Neither party dealing as a consumer |
|---|---|---|
| Title (s. 12) | Invalid | Invalid |
| Sale by description (s. 13) | Invalid | Valid if reasonable |
| Satisfactory quality (s. 14(2)) | Invalid | Valid if reasonable |
| Fitness for purpose (s. 14(3)) | Invalid | Valid if reasonable |
| Correspondence with sample (s. 15) | Invalid | Valid if reasonable |

## The meaning of 'reasonableness'

Clauses which are subject to reasonableness by UCTA obviously only apply if the courts decide it is reasonable for them to do so. The Act gives some guidelines as to the meaning of reasonableness for these purposes, and the concept has been interpreted by the courts. The onus of proving that a term is reasonable is always on the party seeking to benefit from the term (s. 11(5)). Under s. 11(1) the court should ask itself whether the term in question is 'a fair and reasonable one to be included having regard to the circumstances which were, or ought reasonably to have been, known to or in the contemplation of the parties when the contract was made'. Therefore, if the term was a fair and reasonable one in view of the parties' knowledge at the time the contract was made, it will not become unreasonable as a result of subsequent events.

Section 11(2) refers to Schedule 2 to UCTA, which lays down a number of issues that the court may consider when deciding whether a term is reasonable for the purposes of ss. 6 and 7. These are:

- the relative strengths of the parties' bargaining positions and other means by which the customer's requirements could have been met;
- whether the customer received an inducement to agree to the term (for example, if goods were offered more cheaply if the exclusion clause was accepted), or could have entered into a similar contract with another party without agreeing to that term;
- whether the customer knew, or ought reasonably to have known, about the term, bearing in mind any trade custom or previous course of dealing;
- where an exemption clause only comes into operation if a particular condition is not fulfilled, whether it was reasonable at the time of contracting to expect that it would be feasible to comply with that condition; and
- whether the goods concerned were made or adapted to a special order.

Although the Act specifies that these issues are to be considered in relation to ss. 6 and 7, the courts have in practice used the same guidelines when considering reasonableness in relation to other parts of the Act.

UCTA also specifies in s. 11(4) that where the reasonableness of limitation clauses is being considered, the courts should bear in mind the resources which the party putting forward the term could expect to be available for meeting the liability if it should arise, and also how far it was practicable to take out insurance against the liability.

## Key Case  George Mitchell (Chesterhall) Ltd *v* Finney Lock Seeds Ltd

The first case on the issue of reasonableness under UCTA to reach the House of Lords was **George Mitchell (Chesterhall) Ltd** *v* **Finney Lock Seeds Ltd** (1983). The defendants were seed merchants who sold to the claimants 30 pounds of Dutch winter cabbage seed for £192. After planting, it became obvious that the seed was both a different kind from that stated (a spring rather than winter variety) and defective. The 63-acre crop was a complete failure, and the claimants sought compensation of £60,000, the value of the crop which they had lost. The defendants relied on a clause in their invoice, which purported to limit liability to replacing the seed or refunding the price. The House of Lords held that the clause was not reasonable, largely on the grounds that the defendants themselves admitted that in similar situations they had commonly made *ex gratia* payments to compensate farmers who had suffered losses, and their Lordships felt this suggested that the defendants recognised the clause could operate unreasonably. Other factors thought relevant were that the breach was serious, the defendants had been very careless and that it was easier for the sellers to insure against the risk than for the buyers.

### Legal Principle
A term is unreasonable for the purposes of UCTA if it was unfair in view of the parties' knowledge at the time the contract was made.

In determining the issue of reasonableness, recent cases have emphasised the question of whether the contract is made between two businesses of equal bargaining power, or a business and a vulnerable consumer. Thus, in **Watford Electronics Ltd** *v* **Sanderson CFL Ltd** (2001), there was a claim for damages for breach of a contract to supply software. The contract was made on the defendant's standard terms and included two clauses limiting its liability to the price paid for the software of £104,600. The software proved to be faulty and the claimant sought £5.5 million damages. The trial judge held that the exemption clauses were unreasonable. However, the Court of Appeal considered the clauses to be reasonable because the contract had been negotiated between experienced businessmen of equal bargaining power and skill. It stated that in such circumstances a court should be very cautious in interfering with the negotiated contract:

> Unless satisfied that one party has, in effect, taken unfair advantage of the other – or that a term is so unreasonable that it cannot properly have been understood or considered – the court should not interfere.

A similar approach was taken in **Granville Oil & Chemicals Ltd** *v* **Davies Turner & Co Ltd** (2003), where the Court of Appeal stated:

> The 1977 Act obviously plays a very important role in protecting vulnerable consumers from the effects of draconian contract terms. But I am less enthusiastic about its intrusion into contracts between commercial parties of equal bargaining strength, who should generally be considered capable of being able to make contracts of their choosing and expect to be bound by their terms.

In **Phillips Products** *v* **Hyland** (1987) the claimant hired from the defendant a digging machine with driver. The driver's negligence caused damage to the claimant's property, but the hire company claimed they were protected by an exclusion clause in their standard contract, under which the claimant was responsible for any damage caused by the digger. Under UCTA, s. 2 the clause was subject to the test of reasonableness, and the court held that it was not reasonable, on the grounds that the claimant did not regularly hire digging machinery, so was not likely to be familiar with the terms; the hiring was at short notice, with no time to negotiate the terms; and the claimant had no control over the risk for which he was expected to assume liability, since he did not choose the driver and knew nothing about operating the machine.

A further factor was introduced in **Smith** v **Eric Bush** (1990) which concerned a surveyor who was trying to limit his liability for an inaccurate report on the claimant's house. As well as echoing some of the factors considered in previous cases, such as the availability of insurance to each party, the court suggested that the difficulty of the task could be taken into account. In this case, surveying an ordinary house was not especially difficult, and this, combined with other factors, made it unreasonable for the surveyor to limit his liability as he was trying to do; but the court said that such limitation might be reasonable where the task was unusually difficult or complex.

In **Woodman** v **Photo Trade Processing** (1981) a photo processing contract provided that if the film sent for processing was lost, the processor's liability was limited to providing a replacement film. The court stated that on the facts of the case, the clause was unreasonable, but said that a similar clause might be reasonable if the processor also offered a premium service, which cost more but offered better protection.

## Topical Issue

### Fizzy drinks

Young people are drinking increasing quantities of sweet fizzy drinks, despite the warnings about the impact these drinks are having on their health. Perhaps the case of **Britvic Soft Drinks Ltd** v **Messer UK Ltd** (2002) might help to discourage their consumption. In that case the claimants manufactured soft drinks. They bought from the defendant carbon dioxide, which is used to create the bubbles in fizzy drinks. The carbon dioxide contained benzene. In large quantities benzene can damage a person's health, but the amount of benzene was very small and therefore did not pose a health risk. However, to reassure the public, the claimant had to recall from the shops a large amount of soft drinks containing the contaminated carbon dioxide. They then brought this action for breach of contract, to recover damages for the losses they had incurred as a result of this product recall.

The purchase of the carbon dioxide was on the seller's standard terms. Normally, a contract for the sale of goods contains an implied term under s. 14 of the Sale of Goods Act 1979 that the goods are of a satisfactory quality. A clause of the contract sought to exclude this implied term. This exclusion would only be effective if it was reasonable according to s. 6 of the Unfair Contract Terms Act 1977 (see p. 170 above). The Court of Appeal found that this exclusion of liability was unreasonable, even though the parties were of equal bargaining power. It pointed out that when making the contract the parties would not have expected the buyer to carry the risk of a defect arising from a manufacturing error.

# Unfair terms

Following the Maastricht Treaty, the European Union made the Directive on Unfair Terms in Consumer Contracts (1993). This instructed member states to pass domestic legislation to provide consumer protection. As a result, the UK Government made the Unfair Terms in Consumer Contracts Regulations 1994, which have now been replaced by the Unfair Terms in Consumer Contracts Regulations 1999.

# Unfair Terms in Consumer Contracts Regulations 1999

These Regulations revoke and replace the Unfair Terms in Consumer Contracts Regulations 1994. The main aim of the 1999 Regulations is for UK law to be drafted more closely to the wording of the European legislation, to prevent potential discrepancies between the two. In most respects the 1999 Regulations are the same as those passed in 1994, the principal change being that more institutions are now able to enforce the legislation, beyond the Director General of Fair Trading.

## Application of the 1999 Regulations

The Regulations render ineffective certain unfair terms in contracts between sellers or suppliers and consumers (reg. 4(1)). Like UCTA, the Regulations can control the use of exemption clauses, but they can also control other clauses in the contract where they are considered unfair.

'Seller or supplier' is defined as 'any natural or legal person . . . acting for purposes relating to his trade, business or profession, whether publicly owned or privately owned'. 'Consumer' is defined as 'any natural person . . . acting for purposes outside his trade, business or profession' (reg. 3). The meaning of a consumer in this context was considered by the Court of Appeal in **Standard Bank London Ltd** v **Apostolakis** (2003). The defendants were a wealthy lawyer and civil engineer who had entered into a contract with a bank in Athens (where they were residents). Under this contract the bank was to use some of the men's private funds on the foreign exchange market. The two men expected to receive a profit from these transactions. A dispute arose and the court had to consider whether a clause of the contract was unfair under the 1999 Regulations. It was held that this was a consumer contract:

> It is certainly not part of a person's trade as a civil engineer or a lawyer . . . to enter into foreign exchange contracts. They were using the money in a way which they hoped would be profitable but merely to use money in a way which they hoped would be profitable is not enough . . . to be engaging in trade.

The Regulations apply to contract terms that have not been individually negotiated, or, under reg. 5(3):

> Notwithstanding that a specific term or certain aspects of it in a contract has been individually negotiated, these Regulations shall apply to the rest of a contract if an overall assessment of it indicates that it is a pre-formulated standard contract.

There are two important exceptions in this context that are laid down in reg. 6(2). Where terms are in plain, intelligible language the assessment of fairness shall not relate to:

- core contractual terms; or
- the adequacy of the price or remuneration for goods or services provided.

In **Office of Fair Trading** v **Foxtons** (2009) the High Court noted that plain, intelligible language is language which is 'sufficiently clear to enable the typical consumer to have a proper understanding' of the contractual term. Where terms make cross-references between clauses they risk failing the plain and intelligible test. Words which can have different meanings should be avoided or defined.

By excluding assessments of the adequacy of the price of goods or services, the courts are not able to explore whether the parties have made a good, commercial bargain. Any payment required under the contract falls within this exclusion; it does not need to be a price for a core or essential service: **Abbey National and others** v **The Office for Fair Trading** (2009).

Core terms are usually those laying down the price or defining the subject matter of the contract. The purpose of the Regulations is to protect consumers from hidden injustice. When a person shops, they generally make sure that they are happy with the quality of the goods and the price of the goods, so these two things did not need to be controlled by the Regulations. For example, if I was a great admirer of the pop star Madonna and decided to pay £300 to buy a ticket for her concert, I would not be able to rely on the Regulations to argue later that I had paid an unfair price.

The Regulation fails to lay down a clear definition of a core term. An illustration of the concept is provided by the Directive which cites a contract for insurance: the 'core' of an insurance contract consists of those terms which 'define or circumscribe the insured risk . . . since these restrictions are taken into account in calculating the premium paid by the customer'. A term such as that in **Thornton** v **Shoe Lane Parking** (1971) seeking to exclude liability for personal injury might not be considered as dealing with the main subject matter of the contract, which was the provision of parking facilities for a fee. By contrast, on the facts of **Houghton** v **Trafalgar Insurance Co** (1954) the exclusion clause in the car insurance policy limited liability where an excessive load was being carried and could be considered as a core term to which the test of fairness would not apply.

In addition, the Office of Fair Trading has stated that:

> In our view, it would be difficult to claim that any term was a core term unless it was central to how consumers perceived the bargain. A supplier would surely find it hard to sustain the argument that a contract's main subject matter was defined by a term which a consumer had been given no real chance to see and read before signing . . .

**Key Case**     Director General of Fair Trading v First National Bank

The case of **Director General of Fair Trading** v **First National Bank** (2001) concerned a contractual term in the bank's standard loan agreement. The term attempted to allow the bank to claim interest on judgments made in the bank's favour. The Bank argued in the House of Lords that the clause was excluded from the Regulations on the basis that it 'defined the subject matter of the contract or concerned the adequacy of the price or remuneration, as against the services supplied'. This argument was rejected by the House, which noted that the clause only came into operation after the borrower was already in default. The House of Lords explained that the 'core terms' provisions must be restrictively interpreted, otherwise virtually anything could be construed as dealing either with the main subject matter of the contract or the price paid by the consumer, leaving 'a gaping hole in the system' of consumer protection under the Regulations.

> **Legal Principle**
>
> The Unfair Terms in Consumer Contracts Regulations 1999 do not apply to core contractual terms, but the courts will interpret narrowly the concept of a 'core term'.

In **Bankers Insurance Co Ltd** *v* **South** (2003) the claimant had bought travel insurance when she was going on holiday in Cyprus. While on holiday she had seriously injured a person when driving a jet ski. She was subsequently sued and made a claim under her insurance for the cost of this litigation. The insurance policy included a clause that excluded liability for accidents caused by 'motorised waterborne craft'. The claimant argued that this clause was unfair. The High Court held that the court was unable to review this provision under the 1999 Regulations because they were a core term.

Unlike the 1994 Regulations, the 1999 Regulations can apply to contracts relating to succession, family law and the incorporation and organisation of companies. While there is no longer an express exclusion of employment contracts, these are excluded by the Directive and the Regulation will be interpreted in the light of the Directive.

## Topical Issue

### Joining a gym

We are all anxious to keep fit and often join a gym, optimistic we will go regularly, but soon find that our enthusiasm has waned and we stop going. In **Office of Fair Trading** *v* **Ashbourne Management Services** (2011), the Office of Fair Trading (OFT) was concerned that some of the standard terms for gym membership used by Ashbourne Management Services (AMS) were unfair. In particular, the standard contract required people to sign up for a minimum of one to three years. If a person tried to terminate the contract before this period, they would still have to pay the full gym membership fee for the whole minimum membership period, and they would be liable to pay this immediately, not in instalments over the minimum period. The OFT also argued that the contract was not in plain English so it would not be clear to gym users the total sum they were contracting to pay. AMS argued that these terms were not unfair because the price of membership was significantly cheaper than paying per visit or per month, which were also options open to people wanting to use the gyms. AMS pointed out that the contract could be terminated without paying for the whole minimum period in certain circumstances, such as if someone lost their job. The High Court held that these terms did in fact breach the Unfair Terms in Consumer Contracts Regulations. The Court stated:

> In all these circumstances I believe that the defendants' business model is designed and calculated to take advantage of the naivety and inexperience of the average consumer

using gym clubs at the lower end of the market. The defendants' standard form agreements contain a trap in which the average consumer is likely to fall.

The High Court considered whether the term about minimum membership periods was a core term (and therefore within the ambit of reg. 6(2)) or an ancillary term. It held that this was a core term and therefore did fall within the scope of reg. 6(2), but this did not prevent the term from being assessed for fairness. This is because its fairness did not relate to the definition of the main subject matter, but instead related to the consequences to members of early termination:

> [I]t is not the term itself which is excluded from assessment. Rather the term is excluded from certain forms of assessment . . . But it can be subject to challenge on other grounds.

In other words, it was not the minimum term as such that was the problem but the consequences of early termination in the light of it. So even if a term falls within reg. 6(2), the term can still be open to potential attack on other grounds. This distinction between a core term and matters contained in the same clause but ancillary to it is difficult to draw in practice. In reality, the consequences of termination look suspiciously like a dispute over the 'adequacy of the price or remuneration, as against the goods or services supplied in exchange' which are expressly excluded by reg. 6(2)(b) from the scope of the Regulations.

## Defining an 'unfair term'

The definition of an unfair term is provided by reg. 5(1). This states:

> A contractual term which has not been individually negotiated shall be regarded as unfair if, contrary to the requirement of good faith, it causes a significant imbalance in the parties' rights and obligations arising under the contract, to the detriment of the consumer.

In addition, reg. 6 states that

> the unfairness of a contractual term shall be assessed, taking into account the nature of the goods or services for which the contract was concluded and by referring, at the time of conclusion of the contract, to all the circumstances attending the conclusion of the contract and to all the other terms of the contract or of another contract on which it is dependent.

Schedule 2 contains an indicative list of terms which may be regarded as unfair. This is identical to the list that was contained in the 1994 Regulations except in one respect. In the earlier Schedule, the list referred to clauses which enabled a business to alter unilaterally the contract terms without a valid reason being specified in the contract. This was then qualified to exclude changes in interest rates in contracts with a supplier of financial services. This exception has now been removed, so consumers have a better chance of challenging the fairness of a clause in a contract for the provision of financial services.

Unlike the 1994 Regulations, there is no list of factors to be taken into account when assessing the issue of good faith or unfairness. The 1999 Regulations simply provide that the assessment of unfairness will take into account all the circumstances attending the conclusion of the contract. As the fairness of a term is decided in the light of the circumstances at the time of making the contract, the issue is not whether any actual detriment to the consumer has occurred as a result, but rather its potential to do so.

For a term to be unfair, the 'significant imbalance' it generates must be 'contrary to good faith'. The concept of good faith is not one which is familiar to lawyers in England and Wales, but in the light of the law in other European countries it is likely to require that contracting parties deal with each other in an open, honest way, taking into account their relative bargaining strengths. Bingham LJ observed in **Interfoto Picture Library Ltd** v **Stiletto Visual Programmes Ltd** (1989):

> In many civil law systems . . . [good faith] does not simply mean that they should not deceive each other, a principle which any legal system must recognise; its effect is perhaps most aptly conveyed by such metaphysical colloquialisms as 'playing fair', 'coming clean' or 'putting one's cards face up on the table'. It is in essence a principle of fair and open dealing.

The meaning of good faith was considered by the House of Lords in **Director General of Fair Trading** v **First National Bank** (2001). The case concerned a clause in the bank's standard loan agreement which stated:

> Interest on the amount which becomes payable shall be charged in accordance with Condition 4, at the rate stated in Paragraph D overleaf (subject to variation) until payment after as well as before any judgement (such obligation to be independent of and not to merge with the judgement).

The Office of Fair Trading took exception to the provision that the bank should be entitled to interest after judgment. Normally, the law does not require the payment of interest on such sums. At first instance the trial judge decided that the term was not unfair. The judge took the view that the borrower would have been surprised to find that his financial obligations were lessened where the bank obtains a judgment against the borrower, which would be the effect of the law if the term did not apply. The Court of Appeal disagreed in the light of the inequality of bargaining power between the contracting parties and took a broad approach to the issue of fairness. It considered that while logically there was no reason why a person should be better off because a judgment had been obtained against them, in this case fairness and logic did not coincide. The statutory provisions might not be logical, but they served the socially desirable purpose of preventing those already in debt from finding their problems made even worse. It was therefore unfair for the bank to attempt to exclude it. The court commented:

> The Bank, with its strong bargaining position as against the relatively weak position of the consumer, has not adequately considered the consumer's interests in this respect. In our view the relevant term in that respect does create unfair surprise and so does not satisfy the test of good faith, it does cause a significant imbalance in the rights and obligations of the parties . . . and it operates to the detriment of the consumer.

The case went up to the House of Lords and the House allowed the appeal, accepting the original trial judge's approach to the case. The relevant term was not, when properly considered, unfair within the meaning of the Regulations, as it did not cause a significant imbalance in the parties' rights and obligations under the contract to the detriment of the consumer in a manner or to an extent that is contrary to the requirement of good faith.

Lord Bingham held that the issue of good faith was essentially a requirement of 'fair and open dealing'. He concluded that:

> Good faith in this context is not an artificial or technical concept; nor . . . is it a concept wholly unfamiliar to British lawyers. It looks to good standards of commercial morality and practice.

### Estate agents

Estate agents have developed a reputation in our society for using cut-throat business practices to make money from the property market. Such concerns have led to some interesting litigation in the courts.

In **Bairstow Eves London Central Ltd** v **Adrian Smith** (2004) the appellant was an estate agent which had entered into a contract to sell the respondent's house. The agreement stated that the respondent would have to pay 1.5 per cent commission if the commission was paid within ten working days of the contract being completed. If payment was not received within this time the commission would be increased to 3 per cent. The respondent had instructed a firm of solicitors to handle the sale and had told them to pay the commission within ten working days. When the sale was successful the solicitors failed to make the commission payment in time. The estate agents sought payment of the higher level of commission. The Court of Appeal held that the clause requiring payment of 3 per cent commission was unfair, in breach of the 1999 Regulations.

The Office of Fair Trading challenged the fairness of contractual terms in **Office of Fair Trading** v **Foxtons** (2009). The contractual terms entitled Foxtons to make certain charges including a commission where a tenant renewed a tenancy after the fixed tenancy agreement had expired, even where Foxtons no longer managed the property or the landlord had sold the property. Commissions also had to be paid where a land-lord sold a property to a former tenant introduced by Foxtons, even though Foxtons was not in any way involved in negotiating or assisting the sale or renewal. These contract terms were contained in contracts where the owner had opted for a letting-only service to help them find a tenant (rather than full property-management service). The High Court held that the terms were unfair under the Unfair Terms in Consumer Contracts Regulations 1999. The commissions on sales and renewals were held not to be 'core' terms. The court considered that the terms in question were not in plain and intelligible language and the sums payable as commission were not commensurate with the services being received. The High Court held that the clauses created an imbalance and were not the sort of clause consumer landlords expected when they went to a letting agent to get a tenant for their property. The High Court suggested that all contentious terms should be emphasised by printing them in bold or putting them in a separate box.

## Effect of the 1999 Regulations

Under the 1999 Regulations, unfair contract terms are not binding on the consumer. The rest of the contract remains perfectly valid provided that it is capable of continuing in existence without the unfair term.

## Enforcement

The Office of Fair Trading can take the initiative to contact a business to challenge terms contained in their standard contracts. In addition, it is required to consider any complaint made to it about the fairness of a contract term drawn up for general use. It can require traders to produce copies

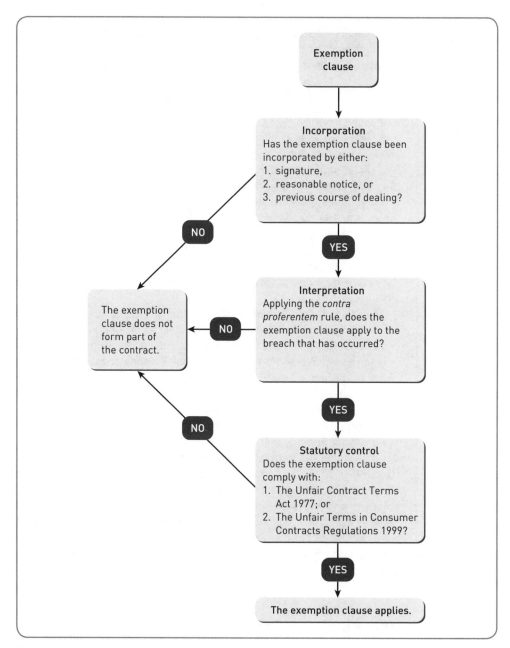

**Figure 8.3** Contractual status of exemption clauses

of their standard contracts and give information about their use, in order to facilitate the investigation of complaints and ensure compliance with undertakings or court orders. Generally, companies challenged by the Office of Fair Trading tend either to accept its suggested changes, or to negotiate a compromise.

Where there is a breach of the Regulations, Part 8 of the Enterprise Act 2002 provides that the Office of Fair Trading and certain other 'enforcers' may apply for an enforcement order. Such an

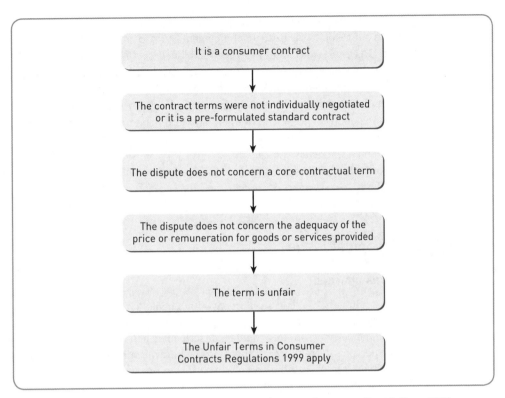

**Figure 8.4** Application of the Unfair Terms in Consumer Contracts Regulations 1999

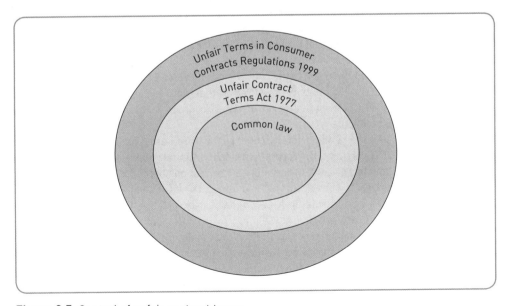

**Figure 8.5** Control of unfair contract terms

order may be made where the infringement harms the collective interests of consumers. The order seeks to put a stop to the existing infringement and also prevent future breaches of the legislation.

The Office of Fair Trading has now established an Unfair Contract Terms Unit. Rather than invoking the power to go to court it has generally adopted an educative and negotiating strategy. The Unit publishes regular bulletins reporting on and explaining its work. In its report in September 1996 it observed that unfair terms were widely in use by the majority of businesses. Such terms appear frequently in home improvement and furnishing businesses, and where goods are sold in the home, such as double-glazing. They were also frequently found in contracts for holidays, mobile phones, funerals and cars.

Through the work of the Office of Fair Trading, the 1999 Regulations (and the earlier 1994 Regulations) have had a considerable impact in securing changes to unfair contract terms.

## Topical Issue

### Bank charges

Most adults have a current account with a bank. In the UK the banks do not generally charge a person for having a current account, but they charge a person if their account becomes overdrawn: this could be described as a 'free-if-in-credit' charging structure. If a person's current account becomes overdrawn without their bank's permission, then the bank can charge the person a heavy sum (for example £40). This can seem rather unfair, because the poorest people who are most likely to find themselves overdrawn are subsidising the free banking of the richest. This has caused considerable dissatis-faction among bank customers who feel that such bank charges are disproportionate and unfair. The public rebellion gained momentum and specialist websites were set up providing standard letters and documents for use in complaining and ultimately launch-ing proceedings for reclaiming bank charges. With an increasing number of complaints, even the Financial Ombudsman Service published a draft letter which consumers could send to their own bank or building society. Many letters of complaint were sent and cases commenced in the courts regarding these charges. The banks initially often chose to refund the sums charged rather than defend the claims; for example, in 2007 HSBC repaid £116 million worth of unfair charges to customers, while Barclays paid back £87 million.

All the pending county court cases were put on hold while the Office of Fair Trading (OFT) carried out a formal investigation into the fairness of the bank charges of eight high street banks (who together are responsible for 90 per cent of current accounts in the UK). In **Abbey National and others** v **The Office of Fair Trading** (2009) the OFT asked the courts to rule on a preliminary issue relating to the investigation: whether such bank charges could fall within the 1999 Regulations, or whether they were excluded because under reg. 6(2) they were in plain, intelligible language and related to the ad-equacy of the price for services (see p. 175). The Supreme Court ruled in favour of the banks. It held that the unauthorised overdraft charges constituted part of the price for the banking services and as long as they were in plain and intelligible language, the courts were not entitled to assess their fairness (comparing the price charged to the service provided). Any payment required under the contract falls within the exclusion laid down in reg. 6(2); it does not need to be a price for a core or essential service. It did not matter that the majority of customers did not incur such charges or that they were only payable in certain circumstances. The court felt that the bank charges had to form part of the price for running the current account because they made up a third of the banks' revenue from running the accounts. Thus, one could say that the banks won on a technicality: the bank charges might well be unfair, but the courts were not entitled to look at this issue because of the limitations in the 1999 Regulations. The case highlights the limits to the protection provided to consumers by the Regulations.

The Supreme Court refused to allow the OFT to appeal to the European Court of Justice on the interpretation of the Directive on Unfair Terms in Consumer Contracts (1993) which had been the reason for the UK Government passing the 1999 Regulations. The OFT subsequently announced that in the light of this judgment it will not pursue its investigation into bank charges under the Unfair Contract Terms Regulations. Instead it will urge the banks to take voluntary action to make their terms clearer and more transparent and will press for legislative change so that consumers are better protected from unfair bank charges. The OFT remains concerned that the market for personal current accounts is not working well for consumers and does not give banks sufficient incentives to compete.

## Comparison between the 1999 Regulations and UCTA

There is a large area of overlap between the scope of the 1999 Regulations and UCTA. We have already noted that UCTA is primarily concerned with controlling exemption clauses, while the Regulations have a much broader application (though they do not cover the core terms referred

**Table 8.2** Comparison between UCTA and the 1999 Regulations

|  | UCTA | 1999 Regulations |
|---|---|---|
| Parties protected | Consumer contracts and some business-to-business contracts, particularly when on written standard terms | Consumer contracts |
| Definition of consumer | A company can be a consumer | Only human beings can be consumers |
| Type of term covered | Exemption clauses, and clauses allowing a business to change the substance of its own performance (s. 3) | Most terms (except core terms and those individually negotiated) |
| Test applied | Unreasonable and some terms automatically ineffective | Unfair |
| Burden of proof | Party claiming that exemption clause valid has to show it satisfies requirement of reasonableness where relevant | Burden on consumer to prove term unfair |
| Enforcement | By the parties | By the parties or by enforcers, such as the Office of Fair Trading, which have preventative powers |

to in reg. 3(2)). The Regulations are restricted to contracts between 'consumers' and 'sellers or suppliers', and a consumer can only be a human being, not a company. UCTA takes a broader approach to who 'deals as consumer', recognising that a consumer can be a company. In addition, the provisions of UCTA extend to some contracts between businesses. There is no requirement in the Regulations that the terms be 'written', although it will only be in rare situations that this is not the case.

UCTA subjects exemption clauses to a test of reasonableness. The test applied under the Regulations is that of unfairness. The Regulations, through the Office of Fair Trading and other qualifying bodies, provide more flexible powers of enforcement.

# Other legislative controls

## Product liability

Under Part I of the Consumer Protection Act 1987, where products are found to have defects which make them unsafe, manufacturers and certain other persons engaged in the distribution of products are liable in tort if the defect causes death, personal injury, or specified types of damage to property (this is called product liability). Section 7 of the Act provides that product liability cannot be limited or excluded by any contract term, notice or other provision.

## Dangerous goods

Under Part II of the Consumer Protection Act 1987, it is an offence to supply goods which do not comply with the safety standard laid down by the Act and secondary legislation arising from it. Committing such an offence gives rise to a civil remedy for any person affected by the dangerous goods, and liability to that person cannot be excluded by any contract term, notice or other provision.

# Reform

The law on unfair contract terms is complex and confused at the moment because there are two pieces of overlapping legislation (UCTA and the 1999 Regulations) covering the same subject but taking slightly different approaches. This makes the law inaccessible to consumers who need its protection. In 2001 the Government asked the Law Commission to consider the desirability and feasibility of replacing UCTA and the 1999 Regulations with a single piece of legislation. This new legislation had to be clearer and more accessible to the reader. In addition, the Law Commission was asked to consider extending the protection currently provided to consumers by the 1999 Regulations to businesses, particularly small businesses. There was concern that small businesses frequently found themselves signing contracts that contained unfair terms which could not be challenged under the current law. For example, a small farmer contracting with a supermarket may accept variations of price after the contract has been agreed. They may find that the supermarket has reserved the right to terminate a contract at will, or for only a minor default, while the small farmer is bound more rigorously by the contract.

The Law Commission issued a report, *Unfair Terms in Contracts* (2005). It recommended the introduction of a single Act which would replace UCTA and the 1999 Regulations. The proposed legislation would extend slightly the protection offered by the current law. It would protect both consumers and small businesses, which are businesses with nine or fewer staff, although certain types of contracts with small businesses would be excluded, such as contracts for financial services, contracts over £500,000 and contracts for land. The legislation would subject all terms to a test of whether they were fair and reasonable. Transparent core terms would not fall within the new legislative regime. With contracts made between a business and a small business, only those terms that had not been individually negotiated would be covered. The Law Commission was of the view that it was not possible to draft legislation on the subject which would be understood by business people and consumers. Instead, they hoped that their proposed piece of unified legislation would be accessible to consumer advisers (many of whom are not legally qualified), and business people who have some experience of contracting.

Following the Law Commission's recommendations, the Consumer Rights Bill is now being considered by Parliament. This contains many of the Law Commission's recommendations but with some amendments. The Bill is expected to be enacted in 2015. If passed, the Bill will repeal the 1999 Regulations. The business-to-consumer rules on unfair exclusions contained in the Unfair Contract Terms Act 1977 will be replaced by the provisions in the Bill. The 1977 Act would continue to apply to contracts between businesses.

If passed in its current form, the Consumer Rights Bill would apply to contracts for financial services as well as other consumer contracts. The unfair term provisions would cover terms that have been individually negotiated, as well as standard terms. The main subject matter and/or price terms will only be exempt from an assessment of fairness where such terms are 'transparent and prominent'. For a term to be prominent, it must be presented in such a way that the 'average consumer' would be aware of the term. A term is transparent if it is expressed in plain and intelligible language and (in the case of a written term) is legible. Any terms not covered by the main subject matter and/or price term exemptions mentioned above, would need to be assessed using the already established fairness test. A number of additional illustrative terms, which may be regarded as unfair, have also been included in the Bill, and are not currently included in the 1999 Regulations. Where terms included in this list are contained in a consumer contract, such terms will not be able to benefit from the exemption from assessment of fairness provisions.

# Answering questions

When answering a problem question in this field, there are three basic questions which you need to consider:

1  Incorporation: is the clause part of the contract?
2  Construction: does the clause cover the factual situation that has occurred?
3  Legislation: is the clause affected by UCTA, the 1999 Regulations or both?

 Amanda is a successful businesswoman, who breeds pedigree cats as a hobby. She regularly buys three months' supply of cat food at a time from Happycat Ltd. The contract of sale provides that (a) the buyer must inform Happycat of any defects in the product within a week of purchase, and (b) any liability for defective products is limited to the contract price. Amanda's latest batch of cat food turns out to be defective, and most of her cats become ill and die within a month of eating it. Advise Amanda.

 This question raises issues concerning implied terms in contracts of sale, and the use of exclusion clauses; this is a common combination, so if you choose to revise one of these, it would be wise to do the other one as well. The facts of this case raise no difficulties in relation to incorporation under common law.

The next stage is to determine whether Amanda would have a claim if the exclusion clauses were not there – in other words, have Happycat breached the contract? Here you look to the terms implied into contracts by the Sale of Goods Act 1979; it seems clear that Happycat are in breach of the implied terms on fitness for purpose and satisfactory quality (see Chapter 16).

The question then is whether terms (a) and (b) of the contract have any effect on Happycat's liability for these breaches. Taking (b) first, this is a clear attempt by Happycat to limit their liability for breach of the implied terms on fitness for purpose and satisfactory quality. Section 6 of UCTA provides that where the buyer is dealing as a consumer, such liability cannot be restricted at all; where the buyer is not dealing as a consumer, such restrictions are subject to reasonableness. Do not be deceived by the description of Amanda as a businesswoman; we are told that breeding cats is her hobby, and therefore in this transaction she appears to be dealing as a consumer and the limitation clause would be invalid.

Term (a) does not exclude liability, nor reduce the amount which can be claimed, so does not fall within the protection of s. 6. However, s. 13 provides that where UCTA prevents the limitation of a liability, it also prevents making enforcement of that liability subject to restrictive or onerous conditions; assuming the cats did not begin dying within a week of purchase, expecting complaints to be notified within that time would seem to be an onerous condition.

It seems therefore that both terms are made ineffective by UCTA, and Amanda can claim damages for the death of her cats. Incidentally, do not be tempted to try to apply s. 2 of UCTA, concerning the restriction of liability for death or personal injury, to a problem concerning the death of animals; that provision only applies to people. Amanda's loss would be seen by the law as loss of or damage to property.

Although UCTA seems to cover this problem adequately, you can earn yourself extra marks by looking at the exclusion clauses in the light of the 1999 Regulations as well, and discussing whether the terms would be unenforceable against Amanda under their provisions.

 Mary regularly parks her car in the customers' 'pay and display' car park at Jones Ltd department store. Inside the car park at all exit points are large notices stating in bold lettering, 'Cars parked at owners' risk'. Underneath is displayed in smaller letters a series of terms and conditions. One of the terms states:

> The company, its employees and agents accept no responsibility for any damage to customers' vehicles whatsoever and howsoever caused. Any term, condition or warranty whether express, implied or statutory covering damage to customer vehicles is hereby specifically excluded.

The next occasion Mary uses the car park she fails to see a notice placed at the entrance and before the automatic ticket barrier which states:

> Jones Ltd regrets the inconvenience caused to customers during the refurbishment and modernisation work. Customers are strongly advised to seek alternative parking during this period but may still use areas of the car park facility not undergoing refurbishing on the clear and express understanding that they do so entirely at their own risk and that the company, its employees and agents accept no responsibility whatsoever for any losses or damage howsoever caused.

Mary takes her ticket from the automatic machine and enters the car park. She suffers facial injuries and damage to the car when a brick is dropped through the car windscreen.

Advise Mary whether she can recover damages for her own injuries and for the damage to the car. *AQA*

 An answer could be structured by looking firstly at the question of incorporation of the two notices into the contract, secondly their construction, thirdly their validity under the Unfair Contract Terms Act 1977 and finally the implications of the Unfair Terms in Consumer Contracts Regulations 1999. On all of these issues, each notice would need to be considered in turn.

Looking first at the question of incorporation of the notice placed at the exit points, this would not have been incorporated through the ordinary principles of reasonable notice, as the information would need to have been given before or at the time of contracting: **Thornton** *v* **Shoe Lane Parking**. However, it may have been incorporated as a result of the course of dealings between Mary and Jones Ltd, since we are told that Mary regularly parks her car in the car park. In **Hollier** *v* **Rambler Motors (AMC) Ltd** there was found to have been no course of dealing, but there the claimant had only visited the garage three or four times in the previous five years. This could therefore be distinguished, and **Spurling** *v* **Bradshaw** relied upon. The fact that the details of the exemption clause are in smaller print would not prevent it from being incorporated, as the exemption is not particularly onerous or unusual – **Thornton** observed that it was fairly common for car park conditions to exclude damage to cars (see p. 160). The notice placed at the entrance point would be incorporated as it was visible before the time of contracting.

On the issue of interpretation, the terms of the first notice placed at the exit points seem clear and straightforward so there seems little scope for the *contra proferentem* rule. The terms of the second notice are, however, ambiguous, as they refer to parking being 'entirely at their own risk' and excluding liability for 'any losses or damage'. This does not clarify whether this is referring purely to losses or damage to property or whether it includes personal injury. This might be interpreted by a court under the *contra proferentem* rule to cover merely damage to property.

The Unfair Contract Terms Act 1977 would apply to this contract. Under s. 2(1) of this Act, any attempt under the notice placed at the exit point to exclude liability for personal injury will be ineffective if the facial injuries were caused by negligence. The exclusion of liability for damage to property resulting from negligence will only be applicable if it is reasonable (s. 2(2)). It would be up to Jones Ltd to prove that they were reasonable. A court will interpret this concept in the light of Article 11 and relevant cases, such as **George Mitchell (Chesterhall) Ltd** *v* **Finney Lock Seeds Ltd**.

Finally, consideration could be given to the Unfair Terms in Consumer Contracts Regulations. These would apply here as this is a contract between a consumer and a supplier; the terms of the contract have not been individually negotiated, and we are not concerned with core contractual terms within the meaning of reg. 6(2). The concept of fairness would be interpreted in accordance with reg. 5 and Schedule 2. It is unlikely that a court would find it unfair to exclude liability for damage to property, but they are likely to consider it unfair to exclude liability for personal injury.

## Summary of Chapter 8

Sometimes, contract terms are considered to be so unfair to one of the contracting parties that the legislature or the courts have been prepared to intervene to prevent an injustice.

### EXEMPTION CLAUSES

In some cases, one party to a contract may seek to avoid incurring liability for certain breaches of the contract, or may specify that their liability for such a breach will be limited, usually to a certain amount in damages. This is called a limitation clause. A clause which seeks to exclude all liability for certain breaches is called an exclusion clause. The term 'exemption clause' is commonly used to cover both limitation and exclusion clauses, and we have used it in that sense here.

### Common law controls

The courts have found two ways to regulate exclusion clauses: first, they may question whether a clause has actually been incorporated into the contract; and, secondly, they may question whether the words used in the clause can be construed as covering the alleged breach.

#### Incorporation

There are three ways in which written exemption clauses may be incorporated into a contract: by signature; by reasonable notice; and by a previous course of dealing.

##### Incorporation by signature

If a document is signed at the time of making the contract, its contents become terms of that contract, regardless of whether they have been read or understood. This principle is known as the rule in **L'Estrange** *v* **Graucob** (1934). The rule does not apply where there is any misrepresentation as to the nature of the document signed: **Curtis** *v* **Chemical Cleaning & Dyeing Co** (1951).

##### Incorporation by reasonable notice

If separate written terms are presented at the time a contract is made, those terms only become part of the contract if it can be said that the recipient had reasonable notice of them: **Parker** *v* **South Eastern Railway** (1877). In deciding whether reasonable steps have been taken, the courts will look at when the notice was given, what form it took, and how serious and unusual the effect of the exemption clause is.

- *Time of notice* As a rule, an exemption clause is only incorporated into the contract if notice is given before or at the time of contracting: **Thornton** *v* **Shoe Lane Parking** (1971).

- *Form of notice* In general, notice of an exemption clause will only be considered reasonable if it is given in a document which a reasonable person would expect to contain contractual terms: **Chapelton** *v* **Barry UDC** (1940). A document will be considered to be contractual if the party to whom it is given knows it is intended to have this effect, or if the circumstances in which it was delivered provide reasonable notice of the fact that it contains conditions.
- *Effect of the clause* Modern cases have stressed that the more unusual or onerous a particular term is, the greater the degree of notice required to incorporate it: **Interfoto Picture Library** *v* **Stiletto Visual Programmes Ltd** (1988).

### Incorporation by a previous course of dealing

If two parties have previously made a series of contracts between them, and those contracts contained an exemption clause, that clause may also apply to a subsequent transaction, even if the usual steps to incorporate the clause have not been taken: **Spurling** *v* **Bradshaw** (1956).

## Interpreting exemption clauses

If it is established that an exemption clause has been incorporated into a contract, the courts will then check to see whether the clause actually covers the breach that has occurred. In doing so, they apply what is called the *contra proferentem* rule, which essentially means that where the words of an exemption clause are ambiguous, they will be interpreted in the way least favourable to the party relying on them. Technically, the *contra proferentem* rule applies to all exemption clauses, but the courts tend to apply it less rigorously to those which merely limit liability, rather than exclude it completely.

### Special applications of the **contra proferentem** *rule*

The *contra proferentem* rule is applied particularly strictly where a party relies on an exemption clause to protect them from liability for negligence. Many clauses purporting to exempt a party from liability for negligence are inoperative under the Unfair Contract Terms Act 1977 (UCTA), and even where it remains possible to exclude liability for negligence, extremely clear words must be used for this purpose. Where a clause expressly refers to negligence, or uses a term that means the same, it will be effective. Clauses written in general terms, without express reference to negligence, will only allow the party concerned to avoid liability for negligence if the clause could not be interpreted as referring to any other kind of liability.

## Other common law controls

There are a number of other common law limitations on the effectiveness of exemption clauses.

### Misrepresentation

Where the party putting forward an exemption clause misrepresents its effect, the clause will not be binding on the other party: **Curtis** *v* **Chemical Cleaning & Dyeing Co Ltd** (1951).

### Inconsistent oral promise

An exclusion clause can be made wholly or partly ineffective by an oral promise, given at or before the time of the contract, that conflicts with it: **Mendelssohn** *v* **Normand Ltd** (1970).

### Third parties

As a result of the doctrine of privity, under the common law third parties cannot be protected by an exemption clause in that contract, even if the clause is stated to apply to them: **Scruttons Ltd** *v* **Midland Silicones Ltd** (1962). They may, however, get the benefit of an exemption clause by relying on the Contracts (Rights of Third Parties) Act 1999.

## Statutory controls

The most important limitations on exemption clauses are statutory, and most are contained in UCTA.

### Unfair Contract Terms Act 1977

This Act controls the use of clauses excluding or limiting liability for breach of contract, particularly where one of the parties is a consumer.

#### Dealing as a consumer

Many of the provisions of UCTA apply only where one of the contracting parties was dealing as a consumer. Section 12 explains that a party is 'dealing as a consumer' where they are not making the contract in the course of a business, and do not suggest that they are doing so, and the other party does act in the course of a business: **R & B Customs Brokers Co Ltd** *v* **United Dominions Trust Ltd** (1988).

#### The main provisions of UCTA

UCTA uses two methods of controlling exemption clauses: declaring them ineffective, and making them subject to reasonableness. The following are the more important provisions of UCTA:

- *Liability for negligence (s. 2)* Liability for death or personal injury resulting from negligence cannot be excluded or limited – clauses purporting to do so will simply be ineffective (s. 2(1)). Responsibility for negligence which causes some harm short of death or personal injury can only be limited or excluded where it is reasonable to do so (s. 2(2)). Both these provisions apply, regardless of whether one party is dealing as a consumer.
- *Non-performance (s. 3)* In a consumer contract, or when dealing on one party's standard business terms, a contract term cannot exclude or restrict liability for non-performance or for performance which is substantially different from what was agreed, unless it is reasonable to do so (s. 3).
- *Indemnity clauses (s. 4)* Indemnity clauses in consumer contracts are only valid if they are reasonable.
- *'Guarantees' of consumer goods (s. 5)* Exemptions in consumer guarantees are ineffective.
- *Implied terms in sale and hire-purchase contracts (s. 6)* The implied condition that the seller has the right to sell the goods in s. 12 of the Sale of Goods Act 1979 can never be excluded. Other terms implied by ss. 13–15 of the Sale of Goods Act cannot be excluded if one party deals as a consumer. Where neither of the parties is dealing as a consumer the exclusion clause will be subject to a requirement of reasonableness.
- *Implied terms in miscellaneous contracts (s. 7)* For certain contracts which are not contracts for the sale of goods or hire-purchase contracts, such as building contracts, s. 7 of UCTA contains similar controls as those contained in s. 6.
- *Misrepresentation (s. 8)* Contractual terms in any type of contract, which seek to exempt a contracting party from liability for misrepresentation, are subject to a test of reasonableness.

#### The meaning of 'reasonableness'

The onus of proving that a term is reasonable is always on the party seeking to benefit from the term (s. 11(5)). Under s. 11(1) the court should ask itself whether the term in question is 'a fair and reasonable one to be included having regard to the circumstances which were, or ought reasonably to have been, known to or in the contemplation of the parties when the contract was made'. Section 11(2) refers to Schedule 2 to UCTA, which lays down a number of issues that the court may consider when deciding whether a term is reasonable for the purposes of ss. 6 and 7.

## UNFAIR TERMS

The Unfair Terms in Consumer Contracts Regulations 1999 render ineffective certain unfair terms in contracts between sellers or suppliers and consumers (reg. 4(1)). The Regulations apply to contract terms that have not been individually negotiated, or, under reg. 5(3), to parts of a contract which have not been individually negotiated. Under reg. 6(2), where terms are in plain, intelligible language the assessment of fairness shall not relate to:

- core contractual terms; or
- the adequacy of the price or remuneration for goods or services provided.

### Defining an 'unfair term'

Under reg. 5(1):

> A contractual term which has not been individually negotiated shall be regarded as unfair if, contrary to the requirement of good faith, it causes a significant imbalance in the parties' rights and obligations arising under the contract, to the detriment of the consumer.

In addition, reg. 6 states that

> the unfairness of a contractual term shall be assessed, taking into account the nature of the goods or services for which the contract was concluded and by referring, at the time of conclusion of the contract, to all the circumstances attending the conclusion of the contract and to all the other terms of the contract or of another contract on which it is dependent. Schedule 2 contains an indicative list of terms which may be regarded as unfair.

### Effect of the 1999 Regulations

Under the 1999 Regulations, unfair contract terms are not binding on the consumer. The rest of the contract remains perfectly valid provided that it is capable of continuing in existence without the unfair term.

# Reading list

Atiyah (1986) *Essays on Contract*, Oxford: Clarendon Press

Chen-Wishart 'Transparency and Fairness in Bank Charges' (2010) 126 Law Quarterly Review 157

Macdonald, 'The duty to give notice of unusual contract terms' (1988) Journal of Business Law 375

Macdonald, 'The Emperor's old clauses: unincorporated clauses, misleading terms and the unfair terms in consumer contracts regulations' (1999) 58 Cambridge Law Journal 413

Mason, 'Contract, good faith and equitable standards in fair dealing' (2000) Law Quarterly Review 66

Mitchell, 'Unfair terms in consumer contracts' (2000) Law Quarterly Review 557

Spencer, 'Signature, consent and the rule in *L'Estrange v Graucob*' (1973) Cambridge Law Journal 103

Whittaker, 'Unfair terms, public services and the construction of a European conception of contract' (2000) Law Quarterly Review 95

## Reading on the internet

The Law Commission Report *Unfair Terms in Contracts* (2005) is available on its website at:

http://www.lawcom.gov.uk/docs/lc292.pdf

The Office of Fair Trading provides information to the public on the subject of unfair terms in consumer contracts:

http://www.oft.gov.uk/Business/Legal/UTCC/default.htm

The Unfair Terms in Consumer Contracts Regulations 1999 are available on the website of the Office of Public Sector Information at:

http://www.opsi.gov.uk/si/si1999/19992083.htm

The House of Lords' judgment of **Director General of Fair Trading** v **First National Bank** (2001) is available at:

http://www.publications.parliament.uk/pa/ld200102/ldjudgmt/jd011025/fair-1.htm

# Part 3
## Vitiating factors

Even where a contract meets the requirements of offer and acceptance, consideration and intent to create legal relations, it may still not be binding if, at the time the contract was made, certain factors were present which mean there was no genuine consent. These are known as vitiating factors (because they vitiate, or invalidate, consent). The vitiating factors which the law recognises as undermining a contract are misrepresentation, mistake, illegality, duress and undue influence. They will be dealt with in turn in the following chapters.

As we have seen, contracts are enforced by the law because they are expressions of the parties' own free will; the parties have consented to their contractual obligations. The reason why the vitiating factors undermine a contract is that they all in some way render invalid the parties' consent to their agreement – for example, if one party agrees to a contract because the other has threatened him or her, he or she cannot be said to have exercised free will.

The presence of a vitiating factor usually makes a contract either void or voidable, depending on which vitiating factor is present. Where a contract is declared void, the effect is that there was never a contract in the first place, so neither party can enforce the agreement. If a contract is voidable a contract comes into existence and the innocent party can choose whether or not to end the contract.

**Void** = never a contract in the first place

**Voidable** = a contract comes into existence. The innocent party can choose whether or not to end the contract

# Chapter 9
## Misrepresentation

### This chapter discusses:

how a misrepresentation is an untrue statement of fact by one party which induces the other to enter into the contract. The courts will find a misrepresentation if one party:

- made an untrue statement;
- it was a statement of fact; and
- it induced the innocent party to enter into the contract.

The courts recognise four types of misrepresentation:

- fraudulent misrepresentation;
- negligent misrepresentation at common law;
- negligent misrepresentation under statute; and
- innocent misrepresentation.

Where there has been a misrepresentation the contract is voidable and the innocent party may have a right to damages.

# What is a misrepresentation?

A misrepresentation is an untrue statement of fact by one party which has induced the other to enter into the contract. A misrepresentation renders the contract voidable and it may also give rise to a right to damages depending on the type of misrepresentation that has occurred. For a misrepresentation to be actionable, it has to fulfil three requirements: there must be an untrue statement; it must be a statement of fact, not mere opinion; and it must have induced the innocent party to enter the contract.

## An untrue statement

An untrue statement of fact must have been made by the other contracting party (or by their agent acting within the scope of their authority), or the other contracting party must have known of the untrue statement. The statement may be in any form – spoken, written or by conduct.

### A continuous representation

A representation made to induce a party to enter into a contract will generally be treated as a 'continuing representation'. Once a representation is made it can become a continuous representation if it has a continuing effect on the receiver of the representation and has not been withdrawn. The Supreme Court reached this conclusion in **Cramaso LLP v Ogilvie-Grant and others** (2014). The Earl of Seafield owned moorland in Scotland used for shooting grouse (a type of bird). A man called Mr Erskine was interested in buying a lease of this moorland as a commercial investment. During the contractual negotiations an e-mail was sent containing information about the estimated number of grouse on the moor. This information was misleading as it honestly but negligently overestimated the grouse population. Relying on this misinformation, Mr Erskine decided to buy the lease and created a limited liability partnership, Cramaso LLP, to become the legal owners. Cramaso LLP did not exist when the misleading e-mail had been sent. Upon discovering that the information was misleading, Cramaso LLP brought proceedings against the Earl of Seafield, claiming that it had been induced to enter into the lease by a negligent misrepresentation contained in the e-mail.

The claim was unsuccessful in the lower courts but succeeded in the Supreme Court. The Supreme Court held that the Earl of Seafield would be liable for the misrepresentation made to Mr Erskine. The representation contained in the critical e-mail was a 'continuing representation'. Although the representation was made over a month prior to the contract being signed, it continued even after the purchasing party changed and was still operative when the contract of sale was signed. As this representation had not been withdrawn, the Earl of Seafield implicitly asserted to Cramaso LLP the accuracy of that representation. The Supreme Court commented:

> [T]he change in the identity of the prospective contract party did not affect the continuing nature of the representation, or the respondent's continuing responsibility for its accuracy . . . Neither party drew a line under the previous discussions, after the appellant was formed, in order to begin afresh. Neither party disclaimed what had previously been said in the course of their discussions.

As a result of this decision, liability for misrepresentation can extend to parties who did not exist at the time of the misrepresentation. Any misrepresentation made by a company or its agents during pre-contractual negotiations may result in liability, even when an interval of time has passed between the misrepresentation and the formation of the contract. Where the representation had a continuing effect and a contract was concluded in reliance on it, the law might impose a continuing responsibility on the representor in respect of its accuracy. A representation might continue to have effect even where one of the contracting parties changed. An inference might be drawn from the parties' conduct that they proceeded with the negotiation and conclusion of the contract on the basis of the accuracy of that representation, implicitly if not expressly, after the identity of the prospective contracting party changed.

## Silence

It is natural that a sales person will sing the praises of goods being sold, while remaining silent about their weaknesses. Mere silence will not usually amount to a false statement, even though it may involve concealing some fact which is highly significant. Under the traditional rule of *caveat emptor* (Latin for 'let the buyer beware'), a purchaser is required to ask questions about important matters if necessary – the seller is not usually expected to volunteer information which may put the buyer off.

Even if one contracting party knows that the other has misunderstood some aspect of the situation, there is no duty to point this out. In **Fletcher** v **Krell** (1873) a woman applied for a post as a governess, without revealing the fact that she had previously been married. At that time, this may well have been a factor that would have affected the employer's decision to employ her. Despite this, the court held that her silence did not amount to a misrepresentation.

It should be noted, however, that in the specific context of consumer contracts, under the Consumer Protection from Unfair Trading Regulations 2008, a criminal offence will be committed by a retail trader (usually a shop) that unfairly misleads a consumer by failing to give information (reg. 10).

In addition, there are five types of situation where the law does impose a duty to disclose information. To remain silent about a material fact in any of these circumstances can therefore amount to a misrepresentation.

### Contracts requiring utmost good faith

These are often known as contracts requiring *uberrimae fidei*, which is Latin for 'utmost good faith'. Examples are contracts for insurance, the sale of shares in a company, the sale of land (where utmost good faith is required on matters affecting title to the land, although not physical defects) and certain family arrangements. Failure to disclose a matter regarding which utmost good faith is required allows the innocent party to rescind the contract, although damages are not available.

The way the rule on utmost good faith works can be seen most clearly in insurance contracts, where the party taking out the insurance policy must tell the insurance company of **any** fact he or she knows about which might affect the company's decision on whether or not to accept the insurance risk, and what premium to charge. If the insured party fails to disclose any fact that affects those decisions, the contract is voidable, and the company is not required to pay out against a claim, even if that claim has no connection with the fact that was not disclosed. For example, if a client takes out a life insurance policy without revealing that they have a heart condition, and is then killed in a car accident which has no connection with the illness, any dependants will not be able to claim against the policy.

The basis for the rule is that the relevant facts are likely to be difficult or impossible for the other party to find out for themselves, so the law should ensure that one party does not have an unfair bargaining position over the other. It was applied by the High Court in **International Management Group UK Ltd** v **Simmonds** (2003). The case concerned an annual cricket tournament (the Sahara Cup) between India and Pakistan. A company known as IMG paid to have the television rights to the matches. The 1999 tournament was not held as the Indian Government refused permission for the Indian team to participate. Given the unstable relationship between India and Pakistan, IMG decided to take out insurance against the risk of the 2000 tournament being cancelled. In negotiating the insurance policy, IMG failed to disclose that it had been informed that some well-placed and well-informed people were of the view that the Indian Government would refuse to allow India to play in the 2000 tournament. By a letter dated 10 August 2000, the Indian Government proceeded to refuse permission for the Indian team to play in the Sahara Cup. IMG claimed compensation under their insurance policy. Their claim was rejected and they brought an action for payment before the British courts. The action was unsuccessful. The High Court held that the insurance contract required utmost good faith and this requirement had been breached by failing to disclose these rumours to the insurance company when entering the contract.

The rule on utmost good faith is subject to the provisions of the Rehabilitation of Offenders Act 1974, which states that under certain circumstances a person cannot be required to disclose past convictions and sentences.

## Topical Issue

### Insurance contracts

English insurance law unfairly favours the insurer and needs to be rebalanced in favour of the insured to fall in line with the law in other European countries. Some insurance companies are themselves keen to remove any impression of bias in their favour and for the law to be modernised so that it remains competitive and fit for the needs of twenty-first-century business.

Current UK insurance law imposes heavy responsibilities on those applying for insurance. Insurance contracts are based on the principle of *uberrimae fidei*, requiring the contracting parties to act with the utmost good faith. This includes a duty on a party taking out insurance to disclose information relevant to calculating the risks involved in the insurance policy. If the duty is not met, the consequence can be that all insurance cover is lost. In particular this duty requires the insured to give full disclosure of all material facts when entering into the insurance contract. If the policyholder fails in this duty, the insurer may avoid the policy and it will be as if the policy never existed, regardless of whether the breach was made innocently, negligently or fraudulently and regardless of whether the breach was subsequently corrected. This can be very unfair in practice, particularly as the remedies currently available to the insurance company can be disproportionate. For example, in **Lambert** v **Co-operative Insurance** (1975) Brenda Lambert arranged some insurance for her valuable jewellery. Some of the jewellery was subsequently lost or stolen and she submitted an insurance claim. The insurance company refused to pay under the policy because it discovered that Brenda

Lambert's husband had been convicted of offences of dishonesty and this had not been mentioned on the application form. At no point had the insurer indicated it wished to be informed of such convictions but it could avoid paying under the policy on the basis of non-disclosure.

Much of the law on insurance contracts was developed during the eighteenth century in the context of contracts made between businessmen face to face and, it does not work well when applied to consumer contracts for household insurance or motor insurance which are frequently made online or over the telephone.

The Law Commission has therefore carried out a review of this area of the law. It has published a report *Consumer Insurance Law: pre-contract disclosure and misrepresentation* (2010), which proposes different reforms for consumer and business insurance agreements. As regards consumer contracts, the Law Commission suggests that the general duty to volunteer information should be abolished and replaced by a duty to answer questions honestly and reasonably. It would be up to the insurance companies to ask the appropriate questions, and if they failed to do so they would not be able to avoid a consumer policy for non-disclosure.

If a consumer made a misrepresentation which induced the insurer to enter a contract and a reasonable person in the circumstances would not have made the misrepresentation, then the remedy available to the insurer would depend on the type of misrepresentation: fraudulent, negligent or innocent. Where there has been a fraudulent misrepresentation, the insurance company would be able to avoid the policy. For negligent misrepresentation the remedy would put the parties back in the position they would have been in if the misrepresentation had not been made. So the remedy would be proportionate to the gravity of the misrepresentation and depend on what the insurer would have done if it had known the true facts. If the insurer would, for example, have charged more, then the claim would be reduced proportionately, or, if the insurer would have declined the risk altogether, then the insurer would not have to pay anything to the insured under the policy. The insurer would receive no remedy for innocent misrepresentations, as in such situations the consumer has behaved both honestly and reasonably. The consumer would therefore still be protected by the insurance policy and the insurance company would be required to pay out on any claims.

The impact of the Law Commission proposals on business insurance contracts would be less dramatic than on consumer contracts, as the duty of disclosure would continue to apply for businesses, although the duty would be modified to apply only to material facts (those that the insured knew or ought to have known the insurer wanted to know).

The Consumer Insurance (Disclosure and Representations) Bill is currently being considered by Parliament and contains the Law Commission's key recommendations.

## Subsequent falsity

A misrepresentation may occur where a statement was true when it was made, but because of a change of circumstances has become incorrect by the time it is acted upon. Keeping silent about the change can amount to misrepresentation.

### Key Case · With v O'Flanagan

In **With v O'Flanagan** (1936) a doctor was selling his medical practice. He told a prospective purchaser that it was worth £200 per annum, which was true at the time. The seller then fell ill, and was unable to keep up with his work. Patients left the practice, and by the time the contract of sale was signed, four months later, there was almost no income. It was held that the failure of the seller to tell the buyer what had happened amounted to a misrepresentation.

**Legal Principle**
Keeping silent about a change of circumstances can amount to a misrepresentation.

### Partial revelation

If one party makes a statement which is itself true, but which misrepresents the whole situation because of what is left unsaid, the statement may amount to a misrepresentation. In **Dimmock v Hallett** (1866) a seller of land told a prospective buyer that the farms on the land were let, but did not mention that the tenants were about to leave. Omitting this fact presented such a distorted picture of the true situation that the court held there had been a misrepresentation.

### Fiduciary relationship

Sometimes it is the existing relationship between the parties, rather than the type of contract concerned, which gives rise to a duty to disclose important facts about a contract. The main types of relationship accepted by the courts as imposing such a duty (called fiduciary relationships) are those between parent and child, solicitor and client, trustee and beneficiary, and principal and agent. The courts have stressed that this list is not exhaustive, and it is always open to a party to show that the relationship between him or her and the other contracting party is such that one party necessarily places some trust in the other, and that other therefore has influence over them.

### Voluntary assumption of responsibility

In **Banque Financière de la Cité v Westgate Insurance** (1989) the Court of Appeal suggested that a party might incur liability for remaining silent where the courts found:

- there was a voluntary assumption of responsibility by one party, and
- reliance on that voluntary assumption by the other.

This will be difficult to show in normal commercial negotiations. The court gave the example of a father who engaged an estate agent to advise his son regarding the purchase of a property. The estate agent would be regarded as having assumed responsibility to the son.

That interpretation of the law was accepted by the House of Lords in **Hamilton v Allied Domecq** (2007). The claimant owned rights to some mineral water. He had begun to produce bottled water but wanted to expand the business. He entered into negotiations with the defendants with a view to them investing in the company, marketing and distributing the product. Mr Beatty was employed by the defendants and carried out the contractual negotiations on their behalf. The claimant apparently thought it was very important that the product should be marketed first in the catering sector (hotels, restaurants and pubs), before being sold in shops, in order to establish the brand as a quality product. After the contract was signed, the product was initially distributed to shops and was never marketed to the catering sector. The business was not successful and the claimant commenced civil proceedings, arguing that Mr Beatty had mis-represented that his company would market the water in the catering sector first. The defendants contended that no such representations had ever been made. The House of Lords believed the defendants. It concluded that the defendants had effectively remained silent on this issue and, as there was no evidence they had voluntarily assumed responsibility towards the claimant, no liability had been incurred for this silence. Mr Beatty was not under a duty to tell the claimant about the defendants' distribution strategy when it differed from the one favoured by the claimant. The House of Lords noted:

> A failure on the part of Mr Beatty to speak might be regarded as morally questionable. But that is different from saying that he was under a legal duty to speak.

## A statement of fact

The statement must be one of fact; merely delivering an opinion will not create an actionable misrepresentation. In **Bisset** v **Wilkinson** (1927) Bisset was selling land in New Zealand to Wilkinson, who planned to use it for sheep farming. The land had not previously been used as a sheep farm, but during the negotiations Bisset expressed the view that if the land were worked properly, it could support 2,000 sheep. This was not actually the case.

On the face of it, the statement looked likely to constitute a misrepresentation; a farmer's description of the quality of his land sounds exactly like a statement of fact. However, in this case it was regarded as no more than a matter of opinion, on the grounds that both parties were aware that the land had never been used for sheep farming, and therefore neither could expect the other to know, as a matter of fact, how many sheep it could support.

There are some cases in which what looks like a statement of opinion will be considered by the courts to be a statement of fact. An example is where one party falsely states their opinion. For example, Ann wants to sell a clock to Ben, and says she thinks the clock is 200 years old, when in fact she knows it was made the week before. Her state of mind is a fact, and she is lying about it; therefore she is making a misrepresentation of fact. This rule was laid down in **Edgington** v **Fitzmaurice** (1885).

**Key Case**   Edgington v Fitzmaurice

In **Edgington** v **Fitzmaurice** (1885) a prospectus inviting loans from the public stated that the money would be used to improve the buildings and extend the business. The Court of Appeal held that this statement was a fraudulent misrepresentation of fact, since the person issuing the prospectus did not intend to use the money as suggested, and had therefore mis-represented the state of his mind. Bowen LJ commented that: 'The state of a man's mind is as much a fact as the state of his digestion.'

### Legal Principle
A statement about what a person is thinking is a statement of fact, and if it is false it can amount to a misrepresentation.

In addition, where circumstances are such that the party giving an opinion appears to be in possession of facts upon which the opinion can reasonably be based, that party is effectively stating that he or she **is** in possession of such facts, and if this is not the case, the statement will be a misrepresentation. In **Smith** v **Land and House Property Corporation** (1884) the claimants were trying to sell a hotel and claimed that it was 'let to Mr Frederick Fleck (a most desirable tenant)'. In fact, Mr Fleck had been seriously in arrears with his rent, and only paid 'by driblets under pressure'.

The Court of Appeal held that the description of Mr Fleck as 'a most desirable tenant' was not a mere expression of opinion. Since the claimants were clearly in a position to know Mr Fleck's record as a tenant, their statement suggested that they were unaware of any facts which could be regarded as making him an undesirable tenant, which was clearly untrue. The statement was therefore an actionable misrepresentation. Bowen LJ stated that:

> In a case where the facts are equally well known to both parties, what one of them says to the other is frequently nothing but an expression of opinion . . . But if the facts are not equally well known to both sides, then a statement of opinion by the one who knows the facts best involves very often a statement of material fact, for he impliedly states that he knows facts which justify his opinion.

To be an actionable misrepresentation, a statement must refer to an existing fact, not something in the future. The exception is a statement of intention, since this comes under the rule that a statement about the state of one's mind is a statement of fact: saying you intend to do something in the future implies that the intention already exists (**Edgington** v **Fitzmaurice**).

Mere 'sales talk' used to recommend a product to a potential customer will not amount to a statement of existing fact. In **Dimmock** v **Hallett** (1866) land for sale was described as 'fertile and improvable': this was held to be simply sales talk, and not a representation of fact. Clearly, this distinction will be difficult at times, but, in general, vague praise will be seen as mere sales talk, while more precise claims are likely to be viewed as misrepresentations of fact.

Statements of the law are not sufficient to amount to an actionable misrepresentation. In practice, it is not always clear when a statement is one as to law or as to fact. We will see in the next chapter that the distinction between mistakes of law and mistakes of fact has been removed by the House of Lords (p. 224). There is now a strong case for reconsidering this distinction in the context of misrepresentations.

## Inducement

The misrepresentation will only be actionable under contract law if it is at least one of the reasons for which the claimant entered into the contract. So if the claimant was not aware that the statement had been made, or knew it was untrue, or it did not affect the decision to enter into the contract, the misrepresentation will not be actionable. The untrue statement must have been made before or at the time of making the contract, because otherwise it cannot have induced the contract to be made. The representation may later be repeated in the contract.

Knowledge that another party's statement was untrue will only prevent that statement from being an actionable misrepresentation if it is genuine knowledge: mere suspicion, or possession of information which could reveal the lie if checked, are not enough. In **Redgrave** v **Hurd** (1881) a solicitor wanted to sell his law practice. He told the buyer that it was worth £300 a year and invited him to check this by inspecting the papers in his office. Had the buyer done this, he could have learnt that the practice was actually worth no more than £200 a year. However, the Court of Appeal held that the buyer had relied on the seller's word, and was entitled to do so, even if he had the means to discover that it was untrue.

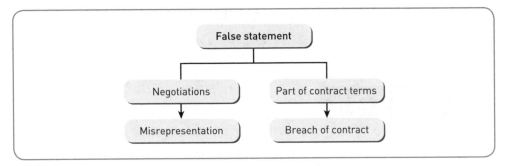

**Figure 9.1** False statement

Where the innocent party does not rely on the other's statement, and instead conducts their own investigations, or simply relies on their own judgement, the party making the misrepresentation will not be liable. In **Attwood** v **Small** (1838) the owners of a mine made rather exaggerated statements as to its earning capacity to the prospective buyers. The purchasers had these statements checked by their own surveyors, who wrongly reported that they were correct. The House of Lords held that the claimants had been induced to enter the contract by their surveyors' report and not by the vendor's statements; if they had believed those statements they would not have had them checked.

A fraudulent misrepresentation does not need to be the only reason why the innocent party entered the contract. In **Edgington** v **Fitzmaurice** (see p. 201 above) the claimant was induced to loan money to the company, partly by a misstatement in the prospectus and partly by his own (mistaken) belief that the contract would give him some rights over the company's property. The claimant admitted that he would not have lent the money if he had not believed he would gain rights in the property, but the court nevertheless held that the statement made in the prospectus was still an actionable misrepresentation.

The House of Lords suggested in **Standard Chartered Bank** v **Pakistan National Shipping Corp (No 2)** (2002) that the rule in **Edgington** v **Fitzmaurice** 'probably' applies only to fraudulent misrepresentations. Therefore, the existence of other negligent or irrational beliefs for entering into the contract alongside the misrepresentation might prevent the courts finding an actionable innocent or negligent misrepresentation. These different forms of misrepresentation are discussed below.

### Constructive knowledge

In some situations a party to a contract may not have actual knowledge of a misrepresentation but for public policy reasons they will be treated as if they did have that knowledge, known as constructive knowledge. The issue of people being placed on inquiry and avoiding constructive knowledge is discussed in detail in the context of undue influence (see pp. 276–8).

## Types of misrepresentation

There are four types of misrepresentation: fraudulent misrepresentation; negligent misrepresentation at common law; negligent misrepresentation under statute; and innocent misrepresentation. Which category a misrepresentation falls into depends on the state of mind of the person making the statement. The reason why the category matters is that the remedies for each type differ.

## Fraudulent misrepresentation

This is also known as the tort of deceit. It was defined by Lord Herschell in **Derry** v **Peek** (1889).

> **Key Case** Derry v Peek
>
> The case of **Derry** v **Peek** (1889) involved a company which had procured the passing of an Act of Parliament which allowed it to run horse-drawn tramcars in Plymouth and, subject to the consent of the Board of Trade, to run tramcars powered by steam. The company's directors thought that obtaining the consent of the Board of Trade was a mere formality, and their share prospectus falsely stated that they had authority to run steam-driven tramcars. Relying on this assertion, the claimant, among others, bought shares in the company.
>
> In fact the Board of Trade refused consent to steam-powered trams, and the company was wound up, with many investors losing money. The directors were sued in the tort of deceit. The House of Lords held that as the directors believed that the consent of the Board of Trade was more or less inevitable, given the passing of the Act, they were inaccurate, but not dishonest, and there was therefore no fraudulent misrepresentation. Their Lordships defined fraudulent misrepresentation as a false statement that is made '(i) knowingly, or (ii) without belief in its truth, or (iii) recklessly as to whether it be true or false'. In practice, a successful claim for fraudulent misrepresentation is rare because it is difficult to prove a defendant had one of these three states of mind, particularly where the defendant is a large, well-established business.
>
> **Legal Principle**
> If a person makes a false statement which he or she does not at the time believe to be true, this is a fraudulent misrepresentation.

## Negligent misrepresentation at common law

Negligent misrepresentation at common law was established by the House of Lords in **Hedley Byrne** v **Heller & Partners** (1964).

> **Key Case** Hedley Byrne v Heller & Partners
>
> The House of Lords stated, *obiter*, in **Hedley Byrne** v **Heller & Partners** that in certain circumstances damages may be recoverable in tort for a negligent misstatement which causes financial loss. The claimant company had entered into some advertising contracts, on behalf of another company, called Easipower. Under the agreement, the claimants were liable if Easipower failed to pay, so the claimants wanted to check Easipower's creditworthiness. They contacted Easipower's bankers, who provided a credit reference. Unfortunately, Easipower did in fact default in their payment, so the claimants sued the bankers.
>
> The claimants lost, because the reference was given with a disclaimer that it was 'without responsibility' (such a disclaimer would probably be inoperable today because of the

Unfair Contract Terms Act 1977). However, the House of Lords stated *obiter* that there could be liability for negligent misrepresentation on the normal principles of tort, where there was a 'special relationship' between the parties.

> **Legal Principle**
> The House of Lords stated, *obiter*, that there can be liability for negligent misrepresentation on the normal principles of tort, where there was a special relationship between the parties.

It is still not completely clear what precisely is a 'special relationship' but, broadly speaking, it appears that such a relationship will only arise where the maker of a false statement has some knowledge or skill relevant to the subject matter of the contract, and can reasonably foresee that the other party will rely on the statement. This was held to be the case in **Esso Petroleum Co Ltd v Mardon** (1976). Esso's sales representative, who had 40 years' experience in the industry, had assured the defendant that a new petrol station would be able to sell around 200,000 gallons of petrol a year. After this statement was made, the local authority insisted on changes to the plans of the site, and these meant the sales potential of the site was less than that detailed by the representative. Lack of care on Esso's behalf meant that this change was not communicated to the defendant, and in reliance on the representative's estimate, he signed a three-year tenancy agreement.

In fact petrol sales were less than half the estimate, and the defendant lost a lot of money. When Mardon fell into arrears with his rent, Esso sued him, so Mardon counter-claimed for damages for negligent misrepresentation. The court applied the **Hedley Byrne** principle and Mardon recovered on his counter-claim.

## Misrepresentation under statute

Section 2(1) of the Misrepresentation Act 1967 states:

> Where a person has entered into a contract after a misrepresentation has been made to him by another party thereto and as a result thereof he has suffered loss, then, if the person making the misrepresentation would be liable to [pay] damages in respect thereof had the misrepresentation been made fraudulently, that person shall be so liable notwithstanding that the misrepresentation was not made fraudulently, unless he proves that he had reasonable ground to believe and did believe up to the time the contract was made that the facts represented were true.

Put more concisely, the section provides that where one party enters into a contract as a result of a misrepresentation by the other, the innocent party can claim damages, unless the other party can prove that at the time the contract was made, they believed the statement to be true, and had reasonable grounds for that belief. This effectively creates a type of negligent misrepresentation, but with the burden of proof reversed so that the person making the statement has to prove they were not negligent.

The fact that the party making the misrepresentation bears a heavy burden of proof under s. 2(1) is illustrated by **Howard Marine and Dredging Co Ltd v A Ogden and Sons (Excavations) Ltd** [1978]. The claimants were involved in major excavation work and needed to dispose of the clay that they had dug up. Having decided to dump it in the sea, they negotiated to hire two seagoing barges. The carrying capacity of these barges was crucial, since it would dictate how quickly the work could be done. The barge owners' representative misrepresented their carrying capacity, saying it was higher than it actually was; he had got his information from an official register of ships, which was usually accepted as an accurate source of such information, but on this occasion was wrong. The correct information was on file at the barge owners' head office. The Court of Appeal held that there was liability under s. 2(1); the defendants had failed to prove they had not been negligent. According to Bridge LJ, 'the statute imposes an absolute obligation not to state facts which the representor cannot prove he had reasonable ground to believe'.

## Topical Issue

### The Spice Girls

A widely publicised case involving a s. 2(1) misrepresentation is that of **Spice Girls Ltd** v **Aprilia World Service** (2002). Spice Girls Ltd was a company formed to promote a pop group called the Spice Girls. At the start of 1998 there were five members of the group but one, Geri Halliwell, left on 29 May of that year. Aprilia is an Italian company which manufactures motorcycles and scooters for sale in Europe and the US. At the time of Ms Halliwell's departure the Spice Girls were in the final stages of a tour which, under a written agreement signed on 6 May 1998, was sponsored by Aprilia in return for the rights to use the Spice Girls' images and logos. The agreement referred to the group 'currently comprising' the five members and required the members to participate in filming a commercial for scooters which could be shown until March 1999. The commercial shoot took place on 4 May 1998.

Aprilia subsequently failed to pay for the advertising campaign and Spice Girls Ltd sued for payment. A counter-claim was brought by Aprilia that the contract had been induced by a misrepresentation. It argued that Ms Halliwell had declared her intention to leave the group before the agreement was signed and that Aprilia had not been told about this. As a result it had incurred expenditure and suffered loss by making the commercial shoot, and having to abandon plans for a limited edition of 'Spice Sonic' motor scooters featuring images of all five members. Aprilia asserted that, had it known of Ms Halliwell's intention to leave, it would not have signed the agreement.

The Court of Appeal ruled that by allowing a member of a singing group to participate in filming a television commercial, the group represented that she would remain a member for the period in which the commercial was to be used. As the group knew she intended to leave during that period it was a misrepresentation. Spice Girls Ltd were ordered to pay Aprilia damages.

## Innocent misrepresentation

Before **Hedley Byrne** v **Heller**, the phrase 'innocent misrepresentation' was used to describe all misrepresentations which were not fraudulent. The appearance of two classes of negligent misrepresentation, one in **Hedley Byrne** and the other in the Misrepresentation Act 1967, means that innocent misrepresentation now applies only to misrepresentations that are made entirely without fault. Where one party has entered into a contract because of the other's false statement, the other party can avoid liability for damages by proving that at the time the contract was made they believed the statement to be true, and had reasonable grounds for that belief – this is the statutory defence laid down in s. 2(1) of the Misrepresentation Act 1967.

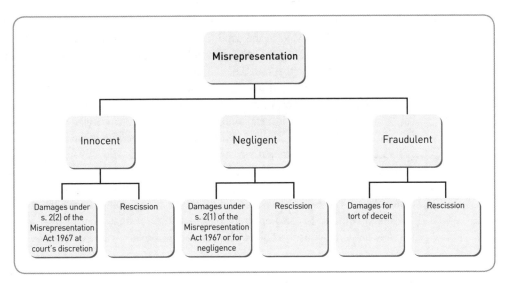

**Figure 9.2** Remedies for misrepresentation

## Topical Issue

### The horsemeat scandal

The recent publicity surrounding the finding of horsemeat for sale labelled as beef in major supermarkets caused outrage and controversy. If consumers wanted to seek a remedy for having bought some of these products they could look at the law of misrepresentation. The packaging of the products represented that the food was beef and this induced the buyer to enter the contract of sale. However, in practice it could prove difficult for consumers to prove that they purchased one of the relevant items as they are unlikely to have kept the receipts, and any award of damages is likely to be very small and inadequate to justify the time and effort of bringing such proceedings. Alongside any claim in contract law, they may have a claim for negligence or under consumer law.

# Remedies for misrepresentation

The effect of a misrepresentation is generally to make a contract voidable, rather than void, so the contract continues to exist unless and until the innocent party chooses to have it set aside by means of rescission. Where a contract is entirely executory, the innocent party may simply choose not to perform their side of the bargain; the misrepresentation prevents the other party from forcing the innocent party to perform. In some cases, damages may be available, either instead of or (in certain cases) as well as rescission.

## Rescission

Rescission is an equitable remedy, which sets the contract aside and puts the parties back in the position they were in before the contract was made. It is available for all four types of misrepresentation.

An injured party who decides to rescind the contract can do so by notifying the other party or, if this is not possible owing to the conduct of the defaulting party, by taking some other reasonable action to indicate the intention to rescind. In **Car and Universal Finance Co Ltd** *v* **Caldwell** (1965) the defendant sold and delivered a car, and was paid by cheque. The cheque bounced, by which time both the car and the buyer, whom we will call X, had disappeared. The defendant immediately notified the police and the Automobile Association, and asked the police to find the car. While the police were investigating, X sold the car to a car dealer, who knew that the car was not X's to sell. Finally, the car dealer sold the car to the claimants, who bought it in good faith. The Court of Appeal held that by contacting the police and the Automobile Association, the defendant had made his intention to rescind the contract sufficiently clear. As soon as he did this, the ownership of the car reverted to him. This meant that at the time the car was 'sold' to the claimants, the car dealer had no legal right to sell it, and so it did not belong to the claimants.

An injured party can also apply to the courts for a formal order of rescission, which provides that any property exchanged under the contract reverts to its former owner.

## Bars to rescission

Rescission is quite a drastic remedy as it brings the whole contract to an end. Restrictions have therefore been placed on its availability. The wronged party may lose the right to rescission when it is unreasonable or impossible to put the contracting parties back into their pre-contractual position. The four circumstances in which this will be the case are where:

- the innocent party affirms the contract (affirmation);
- there is a lapse of time;
- the parties cannot go back to their original, pre-contractual position; and
- rescission would deprive an innocent third party of rights acquired over the property which is the subject of the contract.

If rescission is barred the contract will continue to exist. The four bars to rescission will now be considered in detail.

### Affirmation

Once the innocent party becomes aware of a misrepresentation, it can choose to rescind or affirm the contract. For a contract to be affirmed, the innocent party must have full knowledge of the misrepresentation and either declare their intention to proceed with the contract (express affirmation) or do some act from which such an intention may reasonably be inferred (implied affirmation). For example, the representee's continued use of the subject matter of the contract may amount to an implied affirmation. In **Long** *v* **Lloyd** (1958) the purchaser of a lorry undertook a long journey after discovering serious defects in the lorry. It was held that he had affirmed the contract. A number of cases have been reported involving contracts for the sale of shares. A person who applies for and obtains shares upon the faith of a prospectus containing a misrepresentation is entitled to rescind the contract and to recover the price paid; but if after learning of the misrepresentation, he or she, for example, attempts to sell the shares, the right to rescind is lost, since these acts show an intention to treat the contract as still existing (**Re Hop and Malt Exchange and Warehouse Co, exp Briggs** (1866)). They are acts of ownership over the shares which are inconsistent with an intention to repudiate the contract.

If an innocent party, aware of the misrepresentation, expresses an intention to continue with the contract, or does something suggesting an intention to continue with it, that party is considered to have affirmed the contract; the innocent party will not be allowed to change his or her mind later and rescind unless the position of the other party was unaffected by the potential affirmation. In **Habib Bank Ltd** v **Nasira Tufail** (2006), Habib Bank sought to enforce a mortgage given by Nasira as security for her son's debts but induced by the son's misrepresentation. Nasira affirmed the mortgage but was later allowed to rescind because the position of the bank had not changed as a result of the potential affirmation. To prevent rescission the bank had to show that in reliance on Nasira's conduct it acted to its detriment.

Strictly speaking, simply doing nothing about a contract does not amount to affirmation but if, once the innocent party knows about the misrepresentation, he or she takes no action for a long period of time to rescind the contract, this may be treated as evidence that the contract has been affirmed. Lapse of time without any step towards repudiation being taken does not in itself constitute affirmation, but it may be treated as evidence of affirmation, and when the lapse of time is great it probably would in practice be treated as conclusive evidence that the contract has been affirmed.

## Lapse of time

In the case of non-fraudulent misrepresentation, lapse of time can operate as a separate bar to rescission where the innocent party has no knowledge of the misrepresentation and so cannot be treated as having implicitly affirmed the contract. Claimants are barred from rescinding a contract if a long time has passed after the contract was made. Where there is a fraudulent misrepresentation, lapse of time is merely evidence of affirmation (discussed above), as time only starts to run from the discovery of the truth.

In **Leaf** v **International Galleries** (1950) the claimant bought a painting of Salisbury Cathedral, which the seller said was by Constable. When, five years later, he tried to sell it, he discovered that it was not a Constable at all, and so he immediately applied for the contract to be rescinded. The original seller's assertion that it was by Constable was not a term of the contract, and there was no suggestion that it had been made fraudulently.

The Court of Appeal refused to grant rescission, stating that 'it behoves the purchaser either to verify or, as the case may be, to disprove the representation within a reasonable time, or else stand or fall by it'. It is important to remember that rescission is an equitable remedy, and the courts therefore have a discretion to refuse rescission where it is equitable to do so – in this case, for example, it might seem unfair to the original seller, who had not been trying to deceive the buyer and, five years on, had every reason to believe that the picture had been accepted. The position may well have been different if the misrepresentation had been fraudulent – in that case, the courts would probably have taken account of the time that lapsed between discovering the misrepresentation and the application for rescission, rather than the time since the contract was made.

In **Zanzibar** v **British Aerospace (Lancaster House) Ltd** (2000) the Zanzibar Government had purchased a jet from British Aerospace in 1992. It later failed to pay the full price of the plane which was repossessed and sold. Several years after the original purchase of the plane, the Zanzibar Government initiated proceedings against British Aerospace, claiming it had been induced to purchase the jet by virtue of representations made by British Aerospace as to the type of jet and its airworthiness, which were untrue. It sought to rescind the contract. The action was unsuccessful because the Zanzibar Government had delayed bringing the proceedings for several years after receiving the plane, so their right to rescission had been lost.

## Impossible to return to pre-contractual position

Rescission will not be ordered where it is impossible to return the parties to their original, pre-contractual position (known as counter-restitution). The most common practical reason why the parties cannot be restored to their original position is that the subject matter of the contract has been used up or destroyed. In **Vigers** v **Pike** (1842) the contract concerned a mine, and by the time rescission became an issue, it had been 'worked out' – there was nothing left in it to mine. Therefore rescission was impossible.

Substantial restitution must be possible. If most of the subject matter of the contract can be restored to the other party, or if it can be restored, but not in its original condition, a court may order the return of the property (rescission), along with financial compensation for the partial loss of value. This happened in **Erlanger** v **New Sombrero Phosphate Co** (1878) where the subject matter was again a mine, but where it had only been partially worked.

This issue was considered by the Court of Appeal in **Halpern** v **Halpern** (2007). The case concerned a dispute between four children over the division of their inheritance from their father. The dispute was referred to a Jewish arbitration procedure where a settlement was reached and it was agreed that all the documents produced at the arbitration should be destroyed. Unfortunately, the compromise agreement was not honoured and the claimant brought legal proceedings for its enforcement. At those proceedings, the defendant argued that the settlement agreement should be set aside because it was entered under duress. The claimant counter-argued that the remedy of rescission for duress was not available because the parties could not be returned to their pre-settlement position since all the documents produced at the arbitration hearing had been destroyed. The Court of Appeal accepted that an inability to make counter-restitution would block a remedy of rescission but it would be very rare that counter-restitution would be found to be impossible. The court approved the approach taken in **Erlanger** and suggested that the loss of the documents could be compensated financially.

## Third party rights

Rescission is not possible after a third party has acquired rights under the contract. The third party must be a bona fide purchaser for value, which means that he or she must have provided consideration and have been unaware of the earlier misrepresentation. In some ways this is simply a further example of the bar based on impossibility of restitution.

A common example of this limitation on rescission is where a car has been bought pretending that payment is with a valid cheque, when actually the cheque book has been stolen. Problems then arise if the fraudster sells on the car to an innocent third party. The contract between the fraudster and the original owner is merely voidable for misrepresentation and if the contract is not rescinded before the car is sold to the innocent third party, the courts will not return the car to the original owner. A contract is voidable for misrepresentation and not void. The title to the car obtained by the fraudster is valid until the contract has been rescinded, and any sale of it made before this to an innocent third party for valuable consideration cannot be defeated by the original owner. On the other hand, if the fraud makes the contract void at common law on the grounds of mistake (discussed in Chapter 10) no title passes to the fraudulent person and the latter can pass none to any third party, however innocent this third party may be.

For example, in **White** v **Garden** (1851) Parker bought fifty tons of iron from Garden by persuading him to take in payment a bill of exchange which had apparently been accepted by a person called Thomas of Rochester. Parker resold the iron to White, who acted in good faith and Garden delivered the iron to White using a barge to transport it. Garden discovered that the bill of exchange was worthless because there was no such person as Thomas of Rochester. He therefore removed part of the iron that was still in the barge. Garden was held liable to White for the value of the iron removed. The title to the iron had passed to Parker under a contract that was temporarily valid and had been passed to an innocent purchaser.

## All or nothing

Partial rescission is not possible. In **De Molestina** v **Ponton** (2002) the High Court stated that the victim of a misrepresentation was permitted to rescind the whole of a contract but not part of one. If the whole of the contract could not be rescinded then it could not be rescinded at all; instead an award of damages would generally be made. This is because rescission is supposed to put the parties back into the position they were in before the contract was made; it should not create a completely new agreement.

## Indemnity payment

The courts can order a payment of money known as an indemnity. It is important to note that this payment is not damages; it is designed to put the parties back into their former positions, and is only available for obligations necessarily and inevitably created by the contract.

The distinction between an indemnity and damages can be seen in **Whittington** v **Seale-Hayne** (1900). The claimant was a poultry breeder, who carried out his business on a farm leased from the defendants. The defendants had told the claimant that the premises were in a hygienic condition, although this statement was not contained in the lease and therefore not a term of the contract. In fact, the water supply was poisoned. As a result, the poultry died, the manager of the farm became seriously ill and the local council ordered the claimant to repair the drains. The claimant sued for his lost livestock, loss of profits, the cost of setting up the poultry farm and medical expenses, which amounted to £1,525. The defendants offered £20 to pay for the rent, rates and repairs to the drains (which under the terms of the lease the claimant was bound to pay). The court held that this was sufficient: the remainder of the claimant's claim did not inevitably arise under the terms of the lease, as the contract imposed no obligation to appoint a manager or stock the premises with poultry. Only expenses which inevitably arise from a contract will be compensated by indemnity (on the facts of this case, a different decision might be reached today if, for example, the defendants' statement was a negligent misrepresentation allowing an award of damages, but the case still provides valid authority on the distinction between damages and indemnity).

Where a misrepresentation is found to be fraudulent, an innocent party who rescinds the contract does not have to hand back whatever was received under the contract. So if someone defrauds an insurance company when taking out a policy, the insurance company is not only entitled to refuse payment of a claim against the policy, but also to keep any premiums paid.

## Damages

Clearly there will be some cases in which the innocent party suffers a loss that cannot be put right by rescission, even if an indemnity payment is ordered. Suppose a food manufacturer buys a packaging machine, having been assured that it will keep products fresh for six months. In fact, the packaging only gives a shelf-life of two months, and everything goes off before it can be sold. Being told that the buyers can give back the machine and get their money back is not going to provide a satisfactory solution – their loss can only be compensated for by damages.

Where a party is induced to enter a contract by misrepresentation, they have a right to damages for any loss, unless the misrepresentation is innocent, where an award of damages is at the judge's discretion (see below).

Damages for misrepresentation are calculated using the tort measure, rather than the contract measure. Contract damages are designed to put claimants in the position they would have held if the contract had been performed as agreed, so they aim to provide any (foreseeable) financial benefit that successful performance of the contract would have provided. Tort damages aim to put the claimant back in the position held before the tort was committed (which, in the case of damages for misrepresentation, means the position at the time of the false statement before the contract was made), by making good any losses caused by the misrepresentation.

It is often said that as a result, tort protects a bad bargain and contract a good one. To illustrate the difference, imagine that Ann makes the following bad bargain. She wants to buy a particular type of vase to complete her collection of Wedgwood. Ben claims to be selling such a vase, which would normally be worth £500; realising how much Ann wants it, Ben asks for £1,000 and Ann pays that sum. In fact, the vase is not a Wedgwood at all, and is only worth £100. On these facts, the damages for misrepresentation, calculated on the tort measure, would be £900 – Ann already has a vase worth £100, and receiving the £900 takes her as nearly as possible back to the position she started in. If contract damages were payable, she would receive £400 – if the contract had been performed as agreed (meaning if the misrepresentation had been true), she would have ended up with a vase worth £500, so the £400 tops up the value of the vase she has, to put her as near as possible to the position she would have been in. If, on the other hand, Ann had made a good bargain, contract damages would be more helpful. Suppose the vase would have been worth £1,500 if the representation was true, and Ann paid £1,000 for it, and then discovered that representation was false, and the vase was only worth £900. In tort, all she can recover is £100, whereas in contract she could recover £600.

## Remoteness of damages

The courts will make a more generous award of damages where there has been fraudulent misrepresentation and misrepresentation under s. 2(1) of the Misrepresentation Act 1967, than for common law negligent and innocent misrepresentations. This is because in the former they apply a generous remoteness test, whereas in the latter the remoteness test is narrower. In the case of **Doyle** v **Olby (Ironmongers) Ltd** (1969) it was stated that for fraudulent misrepresentation a person can be compensated for 'all the actual damage directly flowing from the fraudulent inducement'. It does not matter that the loss was not foreseeable; essentially all that is required is that the misrepresentation caused the loss. So a person claiming for fraudulent misrepresentation will frequently be able to claim for lost profits.

The House of Lords was concerned with the calculation of damages for fraudulent misrepresentation in **Smith New Court Securities Ltd** v **Scrimgeour Vickers (Asset Management) Ltd** (1996). The claimants had bought over £23 million of shares in the Italian company Ferranti at a price of 82.25p per share. They were induced to buy the shares by fraudulent representations that there were other possible purchasers actively in the market, which was not actually the case. At the date of the transaction, the shares were trading on the Stock Exchange at about 78p per share. Unknown to either party, the shares in the company were worth far less than the market price, because Ferranti had itself been the subject of a highly sophisticated fraud by a gentleman who had managed to sell Ferranti a worthless company for a large amount of money. Once this became known, the market in Ferranti shares took a steep downward turn and the claimants were forced to sell their shares at a loss in excess of £11 million.

The question before the House of Lords was whether the claimants' damages should be restricted to 4.25p per share which they had paid above the market price, or whether they could recover the whole of the loss they had suffered, including the much bigger loss caused by the hidden defect in the shares. The House held that the claimants could recover the larger sum, stating that the damages had to be assessed to include all the losses flowing naturally from the original fraud.

There has been much debate as to the appropriate remoteness test for damages awarded under s. 2(1) of the Misrepresentation Act 1967. In **Royscot Trust Ltd** v **Rogerson** (1991) the Court of Appeal held that the same remoteness test should apply as for fraudulent misrepresentation. The result is that the measure of damages under s. 2(1) is now as good as where there is a fraud, without the difficulties of having to prove a fraud. In **Smith New Court Securities Ltd** v **Citibank** the House of Lords appeared to have reservations about the correctness of this approach.

The remoteness test for damages for common law negligent misrepresentation is that the loss must have been a reasonably foreseeable consequence of the misrepresentation (**The Wagon Mound (No 1)**). Unlike the position with regard to fraudulent misrepresentation, it is clear that liability is limited to the position assessed at the date of the wrong. The same remoteness test applies to awards of damages for innocent misrepresentation.

## Damages or rescission?

Rescission is available to the innocent party regardless of which category the misrepresentation falls into. In the past, damages were only available for fraudulent misrepresentation. The case of **Hedley Byrne** made it clear that damages were available for negligent misrepresentation at common law, and the Misrepresentation Act 1967 further extended the availability of damages. First, under s. 2(1), a misrepresentor will be liable in damages unless they can prove reasonable grounds for believing the statement to be true. Secondly, under s. 2(2), the court has a discretion to award damages instead of rescission where the misrepresentation was not fraudulent 'if of the opinion that it would be equitable to do so'.

The practical result seems to be that there is a right to damages (assuming loss can be proved) for fraudulent and both types of negligent misrepresentation. Where a misrepresentation is innocent, the award of damages is at the court's discretion.

**Table 9.1** Misrepresentation and remedies

| | Fraudulent misrepresentation: **Derry** v **Peek** | Negligent misrepresentation at common law: **Hedley Byrne** v **Heller** | Misrepresentation under s. 2(1) Misrepresentation Act 1967 | Innocent misrepresentation |
|---|---|---|---|---|
| Rescission | Yes | Yes | Yes | Yes |
| Indemnity payment | Yes | Yes | Yes | Yes |
| Damages | Yes. Liable for all the actual damage directly flowing from the misrepresentation | Yes. Liable for any loss that was a reasonably foreseeable consequence of the misrepresentation | Yes. Liable for all the actual damage directly flowing from the misrepresentation | Yes. Damages instead of rescission can be awarded under s. 2(2) of the Misrepresentation Act 1967 |

## Misrepresentation and terms

Section 1 of the Misrepresentation Act 1967 provides that where a misrepresentation becomes a term of the contract, the innocent party may bring an action for both misrepresentation and breach of contract.

## Excluding liability for misrepresentation

### Topical Issue

**Dishonest salesmen**

Companies need to make sure that their salesmen behave honestly and do not go beyond honest sales patter in their desire to earn commissions. This issue arose in **BSkyB** v **EDS** (2010). In 2000 EDS had successfully tendered to design and implement a new computer software system, known as a customer relationship management system (CRM) for BSkyB. BSkyB agreed to pay EDS £46 million for the system. The project ran into difficulties and in 2004 BSkyB sued EDS alleging that EDS had made fraudulent misrepresentations when it tendered for the contract which meant that EDS was selected to carry out the work instead of competing bidders. The contract between the parties contained a clause that EDS's liability under the contract was limited to £30 million. BSkyB claimed that it had actually suffered £710 million of damage as a result of the misrepresentations. If the misrepresentations were merely innocent or negligent the limitation clause would apply, but if the misrepresentation was fraudulent then the limitation clause could not apply. The trial lasted for a full court year, over 500,000 documents were produced and 70 witnesses called. The final judgment was almost 500 pages long and was handed down 18 months after the trial had ended.

It is very difficult, in practice, to prove fraudulent misrepresentation, particularly by an established and respected company. However, in the case the High Court allowed the claim, accepting that EDS had fraudulently misrepresented the timescales in which it could deliver the CRM. An EDS employee, Joe Galloway, had been the lead salesman on the bid. Galloway's credibility had been destroyed in the witness box. He was found to have lied about his qualifications. He had stated repeatedly that he had received an MBA from Concordia College on St Johns Island in the US Virgin Islands. He lied that he had attended tutorials at the College, because in fact it has no buildings on St Johns and provides online degrees to anyone who makes an application and pays the fee. The barrister for BSkyB exposed the lie during cross-examination by demonstrating that his own pet dog, Lulu, had made an online application for a degree from Concordia College and graduated with marks higher than those awarded to Joe Galloway. He was subsequently sacked by EDS during the course of the trial. The trial judge stated:

> Joe Galloway's credibility was completely destroyed by his perjured evidence over a prolonged period.

The judge found that Joe Galloway, who was the main person involved in calculating the time estimates for how long it would take EDS to deliver the CRM system, had no honest belief in the timeframes he advanced to BSkyB. He had approached the time estimates in a cavalier manner and ignored the need for analysis to establish whether EDS could realistically deliver the CRM in the nine months timescale requested by BSkyB. As a result, EDS could not provide any paperwork to show how it had calculated the time estimates. Galloway had simply proffered timescales which he thought BSkyB wanted, knowing that he had no reasonable basis for these time estimates. The trial court judge considered that his behaviour was more than just careless or grossly careless, it was dishonest. He intended BSkyB to rely on these timeframes and BSkyB did so. The requirements for fraudulent misrepresentation had been made out. The case highlights the importance of salesmen, when delivering their sales pitch, to behave honestly because exaggerated sales talk could amount to a misrepresentation.

In **AXA Sun Life** v **Campbell Martin** (2011) the Court of Appeal observed that any exclusion of liability for misrepresentation has to be clearly stated. Various techniques can be used to try and avoid liability for a misrepresentation. The contract might state that:

- no representations were made before the contract was signed;
- no representations were relied upon (a non-reliance clause);
- liability for a misrepresentation is excluded or limited; and
- the written contract contains the entire agreement (an entire agreement clause).

A non-reliance clause operates as an estoppel, preventing a subsequent claim for misrepresentation by the representee. In **Springwell Navigation Corp** v **JP Morgan Chase Bank** (2010) the Court of Appeal held that where parties to a contract agree that a certain state of affairs forms the basis of the transaction, they are estopped from asserting that the true facts were different.

Under common law, for public policy reasons, it is not possible to exclude liability for fraudulent misrepresentation: **S Pearson and Son Ltd** v **Dublin Corporation** (1907). Liability for other forms of misrepresentation is regulated by legislation. The Misrepresentation Act 1967, s. 3 provides:

If a contract contains a term which would exclude or restrict—

(a) any liability to which a party to a contract may be subject by reason of any misrepresentation made by him before the contract was made; or

(b) any remedy available to another party to the contract by reason of such a misrepresentation, that term shall be of no effect except in so far as it satisfies the requirement of reasonableness as stated in section 11(1) of the Unfair Contract Terms Act 1977; and it is for those claiming that the term satisfies that requirement to show that it does.

Thus, the exclusion clause will only be effective if the person seeking to rely on it can prove that the clause was reasonable at the time the contract was made. The meaning of 'reasonableness' is considered in the Unfair Contract Terms Act 1977, s. 11, and discussed at p. 171.

This legislation was applied in **Walker** v **Boyle** (1982). The seller of the house told the buyer that there were no disputes regarding the boundaries of the property. Unknown to the seller, this was not true. The innocent misrepresentation appeared to entitle the buyer to rescind the contract, but the contract contained a clause stating that 'no error, mis-statement or omission in any preliminary answer concerning the property . . . shall annul the sale'. The court granted rescission, stating that the clause was unreasonable.

In addition, a clause which purports to limit liability for misrepresentation in a consumer contract may be voidable as an unfair term under the Unfair Terms in Consumer Contracts Regulations 1999 (discussed at p. 174).

## Entire agreement clauses and misrepresentation

Some written contracts have a provision that the written document contains all the terms of the contract. This provision is known as an 'entire agreement clause' (see p. 142). Where a contract contains an 'entire agreement clause', which expressly states that the only terms binding on the parties are terms contained in the actual agreement, any pre-contractual negotiations or even promises are taken to fall outside the contract. In recent cases the courts have demonstrated a desire to limit the operation of entire agreement clauses. Such a clause will only avoid liability for misrepresentation if it is broadly drafted to include a non-reliance clause stating that the parties have not relied on any representations when entering into the contract. In addition, no contractual clauses will usually succeed in excluding liability for fraudulent misrepresentations.

In **AXA Sun Life** v **Campbell Martin** (2011) AXA had entered into a contract with Campbell Martin on AXA's standard terms. This included an entire agreement clause in the following terms:

> This agreement and the schedules and documents referred to herein constitute the entire agreement and understanding between you and us in relation to the subject matter thereof.
>
> Without prejudice to any variation as provided in clause 1.1, this agreement shall supersede any prior promises, agreements, representations, undertakings or implications whether made orally or in writing between you and us relating to the subject matter of this agreement but this will not affect any obligations in any such prior agreement which are expressed to continue after termination.

When the contract was terminated, AXA brought a claim for the return of money it alleged was owed by Campbell Martin under the contract. As part of its defence, Campbell Martin argued that AXA had made a number of misrepresentations which had induced them to enter into the contract. In response, AXA relied on the entire agreement clause which, it argued, prevented the defendants from relying on the misrepresentations alleged in their defences. The Court of Appeal unanimously held that the entire agreement clause did not exclude liability for misrepresentations, even though the clause referred expressly to 'representations'. The entire agreement clause was concerned with agreements rather than misrepresentations. Although the word 'representations' did appear in the entire agreement clause it was surrounded by the words 'promises, agreements . . . undertaking or implications' which essentially equate to forms of agreement, rather than misrepresentations. Therefore, it was held that the reference to 'representations' in the entire agreement clause was a reference to statements which were agreed upon and would have formed part of the contract had it not been for the entire agreement clause; it was not a reference to all forms of representation generally and would not include an inaccurate statement made from one party to another. To encompass 'representations for all purposes' the language used must go further and express clearly the parties' intentions to this effect.

As far as possible the courts will respect the agreement that the parties have chosen to enter. In **Springwell Navigation Corporation** v **JP Morgan Chase Bank** (2010) the Court of Appeal stated:

> If A and B enter into a contract then, unless there is some principle of law or statute to the contrary, they are entitled to agree what they like [. . .] there is no legal principle that states that parties cannot agree to assume that a certain state of affairs is the case at the time the contract

is concluded or has been so in the past, even if that is not the case, so that the contract is made upon the basis that the present or past facts are as stated and agreed by the parties.

While an entire agreement clause is not a traditional exemption or limitation clause, its impact can potentially be much the same with regard to avoiding liability for misrepresentation. In **Raiffeisen Zentralbank Osterreich** *v* **Royal Bank of Scotland** (2010) the High Court stated, the key question was to decide whether the clause was simply trying to make clear the basis on which the parties were entering the contract to avoid any uncertainty or whether the clause 'attempts to rewrite history or parts company with reality'.

If the clause is rewriting history and the parties are not of equal bargaining power, it will be viewed as attempting to exclude liability for misrepresentation and will be interpreted as subject to s. 3 of the Misrepresentation Act 1967 and its requirement of reasonableness:

> If sophisticated commercial parties agree, in terms of which they are both aware, to regulate their future relationships by prescribing the basis on which they will be dealing with each other and what representations they are or are not making, a suitably drafted clause may properly be regarded as establishing that no representations (or none other than honest belief) are being made or are intended to be relied on . . . [P]er contra, to tell the man in the street that the car you are selling him is perfect and then agreeing that the basis of your contract is that no representations have been made or relied on, may be nothing more than an attempt retrospectively to alter the character and effect of what has gone before, and in substance an attempt to exclude or restrict liability.

In **AXA** the Court of Appeal stated that while an entire agreement clause could be subject to the UCTA reasonableness test 'in appropriate circumstances', it will not automatically be deemed unreasonable. The reasonableness of the clause is a question of fact and degree. The court's findings will depend upon the nature and bargaining power of the contracting parties, the type of transaction and the precise wording of the entire agreement clause. The relevant clause in **AXA** was required to pass the reasonableness test, and on the facts it did satisfy that test. A contract clause can exclude liability for misrepresentation if the contract clearly states this is the parties' intention.

Therefore, for an entire agreement clause to exclude liability for misrepresentation, express words to this effect will have to be used to show the clear intention of the parties.

# Reform

The Law Commission has published a paper entitled *Consumer redress for misleading and aggressive practices* (2011). It considered that the current law on misrepresentation left a gap, leaving consumers vulnerable to misleading and aggressive sales practices. It suggested that legislation should be passed imposing liability on traders where the overall presentation of a product or service would be likely to mislead the average consumer. Where the misleading or aggressive practice was a significant factor in the consumer's decision to enter into the contract or make the payment he or she would be entitled to a remedy. The Law Commission considered that the remedies available following a misrepresentation are too uncertain. While the remedy of rescission is essentially a right to unwind the contract (putting the person in the position they were in before they entered into the contract), it is unclear how quickly the right must be exercised or how far the consumer must return goods or services. Where the right to rescission has been lost, it is unclear what other remedy the consumer might be entitled to. As a result, it is recommending that legislation should be passed laying down clearer remedies for misrepresentations made to a consumer. The Law Commission recommended that the main remedy should involve 'unwinding' the contract. This right would normally last for three months. After that period, consumers would have a right to receive a discount on the price along with damages for consequential loss, distress and inconvenience. Ultimately it is hoped that these rights would be included in a Consumer Bill of Rights.

## Answering questions

Shirley wishes to set up an airplane service for business people flying between London and Rome. She answers an advertisement in a trade paper for the sale of a light aircraft. Two weeks before completing the contract Shirley is advised by the seller, Dorianne, that the fuel capacity of the aircraft will enable her to fly between the two cities without the need to refuel. She purchases the airplane for £500,000 and sets up her business, Exec Jet Ltd. On a trial flight to Rome, she is forced to land and refuel before she reaches her destination. Further investigation reveals that the aircraft is only suitable for short flights and does not have the capacity to fly the distance she requires on a single tank of fuel. As a result Shirley is forced to abandon her business plans. The aircraft is worth £100,000 less than Shirley paid for it and, in addition, she has incurred considerable expense in setting up her business, which was expected to earn a substantial profit.

Advise Shirley whether she can recover any or all of her losses. *Oxford*

The main issue here is misrepresentation: Dorianne has made an untrue statement of fact which induced Shirley to enter the contract. Once you have established this, you need to look at the possible remedies. First, Shirley could rescind the contract, but this alone would not go far to solve her problems; she would get her £500,000 back, but would still have lost both the money spent on setting up the business and the potential profit. Nor would an indemnity be any help, as the case of **Whittington** shows, because none of her other losses arose inevitably from her contract with Dorianne.

As a result, Shirley will want to claim damages, and her ability to do this will depend to some extent on the type of misrepresentation. If Dorianne made the misrepresentation innocently, Shirley will not be able to claim damages as of right. However, the Misrepresentation Act 1967 and the case of **Howard Marine** make it clear that it will be difficult for Shirley to prove negligent misrepresentation. If she cannot, the court has a discretion to award damages where it would be equitable to do so, so Shirley may succeed in this claim. If the misrepresentation was made fraudulently or negligently under the Misrepresentation Act 1967 (you should briefly define each type), Shirley definitely will be able to claim damages.

You now need to consider how much of her loss she will be able to claim in damages, bearing in mind that damages for misrepresentation are calculated using the tort measure, so the aim is to put Shirley in the position she held before the contract was made.

You should also consider the possibility that Dorianne's statement may be a term of the contract (applying the common law rules on incorporation), and point out that if this were the case, Dorianne's breach of that term would allow Shirley to reclaim all her foreseeable losses, because of the fact that contract damages are calculated to put her in the position she would have enjoyed had the contract been performed as agreed.

Critically assess the remedies available to a party who has made a contract on the basis of a misrepresentation.

The first thing to note here is that this question is very specific. However much you know about what misrepresentation is, if you know very little about the **remedies** for misrepresentation, then choose another question. You can pick up some marks at the beginning of your essay for a **brief** definition of misrepresentation, including an explanation of the different types, as defined in the Misrepresentation Act 1967 and common law, but you must devote the bulk of your essay to remedies.

Note too that your examination is required to be critical – merely listing the remedies is not going to get you a good mark. As well as pointing out any problems with remedies for rescission – such as the apparent unfairness in **Leaf** – you could, for example, contrast the availability of rescission and the availability and measure of damages for misrepresentation with those for breach of contract, pointing out the way in which tort protects a bad bargain and contract a good one.

# Summary of Chapter 9

## What is a misrepresentation?

A misrepresentation is an untrue statement of fact by one party which has induced the other to enter into the contract. For a misrepresentation to be actionable, it has to fulfil three requirements: there must be an untrue statement; it must be a statement of fact, not mere opinion; and it must have induced the innocent party to enter the contract.

## An untrue statement

An untrue statement of fact must have been made by the other contracting party (or by their agent acting within the scope of their authority), or the other contracting party must have known of the untrue statement. Silence does not usually amount to a misrepresentation. There are, however, five types of situation where the law imposes a duty to disclose information. To remain silent about a material fact in any of these circumstances can therefore amount to a misrepresentation.

### Contracts requiring utmost good faith

Where a contract requires utmost good faith, such as a contract for insurance, failure to disclose a matter regarding which utmost good faith is required allows the innocent party to rescind the contract, though damages are not available.

### Subsequent falsity

A misrepresentation may occur where a statement was true when it was made, but owing to a change of circumstances has become incorrect by the time it is acted upon. Keeping silent about the change can amount to a misrepresentation: **With v O'Flanagan** (1936).

### Partial revelation

If one party makes a statement which is itself true, but which misrepresents the whole situation because of what is left unsaid, the statement may amount to a misrepresentation: **Dimmock v Hallett** (1866).

### Fiduciary relationship

Sometimes it is the existing relationship between the parties, rather than the type of contract concerned, which gives rise to a duty to disclose important facts about a contract.

*Voluntary assumption of responsibility*

One contracting party can occasionally incur liability for remaining silent when he or she has accepted responsibility for the other party.

## A statement of fact

The statement must be one of fact; merely delivering an opinion will not create an actionable misrepresentation: **Bisset** *v* **Wilkinson** (1927). There are some cases in which what looks like a statement of opinion will be considered by the courts to be a statement of fact. An example is where one party falsely states their opinion: **Edgington** *v* **Fitzmaurice** (1885). Mere 'sales talk' used to recommend a product to a potential customer will not amount to a statement of existing fact.

## Inducement

The misrepresentation will only be actionable under contract law if it is at least one of the reasons for which the claimant entered into the contract: **Redgrave** *v* **Hurd** (1881).

*Constructive knowledge*

In some situations, a party to a contract may not have actual knowledge of a misrepresentation but for public policy reasons they will be treated as if they did have that knowledge, known as constructive knowledge.

### Types of misrepresentation

There are four types of misrepresentation:

## Fraudulent misrepresentation

A party makes a fraudulent misrepresentation if they make a false statement and, at the time of making it, do not believe it to be true: **Derry** *v* **Peek** (1889).

## Negligent misrepresentation at common law

Negligent misrepresentation at common law was established by the House of Lords in **Hedley Byrne** *v* **Heller & Partners** (1964). The House of Lords stated, *obiter*, that there could be liability for negligent misrepresentation on the normal principles of tort, where there was a 'special relationship' between the parties.

## Misrepresentation under statute

Section 2(1) of the Misrepresentation Act 1967 provides that where one party enters into a contract as a result of a misrepresentation by the other, the innocent party can claim damages, unless the other party can prove that at the time the contract was made they believed the statement to be true, and had reasonable grounds for that belief.

## Innocent misrepresentation

Where one party has entered into a contract because of the other's false statement, the other party can avoid liability for damages by proving that at the time the contract was made they believed the statement to be true, and had reasonable grounds for that belief – according to s. 2(1) of the Misrepresentation Act 1967.

## Remedies for misrepresentation

The effect of a misrepresentation is generally to make a contract voidable, rather than void, so the contract continues to exist unless and until the innocent party chooses to have it set aside by means of rescission.

## Rescission

Rescission is an equitable remedy, which sets the contract aside and puts the parties back in the position they were in before the contract was made. It is available for all four types of misrepresentation.

## Indemnity payment

The courts can order a payment of money known as an indemnity. This payment is designed to put the parties back into their former positions.

## Bars to rescission

There are some circumstances in which it is unreasonable or impossible to put the contracting parties back into their pre-contractual position, and in these cases the injured party may lose the right to rescission. The four circumstances in which this may occur are where the innocent party affirms the contract; there is a lapse of time; the parties cannot return to their pre-contractual position and where rescission would deprive an innocent third party of acquired rights.

## Damages

Where a party is induced to enter a contract by misrepresentation, they have a right to damages for any loss, unless the misrepresentation is innocent, where an award of damages is at the judge's discretion (see below). Damages for misrepresentation are calculated using the tort measure, rather than the contract measure.

### Remoteness of damages

The courts will make a more generous award of damages where there has been fraudulent misrepresentation and misrepresentation under s. 2(1) of the Misrepresentation Act 1967 than for common law negligent and innocent misrepresentations.

# Reading list

Beale, 'Points on misrepresentation' (1995) 111 Law Quarterly Review 385

Brinkworth and Powell, 'Fraudulent misrepresentation: dead or simply resting?' (1992) 13 Business Law Review 3

Cartwright (2002) *Misrepresentation*, London: Sweet and Maxwell

Hooley, 'Damages and the Misrepresentation Act 1967' (1991) 107 Law Quarterly Review 547

Soyer, 'Reforming the assured's pre-contractual duty of utmost good faith in insurance contracts for consumers: are the Law Commissions on the right track?' [2008] Journal of Business Law 385

# Chapter 10
## Mistake

### This chapter explains:

that where one party (or both) is mistaken about some aspect of the contract, there will sometimes be no valid contract. In law there are two types of mistake:

- common mistake, where both parties make the same mistake; and
- cross-purposes mistake, where each party has a different view of the contractual situation.

In order to have an impact on the contract, the mistake must:

- precede the contract; and
- induce the contract.

Where the mistake relates to a written document there are two special remedies:

- *non est factum*; and
- rectification.

As we have seen, vitiating factors operate to prevent a contract being fully binding where one party has not given genuine consent of their own free will. From this it might appear obvious that where one party (or both) is mistaken about some aspect of the contract being entered into, that party cannot be said to be consenting to it – they think the consent is to something different. However, the common law rules of contract take a rather restrictive view of the sort of mistake which negatives consent to, and there are many types of mistake which, to the ordinary person, would suggest that one party was not truly agreeing to the contract, but which would not in law prevent the contract from being legally binding.

In the past, separate rules developed in equity that ran alongside the common law rules. Where a contract was found to be valid in common law despite the existence of a mistake, equity could intervene and render the contract voidable. This approach has now been rejected by the Court of Appeal in **Great Peace Shipping Ltd** v **Tsavliris Salvage (International) Ltd** (2001), as the court considered that this amounted to equity conflicting with the common law rather than supplementing it. There had been confusion as to when equity could intervene in practice. As a result this area of law is now purely governed by the common law.

## General principles

There are two types of mistake: common mistake and cross-purposes mistake. We will discuss each in turn, but the following general rules apply to both.

### Objective principle

As always in contract law, when deciding whether or not there has been a mistake sufficient to make the contract void the courts will look at the facts objectively. They do not ask what the parties themselves believed they were agreeing to, but what an onlooker would have thought each was agreeing to.

**Key Case**  Smith v Hughes

In **Smith** v **Hughes** (1871) the defendant wanted to buy some old oats – for some reason new ones were of no use to him. The claimant apparently knew this, but still sold him new oats. There was no fraud, and the claimant had not done anything to suggest to the defendant that the oats were old but, nevertheless, that was what the defendant believed he was buying. The court held that the contract was binding, despite the defendant's mistake, because any reasonable onlooker would conclude that the parties were in agreement about what was being sold. Blackburn J said:

> If whatever a man's real intention may be, he so conducts himself that a reasonable man would believe that he was assenting to the terms proposed by the other party, and that other party upon that belief enters into the contract with him, the man thus conducting himself would be equally bound as if he had intended to agree to the other party's terms.

**Legal Principle**
When deciding whether or not there has been a mistake sufficient to make the contract void, the courts will look at the facts objectively.

## The mistake must precede the contract

In order to make a contract void, a mistake must be made before the contract is completed. In **Amalgamated Investment & Property Co Ltd** v **John Walker & Sons Ltd** (1977) a contract was made for the sale of a warehouse for £1,710,000. The sellers knew that the purchasers were buying the warehouse with the intention of redeveloping it. The day after the contract was signed, the Department of the Environment made the property a listed building (a device used to protect buildings of important historical interest from inappropriate alterations). This made it more difficult for the buyers to get permission to redevelop; without such permission, the warehouse would only have been worth £210,000. Neither party had been aware that the Department of the Environment was going to list the building.

The Court of Appeal held that the contract was valid; at the time of the agreement both parties were perfectly correct in their belief that the building was not listed, so there was no operative mistake (in fact it is quite likely that the mistake made in this case would not have made the contract void even if it had been made before the contract was completed).

## Mistake must induce the contract

A mistake can only negate consent if it induced the mistaken party to enter into the contract. If a party thinks there is a possibility that they may be mistaken, but takes the risk, or is indifferent about that particular matter, the validity of the contract will not be affected.

## Mistake of fact or law

In the past, only a mistake of fact could affect the validity of a contract; a mistake of law was not sufficient. Thus, if you made a mistake as to the cost of an item in a shop, you might expect the shop to refund the excess amount when you discovered the mistake. However, in law, the shop would only have been obliged to refund you if you had made a mistake of fact (you thought the price was £50 when in fact it was £5). It would not have been obliged to refund the money if you had made a mistake of law (you thought you had to pay VAT on top of the price of the item). The Law Commission has pointed out in its report, *Restitution: Mistakes of Law and Ultra Vires Public Authority Receipts and Payments*, that this distinction was 'notoriously difficult to make' and led to a 'perceived unfairness'. The House of Lords abolished the distinction in 1998 in **Kleinwort Benson Ltd** v **Lincoln City Council** (1999). It ruled that the remedy of restitution would now be available where there had been a mistake of law (for a discussion of restitution, see p. 374).

**Key Case**    Kleinwort Benson Ltd v Lincoln City Council

In **Kleinwort Benson Ltd** v **Lincoln City Council** a bank had paid money to local authorities under certain financial transactions which had been thought to be legal, but were later ruled by the courts to be illegal. The banks had made a mistake of law rather than fact in handing over this money, but the House of Lords accepted that the local authorities should pay the money back. They justified the overturning of the established principle that mistake of law was insufficient for these purposes, on the ground that the distinction between a mistake of law and a mistake of fact was not always clear-cut, and that in order to do justice the money should be paid back. Other Commonwealth countries had already abolished the rule against mistakes of law and no such rule existed in many European systems. The experience of these countries showed that the fear of a flood of litigation resulting was unfounded so the House of Lords was prepared to adopt this reform.

**Legal Principle**
The remedy of restitution is available for a mistake of law.

One of the first cases to explore the implications of the House of Lords' ruling in **Kleinwort Benson Ltd _v_ Lincoln City Council** was **Nurdin _v_ Peacock** (1999). In that case the claimant had leased premises belonging to the defendant. The lease provided that an annual rental had to be paid of £207,000, which was payable in quarterly instalments. An additional £59,000 rent had to be paid for the fourth and fifth years of the lease. There was to be a rent review at the end of the fifth year, when the rent could be increased. No rent review took place, so the rent due reverted to the earlier £207,000. Nevertheless, the defendant continued to demand, and the claimant continued to pay, rent at the higher rate which had been payable in years four and five. Two years later, the claimant realised his mistake and informed the defendant that he would pay only at the lower rate and would set off the overpayments already made against future rent. Soon afterwards, the claimant received legal advice to continue paying at the higher rate and without set-off until the matter had been resolved through arbitration or through the courts, because otherwise the lease might be terminated. The legal advice was that, if successful in those proceedings, the claimant would be entitled to a full refund of any overpayment. The claimant thus paid, in May 1997, the quarterly rental at the higher rate. In fact the claimant had no legal right to recover that over-payment since he was aware that it might not have been due. In the proceedings, the claimant sought to recover all the overpayments. The court had no difficulty in ordering repayment of the excess payments made during the first two years before the claimant realised that he had made a mistake. These payments had been made under a mistake of fact and had to be paid back. The difficult issue was the payment made in May 1997. At that time the claimant was no longer suffering from a mistake of fact, as he knew that the money was not due. The claimant sought to recover the overpayment made in May 1997 on the basis that he had been labouring under a mistake of law, namely that he would be entitled to recover that overpayment. The defendant counter-argued that money paid under a mistake of law could only be reclaimed if the mistake consisted of the claimant believing he was liable in law to make the payment. This argument of the defendant was rejected by the High Court. The money had been made under a mistake of law and, therefore, since **Kleinwort Benson Ltd _v_ Lincoln City Council**, it was recoverable. It made no difference that the claimant's mistake was not about his liability to make the payment but about his right to recover the payment, since it was undesirable for the issue of recoverability to turn on an analysis as to the precise nature of the mistake. The key issue was that the payment would not have been made but for the mistake of law.

While this is a sensible approach, the decision does look peculiar if its logic is followed through. The legal advice to the claimant was that overpayment in May 1997 was recoverable. The advice was wrong. The claimant followed that advice. Therefore, the claimant paid under a mistake of law. Therefore, the money was recoverable as paid under a mistake of law. So in actual fact, the advice was right. So, no mistake was made. The court held that that unusual logical problem did not stand in the way of the conclusion it had reached.

The principle in **Kleinwort Benson** has been applied by the House of Lords where a company, because of a mistake of law, paid too much tax: **Deutsche Morgan Grenfell Group plc** v **Inland Revenue Commissioners** (2006).

# Common mistake

This is also known as identical mistake, shared mistake or mutual mistake. In this situation, both parties make the same mistake – for example, if Ann buys a painting from Ben, which both parties believe is by Picasso, but which is in fact a fake, they have made a common mistake.

## Application of the doctrine of common mistake

A contract will not be void for common mistake if the mistake is due to the fault of one of the parties. In addition, if the contract allocates the risk of the mistake occurring on one of the parties then the doctrine of mistake will not apply. Only if the contract is silent on the point is there scope for invoking mistake. For example, a contract may contain a warranty for the existence of a state of affairs. If the parties have made a mistake and the state of affairs does not actually exist, there is a breach of contract (the parties having allocated the risk to the party providing the guarantee), and the legal doctrine of mistake does not apply. A case on this point is **McRae** v **Commonwealth Disposals Commission** (1951), which was decided by the Australian courts. The defendants sold to the claimant a wrecked oil tanker which was said to be 'on Jourmand Reef'. In fact the oil tanker did not exist, but the claimant did not discover this until he had spent a great deal of time and money searching for it. Consequently, he brought an action to recover the money he had spent on the search. The defendants argued that since there was no tanker, the contract was void for mistake, and they owed him nothing. However, the High Court of Australia rejected this view. They stated that the contract contained an implied warranty that the subject matter was in existence. The defendants had breached that implied term and so the claimant could claim damages. The court's decision may well have been influenced by the fact that the defendants appeared to have been grossly negligent on the facts – they were in possession of information which should have told them there was no tanker. As the court pointed out: 'In those circumstances it seems out of the question that they should be able to assert that no contract was concluded.'

The doctrine of mistake did not apply in **William Sindall plc** v **Cambridgeshire County Council** (1994). The Court of Appeal refused to rescind a contract to purchase land for common mistake as to the existence of an undisclosed sewer under the land. The contract itself allocated the risk of all unknown easements and incumbrances affecting the land to the purchaser.

## Fundamental mistake

A shared mistake will only render a contract void if it amounts to a fundamental mistake. A mistake is fundamental if it renders the performance of the contract essentially and radically different from what the parties had supposed it to be. The Court of Appeal in **Great Peace Shipping Ltd** v **Tsavliris Salvage (International) Ltd** (2002) goes as far as suggesting that the mistake must have rendered performance impossible or devoid of purpose. In determining this issue Lord Diplock's test in **Hong Kong Fir Shipping Co Ltd** v **Kawasaki Kisen Kaisha Ltd** (1962) (discussed at p. 145 in the context of innominate terms) was applied. This asks whether the occurrence of the event deprives the party who has further undertakings still to perform, of substantially the whole benefit of what he or she should have obtained under the contract.

## Key Case    Bell v Lever Brothers

The leading House of Lords' case on common mistake is **Bell v Lever Brothers** (1932). In that case, Bell and Snelling had been appointed chairman and vice-chairman of a company controlled by Lever Brothers. Their contracts were for five years but, before that time was up, a company merger occurred, which meant that there was no longer enough work for the two men. Consequently, at Lever Brothers' suggestion, Bell and Snelling agreed that their contracts should be terminated, and that they would be paid a total of £50,000 compensation.

Lever Brothers later discovered that both men had committed breaches of their contract, and so could have been dismissed without compensation. The company then sued the men to get the £50,000 back, arguing that their agreement was void for mistake, because they had made the compensation agreements in the belief that the service contracts were valid, when in fact they were voidable because of the breaches by Bell and Snelling. Both men had forgotten about the breaches, so they too were under the impression that their contracts were valid, and had not tried to defraud Lever Brothers in any way.

The House of Lords rejected Lever Brothers' argument, stating that the mistake made was not sufficiently fundamental to the parties' agreement to render the contract void.

**Legal Principle**
A shared mistake will only render a contract void if it amounts to a fundamental mistake.

A rare recent example of a fundamental mistake rendering a contract void is the Court of Appeal's judgment in **Nutt v Read** (2000). The claimants had made two agreements with the defendants. First, they had agreed to sell them a chalet. Secondly, they had agreed to rent to the defendants its pitch on a caravan site in Surrey for a monthly rent. Both parties to the contract had made a common mistake that the chalet was a chattel which could be sold independently of its pitch. The defendants failed to pay the rent and the claimants sought to eject them from the site. The defendants argued in their defence that the contracts were void for common mistake because the chalet could not in law be sold independently of its pitch. The Court of Appeal accepted this argument and the case of **Bell v Lever Brothers** was applied. The purchase price therefore had to be returned to the defendants.

There are two specific situations where the courts will find a fundamental mistake: where the parties have made a mistake about the existence of the subject matter, and where they have made a mistake as to title. In exceptional circumstances a mistake as to quality may also be sufficient.

## Mistake as to the existence of the subject matter

The courts will find a fundamental mistake, where there has been a mistake as to the existence of the subject matter of the contract. This kind of mistake will usually concern goods to be sold – if, for example, Ann purports to sell her car to Ben, and it is then discovered that the car has been destroyed by fire, the contract will not be valid. However, it applies equally to other kinds of subject matter. In **Scott** v **Coulson** (1903) a life insurance policy was taken out, covering a Mr A.T. Death, who both parties believed was alive. In fact, Mr Death was, appropriately enough, dead. The agreement was held to be void at common law and the contract was set aside.

It is not always the case that the non-existence of the subject matter will render a contract void, and there are several cases which make this area of the law difficult and rather unclear. A leading case is **Couturier** v **Hastie** (1856), which involved a contract to buy a cargo of corn which, at the time the contract was made, was supposed to be on a ship sailing to England from the Mediterranean port of Salonica. In fact, by that time, the corn had already been sold by the master of the ship, to a buyer in Tunis, because it had begun to go off – this was a common occurrence in the days before refrigerated transport, and the master's action was the usual solution. As far as the contract was concerned, the corn had therefore ceased to exist.

The sellers claimed that the buyer still had to pay; this may seem odd, but is explained by the fact that in such a transaction, which was always risky, the buyer would usually take out insurance against the goods not reaching their destination, and could simply reclaim the price paid from the insurers. In this case the buyer did not have the appropriate insurance. The House of Lords held that the buyer did not have to pay for the corn: the contract was clearly assumed by both parties to refer to 'goods supposed to exist', and not to 'goods lost or not lost' (the terminology usually used in marine insurance policies). The court did not specifically mention mistake as to the existence of the subject matter, but that is widely thought to be the basis of the decision.

The decision in **Couturier** v **Hastie** was put into statutory form and is now contained in s. 6 of the Sale of Goods Act 1979. This states:

> Where there is a contract for the sale of specific goods, and the goods without the knowledge of the seller have perished at the time when the contract is made, the contract is void.

## Mistake as to title

A mistake as to title is also sufficient to amount to a fundamental mistake. Very rarely, a situation will arise in which one party agrees to transfer property to the other, but, unknown to both of them, the latter already owns that property. In such a case, the contract will be void for mistake. In **Cooper** v **Phibbs** (1867) the House of Lords set aside an agreement whereby one party had agreed to lease a fishery to the other, but, unknown to either, the fishery already belonged to the party taking out the lease.

## Mistake as to quality

In most cases a mistake as to the quality of the subject matter will not affect the validity of a contract. This is so even where the quality of the goods is a major factor in the decision to buy. In **Harrison & Jones** v **Bunten & Lancaster** (1953) the contract concerned the sale of some kapok (used to fill stuffed toys), which both parties believed to be of a certain standard of purity. In fact it fell below this standard and, as a result, was of no use to the buyer, but the contract was nevertheless held to be valid.

Occasionally a mistake as to the quality of the subject matter of the contract will be sufficiently fundamental to render the contract void. In **Bell** v **Lever Brothers** Lord Atkin said that a contract would be void if both parties were mistaken 'as to the existence of some quality which makes the thing without the quality essentially different from the thing as it was believed to be'.

In **Nicholson and Venn** *v* **Smith-Marriott** (1947) the defendants put up for auction some table napkins, described as 'with crest of Charles I and the authentic property of that monarch'. The napkins were bought, on the strength of this description, for £787 10s. They turned out to be Georgian, and consequently only worth £105. The buyer recovered damages for breach of contract, but Hallett J also suggested that the contract could have been treated by the buyer as void for mistake. If that approach had been taken, he said, the question would have been what the parties intended to achieve by the transaction. If their intentions were simply to buy and sell antique table linen, that was what they had done, and the fact that they had been mistaken as to its exact age, provenance or value would not be fundamental. If, by contrast, they intended to buy and sell an item associated with Charles I, their mistake was fundamental, and so made the contract void.

## Abolition of common mistake in equity

Until 2002, it had been thought that, alongside the common law rules on common mistake, there existed separate rules in equity, which could intervene to soften the approach taken in common law and render a contract voidable in circumstances where the common law was not prepared to render the contract void. One problem with the equitable law on this subject was that in **Solle** *v* **Butcher** (1950) Lord Denning laid down a test for common mistake in equity that required a fundamental mistake, which appeared on the surface to be the same test laid down in **Bell** *v* **Lever Brothers** for the common law. Lord Denning stated:

> A contract is also liable in equity to be set aside if the parties were under a common misapprehension either as to facts or as to their relative and respective rights, provided that the misapprehension was fundamental and that the party seeking to set it aside was not himself at fault.

It was therefore difficult to see when the equitable doctrine should apply and when the common law should apply. On the facts of the case it seems that Lord Denning felt that as a matter of public policy the contract should not be void under common law, but equity could still apply. The defendant had agreed to let a flat to the claimant, at a rent of £250 a year. Both parties believed that the flat was not subject to the Rent Acts, but they were mistaken; under the Acts, the maximum rent to be charged was £140. Lord Denning felt that the contract should not be rendered void under common law because:

> it would mean that in the many cases where the parties mistakenly think the house is outside the Rent Acts when it is really within them, the tenancy would be a nullity, and the tenant would have to go, with the result that tenants would not dare to seek to have their rents reduced . . . lest they be turned out.

Consequently, equity stepped in to do justice because it could rescind the contract on terms. The Court of Appeal ruled that either the claimant should give up the flat or stay on at the maximum rent chargeable under the Rent Acts.

In a recent case, **Great Peace Shipping Ltd** *v* **Tsavliris Salvage (International) Ltd** (2002), the Court of Appeal dramatically held that there were no separate rules in equity on common mistake. The case of **Solle** *v* **Butcher** was considered wrong and Lord Denning's judgment criticised.

**Key Case** Great Peace Shipping Ltd *v* Tsavliris Salvage (International) Ltd

The case of **Great Peace Shipping Ltd** *v* **Tsavliris Salvage (International) Ltd** (2002) concerned a ship, called the *Cape Providence*, which was sailing from Brazil to China with a cargo of iron. She suffered serious structural damage in the South Indian Ocean. Fearing for the safety of the crew, the defendants sought another ship, the *Great Peace*, that was sailing nearby, to assist. This ship belonged to the claimants. Both contracting parties thought that the *Great Peace* was only about 35 miles away from the damaged ship. Negotiations between the defendants and the claimants resulted in a hire contract for a minimum of five days to escort and stand by the damaged vessel for the purpose of saving life. The agreement contained a cancellation clause giving a right to cancel on payment of five days' hire. When it was discovered that the vessels were in fact 410 miles apart, not 35 miles as previously understood, the defendants found an alternative ship and cancelled the contract. They then refused to pay for the hire of *Great Peace*.

The claimants brought an action claiming $82,500 for the five days' hire, or as damages for wrongful repudiation. The defendants argued that the purported contract had been entered into because of a fundamental mistake. This mistake was the erroneous belief that the two ships were near each other. The mistake either rendered the contract void at common law or voidable in equity. The trial judge ruled in favour of the claimants and awarded the sum claimed. The Court of Appeal agreed with the trial judge and rejected the appeal. The issue in relation to common mistake turned on the question of whether the mistake as to the distance apart of the two vessels meant that the services which the *Great Peace* was in a position to provide were essentially different from those to which the parties had agreed. The Court of Appeal held that, although the *Great Peace* was some distance from the *Cape Providence*, performance of the contract was still possible. The *Great Peace* could still have arrived in time to provide several days of escort service. Thus the mistake was not sufficiently fundamental to satisfy the doctrine of common mistake in common law. Most importantly, it went on to say that there was no separate doctrine of common mistake in equity which could soften the tough stance taken by the common law. Thus, the contract was a valid contract and the defendants were required to pay the money due under it:

> Our conclusion is that it is impossible to reconcile **Solle** *v* **Butcher** with **Bell** *v* **Lever Brothers**. The jurisdiction asserted in the former case has not developed. It has been a fertile source of academic debate, but in practice it has given rise to a handful of cases that have merely emphasised the confusion of this area of our jurisprudence . . . If coherence is to be restored to this area of our law, it can only be by declaring that there is no jurisdiction to grant rescission of a contract on the ground of common mistake where that contract is valid and enforceable on ordinary principles of contract law.

**Legal Principle**
There is no separate doctrine of common mistake in equity.

The Court of Appeal has therefore taken the view that there is no role for equity, because wherever the contract is valid under the common law it should also be valid under equity. But this creates an all-or-nothing approach to common mistake. Allowing equity to intervene enabled the law to rescind on terms. So, for example, in **Nutt** *v* **Read** (discussed on p. 227), the purchasers of the chalet had spent over £15,000 making improvements to the chalet. When the contract for the rental of the pitch was rescinded in equity for common mistake, the court could have chosen to ask the sellers to compensate this money that had been spent on the chalet. In fact, the defendants had not asked for this compensation and the Court of Appeal therefore decided not to order it.

The Court of Appeal in **Great Peace Shipping** did itself recognise that equity had the advantage of creating flexibility and suggested that Parliament should legislate 'to give greater flexibility to our law of mistake than the common law allows'. In practice, Parliament rarely finds the time to legislate on general common law principles, and it would have seemed more desirable for the Court of Appeal to have clarified the equitable rules which undoubtedly allowed some flexibility in the law, rather than abolishing that route and then complaining that Parliament needed to legislate.

# Cross-purposes mistake

This is also known as non-identical mistake and mistake negativing consent. It occurs where each party has a different view of the situation – where, for example, Ann thinks she is buying Ben's Rolls-Royce, when in fact it is his Daimler that is for sale. Two types of cross-purposes mistake are possible:

- *mutual mistakes*,  where each party makes a mistake but they are different mistakes; and
- *unilateral mistakes*,  where only one party is mistaken. The other either knows of the mistake or ought to know of it.

Where this type of mistake occurs, the parties have not reached an agreement, and the contract is not formed. Some textbooks prefer to view this topic as one about the existence of a valid offer and acceptance in the earlier chapters about the formation of a contract. It is rare for a cross-purposes mistake to make a contract void at common law. The courts will simply decide whether a reasonable onlooker would have understood the contract to mean what one party thought it meant, or what the other party thought it meant. In **Wood** v **Scarth** (1855) the defendant was going to lease a pub to the claimant for £63 a year, and thought that his clerk had made it clear to the claimant that there would be an additional one-off charge of £500. In fact the clerk had failed to do this. The court held that the agreement was valid: as far as any reasonable onlooker was concerned, the defendant had made a precise and unambiguous offer, which the claimant had accepted, and the mistake did not negative that.

Occasionally, even viewed objectively it will be impossible to find a contract. In **Scriven Bros & Co** v **Hindley & Co** (1913) bales of hemp and tow were put up for auction. Both hemp and tow are fibres used for making rope, but tow is of much lower quality than hemp. They were put into two lots, one of 176 bales of hemp, the other of the same amount of tow. Unusually, both lots bore the same markings. When the lot of tow came up for sale, the claimant thought it was hemp, and bid a price that was appropriate for hemp, which, not surprisingly, was immediately accepted. The contract was therefore concluded with one party thinking, correctly, that he was selling tow, and the other, wrongly, that he was buying hemp – neither was aware that they were at cross-purposes. There was no genuine consensus between the parties, but was there a contract when the transaction was viewed objectively? The court thought not as, in the circumstances, it was impossible to say that one or other commodity was being contracted for.

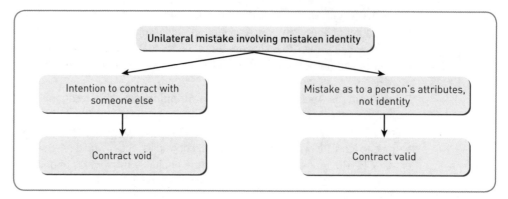

**Figure 10.1** Unilateral mistake involving mistaken identity

There are three situations where a cross-purposes mistake can make a contract void:

- the mistake was negligently induced by the other party;
- the parties are at such cross-purposes that a reasonable observer would not be able to say what they had agreed; and
- one party knew of the other's mistake (a unilateral mistake) regarding their identity or the terms of the contract, and the mistake was fundamental. A unilateral mistake about the quality of the subject matter of the contract is not sufficient.

We will now look in more detail at where unilateral mistakes will render a contract void.

## Unilateral mistake over the terms of the contract

Where one party is mistaken as to the terms of the contract and the other knows this, the contract will be void, regardless of whether the term is fundamental. In **Hartog** v **Colin and Shields** (1939) the defendants had some animal skins for sale, which they intended to sell at a certain price 'per piece', as was apparently the custom in the trade. By mistake, they offered them at the same price 'per pound' instead of 'per piece', which, at about three skins to the pound, obviously worked out much cheaper. The buyers accepted this offer. When they realised their mistake, the sellers refused to deliver the skins and were sued by the buyers for breach of contract. The court held that there was no contract, because the buyers were aware of the seller's mistake.

By contrast, in **Centrovincial Estates plc** v **Merchant Investors Assurance Co Ltd** (1983) a landlord offered, by mistake, to renew his tenant's lease at a rent of £65,000 a year; he had meant to offer it at £126,000. The tenant, unaware of the mistake, accepted the offer. The Court of Appeal held that the mistake had no effect upon the contract, because the tenant did not know of it, and the contract was therefore binding.

## Unilateral mistake involving mistaken identity

Unilateral mistake is frequently relied upon where there is a mistake as to the identity of one of the contracting parties. A genuine mistake of this nature, where the identity of the other party is of fundamental importance, will render the contract void. The law draws a fine distinction between where a person intended to contract with someone else (the mistake renders the contract void), and a mistake which is merely as to a person's attributes rather than as to their identity. A mistake as to a person's attributes, such as thinking that they are creditworthy when they are not, can leave the contract intact.

## Key Case — Shogun Finance v Hudson

The leading case on unilateral mistake involving mistaken identity is **Shogun Finance v Hudson** (2003). A fraudster visited the showrooms of a car dealer in Leicester and agreed to buy a Mitsubishi Shogun for £22,250 on hire-purchase terms. The fraudster signed a draft finance agreement in the name of Durlabh Patel, presenting a stolen driving licence as proof of his name and address. The dealer sent the signed document and a copy of the licence to Shogun. Shogun confirmed the credit rating of Durlabh Patel and approved the sale. The fraudster paid a 10 per cent deposit and was allowed to drive the car away with its paperwork.

Because of the finance arrangements, the dealer sold the car to the finance company, who in turn hired it to the customer under the hire-purchase agreement. Thus, the finance company became the new owner, and the customer only had possession of the car with an option to purchase it after paying all the hire charges. In fact, the fraudster immediately sold the car for £17,000 to an innocent purchaser, Mr Hudson, and disappeared. Shogun later found out about the fraud and traced the car to Mr Hudson. As they were the owners, they sued him for the return of the car, or its value. They were successful before the Court of Appeal. Mr Hudson appealed to the House of Lords. The House of Lords rejected the appeal. Shogun was entitled to the return of the car. The hire-purchase contract was void. The fraudster could therefore pass no title on to Hudson, as he had no title to pass.

It is a fundamental principle of the English law that vendors cannot convey to purchasers a better title to property than that which they themselves enjoy. There are, however, exceptions to this rule. One arises under the Hire Purchase Act 1964, as re-enacted in the Consumer Credit Act 1974. Under this legislation, an innocent private purchaser of a motor vehicle subject to hire-purchase obtains good title. The critical issue in this case was, therefore, whether a hire-purchase agreement had been concluded between Shogun and the fraudster. If an agreement had been concluded, then the fraudster was the 'debtor' under s. 27 of the 1964 Act and passed good title in the vehicle to Mr Hudson. If no agreement had been concluded, then the fraudster could not pass ownership in the car to Mr Hudson.

Shogun argued that the Hire Purchase Act could not apply because the hire-purchase agreement in question was void. In particular, they argued that the agreement was void for mistake because they had intended to contract not with the rogue, but with Durlabh Patel. In order to decide this issue, the House of Lords ruled that they had to focus on the written agreement and determine whether, in the light of the written agreement, interpreted applying the objective principle, the contract was void.

The House found that there was no agreement between the finance company and the fraudster or the finance company and the real Mr Patel. The offer of finance was made to Durlabh Patel, but Durlabh Patel knew nothing of the offer and did not therefore authorise any acceptance. There was therefore no contract. The hirer/debtor under the hire-purchase 'agreement' was Mr Durlabh Patel, not the fraudster. The Hire Purchase Act 1964 did not apply and the title to the car remained with the finance company.

### Legal Principle
Where a party makes a unilateral mistake as to the identity of the other contracting party, the contract is void.

## Face-to-face principle

Under the face-to-face principle, where there has been face-to-face contact between the contracting parties, there is a strong presumption that each party intends to contract with the other person present. The vendor's intention is treated as being to sell to the person present, and identified by sight and hearing. This presumption applies even where the buyer assumed a false name, or practised any other deceit to induce the vendor to sell. Where the parties make a contract at a distance (such as through the post or over the telephone) it will be easier to establish a mistake as to identity, because the identity of the person placing an order has to be known in order to deliver the goods and it is therefore easier to prove that it was of crucial importance to the making of the contract.

In **Shogun Finance** the defendant, Hudson, argued that the hire-purchase agreement was not void for mistake. He submitted that the contract fell within the 'face-to-face' principle. Negotiations between the rogue and Shogun were conducted primarily by written correspondence, and the fraudster never had any face-to-face dealings with the finance company; he dealt with it solely by submitting written documents. The fraudster's only contact was with the car dealer. Hudson argued that the car dealer was Shogun's agent and therefore dealing face to face with the car dealer was equivalent to dealing face to face with Shogun. This argument was rejected by the majority of the House of Lords because they did not accept that the car dealer was Shogun's agent. The car dealer was not Shogun's agent with the authority to make a contract on their behalf; he was merely a go-between whose role was to obtain and communicate information about the hirer to the claimant. Thus, the face-to-face principle could not apply.

The only case which was out of line with the face-to-face principle was **Ingram** v **Little** (1961) and this case was overruled by the House of Lords in **Shogun Finance**. The Ingrams were two elderly sisters who advertised a car for sale. A man came to see it, and made an offer, stating that he would pay by cheque. The sisters refused this, and the man then gave the name of P. Hutchinson, and an address. The sisters checked the telephone directory and, finding that a P. Hutchinson was listed at that address, agreed to take the cheque. The cheque bounced, and the sisters discovered that the man was not who he claimed to be but, by this time, he had disappeared and the car had been sold to a dealer. The court held that the sisters' contract with the fraudster was void for mistake. They had made their offer to P. Hutchinson and, since the fraudster was someone else, there was no offer for him to accept. The judgment stated that the mere presence of an individual did not necessarily mean that the contract was being made with him or her: 'if he was disguised in appearance to represent someone else, and the other party deceived by his appearance, dealt with him on the basis that he was that person and would not have contracted had he known the truth', there was no contract. Therefore, the court held, the same should apply where a person uses words to disguise their true identity. The House of Lords in **Shogun Finance** considered that **Ingram** v **Little** was wrongly decided.

The face-to-face principle creates a strong presumption that the offer was accepted by the person to whom it was physically addressed, and exceptions to it are rare and have been significantly restricted by the decision of the House that **Ingram** v **Little** was wrongly decided. An exception would apply where a rogue attempts, face to face, to deceive someone personally acquainted with the individual whom the rogue is impersonating. Impersonation of that sort is very rare, and unlikely to succeed unless the senses of the deceived person are impaired (for example, he or she is blind).

Where a contract is made face to face, the courts are likely to conclude that the parties intended to contract with the person in front of them and the only mistake was a mistake as to attributes. An illustration of this is **Lewis** v **Averay** (1972). The claimant had advertised his car for sale. A potential buyer introduced himself as Richard Greene, a film actor who was well known at the time for playing the part of Robin Hood. Agreeing to buy the car, he signed the cheque 'R.A. Green', and, when the claimant asked for evidence of identity, he produced a Pinewood Studios pass with his name and photograph on it. The claimant handed over the car, but a few days later was told by his bank that the cheque was worthless. In the meantime, the fake Richard Greene had disappeared after selling the car to Mr Averay (who bought it in good faith and had no knowledge of the fraud). The question then became whether or not Mr Lewis's contract with the fake Richard Greene was valid; if it was, title to the car could pass to Mr Averay through the subsequent sale; if it was not, the car still belonged to Mr Lewis.

The Court of Appeal found that there was a contract, and Lord Denning based his judgment on the fact that Mr Lewis had reached an agreement with the person who turned up on his doorstep, and there was no evidence that he intended to contract with someone other than that person. He also seemed to be influenced by the idea that it was wrong to deprive the innocent purchaser, when he had 'acted with complete circumspection', and it was the seller who allowed the rogue to take the car. The result was that the contract between the seller and the fraudster was voidable for misrepresentation, but, as he had failed to avoid it before a third party, Mr Averay, acquired rights in the property, title to the car had indeed passed to Mr Averay and the car was his to keep.

A second reason for the decision in **Lewis** v **Averay** was given by Megaw LJ, who based his judgment on the fact that the identity of the buyer was not of fundamental importance to Mr Lewis; the only matter of importance was that he assumed a famous film actor would be creditworthy. This was not enough to make the contract void for mistake.

Another case involving a contract made face to face is **Phillips** v **Brooks Ltd** (1919). A rogue went into a jewellery shop and examined some jewellery. He said his name was Sir George Bullough, and gave an address in St James's Square. He was allowed to take away the ring on credit without paying for it after the claimant had checked that a Sir George Bullough lived at the address given. The rogue then sold the ring to a third party and failed to pay for it. The claimant brought an action to recover the ring from the third party. The court rejected the claim, stating that the contract was valid as the claimant had intended to make the contract with the person in front of him in the shop. The mistake had been merely about the creditworthiness of the rogue, rather than as to his identity.

## Interpreting a written contract

When a person is clearly identified as a party on the face of a written agreement, other evidence cannot be adduced to assert that the agreement was, in fact, with someone else.

The majority of the House of Lords in **Shogun Finance** considered that, under established law, they were required to focus on the written agreement to decide this case. Normally, when interpreting a contract, the courts are looking for the intention of the parties, though the intention in this context is the intention that they objectively appear to have. Applying a test of intention to determine the parties to a contract causes problems where there is some form of personal contact between the parties, and where one lies as to their identity. In this situation, innocent parties will have in mind, when considering with whom they are contracting, both the person with whom they are in contact and the third party whom they imagine that person to be.

Where the contract is exclusively in writing, these difficulties are resolved by the court purely focusing on the written contract. In **Shogun** Lord Phillips stated that

> the identity of a party to a contract in writing falls to be determined by a process of construction of the putative contract itself . . . The process of construction will lead inexorably to the conclusion that the person with whom the other party intended to contract was the person thus described. (para. 154)

Because the contracting parties were specifically identified in the document, oral and other extrinsic evidence was not admissible to prove that one of the contracting parties was actually the fraudster and not Mr Durlabh Patel. Thus, evidence that the fraudster was the person who came into the dealer's office, negotiated a price with the dealer and signed the form in the presence of the dealer, would not be taken into account by the court.

In **Cundy** v **Lindsay** (1878) the claimants received an order by post for a large number of handkerchiefs from a Mr Blenkarn of 37 Wood Street, Cheapside. Mr Blenkarn rented a room at that address, and further down the road, at number 123, were the offices of a highly respectable firm called Blenkiron & Co. On the order for the handkerchiefs, Blenkarn signed his name so that it looked like Blenkiron. The claimants sent off the goods, addressed to Blenkiron & Co; Mr Blenkarn received them, and by the time the fraud was discovered, he had sold most of them to the defendant, Cundy, who bought them in good faith. The claimants sued the defendant to get the goods back, and whether they could be successful in this depended on whether there was a contract between the claimants and Blenkarn. If there was, Blenkarn would have become the owner of the goods and so would have been able to transfer ownership to the defendant; if not, the claimants would be able to get their goods back. The House of Lords held that there was no contract between Blenkarn and the claimants, because they had intended all along to deal with Blenkiron & Co, and not with a Mr Blenkarn, of whom they had after all never heard.

> ...how is it possible to imagine that in that state of things any contract could have arisen between the Respondents and Blenkarn, the dishonest man? Of him they knew nothing, and of him they never thought. With him they never intended to deal. Their minds never, even for an instant of time, rested upon him, and as between him and them there was no *consensus* of mind which could lead to any agreement or any contract whatever.

An exception, where the courts will look beyond the written agreement, is where the fraudster has used a 'simple alias' to disguise his or her identity, rather than pretending to be an existing person. In the former situation, there may be a contract with the fraudster.

An example of a simple alias being used is the case of **King's Norton Metal** v **Edridge Merrett & Co** (1897). In that case a Mr Wallis ordered by post some goods from the claimants,

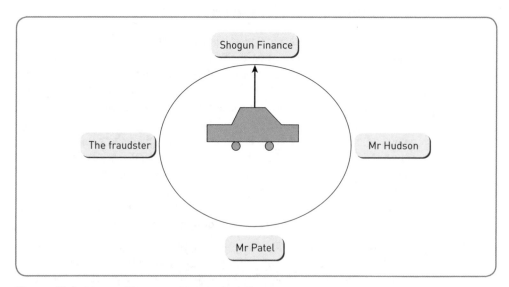

**Figure 10.2 Shogun Finance** v **Hudson** (2003)

using the name 'Hallam & Co', and placing the order on stationery showing a large factory, and claiming that Hallam & Co had depots and agencies in Belfast, Lille and Ghent. The goods were delivered on credit but were never paid for. Again, the issue was whether there was a contract between them. The Court of Appeal held that there was: the claimants intended to contract with the writer of the letter, and that they had done. The importance of their mistake did not concern the identity of the customer, but his attributes, in particular his creditworthiness. **Cundy** was distinguishable because in that case the claimants had a different customer in mind, not merely a different type of customer. The mistake in **King's Norton** was not sufficient to render the contract void, although in fact the agreement would be voidable for fraudulent misrepresentation. A contract had been concluded between the claimants and Wallis, under which property in the goods had passed. The Court of Appeal observed:

> The question was, with whom, upon this evidence, which was all one way, did the plaintiffs contract to sell the goods? Clearly with the writer of the letters. If it could have been shown that there was a separate entity called Hallam and Co. and another entity called Wallis then the case might have come within the decision in **Cundy** v **Lindsay**. In his opinion there was a contract by the plaintiffs with the person who wrote the letters, by which the property passed to him. There was only one entity, trading it might be under an *alias*, and there was a contract by which the property passed to him.

In **Shogun Finance** the fraudster had not used a simple alias; he had pretended to be another existing person. Before entering into the agreement, Shogun checked that Mr Patel existed and that he was creditworthy. On that basis they decided to contract with him and with no one else. The real Mr Patel was technically the hirer under the agreement.

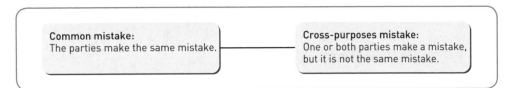

**Figure 10.3** Common and cross-purposes mistake

# Mistakes relating to documents

The parties may agree orally that the goods will cost £98 but accidentally write the price down in a written contract as £89. Where a mistake relates to a written document there are two special remedies: *non est factum* and rectification.

## Non est factum

We have seen that, as a general rule, a person who signs a contractual document is bound by it, regardless of whether he or she has read or understood it (**L'Estrange** v **Graucob** (1934), see p. 158). However, where a person signs a document believing it to be something totally different from what it actually is, the common law remedy of *non est factum* (Latin for 'this is not my deed') may make the contract void. In order to do this, the person seeking the remedy must prove three things: that the signature was induced by a trick or fraud; that they made a fundamental mistake as to the nature of the document; and that they were not careless in signing it.

The mistake made by the signer must concern the actual nature of the document, not just its legal effect. In **Saunders** v **Anglia Building Society** (1971) (also known as **Gallie** v **Lee**) an elderly widow had left her house to her nephew, a Mr Parkin, in her will. When he needed to raise some money, she handed over the deeds to the house for him to use as security. Parkin and an acquaintance called Lee came and asked her to sign a document, which they said transferred the title of the house to her nephew, so that he could raise the money he needed; she did not object to him doing this. In fact, the document was a deed of sale to Mr Lee, but the old lady did not read it because she had broken her glasses. Mr Lee later mortgaged the house to a building society and kept all the money, paying nothing to either the old lady or Parkin. Lee then defaulted on the mortgage repayments, and the building society sought possession of the house. By that time the widow had died, and Saunders, who was dealing with her affairs, sought a declaration of *non est factum* to make the agreement with Lee void. The House of Lords refused to issue this declaration. They agreed that the widow had been tricked into signing, but held that she was not mistaken as to the nature of the document, only as to its exact legal effect. In signing the document she intended to help her nephew raise money, and this was exactly what the document she did sign would have achieved if Lee had not been dishonest. A second reason for the decision was that the woman was careless in signing the document. Lord Reid said:

> The plea cannot be available to anyone who was content to sign without taking the trouble to find out at least the general effect of the document . . . the essence of the plea non est factum is that the person signing believed that the document he signed had one character or one effect, whereas in fact its character or effect was quite different. He could not have such a belief unless he had taken steps or had been given information which gave him some grounds for his belief. The amount of information he must have and the sufficiency of the particularity of his belief must depend on the circumstances of each case.

## Rectification

Where part of a written document is alleged not to reflect accurately the intention of the parties, the equitable remedy of rectification may in certain circumstances allow the written document to be altered so that it coincides with the true agreement of the parties. The legal requirements for rectification were confirmed by the House of Lords in **Chartbrook** v **Persimmon Homes** (2009). The remedy of rectification only applies where the following conditions are satisfied:

- the parties had a common intention (whether or not amounting to an agreement) on the relevant term of the contract which continued to exist when the contract was put down in writing;
- the contract was put down in writing;
- a mistake was made when writing down the particular term of the contract so the contract did not reflect that common intention.

If the parties have simply overlooked the issue, and therefore not reached any agreement on it, then the remedy of rectification is not available: the written agreement will simply be interpreted as it stands. Regarding the parties' intention, the question is what the objective observer would have thought the intention of the parties to be; their actual, subjective intentions are irrelevant. Lord Denning observed in **Frederick Rose** v **William Pim** (1953):

> . . . in order to ascertain the terms of their contract, you do not look into the inner minds of the parties – into their intentions – any more than you do in the formation of any other contract. You look at their outward acts, that is, at what they said or wrote to one another in coming to their agreement, and then compare it with the document which they have signed.

In the case of **Chartbrook v Persimmon Homes**, Persimmon Homes were property developers who had agreed to buy land for development from Chartbrook. The price to be paid for the land included an 'Additional Residential Payment'. A dispute arose as to how the Additional Residential Payment was supposed to be calculated under the contract. On the facts of the case, the House of Lords decided to correct the mistake in drafting the contract to give it commercial sense by using its rules on contractual interpretation. But it noted that if this option had not been available it would have applied the equitable remedy of rectification.

If all the conditions are satisfied, equity will rectify the written document, and order specific performance of the rectified document. For example, in **Craddock Bros v Hunt** (1923) one party agreed to buy the other's house. While their oral agreement excluded an adjoining yard from the sale, the eventual written contract included it. Equity granted rectification of the document, so the buyer was not allowed to keep the yard.

Rectification will not be available where the written document accurately records the agreement, but the agreement is based upon a mistake. In **Rose v Pim** (1953) Frederick Rose was asked to supply a customer with 'feveroles'. Not knowing exactly what these were, Frederick Rose asked his suppliers, the defendants, who replied 'feveroles means just horsebeans'. This was genuinely the defendants' belief, but in fact 'feveroles' were a specific type of horsebean of a superior quality. The parties then made their written contract, using the term 'horsebean'. When the beans were supplied, they turned out to be another type of horsebean, and not feveroles at all. Frederick Rose was sued by his customer and, in order to cover his loss, Frederick Rose sought to rectify the written contract between him and the defendants. His application was refused on the grounds that the written contract did accurately reflect the parties' agreement. In considering an application for rectification, the parol evidence rule does not apply, so that, for example, pre-contractual oral negotiations may be considered.

Following the case of **Chartbrook v Persimmon Homes**, which increased the possibility of correcting contracts through the rules on contractual interpretation, there had been suggestions that there would as a result be only a limited future for the more rigid rules on rectification. However, in **Cherry Tree Investments v Landmain** (2012) the Court of Appeal stated that reports of rectification's death were exaggerated and there was still a role for it in contract law.

## Rectification and unilateral mistake

Rectification is only occasionally available when there has been a unilateral mistake. If the mistake is one-sided, rectification will be available if the person who realised the other was mistaken, dishonestly failed to tell the other of their mistake.

## Topical Issue

### The housing market

The housing market has been central to growth in the UK economy in recent years and Wimpey are well-known builders who have built a large number of new houses across the United Kingdom. Considerable sums of money are involved in the housing and construction industry and inevitably legal disputes can arise regarding the detail of the relevant contracts. In **George Wimpey UK Ltd v V I Construction Ltd** (2005) the vendor was selling Wimpey a piece of land that ran along the side of a river. Wimpey intended to build 231 flats on the land and had agreed to pay the vendor £2,650,000. During the contractual negotiations it was also agreed that Wimpey would pay an additional sum of money to the vendor if they made more profit from the flats than currently envisaged, resulting in particular from changes to the planning permission. The early versions of the relevant contractual clause referred to the 'value of enhancements' to each flat, for example, whether the flat had a car parking space and a view of the river. When the vendor sent an amended version of this clause, it made no mention of the value of enhancements. Wimpey did not notice this omission and signed the contract. The omission effectively meant that Wimpey had to pay an extra £800,000 for the land. Wimpey went to court to try to get the contract rectified to make express mention to the 'value of enhancements'. The Court of Appeal rejected this claim. It was not satisfied that the vendor had known that Wimpey had made a mistake and pointed out that Wimpey was a powerful construction company that was much more experienced than the vendor in such matters.

# Criticism and reform

The last decade has seen a minor revolution in the law of mistake, with radical changes being made by the courts, which is quite exceptional for the usually calm waters of the law of contract. First, in 1998, the House of Lords ruled in **Kleinwort Benson Ltd** v **Lincoln City Council** (1992) that the remedy of restitution would be available for both mistakes of fact and mistakes of law. In 2002, the Court of Appeal announced in **Great Peace Shipping Ltd** v **Tsavliris Salvage (International) Ltd** (2002) that there was no equitable doctrine of common mistake, and in **Shogun Finance** the House of Lords refined the law in relation to unilateral mistakes.

While **Kleinwort Benson Ltd** seems to have been a step in the right direction in achieving justice for the parties, and avoiding undue enrichment, the latter two cases both risk causing injustice, and this injustice seems to have the same source. In both cases the courts placed considerable emphasis on the importance of certainty for commercial law and tried to achieve this by making their starting point the interpretation of the contract itself. In interpreting the contract, it seems perfectly reasonable to look for the intention of the parties in its express terms, so that the parties can determine for themselves where the risks should lie. The danger is that if an objective approach to interpretation is taken to its extreme, the courts can find a contractual intention, where this was clearly not the subjective intention of the parties. The subsequent interpretation given to the contract can appear very artificial and unfair. Thus, in **Shogun Finance** the finance company was treated as contracting with a member of the public who had no knowledge that the contract was being made, while the person who was actually physically present and signed the contract was not treated as a party to the contract at all. In **Great Peace Shipping Ltd** no term was implied that required the *Great Peace* to be close to the sinking ship that needed to be salvaged, despite the fact that the physical location of the ship was at the heart of the contract. If they had not thought that the *Great Peace* was close there would have been no reason for entering into the contract in the first place.

The result is a risk of injustice where mistakes have, as a matter of fact, been made but the objective interpretation of the contract allows the court to ignore this. Where the issue of mistake is raised before the courts, they may determine that no legally significant mistake was made, by applying an objective interpretation of the contract. By obstinately ignoring the reality of the transaction, relying on the justification of contractual certainty and the tradition of an objective analysis, the danger is that the courts are not achieving justice on the actual facts of the case. Clearly, contractual certainty is important, but this is only one aspect of the more important and fundamental goal of justice.

In addition, the court in **Shogun Finance** was only achieving certainty for the company; for future consumers their position has been made very uncertain. The artificial interpretation of the original contractual process led, in **Shogun Finance**, to a subsequent injustice to the innocent purchaser of the dishonestly obtained car. Mr Hudson, the innocent purchaser, was forced to return the car that he had paid for to the finance company, leaving him £17,000 out of pocket. But in fact it was the finance company that had given possession of the car to the fraudster without making sufficient checks about who he really was. Usually the person selling to a fraudster is in a stronger position to check their credentials than the person who buys from a fraudster, and the law should take this into account. Shogun's procedures were lax: they allowed the fraudster to take the car away on credit terms without verifying that he was the person named in the driving licence. In his dissenting judgment in the Court of Appeal, Sedley LJ had been highly critical of Shogun's procedures. Their credit checks were clearly an inadequate basis for giving £20,000 of credit. It is the innocent customer who is penalised for the mistakes of the finance company. A better approach would have been for the House of Lords to have recognised that a contract had been made between the fraudster and the finance company, because of the finance company's lax credit checks, and refused an order of repossession from innocent purchasers on such facts. This would force credit companies to make more stringent credit checks in the future, which all contracting parties would benefit from.

The dissenting judgments of Lord Nicholls and Lord Millett in **Shogun Finance** are very persuasive. They point out the illogicality, when interpreting contracts, of applying a special approach to face-to-face dealings. There is, for example, no difference of substance between contracts made face to face and contracts made over the telephone, by videolink or even by post. Lord Nicholls and Lord Millett therefore proposed that where two individuals deal with each other, by whatever medium, and agree terms of a contract, then a contract will be concluded between them, notwithstanding that one has deceived the other into thinking that he/she has the identity of someone else. They would overrule the case of **Cundy v Lindsay** (1878).

The current legal analysis of this type of factual scenario is also artificial in relying on mistake rather than misrepresentation. Where there has been a fraud that has induced a supplier of goods to hand over their property to a fraudster, the logical argument of the supplier of the goods is that their property was obtained by a fraudulent misrepresentation. But this argument does not provide the remedy that the innocent supplier needs, and so the supplier's argument must centre instead on the issue of whether there was a unilateral mistake which rendered the contract void. The law should reflect the reality of the situation: the heart of the problem is that there has been a fraud, and it is undesirable that the litigation focuses on how far the fraudster's conduct caused the innocent party to make a mistake.

As a result of the law on mistake being given a very narrow interpretation in contract law, the law on misrepresentation has increased in importance. The law on misrepresentation can be applied where mistakes have been induced by the other party. But where an innocent third party has acquired goods which are the subject of a disputed contract, the remedy available for misrepresentation can be inadequate, and then the inadequacies of the law on mistake are more conspicuous.

The Law Reform Committee, in its report *Transfer of Title to Chattels* (1966), proposed abolishing the distinction between contracts void for mistake and those voidable for misrepresentation.

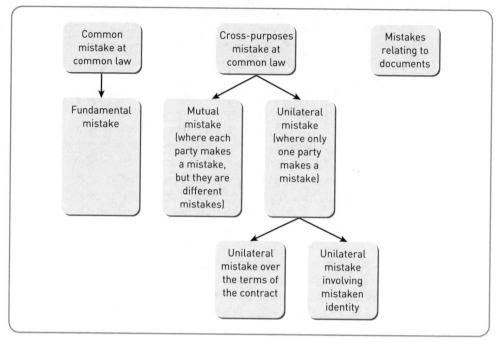

**Figure 10.4** Mistake

Instead, it recommended that where goods are sold under a mistake as to the buyer's identity, the contract should be voidable, and not void. This solution would favour innocent purchasers because they would obtain good title, provided the fraud had not been discovered and the contract rescinded before they purchased the goods.

## Answering questions

The concept of mistake is unsatisfactory as its application through decided cases has led to confusion rather than clarity.

Discuss, in the light of this statement, the ways that courts have developed the concept of mistake both at common law and in equity. *London External LL.B*

You need to consider how far the law on mistake is confused. Central to your answer would be the case of **Great Peace Shipping**. This has tried to simplify the law by removing the role of equity altogether. There certainly has been some confusion in the past as to what was the difference between a fundamental mistake at common law and a fundamental mistake in equity, which determined when the common law would intervene, and when equity would intervene. By abolishing the role of equity in the doctrine of mistake, **Great Peace Shipping** has removed this confusion, but this simplification may have been at the expense of justice. With the abolition of the role of equity, the flexible remedies available in equity have been removed and the doctrine of common law mistake is very narrow.

In your opinion, does English contract law deal adequately with problems of common mistake?

 Note that this question only requires you to deal with **common** mistake. Because of the large amount of law in this area, questions are often confined to certain types of mistake, and you will waste time if you discuss areas not specified.

Start your essay by defining what common mistake is. Then discuss where the doctrine of common mistake applies. You are being asked about the success of the law so, as you explain it, you must highlight any problems. (Some useful critical material is provided at p. 228.) In addition, you could point to the very strict rules on mistake as to quality, which can seem unfair to buyers who end up with goods for which they have no use; or to the defendants in **Bell** v **Lever Bros** who were held to a payment they had no moral obligation to make. The last part of your essay could point out that in the past equity sought to relieve some of the problems caused by the common law doctrine, but the case of **Solle** v **Butcher** was overruled by the Court of Appeal in **Great Peace Shipping Ltd** v **Tsavliris Salvage (International) Ltd** (2002).

---

 Faridah wishes to sell her valuable violin, so advertises it for sale. Germaine visits Faridah, explaining that she would like to buy the violin and they agree on a price. Germaine procures a cheque book, but Faridah hesitates, saying that she would prefer cash. Germaine then replies, 'Look, you can see who I am', and produces various items of identity, bearing the same surname as a famous musician. Faridah is embarrassed and agrees to take the cheque, handing over the violin to Germaine.

A few days later Faridah is contacted by her bank, who informs her that the cheque from Germaine is worthless, and that Germaine cannot be traced. Faridah is upset at this, but, to her surprise, a few days later she sees 'her' violin for sale in the window of a musical instrument supplier, Humbuskers. She tries to recover the violin from Humbuskers, but they claim that they paid a good price for it from someone going abroad, and would certainly not be prepared just to give it back to her.

(a) Advise Faridah as to whether she has any legal right to claim the return of the violin. *(40 marks)*

(b) If Faridah wishes to take legal action against Humbuskers, advise her as to how she may be able to get help with the cost of such an action. *(10 marks)*
*(Total 50 marks) OCR*

 (a) This question raises the issue of a unilateral mistake as to the identity of the contracting party. The law draws a fine distinction between where a person intended to contract with someone else (where the mistake renders the contract void) and a mistake which is merely as to a person's attributes rather than as to their identity. A mistake as to a person's attributes, such as thinking that they are creditworthy when they are not, will leave the contract intact. In determining this issue it is important to note that the contract between Faridah and the purchaser was made face to face. Where the contract is made face to face the courts are likely to conclude that the parties intended to contract with the person in front of them, and the only mistake was a mistake as to attributes. On the other hand, we are told that Faridah entered the contract because she was embarrassed, and this may have been because she thought she was in the presence of a famous musician. You would need to consider cases such as **Shogun Finance** *v* **Hudson**, **Lewis** *v* **Averay** and **Phillips** *v* **Brooks Ltd**. If the court accepts that Faridah made a unilateral mistake as to identity, then the contract will be void and the third party, Humbuskers, will not have gained good title. Faridah will therefore be able to insist on the violin being returned. If the court decides that Faridah had merely made a mistake as to attributes, then there will be a valid contract with the purchaser, who will have passed on good title to Humbuskers, and who will therefore be able to keep the violin.

**Shogun Finance** *v* **Hudson** is the leading case on this subject, but note that its facts are slightly different from the present case. In **Shogun Finance** the contract was not made face to face and the contract was put down in writing. The court concluded on the facts that no contract had been made with the fraudster and the car had to be returned to the original owner (Shogun Finance). The outcome in the present case is likely to be different. Here, a court would probably conclude that the contract was made face to face and therefore between the two people present. The fraudster could as a result pass on a good title to Humbuskers, and Humbuskers will not be required to return the violin to Faridah. This conclusion is strengthened by the fact that the case of **Ingram** *v* **Little**, which reached a different conclusion, was overruled by **Shogun Finance**.

While the purchaser has made a misrepresentation, proving the existence of a fraudulent misrepresentation will not provide the remedy that Faridah needs. Fraudulent misrepresentation would only render the contract voidable, and Humbuskers would have already obtained a good title before the contract had been rescinded.

(b) This question is beyond the scope of a contract law book, and raises issues discussed in the authors' book on the English legal system, and, in particular, the availability of state funding and conditional fee agreements.

# Summary of Chapter 10

## General principles

There are two types of mistake, common mistake and cross-purposes mistake. The following general rules apply to both:

### Objective principle

When deciding whether or not there has been a mistake sufficient to make the contract void, the courts will look at the facts objectively: **Smith** *v* **Hughes** (1871).

### The mistake must precede the contract

In order to make a contract void, a mistake must be made before the contract is completed: **Amalgamated Investment & Property Co** *v* **John Walker & Sons** (1977).

### Mistake must induce the contract

A mistake can only negate consent if it induced the mistaken party to enter into the contract.

### Mistake of fact or law

In the past, only a mistake of fact could affect the validity of a contract; a mistake of law was not sufficient. The House of Lords abolished this distinction in 1998 in **Kleinwort Benson Ltd v Lincoln City Council** (1999).

## Common mistake

In this situation, both parties make the same mistake. A contract will not be void for common mistake if the mistake is due to the fault of one of the parties. In addition, if the contract allocates the risk of the mistake occurring on one of the parties then the doctrine of mistake will not apply. Only if the contract is silent on the point is there scope for invoking mistake: **McRae v Commonwealth Disposals Commission** (1951).

### Fundamental mistake

A shared mistake will only render a contract void if it amounts to a fundamental mistake. A mistake is fundamental if it renders the performance of the contract essentially and radically different from what the parties had supposed it to be: **Bell v Lever Brothers** (1932). There are two specific situations where the courts will find a fundamental mistake: where the parties have made a mistake about the existence of the subject matter, and where they have made a mistake as to title (**Cooper v Phibbs** (1867)). In exceptional circumstances a mistake as to quality may also be sufficient: **Nicholson and Venn v Smith-Marriott** (1947).

### Abolition of common mistake in equity

Until 2002, it had been thought that, alongside the common law rules on common mistake, there existed separate rules in equity, which could intervene to soften the approach taken in common law. In a recent case, **Great Peace Shipping Ltd v Tsavliris Salvage (International) Ltd** (2002), the Court of Appeal dramatically held that there were no separate rules in equity on common mistake.

## Cross-purposes mistake

Cross-purposes mistake occurs where each party has a different view of the situation. Two types of cross-purposes mistake are possible:

- *mutual mistakes*, where each party makes a mistake but they are different mistakes; and
- *unilateral mistakes*, where only one party is mistaken. The other either knows of the mistake or ought to know of it.

Where this type of mistake occurs, the parties have not reached an agreement, and the contract is not formed. It is rare for a cross-purposes mistake to make a contract void at common law. The courts will simply decide whether a reasonable onlooker would have understood the contract to mean what one party thought it meant, or what the other party thought it meant. Occasionally, even viewed objectively it will be impossible to find a contract. There are three situations where a cross-purposes mistake can make a contract void:

- the mistake was negligently induced by the other party;
- the parties are at such cross-purposes that a reasonable observer would not be able to say what they had agreed; and

- one party knew of the other's mistake (a unilateral mistake) regarding their identity or the terms of the contract, and the mistake was fundamental. A unilateral mistake about the quality of the subject matter of the contract is not sufficient.

### Unilateral mistake over the terms of the contract

Where one party is mistaken as to the terms of the contract and the other knows this, the contract will be void, regardless of whether the term is fundamental: **Hartog v Colin and Shields** (1939).

### Unilateral mistake involving mistaken identity

Unilateral mistake is frequently relied upon where there is a mistake as to the identity of one of the contracting parties. A genuine mistake of this nature, where the identity of the other party is of fundamental importance, will render the contract void. The law draws a fine distinction between where a person intended to contract with someone else (the mistake renders the contract void), and a mistake which is merely as to a person's attributes rather than as to their identity. A mistake as to a person's attributes, such as thinking that they are creditworthy when they are not, can leave the contract intact. The leading case on the subject is **Shogun Finance v Hudson** (2003).

#### Face-to-face principle

Under the face-to-face principle, where there has been face-to-face contact between the contracting parties, there is a strong presumption that each party intends to contract with the other person present. The vendor's intention is treated as being to sell to the person present, and identified by sight and hearing and the only mistake was a mistake as to attributes.

#### Interpreting a written contract

When a person is clearly identified as a party on the face of a written agreement, other evidence cannot be adduced to assert that the agreement was, in fact, with someone else. An exception, where the courts will look beyond the written agreement, is where the fraudster has used a 'simple alias' to disguise his or her identity, rather than pretending to be an existing person. In the former situation, there may be a contract with the fraudster.

## Mistakes relating to documents

Where a mistake relates to a written document there are two special remedies: *non est factum* and rectification.

### Non est factum

Where a person signs a document believing it to be something totally different from what it actually is, the common law remedy of *non est factum* (Latin for 'this is not my deed') may make the contract void. In order to do this, the person seeking the remedy must prove three things: that the signature was induced by a trick or fraud; that they made a fundamental mistake as to the nature of the document; and that they were not careless in signing it.

### Rectification

Where part of a written document is alleged not to reflect accurately the intention of the parties, the equitable remedy of rectification may in certain circumstances allow the written document to be altered so that it coincides with the true agreement of the parties. The remedy of rectification only applies where the contract has been put down in writing. The parties must have been in complete agreement on the terms of their contract but by an error wrote them down wrongly: **Rose v Pim** (1953).

**Reading list**

Chandler, Devenney and Poole, 'Common mistake: theoretical justification and remedial inflexibility' (2004) Journal of Business Law 34

Coulter, 'Property: claims of rectification' (2012) Solicitors Journal

Friedman, 'The objective principle and mistake and involuntariness in contract and restitution' (2003) 119 Law Quarterly Review 68

Hare, 'Identity mistakes: a lost opportunity' (2004) 67 Modern Law Review 993

Phang, 'Mistake in contract law – two recent cases' (2002) Cambridge Law Journal 272

Slade, 'The myth of mistake in the English law of contract' (1954) 70 Law Quarterly Review 385

## Reading on the internet

The House of Lords' judgment of **Kleinwort Benson Ltd** v **Lincoln City Council** (1998) is available at:

http://www.publications.parliament.uk/pa/ld199798/ldjudgmt/jd981029/klein01.htm

The House of Lords' judgment of **Shogun Finance** v **Hudson** (2003) is available at:

http://www.publications.parliament.uk/pa/ld200203/ldjudgmt/jd03111/shogun-1.htm

# Chapter 11
## Illegality

### This chapter explains:

that contracts may be illegal either:

- at the time of their formation; or
- because of the way they have been performed.

A contract is illegal where its formation, purpose or performance involves the commission of a legal wrong. The violation may be of either:

- a statutory rule;
- the common law; or
- the public interest.

Under common law the general principle is that an illegal contract is void and unenforceable, but certain exceptions to this have been developed by the courts. Where the contract is illegal because of a statute, the impact of this illegality will depend on the terms of the statute.

# Introduction

An agreement may possess all the requisite elements of a valid contract, such as offer and acceptance and consideration, but be unenforceable because it is illegal. The diversity of legal rules that can be breached and the wide scope of public policy make this branch of the law of contract rather complex. Contracts may be illegal at the time of their formation or because of the way they have been performed.

## Illegal at time of formation

Contracts may be illegal when entered into because they cannot be performed in accordance with their terms without the commission of an illegal act. For example, the contract may involve a breach of the criminal law, or it may be a statutory requirement for the parties to the contract to have a licence which they do not possess. This type of illegality is illustrated by **Levy v Yates** (1838). There used to be a statutory rule that a royal licence was required to perform a play within 20 miles of London. In that case the contract was between a theatre owner and an impresario, for the performance of a theatrical production where no royal licence had been obtained. The contract was illegal at the time of its formation.

## Illegal mode of performance

In some cases, a contract may be perfectly legal when it is made, but may be carried out in an illegal manner. This was the case in **Anderson Ltd v Daniel** (1924) where a statute provided that a seller of artificial fertiliser had to supply buyers with an invoice detailing certain chemicals used in its manufacture. The sellers failed to provide the necessary invoice. It was not against the law to sell artificial fertiliser, but it was against the law to sell it without following the statutory rules. As a result, the sellers were unable to claim the price when the defendants refused to pay.

## Illegality and remoteness

A contract may be entered into with the intention of using it to achieve an illegal purpose, but, if that illegal purpose is remote from the contract itself, the contract will not be tainted by that illegality and will still be valid. Thus in **21st Century Logistic Solutions Ltd v Madysen Ltd** (2004) a contract for the sale of goods was entered into. The purchaser intended to defraud the Government of VAT. The High Court held that this intention to defraud the Government was not sufficient to render the contract itself void for illegality, as this contract was just a standard contract for the sale of goods. The contract itself was lawful and merely provided the opportunity for the individual behind the intended fraud to profit from it. While it is true that there must reach a point at which an intention to do an illegal act is too remote from the original contract, the authors would question whether this point had been reached on the facts of the actual case.

# Violation of legal rules and public policy

A contract is clearly illegal where its formation, purpose or performance involves the commission of a legal wrong. But the law relating to illegal contracts extends beyond this. A contract is also regarded as being illegal where it involves conduct which the law disapproves of as contrary to the interests of the public, even though that conduct is not actually unlawful. In both cases the transaction is treated as an illegal contract and the courts will not enforce it. We will consider first where an agreement violates a legal rule and secondly where it is against public policy.

## The contract violates a legal rule

The contract may constitute a crime or a tort. The violation may be of a statutory rule or of common law.

### Breach of common law

There are a number of factors which may make a contract illegal at common law, the most important being where there is a contract to commit a crime or a tort. There are obvious reasons why the law would not want to uphold a contract between, for example, a contract killer and his or her client. Clearly, it is unlikely that many people employed to commit a criminal offence would sue for their fees, but this was effectively what happened in **Everet v Williams** (1725). Two highwaymen had agreed to share the spoils of their crime and when one tried to evade the agreement, the other sued for his share. Needless to say, he was unsuccessful. Of particular interest in practice are contracts in restraint of trade.

### Contracts in restraint of trade

This issue is highly important in practice. Restraint of trade concerns contracts which limit an individual's right to use his or her skills for payment, or to trade freely. Such contracts fall into four groups:

* Contracts for the sale of a business where the vendor promises not to compete with the purchaser. This might arise where, for example, Ann buys a shop from Ben, and seeks to prevent Ben from opening up another similar shop just around the corner, which might attract the old shop's potential customers.
* Contracts between businesses by which prices or output are regulated. This category is now largely governed by legislation (as discussed on pp. 252–3).
* Contracts in which an employee agrees that on leaving the company, they will not set up in business or be employed in such a way as to compete with that employer. This is common in businesses where personal skills and reputation attract custom, such as hairdressing or advertising. Such contracts tend to provide that the employee should not set up a competing business, or take a job with a competitor, within a certain geographical area and/or within a certain period of time after leaving. The main reason for such contractual terms is the concern that the employee may take customers with them to the new employer or business.
* Contracts where a person agrees to restrict their mode of trade by, for example, only accepting orders from one particular company. This is sometimes called a *solus agreement*, and is frequently used for petrol stations; in return for the land or a lease, the trader promises to buy only the goods of the mortgagee or lessor.

Any of these types of contract may amount to what is called a general restraint, if the contract completely prohibits trading, or a partial restraint if it limits trading to a certain time or area. In **Nordenfelt v Maxim Nordenfelt Guns and Ammunitions Co** (1894) it was held that either type of restraint is contrary to public policy and therefore void, unless it can be shown that it is reasonable with regard to the parties, and is not unreasonable with regard to the public interest. If this can be done, the contract will be valid.

The court must be satisfied that the party making the restriction actually needs to protect their interests. The only legitimate interests employers may seek to protect are their relationship with customers and their trade secrets. Restrictions designed simply to prevent competition will not be upheld.

In considering reasonableness, the court must be satisfied that the agreement is no wider than is necessary to protect those interests, and the scope of the restraint and the area and period of time it covers are all properly balanced against one another. Thus a restriction might be held void if applied over a large geographical area, or for a long time, but it might equally be valid if it only covered a small area or was to last for a short time.

In **Mason** v **Provident Clothing Co** (1913) the House of Lords held that a restriction on an employee which prevented him from working in the same trade within 25 miles of London was wider than was necessary to protect his former employer's business, and was therefore void. Similarly, in **Esso Petroleum Co Ltd** v **Harper's Garage (Stourport) Ltd** (1968) the owner of two garages entered into a contract in which he agreed, among other things, to sell only Esso petrol, in return for a discount on the price per gallon. This restriction was to run for nearly four and a half years on one garage, but 21 years on the other. The House of Lords upheld the four-and-a-half-year agreement, but said the 21-year contract was unreasonable, because it was much longer than was necessary to protect Esso's interests, and therefore void. In reaching this decision the House of Lords took into account the recommendations of a report by the Monopolies Commission, published in 1965, which recommended a five-year limit on all 'tied garage' agreements.

The purpose of invalidating agreements in restraint of trade is to promote competition, but there are cases in which it is recognised that it may be desirable to allow people to bind themselves not to compete. For instance, with the sale of certain types of business, it would simply be impossible to sell if you could not assure the buyer that you would not set up in competition and gain all their potential customers.

## Topical Issue

### Wayne Rooney's image rights

In **Proactive Sports Management Ltd** v **Rooney** (2010) the footballer, Wayne Rooney, had entered into a contract in 2003 with Proactive Sports (sports agents) when he was only 17 years old and had not received any prior legal advice about the contract. Under this agreement, Wayne Rooney gave Proactive Sports the exclusive rights to exploit his image for eight years and Proactive would keep a commission of 20 per cent of any money paid to use those rights. The Football Association recommends that such contracts should be for only two years. Rooney sought to terminate the contract in 2009 and Proactive Sports sued Rooney for breach of contract, claiming over £4 million in compensation. Rooney argued that the contract was illegal for unreasonable restraint of trade. The Court of Appeal accepted this argument. The contract would have imposed substantial restraints on Mr Rooney's freedom to exploit his earning ability over a long period of time, on terms which were not commonplace in the market. The restraint of trade imposed on Rooney was not reasonable, particularly given the very substantial imbalance in bargaining power of the parties. The agreement was unfair and oppressive. It did not matter that Rooney's main trade was as a footballer and that was how he earned most of his money, with his image rights just a sideline. Where businesses seek to contractually restrain the trade of others they should ensure such clauses only protect legitimate business interests and are not unreasonably wide.

## Breach of legislation

Some types of contract are expressly declared void by statute. An example of a contract that was illegal because of legislation is **Cope** v **Rowlands** (1836). The claimant, a stockbroker, did some work for the defendant, but the defendant failed to pay. Under statute, it was an offence for a stockbroker to work within the City of London without a licence, and the claimant did not have such a licence. As a result, his action was dismissed, on the grounds that the statute prohibited him acting as a broker, and therefore the courts could not enforce a contract that involved him doing so.

The most important types of contract expressly declared void by statute are contracts which discriminate and contracts in restraint of trade which breach competition law.

## Contracts which discriminate

Under the Equality Act 2010 certain contracts can be found to be illegal because they discriminate either directly or indirectly against people with protected characteristics. The protected characteristics are: age, disability, gender reassignment, marriage, civil partnership, pregnancy, maternity, race, religion or belief, sex and sexual orientation. The Act prohibits discrimination in relation to the provision of public services (which includes the provision of both goods and services); the disposal of premises; work (both employment and partnerships); education and associations. Section 142 of the Act states:

> (1) A term of a contract is unenforceable against a person in so far as it constitutes, promotes or provides for treatment of that or another person that is of a description prohibited by this Act.

## Competition law

We have seen that the common law lays down some controls on contracts in restraint of trade. But these controls give only limited protection to third parties who may be adversely affected by these contracts. A more comprehensive approach to this problem has, since 1956, been made by legislation. One of the main goals of the European Union is to promote free trade between member states, and clearly restrictive trade agreements can affect this policy. Where a restrictive trade agreement could affect trade between member states, it will only be valid if allowed under both European Union and English law; if there is a conflict, European law should prevail, with the main provision contained in Article 85(1) of the European Community Treaty. Where an agreement is invalid under both, problems may arise as to which should determine the consequences of invalidity, but again, European law should, in theory, prevail.

The relevant UK legislation is now contained in the Competition Act 1998. This Act prohibits a number of anti-competitive practices; it does so in words which closely follow those of Article 85 of the European Community Treaty. The main difference between the two sets of provisions lies in their geographical scope. The Act applies to trade in the UK while Article 85 applies to trade in the whole of the European Union.

The 1998 Act applies to agreements between undertakings, decisions by associations of undertakings or concerted practices, which (a) may affect trade and (b) have as their object or effect the prevention, restriction or distortion of trade. Prohibited agreements are in general void unless an exemption is granted by the Director-General of Fair Trading (under the 1998 Act) or the European Union authorities (under the Treaty).

Prohibitions under the 1998 Act and Article 85 only apply where the agreement has an appreciable effect on competition, and not where that effect is insignificant. The crucial factor in determining whether the effect is appreciable is the percentage of the share of the market affected by it: a share of less than 5 per cent is probably not sufficient. Many of the agreements dealt with by the common law rules discussed earlier in this chapter would not have a sufficiently 'appreciable' effect to be prohibited by the legislation. This seems to reflect the different purpose of the two sets of rules. The legislation is concerned with the effect of agreements on the economy as a whole, while under the common law rules an agreement may be void by reason of its adverse effect on the party restrained by it.

## Gambling

In the past contracts concerned with betting were not enforceable. However, the law in this area was changed by the Gambling Act 2005 and the old legislation was repealed. Under s. 335 of the 2005 Act, contracts concerned with gambling are now usually legal and enforceable provided they comply with the general contractual rules discussed in this book. Thus, contracts made for gambling purposes are to be treated in the same way as contracts made for other purposes. In particular, any debts that arise from gambling will now be enforceable.

The Gambling Commission, which has responsibility for regulating gambling in Great Britain, has the power to void a betting contract if it is satisfied that the bet was substantially unfair. In these circumstances any money paid in relation to the bet must be returned to the person who paid it. The power to void a bet is available to the Commission for six months from the day on which the result of the bet is determined, except where there has been a conviction for cheating, in which case there is no time limit.

## The contract is against public policy

Public policy is notoriously difficult to define, but essentially it assumes that there are some interests which are shared by most of society, which promote the smooth running of the type of society we have, and which should therefore be protected.

That does not mean that we all agree on exactly what those interests are, though most of us may agree on many of them. Although public policy is not the policy of any particular government or political party, it does involve political choices. For example, take the idea that it is public policy to promote free trade and competition, which is clearly accepted in English law. If you agree that free competition is the best way to ensure a balance of supply and demand, in which producers can only charge what the public are willing to pay, then you will agree that it is public policy to promote free trade and to limit the restrictions that can be placed on who makes what, and what they charge for it. On the other hand, you may feel that such a policy gives too much power to producers, especially where they are a small group of big organisations. If they all charge high prices, where does that leave the consumer? You might feel that rather than allowing them to trade freely, you want to restrict the prices they can charge. In that case, you would not consider it public policy to prevent such a restriction. Or you might consider it to be public policy to allow some restrictions and not others. This type of discussion has taken place recently in the context of car prices in the UK.

On almost any area of public policy there will be disagreements within society – even the idea that it is against public policy to uphold contracts with hitmen might be resisted by those who earn their living as contract killers! It is the job of Parliament and the judiciary to employ such public policy as will command the support of most people, though considering the elite background and conservative views of many judges, it is debatable whether this is always achieved.

Public policy changes over time as views and beliefs change. For example, in **Cowan** v **Milbourn** (1867) a contract for leasing a hall for a meeting of atheists was held to be illegal. Some 50 years later, in **Bowman** v **Secular Society** (1917), it was held that such a contract was not illegal at all, and today many people would regard even the suggestion that it might be as ridiculous.

It has been suggested that it is not open to the courts to find new ways in which a contract may be illegal on the grounds of being contrary to public policy. Given the rate at which social values have changed even in the last two or three decades – the position of women is an obvious example – this seems unlikely and undesirable. It may be, for example, that in the future a contract which involved discrimination on sexual or racial grounds could be deemed against public policy.

There are a range of contracts which are considered to be illegal because they are against the interests of public policy. The main categories of contract will be considered here.

## Contracts promoting sexual immorality

In **Pearce** v **Brookes** (1866) the claimant had hired a carriage to a prostitute knowing that she would use it to see clients. He was unable to enforce the contract when she failed to pay the hire charge. But as our society has become more liberal, the courts seem to be less willing to treat a contract as illegal on this ground. **Armhouse Lee Ltd** v **Chappell** (1996) concerned a contract under which the defendants paid the claimant to place adverts for telephone sex lines in magazines. When regulation of such publicity was increased the defendants terminated the contract as they no longer wished to advertise their services in this way. The claimant brought an action for the money due under the contract, but the defendants argued that the contract was illegal and therefore unenforceable as it promoted sexual immorality. This defence was rejected by the Court of Appeal. The court stated that though the adverts were distasteful, the sex lines were generally accepted by society and were regulated by the telephone industry. There was no evidence that any 'generally accepted moral code condemned these telephone sex lines'. It considered that contracts should only be found illegal under this heading if an element of public harm clearly existed. Thus, in the light of today's society, the courts will probably only treat a contract as illegal for promoting sexual immorality where the behaviour concerned amounts to, or involves, a criminal offence such as prostitution.

## Contracts prejudicial to the status of marriage

This category makes void any contract which seeks to restrict someone's right to marry or to choose their own partner, to charge for procuring a marriage partner, or to provide for the future separation of a married couple. For example, in **Hermann** v **Charlesworth** (1905) the claimant paid a special client's fee of £52 to the defendant under a so-called 'marriage brokerage' contract. Despite being introduced to several men by the defendant, the claimant did not become engaged or married to any of them. The Court of Appeal decided that this contract was invalid as it was contrary to public policy to enforce marriage brokerage contracts.

### Pre-nuptial agreements

A pre-nuptial agreement seeks to lay down how a couple's wealth will be divided should a marriage break down. Such an agreement made after a couple have married is known as a post-nuptial agreement. The law in England on both pre and post-nuptial agreements is now the same and so we will refer to these together as nuptial agreements. The Privy Council in **MacLeod** v **MacLeod** (2008) had suggested that post-nuptial agreements were more likely to be applied by the courts than pre-nuptial agreements, but this distinction has been rejected by the Supreme Court in **Radmacher** v **Granatino** (2010) and **MacLeod** is now bad law on this point.

In some countries, including America and many European countries, nuptial agreements have become popular when wealthy individuals decide to get married. For public policy reasons, such agreements have not traditionally been recognised as binding contracts in England in order to protect the status of marriage. However, a shift in the English courts' approach can be seen in the leading Supreme Court case of **Radmacher** v **Granatino** (2010).

**Key Case**    Radmacher v Granatino

The Supreme Court in **Radmacher** v **Granatino** (2010) took the view that judges are not obliged in law to give effect to nuptial agreements, but often they would be prepared to give them decisive weight. When dividing up a couple's assets upon divorce, the courts are applying family law rather than contract law. The Matrimonial Causes Act 1973, s. 25 requires the judges to exercise judicial discretion to achieve fairness in these cases. Thus, the Supreme Court stated in **Radmacher**:

> The court should give effect to a nuptial agreement that is freely entered into by each party with a full appreciation of its implications unless in the circumstances prevailing it would not be fair to hold the parties to their agreement.

Nuptial agreements will not, therefore, be applied by the courts if they are unfair. Deciding whether a nuptial agreement is unfair:

> will necessarily depend upon the facts of the particular case, and it would not be desirable to lay down rules that would fetter the flexibility that the court requires to reach a fair result.

An agreement may make provisions that conflict with what a court considers fair and the existence of the agreement is capable of altering what is fair. In order to be fair:

- the husband and wife must have entered into the agreement of their own free will and without any undue influence, duress or pressure;
- both parties should be fully informed of the impact of entering into the agreement;
- there must not have been a material lack of disclosure so that both parties have all the relevant information (including financial information) to understand the impact of the agreement. Legal advice is not a necessity but it is 'obviously desirable';
- the parties should intend that the agreement will govern the financial consequences of the marriage coming to an end.

According to the Supreme Court there is nothing inherently unfair about an agreement that seeks to protect what might be called 'non-matrimonial property', such as a family inheritance and other assets owned prior to the marriage.

Generally, the longer a marriage lasts following the signing of a pre-nuptial agreement, the more likely the agreement will be unfair, due to unforeseen changes in circumstances, particularly where a young couple start marriage with only a few assets. The Supreme Court stated:

> The circumstances of the parties at the time of the agreement will be relevant. Those will include such matters as their age and maturity, whether either or both had been married or been in a long-term relationship before. What may not be easily foreseeable for less mature couples may well be in contemplation of more mature couples.

The requirement of fairness takes into account need, compensation and sharing. If the effect of an agreement would be to leave a party with less than he or she needs, then this is likely to be unfair. If one party has a valid case for an element of compensation (for example, for loss of earning power following a joint decision that a wife give up her career to look after the children), then an agreement which ignores such compensation is likely to be unfair. An agreement should not be allowed to prejudice the reasonable requirements of any children of the family.

The pre-nuptial agreement will be given varying weight and significance depending on the circumstances of each individual case. In appropriate cases the pre-nuptial agreement will have 'decisive weight'.

In **Radmacher** v **Granatino**, Ms Radmacher was a wealthy German heiress to a paper-making business who had inherited about £100 million. She married a French investment banker, Mr Granatino, in London in 1998. In 2003 he gave up his well-paid job as a banker where he was earning up to £300,000 a year with JP Morgan to study for a doctorate at Oxford University. He subsequently became a researcher at the University earning £30,000 a year. They had two daughters but divorced eight years later. Before marrying, the wife had asked her future husband to sign a pre-nuptial agreement. This was concluded in Germany and subject to German law. It provided that neither party was to gain financially should they get divorced. This agreement was binding under German and French law. The Supreme Court gave full weight to the pre-nuptial agreement because it was entered into willingly and knowingly by responsible adults. The husband had the opportunity to obtain independent legal advice and had decided not to do so; he was fully aware of the extent of the financial restrictions in the agreement; he knew his wife had substantial wealth and he did not need to know all the details; he was very intelligent and well established in banking when he signed the pre-nuptial agreement; he chose not to negotiate the terms of the agreement; it was understood at the time of signing the agreement that the couple intended to have children; and a pre-nuptial agreement is standard practice in France and Germany. While the pre-nuptial agreement was not enforceable under contract law, it was a decisive circumstance of the case under s. 25 of the Matrimonial Causes Act 1973. As a result, Mr Granatino was only awarded £1 million, instead of the £10 million he had been seeking. The husband's needs were covered by his earning capacity and indirectly by the financial provision ordered for the benefit of the children to which he would have access and which would provide him with accommodation and funds until the youngest daughter was aged 22. The Supreme Court approved the use of pre-nuptial agreements, stating that the courts should give due weight to the financial arrangements adults chose to make. Thus, in the absence of fraud, misrepresentation or undue influence, pre-nuptial agreements are likely to be followed by the courts.

On the facts of the case, the pre-nuptial agreement was given 'decisive weight'. It is slightly surprising that the agreement was found to be fair when there had been no disclosure of assets and no negotiation of the terms. The husband had neither a translation of the document nor independent legal advice and there was no provision in the document for any children.

The case brings England closer to the rest of Europe but does not actually make pre-nuptial agreements legally binding as the fairness of the agreements will be assessed by judges on a case-by-case basis.

### Legal Principle
Courts will give effect to a nuptial agreement that is freely entered into unless this would be unfair.

The earlier case law on the subject is of interest, but now has to be considered in the light of the **Radmacher** case. In **Crossley** v **Crossley** (2007) the Court of Appeal ruled:

> This is a childless marriage of very short duration, for a substantial portion of which the parties were living apart. The marriage was between mature adults, both of whom had been previously married and divorced; both parties have and had prior to the marriage very substantial independent wealth. The pre-nuptial agreement provides for the retention by each of the parties of their separate properties and division of joint property if any, and finally that there is no such joint property . . . If ever there is to be a paradigm case in which the court would look to the pre-nuptial agreement as not simply one of the peripheral factors but as a factor of magnetic importance, it seems to be that this is just such a case.

Ultimately the courts retain an absolute discretion to decide what is a fair outcome in each case and the decision in each case is very fact specific. The emphasis of the courts is to achieve fairness by making sure the needs of the parties and their children are catered for. If the pre-nuptial agreement fails to provide for their needs then the agreement will be ignored. A pre-nuptial agreement is more likely to be followed if the parties obtained prior legal advice and were fully informed about the other parties' wealth and the intended impact of the agreement. In **Z** v **Z** (2011) the couple were highly intelligent and well educated. No formal legal advice was given prior to entering the pre-nuptial agreement and the wife did not know all the detail of her husband's financial assets, though she had a general understanding of his financial position. The pre-nuptial agreement was applied but at the same time the wife received around 40 per cent of the total assets to meet her needs.

In **Kremen** v **Agrest** (2012) a Russian couple who had been married for 17 years had entered into a post-nuptial agreement when living in Israel. The High Court disregarded the agreement entirely as it severely prejudiced the reasonable needs of the children. The judge also held that the wife did not have a full appreciation of the implications of the agreement due to a lack of independent legal advice.

## Contracts prejudicial to public safety

The main types of contract made illegal on this ground are transactions with those living in an enemy country during wartime, contracts to perform acts which are illegal in a friendly foreign country and contracts which are damaging to foreign relations. An example of the latter is **Foster** v **Driscoll** (1929) where a contract to smuggle whisky into the USA, when the sale of alcohol was prohibited in that country, was illegal. The case of **Royal Boskalis Westminster NV** v **Mountain** (1997) arose from the Gulf War. The claimant was a company which had been working in Iraq when Kuwait was invaded in 1990. The United Nations imposed sanctions on Iraq and, in retaliation, the Iraqi Government seized the company's employees and assets based in their country. The company reached a deal with Iraq for the release of its employees and some of its assets, in return for making a lump sum payment to Iraq and waiving the money that was due for the work the company had carried out there. The lump sum payment was in breach of UN sanctions.

The claimant was insured by the defendant against the risks of war and sought reimbursement of the value of the waived claims, estimated at £84 million. The action was rejected and the Court of Appeal stated clearly that the agreement would not be given effect to by an English court as, by breaching the UN sanctions, it was contrary to public policy and illegal.

## Contracts prejudicial to the administration of justice

An example of an agreement the courts would find prejudicial to the administration of justice would be an agreement not to report a criminal offence in return for payment. In the past the courts have treated agreements to fund another's litigation with a view to sharing the winnings, as contrary to public policy. Such arrangements are described as 'champertous'. The courts are taking an increasingly restrictive view of the scope of the rules on champerty, particularly with the cuts to the availability of legal aid so that parties are having to look at alternative sources of finance. In **Morris** v **Southwark London Borough Council** (2011) a council tenant brought an action against the council alleging failure to perform its repairing obligations. She instructed solicitors under a 'no win, no fee' agreement, known formally as a conditional fee agreement. This is allowed under the Courts and Legal Services Act 1980, but the contract did not just agree to pay the solicitor a success fee which is expressly allowed by the Act, but also the solicitor undertook to pay the client's costs if she lost the case and had not been able to take out insurance to cover this expense. The Court of Appeal held this agreement was not (and never had been) champertous because it was not an agreement to share in success but to bear the costs of failure. The court noted that modern public policy was to facilitate access to civil justice and accordingly it was hard to accept it was against public policy for a lawyer to agree to shoulder the risk of an adverse order for costs.

### Contracts to oust the jurisdiction of the courts

A contract which purports to deprive the courts of a jurisdiction which they would otherwise have is not enforceable. An example of this was **Bennett** v **Bennett** (1952) where a wife promised her husband that she would not apply to a divorce court for maintenance.

### Contracts tending to encourage corruption in public life

A contract was held illegal on this ground in **Parkinson** v **College of Ambulance Ltd and Harrison** (1925). The claimant had given a charity £3,000 after receiving assurances from its secretary that it could secure him a knighthood. It failed to do so, but he was not allowed to claim back his money because of the illegality of the transaction.

## The effect of an illegal contract

The effect of an illegal contract will depend on whether it is illegal because of a statute or because of the common law. Where the contract is illegal because of a statute, in some cases the statute provides for the consequences of any illegality.

Under common law the general principle is that an illegal contract is void and unenforceable. This general principle was laid down in 1775 in the case of **Holman** v **Johnson**. Thus, a court will never 'enforce' an illegal contract, in the sense of ordering a party actually to do something that is unlawful or contrary to public policy. The courts have, however, developed certain exceptions to the general principle of the unenforceability of an illegal contract. The precise effects of an illegal contract depend on whether the contract is illegal at the time of its formation or is illegal because of the way in which it is performed.

### Contracts illegal at time of formation

In this case the contract is treated as if it was never made, so the illegal contract is unenforceable by either party. Where the making of the contract is unlawful, neither party can sue on it, not even one who is unaware of the facts which make it illegal and has been deceived by the other.

An example of this basic principle is **Re Mahmoud and Ispahani** (1921). The sale of linseed oil was prohibited by legislation unless both the seller and the buyer had a licence. The claimant, who had a licence to sell, asked the defendant whether he had a licence to buy. The defendant replied untruthfully that he did. Relying on that representation, the claimant agreed to sell linseed oil to the defendant. The defendant refused to accept delivery and, when sued for damages for non-acceptance, successfully pleaded the illegality of the contract. The contract was expressly forbidden and the court would do nothing to enforce it. Another example is **Ashton** v **Turner** (1981) where two people had agreed (when drunk) to commit a burglary. One of them was injured when the other negligently drove the getaway car, and sued for damages. The action failed as it would have been obviously contrary to public policy to allow such a claim.

Because the contract is unenforceable, property handed over under an illegal contract cannot be recovered, a point illustrated by the case of **Parkinson** v **College of Ambulance Ltd and Harrison** which concerned a donation made to a charity in order to get a knighthood (mentioned above).

There are two main exceptions to the general principle that the contract is unenforceable. The first exception applies where one party is more at fault than the other (they are described as not being *in pari delicto*). In such a situation the courts may be prepared to view the less guilty party as the victim of the transaction and allow them to recover property transferred to the more guilty party.

The second exception to the general rule that a contract illegal at the time of its formation is unenforceable, allows one person to recover their property which is the subject of the agreement tainted by illegality. This is possible if they can rely on some other cause of action not involving the illegal contract, for example, by relying on an independent tort.

In **Bowmakers** v **Barnet Instruments Ltd** (1945) Bowmakers supplied certain machine tools to the defendants under three hire-purchase contracts. These contracts were illegal as they breached wartime regulations. The defendants, having failed to make all the hire-purchase payments, sold some of the tools and refused to return the others. They subsequently argued that Bowmakers had no remedy against them, because the hire-purchase contracts were illegal. The Court of Appeal allowed the claimants' claim, holding that they did not need to rely on the illegal contracts as, being the owners of the goods, they had a separate cause of action for conversion (a civil wrong which occurs when a party treats someone else's property as their own).

This approach was followed by the House of Lords in **Tinsley** v **Milligan** (1993). Two women lived in a house together. Both of them had provided money to buy it, but they had agreed for ownership to be in Tinsley's name only, so that Milligan could make false claims for social security payments (from which they both benefited). Despite this, there was an understanding that the house was jointly owned. They later quarrelled and Tinsley sought sole possession of the house, arguing that any earlier agreement between them was unenforceable because of its illegal nature. The House of Lords found that Milligan had rights to the house independent of any illegal contract. By contributing to the purchase price of the house and agreeing between themselves that the house was jointly owned, a right in equity (known as a trust) had been created in favour of Milligan.

## Contracts illegal as performed

We have seen that a contract, perfectly lawful when made, may be carried out in an illegal manner. It will be possible to enforce the illegal contract if the illegal act was merely incidental to the performance of the contract. For example, a contract for the delivery of goods may not be tainted by illegality when the lorry driver who delivered the goods is caught speeding or parking his vehicle illegally during the delivery. In **St John Shipping Corp** *v* **Joseph Rank Ltd** (1957) the claimant had carried grain for the defendants from Alabama to England. In doing so, the claimant had overloaded its ship so that the load line was submerged. That was a statutory offence, and the claimant was prosecuted and fined for it. The defendants then sought to withhold part of the payment due, on the basis that the claimant had carried out the contract in an unlawful manner. Devlin J held that the claimant was entitled to full payment as the illegal act was merely incidental to the performance of the contract.

Where the contract is merely illegal because of the way it has been performed, it is possible for either both or only one of the parties to intend illegal performance. It is customary to distinguish between the situation where the legally objectionable features were known to both parties and where they were known to only one of them.

## Both parties aware of illegal performance

If both parties are aware that its performance is illegal, the consequences for this type of contract are the same as for a contract that is illegal at the time of its formation: neither party can enforce it. In **Ashmore, Benson, Pease & Co Ltd** *v* **AV Dawson Ltd** (1973) the defendants agreed to transport two boilers belonging to the claimant, and did so by carrying the boilers on lorries which could not lawfully carry the loads in question. The goods were damaged in the course of transit, but the claim of the owner for damages was rejected; the owner of the goods not only knew that the goods were being transported in an illegal manner, but had actually 'participated' in the illegality in the sense of assisting the defendant carrier to perform the contract in an illegal manner. Another example is **Pearce** *v* **Brookes** (above) where the claimant knew that the prostitute was going to use the carriage for the purposes of her trade and therefore he was unable to enforce the contract.

## Only one party aware of illegal performance

When one party did not know of the illegal performance of the contract by the other party, the innocent party can enforce it. An example might be where a person hires out their car, not knowing that it is going to be used to carry stolen goods. In such a case, all the usual contractual remedies are at the disposal of the innocent party, so long as they repudiate the contract or refuse to continue with it as soon as they know of the illegality.

Thus, in **Archbolds (Freightage) Ltd** *v* **S Spanglett Ltd** (1961) the A company agreed with the B company to carry goods in a van which, unknown to the B company, was not licensed for the purpose. The contract involved the commission of a criminal offence by the A company in using the van for this purpose. But since the B company was unaware of this fact, it was not prevented from suing the A company for failure to deliver the goods.

Where the innocent party has provided any performance of the contract, they may sue on a *quantum meruit* for its value (see p. 376). In **Clay** *v* **Yates** (1856) a printer had contracted to print a book for the defendant. During the printing, he discovered that part of the book was libellous and left out that part. The defendant refused to pay for the printing because of the omission, but the court held that the printer was entitled to be paid for the work he had carried out.

Where one party is completely innocent, the guilty party in these circumstances cannot sue on the contract for damages, or recover any property handed over, unless this can be done without relying on the illegal contract. In **Cowan** *v* **Milbourn** (1867) the defendant agreed to let rooms to the claimant, but later refused to carry out the contract when he learnt that the rooms were to be used for giving blasphemous lectures. As this was an unlawful purpose, the claimant, who was the guilty party, had no remedy.

## Severance

In some cases, it is possible to divide the illegal part of a contract from the rest, and enforce the provisions which are not affected by the illegality – this is called severance. It appears that the illegal parts of a contract can be severed if they are relatively unimportant to the contract and if the severance leaves the nature of the contract unaltered, because the words can be simply lifted out of the contract with no rewording required. If the unlawful part of a contract cannot be severed, the whole contract will be void. For example, in **Goldsoll** *v* **Goldman** (1915) the claimant bought the business of the defendant, who traded in imitation jewellery in the UK. It was a term of the contract that the defendant would not trade in either imitation or real jewellery in the UK, or in a number of specified foreign countries. The Court of Appeal decided that it was unreasonable for the claimant to restrict the defendant from trading in real jewellery, or from trading in either type of jewellery abroad, since the business interests he sought to protect were limited to selling imitation jewellery in the UK. Nevertheless, they said that this did not make the agreement void; the unreasonable parts could be severed from it and the remaining agreement could be enforced.

# Criticism

The Law Commission has criticised this area of law for its complexity, its potential to give rise to unjust decisions and its lack of certainty (Law Commission, *Illegal transactions: the effect of illegality on contracts and trusts* (2000)).

## Complexity

The Law Commission considers the law to be too complex because the courts have started with draconian principles, such as that illegal contracts are unenforceable, and have then had to develop a large number of exceptions to these principles in order to do justice. According to the Law Commission, '[t]he law has thereby been rendered needlessly complex, technical and difficult to justify'.

## Injustice

The Law Commission has argued:

> it has been widely recognised that the illegality rules may lead to injustice and, in particular, to the unjust enrichment of the defendant at the plaintiff's expense. Lord Mansfield made it clear in **Holman** *v* **Johnson** (1775) that an unmeritorious defendant could raise the illegality defence against the plaintiff's claim, despite the defendant's own involvement in the illegal act or purpose and even if the success of the defendant would leave the defendant with an unearned windfall.

Lord Goff commented in a dissenting speech in **Tinsley** *v* **Milligan**:

> It is important to observe that . . . the principle is not a principle of justice; it is a principle of policy, whose application is indiscriminate and so can lead to unfair consequences as between the parties to litigation.

This approach to the illegality of a contract was challenged in **Shanshal** *v* **Al-Kishtaini** (2001) on the basis that it violated Article 1 of the First Protocol of the European Convention on Human Rights, which has been incorporated into national law by the Human Rights Act 1998. This states that 'every natural or legal person is entitled to the peaceful enjoyment of his possessions. No one shall be deprived of his possessions except in the public interest and subject to law.' The claimant had entered into contracts to lend money to Iraqi citizens. This was in breach of United Nations sanctions in force at the time which prohibited trade with Iraqi nationals. As a result the contracts were illegal and the claimant was not entitled to recover the money he had handed over under the contracts. The Convention had not been breached because these facts fell within the 'public interest' exception.

The courts frequently fail to take into account the gravity of the illegality and the culpability of the parties when determining the effects of the illegality. This was the case in **Mohamed** *v* **Alaga & Co** (1998) where the claimant entered into an oral agreement with the defendant solicitor. Under this agreement, the claimant would refer clients (Somali refugees) to the solicitor and assist the solicitor in preparing the clients' asylum applications in return for a share in the solicitor's fees from the Legal Aid Board. This agreement breached rules made under the Solicitors Act 1974, although the claimant did not know this. After making several referrals and carrying out the agreed work, the claimant claimed payment under the contract. Despite the trial judge's finding that it was highly blameworthy of the defendant to enter into such a contract, the claimant's claim was refused. The (guilty) defendant therefore benefited from the (innocent) claimant's work without being required to make any payment for it.

### Uncertainty

There are several areas of the law on illegality where it is not possible to state with any certainty what the relevant rules are.

# Reform

### The Law Commission on Illegality

In 1999 the Law Commission published a consultation paper *Illegal Transactions: the effect of illegality on contracts and trusts*, in which it suggested that legislation should be passed to reform the rules governing the effect of illegality. It considered that the existing technical and complex rules should be replaced by a judicial discretion. It proposed that where a contract involved an element of illegality, the court should have a structured discretion whether to enforce it. Under that discretion the court would decide whether or not to enforce an illegal transaction, to recognise that property rights had been transferred or created by it, or to allow benefits conferred under it to be recovered. Illegality would continue to be used only as a defence to claims under contract. It did not, however, recommend that the court should have an open-ended discretion to produce whatever it considered to be the just solution. Instead the proposed discretion would be structured in order to provide greater certainty and guidance. In exercising its discretion, a court would consider:

- the seriousness of the illegality involved;
- the knowledge and intention of the party seeking to enforce the illegal transaction;
- whether refusing to allow standard rights and remedies would deter illegality;
- whether refusing to allow standard rights and remedies would further the purpose of the rule which renders the transaction illegal; and
- whether refusing to allow standard rights and remedies would be proportionate to the illegality involved.

Where, however, a statute had expressly provided what should be the effect of the involvement of illegality on a transaction, the Law Commission recommended that the proposed discretion should not apply. In other words, it did not want the courts to be able to use the discretion to override the express provisions of a statute.

It hoped that its proposals would have two major advantages over the present law. First, a court would be able to reach its decision on the facts of a particular case using open and explicit reasoning, giving full effect to the relevance of the illegality on the transaction. Secondly, the proposals would result in illegality being used less frequently to deny claimants their usual rights or remedies. That is, under the discretion, illegality would only act as a defence where there was a clear and justifiable public interest that it should do so.

The Law Commission published its final report *The Illegality Defence* in 2010. In this report the Law Commission took a very different view of the subject and concluded that it no longer considered it necessary to introduce general legislative reform in this area. Instead, it considered that the law should be left to develop through the case law. It considered that recent cases such as the House of Lords' case of **Stone & Rolls** *v* **Moore Stephens** (2009) showed a willingness of the courts to take into account the policy factors which lie behind the illegality defence and to explain their reasoning accordingly.

There was just one area where it thought Parliament should intervene and that was to tackle problems which had arisen as a result of the case of **Tinsley** *v* **Milligan** (1993), discussed on p. 259. While the courts may have achieved a satisfactory outcome on the facts of that particular case, the legal principles that the case developed had caused problems in different contexts. The case enabled people to profit from their criminal agreements, such as agreements to engage in money laundering. The Law Commission therefore recommended that where a trust has been set up to conceal the beneficiary's interest in order to commit a criminal offence, legislation should provide the judges with a discretion to deprive the beneficiary of their interest in limited circumstances. In most cases the beneficiary would be able to rely on their normal legal right to enforce the trust, but a court would have a discretion to deny the beneficiary this right in exceptional circumstances. The type of factors for the court to consider when exercising its discretion are laid down in a draft Bill and include the conduct of the parties; the value of the interest at stake; whether refusing the claim would act as a deterrent; and the interests of third parties. The Law Commission noted that it is unmarried couples who are most likely to be affected by this reform as when they buy a home together less than half register the property in their joint names, which can then give rise to problems if they subsequently separate.

## Topical Issue

### Pre- and post-nuptial agreements

Pre- and post-nuptial agreements are binding in America, Australia and most of Europe. On her successful legal proceedings in the Supreme Court in **Radmacher v Granatino** (2010), Ms Radmacher commented:

> We made a promise to each other that, if anything went wrong between us, both of us would walk away without making financial claims on each other. The promise made to me was broken. I know some people think of pre-nuptial agreements as being unromantic, but for us it was meant to be a way of proving you are marrying only for love.

Church leaders are, however, opposed to these agreements on the basis that they undermine marriage and encourage easy divorces. The Law Commission suggests that some wealthy people are actually being deterred from getting married because of the financial risks the current law exposes them to. It is arguable that in any pre-nuptial or post-nuptial agreement there will be improper pressure, given the financial and social inequality between men and women both before and after marriage. In practice, nuptial agreements are generally used by wealthy members of society in an attempt to protect their wealth; for example, when marrying for a second time, to protect the inheritance of their children from the first marriage. They are often protecting the wealth of a rich man from a less wealthy and less powerful future wife.

The Conservative Party's manifesto in 2010 stated that once in office it would legislate to make pre-nuptial agreements legally binding, though this reform has not yet been included in Parliament's legislative programme.

The Law Commission has published a report entitled *Matrimonial property, needs and agreements* (2014). At the moment, following **Radmacher v Granatino** (2010), the courts decide on a case-by-case basis how much weight to give to such agreements. This can lead to uncertainty and expensive litigation. The Commission has recommended that legislation should be passed on the subject, with nuptial agreements being enforceable with suitable safeguards. The agreement would have to make a sufficient provision for both parties' financial needs, as well as the needs of any children.

To be binding the agreement would have to satisfy a number of safeguards. The agreement would have to be:

- compliant with the traditional contractual rules (for example, no duress, misrepresentation or mistake in entering the contract);
- entered after the parties had received independent legal advice;
- entered after full disclosure of material information about the parties' financial situation;
- in writing;
- signed at least 28 days before the wedding or civil partnership; and
- made by deed and contain a statement that the parties understand that the marital agreement will partially remove the court's discretion to make financial orders.

Qualifying pre-nuptial agreements would then be binding on the couple, giving them autonomy and control and making the financial outcome of separation more predictable.

The debate over nuptial agreements is primarily of interest to wealthy couples. For the majority of people getting a divorce, there are only limited assets and income and these will be divided purely on the basis of the parents' and children's needs for housing and subsistence. Most couples have just enough to support two separate lives, with nothing left to divide up through any nuptial agreement.

## Answering questions

 Jack agrees to sell his plumbing business in Wetherbridge to Nicola for £10,000. The written contract between them includes a term stating that Jack will not open a rival plumbing business within 25 miles of Wetherbridge for ten years, nor, during that period, will he approach any customers of the business now owned by Nicola. Jack does not read the contract until after he has signed it. Five years later, Jack plans to set up a plumbing business in Maltham, five miles from Wetherbridge. Advise Nicola.

 Nicola clearly wants to know whether she can enforce the contractual terms mentioned, and either prevent Jack setting up his new business by means of an injunction (discussed at p. 380), or claim damages for any effect it has on her own business. There seems little doubt that the clauses are part of the contract, even though Jack did not read them – see the rule in **L'Estrange** *v* **Graucob**.

Are they void for restraint of trade? Here you need to refer to the presumption set up in **Nordenfelt** *v* **Maxim Nordenfelt Guns and Ammunitions Co**, and the factors which dictate whether this presumption can be rebutted. Are the clauses reasonable with regard to the parties? Are they unreasonable with regard to the public interest – bearing in mind that the public interest includes competition in the marketplace? Is Nicola protecting a legitimate interest, or just trying to prevent competition? Are the clauses wider than is needed to protect her interests, and is the scope of the restraint and the area and period of time it covers properly balanced against one another? Whether Nicola can enforce the agreement will depend on the answers to these questions.

## Summary of Chapter 11

### Introduction

An agreement may be unenforceable because it is illegal. Contracts may be illegal at the time of their formation or because of the way they have been performed.

### Illegal at time of formation

Contracts may be illegal when entered into because they cannot be performed in accordance with their terms without the commission of an illegal act.

### Illegal mode of performance

A contract may be perfectly legal when it is made, but may be carried out in an illegal manner.

### Illegality and remoteness

A person may enter into a contract with the intention of using it to achieve an illegal purpose, but if that illegal purpose is remote from the contract itself, the contract will not be tainted by that illegality and will still be valid.

## Violation of legal rules and public policy

A contract is illegal when it violates a legal rule. In addition, a contract is regarded as being illegal where it involves conduct which the law disapproves of as contrary to the interests of the public, even though that conduct is not actually unlawful.

### The contract violates a legal rule

The contract may constitute a crime or a tort. The violation may be of a statutory rule or of common law.

#### Breach of common law

There are a number of factors which may make a contract illegal at common law, the most important being where there is a contract to commit a crime or a tort. Of particular interest in practice are contracts in restraint of trade.

#### Breach of legislation

Some types of contract are expressly declared void by statute, most notably contracts which discriminate and contracts in restraint of trade.

### The contract is against public policy

Public policy is notoriously difficult to define, but essentially it assumes that there are some interests which are shared by most of society, which promote the smooth running of the type of society we have, and which should therefore be protected. There are a range of contracts which are considered to be illegal because they are against the interests of public policy. The main categories of contract are:

- contracts promoting sexual immorality;
- contracts prejudicial to the status of marriage;
- contracts prejudicial to public safety;
- contracts prejudicial to the administration of justice;
- contracts to oust the jurisdiction of the courts;
- contracts tending to encourage corruption in public life.

## The effect of an illegal contract

The effect of an illegal contract will depend on whether it is illegal because of either a statute or the common law. Where the contract is illegal because of a statute, in some cases the statute provides for the consequences of any illegality. Under common law the general principle is that an illegal contract is void and unenforceable. The precise effects of an illegal contract depend on whether the contract is illegal at the time of its formation or is illegal owing to the way in which it is performed.

### Contracts illegal at time of formation

In this case the contract is treated as if it was never made, so the illegal contract is unenforceable by either party. There are two main exceptions to the general principle that the contract is unenforceable. The first is that a person will be able to recover their property if they can rely on some other cause of action which does not involve the illegal contract, for example, by relying on an independent tort. The second exception applies where one party is more at fault than the other.

### Contracts illegal as performed

We have seen that a contract, perfectly lawful when made, may be carried out in an illegal manner. It will be possible to enforce the illegal contract if the illegal act was merely incidental to the performance of the contract. Where the contract is merely illegal because of the way it has been performed, it is possible for either both or only one of the parties to intend illegal performance. It is customary to distinguish between the situation where the legally objectionable features were known to both parties and where they were known to only one of them. If both parties are aware that its performance is illegal, the consequences for this type of contract are the same as for a contract that is illegal at the time of its formation: neither party can enforce it. When one party did not know of the illegal performance of the contract by the other party, the innocent party can enforce it.

### Severance

In some cases, it is possible to divide the illegal part of a contract from the rest, and enforce the provisions which are not affected by the illegality – this is called severance.

## Reading list

Buckley, 'Illegal transaction: chaos or discretion?' (2000) 20 Legal Studies 155

Buckley (2002) *Illegality and Public Policy* London: Sweet and Maxwell

Creighton, 'The recovery of property transferred for illegal purposes' (1997) 60 Modern Law Review 102

Enonchong, 'Title claims and illegal transactions' (1995) 111 Law Quarterly Review 135

Molan and Boyle, 'Marital agreements: who's got it right?' (2012) 162 New Law Journal 1304

Rose, 'Reconsidering illegality' (1996) 10 Journal of Contract Law 271

Todd, 'The inevitable triumph of the ante-nuptial agreement' (2006) Family Law 539

Vine, 'Family: a new direction?' (2012) 162 New Law Journal 1344

Virgo, 'Withdrawal from illegal transactions – a matter for consideration' (1996) Cambridge Law Journal 23

### Reading on the internet

The Law Commission's Report *The Illegality Defence* (2010, Law Com. No. 320) is available on the Law Commission's website at:

http://www.lawcom.gov.uk/docs/lc320.pdf

Law Commission Consultation Paper *Illegal transactions: the effect of illegality on contracts and trusts* (1999) is available at:

http://www.lawcom.gov.uk/docs/cp154.pdf

# Chapter 12
## Duress and undue influence

### This chapter explains:

that a contract is voidable where it has been obtained by duress or undue influence. Duress exists where illegitimate pressure was exerted on a contracting party which induced that party to enter the contract. The courts will find undue influence where one party uses their influence over the other to persuade them to make a contract. There are two types of undue influence:

- actual; and
- presumed.

Where a court finds that a contract was made as a result of undue influence, it may set it aside or modify its terms so as to mitigate the disadvantage.

Since a contract will only be binding if the parties voluntarily consent to it, it is obvious that where one party is forced to consent by threats or undue persuasion by the other, that consent should be invalid. The law has developed two doctrines to deal with this issue: the common law of duress, and the equitable one of undue influence. Both render a contract voidable.

# Duress

Five conditions need to be satisfied in order for there to be a finding of duress:

1 Pressure was exerted on the contracting party.
2 This pressure was illegitimate.
3 The pressure induced the claimant to enter the contract.
4 The claimant had no real choice but to enter the contract.
5 The claimant protested at the time or shortly after the contract was made.

Each of these conditions will be considered in turn.

## Pressure exerted on the contracting party

Pressure must have been exerted on the innocent contracting party, which amounted to a compulsion of the will. Traditionally, the common law doctrine of duress would only make a contract voidable where one party had obtained the other's consent by means of physical violence or threats of it, or unlawful constraint. Over the past 25 years, the courts have extended the scope of the doctrine to include what has come to be known as economic duress. Although still a relatively new doctrine, in modern times it appears to have more practical significance than the traditional concept of duress.

Economic duress occurs where one party was forced into the contract because of economic pressure. Of course, very few contracts are made without any economic pressure at all. How many of us would enter into employment contracts, for example, if we did not need to earn a living? Therefore, to constitute economic duress, economic pressure must go a great deal further than

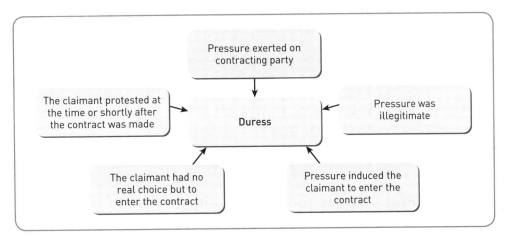

**Figure 12.1** Duress

the ordinary pressure of the market, and most of the cases on the subject have been attempts to define just how much further.

### Key Case — North Ocean Shipping Co *v* Hyundai Construction Co (*The Atlantic Baron*)

Economic duress first arose in **North Ocean Shipping Co *v* Hyundai Construction Co** (*The Atlantic Baron*) (1979) which concerned a contract for the building of a ship. As is commonly the case where duress is raised, the dispute concerned not the initial formation of the contract, but a purported modification of its terms. Such modifications are treated in law as if they were the formation of a new contract. All the usual requirements for the formation of a contract must therefore be satisfied. Both parties must agree to the changes. If one party's consent is achieved by duress, the modification is not binding.

Although the price of the ship had been fixed at the outset, while it was being built the sellers decided to raise the price by 10 per cent, because of a drop in the exchange rate of the dollar. The buyers were not happy about this, but were unwilling to risk delaying completion of the ship, as they were already negotiating for it to be chartered (which means rented) by a major oil company. They therefore agreed to pay the increased price.

Eight months after the ship was delivered, the buyers tried to sue the sellers, claiming back the extra 10 per cent paid because, they said, it had been extracted from them under duress. The judge agreed that economic pressure such as that applied could constitute duress; the question was whether there had been any 'compulsion of the will', and this compulsion could stem from economic pressure as much as from physical force. In this particular case the buyers were not allowed to recover the extra 10 per cent. This was not because there was no duress – in fact the court held that there probably was – but because by waiting so long after delivery, they had effectively affirmed the modification.

> **Legal Principle**
> Duress arises when there is a compulsion of the will from economic or physical pressure.

The principle that economic pressure could amount to duress was confirmed in **Pao On *v* Lau Yiu Long** (1979), a rather complex case in which the claimants threatened to break a contract to buy shares in a company unless the defendants, who were shareholders in that company, guaranteed them against losses which might arise when the value of the shares fluctuated. The defendants gave the guarantee, because they were concerned that if the contract did not go ahead, there might be a loss of confidence in their company. Applying the approach of *The Atlantic Baron*, the Privy Council held that there had been no 'compulsion of will', merely economic pressure that fell within the normal standards of business. Lord Scarman explained that a threat to break a contract was not in itself enough to constitute duress: 'It must be shown that the payment made or the contract entered into was not a voluntary act.'

## Pressure exerted was illegitimate

Illegitimate pressure must have been exerted on the other contracting party. A threat to do an unlawful act (which includes breaking a contract) will always be illegitimate, but a threat to do a lawful act will only be illegitimate if the threat is unreasonable, which will depend on the circumstances. This appears to have been the approach taken in **Atlas Express Ltd v Kafco (Importers and Distributors) Ltd** (1989). Here a small basketware company had secured a valuable contract to supply its products to Woolworths. They then contracted with a national firm of carriers to transport their products. After the contract with the carriers was made, the carriers insisted on raising their charges, threatening to stop deliveries unless the higher price was paid. This happened at a vulnerable time for Kafco, when the shops were beginning to require deliveries for the Christmas period, so they had no time to find an alternative carrier. They reluctantly agreed to the new terms, but later refused to pay the extra.

The court held that Kafco's agreement to pay extra had been obtained by duress, and was therefore not binding. The pressure applied was illegitimate, and Kafco had no realistic alternative but to agree. Had they had more time, they might have been expected to find an alternative carrier and then sue Atlas for breach, but in the circumstances this was completely impractical.

In **CTN Cash and Carry v Gallaher** (1994) the defendants were a cigarette supplier, who had a monopoly on the supply of the best-known brands. They supplied the claimant on credit terms. One of the claimant's orders was mistakenly delivered to the wrong warehouse, and when the claimant complained about this, the defendants admitted responsibility and agreed to redeliver them to the correct address. Unfortunately, the consignment was then stolen before the defendants had a chance to redeliver it. They supplied a new consignment to the correct address, and were paid for it, but then demanded payment for the stolen consignment as well. The claimant refused at first, but agreed when the defendants threatened that, unless the payment was made, they would withdraw credit facilities. The claimant argued that their agreement to make that payment was obtained by duress, but the court held that this was not the case. The defendants had not threatened to break their contract, only to alter its terms, which was not unlawful. The court stated that a lawful act could constitute duress, but that it was unlikely to do so in a commercial situation.

## Topical Issue

### Bravo Two Zero

During the Gulf War in 1991, eight SAS soldiers were dropped behind enemy lines to carry out a mission known as 'Bravo Two Zero'. The men had to search for and destroy Scud missiles and communication cables. Sadly, three SAS soldiers were killed, and of the five who survived, four were captured and tortured. The commanding officer of the group wrote a book, of which Bravo Two Zero formed a chapter. Two other survivors wrote books which were made into films: *Bravo Two Zero* and *The One that Got Away*. This raised concern in the Ministry of Defence that these publications were undermining the tradition of secrecy and solidarity among members of the SAS. It therefore prepared confidentiality contracts which forbade members of the Special Forces from making unauthorised disclosures of their work and secrets.

In **R v Attorney General for England and Wales** (2003) the defendant had been one of the soldiers who had survived the Bravo Two Zero mission and had not initially written about his experience. In May 1996 he was told by his commanding officer that if he wished to remain in the regiment he had to sign a confidentiality contract. If he refused to sign he would cease to be a member of the Special Forces, but would merely serve as an ordinary soldier. This would have involved a reduction in his pay and status. Such demotion only usually occurred where a disciplinary offence had been committed, or where a person was unsuitable for the Special Forces. The Ministry of Defence considered that a person who refused to sign the contract was unsuitable for this reason. The defendant was either informed that he could not obtain legal advice, or was not given the opportunity to do so. He was not allowed to read the contract in advance, although he had time to consider its subject matter before signing. He signed the contract but, soon after, he left the army and moved to New Zealand. In 1998 he entered into a contract with a New Zealand publisher to write his own account of the Bravo Two Zero mission.

The British Attorney General commenced proceedings in New Zealand for breach of the confidentiality contract that the defendant had signed. The Attorney General sought an injunction to block publication. The trial judge in New Zealand held that the defendant had been given an order to sign the confidentiality contract, and this order was unlawful (as it restricted his activities after he had left the army). The judge considered that the unlawful order combined with the threat to demote him amounted to duress.

The Court of Appeal in New Zealand allowed the Attorney General's appeal. It concluded that no order had been given, as the defendant had the option of refusing to sign and becoming an ordinary soldier. This choice put pressure on him, but was not unlawful. Although the Attorney General's appeal was technically successful, the Court of Appeal refused to order an injunction banning publication.

The case went up to the Privy Council where the appeal was dismissed. Pressure had been exerted on the defendant which had amounted to a compulsion of the will. No military order had been given (which had to be obeyed under military law), but the threat of demotion meant that in practice the defendant had no choice but to sign. However, this pressure was not illegitimate. The threat to remove the defendant from the Special Forces was not unlawful, as the Ministry of Defence had the right to do this. A threat to carry out a lawful act can still amount to illegitimate pressure if the threat is unreasonable. On the facts the threat was not unreasonable and therefore the pressure was not illegitimate. The demand that the defendant agree to keep activities of the Special Forces secret was justifiable. The Ministry of Defence had legitimate concerns that publications might undermine the effectiveness of the Special Forces.

## Pressure induced the claimant to enter the contract

Duress must be one of the reasons for entering (or modifying) a contract, but it does not have to be the only or even the main reason. In the Australian case of **Barton** v **Armstrong** (1975) Armstrong, a former chairman of a company, threatened to kill Barton, its managing director, if Barton did not agree to buy Armstrong's shares on terms which were decidedly favourable to Armstrong. Barton bought the shares, but there was some evidence that he in fact did so because it looked like a good business deal at the time. Nevertheless, the Privy Council decided that the contract was voidable for duress. Armstrong's threats had contributed to Barton's decision to sign the deed, even if they were not the only reason. This could be described as a 'but for' test of causation: but for the illegitimate pressure the claimant would not have entered the contract or made a payment.

## Claimant had no real choice but to enter the contract

**Universe Tankships** v **International Transport Workers' Federation (*The Universe Sentinel*)** (1983) concerned an industrial dispute. The ITWF insisted on a payment being made to its welfare fund before it would call off a strike, which was affecting a ship belonging to the claimant. The payment was made and, once the strike was lifted, the shipowners sought to reclaim it, as having been paid under duress. In deciding that the payments had indeed been made under duress, Lord Diplock further defined the test. He suggested that compulsion of will alone could not form the basis of duress, since in all cases there is a choice, even though it may be between two unpleasant options – in other words, the shipowners had the choice of paying the money or losing revenue while the ship was stuck in port; they were not actually compelled to pay the money. He suggested that the issue should be whether they had any practical alternative to complying with the threat, and whether the pressure applied would be regarded by the law as illegitimate.

It now appears that economic duress will be present where there is compulsion of the will to the extent that the party under threat has no practical alternative but to comply.

## Claimant protested at the time or shortly after the contract was made

In **The Atlantic Baron** (discussed on p. 270) it was because the claimant waited eight months after the ship was delivered that the claim for duress was unsuccessful.

# Undue influence

Undue influence is an equitable doctrine, which applies where one party uses their influence over the other to persuade them to make a contract. Where a court finds that a contract was made as a result of undue influence, it may set it aside, or modify its terms so as to mitigate the disadvantage. The leading case on the subject is the House of Lords' judgment of **Royal Bank of Scotland v Etridge (No 2)** (2001). There are two types of undue influence: actual and presumed.

## Actual undue influence

This arises where the claimant can prove that they entered the transaction as a result of undue influence from the other party. In these cases, the influence tends to be of a kind which is similar to, but falls short of, duress. An example might be where a person promises to pay money to someone as a result of a threat to report them for a criminal offence. This falls short of duress,

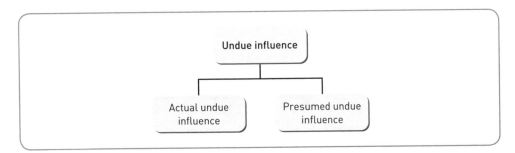

**Figure 12.2** Undue influence

since we cannot say there is no practical alternative but to comply, nor that the pressure applied is illegitimate, but it might still be considered inequitable to uphold the promise. This form of undue influence is rare in practice.

## Presumed undue influence

In certain circumstances an evidentiary presumption will be applied that shifts the burden of proof from the claimant to the defendant, so that it is up to the defendant to disprove the existence of undue influence. If the presumption of undue influence applies, this does not mean that undue influence exists, but rather that the burden of proof falls on the alleged wrongdoer to show that the transaction was not caused by undue influence. The alleged wrongdoer may satisfy this burden of proof and show that they did not exercise any undue influence over the other contracting party.

Undue influence may be presumed where there is a pre-existing relationship of confidence between the two parties to a contract, as a result of which one places trust in the other, and the contract between them is manifestly disadvantageous to the party who places trust in the other. Such a relationship of trust is called a fiduciary relationship, and it may arise in two ways. First, it may fall into one of several categories in which a relationship of trust is automatically presumed to exist. These categories are:

- parent and child;
- religious adviser and disciple;
- guardian and ward;
- solicitor and client;
- trustee and beneficiary; and
- doctor and patient.

Where the relationship does not come within one of these categories, a relationship of trust may nevertheless be established on the facts. In principle, any kind of relationship could be regarded as one of trust if this is justified by the circumstances of the case. Contracts between married couples or cohabitees can fall within this category or within actual undue influence depending on the facts of the case.

The defendant can rebut the presumption of undue influence by showing that the claimant entered into the contract freely, and this is usually done by establishing that independent advice was taken.

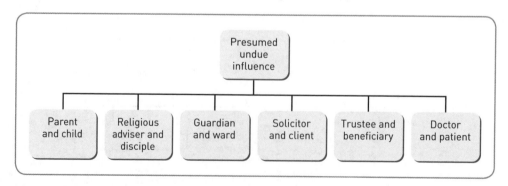

**Figure 12.3** Presumed undue influence

An example of a fiduciary relationship arising on the facts can be seen in **Lloyds Bank** v **Bundy** (1974). The claimant and his son both used the same bank. The son ran into business difficulties, and his father was asked to guarantee the son's overdraft, putting up his own farm as security. He did this, and when the son was unable to pay, the bank tried to possess the farm. The farmer claimed that the contract had been obtained by undue influence, on the basis that he had banked with Lloyds for a long time, and in that time had placed considerable trust in their advice, yet they had made no effort to warn him that it was not in his interest to give the guarantee. The Court of Appeal agreed that the presumption of undue influence had been raised; there was a relationship of trust on the facts, and the transaction was obviously disadvantageous. The bank was unable to rebut the presumption.

In **National Westminster Bank** v **Morgan** (1985) Mrs Morgan jointly owned the family home with her husband. As a result of his business problems, their mortgage payments fell into arrears, and the bank started to seek possession. Mr Morgan approached the bank to arrange a refinancing loan (this works as follows: if Mr Morgan's original mortgage was for £50,000, and he owed arrears of £5,000, he could replace the mortgage with a refinancing loan of £55,000, and start afresh). Mrs Morgan's signature was required to use the house as security for the extended loans. The bank manager went to see her, in the presence of Mr Morgan; she made it clear that she had little confidence in her husband's business, and wanted to talk to the manager alone, but this did not happen, and she eventually signed to prevent the house being repossessed.

The loan was not repaid, and Mr Morgan later died. When the bank tried to take possession of the house, Mrs Morgan pleaded undue influence, on the basis of **Lloyds Bank** v **Bundy**. The House of Lords held that there was no undue influence. The relationship between Mrs Morgan and the manager was no more than the ordinary one between banker and client; no relationship of trust had arisen, and so there was no duty to insist that she took independent advice. Nor was the transaction obviously to her disadvantage – as Lord Scarman pointed out, it could have been a means of saving her home.

Many of the recent cases have raised the issue of wives who allow the family home to be used to guarantee the husbands' debts or the debts of the husbands' business. This is important in practice as the family home is often the family's most valuable asset and frequently provided as surety to finance small businesses (with small businesses making up 95 per cent of all businesses in the UK). The law has to protect wives from being put under undue influence from their husbands to provide the house as surety, as the danger for the wife is that she and her family may find themselves homeless if the husband falls into financial difficulty.

In **Royal Bank of Scotland** v **Etridge (No 2)** (2001) the House of Lords indicated that, in normal circumstances, a wife's agreement to charge the matrimonial home as security for her husband's business debts is not a transaction that calls for explanation. Undue influence connotes impropriety, and should only be found where the husband's influence has been 'misused'.

## A transaction calling for an explanation

Where a party seeks to rely on the existence of presumed undue influence, the transaction must be suspicious and 'call for an explanation'. It is not necessary to prove this in the case of actual undue influence because it only helps to prove undue influence and so, by definition, is not needed where this has already been proved (**CIBC Mortgages** v **Pitt** (1993)). In **Allcard** v **Skinner** (1887) the judge stated that the gift must have been 'so large as not to be reasonably accounted for on the ground of friendship, relationship, charity or other ordinary motives on which ordinary men act'. The courts had on occasion suggested that the transaction had to be 'manifestly disadvantageous' (**CIBC Mortgages Plc** v **Pitt** (1994)), but this was criticised as setting a very high hurdle. In 2002 the House of Lords in **Etridge (No 2)** criticised the 'manifestly advantageous' test and reaffirmed the test in **Allcard** but restated it as 'a transaction that calls for an explanation'. The focus of this requirement is that the transaction looks suspicious but not necessarily to the point of being 'manifestly disadvantageous'. This change will probably make little difference in practice. The disadvantageous nature of an agreement is the most obvious reason why it would call for an explanation and, unless the agreement is disadvantageous, there is unlikely to be a complaint afterwards.

Examples of transactions which look suspicious and call for an explanation would include an exceptionally large gift, the sale of goods at bargain prices and loans on unusually generous terms. A transaction will require explanation if it jeopardises one party's future independence. Thus, most undue influence cases involve the loss of the claimant's home or of the vast proportion of their wealth. In **Portman Building Society** v **Dusangh** (2000) guarantees by parents to support loans to their children may be financially unwise for the parents, but do not call for an explanation because of a parent's affection for their child. For the same reason, since **Etridge (No 2)** a wife's guarantee of a husband's debts does not usually call for an explanation. By contrast in **Crédit Lyonnais** v **Burch** the Court of Appeal found that 'it would cause a bank manager to raise his eyebrows more than a little when he was engaged in entering into a contract with a young employee which involved guaranteeing her employer's indebtedness in the sum of £270,000, and mortgaging her home to the bank'.

## Undue influence and third parties

In **Lloyds Bank** v **Bundy** and **National Westminster Bank** v **Morgan** the undue influence was alleged to have been exercised by a bank employee and therefore it was clearly equitable that, if undue influence had been exercised, this could affect the bank's financial position. In **Barclays Bank** v **O'Brien** (1993) the undue influence was alleged to have been exerted by the husband and not the bank. Thus, the question was how far any undue influence by the husband should affect the financial position of the bank. The answer seems to be that the rights of a contracting party are affected by the impropriety of the third party if they knew of it or are deemed to have such knowledge (known as constructive knowledge). In these circumstances, the innocent contracting party is entitled to have the contract set aside.

The facts of **Barclays Bank** v **O'Brien** were that Mr O'Brien wanted to put up the family home, jointly owned with Mrs O'Brien, as security for his business debts. He told her that it would guarantee an overdraft of £60,000, when in fact the true amount was £135,000. Mrs O'Brien was asked to go to a particular bank to sign the agreement; this was not her usual branch, but the manager of her usual branch had given strict instructions that the nature of the transaction should be explained to her and had left a letter for her to read. Owing to a mix-up, these instructions were not followed.

The husband's business later collapsed, and the issue of whether Mrs O'Brien was bound by the contract arose. As Lord Browne-Wilkinson pointed out, the problem was one which seemed to be arising frequently – there had been 11 Court of Appeal cases on similar facts in the previous eight years. Their Lordships decided that the bank had constructive notice of the undue influence. It then had to take steps to show that actually it did not have notice of the undue influence and was therefore still able to enforce the contract. The House found that the transaction had been so extravagantly improvident that it was difficult to explain in the absence of some impropriety, so that the bank was put on inquiry.

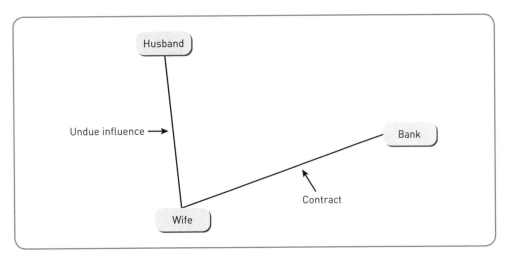

**Figure 12.4** Undue influence and third parties

## Placed 'on inquiry'

It is of course most unlikely that a bank will actually know of impropriety by one of the co-owners and still proceed with the mortgage. In practice, therefore, the courts are concerned with whether the bank had 'constructive knowledge'. It will have constructive knowledge if it had been placed 'on inquiry' that a third party may have committed some impropriety to induce the contract, and it has failed to take action to avoid having constructive knowledge of this impropriety.

Following **Royal Bank of Scotland** *v* **Etridge (No 2)** (2001) a bank will be put on inquiry in every case where the relationship between the surety and the debtor is non-commercial. This will always include where a wife stands surety for her husband's debts. The position is the same for unmarried couples, whether heterosexual or homosexual, where the bank is aware of the relationship. Cohabitation is not essential. A bank will also be put on inquiry where the wife became surety for the debts of her husband's company even where she was a shareholder, director or secretary of the company. This is because the wife's legal status does not always reflect the reality of the situation.

A lender will not be put on inquiry if the person standing surety for another person's debts is providing a commercial service. Banks and other financial institutions will provide this service for a fee. Those engaged in business can be regarded as capable of looking after themselves and understanding the risks involved in the giving of guarantees.

Also, if the loan is made to the parties jointly for their joint benefit, the lender is not put on inquiry unless it is aware that in reality the money is for the wrongdoer's purposes alone.

## Avoiding constructive notice

Where a contracting party is placed on inquiry as to the existence of undue influence, they will only be able to enforce the contract if they can avoid being fixed with constructive notice of the undue influence. A contracting party will avoid having constructive notice by taking reasonable steps to satisfy itself that the other party's agreement had been freely given.

In **Barclays Bank** *v* **O'Brien** the House of Lords ruled that to avoid constructive notice in such cases, the creditor should arrange a private meeting with the wife (the husband must not be present), explain the full implications of the transaction, including the potential extent of her liability, and advise her to take independent advice. If this private meeting did not take place, and the husband did use undue influence (or misrepresentation), the bank's claim on the property would be subject to the wife's interests in it. Lord Browne-Wilkinson added that in exceptional cases where a creditor has knowledge of further facts which render the presence of undue influence not only possible but probable, the creditor, to be safe, will have to insist that the wife is separately advised.

**Key Case**   Royal Bank of Scotland v Etridge (No 2)

The leading case on undue influence and constructive notice is now **Royal Bank of Scotland v Etridge (No 2)** (2001). This case laid down guidelines for the banks on avoiding constructive knowledge of undue influence which apply to any transactions carried out after the date of that judgment. Transactions made prior to that judgment would still be governed by the earlier more flexible guidance laid down in **O'Brien**. **Etridge (No 2)** was a combined appeal of eight different cases which all raised similar issues. In seven of the cases the wife had allowed the matrimonial home in which she had part ownership to be used as surety for her husband's debts or the debts of the husband's company. The wife was thus a guarantor of the husband's debts (a surety) because the money lent by the bank was not given to both husband and wife, but only to the husband (or his company). The husband had got into financial difficulty and the bank had sought possession of the family home. The bank claimed an order for possession of the matrimonial home. The wife raised a defence that the bank had been put on inquiry that her agreement to the transaction had been obtained by her husband's undue influence. The eighth appeal concerned a claim by a wife for damages from a solicitor who acted for her when she provided her house as security for the husband's debts. Five of the appeals were allowed and three were dismissed.

In order to avoid constructive notice of undue influence, a bank had to take reasonable steps to satisfy itself that the wife had been informed, in a meaningful way, of the practical implications of the proposed transaction. Banks are not obliged to hold a personal meeting with the wife.

Ordinarily, it would be reasonable that a bank should be able to rely upon written confirmation from a solicitor, acting for the wife, that he or she had advised the wife appropriately.

**Legal Principle**
Banks can take certain precautions to avoid having constructive notice of undue influence.

## Independent legal advice

In order to avoid having constructive notice of undue influence, the bank can rely on written confirmation from a solicitor that they have given the contracting party (usually the wife) appropriate advice. The bank should take steps to check directly with the wife the name of the solicitor she wished to act for her. The solicitor can also be acting for the bank or the husband of the contracting party. The advantages of a solicitor acting solely for the wife did not justify the additional expense that it would involve for the husband.

Solicitors should obtain from the bank any information needed to advise their client. If the bank failed for any reason to provide the requested information, then the solicitor should refuse to provide confirmation to the bank that the client had been advised. Exceptionally, there might be a case where the bank believed or suspected that the wife had been misled by her husband or was not entering into the transaction of her own free will. If such a case occurred, the bank had to inform the wife's solicitors of the facts giving rise to its belief or suspicion.

Solicitors should see their client in a face-to-face meeting, without the husband being present. They would need to explain to their client the purpose for which they had become involved. Typically, the solicitor would be expected to:

- explain the nature of the documents and their practical consequences for the wife;
- point out the seriousness of the risk involved;
- discuss the wife's financial means, including her understanding of the value of the property being charged;
- discuss the husband's financial position, including the amount of the husband's indebtedness and the amount of his overdraft facility;
- discuss whether the wife or her husband had any other assets out of which repayment could be made if the husband's business should fail; and
- state clearly that the wife had a choice whether or not to proceed with the transaction.

The solicitor should not give any confirmation to the bank without the wife's authority. The House rejected the Court of Appeal's suggestion that where a transaction is not one into which the wife could properly be advised to enter, a solicitor should in effect veto the transaction by declining to act further. The solicitor's duty is only to provide reasoned advice: it is up to the wife to decide whether to proceed. Only in 'exceptional circumstances' where it is 'glaringly obvious' that the wife has been 'grievously wronged' should the solicitor cease to act. If the solicitor considered the transaction was not in the wife's best interest, he would give reasoned advice to the wife to that effect. But, at the end of the day, the decision on whether to proceed was the decision of the client, not the solicitor.

The bank was entitled to proceed on the assumption that a solicitor advising the wife had done his or her job properly, unless it knew or ought to have known that this was not so.

It is not sufficient for a bank to instruct a solicitor to attend to the formalities in the signing of a legal charge, without expressly asking the solicitor to advise the wife. Without such an express request, the solicitor is merely acting for the bank and the wife will probably simply have attended the solicitor's office to sign documents, without receiving advice. This was the basis upon which some of the wives in the **Etridge (No 2)** appeal won their case.

Despite the strong *dicta* in **Etridge (No 2)** that a bank was entitled to assume that a solicitor had advised his client appropriately, in **Pesticcio v Huet and Ors** (2004) the Court of Appeal concluded that a solicitor had not in fact advised his client appropriately, and the relevant contract was tainted by undue influence. The involvement of a solicitor did not guarantee that a contract would be free from undue influence, and on the facts the advice given by the solicitor was inadequate.

In the case of **R v Attorney General for England and Wales** (2003) (the case about the Bravo Two Zero mission discussed on p. 271) the court considered whether the confidentiality contract was voidable on the basis of undue influence. The Privy Council concluded that the contract had not been entered into as a result of undue influence. Of particular interest in this context is the fact that the appellant had not obtained independent legal advice before signing the contract. The Privy Council held that this was 'a matter for regret', but was not fatal to the contract. It was not fatal because the appellant had understood what he was signing and the consequences of doing so. A legal adviser would not therefore have added anything to his understanding and would not have affected the fairness of the transaction.

At the start of his music career, the successful pop singer known as Seal had entered into a contract with a man called Wadlow for management services. After his first album was highly successful, Seal wanted to work with a different manager and entered into a settlement agreement to be released from the earlier contract with his old manager. Seal then failed to pay money owed under the settlement and he argued that this latter contract was invalid because he had been subjected to undue influence. The Court of Appeal rejected this argument, partly because Seal had obtained independent legal advice in relation to the settlement agreement: **Samuel** v **Wadlow** (2007).

## Transferred property

Where undue influence taints one contract, and the relevant property rights are transferred to another property, then the new contract will also be vitiated by the earlier undue influence that had tainted the first contract, if the new contract was made as a condition of discharging the earlier voidable contract. Thus, in **Yorkshire Bank plc** v **Tinsley** (2004) the defendant had agreed to two mortgages being placed over the family home which secured all the husband's current and future debts. These mortgages were voidable because the husband had exerted undue influence over his wife and the bank had constructive notice of this. The marriage subsequently broke down and, as part of the divorce settlement, the family home was sold and the wife bought a new home. This was, again, subject to a mortgage which provided for the new home to be security for all the husband's debts. The Court of Appeal held that this new mortgage was also voidable because of the earlier undue influence exercised at the time of the original contract, even though no further undue influence may have been exerted at the time of buying the new house. The bank could not therefore get possession of the new house to cover the husband's debts. If the new mortgage had been taken out with a different bank, then the new bank could not have been treated as having implied knowledge of the earlier wrongdoing and so the contract with the new bank would have been valid.

## Remedies

The existence of undue influence renders the contract voidable. In **National Commercial Bank (Jamaica) Ltd** v **Hew** (2003), Mr Hew was a long-standing customer of National Commercial Bank, and knew his bank manager well. He owned 150 acres of land in Jamaica. Mr Hew borrowed £1 million from his local bank to develop some of his land. The loan agreement required him to pay a very high rate of interest. The land development proved very slow, and the debt increased dramatically because of the high interest rate. In 1995 the bank demanded repayment, and at the time of the trial Mr Hew owed the bank over £14 million. The trial judge in Jamaica ordered the loan to be set aside for undue influence and the bank was ordered to pay back all the money that Mr Hew had paid under the loan agreement. The bank's appeal was dismissed by the Jamaican Court of Appeal, but the Privy Council allowed their further appeal. It accepted that there was a relationship of influence between the bank manager and Mr Hew, but it did not consider that this relationship had been abused by the bank to obtain an unfair advantage. The loan was unwise, but it was not unfair, as the bank had obtained the same terms that it would have insisted upon with any comparable borrower. On the specific issue of remedies, the Privy Council stated *obiter* that the trial judge's order that the bank should give back to Mr Hew all the money he had paid under the agreement risked leaving Mr Hew unjustly enriched. Instead, if the contract had been set aside for undue influence, the borrower should still have been required to account for the money he had received under the agreement, with interest. The court should merely have reduced the interest rate from the contractual rate to a court rate.

## Bars to relief

As undue influence is an equitable doctrine, relief will be barred on similar grounds to those discussed in relation to the limits on the right to rescission for misrepresentation (see p. 208).

# Inequality of bargaining power

In **Lloyds Bank** *v* **Bundy** Lord Denning suggested that economic duress was simply an example of a general principle of inequality of bargaining power. He argued that this general principle allows English law to give relief to anyone who, without taking independent advice, makes a contract on very unfair terms, or sells property for much less than it is worth, because their own bargaining power is seriously compromised by ignorance, infirmity or need. Clearly, this principle goes further than simple undue influence, since there is no suggestion that the other party had behaved improperly.

Lord Denning's reasoning has produced widely different reactions. Some overseas jurisdictions have regarded it as a bold, creative theory, but in England it has generally been disapproved by other judges. It is interesting to note, though, that in most of the cases where it has been criticised, the judges do nevertheless go to great lengths to analyse whether a transaction is substantively fair.

# Answering questions

Sheila consults her bank manager, Ms Suet, over her plans to sell her house. Sheila is a widow and she frequently consults Ms Suet on financial and personal matters. When told that Sheila intends to sell her house, Ms Suet offers to buy it at the current market price. Sheila accepts the offer and the sale is completed. Six months later house prices have risen by 25 per cent and Sheila is seeking to have the sale of the house set aside, on the grounds that Ms Suet has taken advantage of her position as Sheila's bank manager.

Advise Sheila. *Oxford*

The issue here is undue influence. As you know, this may be either actual or presumed. Actual undue influence requires illegitimate pressure, similar to, but short of, duress. There seems to be no sign of that here – Ms Suet simply makes an offer which Sheila accepts. Is there a presumption of undue influence? Two elements are required: a relationship of trust, and a manifest disadvantage for Sheila in the transaction. As far as the first requirement is concerned, as a matter of fact there does appear to be a relationship of trust and confidence between Sheila and Ms Suet: the cases of **Lloyds Bank** *v* **Bundy** and **National Commercial Bank (Jamaica) Ltd** *v* **Hew** are relevant here.

If a relationship of trust is established – and it seems clear that it can be – the next question is whether the transaction was suspicious and called for an explanation, as discussed in **Bundy**, **Morgan** and **O'Brien**. It is not absolutely clear whether this is the case – on the face of it, being paid the going rate does not seem unusual, but this might depend on whether it was obvious that house prices were going to rise drastically, or whether Sheila had a particular reason for selling at that point. It is perfectly reasonable to state that you would need more information in order to decide this issue, so long as you can state what difference this would make – in this case, that if the transaction was not suspicious, the contract would be valid, and that if it was suspicious, assuming the relationship of trust had been proved, the contract might be set aside, or its terms modified to counteract the disadvantage, unless Ms Suet could disprove the presumption by showing that Sheila had taken independent advice – see **Royal Bank of Scotland** *v* **Etridge (No 2)**.

To what degree does the validity of a contract depend on the relative bargaining strengths of the parties?

Your introduction should set the question in its context, explaining that the basis of contract is voluntary agreement, and that since imbalances in bargaining strength can produce agreements that are not genuinely voluntary, contract law has developed rules aimed at helping the weaker party.

As far as the common law is concerned, the doctrines of duress and undue influence are the most important ways of doing this. Explain the effect of each, and, remembering that the question asks 'to what degree', highlight the limitations on each, using cases to illustrate your points. For example, in explaining that economic duress will only apply where the coercion involves more than mere commercial pressure, you could contrast the cases of **North Ocean Shipping** and **Pao On**, and **Atlas Express** *v* **Kafco** with **CTN** *v* **Gallaher**. Similarly, in relation to undue influence, you can highlight the fact that presumed undue influence will only apply where the transaction is suspicious and requires explanation, contrasting **Bundy** with **O'Brien** and **Morgan**.

You should also point out that statute has intervened to redress the balance between parties of unequal strength, particularly in the area of consumer sales, and describe the ways in which UCTA and the Unfair Terms in Consumer Contracts Regulations 1999 can be used to make contractual provisions invalid.

Janet, a partially sighted invalid, and John Smith, her husband, jointly own the family house which is mortgaged to the County Building Society. John Smith, an optimistic but unsuccessful businessman, is unable to meet the mortgage repayments, so the building society has started proceedings for repossession.

In order to avoid the loss of the house the Smiths approach their bank, the Mid West Bank plc, with a view to refinancing the mortgage. The loans manager of the Mid West Bank visits the Smiths at their home with the relevant documents. Janet Smith makes it absolutely clear that she has no confidence in her husband's business ventures, and will not sign any documents that cover her husband's business liability. The loans manager assures her that the document does not cover any business liability. He also states that if she does not sign, one of the consequences could be the loss of her home and she would therefore become homeless. The loans manager is extremely forceful and persistent in his insistence that she should sign the document. After hesitation and a request that the document be explained to her because she is unable to read it owing to disability and the size of the print, she eventually signs it.

She then discovers that the document secures a charge over the house covering not only the mortgage but also her husband's business debts.

Discuss the various grounds on which Janet Smith might avoid the contract. *AQA*

 The first point to note here is that you are asked to discuss the **various** grounds on which Janet might avoid the contract. The facts of this problem at first glance appear very similar to those in the banking cases on undue influence, and it would be easy to assume that this is all the question is about, when in fact it raises several vitiating factors.

Since undue influence is the most obvious of these, it is probably a good starting point. In deciding whether Janet can rely on it, you need to look at both actual and presumed undue influence. Note that for presumed undue influence, the relationship between bank staff and their clients is not one of those where a fiduciary relationship is presumed to exist, so a fiduciary relationship would have to be established on the facts. We are not told whether Janet has banked with the Mid West Bank for a long time, or was in the habit of consulting them for advice, as was the case in **Bundy**; on the face of it, her relationship with the bank would appear to be more like that of Mrs Morgan in **Morgan**. For presumed undue influence, you also need to consider whether the transaction was suspicious, calling for an explanation; this is not necessary for actual undue influence.

Economic duress is another possibility you should discuss, given that Janet appears to be put under heavy pressure by the loans manager. In the light of **North Ocean Shipping** and **Atlas Express** *v* **Kafco**, you need to consider whether the loans manager was using pressure that would be regarded by the law as illegitimate, and whether Janet had any practical alternative but to comply.

Given Janet's partial sight, and her request to have the document explained to her, you will need to discuss the doctrine of *non est factum*. Note that this is a difficult doctrine to satisfy, as the case of **Saunders** *v* **Anglia Building Society** (see p. 238) shows. To avoid the contract on this ground, Janet would need to prove not only that she was tricked into signing the document, but also that the trick had the result of her being misled as to the nature of the document, not just its legal effect. However, the fact that she asked for it to be explained will count in her favour, since the courts are less likely to allow a claim of *non est factum* where the person making the claim has been careless in some way.

Finally, you should consider misrepresentation. Did the loans manager make an untrue statement of fact, which induced Janet to enter the contract? You will not be expected to know whether the remark about losing her home is true, but it is clear that the claim that the document did not cover John's business debts was untrue, and a statement of fact. It then only needs to be one of the reasons why Janet entered the contract.

# Summary of Chapter 12

Where one party is forced to consent by threats or undue pressure by the other, that consent should be invalid. The law has developed two doctrines to deal with this issue: the common law of duress, and the equitable one of undue influence. Both render a contract voidable.

## Duress

Five conditions need to be satisfied in order for there to be a finding of duress:

1 Pressure was exerted on the contracting party.
2 This pressure was illegitimate.
3 The pressure induced the claimant to enter the contract.
4 The claimant had no real choice but to enter the contract.
5 The claimant protested at the time or shortly after the contract was made.

Each of these conditions will be considered in turn.

### Pressure exerted on the contracting party

Pressure must have been exerted on the innocent contracting party, which amounted to a compulsion of the will. To constitute economic duress, economic pressure must go a great deal further than the ordinary pressure of the market.

### Pressure exerted was illegitimate

Illegitimate pressure must have been exerted on the other contracting party. A threat to do an unlawful act (which includes breaking a contract) will always be illegitimate, but a threat to do a lawful act will only be illegitimate if the threat is unreasonable, which will depend on the circumstances: **Atlas Express Ltd** v **Kafco (Importers and Distributors) Ltd** (1989).

### Pressure induced the claimant to enter the contract

Duress must be one of the reasons for entering (or modifying) a contract, but it does not have to be the only or even the main reason.

### Claimant had no real choice but to enter the contract

Economic duress will be present where there is compulsion of the will to the extent that the party under threat has no practical alternative but to comply.

### Claimant protested at the time or shortly after the contract was made

In **The Atlantic Baron** (1979) it was because the claimant waited eight months after the ship was delivered that the claim for duress was unsuccessful.

## Undue influence

Undue influence is an equitable doctrine, which applies where one party uses their influence over the other to persuade them to make a contract. The leading case on the subject is the House of Lords' judgment of **Royal Bank of Scotland** v **Etridge (No 2)** (2001). There are two types of undue influence: actual and presumed.

## Actual undue influence

This arises where the claimant can prove that they entered the transaction as a result of undue influence from the other party.

## Presumed undue influence

In certain circumstances an evidentiary presumption will be applied that shifts the burden of proof from the claimant to the defendant, so that it is up to the defendant to disprove the existence of undue influence. Undue influence may be presumed where there is a pre-existing relationship of confidence between the two parties to a contract, as a result of which one places trust in the other, and the contract between them is manifestly disadvantageous to the party who places trust in the other. Such a relationship may arise in two ways. First, it may fall into one of several categories in which a relationship of trust is automatically presumed to exist. Secondly, a relationship of trust may be established on the facts.

### A transaction calling for an explanation

Where a party seeks to rely on the existence of presumed undue influence, the transaction must be suspicious and call for an explanation, such as an exceptionally large gift.

## Undue influence and third parties

In **Barclays Bank** v **O'Brien** (1993) the undue influence was alleged to have been exerted by the husband and not the bank. The rights of a contracting party are affected by the impropriety of the third party if they knew of it or are deemed to have such knowledge (known as constructive knowledge).

### Placed 'on inquiry'

A party will have constructive knowledge of undue influence by a third party if it had been placed 'on inquiry' that a third party may have committed some impropriety to induce the contract, and it has failed to take action to avoid having constructive knowledge of this impropriety. Following **Royal Bank of Scotland** v **Etridge (No 2)** (2001), a bank will be put on inquiry in every case where the relationship between the surety and the debtor is non-commercial.

### Avoiding constructive notice

A contracting party will avoid having constructive notice by taking reasonable steps to satisfy itself that the other party's agreement had been freely given. In order to avoid constructive notice of undue influence, a bank has to take reasonable steps to satisfy itself that the relevant party had been informed, in a meaningful way, of the practical implications of the proposed transaction.

### Independent legal advice

In order to avoid having constructive notice of undue influence, the bank can rely on written confirmation from a solicitor that they have given the contracting party (usually the wife) appropriate advice.

## Remedies

The existence of undue influence renders the contract voidable.

**Reading list**

Bigwood, 'Undue influence in the House of Lords: principles and proof' (2002) 65 Modern Law Review 435

Burns, 'The elderly and undue influence inter vivos' (2003) Legal Studies 23, 251

Capper, 'Undue influence and unconscionability: a rationalisation' (1998) 114 Law Quarterly Review 479

Chandler, 'Manifest disadvantage, limits of application' (1999) 115 Law Quarterly Review 213

Halson, 'Opportunism, economic duress and contractual modifications' (1991) 107 Law Quarterly Review 649

Pawlowski and Greer, 'Constructive notice and independent legal advice: a study of lending institution practice' (2001) Conveyancer and Property Lawyer 229

Phang, 'Whither economic duress? Reflections on two recent cases' (1990) 57 Modern Law Review 107

Wong, 'Revisiting *Barclays Bank v O'Brien*: independent legal advice for vulnerable sureties' (2002) Journal of Business Law 456

## Reading on the internet

The House of Lords' judgment of **Royal Bank of Scotland** *v* **Etridge (No 2)** (2001) is available at:
http://www.publications.parliament.uk/pa/ld200102/ldjudgmt/jd011011/etridg-1.htm

# Part 4
## The rights and liabilities of third parties

The people who make a contract and provide consideration for it are the parties to the contract. Other people, who may receive a benefit or a burden from the performance of the contract, are described as third parties. For example, Ann may agree to buy Ben's car for £1,000. Ann may have told her daughter, Claire, that she will be able to drive the car once her mother has bought it. This transaction can be portrayed by the following diagram.

The traditional rule is that only the parties to a contract incur rights and obligations under the contract. This is known as the privity rule. But, increasingly, there are exceptions to this rule.

# Chapter 13
## Third parties

**This chapter explains:**

that a third party to a contract has an interest in the contract, without actually being a party to it. Under the traditional privity rule third parties could not sue or be sued under a contract. A large number of exceptions to the privity rule have been developed and arise under:

- statute, most significantly the Contracts (Rights of Third Parties) Act 1999;
- the common law; and
- equity.

# The privity rule

A third party to a contract is a person who is not a party to the contract and has not provided consideration for the contract but has an interest in its performance. There has been a long-established rule that only the parties to a contract could incur rights and obligations under it. Described as the doctrine of privity, this principle meant that third parties could neither sue nor be sued under a contract.

Even where a contract was made for the benefit of a third party, that party still had no rights under it.

 **Key Case**   Tweddle *v* Atkinson

The privity of contract rule was applied in the old case of **Tweddle *v* Atkinson** (1861). The claimant was engaged to be married, and his father and future father-in-law made a contract providing that each of them would give a certain sum of money to the claimant. Even though the contract expressly provided that the claimant was to be entitled to enforce it, the court held that he could not do so.

**Legal Principle**
Even where a contract is made for the benefit of a third party, under the traditional common law rules, that third party still has no rights under it.

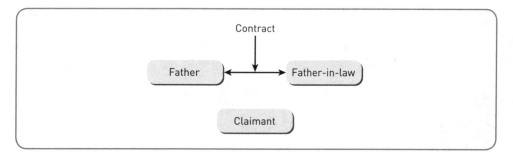

**Figure 13.1 Tweddle *v* Atkinson**

The same approach was taken in the case of **Beswick *v* Beswick** (1968). The claimant's husband sold his business to his nephew in return for an annual allowance to be paid to himself and, after his death, to his widow. Once the husband died, the nephew refused to make payments to the widow. Despite the fact that the husband had clearly intended her to benefit from the contract, it was held that the widow could not sue the nephew on her own behalf, because she was not a party to the contract. However, in this case the court was able to get round the doctrine, because the widow was also the executor of her husband's estate and could, therefore, sue on behalf of the estate.

A large number of exceptions to the privity rule had been developed over the years, to avoid extreme cases of injustice, but these numerous exceptions rendered this area of law extremely complex.

### Topical Issue

#### Top Gear

The case of **BBC** *v* **HarperCollins** (2010) concerned an attempt by the BBC to keep secret the real identity of 'The Stig' who featured in the *Top Gear* television series. The Stig drove cars at speed in this entertainment programme and always wore a driving helmet on the programme to hide his identity. The Stig was actually Mr Ben Collins and he wanted to publish an autobiography which would have included details about his involvement in *Top Gear*. Mr Collins had set up a service company of which he was the company director. The contracts for his services with the BBC were not made between Mr Collins and the BBC, but with the service company and the BBC. Mr Collins had signed those contracts in his capacity as its company director. The contracts contained confidentiality clauses but the High Court held the contract was not binding on Mr Collins because he was not personally a party to the contracts. The company, but not Mr Collins, was bound under the contract to keep the identity of The Stig secret.

# Reform

There are two main aspects to the rule of privity. The first is that the third party cannot be made the subject of a burden imposed by the contract. The second is that a third party cannot enforce a benefit purported to be granted by the contract. The first principle has generally been regarded as just and sensible, as it would be odd if two contracting parties could oblige a third party to build a wall between their homes when the third party has nothing to do with the contract. But the second aspect of the rule has been heavily criticised in the past, and it is this aspect of the rule which has been the subject of a major reform.

There had been many calls for reform of the privity rules over the years. Back in 1937 the Law Revision Committee called for legislation to enable a third party who is expressly given rights under a contract to enforce those rights directly. Lord Scarman commented in 1980 in **Woodar Investment Development Ltd** *v* **Wimpey Construction UK Ltd** that: 'If the opportunity arises, I hope the House will reconsider **Tweddle** *v* **Atkinson** and the other cases which stand guard over this unjust rule.'

The Law Commission issued a report, in 1996, *Privity of Contract: contracts for the benefit of third parties*. This report proposed that, in certain circumstances, the privity of contract rule should no longer apply. This led to a major reform of the law with the passing of the Contracts (Rights of Third Parties) Act 1999, so that now the privity rule has only a very limited application. The Act has made a significant change to the way in which contracts can be enforced by third parties. Under the new Act, Mrs Beswick would probably be able to sue her nephew in her own capacity, rather than only as the executor of her husband's estate.

## Contractual rights conferred on third parties

The privity rule now has only a very limited application following the passing of the Contracts (Rights of Third Parties) Act 1999. The impact of the Act can be understood by looking at the Law Commission's Report, where the Law Commission commented:

> it is important to emphasise that, while our proposed reform will give some third parties the right to enforce contracts, there will remain many contracts where a third party stands to benefit and yet will not have a right of enforceability. Our proposed statute carves out a general and wide-ranging exception to the third party rule, but it leaves that rule intact for cases not covered by the statute.

The rights conferred on third parties by the 1999 Act therefore have the character of a new statutory exception to the common law doctrine of privity. Prior to this Act, statute, common law and equity had all developed exceptions to the privity rule which will still be of interest where the 1999 Act does not apply, or as alternative grounds for founding a legal action. The 1999 Act does not affect any rights which third parties have apart from its provisions: thus it does not deprive third parties of rights which they have because their case falls within one of the other exceptions. Situations may arise in which it will be to the third party's advantage to rely on one of the old exceptions rather than on the new Act. The scope of the doctrine and these other exceptions therefore also need to be examined. The range of third party rights can arise under statute, common law or equity, and will now be considered.

## Statutory rights

### Contracts (Rights of Third Parties) Act 1999

The Contracts (Rights of Third Parties) Act 1999 enables third parties to enforce contractual terms in certain situations. The Act received Royal Assent on 11 November 1999. It applies to contracts made on or after 11 May 2000, or to contracts made during the six-month period after Royal Assent if the contract expressly states that the Act applies.

Under the Act, people who are not parties to a contract can sue on it in two situations:

- the contract expressly provides that they may do so; or
- the contract purports to confer a benefit upon them, unless the parties did not intend it to be enforceable.

#### Express provision in the contract

The first situation is laid down in s. 1(1)(a) which gives third parties a right to enforce the contract if 'the contract expressly provides that he may'. This enables the contracting parties to provide expressly for a third party to be able to enforce a term of the contract. An illustration of when this might be useful is provided by the Law Commission report:

> A (a developer) and B (the client) might wish to designate C (a management company) as having the right to sue to enforce warranties in the construction contract for D–Z (the tenants).

## The contract purports to confer a benefit

The second situation is laid down in s. 1(1)(b). This applies when the term of the contract 'purports to confer a benefit' on the third party. This is subject to an important proviso in s. 1(2), whereby it will not apply 'if on a proper construction of the contract it appears that the parties did not intend the term to be enforceable by the third party'. Thus, if the contracting parties do not want any other persons to have a right to enforce any part of the contract, they can expressly state this in the contract. It seems that a 'benefit' within s. 1(1)(b) can include any performance due under the contract, such as a payment of money, a transfer of property, the rendering of a service, or the benefit of an exclusion or limitation clause (s. 1(6)). The term must, moreover, purport to confer the benefit on the third party, so that it is not enough for third parties to show that they would happen to benefit from its performance. If, for example, Ann agreed to pay Ben £20 for cutting the hedge which grew between her house and Tom's house, a court would probably consider that performance of the contract might benefit Tom, but it did not 'purport to confer a benefit' on Tom.

The first reported case applying the 1999 Act is **Nisshin Shipping** v **Cleaves** (2003). Brokers had negotiated for some shipowners (Nisshin Shipping) to loan their ships to some charterers. The shipowners made contracts with the people loaning the ships (the charterers). These contracts provided that the brokers were entitled to 1 per cent commission of the contract price for their work of negotiating the contracts. The brokers were not themselves a party to these contracts. They sought, however, to rely on these contractual terms by pointing to the 1999 Act. The High Court accepted that the contracts purported to confer a benefit on the brokers for the purposes of s. 1(1)(b). While the contracts did not expressly provide that the brokers could enforce the contractual terms relating to the payment of commission, once it was established that the commission clauses purported to confer a benefit on the brokers within s. 1(1)(b) of the Act, there was a rebuttable presumption that the parties intended the term to be enforceable by the brokers for the purposes of s. 1(2). There was no evidence to rebut that presumption on the facts of this case and the brokers could therefore rely on the relevant contractual terms.

## Identifying the third party

Under either limb it is not necessary for the third party to be specifically named: it is sufficient for him or her to be 'expressly identified in the contract by name, as a member of a class or as answering a particular description' (s. 1(3)). Hence phrases such as 'adjoining occupiers', 'successors in title', 'future owners and occupiers' and 'the owners of nos 1–5 Acacia Avenue' will be capable of conferring rights of enforcement upon these people in appropriate circumstances. Nor need the person be in existence at the time of the contract: rights could be conferred upon a company which is yet to be incorporated, an unborn child or a future spouse.

## Consent to variations

The rights given under s. 1 would be of limited value if the contracting parties could at any time change their minds and remove the promised benefit. Section 2 deals with the issue of amending and cancelling the contract. This states that, unless the contract provides otherwise, the parties to the contract may not rescind the contract, or vary it so as to extinguish or alter the third party's rights, without his or her consent if the third party has either:

- communicated to the promisor their assent to the relevant term;
- relied on the term and the promisor knows of that reliance; or
- relied on the term and the promisor can reasonably be expected to have foreseen that reliance.

If one of these three situations applies, then any variations or cancellation can only take place with the consent of the third party. Take, for example, a situation where Tom has been promised £1,000 by Ann under a contract between Ann and Ben. The fact that he has, in reliance on that promise, spent some of the money he is expecting to receive will be enough to prevent Ann and Ben cancelling the promise, provided that Ann knew or could reasonably be expected to have known that Tom had relied on the promise.

The need for consent to variations can be dispensed with by the court if the third party cannot be traced or is incapable of giving consent (s. 2(4)), and if this occurs the court can order compensation to be paid to the third party (s. 2(6)).

The Act permits the contracting parties to vary the circumstances in which a third party's consent is required, or to exclude its requirement altogether (s. 2(3)).

## Enforcement

Third parties have the same remedies as would be available to them if they were contracting parties, including the rights to damages and specific performance (s. 1(5)). Although the contract is enforceable by the promisee as well as the third party, there cannot be double liability for the promisor (s. 5), so any recovery by the promisee would have the effect of reducing any award subsequently made to the third party.

## Defences

In an action by the third party, the promisor is able to rely on any defence arising out of the contract which would have been available to him or her had the claim been by the promisee (s. 3). Thus, if the promisee induced the promise by misrepresentation or duress, the promisor can use that as a defence to an action by the third party.

The promisor will also be able to rely on any set-off arising between the contracting parties from unrelated dealings. This could arise where Ann contracts with Ben that Ann will pay Tom £1,000 if Ben gives his car to Ann. If Ben owes £700 to Ann under a wholly unrelated contract, Ann could set off that sum against a claim by Tom for the £1,000 and only pay £300.

## Excluding the Act

It must be remembered that the main contracting parties are still in control. They can decide that the provisions of the new Act should not apply and there will be nothing that the third party can do about it.

## Insurance

The Married Women's Property Act 1882 provides that where a husband or wife takes out a life insurance policy for the benefit of their spouse or children, the contract can be enforced by the beneficiary.

The Road Traffic Acts make it obligatory for motorists to insure against liability for injury they may cause to other road users, and in certain circumstances those injured may claim directly against the insurance company, even though they are not a party to any contract with that company.

Similarly, under the Third Parties (Rights Against Insurers) Act 1930, where a person incurs liability to another, and is covered for that liability by an insurance policy, the other person can, in certain circumstances, claim on the policy.

## Covenants relating to land

Under s. 56(1) of the Law of Property Act 1925, privity of contract does not apply to restrictive covenants (which are agreements not to do something) relating to land, providing they are registered in the land register. As an example of why this should be, suppose A sells the field beside her home to B, so that B can build a house there. Naturally, A will want to be sure that B will not build a nightclub instead, so she may make him promise, as part of the contract, that he will only build a house. This will be a restrictive covenant relating to land. In time, B may sell the field and, since A will have no contract with the new buyer, without the protection of s. 56(1) she would have been at risk of a nightclub next door all over again.

## Bills of exchange

Under the Bills of Exchange Act 1882, a third party can sue on a bill of exchange, the most common form of which is a cheque. For example, B does some work for A, who pays by cheque. B happens to owe that amount to C, so endorses the cheque (by signing on the back, so that it becomes payable to whomever she gives it to) and pays C with it. If the cheque bounces, C may sue A on it, even though there is no contract between them. However, the Act does not allow either B or C rights against A's bank.

Section 6 of the Contracts (Rights of Third Parties) Act 1999 states that the Act does not apply to bills of exchange.

# Common law exceptions

## Agency

The term 'agent' has a specific meaning in this context, and applies to an individual who makes a contract on behalf of someone else, who is known as the principal. When the word 'agent' is used in everyday language it does not necessarily have this legal meaning; the fact that in ordinary language a car dealer might be described as a Fiat agent, for example, does not make that person an agent for the purposes of privity, since they will be buying and selling cars on their own behalf, even though all those cars may be made by Fiat.

An agent, in the sense we are using here, is viewed by the law as the intermediary of the principal, rather than a true party to the contract. In practice, one party to a contract made by agency is usually a corporation of some kind, such as a company or local authority, and the agent is their employee.

There are three circumstances in which a person will be treated as being the principal's agent: where there is express authority; where there is implied authority; and where there is apparent (also called ostensible) authority. Express authority is the most straightforward and means that the agent has been specifically asked to make the contract in question. Implied authority arises where the agent is asked to do something which by implication requires the contract to be made. An example might be where a driver is asked to take a car from London to Edinburgh, which would probably imply that the driver should buy petrol on the way on behalf of the principal, so that in the contract for the petrol the driver would merely be the agent.

Apparent authority can cause more problems. It arises where the principal's past behaviour gives the other party to the contract reason to believe that the agent has authority to contract on the principal's behalf. Apparent authority cannot be created solely by the behaviour of the supposed agent. The fact that Ann claims to have authority to make a contract with Ben as the agent of Claire does not in itself make Claire liable on the contract as the principal; it will only do so if Claire has given Ben good reason to believe that Ann has such authority. If this is the case, Claire is liable, even though Ann is lying or mistaken.

Apparent authority was found in **Pharmed Medicare Private Ltd** v **Univar Ltd** (2002). The claimant, Pharmed, manufactured a medicine called GSP, which was used to reduce the symptoms of arthritis. The defendant, Univar, imported and distributed GSP in the United Kingdom. Between January 1999 and July 2000, Univar placed a number of orders with Pharmed for relatively small amounts of GSP (3 tonnes or less per order). Some of these orders were placed by a Mr Somerville, who was employed as an 'Industry Manager' at Univar. On 9 August 2000 Mr Somerville placed an order with the President of Pharmed for the sale of 8 tonnes of GSP per month for 12 months at a price of $18 per kilo. Mr Somerville did not have authority to place such a large order. The market price of GSP fell below $18 per kilo. Univar no longer wanted to buy the medicine at the higher price and argued that there was no contract because Mr Somerville had acted outside his authority. The Court of Appeal found that Mr Somerville had apparent authority to make the contract, and it was therefore binding on Univar. In the series of earlier transactions, Univar had put forward Mr Somerville as a person entitled to make purchases on their behalf. The fact that the particular purchase in this case was for a substantially larger amount was not sufficient to put Pharmed on inquiry as to whether he had authority.

Where an agent is covered by any of the three types of authority, the principal will be bound by any contract made that falls within that authority, as they are treated as having privity of contract. In **Waugh** v **Clifford** (1982) a firm of solicitors was employed to pursue certain litigation. In such circumstances, a solicitor generally has implied authority to negotiate a compromise with the other party, and so reach a settlement, but, in this case, their client had specified that they were not to settle without reference to him. The other party to the litigation was unaware of this instruction, so assumed that the solicitors had the usual authority. The solicitors did in fact settle with the other side, but their client claimed he was not bound by this, because they were acting outside their authority. While the Court of Appeal recognised that the solicitors' implied authority had been terminated, it held that they still had apparent authority, and therefore their client was bound.

Where an agent makes a contract which lies outside the authority granted by the principal, or where the agent in fact has no authority at all, the principal may nevertheless choose to ratify the contract, so long as the agent was purporting to act on the principal's behalf at the time the contract was made, and the principal had the capacity to make the contract at that time. Once a contract is ratified by the principal, it becomes binding on the principal.

## Undisclosed principals

In some cases, an agent may act for a principal without disclosing the principal's identity, or even the fact that there is a principal. English law nevertheless holds that it is the principal with whom the contract is made, so that it is effectively possible to make a contract with someone without even knowing that they exist. This is, of course, in complete contradiction with the usual principles of privity, but is nevertheless the law.

While the principal remains undisclosed, the agent is personally liable on the contract; once the principal is disclosed, if a claim arises, the other party to the contract can choose whether to sue the principal or the agent.

There is one important limitation on the creation of an agency situation where the principal is undisclosed. If the contract is such that it was reasonable to infer that the agent could only have been contracting on their own behalf, there will be no agency, and the purported agent will in fact be liable on the contract. The commonest example of this situation is where a service contracted for is one which relies on personal skill, such as painting a picture.

### Warranty of authority

If an individual purports to make a contract on behalf of someone else, but in fact has no authority to do so, where does that leave the party contracted with? In **Collen** v **Wright** (1857) it was held that in such a situation it may be possible to hold that the purported agent has contracted that he or she does have authority. So the supposed principal would not be liable but the purported agent would be. Thus in **Penn** v **Bristol and West Building Society** (1997) a solicitor had put himself forward as acting as the agent of both the husband and wife who were joint owners of a house. When the house was sold he was found liable by the Court of Appeal for breach of warranty of authority to the building society who had lent money on the sale of the house, when it later transpired that the solicitor was only acting as agent to the husband, and the wife knew nothing about the sale.

## Assignment

It is possible to assign (in effect, to sell) the benefit of a contract without the permission of the other party. A common example is where small businesses, having cash flow problems, sell the debts owed to them by others to what are called factoring houses. The factoring house buys the debt at less than its value, and so makes a profit when it collects from the creditor; the small business may lose a little of what it was owed, but gets its money quicker, and with less effort. Once a debt is assigned, the creditor owes the money to the party to which it was assigned, and not to the party originally contracted with.

It is not possible to assign the burden of a contract without the other parties' permission. There are obvious reasons for this rule; without it, for example, a debtor could simply assign the debt to someone who was bankrupt.

## Negotiability

Certain types of contractual benefit can be assigned merely by being put into a written document and given to another party; the original owner of the benefit need not be notified. The written document is called a negotiable instrument, and the most common examples are banknotes and cheques.

A cheque, for example, represents money 'owed' by the bank to the chequebook holder (in the sense that the bank has in its possession money belonging to the chequebook holder, assuming they are not overdrawn). By writing a cheque to a shopkeeper, the chequebook holder effectively assigns the benefit of the bank's 'debt' to him or her, to the shopkeeper. In most cases, the shopkeeper then banks the cheque, but it is possible for them to endorse it (by signing on the back), and then use it to pay someone else, effectively assigning the benefit of the bank's debt to them. They could in turn do the same, without ever having to notify either the bank or the chequebook holder.

Section 6 of the Contracts (Rights of Third Parties) Act 1999 states that the Act does not apply to negotiable instruments.

## Novation

As we have seen, assignment only transfers the benefits, and not the burdens of a contract. To transfer both burdens and benefits, a novation is required. The effect of novation is that the old contract is destroyed and a new one created. It requires the agreement of both the original parties to the contract, and the third party who is to take on the liability, and consideration must be given for the new contract.

## Damages on behalf of another

One obvious problem with the doctrine of privity occurs when a contracting party buys something on behalf of others – not in the sense of an agent, where the buyer would be paid back, but as, for example, when a woman buys a holiday for herself and her husband, or a mother pays for a meal for the family. Where there is a breach of contract, the rules of privity mean that the party with whom the contract was made can claim for their own loss, but should not be able to claim for that of the other people for whom they have paid.

This problem was addressed in **Jackson** v **Horizon Holidays Ltd** (1975). The claimant bought a package holiday to Sri Lanka for himself and his family. The holiday was a complete disaster, and Horizon were clearly in breach of contract. There was no problem with Mr Jackson's claim for defects in his own holiday, as he was a party to the contract, but clearly his family had lost out as well. Could he claim for their loss? The rules of privity would suggest not, but the Court of Appeal unanimously decided that he could, Lord Denning explaining at some length that Mr Jackson had bought the holiday for the benefit of his family, and should therefore be compensated for their loss as well as his own.

Despite the obvious conflict with the doctrine of privity, it is easy to appreciate the logic of this decision. It was initially disapproved (though not overruled) by the House of Lords in **Woodar Investment Development Ltd** v **Wimpey Construction UK Ltd** (1980). The House accepted that the ultimate decision was correct, but suggested that it should be based on the fact that the loss of enjoyment by his family was itself a loss to Mr Jackson, and it was the loss to him of their enjoyment that should be compensated, rather than the loss to them. Alternatively, they said, it might be that contracts arranged by one person for the benefit of a group should be treated as a special case.

In more recent cases, the courts have been more willing to award damages to reflect the loss of someone other than the claimant.

 **Key Case**   Linden Gardens Trust v Lenesta Sludge Disposals

In **Linden Gardens Trust** v **Lenesta Sludge Disposals** (1994) the House of Lords considered the situation where a building contract was made between parties for the development of a site as shops, offices and flats. Ownership of the site was later transferred to a third party. The building work was not carried out to a satisfactory standard so that the third party was forced to incur expenses remedying the defects. In an action for breach of the building contract brought by the company which originally owned the site, the contractor argued that no loss had been suffered by the original site owner as the property no longer belonged to it when the alleged breaches occurred, and it was therefore entitled to no more than nominal damages. In other words, the defendant argued that while there was a technical breach of contract, the original site owner could not receive substantial damages as the loss had been suffered by the third party. This argument was rejected by the House of Lords. Their Lordships did not say that their earlier decision in **Woodar v Wimpey** was wrong, but instead distinguished it on its facts. Lord Browne-Wilkinson took an exception (to the general principle that claimants can recover damages only in respect of their own loss) that had been developed in shipping law and applied it to contracts in general. He said:

> The contract was for a large development of property which, to the knowledge of both [parties], was going to be occupied and possibly purchased by third parties . . . Therefore, it could be foreseen that damage caused by a breach would cause loss to a later owner and not merely to the original contracting party . . . In such a case, it seems to me proper . . . to treat the parties as having entered into the contract on the footing that [the original owner] would be entitled to enforce the contractual rights for the benefit of those who suffered from defective performance.

Thus the majority's approach was that where many shops, offices and flats are being built it was foreseeable that the site owner does not intend to keep and occupy them all, but intends to sell or rent them at a profit to others on completion. Where it is foreseeable that property will be transferred, the person (usually a builder) contracting to carry out services (usually construction work) on that property would be treated in law as having contracted for the benefit of all persons who might, after the time of contracting, acquire interests in the property. Thus the original owner of that property will be able to sue for breach of contract for loss suffered by the future owner. The loss is treated as having been suffered by the third party rather than by the original site owner, but the original owner can nevertheless receive substantial damages for that loss.

---

**Legal Principle**

In appropriate cases the contracting parties will be treated as having entered into a contract on the basis that a third party is entitled to enforce the contractual rights for the benefit of those who suffer from defective performance of the contract.

---

This decision has subsequently been followed by the Court of Appeal in **Darlington BC v Wiltshier Northern Ltd** (1995). The claimant, a local authority, wished to develop land which it already owned as a recreational centre. It needed to borrow money to finance the project, but central government had imposed restrictions on local government borrowing. It could therefore not accept a direct loan from the bank. Instead two contracts were made. The first one was between the builders and the bank under which the builders undertook to carry out the building work. The second was between the bank and the local authority, under which the bank undertook to assign the completed building and the benefit of any contractual rights against the builders to the local authority. This second contract stated that the bank was not to be liable to the local authority 'for any incompleteness or defect in the building work'.

On completion of the building, the bank, in accordance with the second contract, duly assigned its rights against the defendant to the local authority. The local authority then claimed damages against the building contractor for defects in the work. It was accepted that the local authority could not be put in a better position under the assigned contract than the bank had been under that contract. Therefore the courts had to explore what rights the bank had enjoyed under the contract. The building contractor argued that the bank could not have recovered substantial damages since it had suffered no loss – it was always intended that the building would be transferred to the claimant and the claimant had agreed to pay the bank in full. They claimed, therefore, that the bank was in no way responsible to the claimant for the condition of the building. This argument was accepted by the court of first instance, which awarded only nominal damages, but the decision was overturned by the Court of Appeal. Applying **Linden Gardens**, it held that the bank could have recovered substantial damages from the defendant in respect of the local authority's loss, and therefore the local authority could also do so once that contract was assigned to it.

In **Panatown** v **Alfred McAlpine Construction Ltd** (2000) the House of Lords made it clear that, if the contractual arrangement between the parties in fact provided the third party with a direct remedy against the wrongdoer, the exceptional rule in **Linden Gardens** could not be relied upon.

## Collateral contracts

Where one party makes contracts with two others, the courts will sometimes use the device of 'finding' a collateral contract between the two others to evade the privity rule. An example of this is **Shanklin Pier Ltd** v **Detel Products Ltd** (1951). The claimants owned Shanklin Pier, and needed to have it repainted. They contacted Detel to enquire about the qualities of its paint, and were told that it lasted for between seven and ten years. The claimants then employed contractors to repaint their pier, and specified that Detel's paint should be used. The painting was done, but after three months the paint began to deteriorate. The pier owners could not sue the painters, since it was not they who had promised the paint would last, and the pier owners had no contract with Detel, since the paint was bought by the painters. However, the court held that there was in fact a collateral contract between the pier owners and Detel: Detel had promised that the paint would last and the pier owners' request that the painters should use Detel paint was consideration for that promise.

This device of finding a collateral contract has been used to give a third party the benefit of an exemption clause contained in the main contract to which they are not a party.

 **Key Case** Scruttons Ltd v Midland Silicones Ltd

The leading case on collateral contracts is the House of Lords' decision in **Scruttons Ltd** v **Midland Silicones Ltd** (1962). The case involved a contract to carry a drum of chemicals from the USA to England, which contained a clause limiting the liability of the carriers to $500. The carriers employed Scruttons as stevedores (dock workers) to unload the ship, and the drum was damaged through Scruttons' negligence. Scruttons sought to limit their liability for the damage by relying on the limitation clause in the contract between the owners of the drum of chemicals and its carriers. Lord Reid laid down four conditions which have to be satisfied before the common law will allow a third party to rely on an exemption clause in a contract to which they are not a party:

(first) the bill of lading makes it clear that the stevedore is intended to be protected by the provisions in it which limit liability, (secondly) the bill of lading makes it clear that the carrier, in addition to contracting for these provisions on his own behalf, should apply to the stevedore, (thirdly) the carrier has authority from the stevedore to do that, or perhaps later ratification by the stevedore would suffice, and (fourthly) that any difficulties about consideration moving from the stevedore were overcome . . .

The second condition is essentially that the contracting party was acting as the agent of the third party when entering into the contract. These four conditions were not satisfied on the facts of the case. It was therefore held that the stevedores could not rely on the limitation clause in the contract between the carriers and the owners of the drum, because they were not a party to that contract.

### Legal Principle

In certain circumstances a collateral contract can be found giving a third party the benefit of an exemption clause contained in the main contract to which they are not a party.

In the light of that case, lawyers have attempted to draft exemption clauses which satisfy the four conditions, where their commercial clients wish third parties to get the benefit of these exemption clauses. Such provisions are frequently known as 'Himalaya clauses'. Lord Reid's requirements have been interpreted loosely, so that courts have been prepared to find that any reference in the contract to the third party can give them the benefit of an exemption clause.

There was a Himalaya clause in **New Zealand Shipping Co Ltd** v **Satterthwaite & Co Ltd (*The Eurymedon*)** (1975). The facts of the case were similar to those in **Scruttons**, but the drafting of the relevant contract between the goods' owners and the carriers enabled the Privy Council to find a collateral contract. This collateral contract was between the owners of goods for shipping and the stevedores who unloaded the goods, and was interpreted as incorporating the exclusion clause in the main contract, so the stevedores could get the benefit of this.

This case has subsequently been given a restrictive interpretation in ***The Mahkutai*** (1996). In that case the Privy Council refused to apply ***The Eurymedon*** on the basis that ***The Eurymedon*** was concerned with the application of an exemption clause, and the appeal in the present case was concerned with the application of a jurisdiction clause (that is a clause which decides the country in which litigation can be heard). A cargo of plywood was damaged and an action was brought before the courts in Hong Kong by the owners of the plywood against the ship-owners. The latter argued that the Hong Kong courts did not have jurisdiction to hear the case. In support of this argument, they sought to rely on a term of the contract for the carriage of the plywood entered into by the charterer of their ship, which gave exclusive jurisdiction to the Indonesian courts. They were not a party to this contract, but the contract stated that sub-contractors should have the benefit of 'exceptions, limitations, provisions, conditions and liberties' contained in it. The Privy Council rejected the defendant's argument. Exclusive jurisdiction clauses would not be treated in the same way as clauses exempting or limiting liability for damages to the goods.

Following the enactment of the Contracts (Rights of Third Parties) Act 1999, it is now possible under this legislation for the benefit of an exemption clause to be given to a third party. So third parties will be able to avoid the difficulties in the common law.

# Exceptions in equity

## Constructive trust

A contracting party can specify that the benefit of the contract is held by him or her in trust for a third party, in which case that third party will have enforceable rights to the benefit. At one time, the courts seemed willing to imply such a trust where there seemed to be an intention to create one, even though there was no specific reference to a trust in the contract. In **Les Affréteurs Réunis SA** v **Walford** (1919) Walford, a broker, negotiated a contract for the loan of a ship (a charterparty) between the owners of a ship and a company wanting to hire it. The charterparty provided that the owners would pay Walford a 3 per cent commission on the estimated price of the hire. They failed to pay this, so Walford sued them for it, joining the charterers as parties to the action. The House of Lords upheld his claim, on the basis that even though Walford was not a party to the agreement, he had effectively nominated the charterers to contract on his behalf. The charterers were therefore trustees of the shipowner's promise to pay Walford commission. Walford could bring a joint action with the charterer for payment of the commission by the shipowner. If they had not been willing to help, he could have sued them as co-defendants, the court held.

However, more recent cases have shown the courts unwilling to assume such a trust unless there is a clear intention to that effect; in **Green** v **Russell** (1959) it was held that a mere intention to benefit a third party was not enough by itself. Following **Nisshin Shipping** v **Cleaves** (2003), it is now clear that this type of case, involving the payment of commission to brokers who are not themselves a party to the main contract, can be resolved through reliance on the Contracts (Rights of Third Parties) Act 1999.

## Restrictive covenants

As well as avoiding the rules on privity of contract under statute, restrictive covenants concerning land avoid those rules in equity, following the case of **Tulk** v **Moxhay** (1848).

# Arguments for the privity rule

## Free will

This argument is based on the idea that only the parties to a contract should incur rights and responsibilities since only they have agreed to do so. This 'free will' theory underlies the whole of contract law.

## Lack of reciprocal rights

It can be argued that it would be unjust to allow a party to sue on a contract, if that party could not be sued on it. Yet, as Treitel's *The Law of Contract* (2007) points out, unilateral contracts are a situation in which one party can sue but not be sued – for example, Mrs Carlill could sue the Carbolic Smoke Ball Company on the basis of their offer to pay anyone who used their smokeball and got flu, but the Smoke Ball Company could not have sued Mrs Carlill (or anyone else) for not using the smokeball (**Carlill** v **Carbolic Smoke Ball Co** (1893)). This appears to cause no great problems in unilateral contracts.

In addition, as Hugh Collins has observed in *The Law of Contract* (1993) (London: Butterworths), the promisor has normally had full performance before the prospect of the third party suing arises – for example, in **Beswick** v **Beswick** the nephew already owned the business. Similarly, in **Jackson** v **Horizon Holidays**, it was true that the holiday company would have no right to sue Mr Jackson's family for the price of the holiday, but in practice such a right was not necessary since Mr Jackson was liable for the whole price, and in any case it had already been paid before there was any reason for the family to want to sue.

## Restriction of the contracting parties' rights

Allowing third parties enforceable rights limits the rights of the contracting parties to modify or terminate the contract. Again, this is refuted by Hugh Collins, who argues that contracts could simply provide that third party rights would be lost in the event of modification or termination, with third parties being allowed to claim for any reliance expenditure (see p. 360) if that should happen.

## Making gratuitous promises enforceable

It is also argued that to allow third parties enforceable rights makes gratuitous promises enforceable. It is difficult to see how this could logically be the case. The promise would not be gratuitous, but part of a binding contract, for which consideration has been given; that does not change simply because the beneficiary, rather than the other contracting party, tries to enforce it. In **Tweddle** v **Atkinson**, for example, the promise which the bridegroom tried to enforce was not a gratuitous promise to him, but part of a binding contract with his father.

## The 'floodgates' argument

There have been worries that the Contracts (Rights of Third Parties) Act 1999 exposes promisors to indefinite liability, making it impossible to foresee what they will owe, when and to whom. However, this is an exaggeration. While it is true that a contract must draw the line for the imposition of liability somewhere, there is no reason why that line has to be drawn where a person has the status of a contractual party. Liability can instead be restricted while including third parties identified in the contract.

The construction industry has been particularly worried about the impact of the 1999 Act. Contracts in this field frequently still use collateral warranties (see p. 300) to give third parties rights, rather than falling back on the provisions of the 1999 Act.

## Arguments against the privity rule

## Extended litigation

The privity rule could lead to a chain of contract claims, because it prevented the party with the problem suing the party who actually caused it. A common example is where a consumer buys goods which have been badly manufactured. Because the consumer's contract is usually with the retailer, it is the retailer they must sue, even though the defect has been caused by the manufacturer. The retailer can then in turn sue the manufacturer under their contract, or if the retailer has bought from a distributor, the distributor is next in line to be sued, and the distributor then sues the manufacturer. In most cases this simply makes things a little more complicated and lawyers a little richer, but it can cause practical problems where one party in the chain goes out of business.

## Irrational

While it seems reasonable that someone who is not a party to a contract should not incur obligations under it, it is less easy to understand why English law was so firmly set against allowing third parties enforceable rights under a contract.

## Intention of the parties

One of the arguments in favour of the privity rule was the concept of free will, but this can also work against the rule. Lord Steyn has observed in **Darlington Borough Council** v **Wiltshier Northern Ltd** (1995):

> The case for recognising a contract for the benefit of a third party is simple and straightforward. The autonomy of the will of the parties should be respected. The law of contract should give effect to the reasonable expectations of contracting parties. Principle certainly requires that a burden should not be imposed on a third party without his consent. But there is no doctrinal, logical, or policy reason why the law should deny effectiveness to a contract for the benefit of a third party where that is the expressed intention of the parties.

Hugh Collins further maintains in his book that if we are talking about free will and agreement, why should the law not provide a mechanism for enforcing two parties' agreement that a third party should benefit from their contract? The fact that it does not do so may in fact go against what the parties have agreed and allow one party to revise the agreement without the consent of the other. In **Beswick**, for example, the nephew would have been able to go back on his promise to his uncle if his aunt had not been made executor.

## Unjust enrichment

Cases like **Beswick** show that the doctrine of privity could allow parties to escape their contractual obligations, yet still themselves benefit from the contract. In that case, it was a lucky chance that the widow was made executor; that position could easily have been given to the nephew, in which case he would have been able to keep the business without paying most of the price.

## Justifiable reliance

It can be argued that a contract should protect those who, while not a party to it, incur losses because they reasonably rely on its performance. This principle seems to have been behind the way in which the courts got round the privity rule by the use of collateral contracts, in cases such as **Shanklin Pier** and **New Zealand Shipping**. In the latter case, the owner of the machine had promised in the contract that their rights against the carrier and any sub-contractors would be limited, and it was reasonable for the sub-contractors to rely on this when considering their own insurance coverage.

## International approach

Many modern legal systems have a much more flexible attitude to the issue of who can enforce a contract, including the USA and most European countries. The Contracts (Rights of Third Parties) Act 1999 brings English law into line with these other legal systems.

## Legal complexity

The sheer number of exceptions to the privity rule means that in practice it has caused fewer problems than might be expected, but this in turn has made the law very complex in this field. On the one hand, the 1999 Act adds to the complexity by adding another major exception to the privity rule. On the other hand, it will provide a means for contractors to avoid some of the more complex and legally questionable devices they had been forced to use in the past to avoid the privity rule. The legislation will be particularly important for businesses in the software, construction and oil and gas industries. Companies in these fields had, before the Act, been forced to rely on a web of collateral warranties, agency agreements and trust devices. The construction industry used separate collateral warranties in favour of investors, purchasers and tenants. Now, the relevant rights can be granted by a clause in the building contract. This means, for example, that landowners will be able to pursue sub-contractors for design errors.

## Answering questions

Was Parliament right to vote for the Contracts (Rights of Third Parties) Act 1999?

Reform of the privity rule is likely to be a very popular question with examiners for the next few years following the enactment of the Contracts (Rights of Third Parties) Act 1999. You need to take a critical view of the Act, looking at both its strengths and weaknesses. You could start by explaining that the Act was passed to tackle the perceived problems with the privity rule and briefly explain the privity rule. The main material you will need to analyse whether the Act was required is contained in pp. 302–5. In particular, you could point out that some of the disadvantages of the privity rule were avoided in the past by relying on exceptions that existed prior to the passing of the 1999 Act. You could also discuss in detail the caution of the construction industry to the new legislation and the reasons for their concerns which are discussed at p. 303.

X received an advertisement through the post offering a special discount on cruise holidays if she booked within a month and paid by credit card. In February, she booked a two-week luxury Mediterranean cruise leaving in June. It cost £5,000 for herself, her husband and two children, and she paid a deposit of £500 using her credit card. In late May she received a letter informing her that the cost of the holiday would be £5,500 because of the unforeseeable repairs which had become necessary to the cruise ship. The total cost would now be more than the original would have been without the special discount offer. However, as it was so close to the time of the holiday, X and her family decided that they had no option but to go ahead with the cruise. The entire cruise proved to be very disappointing, as there were thunderstorms every day and the food was extremely poor. A waiter spilled red wine sauce over X's best evening dress worth £600, ruining it, and both children suffered food poisoning which confined them to their cabin for three days of the cruise.

Now that they have returned from the holiday, X, her husband and two children would like to claim compensation for the additional cost of the cruise, and the disappointing cruise. The children want compensation for the food poisoning which they have suffered. Advise each of them as to whether they can claim, and if so, how and from whom. *London*

 The first issue to consider was the formation of the contract and whether the advertisement amounted to an offer or an invitation to treat. As the contract was made by post, the postal rule should be mentioned. It is clear that at the latest a contract was formed once the tendered payment of the £500 deposit had been accepted. The next stage in the question raises issues relating to the discharge of a contract, which are discussed in the next chapter. In summary, it is unlikely that this initial contract was frustrated (discussed at p. 318) by the need for unforeseeable repairs to the boat as these have merely rendered execution of the contract more onerous rather than impossible. Alternatively, by refusing to perform the contract as agreed (i.e. for £5,000) this may have constituted an anticipatory breach. X chose to affirm the contract despite the breach, but this can still leave a claim for damages.

This is a contract for both goods and services and would contain certain implied terms discussed in Chapter 16. Some of the terms of the contract have been broken, and the effect of these breaches will depend on whether they will be treated as conditions or warranties.

As regards the rights to compensation, a full discussion of the cases mentioned under the heading 'Damages on behalf of another' (see p. 298) would be required. Particular emphasis should be placed on **Jackson** *v* **Horizon Holidays** because of the factual similarities. The children and the husband would have no right to bring an action themselves, but if X succeeded in receiving damages to reflect their loss, they may have a right to some of these damages.

This question also raises issues that stretch beyond the scope of this book to tort law and studies of the English legal system. These would consider questions of vicarious liability, the role of the county court and the growing use of methods of alternative dispute resolution such as arbitration by ABTA.

# Summary of Chapter 13

## The privity rule

There has been a long-established privity rule that only the parties to a contract could incur rights and obligations under it: **Tweddle** *v* **Atkinson** (1861). A number of exceptions have developed to the privity rule. The range of third party rights can arise under statute, common law or equity, and will now be considered.

## Statutory rights

### Contracts (Rights of Third Parties) Act 1999

The Contracts (Rights of Third Parties) Act 1999 enables third parties to enforce contractual terms in two situations.

- the contract expressly provides that they may do so; or
- the contract purports to confer a benefit upon them, unless the parties did not intend it to be enforceable.

### Identifying the third party

Under either limb it is not necessary for the third party to be specifically named: it is sufficient for him or her to be 'expressly identified in the contract by name, as a member of a class or as answering a particular description' (s. 1(3)).

### Consent to variations

Section 2 of the 1999 Act states that, unless the contract provides otherwise, the parties to the contract may not rescind the contract, or vary it so as to extinguish or alter the third party's rights, without his or her consent if the third party has either:

- communicated to the promisor their assent to the relevant term;
- relied on the term and the promisor knows of that reliance; or
- relied on the term and the promisor can reasonably be expected to have foreseen that reliance.

### Enforcement

Third parties have the same remedies as would be available to them if they were contracting parties.

### Defences

In an action by the third party, the promisor is able to rely on any defence arising out of the contract which would have been available to him or her had the claim been by the promisee (s. 3).

### Excluding the Act

The contracting parties can state in the contract that the provisions of the 1999 Act should not apply.

## Insurance

Legislation provides that insurance policies can be for the benefit of third parties.

## Covenants relating to land

Under s. 56(1) of the Law of Property Act 1925, privity of contract does not apply to restrictive covenants (which are agreements not to do something) relating to land, providing they are registered in the land register.

## Bills of exchange

Under the Bills of Exchange Act 1882, a third party can sue on a bill of exchange, the most common form of which is a cheque.

# Common law exceptions

## Agency

An agent is viewed by the law as the intermediary of the principal, rather than a true party to the contract. There are three circumstances in which a person will be treated as being the principal's agent: where there is express authority; where there is implied authority; and where there is apparent authority.

Where an agent is covered by any of the three types of authority, the principal will be bound by any contract made that falls within that authority, as they are treated as having privity of contract. Where an agent makes a contract which lies outside the authority granted by the principal, or where the agent in fact has no authority at all, the principal may nevertheless choose to ratify the contract, so long as the agent was purporting to act on the principal's behalf at the time the contract was made, and the principal had the capacity to make the contract at that time.

### Undisclosed principals

In some cases, an agent may act for a principal without disclosing the principal's identity, or even the fact that there is a principal. English law nevertheless holds that it is the principal with whom the contract is made, so that it is effectively possible to make a contract with someone without even knowing that they exist.

### Warranty of authority

If an individual purports to make a contract on behalf of someone else the courts can find that the purported agent has contracted that they do have authority.

## Assignment

It is possible to assign the benefit (but not the burden) of a contract without the permission of the other party.

### Negotiability

Certain types of contractual benefit may be assigned merely by being put into a written document and given to another party; the original owner of the benefit need not be notified. The written document is called a negotiable instrument, and the most common examples are banknotes and cheques.

### Novation

To transfer both burdens and benefits of a contract, a novation is required.

### Damages on behalf of another

Despite the privity rule, in **Jackson** v **Horizon Holidays Ltd** (1975) Lord Denning awarded the claimant damages not only for his own loss but also for the loss of his family, because he had entered the contract for their benefit as well.

### Collateral contracts

Where one party makes contracts with two others, the courts will sometimes use the device of 'finding' a collateral contract between the two others to evade the privity rule. An example of this is **Shanklin Pier Ltd** v **Detel Products Ltd** (1951).

## Exceptions in equity

### Constructive trust

A contracting party can specify that the benefit of the contract is held by him or her in trust for a third party, in which case that third party will have enforceable rights to the benefit.

### Restrictive covenants

As well as avoiding the rules on privity of contract under statute, restrictive covenants concerning land avoid those rules in equity, following the case of **Tulk** v **Moxhay** (1848).

# Reading list

Andrews, 'Strangers to justice no longer – the reversal of the privity rule under the Contracts (Rights of Third Parties) Act 1999' (2001) 60 Cambridge Law Journal 353

Kincaid, 'Privity reform in England' (2000) 116 Law Quarterly Review 43

MacMillan, 'A birthday present for Lord Denning: The Contracts (Rights of Third Parties) Act 1999' (2000) 63 Modern Law Review 721

Roe, 'Contractual intention under section 1(1)(b) and 1(2) of the Contracts (Rights of Third Parties) Act 1999' (2000) 63 Modern Law Review 887

Treitel, 'Damages in respect of a third party's losses' (1998) 114 Law Quarterly Review 527

Treitel and Peel (2007) *Treitel on the Law of Contract*, London: Sweet and Maxwell

## Reading on the internet

The Law Commission Report *Privity of contracts: contracts for the benefit of third parties* (1996) is available on its website at:

http://www.lawcom.gov.uk/docs/lc242.pdf

The Contracts (Rights of Third Parties) Act 1999 is available on the website of the Office of Public Sector Information at:

http://www.opsi.gov.uk/acts/acts1999/19990031.htm

The explanatory notes to the Contracts (Rights of Third Parties) Act 1999 are available on the website of the Office for Public Sector Information at:

http://www.opsi.gov.uk/acts/en1999/1999en31.htm

# Part 5
## Discharge and remedies

A contract is said to be discharged when the rights and obligations agreed in it come to an end. There are four ways in which this can happen: performance, frustration, breach and agreement. Where a contract is breached the innocent party will have a right to a remedy. This will in most cases be limited to financial compensation for loss suffered as a result of the breach, and it is only exceptionally that a court will order a party to fulfil their contractual obligations through an order of specific performance.

# Chapter 14
## Discharge of contract

### This chapter discusses:

the four ways in which a contract can be brought to an end: performance, frustration, breach and agreement.

- The general rule is that **performance** must exactly match the requirements laid down in the contract, and this is known as entire performance. In practice, contracts requiring entire performance are the exception rather than the rule.

- If after a contract is made, something happens, through no fault of the parties, to make its performance impossible, the contract is said to be **frustrated**.

- A contract is said to be **breached** when one party performs defectively, differently from the agreement, or not at all (actual breach), or indicates in advance that they will not be performing as agreed (anticipatory breach).

- In some cases the parties will simply **agree** to terminate a contract, so that one or both parties are released from their obligations.

In this chapter we will look at the four ways in which a contract can come to an end: performance, frustration, breach and agreement.

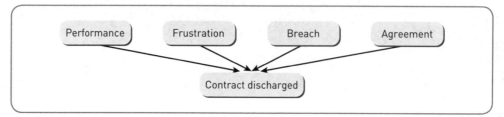

**Figure 14.1** Discharge of contract

# Performance

The most obvious way in which a contract is discharged is by both parties performing their obligations under it. In many cases this is quite straightforward, but there are circumstances in which one party may claim to have performed and therefore, for example, be entitled to payment, yet the other disagrees. As a result, the law has had to address the question of what will amount to performance.

## The entire performance rule

The general rule is that performance must exactly match the requirements laid down in the contract, and this is known as entire performance. If the first party fails to perform entirely, the other need pay nothing at all, even if the shortfall in performance actually causes no hardship.

 **Key Case**   Cutter v Powell

Clearly, the entire performance rule has the potential to cause injustice, as can be seen in the case of **Cutter** v **Powell** (1795). A sailor had contracted to serve on a ship travelling from Jamaica to Liverpool. He was to be paid 30 guineas for the voyage, payable when the ship arrived in Liverpool, but he died during the journey. His widow sued for his wages up until his death, but her claim was unsuccessful. The court held that the contract required entire performance and, as he had not completed performance, she could claim nothing.

**Legal Principle**
If a contract requires entire performance, and a party fails to perform the contract in its entirety, he or she is entitled to nothing under the contract from the other party.

The rule can also allow parties who wish to escape from what has become an unprofitable contract to do so by taking advantage of the most minor departures from its terms. In **Re Moore & Co Ltd and Landauer & Co** (1921) the contract concerned the sale of canned fruits, which were to be packed in cases of 30 tins. On delivery, it was discovered that although the correct number of tins had been sent, about half the cases contained only 24 tins each. This actually made no difference at all to the market value of the goods, but the buyers pointed out that the sale was covered by the Sale of Goods Act, which stated that goods sold by description must correspond with that description. The delivery sent clearly did not, and the buyers were therefore entitled to reject the whole consignment.

# Mitigation of the entire performance rule

In practice, contracts requiring entire performance are the exception rather than the rule, although contracts for the sale of goods are usually entire. There are several ways in which the harshness of the rule is mitigated.

## Substantial performance

Established in **Boone** v **Eyre** (1779) by Lord Mansfield, this doctrine allows a party who has performed with only minor defects to claim the price of the work done, less any money the other party will have to spend to put the defects right. The doctrine will only apply where the claimant has breached a warranty, or has breached an innominate term in a way that is not serious; it cannot be used where the claimant has breached a condition of the contract.

Substantial performance can be understood by contrasting two cases. In the first, **Hoenig** v **Isaacs** (1952), an interior decorator contracted to refurbish a flat for £750. The defendant had paid £400 in advance, but then refused to pay the remaining £350, arguing that the design and workmanship were defective. The court agreed that there were problems with the work done, but the cost of putting these right would only be £56. Consequently it was held that the decorator had substantially performed, and was entitled to the balance of the contract price, less the £56 needed to put right the defects.

In the second case, **Bolton** v **Mahadeva** (1972), a contractor had agreed to install a central heating system for £560. When the work was done, it was found that the system was unable to heat the house adequately, and emitted fumes. It would cost £174 to remedy these defects. The claimant sued for the contract price, less £174, on the basis that he had substantially performed, but the Court of Appeal rejected the claim. The proportion of the contract price required to put the work right was clearly greater than that in **Hoenig**, and the court considered that substantial performance had not taken place. Small domestic building contracts are usually treated as requiring entire performance. Builders carrying out such work have to complete all the work contracted for before they are entitled to be paid.

## Severable contracts

A contract is said to be severable where payment becomes due at various stages of performance, rather than in one lump sum when performance is complete. Most contracts of employment are examples of this: employees are paid weekly or monthly, not all at once when they finally leave the company. Major building contracts usually operate in a similar way, with instalments falling due as various stages of construction are completed.

In a severable contract, the price for each stage can be claimed when that stage is completed, even though the party concerned may be in breach of the contract for not completing subsequent stages – so if you take on a child-minder for the six-week school holidays and pay weekly, the child-minder can claim the first week's pay even if they then refuse to work the following five weeks.

Whether a contract is entire or severable is a question of construction.

## Voluntary acceptance of partial performance

In some cases, while a contract may not originally have been intended to be severable, one party may later agree to accept and pay for part-performance from the other. Where such an agreement can be inferred from the circumstances, the claimant sues on a *quantum meruit*, to recover the cost of such performance as has been provided (see p. 376). The courts will only infer an agreement to accept and pay for part-performance where the party making the promise had a genuine choice – so, for example, this could not apply in **Cutter** *v* **Powell**, because the sailor was hardly in a position to offer the shipowners the choice of accepting part-performance or not.

The principle can be seen in **Sumpter** *v* **Hedges** (1898). A builder agreed to construct two houses and a stable on the defendant's land for £565. However, he abandoned the project after completing £333 worth of work, so the defendant had to complete the building himself, and did so using materials left behind by the builder. The builder claimed on a *quantum meruit* for work done and materials supplied. The claim for the work failed; the defendant was not **choosing** to accept part-performance and finish the job himself; he had no real alternative but to complete the building, which would otherwise be just a useless mess on his land. However, he did not have to use the materials left behind, and so the builder was allowed to claim for these.

## Prevention of performance by other party

Where one party performs part of the agreed obligation, and is then prevented from completing the rest by some fault of the other party, a *quantum meruit* can be used to claim the cost of the work done.

In most of these cases, the innocent party can alternatively claim damages for breach of contract. This may be a higher amount, but there are circumstances in which a *quantum meruit* is more useful. An example is **Planché** *v* **Colburn** (1831) where the claimant was contracted to write a book on costume and ancient armour, for a fee of £100. After he had begun writing, the defendants decided to cease publishing the series of which the book was to form a part. The author was able to recover £50 on a *quantum meruit*.

Where one party cannot perform without the other's cooperation, rejection of an offer to perform (also called a tender of performance) will release the party tendering performance from any further obligation. In **Startup** *v* **Macdonald** (1843) the claimant agreed to sell ten tons of oil to the defendants, to be delivered by the end of March. On the last day of March, the claimant arrived with the oil at 8.30 pm, but the defendants refused to accept the delivery, saying it was too late in the day. The claimant sued for damages, and was successful. The court held that it had done all it could to comply with the contract, and its tender of performance was sufficient basis for the claim (s. 29(5) of the Sale of Goods Act 1979 now provides that delivery must be made at a reasonable hour, so on the same facts a court might take a different approach today).

Slightly different rules apply to the tender of money, rather than goods. The party tendering the money is not obliged to repeat the offer, but the debt remains outstanding and the creditor can demand payment at a future date. Payment must also be of the exact amount due, and in the form of 'legal tender'. This means Bank of England notes for any amount, silver coins up to the value of five pounds, and copper up to the value of 20p – so if you decide to pay back your overdraft in 2p coins just to be annoying, the bank is perfectly free to reject it.

## Breach of terms concerning time

What is the position when one party performs late, but in all other respects as agreed in the contract? Late performance will always amount to a breach of contract giving rise to a right to damages. It will only give rise to a right to terminate the contract if the delay constitutes a substantial failure to perform, or if the time of performance is treated as being 'of the essence'. When time is of the essence, any failure to perform on time justifies the termination of the contract, even if little or no hardship is caused.

There are three main ways in which a contract may be classified as one in which time is of the essence. First, the parties may explicitly state this in their agreement. Secondly, it may be inferred from the nature of the contract, or the circumstances surrounding it. Therefore, in a contract to sell goods which quickly go off, or the price of which fluctuates very rapidly, time is likely to be of the essence. For some types of contract, the rules on time stipulation are made by statute – for example, the Law of Property Act 1925, s. 41 states that time is not of the essence in contracts for the sale of land.

The third situation is where a contract is not originally one in which time is of the essence but, following a delay in performance, a contracting party gives notice of a time limit on performance. The contract then becomes one for which time is of the essence. This was the case in **Charles Rickards Ltd** v **Oppenheimer** (see p. 105).

The current position was developed by the House of Lords in **United Scientific Holdings Ltd** v **Burnley Borough Council** (1978). The defendants in the case were landlords of premises leased by the tenants under a 99-year lease running from 31 August 1962. For the first ten years the rent was to be fixed, but there was provision for periodic rent reviews every ten years after that. If the landlords wished to take advantage of this provision, they were to take steps towards a rent review before the end of each ten-year period. In fact, the landlords did nothing about raising the rent until almost two months after the end of the first ten-year period. The tenant argued that time was of the essence, and that the landlords had therefore lost their chance to raise the rent, but this argument was rejected. Given the nature of the contract, the House of Lords held that there was a presumption that time was not of the essence, and so the landlords were still entitled to use the rent review procedure.

**Figure 14.2** Mitigation of entire performance rule

Where a contract does not specify a time for performance, performance must usually take place within a reasonable time.

# Vicarious performance

Is a contract discharged if the contractual obligations of one of the parties are, at that party's request, performed by someone else? The answer depends on the type of contract. The general rule is that the other party cannot object to such vicarious performance unless it prejudices their interests. If the service contracted for is one which relies on the skill or judgement of one party, the other can insist on personal performance. Obvious examples are employment contracts, or a contract to paint a picture, or perform in a concert.

Clearly, a contract must also be performed personally if that is specified in the terms, or if, by implication, the terms prohibit vicarious performance. In **Davies** *v* **Collins** (1945) the defendant accepted a uniform for cleaning, under a contract stating that: 'Whilst every care is exercised in cleaning . . . garments, all orders are accepted at owners' risk.' The defendant sent the uniform to be cleaned by a sub-contractor, who lost it. It was held that this was a breach of contract, because the words 'every care is exercised in cleaning' excluded the right to perform the cleaning operation vicariously.

Where vicarious performance is permitted, liability for performance nevertheless remains with the original contracting party. In **Stewart** *v* **Reavell's Garage** (1952) the claimant took a 1929 Bentley to the defendants' garage, to have the brakes relined. The defendants suggested that the work should be done by a sub-contractor and the claimant agreed. Unfortunately, the work was done badly, and the brakes failed, with the result that the claimant was injured. The defendants were clearly entitled to perform vicariously, as the claimant had agreed to their doing so, but they were still liable for the sub-contractor's defective workmanship.

# Frustration

The basic principle here is that if after a contract is made, something happens, through no fault of the parties, to make its performance impossible, the contract is said to be frustrated, and the obligations under it come to an end. Although there are many events which may make performance impossible, only certain limited types will allow a contract to be frustrated. Because frustration leads to the automatic discharge of the contract, regardless of the wishes of the parties, the courts use it as a weapon of last resort, which can only be used in exceptional circumstances.

At one time, contractual responsibilities were generally regarded as absolute, and once a contract was made, subsequent events could not justify non-performance. This rule began to be relaxed with the case of **Taylor** *v* **Caldwell** (1863), from which the modern doctrine of frustration developed. The parties in the case had entered into an agreement concerning the use of the Surrey Gardens and Music Hall for a series of 'grand concerts, and day and night fetes'. Six days before the planned date for the first concert, the building was burnt down, making it impossible for the concerts to go ahead. The party planning to put on the concerts sued for breach of contract, arguing that the owners had failed to provide the Music Hall as agreed under the contract. It claimed the money it had wasted on advertisements. The action failed because performance by the owners had become impossible, so the contract had been frustrated.

## Time of frustrating event

A frustrating event which occurs before the contract is made gives rise to the issue of mistake (discussed in Chapter 10) rather than to an issue of frustration. If, for example, the Music Hall in **Taylor** v **Caldwell** had burnt down, without the knowledge of the parties, before the contract was completed, the issue would have been one of mistake, not frustration.

# What will amount to frustration?

It is impossible to compile an exhaustive list of the situations in which a contract will become frustrated, but they fall into three broad categories: events which make performance or further performance impossible; those which make it illegal; and those which make it pointless.

## Impossible

A contract may become impossible to perform in any of the following ways.

- *Destruction or unavailability of something essential for contract's performance.*  **Taylor** v **Caldwell** (1863) is an example of this.
- *Death of either party.*  Contracts which require personal performance (as described above at p. 314) are discharged by frustration on the death of either party.
- *Unavailability of party.*  Contracts requiring personal performance will be frustrated if either party falls ill or is imprisoned, providing that the non-availability of that party substantially affects the performance. In **Robinson** v **Davison** (1871) a piano player was booked to perform, but was ill on the day of the concert. He was sued for breach of contract, but it was held that the contract had been frustrated when his illness made it impossible to perform.
- *Method of performance impossible.*  Where a contract lays down a particular method for performance, and this becomes impossible, the contract may be frustrated. In **Nickoll and Knight** v **Ashton Edridge & Co** (1901) a contract for the sale of cottonseed specified that it was 'to be shipped per steamship *Orlando* from Alexandria during . . . January'. The *Orlando* later ran aground in the Baltic, and could not therefore make the journey to Alexandria in January. A majority of the Court of Appeal interpreted the contract as requiring performance in the stipulated manner, and therefore held that the contract was frustrated since this could not be done. However, there may be cases where although a method of performance is stipulated, the contract can be interpreted as accepting an alternative method if necessary, and, in this case, the contract will not be frustrated if the stipulated method of performance is impossible.

## Illegal

If, after a contract is formed, a change in the law makes its performance illegal, the contract will be frustrated. This happened to many contracts made just before the First and Second World Wars as, once war was declared, it became illegal to trade with enemy countries. In the leading **Fibrosa** case (see p. 323 below) a contract for the sale of machinery which was to be shipped to Poland was frustrated because the port was occupied by the enemy. Trade in various types of goods was also restricted, which again led to contracts concerning those goods being frustrated. Frustration by supervening illegality can of course happen outside wartime situations, but the two world wars appear to have been a fruitful source of cases on this issue.

## Pointless

A contract can be frustrated where a supervening event makes performance of a contract completely pointless, though still technically possible. Another way of putting it is that there has been such a drastic change in circumstances that the contract becomes essentially different from that which was originally agreed. There are very tight limits on this aspect of the doctrine of frustration, and these are best illustrated by a pair of cases associated with the coronation of Edward VII in 1901. The coronation had been planned for a particular date, but in the event had to be postponed because the king fell ill. Since the postponement was made at the last moment, a great many preparations had been made and events organised, and it was from these that the two 'coronation cases' on frustration arose.

In the first case, **Krell** v **Henry** (1903), the defendant had agreed to rent from the claimant a suite of rooms in Pall Mall, for the day on which the coronation was to take place. The room offered a view of the coronation procession, and the defendant had intended to sell tickets to people wanting to watch from its windows. The contract did not mention the coronation, but the price to be paid reflected the significance of the day. Needless to say, when the coronation did not take place, the defendant no longer wanted the room, but the claimant nevertheless sued for the rent. The Court of Appeal held that although the contract was still capable of physical performance, it was frustrated, because the viewing of the procession was the 'foundation of the contract'. The court said that frustration could apply in cases where 'the event which renders the contract incapable of performance is the cessation or non-existence of an express condition or state of things, going to the root of the contract, and essential to its performance'.

The limits of this principle can be seen in the other well-known 'coronation case', **Herne Bay Steam Boat Co** v **Hutton** (1903). Here the defendant had hired a steamboat in order to take passengers to watch the naval review by the king, organised to mark the coronation. When the coronation was cancelled, so was the review, but the Court of Appeal held that the ability to watch the review was not fundamental to the contract; the defendant could still carry out pleasure trips on the boat. The contract was therefore not frustrated.

The distinction between these two cases is obviously an extremely fine one, and perhaps hard to justify.

## What will not amount to frustration?

A particular event will not frustrate a contract if the contract makes provision for such an event; the event merely renders the contract more onerous; it was foreseen or foreseeable; or if it was due to the fault of one of the parties.

## Contractual provision

Some contracts make specific provision for the type of event which might otherwise frustrate a contract. For example, if you buy a house, the contract will often state that the responsibility for buildings insurance rests with the buyer once contracts have been exchanged. This means that if the house burns down between exchange and completion, you cannot say that the contract is frustrated by destruction of the subject matter, because you have already agreed to accept this risk. The contract goes ahead as planned and you claim against your insurance, assuming you have in fact organised it, and you are obliged to pay for the house.

If the potential frustrating event is dealt with in a *force majeure* clause, then the impact of this event will be determined according to this contractual clause, rather than through the doctrine of frustration. The term '*force majeure*' can be literally translated as 'superior forces', thus these clauses are dealing with the impact of unexpected and disruptive events that may have an impact on the performance of the contract. Contracting parties sometimes choose to insert a *force majeure* clause to control what happens when certain events arise, rather than relying on the doctrine of frustration. The parties can agree what types of events to include within the clause (such as terrorism, war, earthquake, flood) and what the impact should be of that event on the contract. If the event that occurs falls outside the *force majeure* clause, then the doctrine of frustration may apply. It is not possible to use contractual terms to exclude frustration by supervening illegality.

## Contract more onerous

A contract is unlikely to be frustrated simply because performance has become more onerous or expensive than expected. This was established in a number of cases arising from the closure of the Suez canal during the 1956 Suez crisis. The canal was – and still is – an important short cut for ships travelling between Europe and Asia and, when it was closed, ships had to follow a much longer route, which was therefore more expensive. Disputes arose where contracts were made before the closure of the canal, in the expectation that the shorter route would be used, but the courts held that if performance was still possible, the fact that it was now more expensive was irrelevant to the issue of frustration. An example of these cases is **Tsakiroglou Co Ltd v Noblee Thorl GmbH** (1962).

Frustration cannot be invoked simply because one party has made what turns out to be a bad deal. This can be seen in **Amalgamated Investment & Property Co Ltd v John Walker & Sons Ltd** (1977) (see p. 224), where the fact that redevelopment of the buildings bought became difficult or impossible did not mean that there was no purpose at all to the contract, only that it was not as lucrative as expected. In **Gold Group Properties Ltd v BDW Trading Ltd (formerly Barratt Homes Ltd)** (2010) BDW argued that a building contract had been frustrated by the fall in property prices. This argument was, predictably, rejected by the High Court. There was no supervening event that could amount to frustration, there was simply a pessimistic forecast about the movement in house prices and the contract itself did allow for the parties to renegotiate the house prices in the contract. A recession can have a severe impact on contracts, but it could only lead to the frustration of a contract if its impact is to render performance impossible, not just impractical or uneconomical.

## Foreseen and foreseeable events

Where the supervening event which interferes with performance is one which the parties foresaw, or could have foreseen, it is generally assumed that they made the contract with the knowledge of what could happen, and shaped their terms accordingly. If, for example, a shipbuilder contracts to build a ship at a time when it is generally thought that the price of raw materials is about to rise, the shipbuilder will usually take this into account when agreeing the price of the ship. In such cases, if the event concerned does happen this should not frustrate the contract. The exception is where the frustrating event is a wartime prohibition on trading with the enemy: the fact that the war was a foreseeable event does not prevent the prohibition from frustrating contracts.

**Key Case** Davis Contractors *v* Fareham UDC

The leading case on frustration and foresight is **Davis Contractors *v* Fareham UDC** (1956). Davis, a building company, contracted to build 78 houses for a local authority. The job was to take eight months, at a price of £94,000. In fact, labour shortages delayed the work, which ended up taking 22 months and costing the builders £21,000 more than they had planned. The defendant was willing to pay the contract price, despite the delay, but, as this did not cover the claimant's costs, Davis sought to have the contract discharged on the grounds of frustration, alleging that the labour shortages made performance fundamentally different from that envisaged in the contract (Davis intended to seek payment on a *quantum meruit* basis to recover its costs).

However, the House of Lords decided that the events which caused the delays were within the range of changes which could reasonably be expected to happen during the performance of a contract for building houses, and the changed circumstances did not make performance radically different from what was expected. It was a contract to build houses, and houses were in fact built. The problems encountered by the builder made his performance more burdensome to him, but they did not change the nature of what he was expected to do, and so the contract was not frustrated. Lord Radcliffe explained:

> It is not hardship or inconvenience or material loss itself which calls the principle of frustration into play. There must be as well such a change in the significance of the obligation that the thing undertaken would, if performed, be a different thing from that contracted for.

**Legal Principle**
Where a supervening event interfering with performance of a contract is one which the parties foresaw, or could have foreseen, it will not frustrate the contract.

In **Four Seasons Healthcare Ltd *v* Maughan** (2004) a nurse employed in a nursing home was suspended for alleged patient abuse pending a criminal trial. He was subsequently convicted and sent to prison for his conduct. The Employment Appeal Tribunal still held that he was entitled to back pay of more than £15,000 for the period while he had been suspended. He had not initially been sacked, but only suspended and was therefore entitled to be paid during the relevant period. His contract had not been frustrated at this stage because his contract of employment expressly foresaw the possibility that he might be accused of abuse and provided for disciplinary proceedings to handle this situation. In order for a contract to be frustrated, the relevant event must have been unforeseen and unforeseeable. The contract was subsequently frustrated when the nurse was convicted and imprisoned, but this frustration could not be backdated to the time of the original accusation.

## Self-induced frustration

A contract will not be frustrated by any supervening event which is the fault of one of the parties. In the Canadian case of **Maritime National Fish Ltd *v* Ocean Trawlers Ltd** (1935) a ship, the

*St Cuthbert*, was chartered for a year from the owners. Both parties were aware that the *St Cuthbert* was a type of ship that required a licence from the Canadian Government before it could be legally operated. The charterers were operating five ships, but were only granted three licences, which they used for three ships that they owned. They then claimed that the charter was frustrated by the Government's refusal to grant more licences. The Privy Council rejected this view, on the grounds that the charterers themselves had a choice, and decided not to use one of the available licences for the *St Cuthbert*.

Similarly, in the **Super Servant Two** (1990) the defendants contracted to carry the claimant's drilling rig in one of their two vessels designed for this purpose, the *Super Servants One* and *Two*. Before the contract was carried out, the *Super Servant Two* sank; the defendants said they could not use the *Super Servant One* because it was needed for another contract, and therefore claimed that the sinking frustrated the contract. The courts denied this claim: the defendants had chosen to use the *Super Servant One* on the other contract. The decision also seems to have been influenced by the fact that the other contract was finalised after the one made with the claimant, and the defendants continued to try to negotiate extra payments before deciding which contract to allocate to the *Super Servant One* – in other words, they seemed to be trying to use frustration to avoid an agreement which had become inconvenient.

# Legal consequences of frustration

Once a court holds that a contract is frustrated, it is automatically terminated from the point at which the frustrating event occurred and the contract is described as being discharged. Obligations which would have arisen from that point on no longer exist, but the contract is not treated as though it never existed, so acts done before the frustrating event may have legal consequences. This can be contrasted with mistake where the contract is treated as void *ab initio* (meaning from the beginning).

## The common law

The common law traditionally took the view that any loss resulting from the frustration should lie where it fell. Thus, if advance payments had been made under the contract prior to the frustrating event they would not be recoverable. This approach was softened slightly in the case of **Fibrosa Spolka Akcyjna *v* Fairbairn Lawson Combe Barbour Ltd** (1943), where the court stated that such advance payments would be recoverable if there had been a total failure of consideration. In that case Fairbairn was contracted to manufacture machinery for Fibrosa, a Polish company, in July 1939. The price was £4,800 and it was agreed that £1,600 should be paid in advance, though in fact only £1,000 was paid over. By September 1940 parts of Poland were under German occupation, including the area to which the machinery was to be delivered, so the contract was frustrated by the ban on trading with the enemy. Fibrosa claimed their £1,000 back. The Court of Appeal held that the money paid could be recovered because Fibrosa had received nothing at all in return for it. However, the court stated that if the party paying in advance had received some benefit under the transaction, even though it might not be complete performance, the money could not be recovered. This 'all-or-nothing' approach clearly had the potential to cause unfairness on both sides. First, where some consideration was given, parties making payment in advance could lose all their money, despite receiving very little benefit. Secondly, where there was a total failure of consideration, allowing the payer to claim back the whole payment could in some circumstances be unfair to the payee, who might have (and in the **Fibrosa** case had) already used the advance payment to finance the initial work on the contract. When the contract was frustrated, that work would be wasted. In other words, there were clearly circumstances in which the losses incurred by frustration were not being fairly allocated.

## The Law Reform (Frustrated Contracts) Act 1943

The Act does not affect the law determining where a contract has been frustrated (that has been discussed on pp. 318–23); it simply alters the legal consequences once the contract is held to have been frustrated under the rules of the common law. It draws a distinction between obligations to pay money and other types of obligation that existed prior to the frustration.

### Obligations to pay money

Section 1(2) of the Act provides that:

> All sums paid or payable to any party in pursuance of the contract before the time when the parties were so discharged (in this Act referred to as 'the time of discharge') shall, in the case of sums so paid, be recoverable from him as money received by him for the use of the party by whom the sums were paid and, in the case of sums so payable, cease to be payable:
>
> Provided that, if the party to whom the sums were so paid or payable incurred expenses before the time of discharge in, or for the purpose of, the performance of the contract, the court may, if it considers it just to do so having regard to all the circumstances of the case, allow him to retain or, as the case may be, recover the whole or any part of the sums so paid or payable, not being an amount in excess of the expenses so incurred.

The principal effect of the subsection is to entitle a person to recover money paid under a contract prior to the frustrating event, and it also removes any obligation to pay money that existed prior to the frustrating event. The court has no discretion over the question whether a sum already paid is recoverable: the only discretion concerns the allowance for expenses.

Section 1(2) goes beyond the common law rule laid down in **Fibrosa** in two respects. First, money paid is recoverable even upon a partial failure of consideration; the common law requirement that the failure be total has therefore been abolished in the case of frustration. Secondly, where the party to whom the money was paid or payable has incurred expenses as a result of the contract before the frustration occurred, the court can order that these expenses, or part of them, be kept back from the money recovered, or claimed from the other party, but only where the contract made provision for advance payment. Expenses may include overheads and the cost of work done.

### Obligations other than to pay money

Section 1(3) states that:

> Where any party to the contract has, by reason of anything done by any other party thereto in, or for the purpose of, the performance of the contract obtained a valuable benefit (other than a payment of money to which the last foregoing subsection applies) before the time of discharge, there shall be recoverable from him by the said other party such sum (if any), not exceeding the value of the said benefit to the party obtaining it, as the court considers just, having regard to all the circumstances of the case and, in particular –

(a) the amount of any expenses incurred before the time of discharge by the benefited party in, or for the purpose of, the performance of the contract, including any sums paid or payable by him to any other party in pursuance of the contract and retained or recoverable by that party under the last foregoing subsection, and

(b) the effect, in relation to the said benefit, of the circumstances giving rise to the frustration of the contract.

Thus, if before the frustrating event one party obtains a valuable benefit (other than money) because of something done by the other in performance of the contract, the party receiving the benefit can be ordered to pay a just sum in return for it. This provision has caused the most problems in practice for the courts. First, a court has to identify the valuable benefit; secondly, it has to award a just sum for that benefit.

As regards identifying the valuable benefit, the courts have had difficulties determining what exactly the benefit was: it could be the 'end product' of the services or the services themselves. In the leading case of **BP Exploration** *v* **Hunt** (1979) Robert Goff J pointed out that the provision of services would often not in itself be a valuable benefit, but the end result might be. He concluded that, in appropriate cases, it was the end product that was to be regarded as the 'benefit'. So, for instance, in a building contract the valuable benefit will not be the provision of so many hours of work, but the value, if any, which this adds to the owner's property. The effect of the frustrating event on the valuable benefit must be taken into account. Thus, if there was a building contract and the frustrating event was a fire, and this destroyed the work the builder had done, the building owner could not be said to have received a valuable benefit, and would not be obliged to pay for it.

In calculating the award of a just sum for the valuable benefit, the courts try to balance out the financial consequences of frustration, in order to prevent the unjust enrichment of one party at the expense of the other. In **Gamerco SA** *v* **ICM/Fair Warning (Agency) Ltd** (1995) the court concluded that there was: 'no indication in the Act, the authorities or the relevant literature that the court is obliged to incline towards total retention or equal division. Its task is to do justice in a situation which the parties had neither contemplated nor provided for, and to mitigate the possible harshness of allowing all loss to lie where it has fallen.' The emphasis is thus placed on the broad nature of the discretion which the court enjoys and the imperative to do justice on the facts of the case.

Regrettably, there is still a gap in coverage for those parties who incur expenses before the frustrating event, but whose contract does not specify advance payment: unless they have provided a valuable benefit, they will be stuck with these losses. The Law Revision Committee, on whose 1939 report the Act was based, argued that this was not a problem, since a contracting party who did not negotiate for advance payment would be voluntarily assuming the risk of such losses. However, since frustration concerns events which cannot be foreseen, it is hard to see how a contracting party could consciously assume the risk that these events might happen.

## Scope of the Law Reform (Frustrated Contracts) Act 1943

Section 1(1) states that the 1943 Act does not apply to contracts concerning the sale of specific goods which are frustrated by the goods perishing, nor to most charterparties or contracts for the carriage of goods by sea or insurance policies. In addition, the parties may agree to place their contract outside the operation of the Act and specify this in the terms of their contract. In such cases the old common law applies.

# The theory of frustration

It is not clear precisely what is the theoretical basis for the doctrine of frustration. Are the courts trying to give effect to the apparent intentions of the parties, as we would expect from the basic principles of contract law, or are they in fact merely imposing the solution which seems to them to be just in the circumstances? Two main schools of thought have developed on this point, known loosely as the 'implied term' and 'imposed solution' theories.

The implied term theory suggests that the contract is discharged because, by implication, the parties have agreed that it will no longer be binding if the frustrating event occurs – in other words, if anyone had asked the parties, at the time of contracting, whether they would consider themselves still to be bound if such an event happened, they would both have said 'Of course not'.

This approach was adopted by Blackburn J in **Taylor** v **Caldwell**, but it has been criticised as being artificial. As Lord Radcliffe pointed out in **Davis** v **Fareham UDC** (1956) there is 'a logical difficulty in seeing how the parties could even impliedly have provided for something which *ex hypothesi* they neither expected nor foresaw'.

Current commentators favour instead the 'just solution' theory, which sees the courts as intervening to impose a fair solution when circumstances make the whole situation completely different from that originally envisaged by the parties. Under this interpretation, the courts ignore the intention of the parties and interfere with the contractual arrangement in order to do justice in a situation which is no fault of either party.

# Breach

A contract is said to be breached when one party performs defectively, differently from the agreement, or not at all (actual breach), or indicates in advance that they will not be performing as agreed (anticipatory breach).

# Actual breach

A simple example of a breach of contract occurred in **Platform Funding Ltd** v **Bank of Scotland plc** (2008). The defendant was a professional valuer, who was asked by a client to estimate the value of '1 Baker's Yard'. This house was on a new development with five plots, none of which was numbered. The valuer mistakenly looked at and valued number 5, thinking it was number 1. The client later claimed it had suffered loss as a result and the Court of Appeal accepted there had been a breach of contract. In deciding whether there had been a breach, it did not matter whether or not the valuer had been negligent, all that mattered was that he had contracted to value number 1 and had actually valued number 5.

Another illustration of an actual breach of contract is **Pilbrow** v **Pearless de Rougemont & Co** (1999). The appellant had telephoned a firm of solicitors and asked to make an appointment with a solicitor. The appointment was arranged with an employee who was not a qualified solicitor. He was not informed that the employee was not a solicitor. The appellant was dissatisfied with the quality of the legal services he had received and refused to pay the outstanding fees. The firm sued for their fees. The Court of Appeal accepted that as a matter of fact the standard of legal services provided had been that of a competent solicitor. But it ruled that there had been a contract not just to provide legal services, but to provide legal services by a solicitor. The firm did not perform that contract at all. No legal services were provided by any solicitor; they therefore had no right to any payment. To avoid this problem in future, professionals should always make clear to the client whether their services are being provided by a qualified professional or not.

A case where breach of contract was not proven was **Modahl *v* British Athletic Federation Ltd** (1999). The claimant was a well-known British international athlete who was suspended from competition by the British Athletic Federation (BAF) because of an allegation that she had taken prohibited drugs to improve her performance. She successfully appealed against the doping allegation and brought an action for breach of contract and damages against BAF. She alleged that her suspension and the initiation of disciplinary proceedings were in breach of her contract with the defendant. She claimed damages for the financial loss suffered because she was unable to compete in international athletics for nearly a year. BAF was a member of the International Amateur Athletic Federation (IAAF). The IAAF had adopted its system of instant suspension followed by disciplinary proceedings in the belief that, although it might sometimes cause injustice in an individual case, it was necessary in the wider interests of the sport. The contract between Modahl and BAF was therefore interpreted as allowing the same procedures and no damages were awarded.

In **Abramova *v* Oxford Institute of Legal Practice** (2011) Ms Abramova took her law school to court. She had been enrolled on a Legal Practice Course with a view to becoming a solicitor. She failed some exams three times. The Law Society only allows students to have a fourth attempt in exceptional circumstances. She sued her Law School on the basis that when she enrolled on the course she entered into a contract for services. This contract included an implied term under s. 13 of the Supply of Goods and Services Act 1982, which states:

> In the contract of supply of the service where the supplier is acting in the course of business, there is an implied term that the supplier will carry out the service with reasonable care and skill.

She claimed that the law school had breached this implied term because, she suggested, the tutors failed to provide her with adequate feedback to enable her to have the best possible chance of succeeding in her resit examinations. The High Court rejected this argument. There would only be a breach of s. 13 if her tutors' acts or omissions had fallen so far below the standard of reasonable tutors that they had been negligent. On the facts Ms Abramova had not satisfied this test.

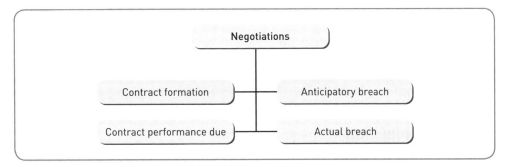

**Figure 14.3** Breach

## Anticipatory breach

Where an anticipatory breach occurs, the other party can sue for breach straight away; it is not necessary to wait until performance falls due. This was what happened in **Frost** v **Knight** (1872). The defendant had promised to marry the claimant once his father had died. He later broke off the engagement while his father was still alive, and when his ex-fiancée sued him for breach of promise (which was a valid claim in those days, though not any longer), he argued that she had no claim as the time for performance had not yet arrived. This argument was rejected and the claimant's claim succeeded.

In **Hochster** v **De la Tour** (1853) the parties had made a contract in April under which the claimant would be a tour leader in Europe for the defendant beginning on 1 June. In May the defendant informed the claimant that his services were no longer required. The claimant started his action for breach of contract on 22 May. The defendant argued that he should be required to wait until the date performance was due, which was 1 June, as there was no breach of contract until that date. The court rejected this argument. The claimant could commence proceedings immediately for damages, even though the date of performance had not yet arrived.

In some cases, the innocent party elects to wait until performance falls due, but this can mean they end up worse off than if they had sued immediately the anticipatory breach was known. In **Avery** v **Bowden** (1856) Bowden chartered Avery's ship and agreed to load up his cargo at Odessa within 45 days. However, Bowden later told Avery that he had no cargo and advised him to take the ship away. This was an anticipatory breach, and Avery could have sued for breach of contract immediately. Instead, he kept the ship available at the port, in the hope that Bowden would eventually fulfil his promise. Before the 45 days were up, the Crimean War broke out between England and Russia, so that performance became illegal and the contract was frustrated. The frustration then prevented Avery from suing for breach.

## Lawful excuse

In some cases, an extraneous event which is not sufficiently serious to frustrate a contract will nevertheless provide an excuse for non-performance. For example, an employee who does not go to work because he is ill is not in breach, even though the illness is not serious enough to frustrate the contract.

## Effect of breach

Any breach of contract will entitle the innocent party to sue for damages, but not every breach allows the wronged party to choose to discharge the contract (in contrast with frustration where the discharge is automatic). If the contract is not discharged, it will still need to be performed. There are three main circumstances in which the innocent party may choose to discharge.

### Repudiation

This is where one party makes it clear that they no longer intend to be bound by the contract, either during its performance, or before performance is due (in practice it is usually the latter, and therefore an anticipatory breach). The courts are slow to find a repudiatory breach. In **Woodar Investment Development Ltd** v **Wimpey Construction Ltd** (1980) Lord Wilberforce stated:

> Repudiation is a drastic conclusion which should only be held to arise in clear cases of a refusal, in a matter going to the root of the contract, to perform contractual obligations.

An old illustration of a repudiatory breach is provided by **Frost** v **Knight** (1872) (see p. 328 above). A more recent illustration is provided by **Vaswani** v **Italian Motors (Sales & Services) Ltd** (1996). The appellant had paid a deposit on a Ferrari car to the respondents, who were sole distributors of such cars in Hong Kong. The price of the car was £179,500, a quarter of which had to be paid in advance by way of deposit. The car had to be specially ordered and took about a month to be delivered to the dealer. The contract of sale allowed the contract price to be increased to take account of increased costs, but the respondents sought to raise the price by £40,300 for a reason not allowed by the contract. They notified the appellant that the car was ready and required payment of the balance quoted at the higher price. Their letter stated that if the car was not collected and paid for by the specified date, they would treat the contract as repudiated and the deposit forfeited. The appellant challenged the respondents' right to do this, arguing that the demand for more money amounted to a repudiation of the contract.

The Privy Council held that, though the sellers did not have the right to demand the higher price, this did not on the facts amount to a repudiation of the contract. This was because they had honestly believed they had the right to increase the price in this way under the contract. In addition, the respondents' conduct had been consistent with the continuation of the contract. They were therefore entitled to keep the buyer's deposit. To avoid losing his deposit the appellant should have tendered the original correct purchase price.

## Topical Issue

### Robbie Williams in court

Following the break-up of the highly successful pop group Take That in 1995, one of its former members, Robbie Williams, unsuccessfully alleged that his manager, Martin-Smith, had committed a repudiatory breach of his management contract: **Martin-Smith** v **Williams** (1999). It seems that after the break-up of the group, a legal dispute had arisen between Robbie Williams and record company BMG. The dispute had been settled when Williams agreed to waive his right to commission payments from BMG in return for being released from Take That's recording agreement. Martin-Smith had been the group's manager and he sued Williams for commission on sums that, but for the compromise, Williams would have received under the recording agreement. Williams counterclaimed that Martin-Smith had been in repudiatory breach of his fiduciary duty arising under the management contract. It seems that after Williams had had a number of disagreements with the other band members in July 1995, he announced his intention to leave the band in January 1996. Two band members had, on Martin-Smith's advice, presented Williams with the choice of reconsidering his decision or leaving the band immediately. The Court of Appeal ruled that the manager of a pop group was authorised to act in the best interests of the whole group in priority to those of any individual member of the group. His advice was not unreasonable, it being in the best interests of all the members that there should be an immediate resolution of disagreements within the group. He had not, therefore, committed a repudiatory breach of the management contract. On the other hand, a waiver in relation to future royalties in the compromise with BMG was in breach of an express term of the management agreement. Even if it had not been, the court would have been prepared to imply a term preventing Williams from doing acts that would have deprived Martin-Smith of the commission for services rendered during the management agreement.

## Breach of a condition

The terms of a contract can be divided into conditions, warranties and innominate terms, according to their importance (as we saw in Chapter 7). Breach of a condition allows the innocent party to terminate the contract; breaches of warranty do not justify termination, although they may give rise to an award of damages. In **Pilbrow v Pearless de Rougemont & Co** (see p. 326) the firm of solicitors was treated as having breached a condition, and the contract was discharged so that the appellant did not have to pay the firm's fees.

## Serious breach of an innominate term

Where the relevant term is classified by the courts as innominate, it will be one which can be breached in both serious and trivial ways, and whether the innocent party is entitled to terminate or not will depend on how serious the results of the breach are. If the results are so serious as to undermine the very foundation of the contract, the innocent party will have the right to terminate.

# Choice to affirm or discharge

Even when one of these three types of breach occurs, the contract is not automatically discharged; the innocent party can usually choose whether or not to terminate. As Viscount Simon stated in **Heyman v Darwins Ltd** (1942):

> Repudiation by one party standing alone does not terminate the contract. It takes two to end it, by repudiation, on the one side, and acceptance of the repudiation, on the other.

In other words, a contract does not come to an end when the contract breaker repudiates liability but only when the innocent party chooses to treat the repudiation as bringing the contract to an end.

If the innocent party opts to treat the contract as discharged, that decision must be made known to the other party in a clear and unequivocal manner. The parties in **Vitol SA v Norelf Ltd** (1996) had entered into a contract under which Norelf sold Vitol goods which were to be shipped from the USA and delivered between 1 and 7 of March. By 8 March loading was still not completed and the buyers, Vitol, sent Norelf a telex rejecting the cargo on the ground that delivery was overdue. It was later found that this telex breached the contract and amounted to a repudiation. The vessel completed loading on 9 March, and Norelf informed Vitol of this two days later, but took no further steps to perform the contract. Some four days afterwards, Norelf sold the cargo for substantially less than Vitol had agreed to pay and, after six months, commenced an action claiming damages for this loss.

The courts had to decide whether the conduct of the innocent party, Norelf, amounted to a clear and unequivocal acceptance of the repudiatory breach (if it did not, Vitol could have withdrawn it before acceptance and so have escaped liability for damages). Norelf had simply remained silent and failed to perform the contract. The Court of Appeal thought that this was not clear and unequivocal: a failure to perform was equally consistent with a misunderstanding by the innocent party of its rights or with indecision or even inadvertence. The House of Lords reversed the decision of the Court of Appeal, finding that the conduct of Vitol did in fact clearly and unequivocally demonstrate that it intended to treat the contract as terminated. The House pointed out that an acceptance of a repudiation required no particular form, and that in some circumstances mere silence and a failure to carry out its contractual obligations under the repudiated contract was sufficient to amount to acceptance of the repudiation. While it was accepted that silence is usually equivocal, Lord Steyn commented that '[s]ometimes in the practical world of businessmen, an omission to act may be as pregnant with meaning as a positive declaration'.

Once the innocent party has made known to the other party that the contract is at an end, the choice is final, taking effect on communication to the other party; the innocent party cannot later decide that the contract should go ahead after all.

The innocent party, once fully aware of the facts, can choose to affirm the contract by indicating with words, acts or even silence, an intention that the contract should continue despite the breach. In this case, apart from any claim for damages, the contract is treated as though the breach had never occurred.

In many cases, the party in breach will prefer the contract to come to an end, but if this is not what the innocent party wants, it is technically possible to continue fulfilling their side of the bargain, and then sue for the price, providing this can be done without cooperation from the other party, and the innocent party has a genuine interest in doing so.

An example of this fairly rare situation occurred in **White and Carter** v **McGregor** (1962) in which McGregor was a garage owner who had entered into a three-year advertising contract under which the claimants would place advertisements for his garage on local litter bins. Later on the very day he made the contract, McGregor decided he wanted to cancel it. He immediately wrote to the claimants informing them of his decision. Even though the claimants were aware that the advertising was no longer required, they went ahead with it, for the full three years, and then successfully sued for the price. The House of Lords held that the claimants had a choice. If they opted to continue with the contract, that was their right no matter how unreasonable. Lord Reid stated:

> The general rule cannot be in doubt . . . If one party to a contract repudiates it in the sense of making it clear to the other party that he refused or will refuse to carry out his part of the contract, the other party, the innocent party has an option. He may accept that repudiation and sue for damages for breach of contract, whether or not the time for performance has come, or he may if he chooses disregard or refuse to accept it and then the contract remains in full effect.

In contract law there is a general duty to take reasonable steps to mitigate one's loss (see p. 358). But this duty only applies where the contract has been discharged. The claimants had made no attempt to mitigate their loss by looking for alternative advertisers. But, on the facts they were under no duty to mitigate because at this stage the contract had not been discharged, but continued to exist. The case is unusual because the claimants were able to perform their side of the contract without any need for cooperation from the other party. Lord Reid justified the decision in the following terms:

> It might be, but never has been, the law that a person is only entitled to enforce his contractual rights in a reasonable way. One reason why that is not the law is no doubt, because it was thought that it would create too much uncertainty to require the court to decide whether it was reasonable or equitable to allow a party to enforce its full rights under a contract.

Lord Reid laid down certain restrictions on when unwanted performance would be compensated. First, it would only be possible where no cooperation for its performance was required from the other contracting party. In most cases, by refusing to cooperate, the other party can be forced to restrict any claim under the contract. Secondly, if the party has no legitimate interest in performing the contract other than claiming damages, they ought not to be entitled to perform.

These two limitations have been applied in some subsequent cases, in order to avoid a strict application of the **White and Carter** principle. Thus, it was emphasised in **Clea Shipping Corp** v **Bulk Oil International Ltd (*The Alaskan Trader*)** (1984) that the innocent party must have a genuine reason for continuing with the contract against the wishes of the other party. The case involved the charter of a rather elderly ship. The charterparty was for a specified period, but before the time was up, the charterers announced that they no longer needed the ship. They were therefore guilty of an anticipatory breach, and the shipowners could have sued for damages. Instead, they chose to behave as though the contract was still in existence, spending £800,000 on having the vessel repaired, and keeping a full crew standing by for the remaining period of the charterparty, after which they sold the vessel for scrap. They then sued for the full price, but the court considered that they had had no legitimate interest in continuing to perform and had simply tried to inflate their damages.

In **Ministry of Sound (Ireland) Ltd** v **World Online Ltd** (2003) the High Court applied **White and Carter** and gave a narrow interpretation to the application of the first of Lord Reid's restrictions in that case. The claimant was one of a group of nightclubs operating under the name 'Ministry of Sound'. The defendant, World Online, was an internet service provider which wished to attract custom by associating itself with the Ministry of Sound brand. They entered into a two-year contract under which World Online was to produce CDs giving access to its internet service. Ministry of Sound would market and package the CDs with its other products. The claimant was to receive eight quarterly payments of £200,000. In the first six months of the contract, World Online produced 650,000 CDs. But then it stopped providing CDs, saying, however, that more CDs would be produced for the second year. World Online continued to pay the amounts due under the contract apart from the last instalment of £200,000. The claimant brought this action to obtain payment of the final sum.

When World Online, in breach of contract, stopped providing the CDs, Ministry of Sound was unable to perform its part of the contract, including marketing, packaging and distributing the CDs, as this performance depended on delivery of the CDs. Ministry of Sound argued that it had not accepted World Online's repudiation of the contract so the agreement remained enforceable in accordance with its terms. World Online submitted that the Ministry of Sound's remedy should be limited to damages for any losses it had made because of World Online's breach of contract. In fact, the Ministry of Sound had suffered no loss because it had received payment for work it had not performed. World Online pointed out that it had produced only about 14 per cent of the CDs due to be produced under the agreement, but Ministry of Sound had received 87.5 per cent of the money due under the contract, even though it had not incurred most of the marketing, packaging and distribution costs for the CDs because World Online had failed to produce them.

In **White and Carter** the court allowed an innocent party to treat a contract as continuing and then sue for the price agreed in the contract. Lord Reid had said that this would not be possible if cooperation for the performance of the contract was required from the other contracting party. He stated:

> . . . in most cases the circumstances are such that an innocent party is unable to complete the contract and earn the contract price without the other party's assent or co-operation . . .

World Online sought to rely on this exception. It submitted that the exception to the general rule that the innocent party can elect to affirm the contract and enforce it applied in a case in which the innocent party cannot perform any outstanding contractual obligation without cooperation. The High Court rejected this broad interpretation of the exception. It pointed to the fact that Lord Reid had not just referred to performance, but had added 'and earn the contract price':

> The words 'and earn the contract price' are equally important and in my view the question is whether the innocent party can, without the other party's assent or co-operation, do whatever the contract requires him to do in order to be entitled to the sum which he is claiming. Whether this involves the performance of all or any outstanding obligations depends on the terms of the contract and the operation of the principle or dependent provisions.

Lord Reid's first exception applied only to cases in which the performance that had been prevented by the breach was a pre-condition to the obligation to pay. This was not the case on the present facts, as the terms of the contract did not link the packaging and distribution of the CDs with the obligation to pay the quarterly sums. As a result, the payments were not 'dependent' on the prior performance of the contractual obligations.

The High Court drew a distinction between contracts where the right to a particular payment under the contract is dependent upon the performance of specific contractual obligations, and contracts where payments are simply due on a specified date. It interpreted this restriction as only applying where the performance prevented was a pre-condition to the right to payment. If the right to the payment claimed is dependent upon the performance of contractual obligations, the prevention of performance by the other party's breach of contract does not alter the position. Thus the matter rests upon the nature of the contractual right, not the circumstances of the breach. The High Court did not think that a right to payment is to be treated as 'dependent' on the performance of services solely because the payment was to be made in return for services. It is dependent only if the right to payment is conditional upon the prior or simultaneous performance of services or other contractual obligations (common examples are contracts for the sale of land or goods). The distinction is between a right to payment which is dependent on performance, and one which is supported only by the other party's promise to perform. It is clear that in most contracts, such as for the sale of goods and the sale of land, there is a presumption that promises are mutually dependent, so that the right to payment arises simultaneously with the transfer of property. The same is true of many contracts for services, for example, building contracts, in which it is common for rights to payment to arise on the completion of the specific stages of the work, so that if the employer prevents the builder from entering the property, he cannot earn any further right to payment.

On the facts of the case the High Court interpreted the contract as not making the right to payment dependent upon performance. The payments were not linked to any specific performance by the Ministry of Sound and were due on specified dates. World Online was therefore obliged to pay the final instalment. The High Court suggested that World Online might, however, be able to bring a counter-claim for some of the money, based on a partial failure of consideration. Though the High Court recognised that, traditionally, such a claim would only be successful where there had been a complete failure of consideration, not just a partial failure. World Online would have the right to recover the payment or part of it on the ground of failure of consideration, which right could be relied upon as a defence.

The decision in **White and Carter** has been criticised as absurd. It allows unwanted performance which can be highly wasteful. But the High Court in **Ministry of Sound** rejected this criticism:

> . . . such a situation is hardly uncommon. For example, if a company leases expensive equipment, with no right to sub-lease, and then has no further use for it, there is no way in which it can force the owner, before the end of the period of the lease, to accept the return of the equipment and minimize its loss by leasing it to another available customer whom it has found, however estimable.

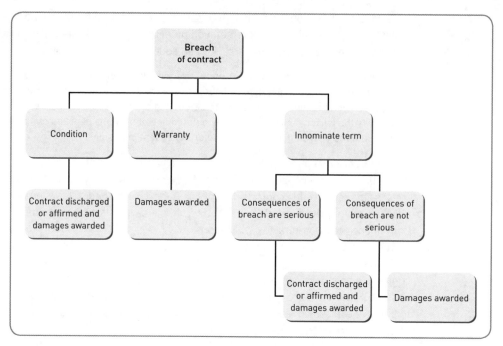

**Figure 14.4** Effect of breach

It would remain liable for the rent for the full period. Nor do I think that the position would be any different if the rent covered both the use of the equipment and the lessor's maintenance obligations which, since they were unwanted, it would not have the expense of performing.

# Agreement

In some cases the parties will simply agree to terminate a contract, so that one or both parties are released from their obligations. A distinction is generally made between bilateral discharge, in which both parties receive a benefit from the discharge, and unilateral, where the change is made for the benefit of one party only.

In general, an agreed discharge will be binding if it contains the same 'ingredients' that make a contract binding when it is formed, and the two which tend to present most problems are formality and consideration.

# Consideration

Consideration is not usually a problem where both parties agree to alter their obligations, since each is giving something in return for the change. For example, Jean, a decorator, contracts to decorate Jack's kitchen and bathroom for £400 and, after the kitchen is finished, Jack decides that in fact he does not want the bathroom done after all. If Jean, perhaps having plenty of other work, agrees, Jack's releasing Jean from the obligation to decorate the bathroom is consideration for her releasing him from the obligation to pay the other £200 and *vice versa*.

Problems are more likely to occur where only one party's obligations change. If the other party agrees to the change, their agreement will only be binding if it is either put in a deed or supported by consideration. Where consideration is provided in return for one party's agreement to change, the agreement is called 'accord', and the provision of consideration for it is called 'satisfaction'; thus the arrangement is often called 'accord and satisfaction'.

Some problems of consideration where contracting parties change their obligations to each other can be avoided by the doctrines of promissory estoppel and waiver (see Chapter 6).

# Formalities

This issue arises in connection with certain types of contract (mainly those concerning the sale of land) which must be evidenced in writing in order to be binding under the Law of Property Act 1925. Does the same requirement apply to an agreement to discharge such a contract? In **Morris** v **Baron** (1918) the House of Lords decided that this depended on how far the parties intended to alter their existing contractual relations, and those intentions had to be inferred from the terms of the discharging contract. There are three possibilities:

- *Partial discharge.* Where the second agreement suggests that the parties only want to modify the terms of their previous contract, without making really substantial changes, the agreed modification must be evidenced in writing. If this is not done, the original contract remains enforceable.
- *Complete discharge.* If the parties intend to abandon completely the original contract, and end their contractual relations, it is not necessary that this agreement be evidenced in writing – an oral agreement is sufficient.
- *Fresh agreement.* If the parties intend to abandon their original contract, but replace it with a new one, an oral agreement will be sufficient to rescind the original contract, but the new one must be evidenced in writing.

In all cases, the question of what the parties intended is determined by the interpretation of the contract.

## Novation

Novation is the name given to a specific type of discharge by agreement. It arises where there are two contracts, and the same person is a debtor under one contract and a creditor under the other – for example, A owes B £100, and C owes A £100. Novation occurs if C agrees to pay B £100 if he will release A from his debt to B; the first two contracts are discharged and a new one is created.

## Condition subsequent

Sometimes contracting parties will agree at the start that if a certain event occurs the contract will come to an end. A common example is a manufacturers' guarantee offering to give a refund if a fault in the goods appears within a specified time. A recent case involving a condition subsequent is **Bland** v **Sparkes** (1999). Bland had been an international swimmer and was engaged as a consultant by the Amateur Swimming Association (ASA) to promote the ASA awards scheme. The consultancy contract allowed the ASA to terminate his engagement if he was convicted of any serious criminal offence or was otherwise guilty of conduct bringing the Association or himself into disrepute (the condition subsequent). The ASA discovered that before the contract was made, the claimant had received bribes or secret commissions to make commercial recommendations to the ASA's clients. It decided to terminate the contract. The claimant sought damages for breach of contract. The Court of Appeal held that the claimant's conduct had brought the ASA into disrepute and the ASA was therefore entitled to terminate the contract.

## Answering questions

It is difficult to ascertain when a frustrating event has occurred. In practice, there are, therefore, few cases of frustrated contracts.

Discuss. *London External LL.B*

This question requires students to focus on when a contract is frustrated. It would not be relevant to the question to look at the legal consequences of frustration. You should divide your answer into two parts, looking first at the positive requirements for finding a frustration, and secondly what factors will prevent a finding of frustration. In your analysis of the case law, you need to consider, in the light of the question, whether the legal rules create uncertainty and whether the tendency of the courts has been to conclude that there was no frustrating event.

Under 'the doctrine of frustration . . . the judges have insisted that the supervening event must destroy a fundamental assumption on which the contract was based; and they have also limited the scope of the doctrine in a number of other ways'. *An Outline of the Law of Contract* by Treitel.

Discuss Treitel's view that the doctrine of frustration is applied narrowly by the judges. *OCR, Advanced GCE Law of Contract 2, 2575, June 2003*

An answer to this question requires a discussion of where the doctrine of frustration applies and where it does not apply. All the material you require on this subject may be found in the sub-section 'Frustration' (see pp. 318–23). Looking closely at the relevant case law, you need to argue whether you consider the law is applied narrowly or not. It does not matter which view you take, as long as you support it with case law. Generally, most academics agree with Treitel that the doctrine of frustration has been given a narrow interpretation.

'The doctrine of frustration is merely an excuse for people to escape from a contract because things have not turned out as they expected.' Discuss. *Oxford*

Start by explaining what the doctrine of frustration is, and its effects on a contract, and illustrate this with some examples of cases in which frustration was successfully argued. You should write why it might not be considered reasonable to escape from an unwanted contract, looking at the importance of binding promises in a market economy, which is discussed in the introduction to this book. You can then go on to debate the accusation made in the quotation, by giving examples of cases which show the strictness of the doctrine – the Suez cases (for example, **Tsakiroglou** *v* **Noblee Thorl**), the ***Super Servant Two***, and **Davis Contractors** *v* **Fareham UDC**. In all these cases, one party can be seen as trying to escape from a contract because of unexpected events which are to their disadvantage, but the courts have not allowed the doctrine to be used in this way. As a final example, you might contrast the two coronation cases, which show that, if anything, the doctrine of frustration can be regarded as leaning too far in preventing escape from contracts, since there was hardly much more point in hiring the steamship without the coronation events than there was in hiring the room overlooking the procession.

A had a contract with B to deliver 30 gallons of petrol weekly to B's garage from A's store. The contract was for a year and was to end in February. In September B told A that he would not take any more petrol but A simply stored the petrol, intending to sue B for breach in February. B objected, pointing out that A could have obtained a good price for the petrol from others. In January there was a fuel crisis and the government, exercising its statutory powers, issued an order confiscating all petrol stores without compensation.

A wishes to claim money from B. What factors would you identify as relevant in considering A's claim? *London*

The first issue here is whether A would have had a claim against B if the government confiscation had not occurred. B is clearly in breach of his contract, and such a breach would entitle A to claim any losses resulting from it. As B's breach is anticipatory, he could have done this as soon as B said he would not be taking any more petrol, and would have been able then to claim, within the usual rules on remoteness of damage, any losses made at that point – so if the market price of petrol had gone down, and he had to sell his stocks at a lower price than that agreed with B, A could claim the difference. However, A chose not to do this, but to continue to perform. Whether he had the right to sue for all the losses thereby incurred will depend on whether the courts feel he has a genuine interest in continuing to perform; the relevant cases here are **White and Carter** *v* **McGregor**, **Clea Shipping Corp** *v* **Bulk Oil International Ltd** (*The Alaskan Trader*) and **Ministry of Sound (Ireland) Ltd** *v* **World Online Ltd**. If B's point about others being willing to pay a good price is true, the courts may well lean in favour of the second case and rule that there was no legitimate reason for A to continue to perform the contract and that therefore he could not claim all the losses which result from him doing so.

If the courts decide there was a genuine reason for continued performance, and that damages could have been claimed as a result, these will be affected by the government confiscation, which appears to have had the effect of frustrating the contract, since it has made further performance impossible. This brings any further obligations under the contract to an end (and this time A definitely has no choice in the matter). As far as obligations incurred before the frustrating event are concerned, A will only be able to claim under the Law Reform (Frustrated Contracts) Act 1943 for expenses incurred in storing the petrol if the contract stipulated advance payment. Since the storage of the petrol provided no valuable benefit to B, A cannot claim any money in respect of this.

Linda was a fashion designer who taught some classes at a college attended by Mark, a wealthy 18-year-old student. Mark became infatuated with Linda and, after his college course finished, he agreed to lend her £10,000 to establish a design business. The terms were very unfavourable to Mark. There was no interest payable on the loan, which was not due for repayment for ten years. Mark was to be entitled to 5 per cent of any annual profits over £20,000. When he discovered that Linda was not really interested in him, Mark began to realise that he might have been foolish to lend her the money.

Linda secured a contract with Nightworks to design and produce clothes for a forthcoming film starring Olivia. She was paid £1,000 in advance, with a further £5,000 to be paid on completion. In preparation, she paid £2,000 for materials to Paul, who assured her that he would be able to deliver within one month. When he gave this assurance, Paul knew that he was having considerable difficulty in getting materials from his supplier. Two months later, while Linda was still waiting for the material from Paul, Olivia died and Nightworks abandoned the film and informed Linda that they would no longer require her services.

(a) Consider whether Mark can terminate his agreement with Linda and recover the £10,000. *(15 marks)*

(b) (i) In view of Paul's statement to Linda about delivery, consider whether Linda has any rights and remedies against Paul in connection with the delay in delivery of materials.

(ii) Discuss the rights and duties of Linda and Nightworks following the decision of Nightworks to abandon the film. *(20 marks)*

(c) Explain and comment on the approach of the law to mistake in contract. *(25 marks) AQA*

 (a) We are told that Mark is 18 years old so he had the capacity to make a binding contract (see p. 71). The only basis on which he could terminate the agreement with Linda and recover his £10,000 is if a court found that he had entered the contract as a result of undue influence. This is an equitable doctrine, which applies where one party uses their influence over the other to persuade them to make a contract. Where a court finds that a contract was made as a result of undue influence, it may set it aside, or modify its terms so as to mitigate the disadvantage. The leading case on the subject is the House of Lords' judgment in **Royal Bank of Scotland** *v* **Etridge (No 2)**.

Mark would need to argue that Linda had exercised undue influence over him. There are two types of undue influence: actual and presumed. Actual undue influence would be found if Mark could prove that he entered the transaction as a result of undue influence from Linda. This form of undue influence is difficult to prove in practice.

As regards presumed undue influence, in certain circumstances an evidentiary presumption will be applied that shifts the burden of proof from the claimant (Mark) to the wrongdoer (Linda), so that it is up to the wrongdoer to disprove the existence of undue influence. Undue influence can be presumed where there is a pre-existing relationship of confidence between the two parties to a contract, as a result of which one party places trust in the other, and the contract between them is manifestly disadvantageous to the first party. Such a relationship of trust is called a fiduciary relationship, and it may arise in two ways. First, it may fall into one of several categories in which a relationship of trust is automatically presumed to exist. The relationship of student/teacher that existed between Mark and Linda does not fall within one of these categories. Secondly, the relationship of trust may nevertheless be established on the facts. We are told that Mark had been one of Linda's students and had become infatuated with her. This would support the existence of presumed undue influence.

The defendant can rebut the presumption of undue influence by showing that the claimant entered into the contract freely, and this is usually done by establishing that independent advice was taken. We are not told that Mark received any such advice.

Where a party seeks to rely on the existence of presumed undue influence, the transaction must be manifestly disadvantageous (see p. 276). The terms of the loan would appear to satisfy this requirement.

As undue influence is an equitable doctrine, Mark will be prevented from terminating the agreement in three circumstances: where there is some practical reason why the parties cannot be restored to their original position; where a third party has gained rights under the contract; and when the innocent party affirms the contract (see p. 208). There is nothing to suggest that any of these three circumstances apply here.

(b) (i) Paul's statement to Linda that he would be able to deliver within one month was a misrepresentation (see p. 196). A misrepresentation is an untrue statement of fact by one party which has induced the other to enter into the contract. Paul's statement was untrue because he was having considerable difficulty in getting materials from his supplier. After two months, Paul had still not delivered the material to Linda. It was a statement of fact and not opinion (see p. 201). It is likely that the statement induced Linda to enter into the contract (see p. 202) though we are not expressly told what her time schedule was to deliver the clothes to Nightworks.

The remedies available to Linda would depend on the type of misrepresentation that was committed. All misrepresentations render the contract voidable. Thus the contract continues to exist unless and until the innocent party chooses to have it set aside by means of rescission. Along with the remedy of rescission, the courts can order a payment of money known as an indemnity. An indemnity payment is designed to put the parties back into their former position, and is only available for obligations necessarily and inevitably created by the contract.

A misrepresentation may also give rise to a right to damages, depending on the type of misrepresentation that has occurred. There are four types of misrepresentation: fraudulent misrepresentation; negligent misrepresentation at common law; negligent misrepresentation under statute; and innocent misrepresentation. Which category a misrepresentation falls into depends on the state of mind of the person making the statement. When Paul made the statement, he knew that he was having considerable difficulty in getting materials from his supplier.

Looking first at fraudulent misrepresentation, it is very difficult to prove fraud. The leading case is **Derry** v **Peek** where it was stated that fraudulent misrepresentation is a false statement that is made: '(i) knowingly, or (ii) without belief in its truth, or (iii) recklessly as to whether it be true or false'. It is possible that Paul made his statement recklessly and that the statement will therefore amount to fraudulent misrepresentation. Alternatively, it was undoubtedly made negligently and would amount to negligent misrepresentation both under statute and under common law. Fraudulent and negligent misrepresentation both give rise to a right to damages.

In addition, it is possible that Paul's statement may have become a term of the contract. Whether a statement is a term of a contract is largely a question of the parties' intentions (see p. 124). In determining the issue, the courts will take into account the importance of the statement, the special knowledge and skill of Paul when he made the statement, the timing of the statement and whether the eventual agreement was made in writing. If Paul's statement has become a term, then it is clear that it has been breached, and the impact of this will depend on whether it was a condition (see p. 144) because time was of the essence (see p. 317). If the statement was a condition, then its breach will give rise to a right to terminate the contract as well as a right to damages.

(ii) Nightworks decided to abandon the film following the death of the leading actress, Olivia, and informed Linda that they would no longer require her services. The death of Olivia may amount to a frustrating event (see p. 318). If, after a contract is made, something happens, through no fault of the parties, to make its performance impossible, the contract is said to be frustrated, and the obligations under it come to an end. In this scenario we do not have the death of one of the contracting parties, but a death which may render performance of the contract between Linda and Nightworks pointless. Performance will be pointless if it was important that Olivia star in the film (see, for example, **Krell** *v* **Henry**). The legal consequences of frustration are discussed in this chapter. Once a court holds that a contract is frustrated, it is automatically terminated from the point at which the frustrating event occurred. Nightworks would therefore have no obligation to pay Linda the remaining £5,000 that was due to be paid on her completing the clothes.

Linda had received an advance of £1,000. Under s. 1(2) of the Law Reform (Frustrated Contracts) Act 1943, Nightworks would be entitled to recover money paid under the contract prior to the frustrating event. But a court can allow Linda to deduct any expenses she has incurred as a result of the contract from this sum. Thus, if Linda is obliged to pay Paul the £2,000 for the materials, she will be able to deduct this as an expense from her advance and thus she would not have to return anything.

If the contract has not been frustrated by Olivia's death, because it was reasonable to have found another actress to star in the film, then Nightworks would be in breach of their contract and would have to pay Linda damages (see p. 346).

(c) The material required to answer this part of the question is contained in Chapter 10 on mistake.

# Summary of Chapter 14

There are four ways in which a contract can come to an end: performance, frustration, breach and agreement.

## Performance

The most obvious way in which a contract is discharged is by both parties performing their obligations under it.

### The entire performance rule

The general rule is that performance must exactly match the requirements laid down in the contract, and this is known as entire performance. If the first party fails to perform entirely, the other need pay nothing at all, even if the shortfall in performance actually causes no hardship.

## Mitigation of the entire performance rule

There are several ways in which the harshness of the entire performance rule is mitigated:

### Substantial performance

Established in **Boone** v **Eyre** (1779) by Lord Mansfield, this doctrine allows a party who has performed with only minor defects to claim the price of the work done, less any money the other party will have to spend to put the defects right. The doctrine cannot be used where the claimant has breached a condition of the contract.

### Severable contracts

A contract is said to be severable where payment becomes due at various stages of performance, rather than in one lump sum when performance is complete. Whether a contract is entire or severable is a question of construction.

### Voluntary acceptance of partial performance

In some cases, while a contract may not originally have been intended to be severable, one party may later agree to accept and pay for part-performance from the other.

### Prevention of performance by other party

Where one party performs part of the agreed obligation, and is then prevented from completing the rest by some fault of the other party, a *quantum meruit* can be used to claim the cost of the work done. In most of these cases, the innocent party can alternatively claim damages for breach of contract. Where one party cannot perform without the other's cooperation, rejection of an offer to perform will release the party tendering performance from any further obligation.

### Breach of terms concerning time

Late performance will always amount to a breach of contract, giving rise to a right to damages. It will only give rise to a right to terminate the contract if the delay constitutes a substantial failure to perform, or if the time of performance is treated as being 'of the essence'.

## Vicarious performance

The general rule is that a contracting party cannot object to vicarious performance unless it prejudices their interests. If the service contracted for is one which relies on the skill or judgement of one party, the other can insist on personal performance.

## Frustration

If after a contract is made, something happens, through no fault of the parties, to make its performance impossible, the contract is said to be frustrated, and the obligations under it come to an end.

### Time of frustrating event

A frustrating event which occurs before the contract is made gives rise to the issue of mistake rather than to an issue of frustration.

## What will amount to frustration?

Events that will frustrate a contract fall into three broad categories: events which make performance or further performance impossible; those which make it illegal; and those which make it pointless.

### Impossible

A contract may become impossible to perform in any of the following ways:

- Destruction or unavailability of something essential for the contract's performance.
- Death of either party.
- Unavailability of a party.
- Method of performance impossible.

### Illegal

If, after a contract is formed, a change in the law makes its performance illegal, the contract will be frustrated.

### Pointless

A contract can be frustrated where a supervening event makes performance of a contract completely pointless, though still technically possible: **Krell** *v* **Henry** (1903).

## What will not amount to frustration?

A particular event will not frustrate a contract if: the contract makes provision for such an event; the event merely renders the contract more onerous; it was foreseen or foreseeable; or it was due to the fault of one of the parties.

## Legal consequences of frustration

Once a court holds that a contract is frustrated, it is automatically terminated from the point at which the frustrating event occurred and the contract is described as being discharged. Obligations which would have arisen from that point on no longer exist, but the contract is not treated as though it never existed, so acts done before the frustrating event may have legal consequences.

### The common law

The common law traditionally took the view that any loss resulting from the frustration should lie where it fell. Advance payments would be recoverable if there had been a total failure of consideration: **Fibrosa Spolka Akcyjna** *v* **Fairbairn Lawson Combe Barbour** (1943).

### The Law Reform (Frustrated Contracts) Act 1943

This Act alters the legal consequences once the contract is held to have been frustrated under the rules of the common law. It draws a distinction between obligations to pay money and other types of obligation that existed prior to the frustration.

#### Obligations to pay money

Section 1(2) of the Act entitles a person to recover money paid under a contract prior to the frustrating event, and removes any obligation to pay money that existed prior to the frustrating event.

#### Obligations other than to pay money

Under s. 1(3), if, before the frustrating event, one party obtains a valuable benefit (other than money) because of something done by the other in performance of the contract, the party receiving the benefit can be ordered to pay a just sum in return for it.

## Breach

A contract is said to be breached when one party performs defectively, differently from the agreement, or not at all (actual breach), or indicates in advance that they will not be performing as agreed (anticipatory breach). Where an anticipatory breach occurs, the other party can sue for breach straight away; it is not necessary to wait until performance falls due.

## Lawful excuse

In some cases, an extraneous event which is not sufficiently serious to frustrate a contract will nevertheless provide an excuse for non-performance.

## Effect of breach

Any breach of contract will entitle the innocent party to sue for damages, but not every breach allows the wronged party to choose to discharge the contract (in contrast with frustration, where the discharge is automatic). If the contract is not discharged, it will still need to be performed. There are three main circumstances in which the innocent party may choose to discharge.

### Repudiation

This is where one party makes it clear that they no longer intend to be bound by the contract, either during its performance, or before performance is due (in practice it is usually the latter, and therefore an anticipatory breach).

### Breach of a condition

Breach of a condition allows the innocent party to terminate the contract; breaches of warranty do not justify termination, although they may give rise to an award of damages.

### Serious breach of an innominate term

Where the relevant term is classified by the courts as innominate, it will be one which can be breached in both serious and trivial ways; and whether the innocent party is entitled to terminate or not will depend on how serious the results of the breach are. If the results are so serious as to undermine the very foundation of the contract, the innocent party will have the right to terminate.

## Choice to affirm or discharge

Even when one of these three types of breach occurs, the contract is not automatically discharged; the innocent party can usually choose whether or not to terminate.

## Agreement

In some cases the parties will simply agree to terminate a contract, so that one or both parties are released from their obligations. A distinction is generally made between bilateral discharge, in which both parties receive a benefit from the discharge, and unilateral, where the change is made for the benefit of one party only.

In general, an agreed discharge will be binding if it contains the same 'ingredients' that make a contract binding when it is formed; and the two which tend to present most problems are formality and consideration.

### Novation

Novation is the name given to a specific type of discharge by agreement. It arises where there are two contracts, and the same person is a debtor under one contract and a creditor under the other; the first two contracts are discharged and a new one is created.

### Condition subsequent

Sometimes contracting parties will agree at the start that, if a certain event occurs, the contract will come to an end.

## Reading list

Carter, Phang and Phang, 'Performance following repudiation: legal and economic interests' (1999) 15 Journal of Contract Law 97

Courtney, 'Termination of a contract by a party in breach' (2008) Journal of Business Law 226

Hall, 'Frustration and the question of foresight' (1984) 4 Legal Studies 300

Haycroft and Waksman, 'Restitution and frustration' (1984) Journal of Business Law 207

Jones, 'The law on repudiation has been given welcome clarification' (2013) 163 New Law Journal 12

Treitel, 'Affirmation after repudiatory breach' (1998) 114 Law Quarterly Review 22

# Chapter 15
## Remedies

### This chapter explains:

that when a contract is breached, there are three different types of remedy that can be available to the innocent party: common law remedies, equitable remedies and remedies agreed between the parties.

- **Common law remedies** are usually damages compensating a financial loss and aim to put innocent parties in the position they would have been in if the contract had been performed. Limits are imposed on these damages under the rules on causation, remoteness and the requirement to mitigate one's loss. In calculating the damages the courts can either focus on the loss of expectation or, less frequently, on what is known as the 'reliance loss'. When calculating the damages, the courts have traditionally not taken into account any profit the party in breach has made by breaking the contract.

- **Equitable remedies** are available at the discretion of the court when the common law remedies are inadequate to compensate the claimant. These remedies are specific performance (compelling someone to perform their obligations under a contract) and an injunction (normally ordering a defendant not to do something).

- **Agreed remedies** are sometimes provided for in the contract itself.

This chapter is concerned with the remedies that are available to the innocent party in the event of a breach of contract. These can be divided into three categories. During the period when the English courts were split into courts of common law and of equity, each branch developed different remedies. Even though the courts are no longer divided in this way, it is still convenient to distinguish between common law and equitable remedies, since their separate histories have led to different rules about when they will be applied. The third category covers remedies which arise from the parties' own agreement.

# Common law remedies

All common law remedies are available as of right if a contract is breached.

# Damages

An award of damages is the usual remedy for a breach of contract. It is an award of money that aims to compensate the innocent party for the financial losses they have suffered as a result of the breach. Damages for breach of contract are available as of right where the contract has been breached. The general rule is that innocent parties are entitled to such damages as will put them in the position they would have been in if the contract had been performed. When a contract is breached, a party may suffer pecuniary loss (that is to say financial loss) or non-pecuniary loss.

## Pecuniary loss

Damages aim to compensate the innocent party for their financial losses that result from not receiving the performance bargained for. In general, such losses include physical harm to the claimants or their property and any other injury to their economic position.

## Non-pecuniary loss

As we have seen, contract damages usually aim to compensate for financial (pecuniary) loss. They have traditionally not been available to compensate non-pecuniary loss, such as mental distress. This has been a key distinction between the law of contract and tort for, while in contract law damages for mental distress have not been available, such damages are available in tort law. In reality, following a breach of contract, a claimant might suffer not only financial loss but also mental distress, such as disappointment, hurt feelings or humiliation, but damages for such non-pecuniary losses are generally not recoverable in contract. The main policy consideration for this seems to be a concern to keep contractual awards down, to provide fair compensation without encouraging unnecessary litigation by offering excessive compensation. In **Hayes v Dodd** (1990) Staughton LJ stated:

> [T]he English courts should be wary of adopting . . . the United States practice of huge awards. Damages awarded for negligence or want of skill, whether against professional men or anyone else, must provide fair compensation, but no more than that. And I would not view with enthusiasm the prospect that every shipowner in the Commercial Court, having successfully claimed for unpaid

freight or demurrage, would be able to add a claim for mental distress suffered while he was waiting for his money.

Damages for mental distress are not awarded for commercial contracts.

**Key Case**   Addis *v* Gramophone Co Ltd

The leading authority on the denial of damages for mental distress in commercial contracts is **Addis *v* Gramophone Co Ltd** (1909). The claimant had been employed as a manager of a company in India. He was wrongfully sacked for alleged dishonesty. He brought an action claiming that the manner of his dismissal had been harsh and humiliating. He had been ostracised by the British community in Calcutta. As a result he had suffered mental pain and anguish. The House of Lords held that he could recover the usual damages for loss of salary and commission, but not for the injury to his feelings caused by the way in which he was sacked.

**Legal Principle**
Damages for mental distress are not awarded for commercial contracts.

However, recent cases have developed the principle that, in a limited number of situations, injury to feelings (generally called mental distress) and loss of amenity will be compensated. Initially, such compensation was limited to cases involving contracts whose whole purpose was the provision of pleasure, relaxation and peace of mind. More recently, the House of Lords has allowed damages for non-pecuniary loss where a major object (though not the whole purpose) of the contract was to provide pleasure, relaxation and peace of mind. Mental suffering can be compensated if it is related to physical inconvenience and discomfort caused by the breach of the contract. In addition, in contracts of employment, breach of the implied duty of mutual trust and confidence can give rise to an award of damages for financial loss resulting from the psychiatric harm caused.

## Contracts where the whole purpose is pleasure, relaxation and peace of mind

**Key Case**   Jarvis *v* Swans Tours Ltd

The leading case on the provision of damages for non-pecuniary loss where a contract for recreation has been breached is **Jarvis *v* Swans Tours Ltd** (1973). The claimant was a solicitor who had booked a two-week winter sports holiday that was described in the brochure as a 'house party'. The brochure stated that there would be a welcoming party, afternoon tea and cakes and a yodelling evening. In the event, there was no welcoming party, the afternoon tea consisted largely of crisps and the yodeller turned out to be a local man who arrived in his working clothes, sang a couple of songs and then left. The 'house party' also left something to be desired, consisting of 13 holidaymakers in the house in the first week, but in the second week Mr Jarvis was the sole member of the 'house party'.

The holiday had cost £63. The holiday company was clearly in breach of contract and the judge at first instance awarded Mr Jarvis half the contract price, on the basis that Mr Jarvis had received some benefit, in the shape of transport and accommodation, and the sum awarded was the difference in value between what he expected and what he got. Not surprisingly, Mr Jarvis appealed. The Court of Appeal raised the damages to £125 on the basis that merely giving him back the cost of the holiday would not adequately compensate his loss, and instead the damages should take account of his disappointment and distress. Lord Denning explained:

> It is true he was conveyed to Switzerland and back and had meals and bed in the hotel. But that is not what he went for. He went to enjoy himself with all those facilities which the defendants said he would have. He is entitled to compensation for the loss of those facilities, and for his loss of enjoyment.

The case was compared with where a man plans to go to an evening opera performance in Glyndebourne. He arranges to hire a car for the night, but the car fails to turn up and he misses the performance. He would be entitled to claim from the car hire company, not just the cost of his ticket, but also for his disappointment at missing the concert.

**Legal Principle**
Where a contract for recreation has been breached, damages for non-pecuniary loss can be awarded.

This case was affirmed in **Jackson** v **Horizon Holidays Ltd** (1975) (discussed on p. 298). In the Scottish case of **Diesen** v **Samson** (1971) the defendant had been booked to take photographs at the claimant's wedding. He failed to attend and damages were awarded to the bride for the distress of having no wedding photographs. This was not a purely commercial contract that fell within the rule in **Addis** v **Gramophone Co**. Instead, it was a contract under which the bride would get pleasure looking at the photographs in the years ahead.

In **Heywood** v **Wellers** (1976) the claimant, Sheila Heywood, was a single parent living in Penge who met a married man with whom she had an affair. Later, they split up, but he began stalking her. The claimant went to the defendants, a firm of solicitors, to seek an injunction against her former companion. The defendants negligently failed to do so, with the result that the claimant had to suffer further harassment. The Court of Appeal held that she could recover for the mental distress caused by the breach of contract.

Where a contract is for the provision of a product for leisure activities and this contract is breached, damages for loss of pleasure and amenity may be awarded.

 **Key Case** Ruxley Electronics and Construction Ltd v Forsyth

In **Ruxley Electronics and Construction Ltd** v **Forsyth** (1995) a contract had been entered into for the construction of a swimming pool for £70,000. The claimant made it clear that one end of the pool had to be 7 ft 6 in deep as he needed this depth to feel safe when diving. In fact, on completion, it was only 6 ft 9 in deep. Mr Forsyth had contracted for a swimming pool for reasons of pleasure, and in this sense his expectation had not been fulfilled. The trial judge awarded the defendant £2,500 for loss of amenity and pleasure, an award that was approved by the House of Lords. This was to compensate the pleasure lost by the defendant by not feeling safe when he dived into the swimming pool.

**Legal Principle**

Where a contract is for the provision of a product for leisure activities and this contract is breached, damages for loss of pleasure and amenity may be awarded.

## Contracts where a major object is pleasure, relaxation and peace of mind

The House of Lords further considered the issue of the award of damages for loss of amenity in **Farley** v **Skinner** (2001).

**Key Case**    Farley v Skinner

Mr Farley was the claimant in the case of **Farley** v **Skinner** (2001), who was thinking of buying a house in the Sussex countryside where he would spend his retirement. He paid a chartered surveyor, Mr Skinner, to look at the property, and specifically instructed him to assess the impact of aircraft noise on the property. The house was 15 miles from Gatwick airport. The surveyor was negligent in carrying out this work and advised Mr Farley that it was 'unlikely that the property will suffer greatly from such noise'. After Mr Farley had spent a considerable amount of money renovating the house and had moved into the property, he discovered that the house was in fact badly affected by aircraft noise, particularly at weekends. It seems that the house was positioned near a navigation beacon and at busy times aircraft flew around this beacon while they waited for a slot to land. Mr Farley's enjoyment of the house was badly affected. He brought an action against the surveyor for the difference in the value of the house between what he paid and what it was worth with the aircraft noise. This part of his claim was unsuccessful because it was found that the price he paid was the market value for the house taking into account the aircraft noise. In addition, he included a claim for non-pecuniary damages for the loss of amenity caused by the aircraft noise. At first instance, the claimant was awarded £10,000 for distress and inconvenience. The House of Lords upheld this award. The House held that it did not matter that the object of the contract with the surveyor was not entirely to give pleasure, relaxation or peace of mind, since this was nonetheless a major and important object of the contract. The surveyor had been specifically asked to report on aircraft noise. It would be perverse to allow someone to recover damages if they had just asked a surveyor to report on aircraft noise, but not where the client (like Mr Farley) had specifically asked the surveyor about that issue as well as some other matter. That would be a distinction of form and not substance. From now on, 'it is sufficient if a major or important object of the contract is to give pleasure, relaxation or peace of mind'. The House emphasised that awards of damages in this area should be modest. While they allowed the trial judge's award of £10,000 to stand, it was noted that this was at the very highest end of the scale. They did not want the award to encourage a litigation culture.

> **Legal Principle**
> Damages will be awarded for loss of amenity where a major object of the contract is pleasure, relaxation and peace of mind.

## Mental suffering caused by physical inconvenience

Mental suffering can be compensated if it is caused by physical inconvenience and discomfort resulting from the breach of contract. In **Perry** v **Sidney Phillips and Son** (1982) the claimant bought a house, relying on a survey prepared by the defendants. Their report stated that the house was in good order, but it was found to have many faults, including a leaking roof and a septic tank that gave off an offensive odour. These problems with the property caused the claimant distress, worry and inconvenience. As well as awarding damages for the reduced value of the property, the Court of Appeal awarded damages for the physical inconvenience and discomfort caused by having to live in the house while the builders were doing repairs and for mental distress.

In **Bailey** v **Bullock** (1950) the claimant brought an action against his solicitor for failing to act to recover possession of a house which had been leased to a third party. As a result of the delay, the claimant was required to live in a small house with his parents-in-law. Damages for discomfort were awarded.

The House of Lords noted in **Farley** v **Skinner** that the concept of physical inconvenience should not be narrowly interpreted, and could include the harmful effects of aircraft noise. The House stated that 'aircraft noise was something which affects the claimant through his hearing and can be regarded as having a physical effect on him'.

## Breach of implied duty of mutual trust and confidence

Contracts of employment include an implied duty of mutual trust and confidence (see **Malik** v **Bank of Credit and Commerce International** (1997), discussed on p. 141). The House of Lords ruled in **Eastwood** v **Magnox Electric plc** (2004) that breach of this implied term can give rise to an award of damages for the financial losses incurred as a result of illness, including psychiatric illness, caused by unfair treatment by an employer in breach of the contract.

## Limitations on awards of damages

The general rule is that innocent parties are entitled to such damages as will put them in the position they would have been in if the contract had been performed, but there are three limitations, which will be considered under the headings of causation, remoteness and mitigation.

### Causation

A person will only be liable for losses caused by their breach of contract. The defendant's breach need not be the sole cause of the claimant's losses, but it must be an effective cause of their loss. It is not enough if the breach merely provided the claimant with the opportunity to sustain loss. Intervening acts between the breach of contract and the loss incurred may break the chain of causation. Those events which were reasonably foreseeable will not break the chain of causation. Sometimes a loss can be caused partly by a breach of contract and partly by some other factor. The general rule is that where breach can be shown to be an actual cause of the loss, the fact that there is another contributing cause will not prevent the existence of causation.

In **County Ltd** v **Girozentrale Securities** (1996) the claimants' bank agreed to underwrite the issue of 26 million shares in a publicly quoted company. The defendants were stockbrokers who were engaged by the claimants to approach potential investors in the shares. The brokers breached the terms of their contract and, in due course, the claimants found themselves with some 4.5 million shares on their hands which, the price of the shares having fallen, represented a loss of nearly £7 million. They sued the stockbrokers, and the main issue in the case was whether the claimants' loss was caused by the defendants' breach of contract. In effect, the claimants would not have suffered their loss if there had not been a concurrence of a number of events, of which the defendants' breach of contract was but one. The Court of Appeal held that the brokers' breach of contract remained the effective cause of the claimants' loss; the breach did not need to be the only cause. The defendants were therefore liable to pay damages.

In **Quinn** v **Burch Bros (Builders) Ltd** (1966) the claimant was an independent sub-contractor carrying out such building work as plastering on a building project. In breach of their contractual undertaking to supply equipment 'reasonably necessary' for the work, the defendant failed to supply a stepladder. The claimant found a folded trestle, and stood on it to do the work. He slipped and broke his hand. The Court of Appeal held that the cause of the claimant's injury was his own choice to use unsuitable equipment. The defendant's breach of contract was only the occasion for the accident, not its legal cause.

## Remoteness

There are some losses which clearly result from the defendant's breach of contract, but are considered too remote from the breach for it to be fair to expect the defendant to compensate the claimant for them. Take, for example, the situation where a taxi driver is booked to take a passenger to the airport in time for a certain flight to New York, where the passenger expects to complete a deal worth £1 million. If the taxi driver breaches the contract by arriving late and makes the passenger miss the flight, the taxi firm may be liable for expenses such as any extra cost for getting the next flight, but is unlikely to be expected to compensate the passenger for the lost £1 million.

**Key Case**   Hadley v Baxendale

The rules concerning remoteness were originally laid down in **Hadley** v **Baxendale** (1854). The case concerned a contract for delivery of an important piece of mill equipment, which had been sent away for repair. The equipment, an iron shaft, was not delivered until some days after the agreed date. This meant that the mill, which could not work without it, had stood idle for that period. The mill owners attempted to sue for loss of the profits they would have made in the time between the agreed delivery date and the actual delivery. The court laid down two situations where the defendant should be liable for loss caused by a breach of contract:

1 Loss which would arise naturally, 'according to the usual course of things', from the breach.

2 Loss 'as may reasonably be supposed to have been in the contemplation of the parties at the time when they made the contract, as the probable result of the breach of it'.

Recovery under the first limb is about determining in advance what, objectively, is likely to happen if breach occurs. Under the second limb, unusual losses resulting from breach can still be recovered if the circumstances giving rise to them were known when the contract was made.

In practice, it is the second 'reasonable contemplation' test which has proved the most important in subsequent cases. In this case, they did not consider the lost profit to fall within either category. The fact that the mill could not work without the equipment was not considered to be a loss that arose in the usual course of things, because there could well have been a spare; nor could such a loss be said to be within the contemplation of the defendants, because the mill owners had failed to make it clear that the mill could not work without the shaft. It is therefore important to inform the other contracting party at the time of contracting of circumstances which affect performance, to prevent a subsequent loss being found to be too remote.

> **Legal Principle**
>
> Damages will be awarded for (1) loss which would arise naturally from the breach of contract and (2) loss which may reasonably be supposed to have been in the contemplation of the parties when they made the contract, as the probable result of its breach.

The approach in **Hadley** v **Baxendale** was reaffirmed in **Victoria Laundry (Windsor) Ltd** v **Newman Industries Ltd** (1949) and then discussed again by the House of Lords in **_The Heron II_** (1969). These two cases addressed the problem of abnormal losses – those which could not be said to occur 'in the normal course of things', but which, on the other hand, the defendant might well have been able to contemplate when making the contract.

 **Key Case**    Victoria Laundry (Windsor) Ltd v Newman Industries Ltd

In **Victoria Laundry (Windsor) Ltd** v **Newman Industries Ltd** [1949] the claimants were launderers and dyers, who needed to buy a large boiler in order to expand their existing business and take on a very well-paid Government contract. They contracted to buy such a boiler, second-hand, from the defendants, making it clear that it was needed for immediate use. As the defendants dismantled the boiler in preparation for delivery, it was damaged, and so the delivery was considerably later than agreed. The launderers claimed loss of profits under two heads: £16 per week for the loss of 'normal' profits, which represented the additional ordinary work they could have taken on with the extra boiler; and £262 per week for the loss of a lucrative dyeing contract with the Government.

Evidence was given that although the defendants knew the claimants wanted the boiler working as soon as possible, they did not know about the Government contract, or the fact that it was so much more lucrative than the laundry's other work. As a result, the Court of

Appeal held that they were liable for the £16 per week, but not for the £262. The court stated that a defendant should only be liable for such losses as were 'reasonably foreseeable' as arising from the breach.

> **Legal Principle**
> A defendant should only be liable for such losses as were 'reasonably foreseeable' as arising from the breach.

**Key Case**   *The Heron II*

In **The Heron II** (1969) the claimant chartered a ship, the *Heron II*, to carry sugar to Basrah, where the cargo was to be sold. The journey was to take 20 days, but the shipowner strayed from the normal route and took 29 days. During the period between the agreed delivery date and the actual delivery, the market price of sugar at Basrah fell significantly. The late delivery put the shipowner in breach of contract, and the claimant sued for the difference between the price he would have got for the sugar had the delivery been made on time and the going price when the delivery was actually made. The shipowner had not been told that the claimant intended to sell the sugar as soon as it arrived in Basrah, but he did know that there was a market for sugar at Basrah. From this the court held that 'if he had thought about the matter he must have realized that at least it was not unlikely that the sugar would be sold in the market at market price on arrival'. In view of this, the House of Lords held that the claimant's intention to sell the sugar at Basrah when the ship arrived was so probable that it should be regarded as arising in the normal course of events, and would therefore be within the contemplation of the parties at the time the contract was made.

> **Legal Principle**
> Loss which arises in the normal course of events should be compensated.

In **Jackson** *v* **Royal Bank of Scotland** (2005) the House of Lords emphasised that the time to determine what was reasonably foreseeable was the time at which the contract was made, not the time at which it was broken. This is because at the time the contract is made the parties can make provision for the distribution of risk in their negotiations if they wished to do so. The parties have the opportunity to limit their liability in damages when they are making their contract. They can at that stage draw attention to any special circumstances outside the ordinary course of things which they ought to have in contemplation when entering into the contract. In **Jackson**, the claimant imported cheap dog biscuits from Thailand and sold them on to its customer, known as Economy Bag, at a considerable profit. Economy Bag did not realise how cheap the biscuits were in Thailand until the defendant bank revealed this information to Economy Bag in breach of its contract with the claimants. Following this revelation, Economy Bag ceased to buy the biscuits from the claimants and bought them directly from Thailand. The claimant sued the bank for the loss of the repeat business with Economy Bag. The bank argued that the losses alleged to have been suffered by the claimant were too remote a consequence of the bank's breach of contract, stating that it had no reason to think that its breach of contract would lead Economy Bag to stop trading with the claimant. The bank argued that when the contract was made the parties' reasonable contemplation would have been that, as Economy Bag knew the identity of the supplier and where it could be contacted, no loss would flow from the disclosure to it of the amount of the claimant's mark-up.

The House of Lords held that the lost business was not too remote. As soon as the confidential information was released, there was no repeat business. All that the claimant had to show was that, at the time of the contract, the contract breaker should have contemplated that damage of the kind suffered would have occurred as a result of his breach. Once it had decided, correctly, that it was a natural and probable consequence of the bank's breach that the claimant would suffer a loss of repeat business, there was no cut-off point. The claimant was entitled to an award of damages to put them in the same position as they would have been if there had been no breach of contract. The question that remains is one of assessment. The bank did not include any provision in the letter of credit limiting its liability for the loss of repeat business to any particular period. So the only limit on the period of its liability is that which the trial judge identified. This is when, on the facts, the question whether any loss has been sustained has become too speculative to permit the making of any award. The bank's liability was open-ended, as it had not limited its liability by the contract to any particular period. There was no evidence that the parties contemplated, at the time of the contract, that knowledge of the supplier's identity and its contact details would lead inevitably to knowledge of the prices which were being charged by it. It was only a matter of time before the harsh reality of doing business persuaded Economy Bag that it should take a closer interest in what its arrangements with the claimant were costing and reduce or eliminate those costs. In determining the amount of damages available, the House of Lords stated that the court had to consider how long it was or should have been in the reasonable contemplation of the parties at the time that the contract was made (and not at the time that it was broken) that the trading relationship would continue. On the facts this was four years. After this time the damages were too speculative to be recoverable.

In *The Heron II* the House of Lords discussed the level of probability required for an event to be considered to be within the contemplation of the parties. They disapproved of the phrase 'reasonably foreseeable', as used in **Victoria Laundry**, on the grounds that it suggested a very low degree of probability (similar to the remoteness test used in tort law). They stated that in order for a claimant to be held responsible for a loss, that loss must be such that both parties would, at the time the contract was made, have regarded it as 'liable to result' from the breach; the fact that they knew there was a very remote chance that the loss might occur would not be enough. Therefore a victim of contract breach may suffer losses which he cannot recover because their occurrence cannot be said to be probable from the outset.

The above two cases make it clear that where a loss only results from a breach because of special circumstances (such as the unusually lucrative contracts in **Victoria Laundry**), defendants will only be liable for that loss if they knew about the special circumstances at the time the contract was made, and contracted on the basis that such circumstances existed. Thus, a party in breach has to pay the bill arising from the consequences of what the parties reasonably contemplated as the probable result of breach, at the time they made their agreement. The assessment is to be made objectively – we are not looking at what the parties actually contemplated, but what they must be taken to have contemplated, taking into account special circumstances known to both parties when they made their contract.

**Key Case**    Transfield Shipping *v* Mercator Shipping (*The Achilleas*)

In **Transfield Shipping** *v* **Mercator Shipping** (*The Achilleas*) (2008) the House of Lords stated that in determining the issue of remoteness the courts had to take into account the parties' apparent intentions as to where responsibility for losses should fall, as this was relevant to determining what losses the parties could have reasonably foreseen. This has become known as the assumption of responsibility test. The case concerned a ship, *The Achilleas*, which was returned late to the owners by the company that had rented it (known as charterers). Before the boat was due to be returned, the owners had arranged for it to be rented to another company for US$39,500 a day. Market hire rates then fell sharply and when the boat was returned nine days late, the owners had to renegotiate the planned hire contract (the follow-on charter) for US$8,000 less a day. Transfield was clearly liable for loss caused to the shipowners as a result of the overrun of its last voyage. The dispute was over how much damages had to be paid for this breach of contract.

In the litigation that followed, the owners claimed US$1.3 million damages for loss of profit calculated by multiplying the US$8,000 loss by the number of days covered by the follow-on charter. There was no reported case in which such a claim had been made, as until this case the courts had assumed damages for late delivery would be calculated on the basis of the difference between the sum paid at the rate of the original contract for the extra days that the boat was used and the higher market rate which the owners could have obtained if the boat had been returned on time. The charterers argued that this traditional calculation for damages should be applied. Under this mode of calculation the damages awarded would only be US$158,301, as this was the loss of income caused to the owners during the extra nine days. However, applying the established principles of damages in **Hadley** *v* **Baxendale** as developed and explained in *The Heron II* one would have expected the owners to be able to recover their entire loss – this type of loss was reasonably foreseeable even if the quantity was not. It was clear that in its ordinary sense this type of loss was foreseeable and within the contemplation of the parties: it is well known that the shipping market is volatile. The actual amount of the owner's loss was surprising but this has traditionally been held not to matter. The House of Lords unanimously accepted the charterer's lower calculation of damages. Two separate strands of reasoning led to this result.

Lord Hoffmann focused on the issue of assumption of responsibility at the time the contract was made. He said it was accepted that the foreseeability of the amount of loss was irrelevant. If the type of loss is reasonably foreseeable at the outset, it is recoverable, but a restrictive view was taken as to what would amount to the same type of loss. The foreseeability of the type of loss suffered was not in its simplified form the correct test. Instead, one should ask: was the loss of a type for which the contract breaker ought fairly to be taken to have accepted responsibility at the time the contract was made? That was what was meant by the court in **Hadley** *v* **Baxendale** when saying that such damages were recoverable 'as may reasonably be supposed to have been in the contemplation of both parties at the time they made their contract as the probable result of breach'.

Lord Hoffmann said that in determining whether damages were too remote, courts should first decide whether the loss was of the kind for which the contract breaker ought fairly to have taken responsibility. The House of Lords noted that the rule in **Hadley** *v* **Baxendale** that a party may recover losses which were foreseeable would not automatically be imposed on every contract. The rule was flexible and sought to give effect to the presumed intentions of the parties. The rule amounted to a 'prima facie assumption about what the parties may be taken to have intended', which would be applicable in the great majority of cases but capable of rebuttal where the 'context, surrounding circumstances or general understanding in the relevant market' (such as banking or shipping) shows that a party would not reasonably have been regarded as assuming responsibility for such losses. Liability for damages in contract had to be founded on the intention of the parties, objectively ascertained, because all contractual liability was voluntarily undertaken. The general understanding in the shipping market was that liability was restricted to the difference between the market rate and the charter rate for the overrun period and any departure from this rule was likely to give rise to a real risk of serious commercial uncertainty which the industry as a whole would regard as undesirable.

> It seems to me logical to found liability for damages upon the intention of the parties (objectively ascertained) because all contractual liability is voluntarily undertaken. It must be in principle wrong to hold someone liable for risks for which the people entering into such a contract in their particular market would not reasonably be considered to have undertaken.

Therefore, the question of whether a given type of loss is one for which a party assumed contractual responsibility involves the interpretation of the contract as a whole against its commercial background. The charterer could not reasonably be regarded as having assumed the risk of the owner's loss of profit on the follow-on charter. On the facts of the case, the parties would have considered such losses of a type for which the charterer was not assuming responsibility.

Lord Hoffmann noted that any other conclusion would have been unfair to the charterers as it would have been impossible for them to quantify losses stemming from the follow-on charter. While the parties to a charter would regard it as likely that the owners would enter into a follow-on charter, they would have no idea when that would be done or what its length or terms would be. On the other hand, if owners could see that the last voyage was bound to overrun and put the follow-on charter at risk, they had the option of refusing to undertake it. If the dates for the last voyage under the charterparty were agreed and this overran, the shipowners would be entitled to be paid for the overrun at the market rate only.

> All this will be known to both parties. It does not require any knowledge of the owner's arrangements for the next charter.

Lord Rodgers's reasoning was very different. He applied the traditional foreseeability test in a novel way. He found that, although the type of loss suffered (loss of an advantageous charterparty if the vessel was delayed) was foreseeable at the time the charterparty was made, the degree of loss suffered in this case was not foreseeable. Lord Rogers based his judgment on the extreme volatility of the market on the relevant dates:

> Back in September 2003 this loss could not have been reasonably foreseen as being likely to arise out of the delay in question. It was, accordingly, too remote to give rise to a claim for damages for breach of contract.

---

**Legal Principle**

In determining the issue of remoteness the courts had to take into account the parties' apparent intentions as to where responsibility for losses should fall, as this was relevant to determining what losses the parties could have reasonably foreseen.

---

Thus, under the traditional view damages will be recoverable which are of a type that could reasonably be contemplated by the parties when they made the contract. In the past, so long as the loss was of a type that could reasonably have been contemplated, the fact that the loss turned out to be much greater than could be foreseen did not prevent the defendant from incurring liability for it. In **Vacwell Engineering Co Ltd** v **BDH Chemicals Ltd** (1971) a scientist dropped an ampoule of chemicals into a bin which caused an explosion, killing both the scientist and a colleague, and causing extensive damage to property. Rees J stated that 'the explosion and the type of damage being foreseeable it matters not in the law that the magnitude of the former and the extent of the latter were not'. But *The Achilleas* potentially represents a tightening up of this approach because some losses could be so great that the size of the loss shifts the loss into a type which was not reasonably contemplated.

The High Court stated in **Sylvia Shipping Co Ltd** v **Progress Bulk Carriers Ltd** (2010) that the assumption of responsibility test in *The Achilleas* should only be applied exceptionally. It suggested that it would apply where the application of the general tests on remoteness would lead to an unquantifiable, unpredictable or disproportionate liability or where there is clear evidence that such a liability would be contrary to market understanding and expectations. On the facts of the actual case, *The Achilleas* was not applied because the court held that the loss from terminating the charterparty early was quantifiable.

It is interesting to note that the Court of Appeal in Singapore has refused to follow *The Achilleas*. Instead it has followed the approach taken in **Hadley** v **Baxendale**.

One way of looking at the two tests laid down in **Hadley** v **Baxendale** is that the first applied to normal losses (where the loss arose in the usual course of things) and the second applied to abnormal losses (where they were within the reasonable contemplation of the parties). In practice, the courts have not favoured this distinction and have preferred to see **Hadley** v **Baxendale** as laying down a single principle. Under this single principle, as the likelihood of the loss occurring diminishes, the degree of knowledge on the part of the defendant must increase for the loss to be recoverable in damages. The House of Lords explained in **Jackson** v **Royal Bank of Scotland** (2005) that the two rules in **Hadley** v **Baxendale** were not actually mutually exclusive. To determine whether a loss arose naturally and in the ordinary course of things, for the purposes of the first rule one needed to consider the terms of the contract, its business context, and the reasonable contemplation of the parties, though the latter issue was laid down in the second rule. Thus, if one contracting party told the other contracting party at the time of making the contract about special circumstances affecting the contract, losses resulting from those special circumstances would actually become the natural consequences of the breach. Lord Reid stated in the House of Lords in **Koufos** v **Czarnikow Ltd** (1969):

> I do not think that it was intended that there were to be two rules or that two different standards or tests were to be applied.

The important issue is what the contract breaker knew or must be taken to have known, so as to bring the loss within the reasonable contemplation of the parties. When that is established, it may often be the case that the first and second parts of the rule overlap, or at least that it seems unnecessary to draw a clear line of demarcation between them.

In **Satef-Huttenes Albertus SpA** v **Paloma Tercera Shipping Co SA,** *The Pegase* (1981) Goff J discussed the two rules laid down in **Hadley** v **Baxendale**. He stated that in the light of the subsequent decisions, the case should now be seen as laying down a single principle, whereby remoteness depended on 'the degree of relevant knowledge held by the defendant at the time of the contract in the particular case'. The test was now whether:

the facts in question came to the defendant's knowledge in such circumstances that a reasonable person in the shoes of the defendant would, if he had considered the matter at the time of making the contract, have contemplated that, in the event of a breach by him, such facts were to be taken into account when considering his responsibility for loss suffered by the claimant as a result of such breach.

In **Balfour Beattie Construction (Scotland)** v **Scottish Power plc** (1994) Balfour Beattie was building a section of motorway near Edinburgh. It needed a continuous supply of electricity to make concrete. The defendants agreed to set up a temporary electricity supply for the concrete plant. When this supply failed, a bridge under construction could not be completed and later had to be rebuilt. Balfour Beattie sued for the cost of rebuilding the bridge. The House of Lords held that the loss incurred was too remote. There was no evidence that Scottish Power knew the concrete plant needed a continuous supply of electricity. The parties had to have reasonable knowledge of the other's business, but not every technical fact particularly of something as vast and complicated as major motorway construction.

## Topical Issue

### Air travel

Air travel is becoming increasingly common, but unfortunately many people experience delays and inconvenience while travelling, as was recently highlighted by problems caused by volcanic ash and heavy snow falls. In **Wiseman** v **Virgin Atlantic Airways Ltd** (2006) the claimant had, in breach of contract, not been allowed to catch his return flight from Nigeria to London. The High Court accepted that he was allowed to receive damages to cover the cost of his hotel and related expenses while he was delayed in Nigeria. These damages satisfied the requirements in **Hadley** v **Baxendale**. However, there had also been certain other, unforeseeable consequences of Dr Wiseman's delay. Because he was late returning to the UK, his fiancée cancelled their engagement. He was robbed during his extended stay in Nigeria and subsequently had problems sleeping because of the trauma. Damages for distress were, however, refused because the distress he suffered was too remote – these events were neither an immediate and necessary result of the breach nor could they have been in the contemplation of the parties when the contract was made.

## Mitigation

Claimants cannot simply sit back and allow losses to pile up and expect the defendant to pay compensation for the whole amount if there is something they could reasonably do to reduce the loss. Claimants are under a duty to mitigate their loss, and cannot recover damages for losses which could have been avoided by taking reasonable steps. For example, if Jane has a contract with David to repair the machines in his factory, and fails to carry out her duties as agreed, David cannot simply keep the factory idle for years and submit a claim for lost profits; he will only be able to claim for such losses as he could not reasonably avoid by taking steps, such as finding a replacement machine, or an alternative source of repairs.

The claimant does not have to prove that reasonable steps have been taken; it is up to the defendant to prove that the loss could have been mitigated, or better mitigated. Nor are claimants expected to make enormous efforts to mitigate the loss; they need only do what is reasonable.

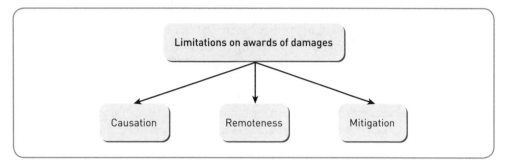

**Figure 15.1** Limitations on awards of damages

In **Pilkington** v **Wood** (1953) the defendant, a solicitor, was in breach of contract for wrongly advising that the title to the claimant's house was good. The defendant argued that the claimant should have mitigated his loss by taking proceedings against the seller of the house for having conveyed a defective title. However, this would have involved complicated litigation, which would not necessarily have succeeded, and the court held that the purchaser was not required to take such onerous and uncertain steps in mitigation.

In the leading case of **Brace** v **Calder** (1895) the defendants, a partnership consisting of four members, had agreed to employ the claimant for two years as manager of a branch of their business. Five months later, two of the members retired and the partnership was dissolved, with the business being transferred to the remaining two. Legally, the dissolution of the partnership constituted wrongful dismissal of the claimant, but the two remaining partners offered to re-employ him, on the same terms as before. He rejected the offer and brought an action for breach of contract, seeking to recover the salary that he would have received had he served the whole period of two years. The claim was refused and only nominal damages awarded, on the grounds that it was unreasonable to have rejected the offer of continued employment.

Another illustration of the requirement of mitigation is **British Westinghouse Electric Co Ltd** v **Underground Electric Rys Co of London Ltd (No 2)** (1912). The appellants had contracted to supply electricity turbines to the respondents' specification. The turbines delivered did not match these specifications, and the respondents replaced them with some other turbines made by a different manufacturer. These turbines were much more efficient, so that the replacement machines paid for themselves in a short time. The respondents claimed damages for the cost of replacing the original turbines, but the House of Lords rejected the claim. The respondents had rightly mitigated their loss, and had been so successful that most of the losses had been eliminated. They were therefore only entitled to compensation for the period of time when the original turbines were running inefficiently.

## Calculating loss

Once it has been established that a loss is one for which the defendant is liable, the court must calculate the sum of damages – what amount will compensate the claimant for the loss? There are two main ways in which the losses of a claimant in a contract action can be calculated: the loss of expectation and the reliance loss.

### Loss of expectation

Where loss of expectation is the basis for calculating damages, the courts aim to put claimants in the position they would have been in if the contract had been performed. Thus the parties would have expected a certain result from the performance of the contract and the damages will compensate for the loss of this expectation. This can be described as the difference in value measure, that is the difference in value between the promised performance and the actual performance. If, for example, a claimant was buying goods with the intention of selling them and the supplier failed to supply the goods, the claimant can claim the profit that would have been made on that sale. A claimant who is forced to sell goods at a lower price when the original buyer pulls out can claim the difference between the contract price and the price at which the goods were eventually sold. Expectation losses provide an incentive to perform a contract: if the party contemplating a breach of contract knows that by failing to perform they will be liable for the full loss of profits, they are discouraged from breaking the agreement.

The usual starting point for the courts in calculating expectation loss damages is the time that the contract was breached (the breach date rule). The breach date rule will not be applied where it would fail to put a party in the same position as if the contract had been performed. Where events after the breach have affected the value of the loss suffered, the courts will look at the loss at the time of assessment. This possibility was accepted by the House of Lords in **Golden Strait Corporation v Nippon Yusen Kubishika Kaisha (*The Golden Victory*)** (2007). In July 1998, the owners of a ship, the *Golden Victory*, had rented it out to the defendant for seven years. In December 2001, the defendant returned the ship four years early, in breach of contract. The contract had contained a war cancellation clause under which either party could terminate the contract in the event of war breaking out between a number of countries including the USA, the UK and Iraq. Such a war broke out in March 2003 (the second Gulf War). The House of Lords held that the shipowner's loss did not extend to the whole four-year period, but only the 15 months until the contract would have been terminated anyway when war broke out. The shipowner could not recover any damages for the period after March 2003. It would have been artificial if the courts had been forced to ignore what had actually happened after the breach. Though the owner had argued that the breach date rule provided certainty in the assessment of damages, the duration of the contract was actually, because of the war clause, uncertain. Even if war had not broken out when the damages fell to be assessed, the courts would still have taken into account the chance that the contract might have ended before the seven years was up because they had to take into account all contingencies which might reduce or extinguish the loss suffered. The House of Lords considered it was more important for the courts to give an accurate assessment of loss rather than prioritising the benefits of certainty of the breach date rule. To apply the breach date rule to such facts would have offended the compensatory principle whereby a party is placed, so far as damages can do so, in the same situation as if the contract had been performed. The owner was seeking to recover compensation which exceeded the value of the contractual benefits of which it had been deprived. Damages should represent the value of the contractual benefits of which the claimant has been deprived – no less but also no more. The shipowners had not suffered any loss for the last three years of the contract, because it would have been terminated anyway by the defendant when war broke out.

## Reliance loss

Where reliance loss is the basis for calculating damages, the damages seek to put claimants in the position they were in before the contract was made. The damages will therefore compensate for the actual wasted expenditure and other losses incurred because of the contract which has been breached. Reliance loss is the normal test in tort law.

The case of **Anglia Television Ltd v Reed** (1972) established that reliance loss compensation can include money spent before the contract was made. The television company had planned to make a film for television, and had signed up an actor called Robert Reed to star in it. Reed signed the contract to perform in the film and then later pulled out in breach of contract. As a result, the film was not made. Clearly, the potential profits on a project such as a film are extremely difficult to predict; it could be a huge success, or sink without trace. Consequently, Anglia sought instead to claim back the money they had spent on making the film.

The amount they had spent after contracting with Reed was clearly recoverable, since it had been spent in reliance on him performing as agreed, but the film company also wished to claim money spent in the preparatory stages, before Reed was signed. It could not be said that this was spent in reliance on Reed, but the court said that there was, nevertheless, no reason why such expenditure should not be recovered, so long as it satisfied the rules on remoteness; if Reed could have been expected to realise that such losses were likely to result from his breach, he was liable for them. As Lord Denning MR pointed out, Reed would have known that money had been spent on the film before he signed up, and that that money would be wasted if the film was not made. Therefore Anglia were allowed to recover all they had spent on the film before and after the contract was made with Reed.

## Choosing between the expectation and reliance principles

As a rule, a claimant can choose whether to base a claim on loss of expectation or on reliance. In **Anglia Television** v **Reed** (1972) Lord Denning stated that a claimant could not claim for both expectation loss and reliance loss because of the risk of being compensated twice for the same loss. This is because wasted expenditure is normally included within a claim for lost performance, as the innocent party's expenditure would be taken into account when calculating how much profit they would have made from the performance of the contract. However, provided the claimant avoided such overlapping claims, there is no reason why they should not claim for both.

In practice, loss of expectation is the usual basis for calculating contract damages. Reliance loss is generally less generous than the loss of expectation measure. However, it may be seen as fairer in that it compensates for actual losses, rather than relying on guesses as to what the future gains from the performance of the contract would have been.

## Limits on the claimant's choice

There are two main restrictions on the claimant's choice between the expectation and the reliance principles. These are the bad bargain rule and the speculative damages rule.

### The bad bargain rule

If the claimant would have made a loss from the contract, then he or she will only be entitled to nominal damages, and will not be entitled to claim their expenses on the basis of reliance loss. To compensate on a reliance basis would mean that the injured party would be placed in a better position as a result of the breach than they would have been in if the contract had been performed. In **C & P Haulage** v **Middleton** (1983) the claimant had a licence to use premises in Watford for six months, with the possibility that the contract could be renewed. He spent money on fixtures and fittings knowing that the contract stated that these could not be removed when the licence expired. When the contract was breached, the court held that the claimant could not recover for his expenditure and was entitled to nominal damages only. He could not claim for his wasted expenditure on the fixtures and fittings, because this would have been wasted even if the contract had been performed as agreed. If Robert Reed in the **Anglia Television** case could have shown that Anglia Television would not have made any money from the film anyway, the television company could not have claimed back the money they spent.

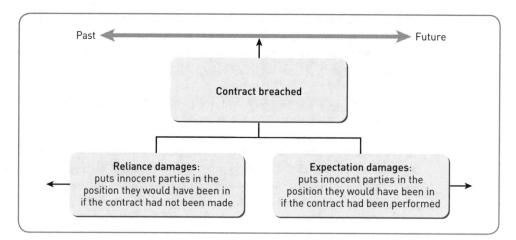

**Figure 15.2** Calculation of damages

### Expectation losses are 'too speculative'

The reliance basis for calculating damages must be used where it is virtually impossible to calculate what profit the claimant would have made if the contract had been performed correctly. In practice, the courts are reluctant to conclude that damages are too speculative and are prepared to base their awards on a certain amount of guesswork.

**McRae** v **Commonwealth Disposals Commission** (1951) was an Australian case heard by the Australian High Court. The claimant had successfully tendered for the salvage rights to an oil tanker, said to be wrecked on a reef approximately 100 miles north of Samarai. Despite being given an exact map reference for the location of the tanker, the claimant's salvage expedition failed to find the tanker, and it was eventually agreed that it was not in fact there at all. The claimant attempted to claim for loss of the profit he expected to make on salvaging the ship, but the court refused to allow this, on the grounds that it was impossible to calculate the value of a ship that did not exist. However, McRae was allowed to recover the wasted costs of the salvage trip – in other words, his reliance loss.

Damages were considered too speculative in **Sapwell** v **Bass** (1910). The claimant was a breeder of racehorses and the defendant the owner of a stallion who was paid £315 so that his stallion could 'serve' the claimant's mares. The defendant sold the stallion to a third party in South America, making it impossible to carry out the contract. The claimant claimed damages for the foals which he had lost, including the possibility he had lost a valuable prize-winning animal. The court held that these damages were too uncertain and instead made a nominal award.

## Quantifying the expectation loss

Contract damages based on expectation loss aim to put the non-breaching party in the position they would have been in had the contract been performed as agreed. In calculating damages, the focus is on the claimant's loss. Claimants cannot recover more than their actual loss. If the claimant suffers no loss, they will only receive nominal damages. An award of damages can include compensation for a loss of profit which would have been made but for the breach of contract. The damages are essentially seeking to compensate the difference in value between the promised performance and the actual performance.

## The market price rule

Where a contract has been breached, the law assumes that the wronged party will immediately mitigate their loss by buying similar goods which they had contracted for from another source or selling the goods which they had contracted to sell to another source. The wronged party will then suffer a loss only if they had to pay more for the substitute goods on the open market than they had originally contracted to pay, or had to sell the goods at a lower price. The buyer's damages will therefore be assessed by subtracting the contract price from the market price at the time of breach. A market price exists when goods can be bought and sold at a price fixed by supply and demand. This mode of calculating loss is expressly laid down for certain breaches of contracts for the sale of goods in ss. 50 and 51 of the Sale of Goods Act 1979, but the principle applies more generally.

As a result of the market price rule, the wronged party will often suffer no loss, as there is often no difference between the market price and the contract price. Take the example where Ann has two bags of flour and contracts to sell them to Ben at the market price of £10 per bag. If Ben later wrongfully refuses to accept the flour, Ann will almost certainly be able to sell them to Claire at the same price. Only nominal damages will be awarded. Ann may argue that she has lost profit because she would have been able to sell another two bags of flour to Claire. This argument may succeed if supply is greater than demand, that is to say that Ann had access to more sacks of flour which could have been sold to Claire, so that there is one lost sale.

An illustration of how the law applies in practice is **Thompson Ltd** v **Robinson (Gunmakers) Ltd** (1955). The buyers of a car were in breach of contract for refusing to accept delivery of the car from the sellers, who were car dealers. The dealers had to sell the car at the manufacturer's list price, which meant the market and contract prices were effectively the same. At the time, there was little demand for the type of car in question and supply was exceeding demand. Realising that they were unlikely to find another buyer, the dealers persuaded their suppliers to take the car back. The buyers admitted that they were in breach, but argued that the claimants had in fact suffered no loss, as there was no difference between market and contract price at the time when they refused to accept delivery. The court disagreed, pointing out that s. 50 of the Sale of Goods Act was merely a *prima facie* rule which did not apply in this situation. The sellers were awarded £61, the profit they would have made on the sale. On the facts the dealers had lost a sale, which could not be mitigated. A contrasting case is **Charter** v **Sullivan** (1957). Here the facts were similar, except that the car was of a type which was in such demand at the time that the sellers admitted that they were easily able to sell every example they could get their hands on. As a result, it was easy to find another buyer, and the sellers were only awarded nominal damages.

### Exclusion of the market price rule

The market price rule will not be used as the measure of loss either where there is no available market or where, in the circumstances, the non-breaching party is not expected to avail itself of the market to mitigate its loss. Where there is no market, the loss has to be quantified by the court estimating the actual value of the goods. There is no market for unique goods because alternative substitute goods cannot be obtained. In **Lazenby Garages Ltd** v **Wright** (1976) the sale of a second-hand car was treated as a sale of a unique item, but it is unlikely that every second-hand car would be treated as unique. There will be no market for goods where they have been specially manufactured to the exact specifications of the buyer, so that it is very unlikely that a different buyer would have ordered precisely the same goods.

### Cost of cure

Cost of cure is the other possible way of calculating expectation loss. In some cases, claimants may have wanted the performance of a contract for personal ('subjective') reasons. These subjective reasons are the value to the consumer of contractual performance which is over and above the market value of that performance. They can be described as the consumer surplus. Thus, an award of damages based on an objective difference in value between the contractual performance and the market value of the performance received will not compensate them for their loss.

The cost of cure may be significantly greater than the difference in value from that contracted for. The question, therefore, is whether the courts should take account of the consumer surplus and award higher cost of cure damages. Cost of cure damages will only be awarded where this would be reasonable. They will not be awarded where they would be out of all proportion to the consequences of the breach and there is a risk of unjust enrichment where the claimant is awarded cost of cure damages but then does not use the money to remedy the breach.

In a US case, **Jacobs & Young** v **Kent** (1921), the claimant had specified in the contract for the construction of a house that a particular brand of piping had to be used for the plumbing work. A different make of piping of identical quality was in fact used. The court refused to allow damages on the basis of cost of cure, and allowed only the difference in value between the two types of pipe, which was purely nominal.

**Key Case**    Ruxley Electronics and Construction Ltd v Forsyth

A leading case on cost of cure damages is **Ruxley Electronics and Construction Ltd** v **Forsyth** (1995). (This case was discussed on p. 348.) The claimant had contracted for the construction of a swimming pool in his garden. He had specified that the pool needed to be 7 ft 6 in deep so that he would feel safe when diving. The completed pool was only 6 ft 9 in deep. The cost of rebuilding the pool (the cost of cure) was out of proportion to the loss suffered and so the House of Lords held that the cost of cure was not recoverable. The House of Lords gave an example of the construction of a house where the owner specifies that some of the lower bricks should be blue. Instead of using blue bricks, yellow bricks are used. To conform with the contractual requirements, the house would have to be knocked down and rebuilt, but this would be disproportionately expensive. It would therefore be unreasonable to award cost of cure damages. By contrast, if a house has been built so defectively that it is not inhabitable, it would be reasonable to award cost of cure damages.

**Legal Principle**

Cost of cure damages will not be awarded where they would be out of all proportion to the consequences of the breach.

The High Court concluded in **Birse Construction Ltd** v **Eastern Telegraph Co Ltd** (2004) that an award of damages calculated on the basis of cost of cure would not be appropriate on the facts of the case. The claimants, Eastern Telegraph Company Ltd (ET) had entered into a contract with Birse Construction Ltd (BCL). Under this contract BCL agreed to build a residential training college for ET. The latter alleged that there were a number of defects with the building, but chose not to put most of them right because it had decided instead to try to sell the building. While there were explanations for not dealing with some of the items (such as inaccessibility), the court was not convinced that there were any items which truly affected the general appearance, comfort and amenity of the college. If there were any such items, then any reasonable owner with resources (and ET had them) would have put them right promptly either at the same time as the main works or soon thereafter. The sale was close to completion and no discount had been required by the buyers to take into account the defects. BCL therefore argued that ET had suffered no loss and should only be awarded nominal damages. The court accepted that, following **Ruxley**, the normal measure of damages for defective works is the cost of putting the defects right (the remedial work). But this was not the measure for damages if this would be unreasonable on the facts of the case. Where the cost of the remedial works would, as a matter of common sense, be out of proportion to the claimant's real loss, then some other measure should be used. This is the case where there has been a modest effect on the utility of the works and where it would be reasonable to assess the loss on the basis of diminution in value. To award ET the cost of putting the defects right would be unreasonable and out of all proportion to ET's loss which appeared to be minimal. There was no evidence that ET's business had suffered or even that the work of any of its students had been affected. Moreover, if the college was sold, which was probable at the date of trial, ET's supposed loss would have been avoided and would not therefore be recoverable. ET was only entitled to nominal damages for the unremedied defects. It was unreasonable to award cost of cure damages as there was no intention to repair the defects and no financial loss had been suffered because the price to be obtained on the sale had not been reduced to take into account the defects. There appeared to be no real loss of amenity as no steps had been taken to rectify the defects.

## Loss of opportunity damages

The loss of an opportunity is recoverable in damages if the lost chance is quantifiable in monetary terms and there was a substantial chance that the opportunity might have come to fruition. Otherwise, the loss of opportunity will be treated as too speculative. The leading case is **Chaplin** v **Hicks** (1911) in which the defendant, Sir Edward Seymour Hicks, was a theatre producer. He advertised a competition in the *Daily Express* for young women to send photographs to the newspaper to be shortlisted by readers for a prize. The winner of the competition would be offered a part in one of the defendant's plays. Six thousand photographs were sent in, each woman paying one shilling to take part in the competition. For the purposes of the competition, the country was divided into four areas, and the winners from each area were to attend the final round. The claimant, Eva Chaplin, came top in her area but was only informed of this at a very late stage, and was then unable to attend the final round. She sued for the loss of the chance to win the competition. The Court of Appeal held that she was entitled to damages for breach of contract. The mere fact that such damages were difficult to assess did not in itself mean that the claimant could not succeed. The court stated that in calculating the damages the jury 'must of course give effect to the consideration that the claimant's chance is only one out of four and that they cannot tell whether she would have ultimately proved to be the winner. But having considered all this they may well think that it is of considerable pecuniary value to have got into so small a class, and they must assess the damages accordingly.'

Lord Reid in **Davies** v **Taylor** (1974) put forward the requirement that there must have been a substantial chance that the opportunity would have come to fruition.

> The issues and the sole issue is whether that chance or probability was substantial. If it was it must be evaluated. If it was a mere possibility it must be ignored. Many different words could be

and have been used to indicate the dividing line. I can think of none better than substantial on the one hand, or 'speculative' on the other.

The distinction between loss of a chance and speculative loss was discussed in **Allied Maples Group Ltd** *v* **Simmons and Simmons** (1995) in which the claimant sued a firm of solicitors for negligence in failing to pursue a claim. The court stated that the claimant could only succeed if the chance was substantial rather than speculative.

## Tax

As we have seen, the aim of contract damages is to put the claimant in the position that they would have been in had the contract been performed. This means that, as a rule, the claimant should not make a profit from the defendant's breach if the profit would not have been made had the contract been performed as agreed. Therefore where a claimant's claim includes money

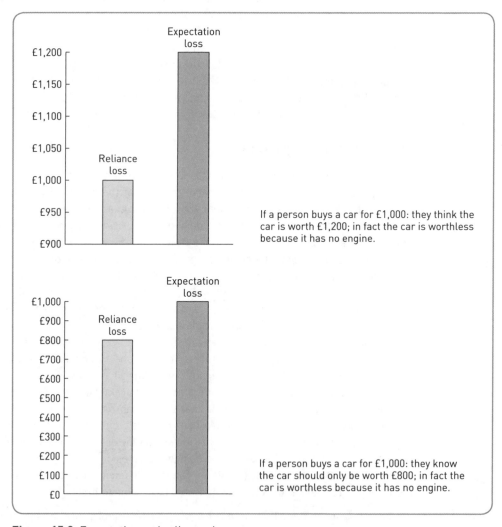

**Figure 15.3** Expectation and reliance damages

on which they would have had to pay income tax if it were earned by performing the contract, the amount of tax payable can be deducted from the damages.

This principle was established in **British Transport Commission** v **Gourley** (1956). This was actually a tort case, but the same principle applies to contract damages. The claimant had been seriously injured as a result of negligence by the defendants and was claiming for lost earnings of £37,000. The court awarded him the sum that he would have earned after paying tax, since that was what he would have received had the injury not occurred.

If the damages will themselves be subjected to tax, then the courts do not have to deduct tax themselves when calculating the damages, because this would lead to tax being deducted twice.

## Profit made by the defendant

Contract damages are not intended to be a means of punishing the party in breach; they are intended to compensate the innocent party for any loss they have suffered as a result of the non-performance of the contract. For this reason, with minor exceptions, when calculating damages, the courts have traditionally not taken into account any profit the party in breach has made by breaking the contract, only the loss caused to the innocent party. So if, for example, Bill, a greengrocer, fails to make a delivery to Jill because a top chef has just come in and bought all his stock at a vastly inflated price, Bill will be liable to compensate Jill for any extra cost she incurred in buying elsewhere, but does not have to hand over the extra profit he made on the sale to the chef.

An award of damages calculated on the basis of a defendant's profit could be described as restitutionary rather than compensatory. Restitution is the remedy available where there has been unjust enrichment, and is not traditionally available for breach of contract (see p. 374). There are circumstances in which a claimant has not suffered any direct financial loss from the defendant's wrongdoing. Under the traditional basis of calculation they could not be compensated. If compensation is calculated to take into account the defendant's profit, then the innocent party, who has suffered no direct loss in the traditional sense, can still receive compensation. It seems that some form of restitutionary damages will be available where compensatory damages do not provide a satisfactory remedy. In the most recent cases the courts now appear to be willing to compensate for a loss of profit in exceptional cases. It is in many ways unsatisfactory to have the two different principles of expectation and restitution simultaneously at work for the calculation of damages. Clear rules will have to be developed to determine when each principle should be relied upon.

In deciding whether to compensate for a loss of profit, the courts have drawn a distinction between where defendants are ordered to hand over part of their profits, and where they are ordered to hand over all their profit (known as 'an account of profits'). The court will now sometimes order the former, but only in very exceptional circumstances order the latter.

### Defendants to hand over part of their profits

Until recently the courts were not prepared to take into account a defendant's profit when calculating an award of damages. The position has now changed and the courts are prepared to make an award of damages that is calculated on the basis of the guilty party being required to return part of their profits.

A case that had originally rejected profit-based damages is **Surrey County Council** v **Bredero Homes Ltd** (1993). The Council sold land to the defendant property developer, who covenanted not to build more than 72 houses on it. Without seeking a variation of the covenant, the developer built an additional five houses. The developer deliberately breached the covenant in order to make more profit. The Council claimed damages based on its estimate of what the defendant would have had to pay as the 'price' for variation of the covenant. While the developer had been 'unjustly enriched', the Council had not suffered any loss. Normal contract damages were not recoverable, because the claimant was already in the position it would have been in had the contract not been breached. The question for the Court of Appeal was whether the deliberate breach of the contract should in some way be sanctioned by making the defendant hand over part of its profit. The court did not think it should.

A different approach was taken in **Wrotham Park Estate Co Ltd** v **Parkside Homes Ltd** (1974). The defendant had built houses on his land which was in breach of a restrictive covenant in favour of a neighbouring property. The neighbour sought an injunction which would effectively have required the houses to be demolished. The courts refused to issue an injunction because this would have been an 'unpardonable waste of much needed houses'. Instead they were awarded damages. If the usual measure of damages had been used, only nominal damages could have been awarded, because the construction of the houses had not caused any financial loss to the claimant – the construction of the houses had not affected the value of the neighbouring property. The court considered as the 'just substitute for a mandatory injunction . . . such sum as might reasonably have been demanded by the plaintiffs from Parkside as a *quid pro quo* for relaxing the covenant'. This was calculated on the basis of 5 per cent of the profit which the defendant made from the breach of covenant. This measure was used because it reflected the sum the neighbour might reasonably have required for the claimant's consent to the development.

The award could therefore be described as compensation rather than restitution, as it was compensation for the lost opportunity to negotiate a release from the covenant. This opportunity had been lost when the covenant was breached unilaterally.

The decision was approved by the House of Lords in **Attorney General** v **Blake** (2000). The House preferred this case over the case of **Surrey County Council** v **Bredero Homes**. It viewed **Wrotham Park** as 'a solitary beacon'. It showed that 'in contract as well as tort damages are not always narrowly confined to recoupment of financial loss', and that in 'a suitable case damages for breach of contract may be measured by the benefit gained by the wrongdoer from the breach. The wrongdoer must make a reasonable payment in respect of the benefit he has gained.'

The House thought that these damages amounted to compensation and not restitution. Compensation seeks to compensate someone for their loss. The House thought that a broad view needed to be taken as to a party's loss – on the facts of the case the claimant's loss did not have to be limited to a loss in value to their property (which had not occurred). The House did not think that the award of damages came within the concept of restitution because it did not amount to the defendant handing back an unjust enrichment. The damages were calculated on the basis of the amount the defendant could have been required to pay for the claimant's consent to the development. The House considered this to be a form of compensation. In **Blake** the House commented that the law was giving effect to the instinctive reaction that, whether or not the appellant would have been better off if the wrong had not been committed, the wrongdoer ought not to gain an advantage for free, and should make some reasonable recompense. In such a context it is natural to pay regard to any profit made by the wrongdoer.

In **Pell Frischmann Engineering Ltd** v **Bow Valley Iran Ltd** (2009) the Privy Council stated that **Wrotham Park** damages were effectively damages being paid instead of specific performance or an injunction (discussed on p. 378).

### Jimi Hendrix's legacy

The case of **Experience Hendrix** v **PPX Enterprises** (2003) concerned the estate of the musician Jimi Hendrix, who died in 1970 at the age of 27. The claimant was a company that was effectively owned by Jimi Hendrix's father, who had inherited Hendrix's estate and held most of the rights to Hendrix's music. Under an agreement that had been signed in 1973, PPX had rights over some recordings of Hendrix's music, which were listed in the agreement. In breach of this agreement, PPX released some unlicensed recordings of Hendrix's music. The claimants therefore brought this action for an injunction requiring the defendant to deliver up the relevant master tapes and provide an account of profits.

The claimants were unable to prove or quantify any loss they had suffered as a result of these breaches. Thus, if the traditional approach to the calculation of damages was taken, they would only have received nominal damages. But if the defendant had obtained permission for the issuing of licences, then they would have been required to pay the claimant royalties. It would therefore be illogical, when the courts had found a breach of the 1973 agreement, that the defendant should pay nothing for the use of these master tapes. The Court of Appeal decided that, as a matter of practical justice, the defendant was required to make reasonable payment for its use of the master tapes. But it was not appropriate to order a full account of all profits that had been made by the defendant. An award of damages calculated on the basis of part of the defendant's profits was appropriate because:

- there had been a deliberate breach by the defendant of its contractual obligations for its own reward;
- the claimants would have difficulty in establishing that they had suffered a financial loss as a result;
- the claimants had a legitimate interest in preventing the defendant from making a profit from its breach of contract.

An injunction was issued to prevent future breaches. For the past breaches, the defendant was ordered to pay a reasonable sum for its use of material in breach of the settlement agreement. These damages would be calculated by setting a royalty rate. That sum was the amount that could reasonably have been demanded by Jimi Hendrix's estate for the use of the material. This was the same approach that was adopted to the calculation of damages in **Wrotham Park**. The Court of Appeal acknowledged that there was an element of artificiality in this process, as the claimant might never have given permission for the material to be used. But the court still favoured taking this approach, because it 'directed the court's attention to the commercial value of the right infringed and of enabling it to assess the sum payable by reference to the fees that might in other contexts be demanded and paid between willing parties'. This remedy of requiring defendants to pay part of their profits to the innocent party is available for ordinary commercial contracts.

In **Lane** v **O'Brien Homes** (2004), a case with similar facts to those in **Wrotham Park**, the High Court ordered the defendant to pay over 50 per cent of their profits to the claimant.

## An account of profits

In exceptional circumstances, the courts will now order a party in breach of a contract to hand over all of the profit they have made from the breach of contract. Such an order will only be made where the other possible contractual remedies are not adequate. This change in the law was made by the House of Lords in **Attorney General** v **Blake** (2000).

**Key Case**  Attorney General v Blake

In **Attorney General** v **Blake** (2000), Blake had been a member of the Secret Intelligence Service. In 1951 he became an agent for the Soviet Union. From that time until his arrest in 1960, he worked as a spy, disclosing valuable secret information. In 1961 he was convicted of committing offences under the Official Secrets Act 1911 and was sentenced to 42 years' imprisonment. Five years later he escaped from Wormwood Scrubs and made his way to the Soviet Union, where he now lives as a fugitive from justice.

The publishers, Jonathan Cape Ltd, agreed to pay the defendant £50,000 on signing a contract to write a book of his experiences, £50,000 on delivery of the manuscript and a further £50,000 on publication of the autobiography. In 1990 the book was published. The information in the book was no longer confidential and nor was its disclosure damaging to the public interest.

By the time the Government knew about the book, Blake had already received £60,000, which could not in practice be recovered. Approximately £90,000 remained payable by the publisher and the present action was brought to prevent its payment to Blake.

In 1944, Blake had signed a declaration under the Official Secrets Act 1911 which included an undertaking not to divulge any official information gained as a result of his employment. The House of Lords held that this undertaking was contractually binding and had been breached by Blake.

The House accepted that following a breach of contract an account of profits could, in exceptional circumstances, be ordered. Under this order the defendant would have to hand over to the claimant any profits received from the breach of contract. This order could be made when the claimant's interest in performance made it just and equitable that the defendant should retain no benefit from the breach of contract. The House of Lords said that such an order would only be made in 'exceptional circumstances'.

> Normally the remedies of damages, specific performance and injunction . . . will provide an adequate response to a breach of contract. It will be only in exceptional cases, where those remedies are inadequate, that any question of accounting for profits will arise. No fixed rules can be prescribed. The court will have regard to all the circumstances, including the subject matter of the contract, the purpose of the contractual provision which has been breached, the circumstances in which the breach occurred, the consequences of the breach and the circumstances in which relief is being sought. A useful general guide, although not exhaustive, is whether the plaintiff had a legitimate interest in preventing the defendant's profit-making activity and, hence, in depriving him of his profit.

Lord Steyn stated that four conditions would need to be satisfied before there could be an order for an account of profits for a breach of contract:

- There must be a breach of a negative stipulation (in this case not to disclose official secrets).
- The contract breaker has obtained a profit by doing the precise opposite of what he promised not to do.
- The claimant has a special interest greater than the financial one of having the contract performed.
- Specific performance or an injunction (both discussed below) would be ineffective remedies.

The House considered that three facts would not in themselves be sufficient grounds for departing from the normal basis on which damages are awarded:

> the fact that the breach was cynical and deliberate; the fact that the breach enabled the defendant to enter into a more profitable contract elsewhere; and the fact that by entering into a new and more profitable contract the defendant put it out of his power to perform his contract with the plaintiff.

### Legal Principle

In exceptional circumstances, where the ordinary contractual remedies are not adequate, the courts will order parties in breach of contract to hand over all of the profit they have made from the breach.

The requirement of exceptional circumstances to order an account of profits was emphasised by the Court of Appeal in **Experience Hendrix** v **PPX Enterprises** (2003):

> The exceptional nature of *Blake's* case lay, first of all, in its context – employment in the security and intelligence service, of which secret information was the lifeblood, its disclosure being a criminal offence . . . Blake had furthermore committed deliberate and repeated breaches causing untold damage, from which breaches most of the profits indirectly derived in the sense that his notoriety as a spy explained his ability to command the sums for publication which he had done . . . Thirdly, although the argument that Blake was a fiduciary was not pursued beyond first instance, the contractual undertaking he had given was 'closely akin to a fiduciary obligation, where an account of profits is a standard remedy in the event of breach'.

The claim in **Experience Hendrix** was not sufficiently exceptional to justify an account of profits. While the claimant had a legitimate interest in preventing the breach of the licences, the case raised no issues of national security and there was no fiduciary relationship.

The Court of Appeal distinguished the High Court judgment of **Esso Petroleum Co Ltd** v **Niad** (2001). The High Court had given a much broader interpretation to the application of **Blake**, applying it to an ordinary commercial contract, an approach which is unlikely to be taken in future in the light of **Experience Hendrix**. In the latter case, the Court of Appeal pointed with approval to a case decided by an arbitration panel: **AB Corporation** v **CD Company (*The Sine Nomine*)** (2002). The tribunal refused an account of profits to charterers in circumstances where owners had wrongfully withdrawn the vessel from a charter after its market value had risen. The tribunal held that an award of wrongful profits was inappropriate where both parties were dealing with a marketable commodity (the services of a ship in that case) for which a substitute can be found on the market.

The Court of Appeal in **Experience Hendrix** stated that it did not regard the facts of the appeal as exceptional to the point where the court should order a full account of all PPX's profits which had been or might in the future be made by its breaches. Here, the breaches, although deliberate, took place in a commercial context. In **Esso Petroleum** v **Niad**, the High Court had ordered an account of profits for breach of a commercial contract, but this case was distinguished, and is unlikely to be followed in the future.

In **Vercoe** v **Rutland Fund Management Ltd** (2010) the High Court emphasised that an account of profits is an exceptional remedy which is more likely to be suitable for breach of a property right, rather than other rights, such as rights to confidential information. It would not be reasonable to buy out certain rights, such as rights to top secret state information in **Blake**, where a particularly high level of protection is appropriate. The remedy is less likely to be available for commercial contracts where a party might be entitled to take a commercial decision about how to behave with regard to performance of the contract. In a commercial context, a degree of self-seeking and ruthless behaviour is accepted. Where there is a fiduciary relationship of trust, rather than a purely commercial relationship, an account of profits is more likely to be available. The fundamental question for the court in choosing a remedy is 'What is the just response to the wrong?' For an account of profits the court must have decided it is just and equitable that the defendant should retain no benefit from the breach of contract. The remedy must not be oppressive and must be proportionate to the wrong done to the claimant.

Occasionally, the courts will even award more than the profits that were actually made by the defendant. This occurred in **Pell Frischmann Engineering Ltd** v **Bow Valley Iran Ltd** (2009). The parties were hoping to enter into a contract with the National Iranian Oil Company. They agreed that the claimant would be the sole person allowed to negotiate directly with the national oil company. The claimant fell out of favour with the Iranians and the parties entered into negotiations to allow the defendants to communicate directly with the national oil company. The negotiations looked at paying the claimant between US$8 million and US$11 million to allow them to do this in breach of their original contract. The negotiations were unsuccessful but the defendant proceeded to communicate directly with the national oil company regardless. It entered into a contract with the oil company but the contract proved less profitable than expected, the profit being no more than US$1.8 million. In the subsequent litigation for breach of contract, the Privy Council awarded the claimant US$2.5 million **Wrotham Park** damages. In calculating these damages the Privy Council considered that the courts would normally put themselves in the position of the parties at the time of the breach and imagine what the parties would have agreed to pay for the right to breach the contract at that time. At the time of the breach, the parties thought the right to breach was more valuable than it actually was and this would be reflected in the award of damages.

## Nominal damages

Nominal damages of a small sum of money (typically £2) can, on occasion, be awarded by a court. Such damages are not intended to compensate the victim but rather are awarded as an acknowledgement that the claimant's rights have been breached. This token award can be made where:

- a legal claim is justified but the claimant has not suffered any real financial loss;
- the claimant suffered economic loss but it cannot be calculated; or
- the claimant has acted in bad faith through lying or deception. In this case, the nominal damages express the court's disapproval of their conduct.

In **Campbell** v **Mirror Group Newspapers** (2004) the supermodel, Naomi Campbell, sued the Mirror Group for breach of her right to privacy when photos were published of her leaving a Narcotics Anonymous meeting. While her claim was successful, she was only awarded nominal damages because her battle with drink and drugs was already in the public domain.

## Exemplary damages

Exemplary damages (sometimes called punitive damages) are only awarded in limited circumstances. Lord Devlin stated in **Rookes** v **Barnard** (1964) that exemplary damages could be awarded where:

- there were oppressive, arbitrary or unconstitutional actions by government servants;
- the defendant's conduct was calculated for personal profit, which could exceed the normal compensation payable to the claimant; or
- the award was authorised by a statute.

In **Kuddus** v **Chief Constable of Leicestershire** (2001) the House of Lords stated that any cause of action can give rise to exemplary damages provided the **Rookes** criteria are satisfied. In the English civil system, there is a growing trend for courts to make awards of exemplary damages in civil claims involving fraud. For example, where someone has sought to make a bogus claim under an insurance policy, the insurance company can sue the wrongdoer and seek exemplary damages.

There is no precise formula or prescribed method for the quantification of exemplary damages – some courts will increase an award by 50 per cent, others will take a more broad-brush approach. If the defendant has already suffered a criminal sanction then the courts may be reluctant to impose exemplary damages on top.

In the USA the award of exemplary damages is more common. Thus, in the legendary case of **Liebeck** v **McDonald's** (1994) Stella Liebeck was awarded $2.7 million after suffering third-degree burns from a scalding cup of coffee. Of this award, $2.6 million was for punitive damages, the rest was to cover actual losses.

# Action for an agreed sum

Where a contract specifies a price to be paid for performance, and payment has not been made, the party who has performed can claim the price owing by means of an action for the agreed sum. Although the claim is obviously for money, this is not the same as a claim for damages. This is a claim for a debt and not a claim for damages. The claimant is not seeking compensation, but simply enforcement of the defendant's promise to pay. However, where the claimant has suffered additional loss, beyond not receiving the agreed price, damages can be claimed alongside the agreed sum and the claim for damages follows the usual rules on remoteness and so on.

There are many advantages of an action for an agreed sum over an action for damages. The amount claimed is known from the beginning, so that questions of quantification, remoteness, causation and mitigation do not arise. In addition, because the issues at trial are frequently uncomplicated, there is a streamlined procedure for claims for unpaid debts (known as a summary judgment).

An action for the agreed sum can only be brought once the duty to pay has arisen, which will depend on the terms of the contract. Where the party failing to pay has wrongfully repudiated the contract, the injured party will have had the choice of terminating the contract or affirming it. If the injured party has chosen to terminate, he or she cannot sue for any sum which, under the contract, only became due after the date of termination. Damages can, however, be claimed for wrongful repudiation, and in calculating these the court may take into account any sums which should have been received under the contract.

# Restitution

Restitution is the remedy available when there has been unjust enrichment. Where money has been paid under a contract, or purported contract, and performance has not been received in return, or has not been adequate, the payer may want to claim the money back, rather than claiming damages (if, for example, no additional loss has resulted from the failure to perform). Restitution is not a remedy for a breach of contract. Rather, restitution seeks to restore money paid or the value of a benefit conferred in circumstances in which no contract exists, or in which there is no longer any obligation to perform under a contract.

Traditionally, contract remedies and restitution do not overlap. In practice, restitution will therefore be available where there is no contract. There may be no contract for one of the following reasons:

- a contract has not been made (e.g. because of a lack of agreement, uncertainty or the absence of consideration);
- the contract has been discharged; or
- the contract was void (e.g. because of illegality).

Restitution will be available, for example, where one party has provided some performance to the benefit of another party in anticipation of a contract being made, but the contract is never made. The recipient of the performance has received a benefit which will have cost the other party to provide, and it would be unjust to allow the benefit to be retained without payment of some kind.

Restitution can apply in many legal contexts, but in the context of contract law, restitution will allow an injured party to recover money paid, or claim the value of benefits conferred for the services rendered at the other's request; this is called a *quantum meruit*.

## Total failure of consideration

In general, restitution will only be possible if there has been a total failure of consideration so that restitution will prevent unjust enrichment. There is a total failure of consideration where one party has provided a benefit to another party, but has received nothing in return. There need not be any breach of contract. In this context, there may have been consideration at the time of the formation of the contract, but in practice the consideration has not actually been performed as promised by the contract. Performance may be impossible because the contract has been frustrated, or because unknown to the parties the subject matter of the contract had been destroyed before the contract was made. In each case, a person may recover money paid in advance even though the failure of performance does not amount to a breach of contract. Where there has been a breach of contract, the appropriate remedy is damages and not restitution.

An example of restitution where there is a total failure of consideration is **Fibrosa Spolka Akcyjna** *v* **Fairbairn Lawson** (see p. 323). The seller of goods was prevented from completing performance of a contract by delivering the goods because of the outbreak of war, and the purchaser was in enemy-occupied territory. The contract was frustrated. The purchaser had paid part of the price of the goods in advance, but had received none of the goods. They were able to claim back these advance payments because of the total failure of consideration under the principles of restitution.

In order for there to be a total failure of consideration, it is not sufficient that one party had received nothing under the contract; what has to be shown is that one party had not performed any of their contractual duties. Thus, in **Stocznia Gdanska SA** v **Latvian Shipping Company** (1998) the defendants had ordered some vessels from the claimants, which were not delivered. The House of Lords considered that the claimants' contractual obligations included designing and building the vessels. Since some of this work had been performed, there had not been a total failure of consideration.

Restitution may be available where a contract is void for illegality where the parties are not equally at fault. Following the House of Lords' judgment of **Kleinwort Benson Ltd** v **Lincoln CC** (1999), if money has been paid under a void contract as a result of a mistake of law, the money can be recovered even though there is no total (or partial) failure of consideration.

## Partial failure of consideration

Where there is only a partial, rather than a total, failure of consideration (for example, if part of a job is done, or part of a consignment of goods supplied), the general rule is that there is no right to recover money paid. There is an exception to this rule: under the Law Reform (Frustrated Contracts) Act 1943, money paid in advance under a contract which is later frustrated can be recovered, even if the failure of consideration is only partial. This is because in such a case the party making payment has no other remedy, since damages cannot be claimed when a contract is frustrated.

There is a second exception where restitution is possible when there is partial or defective performance. This is where a party chooses to give back any benefit received, bringing about a total failure of consideration, so that money paid can be recovered. This is not, however, possible where the nature of the benefit received is such that it cannot be returned to the other party. An example would be a bad haircut.

Where the subject matter can be returned, handing it back will only bring about a total failure of consideration if the injured party has not received a benefit from it, for example, by using the goods, or occupying a property. Simply testing goods does not count as benefiting from them, but any further use may prevent a total failure of consideration. In **Hunt** v **Silk** (1804) an agreement for a lease provided that the tenant would take possession immediately, the landlord would undertake specified repairs and the lease would be executed within ten days, with the tenant paying £10 when it was executed. The tenant duly took possession, and paid his £10, but the landlord failed to do the repairs, or to execute the lease within ten days. The tenant waited a few more days, then left, and claimed the £10 back. His claim was rejected, and the case has generally been taken as establishing a strict rule that, if a party has received any part of the benefit due under the contract, failure of consideration is not total. Although the decision in the case seems reasonable, since the tenant could presumably have claimed damages instead, the rule itself is open to criticism because it has the potential to prevent a claim for the recovery of money even where the benefit received is negligible or of no practical use.

The courts are sometimes prepared to find a sufficient failure of consideration for the purposes of restitution, where that failure appears to be less than total by apportioning the consideration. Consideration is apportioned by finding independent promises, one of which fails totally and can be the subject of restitution. This approach can be seen in **D O Ferguson Associates** v **M. Sohl** (1992).

The defendant employed the claimant as building contractors to renovate shop premises in Kensal Green. The price agreed was £32,194. After disputes between the parties, the builders walked off the site and did not return. They had already been paid £26,738. The defendant employed another firm of builders who completed the work for less than it would have cost under the original contract. The builders brought an action for the rest of the contractual price, and the defendant counter-claimed for damages and repayment of an overpayment made by him. The Court of Appeal held that the claimant had repudiated the contract which was discharged by the defendant's acceptance of the breach. The value of the work done by the claimant was only £22,065. The defendant had therefore overpaid by £4,673. The defendant received £1 nominal damages for the claimant's breach of contract. In addition, the court awarded the defendant restitution of the £4,673 overpayment for work which had not been done. In other words, there was a total failure of consideration of this part of the contract. Hirst LJ stated:

> It matters not that at some stage or other that sum of money formed part of a larger instalment.

The Law Commission in its working paper, *Pecuniary Restitution on Breach of Contract (No 65)*, had provisionally recommended that restitutionary recovery ought to be available in cases of partial failure of consideration. However, it changed its mind in a later report (No 121).

## Quantum meruit

Where work has been done or goods supplied but no payment has been received and cannot be obtained under a contract, an action is available called a *quantum meruit* (Latin for 'as much as is deserved'), under which claimants can claim a reasonable price for their performance. Payment cannot be obtained under a contract where there is no contract, or where the price has not been specified in the contract. A *quantum meruit* is based on restitutionary principles and is different from damages, since it merely aims to pay for performance, not to compensate for loss. So long as there is a contract between the parties, under which the claimant was intended to be paid, the court will order payment of a reasonable sum for the performance rendered – essentially the market price or 'going rate'. Where there is no contract because the contract is void, the court will still be able to order a *quantum meruit* for performance rendered.

In **Sir Lindsay Parkinson & Co Ltd** *v* **Commissioners of Works** (1949) contractors agreed to do some building work. The price was £5 million, but the contract allowed for extra work to be ordered, and also provided that the price paid should provide a profit of between £150,000 and £300,000. In the event, the Commissioner did order extra work, taking the cost to over £6 million. The contractors claimed for extra profit on a *quantum meruit*. The court allowed their claim, stating that the express provision concerning the maximum profit only applied to works worth about £5 million.

A *quantum meruit* based on extra work done or goods supplied will only be allowed if the defendant had the choice of accepting or rejecting the extra benefit. In **Forman & Co Proprietary Ltd** *v* **The Liddesdale** (1900) the contract concerned repairs to a ship, for which a price had been agreed. Materials had been specified in the contract, but the repairer chose to use alternative ones, which were more suitable for the job and more expensive. The shipowner then refused to pay for the work. The Privy Council held that the repairer could recover nothing for the work he had done. He could not claim for the agreed sum, because he had not performed as agreed and he could not use a *quantum meruit* because the shipowner had never been asked whether he wanted the extra benefit.

For an example of the operation of this principle, see **British Steel Corporation** *v* **Cleveland Bridge & Engineering Co Ltd** (1984). Work had begun at the request of the defendants, on the provision of some steel before all the elements of the contract for the steel had been agreed. Both sides confidently expected to reach agreement without difficulty. In fact, final agreement was never reached. The claimants successfully claimed a *quantum meruit* for the work they had done.

The **Cleveland Bridge** case was distinguished in **Regalian Properties plc** v **London Dockland Development Corp** (1995). In that case the claimants had not carried out the work at the request of the defendants, but had done it in order to win the contract from the defendants. The negotiations had been conducted on a subject to contract basis, so that such expenditure was at their own risk. It was not recoverable when they failed to obtain the anticipated contract.

Where there is precise provision for remuneration, a *quantum meruit* cannot usually be used to alter the price, even if extra work is done. In **Gilbert & Partners** v **Knight** (1968) Knight employed a firm of surveyors to supervise building work for a fee of £30. The surveyors did more supervision than Knight had asked for and submitted an account for £30 plus £105 for the additional work. Knight refused to pay the extra £105 and the court upheld his case. The original contract had fixed the payment and it was still in existence.

The following are circumstances in which the courts will allow a *quantum meruit* claim even though a price has been fixed.

## Incapacity

Where necessaries are sold and delivered to a minor, they need only pay a reasonable price for them, even though there may have been an agreement to pay more (see Chapter 4).

## Wrongful prevention of performance

If one party begins performance but is prevented from finishing by the other party's breach, the innocent party can claim a *quantum meruit* at the agreed rate for the work done (see **Planché** v **Colburn**, p. 316).

## Agreed partial performance

Where a party performs only part of their contractual obligation, but this part-performance is voluntarily accepted by the other party, a *quantum meruit* can be used to secure a reasonable payment for the work done. In **Miles** v **Wakefield Metropolitan District Council** (1987) the House of Lords held that a worker on industrial action, in the form of a 'go slow', could not claim his wages under his contract of employment because he was deliberately working in a manner designed to harm the employer. He was, however, entitled to be paid on a *quantum meruit* basis for the value of the reduced work performed and accepted by the employers.

## Contract void

Remuneration on the basis of a *quantum meruit* may be recoverable where performance is rendered under a contract which, unknown to both parties, is void. In **Craven-Ellis** v **Canons Ltd** (1936) the claimant had been appointed and carried out work as a managing director of the defendant company, but it turned out that his contract of employment was void. The Court of Appeal held that he could recover the reasonable value of his work on a *quantum meruit*. This principle would also apply where a contract with a company is void because when the contract was made the company was not yet legally in existence or had been dissolved, and where goods have been supplied under a contract of sale which is void for a mistake as to the purchaser's identity.

### Contract frustrated

Where work is done under a contract before it is frustrated, a *quantum meruit* is not available at common law, but the party can make a claim in respect of a valuable benefit conferred by the work under the Law Reform (Frustrated Contracts) Act 1943. Work done after the frustrating event can be claimed for on a *quantum meruit*, on the principle of **Craven-Ellis** *v* **Canons Ltd**.

# Equitable remedies

Where common law remedies are inadequate to compensate the claimant, there are a range of equitable remedies. However, these are not available as of right, merely because the defendant is in breach. They are provided at the discretion of the court, taking into account the behaviour of both parties and the overall justice of the case.

# Specific performance

An order of specific performance is a court order compelling someone to perform their obligations under a contract. As we have seen, the common law will not force a party in breach to perform (except where the performance is simply paying money), even though this may seem a fairly obvious solution to many contract problems. The equitable remedy of specific performance does compel the party in breach to perform. In practice, specific performance only rarely applies, as the making of such an order is subject to the following restrictions.

## Damages must be inadequate

Specific performance is only granted where damages alone would be an inadequate remedy (though damages may be ordered as well as specific performance). It is not, therefore, applied where the claimant could easily purchase replacement goods or performance. Where the goods that are the subject of the contract are in some way unique, then specific performance can be available. For this reason, specific performance is mainly applied in contracts to sell land (which includes land with buildings), since each piece of land is thought to be unique, and impossible to replace exactly.

Where the damages would only be nominal, specific performance may be ordered to avoid one party being unjustly enriched. The latter circumstance applied in **Beswick** *v* **Beswick** (1968) (discussed at p. 290) where the claimant's husband sold his business to his nephew in return for an annual allowance to be paid to himself and, after his death, to his widow. Once the husband died, the nephew refused to make payments to the widow. Despite the fact that the husband had clearly intended her to benefit from the contract, it was held that the widow could not sue the nephew on her own behalf, because she was not a party to the contract. However, the widow was allowed to sue as the executor of her husband's estate. The circumstances were such that the husband suffered no loss, because he had died before the nephew stopped paying the annuity, so damages would only have been nominal. It was clearly unjust for the defendant to keep the entire benefit of the contract without himself performing much at all. As a result, specific performance was ordered.

## Hardship to the defendant

Because specific performance is a discretionary remedy, the court will not apply it to cases where it could cause the defendant great hardship or unfairness. In **Patel** v **Ali** (1984) the claimant had requested specific performance on a contract for the sale of a house. The claim was delayed by four years (through no fault of either party) and in this time, the seller's husband had gone bankrupt and she had become disabled. As a result, she needed to be near friends and relatives, and moving house would have caused her hardship. Consequently, the court refused specific performance and ordered damages instead.

## Contracts made unfairly

Equity also allows the court to refuse specific performance of a contract which has been obtained by unfair means, even if they do not amount to the sort of vitiating factor which would invalidate the contract. In **Walters** v **Morgan** (1861) the defendant, who had just bought some land, agreed to grant the claimant a mining lease over it. When the party who had asked for the lease tried to enforce the agreement by specific performance, the court refused, on the grounds that the claimant had taken advantage of the fact that the defendant had not really known the value of the lease at the time the agreement was made.

## Contracts unsuitable for specific performance

Some types of contract are, by their nature, unlikely to be the subject of an order for specific performance. The two main types are contracts involving personal services (such as employment contracts), where specific performance would infringe personal freedom, and contracts which involve continuous duties. In the latter case, it is impractical for the courts to supervise proper performance, but more importantly, failure to perform after an order for specific performance can lead to a charge of contempt of court, and the courts are not keen to envisage a series of contempt actions arising from a long-running contract. In **Ryan** v **Mutual Tontine Association** (1893) the lease of a flat promised tenants that a resident porter would be 'constantly in attendance'. The person appointed had other employment, and so was in fact often absent from the flats. The court refused specific performance of this term of the lease because it would require a level of constant supervision beyond that which the court was able to assess.

However, there is flexibility, and the courts are willing to weigh up the degree of supervision required, and the balance of hardships if the order is made against those if it is not. These were said to be the issues taken into account when the court decided to grant specific performance in **Posner** v **Scott-Lewis** (1986) where the tenants of a block of 'luxury' flats sought to enforce their landlords' obligation to provide a resident porter.

In **Co-operative Insurance Society Ltd** v **Argyll Stores (Holdings) Ltd** (1997) the claimants were developers of a shopping centre. They had granted the defendants a 35-year lease to operate a Safeway supermarket in the largest shop unit. This store was central to the success of the centre, as it would attract customers, generating business for the smaller shops. The lease therefore contained a promise to keep the store open as a supermarket during ordinary business hours and only allowed for closure for a maximum of four months during the lease. In 1995, the supermarket was losing money and the defendants informed the claimants that they intended to close it down, despite the fact that 20 years remained on the lease. The claimants in turn proposed that the defendants keep the supermarket open at a reduced rate until they found a suitable tenant to replace them. Without replying, the defendants closed the supermarket, which constituted a serious breach of contract. The claimants sought an order for specific performance to compel the supermarket to come back and carry on the tenancy for the rest of the lease. This had been granted by the Court of Appeal, but was refused by the House of Lords.

The House considered that while it would be difficult to arrive at an accurate figure for the loss which was going to be caused to the claimants over the next 20 years, taking into account the impact on the smaller shops in the centre, this was not sufficient to justify an order for specific performance. Lord Hoffmann, in delivering the principal judgment, was clear that 'the established practice may justify a refusal of specific performance even when damages are not an adequate remedy'. It was settled practice not to make such orders where this would compel someone to carry on a business, since this would require constant supervision by the court. Moreover, the only tool at the court's disposal to ensure compliance was the draconian criminal sanction for contempt of court, which he considered to be an unsuitable rod to hold over a commercial party being compelled to trade. The result of ordering someone to run a business which was uneconomic might well be to cause them loss which was completely out of proportion to that caused to the other party by the original breach of contract. While the Court of Appeal had clearly been influenced by what they considered to have been blatantly dishonest conduct by the defendants, the House of Lords followed the traditional common law path of refusing to treat the nature of the defendants' conduct as relevant. Finally, Lord Hoffmann distinguished between contracts requiring someone to carry on an activity over a period of time and contracts for results. In the latter case, supervision by the courts was less problematic, as the court could often simply view the end result. This distinction was used to explain the fact that specific enforcement had been ordered in the past in relation to building contracts.

Specific performance will not be applied to a contract which is vague as to the performance required, nor to a promise which is only supported by nominal consideration or contained in a deed. It is not used where a contract allows the party concerned to terminate it (since if specific performance were ordered, the party in breach could simply exercise the right to terminate).

An order for specific performance is also subject to the principle of mutuality, which means that it will not usually be ordered against a defendant if it could not have been ordered against the claimant had they been the one in breach. So, for example, specific performance is never ordered when the claimant is a minor, because it cannot be ordered against a minor.

The courts tend to make the order where substitute performance cannot be bought.

# Injunction

An injunction normally orders the defendant not to do a particular thing. For example, Ken, a horse owner, rents a field from Julie, and it is a term of their agreement that no buildings should be put up on the land. If Julie discovers that Ken is about to build a stable, she could apply to the court for an injunction to prevent him doing so. This is called a negative (or prohibitory) injunction.

Where the action has already taken place (if Ken has already built the stable, for example) the court may make a mandatory injunction, which orders the defendant to take action to restore the situation to that which existed before the defendant's breach – so Ken would have to demolish the stable.

When considering an application for a mandatory injunction, the court applies a balance of convenience test, and may refuse the remedy if the defendant would lose a lot more by restoring the original position than the claimant would gain. However, in deciding this issue, they will also take into account the nature of the breach and the circumstances, and a mandatory injunction may be applied even where the defendant's loss in the event of restoration outweighs the claimant's gain – if, for example, the breach was committed knowingly and damages would not be an adequate remedy.

## Injunction and specific performance

As we have seen, specific performance will not be granted for a contract concerning personal services, such as an employment contract. However, there are borderline cases where an injunction has the potential to be used, for all intents and purposes, to bring about the effect of specific performance. Even a negative injunction can have this effect, if the party subject to this injunction cannot effectively offer their services elsewhere once this injunction is in place. In **Warner Bros Pictures Inc** *v* **Nelson** (1937) the actress Bette Davis had signed a contract with Warner Brothers, under which she agreed not to work for any other film company for a year. During this period, she contracted with another company, in breach of the Warner Brothers contract, and Warner Brothers sought an injunction to stop her actually working for the rival company. Although the practical effect was to make Ms Davis work for Warner Brothers, because she could not work for anyone else, the order could be distinguished from specific performance on the grounds that it was an encouragement to work for the claimant, and not a compulsion, because in theory she could have simply made her living in some other way, and not acted in anyone's films.

In practice, the courts place limits on the use of injunctions in such circumstances. Where a contract provides for the provision of personal services, an injunction is less likely to be ordered, because it could force a person to provide the other contracting party those services, or stop working altogether. An injunction is also less likely to be granted when the relationship of trust and confidence, fundamental to a personal contract of services, has broken down. Where the services are of a more commercial nature, then an injunction is more likely to be ordered. In **Page One Records Ltd** *v* **Britton** (1968) the defendants were a pop group called The Troggs, who were at that time very well known. They had engaged one of the claimants as their manager, and agreed not to employ anyone else to do that job. Later, they wanted to terminate the agreement and the claimants responded by seeking an injunction to stop the group from taking on another manager. The injunction was refused, on the grounds that its practical effect would be to force the group to employ the claimants as manager, because without a manager they would not be able to work.

**Warren** *v* **Mendy** (1989) concerned a contract between a boxer and his manager, Warren. The contract gave Warren exclusive rights to manage the boxer for three years, but during that period the boxer apparently lost confidence in Warren and asked advice on his career of Mendy. Warren sought an injunction against Mendy, to prevent him from inducing a breach of Warren's contract with the boxer. The Court of Appeal declined to grant the injunction to enforce the agreement, on the grounds that doing so would indirectly compel performance of the contract. The general view seems to be that an injunction should not be granted unless it leaves the employee with some other reasonable means of earning a living.

The case of **Warren** *v* **Mendy** (1989) was distinguished by the Court of Appeal in **Lauritzencool AB** *v* **Lady Navigation** (2005). The case involved a dispute between the charterers (renting the ships) and the managers of a pool of ships on the one hand, and the owners of two of the ships on the other. The owners claimed that the charterers and managers had breached certain duties under the charter contracts. They wanted to withdraw their ships from the pool of ships before the end of the relevant contracts. The Court of Appeal issued a negative injunction against the shipowners preventing them from withdrawing their ships from the pool until the dispute had been resolved by arbitration. Although not technically amounting to specific performance, the injunction effectively prevented the other party from acting in contravention of the contract and therefore provided compelling financial and practical reasons to perform the contract. The case of **Warren** v **Mendy** was distinguished on the basis that that involved a contract for personal services. By contrast this case was concerned with commercial services between companies. During the litigation, the ships continued to operate normally under the charter contracts.

## Remedies agreed by the parties

Many contracts, particularly commercial ones, specify the kinds of breach which will justify termination, and/or the damages to be paid by each party in the event of certain types of breach. For example, building contracts often contain provision for specified damages to be paid in the event that the building is not completed on time, and holiday contracts often state that the tour company is allowed to keep a percentage of the price paid if the customer cancels at a late stage. This sort of provision allows both sides to know in advance what their liability will amount to, and to plan accordingly.

There are two types of contract clauses concerning damages: liquidated damages clauses and penalty clauses.

## Liquidated damages

Liquidated damages is the term used where a contract specifies the amount of damages to be paid in the event of breach, and this amount represents a genuine attempt to work out what the loss would be in the event of such a breach. In such a case, the court will allow the claimant to recover this amount without proof of actual loss, even if the actual loss is larger or smaller than the sum laid down in the contract. The usual rules as to damages are excluded (damages which are not fixed by a contract, and must be calculated using the rules described in the first part of this chapter, are described as unliquidated damages).

## Penalty clauses

If a contract states that a particular sum is to be paid on breach of the contract, and that sum is not a genuine pre-estimate of the loss that would be suffered in the event of breach, but is designed instead to threaten to penalise a party in breach, this is a penalty clause. Where the damages laid down in a contract amount to a penalty clause, the clause will be found to be invalid and the award of damages will be determined by the ordinary principles of contract law instead, discussed in the first half of this chapter. The courts are reluctant to find that agreed damages amount to a penalty clause in a commercial contract where the parties have comparable bargaining power. Only if the courts find a big difference between the level of damages laid down in the contract and the level of damages that was likely to be suffered will the courts conclude that the pre-estimate was unreasonable.

Guidelines for determining when specified damages should be considered penal were laid down in **Dunlop Pneumatic Tyre Co Ltd** *v* **New Garage and Motor Co Ltd** (1915). The claimants supplied tyres to the defendants, under a contract providing that the defendants would not resell them at less than the list price. If they breached this provision, they were to pay £5 for every tyre sold at less than list price (an arrangement which would now be illegal).

The House of Lords held that the provision was not penal and was in the nature of liquidated damages. Undercutting the list price would have been very damaging to the claimant's business, and although it was impossible to calculate the loss precisely in advance, the sum specified was reasonable in the circumstances.

Lord Dunedin described the factors to be taken into account when deciding whether damages were penal or not. Damages would be regarded as penal if the sum laid down was extravagantly greater than any loss which might conceivably result from the breach. This would include a situation where the breach consisted of not paying a certain sum of money and that sum was smaller than the damages stipulated for not paying it. There is a presumption (but no more) that damages are penal if 'a single lump sum is made payable . . . on the occurrence of one or more or all of several events, some of which may occasion serious and others but trifling damage'.

Lord Dunedin made it clear that even if the parties themselves describe the damages they set as either 'liquidated' or 'penalty' this will not be conclusive, though it may be relevant. The court should look at the substance of the agreement and decide what the terms really amount to; if there was a genuine attempt to pre-estimate the consequences of a breach, damages would not be considered penal, even if such consequences could not be precisely calculated in advance.

The law on penalty clauses only relates to clauses which apply when contracts are breached. This area of law does not therefore cover the requirement to pay high bank charges for an unauthorised overdraft facility: **Berwick** *v* **Lloyds TSB Bank plc** (2007). These charges were not imposed for breach of contract; they were imposed for conduct which fell within the terms of the contract.

# Extinction of remedies

Where one party has a right of action for breach of contract, this right may be extinguished by agreement between the parties, either by a release under seal or by accord and satisfaction (see Chapter 14). Such a right can also be extinguished by the passage of time, under the Limitation Act 1980. The Act lays down various time limits for different kinds of action, and once these have expired the claimant is said to be 'statute-barred' from claiming.

# The statutory time limits

Contract proceedings should normally be brought within six years of when the cause of action accrued. 'Cause of action' means the facts giving rise to the action and will usually be when the contract is breached.

An action based on a contract made by deed must be brought within 12 years of the date on which the cause of action accrued.

There are contract cases where the claimant does not know that there is a cause of action at the time when the situation occurs, and may not know for some time afterwards, possibly even not until the ordinary limitation period has passed. This issue is addressed in the Latent Damage Act 1986, which provides that where the cause of action could not be discovered when it arose, the claimant can sue within three years of the time when it could be discovered. In addition, s. 32 of the Limitation Act 1980 provides that when a claimant is unaware of the cause of action at the time it accrues because of mistake or fraud by the defendant, the period of limitation does not begin until the claimant has discovered the fraud or mistake, or until such time as they could have discovered it by using reasonable diligence.

Section 32 was applied in **Applegate** v **Moss** (1971). The defendant, a builder, was contracted to build a house on a specific type of foundations. He did the work on the foundations very badly, with the result that several years later the house was found to be unsafe to live in. By this time the six-year limitation period was over, but the court held that there had been concealment of the defective foundations and allowed the action to proceed.

Where a claimant is under a disability, for example they are a minor or of unsound mind at the time when the cause of action accrues, the limitation period does not begin until the disability has ceased to operate. Therefore a minor can bring proceedings relating to contractual matters that arose while they were a minor, for six years after their eighteenth birthday.

## Acknowledgement

The limitation period may be extended if, before it expires, the defendant acknowledges the claim or pays part of it (s. 30). If this happens, the limitation period starts again on the date of the acknowledgement or part-payment (s. 29). If, for example, under a contract between A and B, A was due to pay B £300 in December 1987 and failed to do so, B's right to sue would be barred after six years; he would have to sue by December 1993. But if in July 1992 A pays B £50 as part-payment of the debt, or simply acknowledges that she does owe the money, the time limit of six years starts again, so that B now has until July 1998 to sue for the rest of the money.

In order for an acknowledgement to have this effect, it must be in writing, signed by the person making it, and must clearly acknowledge the debt, not just the fact that a dispute exists. It must also apply to a debt or some other liquidated sum.

## Equitable claims

Section 36(1) of the Limitation Act 1980 makes it clear that the statutory limitation periods do not apply to claims for specific performance, an injunction or other equitable remedies. Instead, the equitable doctrine of 'laches' (delay) is applied: if, taking account of all the circumstances of the case, the court considers that the claimant has been too slow in bringing the action, the equitable remedy sought will be refused.

It is not possible to lay down strict rules on when laches will prevent a claim; in each case, it will depend on the length of the delay, how diligent the court believes the claimant ought to have been and the nature of the contract. Thus, where a defendant is seeking specific performance, a lengthy delay will be less acceptable if the contract concerns goods whose value fluctuates rapidly than in a case where prices remain steady.

In **Pollard** v **Clayton** (1855) the defendants agreed to extract all the coal in a particular mine, and sell it to the claimants at a fixed price per ton. They began to perform as agreed, but later refused to deliver any more coal to the claimants, and began selling it elsewhere. Naturally, the claimants objected, but the defendants simply referred them to their solicitors. The claimants waited 11 months, and then made a claim for specific performance. It was refused, on the grounds that too long a delay had occurred between the claimants becoming aware of the breach of contract and bringing their action.

## Problems with remedies

A cursory look at this chapter might suggest that the range of remedies on offer provides a solution for every breach. In fact, there are two main problems with the law's provision for breach of contract.

### The interests protected

The law focuses mainly on one type of loss: financial loss to the party concerned. It generally ignores the mental distress, anxiety and sheer inconvenience which a breach of contract may cause. For example, the directors of large businesses may not lose any sleep over a supplier's failure to deliver, but the situation is very different for a small business, where such a breach may involve the proprietor in extra work finding alternative stock or, if this cannot be done, customers may be disappointed and shop elsewhere. The injured party may be able to claim for the cost of buying goods at a higher price, or the loss of the profit from the goods that should have been supplied, but will not be able to claim for the stress caused by extra work, or for the incalculable long-term damage caused by disappointing customers.

There are kinds of interest which contract law is simply not equipped to consider. Take, for example, a situation where a rich environmentalist, Sue, makes a contract with a farmer, Giles, under which she pays him not to tear up the hedgerows around the farm. What if Giles pulls up the hedges anyway? Sue could probably get her money back, but she has made the contract in order to protect the environment; not only will no damages be payable, as she has suffered no financial loss, but also no damages could restore the position that would have existed had the contract been performed.

The law of contract needs to recognise that consumers tend to contract for reasons other than financial profit, so that remedies which focus entirely on their loss of economic bargain are inadequate.

### Practicalities

Even where the available remedies would provide an adequate solution, there are many situations in which it is completely impractical for the claimant to make a claim, because the costs and/or time and effort involved in litigation are out of proportion to the amount that could be claimed. Because of this, it will frequently be obvious to a party considering breaching a contract that no action will be taken against them if they do, especially where they are the stronger party.

An additional problem is that, in many cases, the injured party does not know they have a right to claim. Even the considerable amount of consumer protection legislation enacted in recent years cannot protect a consumer who does not know what they are entitled to when buying goods or paying for a service.

## Limitation periods

The Law Commission has produced a report, *Limitation of Actions* (2001), in which it has highlighted problems with the current law on statutory time limits. For example, it can be difficult to determine which time limit applies to certain cases. The report recommends a single regime of limitation periods to apply to all claims. There would be a primary limitation period of three years from the date on which claimants knew or ought reasonably to have known the facts relevant to their case. The maximum time possible to bring a claim would normally be ten years from the date on which the relevant events took place. An exception to the maximum ten-year rule would be personal injury, where the three-year rule could be disapplied at the discretion of the court.

## Damages and profit

The decision of **Attorney General** v **Blake** has been criticised as working against the creation of wealth. There is a theory, developed by the academic Posner, which is known as the 'economic theory of efficient breach'. Under this theory, contracts are made to generate wealth. Parties contract on terms that give them a benefit over and above the cost of their performance. Occasionally there will be a change of circumstances, so that more wealth will be generated if the contract is not performed. This could be because one party might find someone else who is willing to pay considerably more for the goods that were to be sold under the contract, so that even after compensating the innocent contracting party they are left with a bigger profit. Under the theory of efficient breach, the defendant should only be required to compensate the innocent party for their loss, and should not be punished for non-performance by, for example, confiscating any profit made from their breach of contract. Such punishment would discourage the parties from generating further wealth. The traditional approach of contract law is therefore to give much greater weight to compensation and mitigation than to ensuring performance. The decision of **Attorney General** v **Blake** is considered to conflict with a healthy market economy. A counter-argument to this is that if the courts are prepared to calculate damages to take into account the wrongdoer's profit, the parties would be encouraged to reach a negotiated agreement for their mutual release from the contract, which would be on favourable terms for both parties.

In its report, *Aggravated, Exemplary and Restitutionary Damages* (1997), the Law Commission considered the question of damages when the contract breaker has profited from their breach. It came to the conclusion that the law in this area should be left to the courts rather than being developed by statute. They pointed out that it would be difficult to draw the distinction between 'innocent' breaches of contract and 'cynical' breaches which were based on the parties' own commercial reasons. Thus any legislative provisions based on this distinction would lead to greater uncertainty in the assessment of damages in commercial and consumer disputes. It would also be difficult to show which profits were a direct result of the breach of contract.

## Restitution

In its 1997 report, *Aggravated, Exemplary and Restitutionary Damages*, the Law Commission considered whether the remedy of restitution should be laid down in legislation. It rejected this suggestion, on the basis that this would 'freeze' the position. Instead, it recommended that the availability of such damages should be left to be developed by the common law. (Restitution was discussed at p. 374.)

# Answering questions

House owners in Larry's neighbourhood were very concerned that the value of their houses would be reduced by the poor state of repair of Larry's house and the appalling condition of his garden. Eventually, Mike, Larry's closest neighbour, promised to paint Larry's house if Larry would promise to repair the garden fence and tidy the garden. Larry agreed to do so. Knowing nothing of this agreement, Nazia, another neighbour, said that she would give Larry £200 towards house improvements if he repaired the garden fence and tidied the garden. Larry did the work on the fence and the garden but, by that time, Mike and Nazia had discovered what had happened. Mike refused to paint the house and Nazia refused to pay any money.

Mike arranged for Oz to demolish and rebuild his (Mike's) brick garage, making it bigger. The day before the work was due to begin, a gas canister stored in the garage exploded and reduced most of the garage to rubble. Mike had previously mentioned to his wife that he thought he could smell gas but he had then put it out of his mind. Mike told Oz that he no longer wanted him to do any work because he proposed simply to create a covered car port. Oz was furious because he had already spent £500 buying materials and hiring equipment, and had turned down another job on which he could have made a profit of about £800.

(a) Consider whether Larry has any legal rights and remedies against Mike and Nazia. *(25 marks)*

(b) Taking account of the rules on termination of contracts by frustration and by breach, consider the rights, duties and remedies of Mike and Oz in connection with the work on the garage. *(25 marks)*

(c) Outline and critically evaluate the rules in any one of the three vitiating factors in contract (mistake, misrepresentation, duress/undue influence). *(25 marks)* AQA

(a) The agreement between Larry and Mike would appear to have the main ingredients for a binding contract: offer, acceptance and consideration. The main issue would be whether there was an intention to create legal relations. The courts would have to decide whether this was a social/domestic agreement to which there is a presumption that the parties do not intend to create legal relations and, if so, whether this presumption had been rebutted.

As regards the agreement between Larry and Nazia, again there appears to be an offer and acceptance but on these facts there could be a problem both with the existence of an intention to create legal relations and with the existence of consideration. The problem with consideration is that Larry has merely promised to do something which he had already promised to do for Mike. This raises issues about the sufficiency of the consideration (see p. 96), and the cases on consideration where there is an existing contractual duty to a third party (see p. 104) could be examined.

If there was a binding contract with Mike or Nazia, then breach of that contract would give rise to a remedy of damages. The remedy of specific performance is unlikely to be ordered (see p. 378).

(b) Mike would seek to argue that the contract had been frustrated by the gas explosion. But, the doctrine of frustration will not apply if it was Mike's fault that the explosion occurred (see pp. 321–2), and note that Mike had smelt gas on an earlier occasion – or if it is still possible for Oz to perform most of the contract, since his agreement was not just to demolish the garage but also to rebuild it.

If the explosion did amount to a frustrating event, then the contract would cease to exist and the Law Reform (Frustrated Contracts) Act 1943 would apply. Under this Act Oz would only be able to reclaim the expenses he had incurred if Mike was already due to have paid some money in advance (s. 1(2)); in which case, these expenses could be deducted from that advance.

If there was no frustration, then Mike's refusal to proceed with the contract would amount to a breach. Oz could then seek a remedy of damages. This would compensate him for the expenses he had already incurred. Whether the missed opportunity to earn £800 from the alternative contract would be recoverable would depend on whether or not this was too remote (see p. 351).

(c) To answer this question you are asked both to outline and to critically evaluate the rules of one of the three vitiating factors. Thus you are required both to outline the law on the subject and to provide some critical analysis. For a critical analysis of mistake you could discuss the case of **Shogun Finance**, the impact of an objective interpretation of the contract, the difficulties in determining what is a fundamental mistake, and the role of equity.

On misrepresentation, you could comment on the complicated distinction between the different types of misrepresentation and the reduced importance of this distinction for the purposes of remedies. You could also discuss the complexities in determining the award of damages according to the type of misrepresentation that has occurred.

On duress and undue influence you could consider how far the law is achieving justice for the parties, looking at the facts of the cases, and considering the position of married women.

---

 Anne-Marie, a joiner, decides to set up her own business. She contracts with John, a builder, to convert her garage into a workshop. The price is £10,000, and the work is to be completed by 1 March. However, problems with labour and materials mean that John does not finish the work until 1 June. Anne-Marie now wants to know whether she can claim damages to cover:

(a) The loss of profit from cancelled joinery jobs for the period between March and June.

(b) The loss of a special contract she had with a local stately home, to make rather expensive shelving for its library.

(c) The mental distress which Anne-Marie's inability to get her business up and running has caused to Anne-Marie and her husband Trevor.

 (a) The question here is whether the loss of profit was something that would arise naturally from the breach, or which 'may reasonably be supposed to have been within the contemplation of the parties at the time when they made the contract' (**Hadley** v **Baxendale**). If the loss falls within this principle, Anne-Marie can claim damages to put her in the position she would have been in had the contract been performed as agreed, which would cover her lost profit.

(b) The cases to consider here are **Victoria Laundry** and *The Heron II*. John will be liable if he knew about the contract with the stately home, or if Anne-Marie's losses through losing the contract were reasonably foreseeable as liable to result from his breach, but not if he is only aware that there is a remote possibility of such a loss.

(c) Here Anne-Marie has little chance of an award for the distress, for three reasons. First, the rule of privity prevents her from claiming for any loss to Trevor, and none of the exceptions to the rule seem to apply here. Secondly, damages for mental distress have so far been confined to cases where peace of mind or enjoyment are the object of the contract, such as **Jackson**. Thirdly, it was specifically stated in **Addis** *v* **Gramophone** that damages for mental distress are not available in commercial contracts; since both John and Anne-Marie are acting for the purposes of their businesses, this would seem to be a commercial contract.

---

Analyse the factors the courts will take into account when awarding damages for breach of a contract, where there is no provision for this in the contract. *Oxford*

The material you need to answer this question is primarily contained in this chapter (see pp. 346–73) and you could follow the same structure for your answer.

You are asked to analyse the law and should therefore take a critical approach, evaluating the current law in the field. You might point out that the law attempts to strike a balance between adequately compensating the claimant and imposing an unfair burden on the defendant, and show how the cases on remoteness of damage and mitigation have achieved this balance. You should highlight any problems with the case law – you may feel, for example, that the rules on damages for mental distress are too harsh, and cite the case of **Addis** *v* **Gramophone Co Ltd**. You could also highlight the problems with contractual remedies (as discussed at p. 385).

---

Amy knew that her friend Claire was thinking of buying a new sofa and armchairs, so she said to her, 'Are you going to sell the ones you already have? If so, I could pay you £100 for them.' Claire said she would think about it. Two weeks later, not having seen or spoken to Amy, who was not on the telephone, Claire posted a short note to Amy which read, 'I am having new furniture delivered tomorrow and I want to take you up on your suggestion that you pay me £100 for my existing sofa and armchairs. Please give me a ring so that we can make the arrangements.'

Shortly after returning from posting the note, Claire received a letter in the post from Amy which informed her that she had gone away for a few days but that, before she did so, she had been able to buy a new sofa and armchairs at a bargain price from a local store.

In fact, when Amy returned home after a three-week holiday, she discovered that the furniture that she had bought in a sale from Princeway Stores was lumpy and uncomfortable, that the material was slightly frayed at the bottom of the back of the sofa, and that there were slight variations in colour between the two armchairs. When she complained to Princeway Stores, she was reminded of the prominent notices displayed on the walls of the store which read, 'No refunds on any sale items'.

(a) Explain the relevant rules on the formation of contracts and apply those rules to determine whether a contract for the sale to Amy of Claire's furniture ever came into existence. *(10 marks)*

(b) Amy made a contract with Princeway Stores for the purchase of the furniture in the sale. Explain what obligations are placed on Princeway Stores under that contract and consider whether any have been broken. *(10 marks)*

(c) Assuming that Amy and Claire had a contract which Amy would not fulfil and that Princeway Stores was in breach of its obligations to Amy, discuss what remedies might be available to Claire against Amy and to Amy against Princeway Stores. In your answer, discuss the effect of the notice displayed in the store. *(10 marks)*

(d) Compare the respective merits of legislation and case law as mechanisms for changing rules of law such as those in contract. *(10 marks)*

(e) How far would you agree that the law has now succeeded in overcoming the problems formerly created by inequalities in bargaining power between parties to contracts? *(10 marks)* *AQA*

 This question covers material from across this book, including issues from the next chapter. Each sub-part of this question will be considered in turn.

(a) A discussion was required of the rules of offer, acceptance and an intention to create legal relations (which were discussed in Chapters 1 and 3). The important thing for a question like this is to have recognised the relevant issues, and to have applied the law logically to the facts. The actual conclusion that is reached as to the existence or absence of a contract is less important, as a court could have reached either conclusion.

On the issue of offer and acceptance, you needed to consider whether Amy's suggestion that she could pay £100 for Claire's furniture was an offer or merely some preliminary stage of negotiation, known as an invitation to treat. If a court did regard it as an offer, it would have to decide whether it remained in existence after two weeks so as to be capable of valid acceptance. No time was specified for how long the offer would remain open, so it would be treated as continuing for a reasonable length of time. As in this instance the offer was concerned with the purchase of non-perishable goods any offer is likely to be treated as still in existence after two weeks. If a court treated Amy's suggestion as an offer and found that it was still in existence after two weeks, the next issue is whether it was validly accepted before Claire received Amy's letter which made it clear that she was no longer interested in buying Claire's furniture. You would need to consider the postal rule, and the fact that under cases such as **Byrne** *v* **Van Tienhoven**, where an acceptance has been posted before a revocation has been received, the acceptance will be binding.

In relation to the requirement of an intention to create legal relations, on the one hand the friendship between Amy and Claire and the probable social occasion on which any offer was made would suggest an initial presumption against such intention. On the other hand, the subject matter of the deal and the apparent seriousness of both parties at various stages of the process offered powerful evidence in rebuttal.

You are asked to discuss only the 'relevant' rules on formation of a contract, and thus only a passing mention needs to be made of the rules of consideration, privity and capacity.

(b) The main issues raised in this part of the question are dealt with in the next chapter. The important obligations placed on Princeway Stores in relation to Amy's purchase of furniture are implied into the contract by the Sale of Goods Act 1979, as amended by the Sale and Supply of Goods Act 1994. So the contract would be subject to terms as to description (s. 13), satisfactory quality (s. 14(2)) and fitness for purpose (s. 14(3)). On whether any of these terms had been broken, it is unlikely that the term as to description had been infringed or that Amy's perception that the furniture was 'lumpy and uncomfortable' was sufficient to render it not fit for its purpose. On the other hand, it might have been argued that the furniture was not of satisfactory quality in view of the fraying of the material and the colour variations, though this would have to be considered in the context that these defects may have been the reason for the 'bargain' price.

(c) To answer this part of the question a distinction should be drawn between the remedies available to Claire and those available to Amy. Claire's remedy would lie in common law for damages, there being no apparent reason why a claim for specific performance should be entertained by a court. The measure of damages awarded would be the difference between what Amy had offered and the price at which Claire could now sell.

By contrast, Amy's remedies against Princeway Stores would have stemmed from the Sale of Goods Act 1979, discussed in the next chapter, and would thus have included rejection, damages, repair, replacement, a price reduction or a full refund. The remedy of rejection will no longer be available if there has been acceptance through use of the furniture or through a lapse in time. The measure of damages in this context would be the difference between the value of the goods contracted for and those actually supplied. Even if the notices displayed on the wall of the shop were found to contain a term incorporated into the contract in accordance with the common law requirements of notice, they would be ineffective owing to the Unfair Contract Terms Act 1977.

(d) This question goes beyond the scope of this book, and is covered by the authors' book on the English legal system. Advantages of legislation include the fact that it is the product of a democratic process that takes place in public, with the possibility of a wide input of information, consultation and advice. The danger is of delays and the problems with interpreting the legislation when it needs to be applied to particular situations. Case law has the advantage of responding directly to problems occurring, and is flexible, providing scope to be adapted gradually to particular circumstances. On the other hand, case law is the product of an unelected judiciary, is dependent on relevant litigation to arise for its development and can produce uncertainty.

(e) Material to answer this question can be found in the introduction to this book. Your point could be illustrated by reference to the consumer protection legislation, such as the Sale of Goods Act 1979 (and amendments), the Supply of Goods and Services Act 1982, the Consumer Protection Act 1987, the Unfair Contract Terms Act 1977 and the 1999 Regulations. You could also discuss the common law attempts to control the use of exemption clauses – the rules on incorporation, restrictive interpretation and the development of devices such as fundamental breach. You could consider the law in relation to minors and the law on duress and undue influence.

Drawing from English legal system material, you could discuss issues concerning access to justice (cost, delays, small claims arbitration, state funding, etc.) as rights and remedies are of no practical significance if parties are effectively denied access to them.

---

Harry had recently opened a fitness centre and was still trying to improve his stock of fitness machines. He knew that his friend, Jim, the manager of another fitness centre, had a spare step-machine and he asked him how much he would sell it for. Jim said, 'Probably £700.' The next day, Harry telephoned Jim's home and left a message on his answering machine saying, 'I will give you £650. No need to reply if that is all right. I will pick it up next week.' Jim kept the machine for Harry and so he was very annoyed when, two weeks later, Harry told him that he had changed his mind and did not want it after all.

Harry agreed with Kevin that Kevin would service all the machines for an annual fee of £5,000. The written contract stated that Kevin would service and repair any machine within 48 hours of being requested to do so, or would supply a replacement. During the first three months, Kevin twice took 55 hours to return machines and did not supply a replacement on either occasion. Harry terminated the contract with Kevin and demanded the return of the £5,000 fee.

(a) Consider whether there is a contract between Harry and Jim for the purchase of the step-machine. Assuming there is a contract, discuss what remedy Jim may pursue. *(25 marks)*

(b) Consider the rights, duties and remedies of Harry and Kevin in connection with the terms of the agreement to service and repair the machines and Harry's decision to end the agreement. *(25 marks)*

(c) How satisfactory are the rules on formation of contracts? *AQA*

(a) Looking first at whether there is a binding contract between Harry and Jim, you need to break down the transaction into the legal concepts of invitation to treat, offer and acceptance. Harry starts the negotiations by asking how much Jim would sell his spare step-machine for. This is merely a request for information. Jim responds, 'Probably £700.' This is too uncertain to amount to an offer. An offer can be defined as a communication which indicates the terms on which the offeror is prepared to make a contract and gives a clear indication that the offeror intends to be bound by those terms if they are accepted by the offeree. The use of the word 'probably' means that the terms on which Jim is prepared to be bound are not certain and he does not appear to intend to be bound by any acceptance. Instead of being an offer, this would be treated as an invitation to treat. You could refer to the cases of **Gibson** *v* **Manchester City Council** and **Harvey** *v* **Facey** to illustrate how the law has been applied in practice.

The next day Harry telephones Jim stating, 'I will give you £650. No need to reply if that is all right. I will pick it up next week.' This is an offer.

Jim then kept the machine for Harry and to determine whether this had led to the formation of a contract, you needed to consider the case of **Felthouse** *v* **Bindley**. In that case an uncle wrote to his nephew offering to pay £30 and 15 shillings, saying, 'If I hear no more about him, I consider the horse mine at that price.' The nephew was on the point of selling off some of his property in an auction. He did not reply to the uncle's letter, but did tell the auctioneer to keep the horse out of the sale. The auctioneer forgot to do this, and the horse was sold. It was held that there was no contract between the uncle and the nephew. The court felt that the nephew's conduct in trying to keep the horse out of the sale did not necessarily imply that he intended to accept his uncle's offer, and so it was not clear that his silence in response to the offer was intended to constitute acceptance.

In **Re Selectmove Ltd** the Court of Appeal stated that an acceptance by silence could be sufficient if it was the offeree who suggested that their silence would be enough to complete the contract.

On the facts before us, like **Felthouse** v **Bindley**, it is the offeror suggesting that silence will be sufficient and not the offeree. The question for the court will therefore be whether Jim has done enough to make it clear that he intended to accept the offer. He does not appear to have done any more than the nephew in **Felthouse** v **Bindley**, so a court is likely to find that he has not effectively accepted the offer and there is therefore no binding contract.

The question asks you to consider what remedies Jim would have if there had been a contract. The main remedy in contract law is damages. This is an award of money that aims to compensate the innocent party for the financial losses they have suffered as a result of the breach. The general rule is that innocent parties are entitled to such damages as will put them in the position they would have been in if the contract had been performed. Here Jim has suffered a pecuniary loss, which the courts are more willing to compensate than non-pecuniary losses.

When calculating the amount of damages to be awarded, three main restrictions apply: causation, remoteness and mitigation. On the issue of mitigation (p. 358), Jim will be required to mitigate his loss, so he cannot recover damages for losses which could have been avoided by taking reasonable steps. On these facts Jim will therefore be expected to have tried to secure an alternative sale of the step-machine. On the issue of remoteness (p. 351), he will only be able to claim for losses which are not too remote. The main question for the court will be whether any loss of profit will be compensable. The test to be applied was laid down in the case of *The Pegase*, which is whether

> the facts in question come to the defendant's knowledge in such circumstances that a reasonable person in the shoes of the defendant would, if he had considered the matter at the time of making the contract have contemplated that, in the event of a breach by him, such facts were to be taken into account when considering his responsibility for loss suffered by the plaintiff as a result of such breach.

The likely basis for the calculation of Jim's loss is his expectation (p. 359). This means that if he manages to sell the step-machine to a third party he will be compensated for the difference in price he received for the machine (the market price) and the £650 that Harry had promised to pay.

(b) Under the contract between Harry and Kevin, there is an express term that Kevin will service and repair any machine within 48 hours of being requested to do so or he would supply a replacement. Kevin has breached this term because on two occasions he has taken 55 hours to return machines and did not supply a replacement on either occasion. The effect of the breach will depend on the type of term that has been breached. Terms can be divided into three types: conditions, warranties and innominate terms (see p. 144).

A term which is clearly an important one, in the sense that a breach of it would have very significant consequences for the innocent party, will usually be regarded by the courts as a condition. Where a condition is breached, the innocent party is entitled to regard the contract as repudiated, and so need not render any further performance, and can also sue for damages. An example of a term deemed by the courts to be a condition can be found in **Bunge Corp** *v* **Tradax Export SA**.

The word 'warranty' usually describes a contractual term which can be broken without highly important consequences. If a warranty is breached the innocent party can sue for damages, but is not entitled to terminate the contract.

Innominate terms are terms which can be broken with either important or trivial consequences, depending on the nature of the breach. If the effects of the breach are serious, the term will act as a condition; if they are minor it acts as a warranty.

It will be up to the court to determine whether the contractual term broken in Harry and Kevin's contract was a condition, warranty or innominate term. The term has been broken in two ways: first, there has been delay and, secondly, no replacement machine has been provided. The effect of delay in performance will depend on whether the time of performance is considered to be 'of the essence' (see p. 317). If this is the case, then late performance will give rise to a right to terminate the contract. Where time is not of the essence, late performance will not justify termination unless it amounts to a substantial failure in performance. It is unlikely that time was of the essence for this type of contract.

(c) To answer this question you could look at the sections headed 'Problems with offer and acceptance', 'How important is intention to create legal relations' and 'Problems with consideration' in this chapter.

## Summary of Chapter 15

The remedies available to the innocent party in the event of a breach of contract can be divided into three categories: common law remedies, equitable remedies and remedies agreed by the parties.

### Common law remedies

All common law remedies are available as of right if a contract is breached.

### Damages

An award of damages is the usual remedy for a breach of contract. It is an award of money that aims to compensate the innocent party for the financial losses they have suffered as a result of the breach. The general rule is that innocent parties are entitled to such damages as will put them in the position they would have been in if the contract had been performed. When a contract is breached, a party may suffer pecuniary loss or non-pecuniary loss.

### Pecuniary loss

Damages aim to compensate the innocent party for their financial losses that result from not receiving the performance bargained for.

### Non-pecuniary loss

Damages for non-pecuniary losses are generally not recoverable in contract. Thus, damages for mental distress are not awarded in commercial contracts: **Addis** v **Gramophone Co Ltd** (1909). Recent cases have developed the principle that, in a limited number of situations, injury to feelings (generally called mental distress) and loss of amenity will be compensated. Such compensation is available where the contract's whole purpose was the provision of pleasure, relaxation and peace of mind (**Jarvis** v **Swans Tours Ltd** (1973)); where a major object of the contract was to provide pleasure, relaxation and peace of mind (**Farley** v **Skinner (No 2)** (2001)); and if the mental suffering is related to physical inconvenience and discomfort caused by the breach of the contract.

### Limitations on awards of damages

The general rule is that innocent parties are entitled to such damages as will put them in the position they would have been in if the contract had been performed, but there are three limitations, which will be considered under the headings of causation, remoteness and mitigation.

#### Causation

A person will only be liable for losses caused by their breach of contract. The defendant's breach need not be the sole cause of the claimant's losses, but it must be an effective cause of their loss.

#### Remoteness

There are some losses which clearly result from the defendant's breach of contract, but are considered too remote from the breach for it to be fair to expect the defendant to compensate the claimant for them. The rules concerning remoteness were originally laid down in **Hadley** v **Baxendale** (1854). The court laid down two situations where the defendant should be liable for loss caused by a breach of contract:

1 Loss which would arise naturally, 'according to the usual course of things', from their breach.
2 Loss 'as may reasonably be supposed to have been in the contemplation of the parties at the time when they made the contract, as the probable result of the breach of it'.

The approach in **Hadley** v **Baxendale** was reaffirmed in **Victoria Laundry (Windsor) Ltd** v **Newman Industries Ltd** (1949) and then discussed again by the House of Lords in *The Heron II* (1969).

#### Mitigation

Claimants are under a duty to mitigate their loss, and cannot recover damages for losses which could have been avoided by taking reasonable steps.

### Calculating loss

There are two main ways in which the losses of a claimant in a contract action can be calculated: the loss of expectation, and the reliance loss.

#### Loss of expectation

Where loss of expectation is the basis for calculating damages, the courts aim to put claimants in the position they would have been in if the contract had been performed. Thus, the parties would have expected a certain result from the performance of the contract and the damages will compensate for the loss of this expectation.

### Reliance loss

Where reliance loss is the basis for calculating damages, the damages seek to put claimants in the position they were in before the contract was made. The damages will therefore compensate for the actual wasted expenditure and other losses incurred because of the contract which has been breached.

### Choosing between the expectation and reliance principles

As a rule, a claimant can choose whether to base a claim on loss of expectation or on reliance. In practice, loss of expectation is the usual basis for calculating contract damages. There are two main restrictions on the claimant's choice between the expectation and the reliance principles. These are the bad bargain rule and the speculative damages rule.

- *Bad bargain rule*: if the claimant would have made a loss from the contract, then he or she will only be entitled to nominal damages, and will not be entitled to claim their expenses on the basis of reliance loss.
- *Expectation losses are 'too speculative'*: the reliance basis for calculating damages must be used where it is virtually impossible to calculate what profit the claimant would have made if the contract had been performed correctly.

## Quantifying the expectation loss

Contract damages based on expectation loss are essentially seeking to compensate the difference in value between the promised performance and the actual performance.

### The market price rule

Where a contract has been breached, the law assumes that the wronged party will immediately mitigate their loss by buying similar goods which they had contracted for from another source or selling the goods which they had contracted to sell to another source. The buyer's damages will therefore be assessed by subtracting the contract price from the market price at the time of breach. The market price rule will not be used as the measure of loss either where there is no available market or where, in the circumstances, the non-breaching party is not expected to avail itself of the market to mitigate its loss.

### Cost of cure

Cost of cure damages will only be awarded where this would be reasonable. They will not be awarded where they would be out of all proportion to the consequences of the breach and there is a risk of unjust enrichment if the claimant is awarded cost of cure damages but then does not use the money to remedy the breach: **Ruxley Electronics and Construction Ltd v Forsyth** (1995).

### Loss of opportunity damages

The loss of an opportunity is recoverable in damages if the lost chance is quantifiable in monetary terms and there was a substantial chance that the opportunity might have come to fruition. Otherwise, the loss of opportunity will be treated as too speculative.

### Tax

Where a claimant's claim includes money on which they would have had to pay income tax if it were earned by performing the contract, the amount of tax payable can be deducted from the damages.

### Profit made by the defendant

When calculating damages, the courts have traditionally not taken into account any profit the party in breach has made by breaking the contract, only the loss caused to the innocent party. In the most recent cases, the courts now appear to be willing to compensate for a loss of profit in exceptional cases. In deciding whether to compensate for a loss of profit, the courts have drawn a distinction between where defendants are ordered to hand over part of their profits, and where they are ordered to hand over all their profit (**Attorney General** v **Blake** (2000)). The court will now sometimes order the former, but only in very exceptional circumstances order the latter.

## Action for an agreed sum

Where a contract specifies a price to be paid for performance, and payment has not been made, the party who has performed can claim the money owed by means of an action for the agreed sum. This is a claim for a debt and not a claim for damages. The claimant is not seeking compensation, but simply enforcement of the defendant's promise to pay.

## Restitution

Restitution is the remedy available when there has been unjust enrichment. Where money has been paid under a contract, or purported contract, and performance has not been received in return, or has not been adequate, the payer may want to claim the money back, rather than claiming damages. Traditionally, contract remedies and restitution do not overlap. In practice, restitution will therefore be available if there is no contract. There may be no contract for one of the following reasons:

- a contract has not been made (e.g. because of a lack of agreement, uncertainty or the absence of consideration);
- the contract has been discharged; or
- the contract was void (e.g. because of illegality).

### Quantum meruit

Where work has been done or goods supplied but no payment has been received and cannot be obtained under a contract, an action is available, called a *quantum meruit*, under which claimants can claim a reasonable price for their performance.

## Equitable remedies

Equitable remedies are provided at the discretion of the court.

## Specific performance

An order of specific performance is a court order compelling someone to perform their obligations under a contract. Specific performance is only granted where damages alone would be an inadequate remedy. A court will not order specific performance to cases where it could cause a party great hardship or unfairness. Specific performance will be refused where a contract has been obtained by unfair means.

### Contracts unsuitable for specific performance

Some types of contract are, by their nature, unlikely to be the subject of an order for specific performance. The two main types are contracts requiring personal services and contracts which involve continuous duties. Specific performance will not be applied to a contract which is vague as to the performance required, nor to a promise which is only supported by nominal consideration or contained in a deed. It is not used where a contract allows the party concerned to terminate it. Specific performance will not usually be ordered against a defendant if it could not have been ordered against the claimant, had they been the one in breach, because of the principle of mutuality.

## Injunction

An injunction normally orders the defendant not to do a particular thing.

## Remedies agreed by the parties

Many contracts specify the kinds of breach which will justify termination, and/or the damages to be paid by each party in the event of certain types of breach. There are two types of contract clauses concerning damages: liquidated damages clauses and penalty clauses.

## Liquidated damages

Liquidated damages is the term used where a contract specifies the amount of damages to be paid in the event of breach, and this amount represents a genuine attempt to work out what the loss would be in the event of such a breach.

## Penalty clauses

If a contract states that a particular sum is to be paid on breach of the contract, and that sum is not a genuine pre-estimate of the loss that would be suffered in the event of breach, but is designed instead to threaten to penalise a party in breach, this is a penalty clause. Where the damages laid down in a contract amount to a penalty clause, the clause will be found to be invalid and the award of damages will be determined by the ordinary principles of contract law instead: **Dunlop Pneumatic Tyre Co Ltd** *v* **New Garage & Motor Co Ltd** (1915).

## Extinction of remedies

Where one party has a right of action for breach of contract, this right may be extinguished by agreement between the parties, either by a release under seal or by accord and satisfaction. Such a right can also be extinguished by the passage of time, under the Limitation Act 1980.

# Reading list

Bridge, 'Mitigation of damages in contract and the meaning of avoidable loss' (1989) 105 Law Quarterly Review 38

Brodie, 'Specific performance and employment contracts' (1998) 27 Industrial Law Journal 37

Campbell and Harris, 'In defence of breach: a critique of restitution and the performance interest' (2002) 22 Legal Studies 208

Chen-Wishart, 'Restitutionary damages for breach of contract' (1998) 114 Law Quarterly Review 363

Coote, 'Contract damages, *Ruxley* and the performance interest' (1997) Cambridge Law Journal 537

Cunnington, 'The assessment of gain-based damages for breach of contract' (2008) 71 Modern Law Review 559

Enonchong, 'Breach of contract and damages for mental distress' (1996) 16 Oxford Journal of Legal Studies 617

Friedman, 'The performance interest in contract damages' (1995) 111 Law Quarterly Review 628

Johnson, 'A sword and a shield: there is a growing trend for courts to make awards of exemplary damages in civil claims where fraud is proven' (2013) 163 New Law Journal 6

Lee, 'Contractual Interpretation and Remoteness' (2010) Lloyd's Maritime and Commercial Law Quarterly 150

Loke, 'Cost of cure or difference in market value? Towards a sound choice in the basis for quantifying expectation damages' (1996) 10 Journal of Contract Law 189

McKendrick, 'Breach of contract and the meaning of loss' (1999) 52 Current Legal Problems 37

Pearce and Halson, 'Damages for breach of contract: compensation, restitution and vindication' (2008) Oxford Journal of Legal Studies 73

Phang, 'The crumbling edifice? The award of contractual damages for mental distress' (2003) Journal of Business Law 341

Robertson, 'The basis of the remoteness rule in contract' (2008) 28 Legal Studies 172

Rowan, 'Reflections on the Introduction of Punitive Damages for Breach of Contract' (2010) 30 Oxford Journal of Legal Studies 495

Rowan, 'For the Recognition of Remedial Terms Agreed Inter Partes' (2010) 126 Law Quarterly Review 448

Unberath, 'Third party losses and black holes: another view' (1999) 115 Law Quarterly Review 535

Wallace, 'Third party damage: no legal black hole?' (1999) 115 Law Quarterly Review 394

Weaver, 'The mane line: what remedy, if any, might be available to consumers duped into eating horsemeat?' (2013) 163 New Law Journal 27

## Reading on the internet

The Law Commission report *Aggravated, Exemplary and Restitutionary Damages* (1997) is available on its website at:

http://www.lawcom.gov.uk/docs/lc247.pdf

The Law Commission report *Compound Interest* (2004) is available on its website at:

http://www.lawcom.gov.uk/docs/lc287.pdf

The House of Lords' judgment of **Farley v Skinner (No 2)** (2001) is available at:

http://www.publications.parliament.uk/pa/ld200102/ldjudgmt/jd011011/farley-1.htm

The House of Lords' judgment of **Attorney General v Blake** (1999) is available at:

http://www.publications.parliament.uk/pa/ld199900/ldjudgmt/jd000727/blake-1.htm

The Law Commission report *Limitation of Actions* (2001) is available on its website at:

http://www.lawcom.gov.uk/docs/lc270(2).pdf

# Part 6
## Consumer protection

Although the common law principles of the law of contract (covering issues such as offer and acceptance, consideration and vitiating factors) apply to all contracts, in recent years there has been increasing intervention by Parliament in certain types of contract, with the result that many are now covered by special rules governing both the way in which they are made and the terms they may include. The three most important types of contract in which Parliament has intervened in this way are employment, landlord and tenant, and consumer contracts; the third is the subject of this chapter. These are the kind of contracts we make when, as an ordinary individual, we buy or hire goods, or pay to have services, such as plumbing or hairdressing, done for us.

The reason for intervention in consumer contracts is a move away from the traditional idea that the parties should be left to negotiate the best possible bargain for themselves, and a recognition that in many modern situations ordinary consumers will be contracting with large, powerful organisations and effectively have no power to negotiate a favourable deal, or sometimes even a fair one. An example of this is the standard form contract offered when you engage in many common transactions, from hiring a car to having clothes dry-cleaned. Often, roughly the same form will be used by all the businesses in a particular industry, and, if unregulated, they have the potential to remove choice from the purchaser, the only options being to contract on those terms or not at all.

# Chapter 16
## Consumer contracts

### This chapter explains:

that since the 1960s Parliament has passed a series of Acts designed to promote the interests of consumers. This chapter discusses:

- contracts for the sale of goods and the impact of the Sale of Goods Act 1979;
- contracts for the supply of services;
- hire contracts;
- the direct liability of manufacturers to consumers;
- restrictions on companies seeking payment for unsolicited goods or services; and
- consumer credit.

# History

Recognition that consumers could be at a disadvantage in contracting with businesses came as early as the nineteenth century. The courts began to imply terms into contracts, especially those for the sale of goods, which made sure the buyer got a fair deal, by, for example, requiring that the goods were fit for their purpose. Unfortunately, the fact that businesses were richer and more powerful than their consumers also meant that they had access to good lawyers, and as fast as the courts found terms to imply into contracts, businesses found ways to draw up contracts excluding themselves from those liabilities.

In 1893 the first Sale of Goods Act was passed, but it merely codified the existing case law and, by the twentieth century, it was clear that more drastic action was needed. The supply of goods and services was by then largely dominated by big companies, who were able to draw up contracts which were extremely favourable to themselves; the consumer had the choice of buying goods and services on those terms or not at all, since even competitor companies would be offering much the same terms. The courts attempted to curtail the power of companies by construing contracts strictly against them, and finding ways round the various exclusion clauses, but it was clear by this time that the common law simply could not provide adequate protection for consumers.

As a result, since the 1960s, Parliament has passed a series of Acts designed to protect the interest of consumers, including the Consumer Protection Act 1961, the Trade Descriptions Act 1968, the Consumer Credit Act 1974, the Unfair Contract Terms Act 1977, the Consumer Safety Act 1978 and the Consumer Safety (Amendment) Act 1986, the Sale of Goods Act 1979, the Supply of Goods and Services Act 1982 and the Sale and Supply of Goods Act 1994. More recently, the European Union has been concerned to harmonise consumer law in the different member states, to facilitate trade across Europe. All of this legislation aims, in varying ways, to even out the balance of power in contracts by providing protection for the individual.

# Contracts for the sale of goods

These are largely covered by the Sale of Goods Act 1979, as amended by the Sale and Supply of Goods Act 1994 and the Sale and Supply of Goods to Consumers Regulations 2002. The Regulations implement the Directive on Certain Aspects of the Sale of Consumer Goods and Associated Guarantees 1999. This Directive was issued by the European Union to try to harmonise the basic provision of consumer protection across Europe. Section 2(1) of the 1979 Act defines a sale of goods contract as one 'by which the seller transfers or agrees to transfer the property in goods to the buyer for a money consideration, called the price'. Thus the Act applies only to goods sold for money and does not cover other kinds of transaction such as the swapping or exchanging of goods.

'Goods' has been interpreted broadly. It has been held to include packaging surrounding goods and instructions appearing on the packaging. It does not cover services, which are covered by the Supply of Goods and Services Act 1982 (see p. 412 below). In **Southwark LBC v IBM UK Ltd** (2011) the High Court held that a contract for the purchase of software did not come within the Act. The software could not be described as goods and there was no transfer of property as required in s. 2(1). If software is sold through a physical medium, for example on a CD, then it might come within the Act, but not if it is sold online.

## In the course of a business

Certain provisions of the 1979 Act apply only when goods are sold 'in the course of a business'. Difficulties have arisen in determining when a sale is in the course of a business. There is clearly a range of different types of sale transactions. At one end of the spectrum is a sale by a retail organisation, like a supermarket selling eggs and cheese, or a clothes shop selling a pair of trousers. There has never been any doubt that such a sale is in the course of a business. At the other end of the spectrum is a purely private sale by a member of the public, like the sale of a private car through an advertisement in the local newspaper. There has never been any doubt that this sort of sale is not in the course of a business and the relevant protections in the Sale of Goods Act 1979 do not apply.

In the middle of the spectrum are sales of goods by a business, where the sale does not fall within the normal business activity of the company. Is this a sale in the course of a business or not? For example, if a solicitors' firm has some old computers that it no longer needs and decides to sell them, is this sale in the course of a business or not? Following the decision of the Court of Appeal in **Stevenson** v **Rogers** (1999), this type of case is now clearly caught by the wording 'in the course of a business'.

### Key Case    Stevenson v Rogers

The defendant in **Stevenson** v **Rogers** was in business as a fisherman. In 1988 he sold his only fishing boat, *The Jelle*, to the claimant and replaced it with *The Marilyn Jane*. The claimant was dissatisfied with *The Jelle* and brought an action against the defendant, complaining that he was in breach of the implied term, incorporated into the sale contract by s. 14(2) of the Sale of Goods Act 1979, that the boat should be of 'merchantable quality' (the contract was made before the 1994 Act came into force, replacing the test of 'merchantable quality' with that of 'satisfactory quality' discussed at p. 406). The implied term only applied to a sale of goods made by the seller 'in the course of a business'. So, as a preliminary issue, the Court of Appeal was required to decide whether the sale of *The Jelle* was made in the course of Rogers's business as a fisherman.

The court gave the phrase a very wide scope, in order to impose as few limitations as possible on the remedies available to a person buying goods as a consumer. It looked at the legislative history of the Sale of Goods Act 1979, including the relevant Law Commission Report and the parliamentary statements and debates recorded in Hansard at the time it was enacted. The court decided that the wording 'in the course of a business' was intended to have a wider meaning than the narrower wording found in earlier versions of the Act, and was thus intended to catch all sales of goods made by businesses, whether or not the sale of such goods was the regular trade of that business. The expression 'in the course of a business' in s. 14 of the Sale of Goods Act did not require any regularity of dealing, or indeed any previous dealing at all. It considered that it was the intention of the legislators that a broad construction should be applied to s. 14, so as to reflect the emphasis on consumer protection which underlies the more recent reforms. It concluded that the sale by the defendant was made in the course of a business and, accordingly, was subject to the implied term as to merchantable quality.

#### Legal Principle
The phrase 'in the course of a business' used in the Sale of Goods Act 1979 refers to all sales of goods made by businesses, whether or not the sale of such goods was in the regular trade of that business.

## Implied terms in contracts for the sale of goods

Whatever the terms agreed by the parties under the Sale of Goods Act 1979, a set of terms concerning the goods is implied into all contracts covered by the Act.

### Title

Under s. 12(1) of the 1979 Act, a condition is implied into any contract for the sale of goods that the seller has a right to sell the goods and is able to pass good title to the buyer. A breach of this condition amounts to a total failure of consideration and the buyer may claim back the price of the goods, even if they have been used for some time.

### Sale by description

Section 13(1) of the 1979 Act states that 'where there is a contract for the sale of goods by description, there is an implied condition that the goods will correspond with the description'.

Sale by description in practice covers all but a minority of transactions, where the parties agree on a specific article without describing it in any way – such as, for example, offering to sell 'my car', without specifying its make, age or colour. Section 13(3) specifies that goods sold by self-selection, as in a supermarket, are included within the category of sales by description (on the basis that they are usually labelled in some way).

In **Beale** *v* **Taylor** (1967) the claimant responded to an advertisement for a 'Herald, convertible, white 1961'. On going to inspect the car, he noticed on the back a disc marked '1200'. In fact the car consisted of the rear of a 1961 Herald 1200 welded to the front part of an older model. The Court of Appeal held that the advertisement and disc together constituted a sale by description and, as the vehicle clearly did not conform to this description, there was a breach of s. 13.

The potential strictness of s. 13 can be seen in **Re Moore & Co Ltd and Landauer & Co** (1921) (see p. 315), where a seller was entitled to reject goods which did not comply with their description, even though that fact caused him no hardship at all and there was no defect in the goods.

In many cases, the implied term as to description will also be an express term of the contract. If you buy a sweater which you are told is cashmere, that is likely to become an express term of the contract, alongside the implied term that the goods correspond with that description.

As s. 13 is not limited to sales 'in the course of a business' it can apply to private sales.

### Satisfactory quality

Under s. 14(2) goods sold in the course of a business should be of 'satisfactory quality'. In the past the statute had required the goods to be of 'merchantable quality' but this phrase was considered to be too imprecise. Goods are of a satisfactory quality if they 'meet the standard that a reasonable person would regard as satisfactory', taking account of any description of the goods, the price (if relevant) and all the other relevant circumstances. Where the buyer deals as a consumer, these relevant circumstances 'include any public statements on the specific characteristics of the goods made about them by the seller, the producer, or his representative, particularly in advertising or in labelling'. Sellers can avoid liability for nonconformity with these public statements, if they can show that, when the contract was made:

- they neither knew nor could reasonably have been aware of the statement;
- the statement had, before the contract was made, been publicly withdrawn or corrected; or
- the decision to buy the goods could not have been influenced by the particular statement.

The quality of the goods takes into account their state and condition, fitness for all the purposes for which goods of that kind are commonly supplied, appearance and finish, freedom from minor defects, safety and durability.

Because the price of the goods can be relevant in determining whether the goods are of a satisfactory quality, there is not a single standard that will be required, for example, for all dishwashers. Instead, the standard required may vary according to the price of the dishwasher. The more expensive the dishwasher, the higher the standard that may be required to satisfy the Sale of Goods Act. The claimant in **Clegg** v **Andersson** (2003) had bought a yacht for £236,000. The yacht's keel was heavier than expected. He rejected the boat and sought the return of his money on the basis that the boat was not of satisfactory quality. The Court of Appeal allowed his claim because it was not sufficient that the boat was fit for its purpose (it could still sail); it was not of a satisfactory quality given the price that had been paid. A purchaser of expensive goods was entitled to expect a high quality product, free from even minor defects.

The requirement of satisfactory quality will not apply where any defect or other matter is specifically drawn to the buyer's attention before the contract is made, or which ought to have been revealed by the buyer's own examination of the goods. There is no obligation for a purchaser to examine the goods, and a cursory look at them – without opening the packaging, for example – is not expected to reveal defects. On the other hand, where a purchaser does examine the goods before buying, any defects he or she should have spotted will not be covered by the implied condition on satisfactory quality. In **Bramhill** v **Edwards** (2004) Mr and Mrs Bramhill had bought a motorhome from Mr Edwards, a second-hand dealer. When buying the vehicle, they had inspected it and commented that it felt very spacious inside. After they had bought the vehicle they discovered that it measured 102 inches wide, when UK law provided that vehicles must be no wider than 100 inches. They subsequently sought to reject the motorhome. One of the reasons why their action was unsuccessful was that the Court of Appeal held that they should

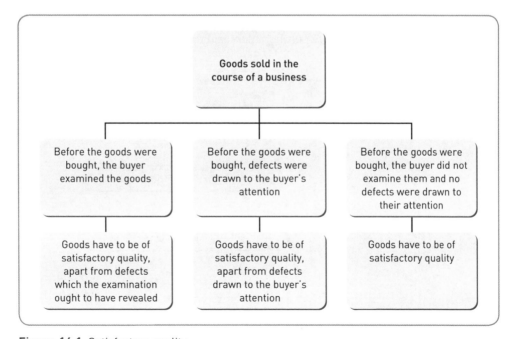

**Figure 16.1** Satisfactory quality

have measured the vehicle before purchasing it, as they knew of the UK legislation concerning the maximum width of such vehicles.

The implied term on satisfactory quality only applies to sales in the course of a business, and so not to private sales (see p. 405).

## Fitness for purpose

Section 14(3) of the Sale of Goods Act 1979 states:

> where the seller sells goods in the course of a business and the buyer, expressly or by implication, makes known . . . to the seller . . . any particular purpose for which the goods are being bought, there is an implied condition that the goods supplied under the contract are reasonably fit for that purpose, whether or not that is a purpose for which such goods are commonly supplied, except where the circumstances show that the buyer does not rely, or that it is unreasonable for him to rely on the skill or judgment of the seller.

This subsection basically means that if a buyer tells the seller the goods are required for a particular purpose, and the seller goes ahead and sells them, they must be fit for that purpose, even if it is an unusual one. So if you buy a very large raincoat, telling the seller you want it for your pet elephant, it must be able to stand up to the strains of such a use, unless it is clear that in making your choice you were not relying on the seller's advice.

For the section to apply, the buyer must make known any special purpose for which the goods are to be used. In **Griffiths** v **Peter Conway Ltd** (1939) a woman with abnormally sensitive skin developed dermatitis as a result of wearing a tweed coat. She sued for breach of the implied condition of fitness for purpose, but failed, because she had not made known to the seller the fact that she was assuming the coat would not irritate her skin.

In summary the key questions for the court are:

- Did the buyer make known to the seller (expressly or impliedly) the purpose for which the goods were being bought?
- Were the goods reasonably fit for that purpose?

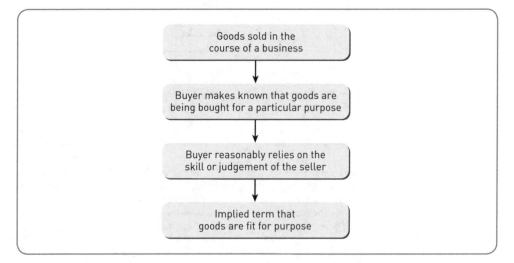

**Figure 16.2** Fitness for purpose

- Did the buyer rely on the seller's skill and judgment?
- Was it reasonable for the buyer to rely on the seller's skill and judgment?

There is often an overlap between the conditions on fitness for the purpose and satisfactory quality. Where the purpose for which the buyer claims to want the goods is their ordinary purpose, the ability of those goods to fulfil that purpose may also be a measure of their satisfactory quality. For example, in **Preist** v **Last** (1903) the buyer asked for 'a hot water bottle', and this request was taken to mean that he wanted goods fit for the purpose of filling with water and heating his bed, without splitting. When the bottle did split, this was therefore a breach of both the implied condition on merchantable quality (and would now be a breach of the requirement for satisfactory quality) and that on fitness for its purpose.

The condition of fitness for purpose will be implied only where the goods are sold in the course of a business.

## Correspondence with sample

Section 15 of the Sale of Goods Act 1979 provides that where goods are sold by sample, there is an implied condition that the bulk of the goods will correspond with the sample, that the buyer will have a reasonable opportunity of comparing the bulk with the sample, and that the goods will be free from any defect, rendering them unsatisfactory, which would not be apparent on reasonable examination of the sample.

**Table 16.1** Sale of Goods Act 1979

| Sale of Goods Act 1979 section number | Implied term |
|---|---|
| 12(1) | Title |
| 13(1) | Sale by description |
| 14(2) | Satisfactory quality |
| 14(3) | Fitness for purpose |
| 15 | Correspondence with sample |

## Remedies for breach of the Sale of Goods Act 1979

The remedies available to consumers where the goods do not conform to the express or implied terms of the contract at the time of delivery have been strengthened by the Sale and Supply of Goods to Consumers Regulations 2002. The Regulations reverse the burden of proof in this context. If goods do not conform with the contract at any time within the period of six months from the date of delivery, they are to be taken not to have conformed at the date of delivery. In these circumstances, the seller has the burden of proving that in fact the goods did conform with the contract at the time of delivery. This reversal of the burden of proof will not apply if it is considered to be incompatible with the nature of the goods or the nature of the lack of conformity. This reversal of the burden of proof helps support consumer rights. Sellers are more likely than consumers to have access to evidence of the contract's conformity or lack of conformity with the contract at the time of delivery.

The Regulations lay down four new remedies:

- repair;
- replacement;
- price reduction; and
- a full refund of the price (known as rescission).

If goods fail to conform to the contract of sale at the time of delivery, then under ss. 48A–48F the buyer has the right to first of all require the seller to repair or replace the goods within a reasonable time and without causing the buyer significant inconvenience. The consumer is not entitled to repair or replacement where either of these remedies is impossible or disproportionate. If repair or replacement is impossible or disproportionate, or if the seller fails to repair or replace the goods within a reasonable time or without significant inconvenience to the buyer, the buyer may then ask for a price reduction or demand a full refund (known as rescission). If rescission is granted, the amount refunded may be reduced to take into account any use that the purchaser has had of the goods.

Before 2002, the purchaser had two other remedies:

- rejection; and
- damages.

These two remedies continue to exist, but the new reversal of the burden of proof in relation to the nonconformity of the goods to the contract does not apply to them.

The Regulations provide for the interaction between the pre-existing rights to reject and terminate and the new remedies of repair and replacement. Where consumers ask for repair or replacement, they cannot reject the goods and terminate the contract until they have given the seller reasonable time to repair or replace. A consumer might prefer to reject the goods and terminate the contract immediately, without giving the seller the opportunity to repair or replace the goods.

Under s. 35(6) of the Sale of Goods Act 1979:

> The buyer is not . . . deemed to have accepted goods merely because . . . he asks for, or agrees to, their repair by or under an agreement with the seller.

Where a seller repairs goods, they have an obligation to explain to the buyer upon request what was wrong with the goods and how they have been repaired so that the buyer can assess whether an effective repair has been carried out. Buyers cannot be treated as having accepted goods until they have been given an opportunity to inspect them after being repaired, and that requires the buyer to be given adequate information to make an informed choice about whether to accept or reject the goods. A failure to give this information will entitle the buyer to reject the goods despite the fact that they have been repaired, as will a failure to repair the goods to a satisfactory standard. This was the opinion of the House of Lords in **J & H Ritchie** v **Lloyd** (2007). In that case, a farmer had bought a piece of agricultural machinery (a harrow for ploughing the fields) which had been defective (it had vibrated a lot because it was missing two ball bearings). The seller had taken back the machine and repaired it to 'factory gate standard'; in other words, it was as good as new. After repairing the machine, the seller had refused to tell the buyer what the problem had been with the machine, but simply stated that it had been repaired to factory gate standard. The farmer discovered informally what the problem had been (by chatting with the defendant's employees). He was concerned that the earlier use of the machine without these ball bearings might have damaged other parts of the machine. In these circumstances, the farmer was entitled to reject the repaired machine and demand his money back.

A breach of an implied term is normally treated as a breach of a condition, giving rise to the right to terminate the contract by rejecting the goods. Under s. 15A of the Sale of Goods Act

1979, however, a breach of an implied term will, in certain circumstances, be deemed to be merely a breach of warranty which does not give rise to a right to reject the goods. These circumstances are that the buyer does not deal as a consumer and breach is so slight that it would be unreasonable to reject the goods. Once the buyer has accepted goods, any breach of the implied terms is only treated as a breach of warranty, so that the buyer cannot reject the goods. Acceptance is deemed to have taken place unless the seller is told otherwise within a reasonable length of time (which must be long enough to give the buyer a reasonable opportunity to examine the goods). Asking for, or accepting, a repair to defective goods does not amount to acceptance, and therefore does not cancel the buyer's right to reject the goods. Because acceptance puts an end to the right to reject the goods, the remedy of rejection is only available for a short time. By contrast, the remedy of rescission is theoretically available for up to six years when the limitation period would then apply (discussed on p. 383). The remedy of rescission will therefore be particularly useful where the fault in the goods has appeared some time after delivery.

An additional protection is provided by s. 11 of the 1979 Act, which states that the restrictions on terminating a contract for breach of an implied term do not apply where there is an express or implied term to the contrary in the contract of sale. So if, for example, a shop claimed that faulty goods could be returned for a refund at any time, it would not matter that, in terms of the legislation, the buyer might be deemed to have accepted them.

## Topical Issue

### Buying a new car

Buying a car is one of the most important purchases made by an individual – with large sums of money at stake the choice of car is very important. When people decide to buy a brand new car instead of a second-hand one they are hoping, among other things, that the extra expense will mean that the car is in a first-rate condition. Unfortunately, in **Fiat Auto Financial Services** v **Connolly** (2007) the defendant had bought a brand new car, a Fiat Stilo, but the car was not of a satisfactory quality. He had ordered a car with a fitted CD player, air conditioning and a refrigerated cool box. When the car was delivered he discovered that it had none of these fittings, and was told by the car dealer that they could only be added at an extra cost to the purchaser. Three days after the car was delivered, there were problems with the engine management system, causing the car to break down a week later. This fault was investigated by the dealer but was never diagnosed and persisted throughout the time the buyer had the car. Over the next nine months the car had steering problems, defective windscreen wipers, a faulty clutch and faulty headlamps. Eventually the buyer had had enough, and returned the car to the dealer, rejecting it on the basis that it was not of a satisfactory quality or fit for purpose. By this time the buyer had used the car as a taxi and it had notched up over 40,000 miles. Despite this, the court of first instance concluded that the car had not been accepted and the buyer was entitled to reject it. A period spent by the buyer waiting for information to enable him to make an informed decision as to whether to reject did not count when considering whether he had had the goods for more than a reasonable length of time to amount to an acceptance. Given that throughout his period of possession the buyer was communicating with the seller regularly regarding his complaints, his continued use of the vehicle did not amount to acts inconsistent with the ownership of the seller.

## Excluding the implied terms in contracts of sale

The Unfair Contract Terms Act 1977 (UCTA) lays down rules concerning the exclusion of terms implied by the Sale of Goods Act 1979 (which are described in Chapter 8). The provisions of UCTA are strengthened by the Consumer Transactions (Restrictions on Statements) Order 1976, as amended. This order makes it a criminal offence to purport to introduce into a consumer transaction a term which is void by virtue of s. 6 of UCTA. The idea behind this provision is to prevent unscrupulous traders from misleading consumers about their rights, by, for example, stating that no refunds will be given. Further protections are provided by the Unfair Terms in Consumer Contracts Regulations 1999 (which are also discussed in Chapter 8, although they cover all types of unfair terms).

## Passing of ownership

The basic rule is that the parties themselves agree on the point at which ownership passes from seller to buyer, but if they do not make such an agreement, the Sale of Goods Act 1979 lays down rules on when ownership will pass. This will usually, but not always, be when the goods are physically delivered or handed over, and from that point the buyer is normally responsible for the goods.

The Sale of Goods (Amendment) Act 1995 amended the 1979 Act, laying down special rules on how ownership passes when there is a contract for a sale of a specified quantity of unascertained goods forming part of an identified bulk, for example, a contract for the sale of a gallon of petrol from a tankload. The buyer of such unascertained goods will now become an 'owner in common' of an identified bulk of goods.

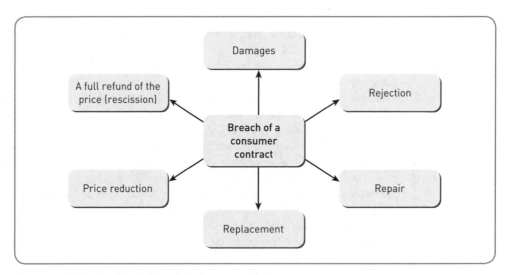

**Figure 16.3** Remedies for breach of a consumer contract

# Contracts for the supply of services

These are largely governed by the Supply of Goods and Services Act 1982. As well as straightforward services, such as hairdressing, window cleaning or plumbing, it covers contracts in which

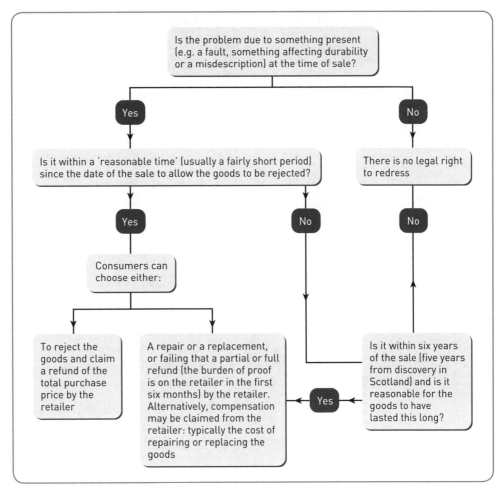

**Figure 16.4** Sale of Goods – simple summary of consumers' rights and remedies
*Source: A Trader's Guide: The Law Relating to the Supply of Goods and Services*, DTI (2005) available at www.berr.gov.uk/files/file25486.pdf. Crown Copyright material is reproduced with permission under the terms of the Click-Use Licence.

a service is performed and goods supplied at the same time, often called work and materials contracts. An example would be the decoration of a house, in which the decorator supplied the wallpaper and paint as well as applying them, or the mending of a car where new parts are provided.

There are some cases where it is difficult to say whether a contract is one for goods or services: for example, in **Lockett** *v* **A & M Charles Ltd** (1938) the contract concerned a restaurant meal, which clearly involved the services of cooking and serving, but the court decided that, on balance, the contract should be seen as one of sale, and would therefore be covered by the Sale of Goods Act 1979. In **Robinson** *v* **Graves** (1935), concerning a contract to paint a portrait, Greer LJ said the contract was one of service because the buyer was essentially purchasing the artist's labour and skill in producing the painting; the fact that some materials, in the form of paint and canvas, might also pass to the buyer was a secondary consideration.

## Implied terms in contracts for services

Under the Supply of Goods and Services Act 1982, the following terms are automatically implied in contracts for the supply of a service.

### Care and skill

Section 13 provides that 'where the supplier is acting in the course of a business, there is an implied term that the supplier will carry out the service with reasonable care and skill'. Note that this does not mean that a job must be carried out successfully. If, for example, you employ someone to cure the damp in your house, and they fail to do so, that will only be a breach of the implied term if the damp could have been cured using reasonable care and skill. If reasonable care and skill would not have solved the problem, there is no breach of the implied term (though there may be breach of an express term, if the firm promised that they could eradicate the damp).

### Time

Section 14(1) provides that in a business transaction, where the parties do not specify a time by which the job should be finished, 'there is an implied term that the supplier will carry out the service within a reasonable time'.

What is a reasonable time is a question of fact, and will obviously depend on the nature of the work done. The section only applies to contracts entered into in the course of a business.

### Price

Section 15(1) states that where the parties have not fixed a price 'there is an implied term that the party contracting with the supplier will pay a reasonable price'. Again, the reasonable price is a question of fact, depending on the nature of the service, and the term only applies to business contracts.

### Property

Where a service contract also involves the transfer of property to the customer (as in the decorating and car repair examples above), ss. 2–5 of the 1982 Act imply terms as to title, description, satisfactory quality, fitness for purpose and sample, which are basically the same as those implied into contracts for sale by ss. 12–15 of the Sale of Goods Act 1979.

## Remedies for breach of the Supply of Goods and Services Act 1982 implied terms

The implied terms in the 1982 Act are referred to as terms. They are therefore treated by the courts as innominate terms and the consequences of breach depend on the seriousness of that breach.

## Excluding the implied terms in service contracts

UCTA lays down rules concerning the exclusion of the implied terms under the 1982 Act (which are described in Chapter 8).

# Hire contracts

The Supply of Goods and Services Act 1982 also covers contracts where goods are hired, and s. 6 defines such a contract as one under which one party gives possession of goods to another, to be used for purposes agreed between them, in return for consideration. The section does not include hire-purchase agreements.

Under ss. 6–10, hire contracts are covered by implied conditions on satisfactory quality, fitness for the purpose and correspondence with description or sample, which are similar to those implied into other service contracts. Under s. 7, there is an implied condition in contracts of hire that the party hiring out the goods has a right to transfer possession of the goods by way of hire, or will have such a right at the time of the hiring.

# Manufacturers' liability

As far as contract law is concerned, consumer protection generally involves rights against retailers, since it is the retailer with whom the contract is usually made (except on the rare occasions when a consumer buys direct from the manufacturer). There are, however, three ways in which manufacturers may be liable directly to the consumer: under a manufacturer's guarantee; as a result of the manufacturer's negligence; and under the provisions of the Consumer Protection Act 1987.

## Guarantees

Many goods come with a manufacturer's guarantee, but in the past the legal status of this guarantee was not clear: was it legally enforceable? The position has now been clarified by reg. 15 of the Sale and Supply of Goods to Consumers Regulations 2002. Where goods are sold to a consumer with a guarantee, this takes effect as a contractual obligation. The guarantee must lay down in plain, intelligible English the contents of the guarantee and the essential information necessary for making claims under it. These include how long the guarantee lasts and the name and address of the company providing the guarantee.

## Negligence

If goods actually harm the end consumer, the manufacturer may be liable for negligence. An important line of cases arising from **Donoghue v Stevenson** (1932) established the principle that a manufacturer of goods is under a duty of care not to put on the market goods which could harm the ultimate consumer, and this line of cases is now backed up by statute. It gives an additional layer of protection in that the consumer is not required to have a contractual relationship with the manufacturer in order to have rights against them.

Manufacturers can defend themselves against a claim for negligence by showing that the goods were manufactured using reasonable care and skill. The burden of proving that the manufacturer is negligent lies on the consumer, and can be extremely difficult to discharge, given the complexity of modern manufacturing processes. A tragic example from the 1960s concerned a drug, Thalidomide, which was used to treat morning sickness in pregnant women. It produced serious deformities in the children who were born to them. Only after three years was it discovered that the deformities were caused by the drug and, even then, negligence by the manufacturer was never actually proved.

The difficulty of proving negligence with regard to products can also be seen in **Daniels** *v* **R White & Sons Ltd** (1938). Mr Daniels bought a bottle of R White's lemonade and a jug of beer from his local pub, took them home and mixed lemonade shandies for himself and his wife. On drinking the shandy, both felt burning sensations in their mouths; the lemonade was later shown to be contaminated with carbolic acid. It was proved that carbolic acid was used in the defendant's bottle-cleaning plant, but the claimant could not show where in the manufacturing process the negligence had occurred and his claim failed. By contrast, Mr Daniels also claimed in contract against the pub licensee, Mrs Tabard, and this claim succeeded. Liability in contract is strict and Mrs Tabard was in breach of the implied condition of merchantable quality, then applied by the legislation governing the sale of goods.

The somewhat unsatisfactory result of the case was that, although both Mr and Mrs Daniels were injured, only Mr Daniels could recover damages (because of privity of contract); and those were recovered from a party, Mrs Tabard, who was not responsible for the problem and could have done nothing to prevent it, as the lemonade was sold in sealed containers.

The courts nowadays tend to impose a less rigorous burden of proof in negligence cases than that borne by the Danielses, and have also imposed stricter responsibilities on manufacturers, such as a duty to carry out research to discover whether a product is dangerous (**Vacwell Engineering Co Ltd** *v* **BDH Chemicals Ltd** (1971)).

Liability for negligence with regard to products only covers damage to person or property, and not economic loss (loss of profits). This was established in **Muirhead** *v* **Industrial Tank Specialities Ltd** (1986) where a fish merchant installed a fish tank to keep lobsters alive out of season. When the motor which powered the tank failed, all the lobsters died, causing substantial loss of potential profit. The supplier of the motor had gone into liquidation, so the fish merchant sued the manufacturer. The court held the relationship was not sufficiently proximate to allow recovery of pure economic loss.

## Consumer Protection Act 1987

This Act was passed as a result of the EC Directive of July 1985, which sought to harmonise the law of member states on liability for defective products. In compliance with this goal, s. 1(1) provides that the Act is to be construed in accordance with the Product Liability Directive.

The Act establishes strict liability for damage caused by defective products. This means that a claimant does not have to establish that the manufacturer was negligent; unless the manufacturer is covered by one of the defences provided by the Act, it will be held responsible for the damage. This obviously makes things easier for the injured party than an action in tort.

### Liability under the Act

Section 2(1) of the Act lays down the basic liability for damages caused by a defective product. 'Product' is widely defined to mean 'any goods or electricity', with only unprocessed agricultural products and game being outside the scope of the Act. Thus the Act applies to all the usual consumer goods.

Liability under the Act cannot be limited or excluded by any term or notice (s. 7). The statute obliges the supplier of a defective product (usually a distributor or retailer) to identify its producer when requested to do so by the victim of the defective product. Suppliers who do not give the name of a person who is primarily liable, or the name of the person who supplied the product to them, will face liability for the damage themselves.

## Who may be liable?

The Act imposes liability on the producer of a product. In most cases this will be the manufacturer, but in the case of 'own brands' (products made by manufacturers but sold under the names of supermarkets and large chain stores) the retailer whose name appears on the pack will be regarded as the producer (s. 2(2)).

## Defects

Section 3(1) states that there is a defect in a product 'if the safety of a product is not such as persons generally are entitled to expect'.

## Damage

'Damage' is defined in s. 5(1) as death, personal injury or loss of or damage to property. It does not include damage to the product itself (s. 5(2)), nor damage worth less than £275 (s. 5(4)). In these cases, any claim must be made on the basis of pre-existing law.

## Defences

The Act offers four defences:

- *Contributory negligence*   The manufacturer will have a defence where the consumer has done something which contributes to the damage – an obvious example might be where the consumer has interfered with the workings of the product.
- *Compliance with legislation*   There is a defence where the defect is a result of the manufacturer's compliance with any Act of Parliament or European Union obligation.
- *The 'development risks' defence*   This is a controversial provision, allowing a defence on the basis that, when the product was being produced, the state of scientific and technical knowledge was insufficiently advanced for the producer to be expected to discover the defect. The implications for a case such as that of the Thalidomide victims are obvious: if the manufacturer can prove that, at the time a drug was made, scientific knowledge was such that they could not be expected to discover that it had side effects, victims could be left with no compensation at all. Opposition to the provision was strong, led by the Consumers' Association, but, not surprisingly, industry, and especially the drug industry, was in favour of it.

  The provision clearly weakens the Act's requirement of strict liability, but some protection for consumers is offered by the fact that the burden of proof to establish this defence is on the producer. The drafting of this defence was found to be in conformity with the Directive it was implementing in **Commission of the European Communities** *v* **United Kingdom** (1997). The argument of the European Commission that the defence was considerably broader than the equivalent provision in the Directive was rejected.
- *Time limits*   A right of action under the Act is extinguished ten years after the date when the product was put into circulation.

## General Product Safety Regulations 2005

The General Product Safety Regulations 2005 have increased the public's protection from dangerous products. The regulations impose a general safety requirement on producers and distributors of goods. Under reg. 5 the producer can place on the market only safe products. Regulation 1 defines 'safe' to mean that the product must present no risk, or 'only the minimum risks compatible with the product's use, considered to be acceptable and consistent with a high level of protection for the safety and health of persons'. In determining whether a product is safe, a court will have regard to the:

- characteristics of the product;
- effect of the product on other products;
- presentation of the product, including labelling, warnings and instructions; and
- categories of consumers at risk when using the product, particularly children and the elderly.

Regulation 7 requires producers to provide consumers with the relevant information to enable them to assess the risks inherent in the product and to take precautions against those risks. There is also a general obligation on the producer to take appropriate measures to check the risks posed by a product and to take the measures necessary to alleviate such risks.

Distributors of products must act with due care to avoid putting unsafe products on the market (reg. 8). When producers or distributers are aware that they have placed an unsafe product on the market, they are obliged by reg. 9 to inform the enforcement authorities (usually the local trading standards officers).

The regulations give the enforcement authorities a wide range of powers, including the power to issue a suspension notice which prevents the product being placed on the market while the safety of the product is evaluated, and a requirement to warn the public that a dangerous product has been placed on the market. The enforcement authorities can require that the risks are marked on a product and, as a last resort, that an unsafe product is recalled from the marketplace. Breach of the regulations does not in itself give rise to a civil action (reg. 42); generally such proceedings would be brought under the Consumer Protection Act 1987 or the Sale of Goods Act 1979.

## Consumer Protection from Unfair Trading Regulations 2008

The European Union is keen to harmonise consumer law in member states in order to facilitate cross-border trade in Europe. With this goal in mind, it passed the Unfair Commercial Practices Directive 2005. The provisions in this Directive have been implemented in the United Kingdom through the Consumer Protection from Unfair Trading Regulations 2008. These regulations were amended by the Consumer Protection (Amendment) Regulations 2014. The legislation replaces a range of provisions which were contained in the Trade Descriptions Act 1968 and the Consumer Protection Act 1987. The regulations seek to prevent misleading and aggressive selling techniques which are unfair to consumers, such as unfair advertising, pressure selling and misleading marketing. They are only concerned with transactions between consumers and businesses and not business-to-business contracts. They contain a general prohibition on unfair commercial practices as well as listing certain specific unfair practices which are banned.

Regulation 8 provides that a trader is guilty of an offence if he 'knowingly or recklessly engages in a commercial practice which contravenes the requirements of professional diligence' and 'the practice materially distorts or is likely to materially distort the economic behaviour of the average consumer'. Thus, the key test is whether a commercial practice has an unfair impact on consumers.

Strict liability is imposed for offences involving misleading actions and aggressive practices. The regulations do not apply to omissions, so consumers will be able to take action against traders who provide inaccurate product or price information, but not against those who fail to inform consumers that goods purchased were reconditioned or do not match their stated needs. Schedule 1 to the Regulations contains a list of 31 specific unfair activities. These include 'creating the impression that the consumer cannot leave the premises until a contract is formed' and 'claiming that the trader is about to cease trading or move premises when he is not' (tackling the problem of a shop having a 'closing down sale' when it is not, in fact, closing down). It also prohibits describing the produce as 'free' when the consumer does actually have to pay something (which might outlaw 'buy one get one free' offers). An unfair contract term might not only be unenforceable (see Chapter 8) but it might also amount to an unfair commercial practice, potentially giving rise to criminal liability.

Regulation 27A sets out when a consumer has a right to redress. The consumer must have entered into a contract with a trader or made a payment to a trader for the sale or supply of a product. The consumer has a right of redress where they themselves have sold goods to the trader, such as jewellery. The trader must have engaged in a prohibited practice in relation to the product. The prohibited practice must have been a significant factor in the consumer's decision to enter into the contract or make the payment. Finally, the consumer must satisfy any specific conditions that apply to the right of redress they are exercising.

The right to redress can be the right to unwind, the right to a discount or to damages. The consumer must exercise the right to unwind within 90 days and while the product remains capable of being rejected. The effect of unwinding such a contract is that it comes to an end and the consumer has a right to a refund. In practice this means the consumer has a right to return the goods or, if they cannot be returned in the same condition, to be refunded any difference between the amount the consumer paid and the amount the goods were worth.

The right to a discount entitles consumers to a 25 per cent, 50 per cent, 75 per cent or 100 per cent discount, depending on the seriousness of the prohibited practice assessed by reference to the behaviour of the trader, the impact of the practice on the consumer and the time that has elapsed. Where the goods cost over £5,000, the discount will be the difference between the market price of the product and the amount paid. The right to damages is available for additional financial losses and alarm, distress, physical discomfort and inconvenience caused by the prohibited practice. This could be useful, for example, where a business targets the old and vulnerable when selling mobility aids at excessive prices.

Traders have a due diligence defence in respect of the right to damages. The new rights to redress do not affect existing causes of action under contract law that consumers may have, but they cannot recover twice for the same loss.

## Topical Issue

### Prize draw scratch cards: if it's too good to be true, it probably is!

In **Purely Creative** v **Office of Fair Trading** (2012) the Office of Fair Trading (OFT) successfully sought a High Court injunction under the Consumer Protection from Unfair Trading Regulations 2008. The injunction was issued against a number of companies and individuals to prevent them from producing various prize draw scratch cards, advertisements and personally addressed letters that it considered misleading. The scratch cards and advertising inserts were distributed in magazines and newspapers. They informed readers that they were entitled to claim one of a number of specified prizes or awards of varying value. To claim the prize, consumers needed to call a premium rate telephone number, send a premium rate text or use the (cheaper) post to find out what they had 'won'. The consumer was not told how long it would take to obtain the necessary information, or that the promoter received £1.21 of the £1.50 cost per minute of the premium rate calls. In some cases, the consumer also needed to pay extra for delivery and insurance. Admittedly there were some prizes of very high value, but often the value of the prize was less than the cost of claiming it.

One promotion involved the consumer winning a Mediterranean cruise for four. To claim the prize, consumers had to fill out a form and pay £14.95 for insurance and delivery. They then received a voucher, and the small print on the voucher showed that the cruise would last three days, leaving from an unspecified port in Tuscany, on unspecified dates, and visiting Corsica and Sardinia. The voucher entitled the consumer to a transfer from England to the departure port and return for £159. There was a supplement for one-bed or two-bed cabins, and the consumer had to pay for food and drink and port fees. It would have cost two couples £399 per person, or £1,596 in total, to participate in the cruise.

Schedule 1 to the Consumer Protection from Unfair Trading Regulations 2008 lists 31 practices that will always be regarded as unfair. Of these, two were particularly relevant to the case:

- describing a product as 'gratis', 'free', 'without charge' or similar if the consumer has to pay anything other than the unavoidable cost of response and collecting or paying for delivery;
- creating the false impression that the consumer has won or will win a prize, when in fact either there is no prize or the consumer would have to pay money or incur a cost to claim it.

The Office of Fair Trading argued that the promotions were unfair because they created the impression that the recipient had won a prize that, in fact, could not be claimed without incurring a cost. The High Court ordered an injunction and an appeal was made to the Court of Appeal. The Court of Appeal sought guidance from the Court of Justice of the European Union (CJEU) on how to interpret the Unfair Commercial Practices Directive 2005, which was implemented by the 2008 Regulations. The European Court stated that consumers must not be told they have already won a prize if anything they must do to claim it (including requesting information about the nature of the prize or taking possession of it) involves paying money or incurring any cost whatsoever. It is irrelevant that the cost imposed on consumers, such as the cost of a stamp, is very small compared with the value of the prize or that the trader does not receive any benefit from it. It is also irrelevant that the business offers consumers a number of methods by which they may claim the prize, at least one of which is free of charge, if any of the other methods would involve consumers incurring a cost to obtain information on the prize or how to acquire it. Businesses must not tell consumers they have won a prize without saying what it is or make the consumer bear any cost to find out. Businesses must be honest about their 'free' prizes.

## The Consumer Contracts (Information, Cancellation and Additional Charges) Regulations 2013

These Regulations implement most of the provisions of the European Consumer Rights Directive 2011. The aim is to provide a high level of protection to consumers to combat unfair practices. They give consumers the right to cancel the purchases they have made online. The Regulations apply to contracts between traders and consumers. They do not apply to contracts for gambling, health services, package holidays, banking or insurance services. Traders must provide certain information to consumers in relation to contracts concluded between them. This information includes the main characteristics of the goods or service, the identity of the trader and the total price. If the contract is concluded off-premises (for example online) the information must include the delivery arrangements, the trader's complaint handling policy and cancellation rights. The trader must provide the consumer with a copy of the signed contract or confirmation of the contract, within a reasonable time after the conclusion of the contract. Regulation 19 provides that a trader is guilty of a criminal offence if the trader enters into an off-premises contract without having provided the information on cancellation rights.

Consumers have a right to cancel the contract within 14 days from the date of conclusion of the contract or the date of delivery, according to the type of contract. The cancellation period may be extended by up to 12 months if the trader does not provide the consumer with the information on cancellation rights. Regulation 34 requires the trader to pay a refund to the consumer within 14 days of being informed of the cancellation or within 14 days of the goods being returned or evidence of return being provided. The trader may deduct from the refund an amount reflecting the diminished value of the goods caused by unnecessary handling by the consumer. Regulation 35 requires the consumer to return any goods to the trader and bear the cost of doing so, unless the trader has agreed to collect the goods or bear the costs of the consumer returning them. The consumer loses the right to cancel where a service or digital content is supplied during the cancellation period, if the consumer acknowledged that the right would be lost in those circumstances. An ancillary contract (such as for insurance) is automatically terminated on cancellation of the main contract.

# Unsolicited goods

Some unscrupulous companies send goods to consumers who have not requested them, and then demand payment for the goods – usually stating that unless the goods are returned or rejected within a specified time, the company will assume the 'customer' wants them. As you will realise by now, under common law this in itself imposes no obligation whatsoever on the consumer – the case of **Felthouse** v **Bindley** (1862) (see p. 24) states that one party cannot make an offer to another and insist that silence will be taken as acceptance.

However, the average consumer has, unfortunately, not read this book, and, as so often happens with consumer transactions, the practice has caused great confusion and anxiety. Some companies found it easy to give the impression that people were obliged either to pay for the goods or return them at their own expense. In other cases, customers assumed that since they had not ordered the goods, they were not bound to pay for them and duly used the goods, only to find that if the common law judged that this amounted to acceptance, they were liable to pay. Consequently, in 1971 Parliament decided to regulate this method of selling and the result was the Unsolicited Goods and Services Act 1971. This Act allowed the recipient of unsolicited goods, after a specified time, to treat the goods as a gift. The provisions of the Act, in so far as they deal with goods sent to consumers, have now been replaced by reg. 24 of the Consumer Protection (Distance Selling) Regulations 2000. These enable the consumer to treat the goods as an unconditional gift as soon as they are received. Moreover, reg. 24 makes it a criminal offence to seek payment for unsolicited goods or services.

# Consumer credit

During the past 20 years, there has been an enormous increase in the number of people using credit to make purchases. Where once credit was only used for major purchases, such as cars or furniture, the advent of easily available credit cards now means that all kinds of everyday purchases are made in this way.

Given that the providers of credit are generally large and powerful organisations, and their customers often ordinary consumers, the inequality of bargaining power could easily lead to transactions which are clearly much more favourable to the credit suppliers. In addition, there is a danger that heavy promotion of credit services may lead consumers to take on more debt than they can realistically afford. For these two reasons, the Consumer Credit Act 1974 was passed to regulate credit transactions.

## Hire purchase

Widely used for cars and other major purchases, hire purchase is generally arranged by the seller of the goods. The buyer chooses a purchase, and fills in a form, which the seller then passes to a finance company (usually the same one for all their transactions). The finance company checks the buyer's creditworthiness and, if satisfied, accepts the deal. The goods are then sold not to the buyer, but to the finance company. The buyer takes possession of the goods, and pays regular instalments to the finance company. The goods remain the property of the finance company until some agreed point (usually when the final payment is made). In effect, what happens is that the finance company hires the goods to the buyer, with an option to buy them. The contract of sale is therefore between the buyer and the finance company, not the buyer and the original seller.

The 1974 Act covers hire-purchase agreements where the credit given is no more than £15,000 – note that does not mean the purchase price must be less than £15,000, as in many cases the buyer will have put down a cash deposit. Interest is also excluded from the £15,000 total.

Where a hire-purchase agreement falls inside this total, there are a number of provisions to protect the consumer. These include strict rules on the formalities of the agreement: it must be in writing, with even the print and paper regulated by the Act, and the consumer must be given at least one copy.

As with any other contract, the consumer can cancel at any time before the offer is accepted by the finance company, but the Act provides an additional means of escape. Where the finance company's negotiator (often the seller of the goods) has made oral representations to the buyer, and the agreement was signed somewhere other than the business premises of the buyer, the seller, the finance company or anyone involved in a linked transaction, the consumer is allowed a 'cooling off' period of five days from receiving a copy of the agreement that was signed. During this time, the consumer may cancel in writing (which takes effect on posting), return the goods and get back any money paid; the transaction is then treated as though it had never been made.

## Enforcement orders

If a trader infringes consumer protection legislation, Part 8 of the Enterprise Act 2002 provides that the Office of Fair Trading and certain other 'enforcers' may apply for an enforcement order. Such an order may be made where the infringement harms the collective interests of consumers. It is intended to put a stop to any existing infringement and also prevent future breaches of the legislation.

## Contract law and consumer protection

As this chapter shows, the majority of consumer protection provisions have been developed not, like most contract law, by the common law, but by legislation. Part of the reason for this is the fundamental clash between the idea of protecting one party against the other and the roots of contract law in the idea that parties should be left alone to make their own agreements and protect their own interests.

There are, however, other reasons why statutory intervention has been needed. First, the fact that criminal sanctions have been seen as the only way to deal with certain trading practices clearly required legislation; there is general agreement that criminal offences should only be created by Parliament.

Secondly, only the highest courts are really involved in developing the common law, and consumer problems rarely reach those courts. The vast majority do not get to court at all, and those that do tend to be dealt with in the lower courts, so there is little opportunity to set new precedents.

Thirdly, much of the pressure for reform has come from consumer groups, notably the Consumers' Association. Such pressure groups cannot directly influence the decisions of the courts, and can only bring about change in the law through publicising problematic issues and then pressing for legislation. Many changes in the law on consumer contracts have been influenced by such campaigns.

Lastly, the European Union has become increasingly involved in the regulation of consumer transactions, with a view to harmonising this area of law and thereby facilitating trade across Europe.

## Reform

A package of reform measures is currently being considered by Parliament and contained in the Consumer Rights Bill. It is expected to be passed in 2015, and if it is brought into force will consolidate existing consumer legislation into a single, user-friendly statute, and repeal, in whole or in part, some of the existing consumer legislation. The Consumer Rights Bill would replace most of the consumer-to-business provisions in the Sale of Goods Act 1979 and the Supply of Goods and Services Act 1982. The 1979 Act and 1982 Act would continue to apply to contracts made between businesses. The Sale and Supply of Goods to Consumers Regulations 2002 would be replaced by the Bill.

## Answering questions

While in a shoe shop owned by E, D tried on a pair of shoes. These were to D's satisfaction and she offered to purchase them for £30. The sales assistant informed D that the shoes were only a sample and not for sale, but that there was an identical pair in the stockroom. D was in a hurry and agreed to take the pair from the stockroom, which were packaged in a box, and she paid the £30. When D opened the box at home, she discovered that, although the shoes were very similar to the pair she had tried on, the soles were of man-made material and not real leather, as the sample pair had been. She also noticed that one of the heels was loose and would soon be torn away after some use. D is concerned that a notice she had read in the shop declared that goods would not be replaced or money refunded to customers under any circumstances.

What are D's rights regarding her purchases? What is the legal effect, if any, of the notice in E's shop? *London*

This question clearly covers the terms in sales contracts implied by the Sale of Goods Act 1979. E appears to be in breach of two of these. First, the requirement that goods sold by sample should correspond with that sample seems clearly to be breached, because there are major differences in quality between the two. You also need to consider whether D was given a reasonable opportunity to examine the shoes she actually bought, as required under s. 15.

Secondly, the requirement for satisfactory quality – look at the problems with the shoes by reference to the kinds of factors which the Act allows the courts to take into account, and remember that price is important.

Assuming one or both of these terms have been breached, what rights does D have? Here you need to talk about remedies – does she have the right to demand a refund, under the amended rules on acceptance (discussed at p. 409 above)?

Finally, analyse the notice in the shop. This is covered by the Unfair Contract Terms Act 1977, and you will find more detailed information in the chapter on exclusion clauses, but essentially the notice has no legal effect as far as D is concerned, because the Sale of Goods Act 1979 implied terms cannot be excluded in consumer sales. You should also discuss the fact that such a notice may make E liable for a criminal offence, under the Consumer Transactions (Restrictions on Statements) Order 1976 (which is discussed at p. 412).

---

'There is no room for a doctrine of freedom of contract in modern consumer protection legislation.'

Critically evaluate this statement in relation to twentieth-century consumer protection legislation. *WJEC*

You should begin by defining what freedom of contract is, with a little of the historical and political background to it – this material can be found in the introductory chapter. Then explain why freedom of contract caused problems for consumers – because of their inequality of bargaining power. Mention the growth of standard contracts and the use of lawyers by big companies to ensure contracts were agreed in their favour. Go on to explain some of the ways in which legislation has protected the consumer by interfering with freedom of contract – discuss the Sale of Goods Act 1979, Supply of Goods and Services Act 1982, Sale and Supply of Goods Act 1994, Sale and Supply of Goods to Consumers Regulations 2002, Unfair Contract Terms Act 1977 and other consumer legislation concerning contract terms referred to in this chapter. You should also mention the Unfair Terms in Consumer Contracts Regulations 1999 (covered in Chapter 8). You might then point out briefly that this approach alone has not been entirely successful, because giving consumers greater rights under contracts only protects those consumers who are aware of their rights, and that, as a result, stronger policing of freedom of contract has been thought necessary, in the form of criminal sanctions, and the new power to ban unfair contract terms without litigation by affected individuals contained in the 1999 Regulations.

Your conclusion should say whether you agree that there is now no place for freedom of contract within consumer contracts and, on the basis of the points you have made, whether this should be considered a good or bad development in the law.

 Henry drove into town to do some shopping and parked his car in a car park which he had used a few times before and which was operated by Safeparks. At the entrance to the car park was a notice which stated: 'For the sole use of customers of the shops in this precinct. Exit by token available from shops with any purchase.' As he walked towards one of the shops, Henry met an old friend who had acquired a token which he did not need and who now gave it to Henry. Henry decided that he no longer needed to buy anything from the precinct shops and, leaving his car in the car park, went off and ordered a dining room carpet from Comfyfloors. When he later tried to leave the car park, he was stopped by security staff doing a spot check on customers and it was discovered that he had not bought anything in the shops, despite having a token. The security staff pointed to a notice displayed at the exit barrier and to a notice at the entrance to the shops (some distance from the entrance to the car park) which stated that exit without a token would cost £25. Henry was told that he could not now go and make a purchase and he had to pay the £25 before the security staff would open the barrier.

Henry engaged Ken, a carpet-fitter, to lay the carpet for him and, after a brief inspection of the completed work, signed a document to say that he was completely satisfied. When he was able to examine the carpet and the fitting more carefully, he discovered that there were variations in the colour and pattern and that Ken had cut it short in three or four places, so that it did not reach the wall. When he complained to Comfyfloors, he was reminded that the delivery note which he had signed informed him that no liability for any defects would be accepted once the carpet had been cut by anyone other than Comfyfloors' employees or authorised agents. Additionally, Henry complained to Ken about the fitting, but Ken rejected the complaint by reminding Henry of the document that he had signed on completion of the work.

(a) Discuss the rights, duties and remedies between Safeparks and Henry arising out of the above incidents. *(15 marks)*

(b) Discuss the rights, duties and remedies arising out of the incidents involving Henry and Comfyfloors and Henry and Ken. *(15 marks)*

(c) Explain the mechanisms, both formal and less formal, which exist for the resolution of the disputes between the various parties. *(10 marks)*

(d) Assess the contribution made by the judges to the development of the rules which you have explained and applied in answering parts (a) and (b) above. *(10 marks) AQA*

 (a) This part of the question concerned the formation of contracts and remedies for breach. A court would be likely to find that Safeparks had made a unilateral offer to all those who wished to park, the terms of which were contained in the notice at the entrance to the car park. Henry accepted this offer by parking his car. The case of

**Thornton** v **Shoe Lane Parking** (discussed at p. 160) is very important on these facts and should be considered in depth. The consideration for this contract would normally be the provision of the car-parking facility and the purchase of merchandise from one of the shops in the precinct. In fact, Henry makes no such purchase and instead obtains a token provided by an old friend, which might be viewed as past consideration (see p. 93). The case of **Chappell & Co Ltd** v **Nestlé Co Ltd** (at p. 96) could also be considered.

In the light of **Thornton** v **Shoe Lane Parking** and **Olley** v **Marlborough Court Ltd**, the notice at the entrance of the car park stating 'Exit by token available from shops with any purchase' is likely to be viewed as a term of the contract. A court would probably interpret this clause to require a purchase to be made by the car user, despite the fact that this is not expressly stated, as this would reflect the purpose of the contract – **Investors Compensation Scheme Ltd** v **West Bromwich Building Society** (p. 134).

The requirement to pay £25 on failing to satisfy the conditions of entrance was not mentioned in the notice at the entrance to the car park. Therefore, in the light of **Thornton** v **Shoe Lane Parking** and **Olley** v **Marlborough Court Ltd**, this has not been incorporated into the contract by giving Henry reasonable notice of the penalty. Consideration could be given as to whether it has been incorporated through a course of dealings (see p. 163), that is to say, by Henry having used the car park in the past. If this was found not to be a term of the contract, then Safeparks would have to rely on the remedies of damages or an injunction.

(b) Your answer should be divided into two parts. First, consider the contract between Henry and Comfyfloors: this would be affected by the Sale of Goods Act 1979. This Act imposes an obligation that the carpet should be of 'satisfactory quality' (see p. 406). Given the importance of the aesthetic qualities of carpets to customers, a court might well find that the deficiencies described do not satisfy this implied term. Under s. 6 of the Unfair Contract Terms Act 1977, liability for breach of this implied term cannot be excluded as Henry was acting as a consumer (see p. 168). You should also consider whether the delivery note was incorporated into the contract under common law and whether its terms would be considered unfair under the Unfair Terms in Consumer Contracts Regulations 1999. If the carpets are not of a satisfactory quality, Henry will have a right to damages. He is unlikely to have a right to reject the goods because, while he has contacted Comfyfloors promptly about the defects, Ken has already cut the piece of carpet delivered (p. 410).

Secondly, the contract between Henry and Ken would be affected by the Supply of Goods and Services Act 1982. This contains an implied term that reasonable care and skill will be used in the provision of services. Again, this term could not be excluded by an exclusion clause (UCTA, s. 6). In addition, the clause would not have been incorporated into the contract as Henry did not sign the document at the time of making the contract (p. 158).

(c) This question requires information that is outside the scope of this book and which is covered in the authors' book on the English legal system. As regards formal mechanisms or resolution, you would need to include a discussion on the courts, including the relevance of the size of the claim to determine which court has jurisdiction, and a discussion of the small claims procedure. As regards less formal procedures, you could explore the trade schemes available for arbitration and the growing importance of alternative methods of dispute resolution.

(d) In answering this part of the question you could draw on material contained in the introductory chapter under the headings 'The origins of contract law', 'Freedom of contract' and 'Contract and fairness'. You could point out that most of the general principles of contract, including those concerning the formation of a contract, were created and developed by the judges as part of the common law. On the other hand, the judges' role in developing consumer protection has been more limited owing to their adherence to the principle of freedom of contract. They tended to restrict their scrutiny of contracts to formalities and avoided assessment of their substance, as can be seen in their approach to exemption clauses. But it should be noted that judicial contribution continues even where there is legislation through their role in statutory interpretation.

# Summary of Chapter 16

## Contracts for the sale of goods

These are largely covered by the Sale of Goods Act 1979.

### In the course of a business

Certain provisions of the 1979 Act apply only when goods are sold 'in the course of a business'. This concept was given a wide interpretation in **Stevenson** v **Rogers** (1999).

### Implied terms in contracts for the sale of goods

A set of terms concerning the goods is implied into all contracts covered by the Act.

### Title

Under s. 12(1) of the 1979 Act, a condition is implied into any contract for the sale of goods that the seller has a right to sell the goods and is able to pass good title to the buyer.

### Sale by description

Section 13(1) of the 1979 Act states that 'where there is a contract for the sale of goods by description, there is an implied condition that the goods will correspond with the description'.

### Satisfactory quality

Under s. 14(2) goods sold in the course of a business should be of 'satisfactory quality'.

### Fitness for purpose

Under s. 14(3) if a buyer tells the seller the goods are required for a particular purpose, and the seller goes ahead and sells them, they must be fit for that purpose, even if it is an unusual one. The condition of fitness for purpose will be implied only where the goods are sold in the course of a business.

### Correspondence with sample

Section 15 of the Sale of Goods Act 1979 provides that where goods are sold by sample, there is an implied condition that the bulk of the goods will correspond with the sample, that the buyer will have a reasonable opportunity of comparing the bulk with the sample, and that the goods will be free from any defect, rendering them unsatisfactory, which would not be apparent on reasonable examination of the sample.

### Remedies for breach of the Sale of Goods Act 1979

Historically, breach of the implied terms gave rise to two possible remedies.

- rejection; and
- damages.

The Sale and Supply of Goods to Consumers Regulations 2002 lays down four new additional remedies:

- repair;
- replacement;
- price reduction; and
- a full refund of the price (known as rescission).

### Excluding the implied terms in contracts of sale

The Unfair Contract Terms Act 1977 (UCTA) lays down rules concerning the exclusion of terms implied by the Sale of Goods Act 1979.

### Passing of ownership

The basic rule is that the parties themselves agree on the point at which ownership passes from seller to buyer, but if they do not make such an agreement, the Sale of Goods Act 1979 lays down rules on when ownership will pass.

## Contracts for the supply of services

These are largely governed by the Supply of Goods and Services Act 1982.

### Implied terms in contracts for services

Under the Supply of Goods and Services Act 1982, the following terms are automatically implied in contracts for the supply of a service.

#### Care and skill
Section 13 provides that 'where the supplier is acting in the course of a business, there is an implied term that the supplier will carry out the service with reasonable care and skill'.

#### Time
Section 14(1) provides that in a business transaction, where the parties do not specify a time by which the job should be finished, 'there is an implied term that the supplier will carry out the service within a reasonable time'.

#### Price
Section 15(1) states that where the parties have not fixed a price 'there is an implied term that the party contracting with the supplier will pay a reasonable price'.

#### Property
Where a service contract also involves the transfer of property to the customer, ss. 2–5 of the 1982 Act imply terms as to title, description, satisfactory quality, fitness for purpose and sample, which are basically the same as those implied into contracts for sale by ss. 12–15 of the Sale of Goods Act 1979.

### Remedies for breach of the 1982 Act implied terms

The implied terms in the 1982 Act are treated by the courts as innominate terms and the consequences of breach depend on the seriousness of that breach.

### Hire contracts

The Supply of Goods and Services Act 1982 also covers contracts where goods are hired. Under ss. 6–10, hire contracts are covered by implied conditions on satisfactory quality, fitness for purpose and correspondence with description or sample, which are similar to those implied into other service contracts.

### Manufacturers' liability

As far as contract law is concerned, consumer protection generally involves rights against retailers. There are, however, three ways in which manufacturers may be liable directly to the consumer: under a manufacturer's guarantee; as a result of the manufacturer's negligence; and under the provisions of the Consumer Protection Act 1987.

 ## Reading list

Bartley, 'Making consumer law fit for purpose' (2013) 156 Solicitors Journal 46

Blyth, 'A heavy burden: a bespoke procedure for personal injury product claims?' (2012) 162 New Law Journal 1523

Clubb, 'Will proposed new legislation improve consumer rights?' (2014) 164 New Law Journal 12

Ervine, 'Satisfactory quality: what does it mean?' (2004) Journal of Business Law 684

Lawson, 'Case law under the Consumer Protection from Unfair Trading Regulations: Part I, Offences' (2013) 177 Criminal Law and Justice Weekly 7

Lawson, 'Case law under the Consumer Protection from Unfair Trading Regulations: Part II, Offences' (2013) 177 Criminal Law and Justice Weekly 8

Low, 'Repair, rejection and rescission: an uneasy resolution' (2007) 123 Law Quarterly Review 536

Stevens, 'Fool's gold – the ECJ's ruling in the first case under unfair trading regulations' (2012) 162 New Law Journal 1529

Truilhek-Marengo, 'Towards a European law of contracts' (2004) 10(4) European Law Journal 463

### Reading on the internet

The Sale and Supply of Goods to Consumers Regulations 2002 are available on the website of the Office of Public Sector Information at:

http://www.opsi.gov.uk/si/si2002/20023045.htm

The General Product Safety Regulations 2005 are available on the website of the Office for Public Sector Information at:

http://www.opsi.gov.uk/si/si2005/20051803.htm

The explanatory memorandum to the General Product Safety Regulations 2005 is available on the website of the Office of Public Sector Information at:

http://www.opsi.gov.uk/si/em2005/utsiem_20051803_en.pdf

# Appendix: Answering examination questions

At the end of each chapter, you will find detailed guidelines for answering exam questions on the topics covered. Many of the questions are taken from actual A-level past papers, but they are equally relevant for candidates of all law examinations, as these questions are typical of the type of questions that examiners ask in this field.

In this section, we aim to give some general guidelines for answering questions on contract law.

## Citation of authorities

One of the most important requirements for answering questions on the law is that you must be able to back up the points you make with authority, usually either a case or a statute. It is not good enough to state that the law is such and such, without stating the case or statute which says that that is the law.

Some examiners are starting to suggest that the case name is not essential, as long as you can remember and understand the general principle that the case laid down. However, such examiners remain in the minority and the reality is that even they are likely to give higher marks where the candidate has cited authorities by name; quite simply, it helps give the impression that you know your material thoroughly, rather than half-remembering something you heard once in class.

This means that you must be prepared to learn fairly long lists of cases by heart, which can be a daunting prospect. What you need to memorise is the name of the case, a brief description of the facts, and the legal principle which the case established. Once you have revised a topic well, you should find that a surprisingly high number of cases on that topic begin to stick in your mind anyway, but there will probably be some that you have trouble recalling. A good way to memorise these is to try to create a picture in your mind which links the facts, the name and the legal principle. For example, in the case of **Routledge** v **Grant** (1828) the defendants made a provisional offer to buy the plaintiff's house at a specified price, 'a definite answer to be given within six weeks from date'. The principle established in the case was that the offeror had the right to withdraw the offer at any moment before acceptance, even though the time limit had not expired. You could remember this case by imagining the actress Patricia Routledge trying to buy a house from the *EastEnders* character Grant Mitchell, with Grant telling Patricia that he has the right to withdraw his offer at any time before acceptance. Or turn the names into objects – you can remember **Fisher** v **Bell**, for instance, by imagining a fisherman trying to sell flick knives to a bell, and the bell replying, 'Putting those knives in your window is not an offer, but an invitation to treat.' The more bizarre the image, the more likely you are to remember it.

Knowing the names of cases makes you look more knowledgeable, and also saves writing time in the exam, but if you do forget a name, referring briefly to the facts will identify it. It is not necessary to learn the dates of cases, though it is useful if you know whether it is a recent or an old case. Dates are usually required for statutes.

You need to know the facts of a case in order to judge whether it applies to the situation in a problem question. However, unless you are making a detailed comparison of the facts of a case and the facts of a problem question in order to argue that the case should or could be distinguished, you should generally make only brief reference to facts, if at all – long descriptions of facts waste time and earn few marks.

When reading the 'Answering questions' sections at the end of each chapter in this book, bear in mind that for reasons of space we have not highlighted every case and statute which you should cite. The skeleton arguments outlined in those sections **must** be backed up with authority from cases and statute law.

## There is no right answer

In law exams, there is not usually a right or a wrong answer. What matters is that you show you know what type of issues you are being asked about. Essay questions are likely to ask you to 'discuss', 'criticise', or 'evaluate', and you simply need to produce a good range of factual and critical material in order to do this. The answer you produce might look completely different from your friend's but both answers could be worth the same marks.

## Breadth and depth of content

Where a question seems to raise a number of different issues – as most do – you will achieve better marks by addressing all or most of those issues than by writing at great length on just one or two. By all means spend more time on issues which you know well, but be sure to at least mention other points which you can see are relevant, even if you can only produce a paragraph or so about them.

## The structure of the question

If a question is specifically divided into parts, for example (a), (b) and (c), then stick to those divisions and do not merge your answer into one long piece of writing.

Law examinations tend to contain a mixture of essay questions and what are known as 'problem questions'. Tackling each of these questions involves slightly different skills, so we consider each in turn.

# Essay questions

## Answer the question asked

Over and over again, examiners complain that candidates do not answer the question they are asked – so if you can develop this skill, you will stand out from the crowd. You will get very few marks for simply writing all you know about a topic, with no attempt to address the issues raised in the question, but if you can adapt the material that you have learnt on the subject to take into account the particular emphasis given to it by the question, you will do well.

Even if you have memorised an essay which does raise the issues in the question (perhaps because those issues tend to be raised year after year), you must fit your material to the words of the question you are actually being asked. For example, suppose during your course you wrote an essay on the advantages and disadvantages of the privity rule, and then in the exam you find yourself faced with the question 'Should the privity rule be abolished?' The material in your coursework essay is ideally suited for the exam question, but if you begin the main part of your answer with the words 'The advantages of the privity rule include . . .' or something similar, this is a dead giveaway to the examiner that you are merely writing down an essay you have memorised. It takes very little effort to change the words to 'Abolition of the privity rule would ignore certain advantages that the current law has . . .' but it will create a much better impression, especially if you finish with a conclusion which, based on points you have made, states that abolition is a good or bad idea, the choice depending on the arguments you have made during your answer.

During your essay, you should keep referring to the words used in the question – if this seems to become repetitive, use synonyms for those words. This makes it clear to the examiner that you are keeping the question in mind as you work.

## Plan your answer

Under pressure of time, it is tempting to start writing immediately, but five minutes spent planning each essay question is well worth spending – it may mean that you write less overall, but the quality of your answer will almost certainly be better. The plan need not be elaborate: just jot down everything you feel is relevant to the answer, including case names, and then organise the material into a logical order appropriate to the question asked. To put it in order, rather than wasting time copying it all out again, simply put a number next to each point according to which ones you intend to make first, second and so forth.

## Provide analysis and fact

Very few essay questions require merely factual descriptions of what the law is; you will almost always be required to analyse the factual content in some way, usually highlighting any problems or gaps in the law, and suggesting possible reforms. If a question asks you to analyse whether consumers are adequately protected by the law when they buy goods, you should not write everything you know about consumer protection and finish with one sentence saying consumers are or are not adequately protected. Instead you should select your relevant material and your whole answer should be targeted at answering whether the protection is adequate, by, for example, pointing out any gaps or problems in it, and highlighting changes which have improved protection.

Where a question uses the word 'critically', as in 'critically describe' or 'critically evaluate', the examiners are merely drawing your attention to the fact that your approach should be analytical and not merely descriptive; you are not obliged to criticise every provision you describe. Having said that, even if you do not agree with particular criticisms which you have read, you should still discuss them and say why you do not think they are valid; there is very little mileage in an essay that simply describes the law and says it is perfectly satisfactory.

## Structure

However good your material, you will only gain really high marks if you structure it well. Making a plan for each answer will help in this, and you should also try to learn your material in a logical order – this will make it easier to remember as well. The exact construction of your essay will obviously depend on the question, but you should aim to have an introduction, then the main discussion, and a conclusion. Where a question is divided into two or more parts, you should reflect that structure in your answer.

A word about conclusions: it is not good enough just to repeat the question, turning it into a statement, for the conclusion. So, for example, if the question is 'Are the rules on offer and acceptance satisfactory?' a conclusion which simply states that the rules are or are not satisfactory will gain you very little credit. Your conclusion will often summarise the arguments that you have developed during the course of your essay.

# Problem questions

In problem questions, the exam paper will describe an imaginary situation, and then ask what the legal implications of the facts are – usually by asking you to advise one of the parties involved.

## Read the question thoroughly

The first priority is to read the question thoroughly, at least a couple of times. Never start writing until you have done this, as you may well get halfway through and discover that what is said at the end makes half of what you have written irrelevant – or at worst, that the question raises issues you have no knowledge of at all.

## Answer the question asked

This means paying close attention to the words printed immediately after the situation is described. If a question asks you to advise one or other of the parties, make sure you advise the right one – the realisation as you discuss the exam with your friends afterwards that you have advised the wrong party and thus rendered most of your answer irrelevant is not an experience you will enjoy. Similarly, if a question asks about possible remedies, simply discussing whether there has been a breach of contract will not be enough – you need to say what the innocent party can claim as a result.

## Spot the issues

In answering a problem question in an examination, you will often be short of time. One of the skills of doing well is spotting which issues are particularly relevant to the facts of the problem and spending most time on those, while skimming over more quickly those matters which are not really an issue on the facts, but which you clearly need to mention.

## Apply the law to the facts

What a problem question requires you to do is to spot the issues raised by the situation, and to consider the law as it applies to those facts. It is not enough simply to describe the law without applying it to the facts. So in a question raising issues of offer and acceptance, for example, it is not enough to say what constitutes an offer and what makes an acceptance. You need to say whether, in the light of those rules, there has been an offer and acceptance in the situation described in the problem.

Do not start your answer by copying out all the facts, or keep referring to them at great length. This is a complete waste of time, and will gain you no marks.

Unlike essay questions, problem questions are not usually seeking a critical analysis of the law. If you have time, it may be worth making the point that a particular area of the law you are discussing is problematic, and briefly stating why, but if you are addressing all the issues raised in the problem you are unlikely to have much time for this. What the examiner is looking for is essentially an understanding of the law and an ability to apply it to the particular facts given.

## Use authority

As always, you must back up your points with authority from case or statute law.

## Structure

The introduction and conclusion are much less important for problem questions than for essay questions. Your introduction can be limited to pointing out the issues raised by the question, or, where you are asked to 'advise' a person mentioned in the problem, what outcome that person will be looking for. You can also say in what order you intend to deal with the issues. It is not always necessary to write a conclusion, but you may want to summarise what you have said, highlighting whether, as a result, you think the party you have advised has a strong case or not.

There is no set order in which the main part of the answer must be discussed. Sometimes it will be appropriate to deal with the problem chronologically, in which case it will usually be a matter of looking at the question line by line, while in other cases it may be appropriate to group particular issues together. If the question is broken down into clear parts – a, b, c and so on – the answer can be broken down into the same parts; whether this is the case varies with different examining boards.

Whichever order you choose, try to deal with one issue at a time. Jumping backwards and forwards gives the impression that you have not thought about your answer. If you work through your material in a structured way, you are also less likely to leave anything out.

# Glossary

**Acceptance** of an offer means unconditional agreement to all the terms of that offer. Acceptance will often be oral or in writing, but in some cases an offeree may accept an offer by doing something (such as delivering goods in response to an offer to buy). The courts will only interpret conduct as indicating acceptance where it seems reasonable to infer that the offeree acted with the intention of accepting the offer.

**Accord and satisfaction** occur where one party's obligations under a contract change and consideration is provided in return for the other party's agreement to the change. The agreement is called 'accord' and the provision of consideration for it is called 'satisfaction'; thus the arrangement is called 'accord and satisfaction'.

**Agent** A person authorised to act on behalf of another who is known as the principal. The principal will be bound by any contract the agent makes, so long as the agent is acting within the authority granted by the principal or apparently granted by the principal.

**Bilateral contract** This is where each party takes on an obligation, usually by promising the other something (for example, where A promises to sell something and B promises to buy it). It can be distinguished from a unilateral contract (discussed below).

**Breach of contract** A contract is said to be breached when one party performs defectively, differently from the agreement, or not at all (actual breach), or indicates in advance that he or she will not be performing as agreed (anticipatory breach).

**Caveat emptor** (Latin for 'Let the buyer beware.') It is a traditional rule that a purchaser is required to ask questions about important matters if necessary – the seller is not usually expected to volunteer information which may put the buyer off.

**Chartered corporation** A corporation set up by Royal Charter, which means that its powers are officially granted by the Crown. Examples are some charities, and some universities and other educational institutions.

**Common mistake** is where both parties to a contract make the same mistake (for example, if A buys a painting from B, which both parties believe is a Constable, but which is in fact a fake, they have made a common or shared mistake).

**Condition** A term in a contract which is an important one, in the sense that a breach of it would have very significant consequences for the innocent party, will usually be regarded by the courts as a condition. Where a condition is breached, the innocent party is entitled to regard the contract as repudiated, and so need not render any further performance, and may also be able to sue for damages.

**Consideration** is something that must be provided by each of the parties in order to make a binding contract. Put simply, this means that there must be some kind of exchange between the parties. If, for example, A says that she will give B her car, and B simply agrees to have it, A has voluntarily made her a promise (called a gratuitous promise) which B cannot enforce if A changes her mind. If, however, A promises to hand over her car to B and B promises to pay A a sum of money in return, they have each provided consideration.

**Contra proferentem rule** This means that where the words, for example of an exemption clause, are ambiguous, they will be interpreted against the party relying on them.

**Contract** In law this means a legally binding agreement, written or unwritten. In order to be legally binding, the agreement has to satisfy certain requirements (see Chapters 1–6) but, with few exceptions, being in writing is not one of these requirements.

**Corporation** A corporation is a legal entity (usually a group of people) which is treated by law as having a separate identity from the person or persons who constitute it.

**Cross-purposes mistake** This occurs where each party to the contract has a different view of the situation – for example, where A thinks he is buying B's Rolls-Royce when in fact it is his Daimler that is for sale.

**Economic duress** occurs where one party is forced into a contract owing to economic pressure, which is much more than the ordinary pressure of the market. To constitute economic duress there must be compulsion of the will to the extent that the party under threat has no practical alternative but to comply, and the pressure used is regarded by the law as illegitimate.

**Exclusion clause** A clause which seeks to exclude all liability for certain breaches of contract (for example, the terms often imposed by holiday companies which exclude liability for holiday problems caused by events beyond the company's control, such as war).

**Exemption clause** This is a term commonly used to cover both limitation clauses (see below) and exclusion clauses (see above).

**Freedom of contract** This doctrine promotes the idea that, since parties are the best judge of their own interest, they should be allowed to make the bargain that suits them without interference from the courts.

**Gratuitous promise** A promise for which no consideration is given in return.

**Implied terms** Terms which are not expressly stated in a contract but which the courts will 'read in'.

**Indemnity clause** Provides that one party will reimburse (indemnify) the other in the event of any loss arising from the contract.

**Innominate terms** These are terms which can be broken with either important or trivial consequences, depending on the nature of the breach.

**Legal tender** The following are regarded as legal tender for the purpose of paying a debt: Bank of England notes for any amount, silver coins up to the value of £5, and copper up to the value of 20p.

**Limitation clause** This is one whereby a party to a contract seeks to limit his or her liability for particular breaches.

**Liquidated claim** This is one for a fixed amount, for example a sum of money lent or the agreed price of goods or services supplied.

**Liquidated damages** This term can be used where a contract specifies the amount of damages to be paid in the event of breach, and this amount represents a genuine attempt to work out what the loss in the event of such a breach would be.

**Minor** A person under the age of 18.

**Misrepresentation** If one party has been induced to enter into a contract by a statement made by the other party, and that statement is in fact untrue, the contract is voidable and the innocent party may also claim damages. For a misrepresentation to be actionable, it has to fulfil three requirements: it must (1) be untrue; (2) be a statement of fact, not mere opinion; and (3) have induced the innocent party to enter the contract.

**Mistake** See **Common mistake**; **Cross-purposes mistake**.

***Non est factum*** (Latin for 'This is not my deed'). Where a person signs a document believing it to be something totally different from what it actually is, the common law remedy of *non est factum* may make the contract void.

**Novation** is an act whereby, with the consent of all the parties, a new contract is substituted for an existing contract and the latter is discharged. Usually it takes the form of the introduction of a new party to the contract and the discharge of a person who was a party to the old contract. For example, if A owes B £100 under one contract and C owes A £100 under another, novation will occur if C agrees to pay B £100 if she will release A from her debt to B. The first two contracts are destroyed and a new one is created.

**Offer** A communication is treated as an offer if it indicates the terms on which the offeror is prepared to make a contract and gives a clear indication that the offeror intends to be bound by those terms if they are accepted by the offeree.

**Parol evidence rule** Under this rule, where there is a written contract, extrinsic (parol) evidence cannot usually change the express terms laid down in that document.

**Privity of contract** This doctrine specifies that only the parties to a contract incur rights and obligations under it – so a person who is not a party to the contract (called a third party) can neither sue nor be sued on the contract. There are a series of exceptions to this rule.

*Quantum meruit* (Latin for 'As much as is deserved.') Where a price has not been specified in a contract between the parties but work has been done or goods supplied under it, an action called a *quantum meruit* is available under which the claimant can claim a reasonable price for the performance rendered.

**Rectification** An equitable remedy under which a document can be altered to correct a mistake.

**Registered company** A company registered under the Companies Act 1985.

**Representation** This is a statement which may have encouraged one party to make a contract but is not itself part of that contract.

**Severable contract** A contract is said to be severable where payment becomes due at various stages of performance rather than in one lump sum when performance is complete.

**Severance** In some cases it is possible to divide the illegal part of a contract from the rest, and enforce the provisions which are not affected by the illegality (this is called severance).

**Speciality contract** An agreement by deed.

**Statutory corporation** A corporation created for particular purposes by an Act of Parliament, for example the Independent Broadcasting Authority.

**Subject to contract** Use of these words in an agreement is usually (though not always) taken to mean that the parties do not intend to be legally bound until formal contracts are exchanged.

**Terms of the contract** describe the duties and obligations which each party assumes under the agreement.

*Uberrimae fidei* (Latin for 'of Utmost good faith.') This is essential to the validity of certain contracts between persons bearing a particular relationship to one another (for example insurer and insured). Failure to disclose a matter regarding which utmost good faith is required allows the innocent party to rescind the contract.

*Ultra vires* (Latin for 'Outside the powers.') A contract, for example, which is outside a company's range of activities is said to be *ultra vires*.

**Unilateral contracts** arise where only one party assumes an obligation, for example W will pay a £100 reward to anyone who finds his dog. Here W is obliged to pay a reward to anyone who finds his dog but nobody is obliged to do so.

**Unliquidated claim** Where the amount of claim is uncertain, it is said to be unliquidated.

**Void contract** Where a contract is declared void, the effect is that there never was a contract in the first place, so neither party can enforce the agreement.

**Voidable contract** is one where an innocent party can choose whether or not to be bound by it.

**Warranty** This describes a contractual term which can be broken without highly important consequences. If a warranty is breached, the innocent party can sue for damages but is not entitled to terminate the contract.

# Index

Emboldened entries refer to terms in the glossary